Positive Political Theory II

MICHIGAN STUDIES IN POLITICAL ANALYSIS

Michigan Studies in Political Analysis promotes the development and dissemination of innovative scholarship in the field of methodology in political science and the social sciences in general. Methodology is defined to include statistical methods, mathematical modeling, measurement, research design, and other topics related to the conduct and development of analytical work. The series includes works that develop a new model or method applicable to social sciences, as well as those that, through innovative combination and presentation of current analytical tools, substantially extend the use of these tools by other researchers.

General Editors: John E. Jackson (University of Michigan) and Christopher H. Achen (Princeton University)

Keith Krehbiel
Information and Legislative Organization

Donald R. Kinder and Thomas R. Palfrey, Editors
Experimental Foundations of Political Science

William T. Bianco
Trust: Representatives and Constituents

Melvin J. Hinich and Michael C. Munger
Ideology and the Theory of Political Choice

John Brehm and Scott Gates
Working, Shirking, and Sabotage: Bureaucratic Response to a Democratic Public

R. Michael Alvarez
Information and Elections

David Austen-Smith and Jeffrey S. Banks
Positive Political Theory I: Collective Preference

Gregory Wawro
Legislative Entrepreneurship in the U.S. House of Representatives

David Austen-Smith and Jeffrey S. Banks
Positive Political Theory II: Strategy and Structure

Positive Political Theory II
Strategy and Structure

David Austen-Smith and Jeffrey S. Banks

THE UNIVERSITY OF MICHIGAN PRESS
Ann Arbor

Copyright © by the University of Michigan 2005
All rights reserved
Published in the United States of America by
The University of Michigan Press
Manufactured in the United States of America
∞ Printed on acid-free paper

2010   2009   2008   2007   5 4 3 2

No part of this publication may be reproduced,
stored in a retrieval system, or transmitted in any form
or by any means, electronic, mechanical, or otherwise,
without the written permission of the publisher.

A CIP catalog record for this book is available from the British Library.

Library of Congress Cataloging-in-Publication Data

Austen-Smith, David.
   Positive political theory II : strategy and structure / David Austen-Smith
and Jeffrey S. Banks.
   p. cm. — (Michigan studies in political analysis)
   Includes bibliographical references and index.
   ISBN 0-472-09894-2 (alk. paper) — ISBN 0-472-06894-6 (pbk. : alk. paper)
   1. Political science—Methodology. 2. Political science—Decision making.
3. Rational choice theory. 4. Social choice. 5. Elections. 6. Voting. I. Title:
Positive political theory two. II. Banks, Jeffrey S. III. Title. IV. Series.

JA71.A763   2005
321.8′01—dc22   2004058014

ISBN 978-0-472-09894-1 (alk. paper)
ISBN 978-0-472-06894-4 (pbk. : alk. paper)

ISBN 978-0-472-02247-2 (electronic)

To the memory of

Jeffrey S. Banks
1958-2000
and
Richard D. McKelvey
1944-2002

You leave us too soon.

Contents

Acknowledgments	xi
Preface	xiii
1 Preliminaries	**1**
1.1 Review	1
1.2 Decision theory	8
1.3 Discussion	16
1.4 Exercises	17
1.5 Further reading	18
2 Strategy-Proof Collective Choice	**19**
2.1 Strategy-proofness on finite sets	20
2.2 Application: The amendment rule	29
2.3 Strategy-proofness and Arrovian aggregation	30
2.4 Single-peaked preferences	33
2.5 Application: The amendment rule revisited	52
2.6 Strategy-proofness in the spatial model	53
2.7 Application: The issue-by-issue rule	61
2.8 Separable preferences	63
2.9 Discussion	66
2.10 Exercises	67
2.11 Further reading	68
3 Implementable Collective Choice	**69**
3.1 Mechanisms and equilibria	70
3.2 The Revelation Principle	74
3.3 Nash implementation	78
3.4 Application: Monotonicity of electoral rules	90
3.5 Quasi-linear preferences	94

3.6	Application: Collective action	104
3.7	Discussion	105
3.8	Exercises	109
3.9	Further reading	110

4 Binary Agendas   113
4.1	Binary agendas and sophisticated voting	114
4.2	Equilibrium outcomes of binary agendas	128
4.3	Application: Agenda independence	138
4.4	Discussion	142
4.5	Exercises	144
4.6	Further reading	146

5 Spatial Voting in Committees   147
5.1	Issue-by-issue voting in the spatial model	148
5.2	Application: Committees and cabinets	158
5.3	Endogenous agendas	166
5.4	Application: Sophisticated sincerity	184
5.5	Discussion	186
5.6	Exercises	188
5.7	Further reading	190

6 Legislative Bargaining   193
6.1	A basic framework	194
6.2	Bargaining over distributions	204
6.3	Application: Pork barrel politics	221
6.4	Bargaining over policy	224
6.5	Application: Coalition government formation	244
6.6	Discussion	248
6.7	Exercises	250
6.8	Further reading	251

7 Two-Candidate Elections   253
7.1	Electoral equilibrium and the core	254
7.2	Application: Ideological convergence	259
7.3	Equilibrium in multidimensional spaces	262
7.4	Application: Progressive taxation	280
7.5	Probabilistic voting	282
7.6	Application: Director's Law	289
7.7	Policy-motivated candidates	293

7.8	Application: Ideological divergence	301
7.9	Turnout	304
7.10	Discussion	322
7.11	Exercises	328
7.12	Further reading	330

8 Multicandidate Elections — 333

8.1	Sincere voting in multicandidate elections	335
8.2	Application: Comparing electoral rules	342
8.3	Strategic voting	344
8.4	Application: Duverger's Law	352
8.5	Candidate entry	353
8.6	Application: Duverger and divergence	379
8.7	Discussion	382
8.8	Exercises	387
8.9	Further reading	388

9 Legislative Elections — 391

9.1	Elections, government and policy	392
9.2	Application: Representative legislatures	413
9.3	Discussion	415
9.4	Exercises	416
9.5	Further reading	417

10 Summary and Conclusions — 419

10.1	Retrospective	421
10.2	A conclusion	427

Bibliography — 429

Index — 445

Acknowledgments

Undeniably the deepest debt is owed to Jeffrey Scot Banks. Although drafts of some sections of the chapters herein already existed, spin-offs from working on *Positive Political Theory I: Collective Preference* [11], we did not begin this volume until September 2000. In October of that year, Jeff was admitted to the hospital, where he remained until his death two months later, on the twenty-first of December 2000. Nevertheless, *Positive Political Theory II: Strategy and Structure* is as much due to Jeff as it is to me; in part because it draws extensively on his work, but mostly because Jeff's view and understanding of the field so deeply influenced my own. With *Positive Political Theory I*, this book completes a collaborative project that almost surely would not have been started without Jeff. I miss him sorely.

In addition to a great many of Jeff's and my friends who offered encouragement and support during the writing of this book, I owe thanks to several people for more specific help with the project. John Duggan graciously allowed me to include some unpublished (at the time of writing) results by (among others) Jeff Banks and himself, patiently responding to what must have seemed like an endless litany of questions about the details and technicalities therein. Richard McKelvey and Raghu Sundaram both provided valuable help at various times. Matthias Dahm, Hulya Eraslan, Maggie Penn, Gregory Pavlov and Razvan Vlaicu all read chapters and offered detailed comments and constructive suggestions. My friends and colleagues at Northwestern University, Steven Callander, Daniel Diermeier, Tim Feddersen, Ken Shotts and Michael Wallerstein, consistently helped me see what I was trying to say at many junctures in the development of the manuscript. Roger Myerson helped me understand his theory of Poisson games, providing a proof within this theory for Theorem 8.3. And despite his experience dealing with us in regard to *Positive Political Theory I*, Bob Turring again translated hand-drawn diagrams into legible figures, tolerating many revisions and last-minute changes without complaint. None of these people, however, can be held responsible for any errors remaining or views expressed in the chapters to follow; that privilege rests with me.

Finally, I could not have managed at all without the love and understanding of my wife, Maggie, and children Clare and Luke, or the friendship and encouragement of Jeff's widow, Shannon, and sons Bryan and Danny. Thank you from both of us.

David Austen-Smith
April 2004

Note added, March 2014. Since the time of publication, varous obscurities and errors in the text, ranging from the essentially typographical to the substantively significant, have been observed. I am grateful to the many people who have brought them to my attention. The text to follow corrects the identified errors including, I hope, all of the more egregious substantive mistakes. I cannot promise, however, that the book is now completely free of mistakes and I retain all responsibility for those that remain.

David Austen-Smith

Preface

As with its precursor, *Positive Political Theory I: Collective Preference*, this book is concerned with understanding the connection between individuals' preferences within any society and the collective choices of that society. Motivated by the canonical rational choice theoretic model of decision-making, *Positive Political Theory I* [PPTI] explores "the possibility that individual preferences are directly aggregated into a collective, or social, preference relation which ... is then maximized to yield a set of best alternatives (where "best" is here defined as being most preferred with respect to the collective preference relation)" [PPTI, p.xi]. To the extent that this is possible, therefore, a theory of political behavior can be built around an appropriate "as if" assumption, whereby the society as a whole is treated anthropomorphically as a single, representative, agent endowed with the social preference relation. Perhaps unfortunately, it turns out that direct preference aggregation yields a well-defined theory of political decisions in this sense only when the environment is relatively simple, having few alternatives or limited heterogeneity in the distribution of individual preferences, or when the political system endows some individuals with veto power over all collective choices. In complex environments or in polities where the approval of some particular individual or individuals is not required for all social decisions, however, the existence of "best alternatives" is not assured and the value of the direct aggregation theory as a positive theory of collective choice is attenuated. But the direct aggregation of individual preferences is not equivalent to the indirect aggregation of preferences through the aggregation of individual actions; in particular, actions to determine the alternatives for collective choice (agenda selection) and actions to determine the choice of an alternative from those available (voting).

The difficulty with using a direct preference aggregation approach to develop positive (that is, explanatory or predictive) accounts of political behavior in relatively complex environments lies with an insistence that acceptable collective decisions respect a minimal democracy constraint, loosely, that no single individual gets his or her way whenever he or she is unanimously opposed by the rest of society. The argument of *Positive Political Theory I* is that, while this sort of constraint does not bind for simple decisions or relatively homogenous populations, it essentially precludes any acceptable compromise when decisions are complex or preferences heterogenous. Moreover, the indirect preference aggregation approach is not immune to this difficulty [PPTI, ch.7].

Developing an indirect preference aggregation theory requires developing a theory of how individual actions are linked, both to individual preferences and to the actions of others. The notion of a "wasted vote" in elections with, say, three candidates for a given office provides a clear example: an individual may strictly prefer candidate A to candidate B, and strictly prefer candidate B to candidate C; but if the individual believes or conjectures that sufficient numbers of other voters are voting for B and C to make A's chances of election negligible, then the individual is better off voting for B to minimize the chance that his or her least favorite candidate, C, wins. At the least, therefore, a coherent explanatory theory of how individuals act in such situations entails some notion of mutual consistency or compatibility among individual actions; without such consistency, every imaginable pattern of behavior is admissible and there is no basis on which to build a systematic account of collective choice. The notions of mutual consistency of concern in the chapters to follow are the equilibrium concepts of game theory. Thus the analogue to exploring the existence and characterization of suitably defined maximal sets of alternatives in the direct theory of collective preference is exploring the existence and characterization of suitably defined equilibrium sets of actions and the collective choices they induce. And it turns out that while equilibrium sets of actions quite generally exist, they occasionally imply some violation of the minimal democracy constraint. That is, an equilibrium outcome can be an alternative that is strictly less preferred to a distinct (non-equilibrium) outcome by all but at most one member of the society. Therefore, the direct (collective preference) and indirect (game-theoretic) "approaches to the study of collective decision-making differ not with respect to existence of solutions *per se* but rather with respect to the implicit trade-off each makes between existence and minimal democracy" [PPTI, p.xv]. Analysing the implications of making this trade-off occupies the chapters to follow.

We are especially interested in indirect preference aggregation through agenda-selection and voting within more-or-less democratic political institutions. The simplest model of indirect preference aggregation falling under this rubric is perhaps that of direct democracy: individuals report a prefer-

PREFACE

ence over alternatives by voting and some rule is used to "add up" votes to arrive at the collective choice. Direct democracy is a special case of a more complicated model with intermediate stages between individual votes and the determination of a final policy or collective choice. In particular, representative systems typically involve first choosing a set of representatives who subsequently make the collective choice. The focus of the book, therefore, is on representative systems, loosely described by a two-stage process, elections and legislative decision-making. And throughout, the concern is with connecting individual preferences to collective outcomes and not with providing a comprehensive descriptive account of all aspects of representative democracy.

After reviewing some salient concepts and notation from *Positive Political Theory I* and elsewhere in Chapter 1, Chapter 2 considers the extent to which direct collective choice procedures provide incentives for individuals to misrepresent their preferences: if there are reasonable procedures that always induce truthful preference revelation, then there is little reason to worry about political outcomes being subject to manipulation as votes are direct representations of individuals' preferences. We argue, however, that the opportunity for strategic manipulation of collective decisions is inherent in any reasonable (nondictatorial and responsive) polity. There are two responses to this result. The first, explored in Chapter 3, is to look for institutions and mechanisms that, conditional on a prior commitment to how outcomes should be associated with lists of individual preferences, offer incentives for individuals to take actions that yield precisely the outcomes chosen under truthful reporting of preferences. Although it is possible to design such mechanisms, they are typically sensitive to details of how individuals are presumed to behave and, at least in the absence of limitations on individual preferences, are peculiarly complicated, bearing at most a cursory resemblance to any observed political institution. Empirical political institutions, therefore, are necessarily more than instruments for identifying and implementing the collective decisions associated with sincerely revealed preferences. The second response, then, is to take the institutions we observe and study the connection between individual preferences, individual actions and collective choices induced through these institutions. We begin with legislatures.

Policy-making within legislatures involves many things and we simplify considerably. Chapter 4 considers committee voting over a fixed agenda and Chapter 5 exploits the analysis of Chapter 4 to provide some understanding of how agendas are formed in a variety of legislative settings. Voting is not the only legislative activity of interest, however, and Chapter 6 develops a theory of bargaining over legislative policy. In the theory, legislators are periodically "recognized" and given the right to offer an alternative for the policy outcome; if a winning coalition of legislators supports the proposal then that fixes the decision and bargaining stops; if a proposal is rejected, another legislator is recognized and the sequence repeats until some decision is reached. An important lesson from the analysis of these three chapters is that having agenda-setting or proposal rights allows legislators to influence final decisions to their particular advantage, even when individuals are otherwise identical up to the description of their preferences over outcomes.

Legislators are elected. The simplest nontrivial election involves two candidates competing for a single elected office and Chapter 7 considers the theory of these elections in some detail. Although some attention is paid to questions of voter turnout and abstention here, the emphasis, consistent with the underlying theme of indirect preference aggregation, is less on accounting for abstention *per se* and more on understanding how abstention affects candidates' selection of electoral platforms. Despite the analytical importance of two-candidate elections, a great many elections involve more than two candidates and, furthermore, assuming any fixed number of candidates precludes any explanation of the number of electoral candidates choosing to compete. Chapter 8, therefore, concerns the theory of multicandidate elections, initially with a fixed and then with an endogenous number of candidates. The results here are complicated by the associated complexity of the voters' decision: with only two candidates, instrumentally rational and policy-oriented voters have a clear decision rule; this is not (as the example of the wasted vote above suggests) true when there are more than two candidates for a given elected office.

In a considerably simplified environment, Chapter 9 ties electoral and legislative stages together with an integrated model of three-party electoral competition for legislative representation, followed by a legislative bargaining process to determine both the governing coalition and final collective choice. It is apparent from Chapter 9 that the mapping that connects individuals' preferences and final collective choices induced through a representative democratic system is subtle. Moreover, the analysis suggests that conclusions for collective choice drawn exclusively on the basis of an electoral or a legislative model are not obviously robust when compared to those drawn on the basis of a model that explicitly includes both stages.

Chapter 10 provides an overview, tying the formal analysis of the text to a recurrent theme of the book, that the indirect approach to preference aggregation is the complement of the direct approach. The direct approach links preferences to outcomes through maximization of a derived social pref-

PREFACE xvii

erence relation; the indirect approach links preferences to outcomes through strategic agenda selection and voting. Both approaches concern mapping individuals' preferences into collective choice.

This book is not a survey. It is, rather, intended as a coherent, cumulative development of a more abstract concern with connecting preferences indirectly to collective choice through strategic behavior. Many aspects of political behavior are therefore ignored, to a large extent excluded as peripheral to this concern; there is, for instance, no consideration of international relations, interest groups, the influence of money in politics or the implications of incomplete information. Similarly, the noncooperative strategic approach we adopt throughout leaves aside important literatures that exploit a more cooperative game-theoretic perspective on a variety of topics as, for example, the cooperative game-theoretic models of coalition formation.

Finally it should be noted that, in common with *Positive Political Theory I*, "although most (but not all) of the results reported were originally derived by others, in the interests of continuity we have chosen to leave the relevant credits to a 'further reading' section at the end of each chapter. If we have missed anyone in this regard, we apologize. With very few exceptions, all of the results are proved explicitly in the text and we have tried to make the formal arguments as transparent and self-contained as possible. Consequently, some of the proofs are less succinct than they might otherwise be and some of the results are not proved in their most general form" [PPTI, p.xv].

Chapter 1

Preliminaries

Positive Political Theory I: Collective Preference concerns the problem of aggregating individual preferences directly into some sort of collective preference or choice. The current book concerns the problem of aggregating individual preferences indirectly, through individual actions, to arrive at a collective choice. These two perspectives, as we argue in *Positive Political Theory I* and elaborate in this text, are far from mutually exclusive. *Inter alia*, much of the analytical apparatus of, and many of the lessons from, the theory of collective preference proves important for the theory of indirect preference aggregation. Before moving on to develop this theory, therefore, it is useful first to review the salient notation, concepts and results from *Positive Political Theory I* (where a more detailed discussion of the material can be found) and to introduce the necessary decision theory for the chapters to follow.

1.1 Review

Let X be a (finite or infinite) set of alternatives and let $\mathcal{X}$ be the family of all nonempty subsets of X. A *binary preference relation* R on the set X describes the relative merits of pairs of outcomes in X: for any two alternatives $x, y \in X$, the statement xRy means that (with respect to R) "x is at least as good as y". Define the asymmetric part of R, the strict preference relation, P, by xPy ("x is strictly better than y") if and only if xRy and $\sim[yRx]$, all $x, y \in X$; similarly, define the symmetric part of R, the indifference relation, I, by xIy ("x and y are at least as good as each other") if and only if xRy and yRx, all $x, y \in X$. The relation R is a *weak preference order* on X if R is *reflexive* (for all $x \in X$, xRx), *complete* (for all $x, y \in X$, xRy or yRx or both) and *transitive* (for all $x, y, z \in X$, xRy and yRz implies xRz). Let $\mathcal{R}$ (respectively, $\mathcal{P}$) denote the set of all weak (respectively, strict) preference orders on X.

Suppose the set of feasible alternatives X is a subset of some k-dimensional Euclidean space, $X \subset \Re^k$; assume X is *convex* (for all $x, y \in X$ and $t \in [0, 1]$, $[tx+(1-t)y] \in X$) and *compact* (X is closed and bounded). Fix a preference relation R on X and, for all $x \in X$, define the sets

$$P(x) = \{y \in X : yPx\}$$
$$P^{-1}(x) = \{y \in X : xPy\}.$$

Thus $P(x)$ is the set of alternatives that are strictly preferred to x and $P^{-1}(x)$ contains all those alternatives to which x is strictly preferred; these are sometimes referred to as the (strict) *upper* and *lower contour sets*, respectively, associated with R. The weak upper and lower contour sets, $R(x)$ and $R^{-1}(x)$ respectively, are defined analogously. A binary relation R is said to be *continuous* on X if, for all $x \in X$, both $P(x)$ and $P^{-1}(x)$ are open relative to X. A virtue of continuous preference orders on convex and compact sets of alternatives is that they admit continuous numerical representations. A *utility function* $u : X \to \Re$ represents R if and only if, for all $x, y \in X$,

$$xRy \Leftrightarrow u(x) \geq u(y).$$

In other words, u represents R if and only if it assigns higher numbers to strictly more preferred alternatives and assigns the same number to any pair of alternatives that are indifferent to each other. As defined, u is an ordinal representation; all that matters is whether, say, $u(x)$ is bigger or smaller than $u(y)$ and their particular cardinal values have no meaning whatsoever.

A preference ordering R on a convex set of alternatives $X \subseteq \Re^k$ is *convex* if xRy and $x \neq y$ imply $[tx+(1-t)y]Ry$ for all $t \in (0, 1)$; if $[tx+(1-t)y]Py$ for all $x \neq y$ and all $t \in (0, 1)$, we say R is *strictly convex*. Every continuous and convex preference relation R has a continuous *quasi-concave* representation, u; that is, for all $x, y \in X$ and all $t \in (0, 1)$,

$$u(tx + (1-t)y) \geq \min\{u(x), u(y)\}.$$

If R is strictly convex, the weak inequality can be replaced by a strict inequality and u is said to be strictly quasi-concave. An important feature of quasi-concave utilities is that, for all $r \in \Re$, the upper contour sets $\{x \in X : u(x) \geq r\}$ are convex. Let $\mathcal{R}_{cs} \subset \mathcal{R}$ denote the set of all continuous and strictly convex weak preference orders on X.

1.1. REVIEW

Let $N = \{1,\ldots,n\}$ be a finite set of individuals, $n \geq 2$. We assume throughout that each individual $i \in N$ is endowed with a weak preference order $R_i \in \mathcal{R}$ on X. A *preference profile* is then an n-tuple of weak orders $\rho = (R_1,\ldots,R_n)$ describing the preferences of all individuals. The set of all preference profiles is $\mathcal{R}^n$; for any $\rho \in \mathcal{R}^n$ and nonempty subset of alternatives $S \in \mathcal{X}$, let $\rho|_S = (R_1|_S,\ldots,R_n|_S)$ denote the restriction of ρ to the set S, i.e. $\rho|_S$ describes the individuals' preferences only over those alternatives in S. For any profile $\rho \in \mathcal{R}^n$ and any $x,y \in X$, let $P(x,y;\rho) \equiv \{i \in N : xP_iy\}$ be the set of individuals who strictly prefer x to y at profile ρ; the sets $R(x,y;\rho)$ and $I(x,y;\rho)$ are defined similarly. Finally, let $\mathcal{B}$ denote the set of all reflexive and complete binary preference relations on X.

Definition 1.1 *For any subset of profiles $\mathfrak{D} \subseteq \mathcal{R}^n$, a preference aggregation rule on $\mathfrak{D}$ is a map, $f : \mathfrak{D} \to \mathcal{B}$.*

Thus a preference aggregation rule assigns to every possible preference profile within the domain $\mathfrak{D}$, a reflexive and complete binary relation, which we can think of as the social or collective preference relation $f(\rho)$. Given $f(\rho) \in \mathcal{B}$ and $x,y \in X$ we occasionally denote the weak social preference as $xR_{f(\rho)}y \equiv xf(\rho)y$; thus, $xP_{f(\rho)}y \equiv (xf(\rho)y \ \& \sim [yf(\rho)x])$ and $xI_{f(\rho)}y \equiv (xf(\rho)y \ \& \ yf(\rho)x)$. And for notational ease we often leave the underlying preference domain or profile as understood, simply writing xRy and so on.

Example 1.1 Examples of preference aggregation rules on $\mathfrak{D} = \mathcal{R}^n$ are
 (1) *Simple majority rule*: $\forall x,y \in X$, xPy if and only if $|P(x,y;\rho)| > n/2$.
 (2) *q-rules*, $n/2 < q \leq n$: $\forall x,y \in X$, xPy if and only if $|P(x,y;\rho)| \geq q$.
 (3) *Plurality rule*: $\forall x,y \in X$, xPy if and only if $|P(x,y;\rho)| > |P(y,x;\rho)|$.
 (4) *Pareto extension rule*: $\forall x,y \in X$, xPy if and only if $R(x,y;\rho) = N$ and $P(x,y;\rho) \neq \emptyset$. □

If the domain of an aggregation rule f is $\mathfrak{D} = \mathcal{R}^n$, we say that f satisfies *unrestricted domain*. When $X \subseteq \Re^k$ is a continuum, the domain of continuous and strictly convex preference profiles on X, $\mathfrak{D} = \mathcal{R}^n_{cs}$, plays an important role. To avoid trivialities, assume throughout that there is at least one pair of alternatives $\{x,y\} \subseteq X$ on which $\mathfrak{D}|_{\{x,y\}} = \mathcal{R}^n|_{\{x,y\}}$. Other important possible properties of aggregation rules include the following [PPTI, ch.2]:

Definition 1.2 *A preference aggregation rule $f : \mathfrak{D} \to \mathcal{B}$ is*
 (1) Weakly Paretian if, for all $\rho \in \mathfrak{D}$ and any $x,y \in X$, $P(x,y;\rho) = N$ implies xPy;

(2) Independent of Irrelevant Alternatives if, for every $\rho, \rho' \in \mathfrak{D}$ and for any $x, y \in X$, $\rho|_{\{x,y\}} = \rho'|_{\{x,y\}}$ implies $f(\rho)|_{\{x,y\}} = f(\rho')|_{\{x,y\}}$;
(3) Transitive on X if, for all $\rho \in \mathfrak{D}$, $f(\rho)$ is transitive;
(4) Acyclic on X if, for all $\rho \in \mathfrak{D}$, for all alternatives $a_1, \ldots, a_r \in X$,

$$a_1 P_{f(\rho)} a_2 P_{f(\rho)} \ldots P_{f(\rho)} a_r \text{ implies } a_1 R_{f(\rho)} a_r.$$

In words, weakly Paretian aggregation rules respect pairwise unanimous preference, ranking an alternative x over an alternative y whenever all individuals strictly prefer x to y; rules that are independent of irrelevant alternatives evaluate any pair of alternatives exclusively on the basis of ordinal preference information over that pair, thus precluding any interpersonal comparisons or consideration of preference intensity; and, finally, transitive and acyclic aggregation rules exhibit degrees of internal consistency at all possible profiles in their domain, with transitivity being a more demanding consistency property than acyclicity [Exercise].

Hereafter, unless explicitly stated otherwise, assume an aggregation rule f satisfies unrestricted domain, $\mathfrak{D} = \mathcal{R}^n$. A set or coalition of individuals $L \subseteq N$ is a *decisive coalition* under the preference aggregation rule f, if for every profile $\rho \in \mathcal{R}^n$ and for all $x, y \in X$, $[xP_i y$, all $i \in L]$ implies xPy. A *dictator* for f is a decisive set consisting of exactly one individual $i \in N$. The family of decisive coalitions associated with an aggregation rule f, denoted $\mathcal{L}(f)$, is defined by

$$L \in \mathcal{L}(f) \Leftrightarrow [\forall x, y \in X, \ \forall \rho \in \mathcal{R}^n, \ xP_i y \ \forall i \in L \Rightarrow xPy].$$

It can be checked that if f is a preference aggregation rule then $\mathcal{L}(f)$ is *proper* ($L, L' \in \mathcal{L}(f)$ implies $L \cap L' \neq \emptyset$) and *monotonic* ($L \subset L'$ and $L \in \mathcal{L}(f)$ imply $L' \in \mathcal{L}(f)$) [Exercise]. Properness means that two distinct decisive coalitions cannot insist on contradictory collective preferences (otherwise there must be some individual who strictly prefers both x to y, say, and y to x); and monotonicity means that adding individuals to a decisive coalition results in a decisive coalition. For any family of coalitions $\mathcal{L} \subseteq 2^N$ we can define an aggregation rule induced by $\mathcal{L}$, denoted $f_{\mathcal{L}}$, as

$$\forall x, y \in X, \ xP_{\mathcal{L}} y \Leftrightarrow [\exists L \in \mathcal{L} : \forall i \in L, \ xP_i y].$$

Note that the induced aggregation rule $f_{\mathcal{L}}$ is only well-defined if $\mathcal{L}$ is proper.

Now consider the relationship between $f_{\mathcal{L}(f)}$, i.e. the aggregation rule generated by the decisive sets of an aggregation rule f and the original rule f itself.

1.1. REVIEW

Definition 1.3 *An aggregation rule f is a simple rule if $f = f_{\mathcal{L}(f)}$.*

Not all aggregation rules are simple. For example, consider simple plurality rule, f_p, defined on $\mathcal{R}^n$ by

$$x f_p(\rho) y \Leftrightarrow |P(x,y;\rho)| \geq |P(y,x;\rho)|$$

for all $x, y \in X$, and simple majority rule, f_m, defined on $\mathcal{R}^n$ by

$$x f_m(\rho) y \Leftrightarrow |P(x,y;\rho)| \geq n/2$$

for all $x, y \in X$. Then it is easy to check

$$\begin{aligned}\mathcal{L}(f_p) &= \{L \subseteq N : |L| > n/2\} \\ &= \mathcal{L}(f_m).\end{aligned}$$

Hence, $f_{\mathcal{L}(f_p)} = f_m$ but $f_p(\rho) \neq f_m(\rho)$ for at least some profiles; for instance, any profile such that $\rho|_{\{x,y\}} = (xP_1y, xI_2y, \ldots, xI_ny)$.

Many important properties of simple rules can be understood with the idea of the *Nakamura number* [PPTI, Definition 3.5]. A (not necessarily simple) preference aggregation rule f is *collegial* if there is at least one individual $i \in N$ who is a member of all of the decisive coalitions induced by f, $\bigcap_{L_i \in \mathcal{L}(f)} L_i \neq \emptyset$; the rule f is *noncollegial* otherwise.

Definition 1.4 *The Nakamura number of a simple rule f, labeled $s(f)$, is equal to ∞ if f is collegial; otherwise,*

$$s(f) \equiv \min\{|\mathcal{L}'| : \mathcal{L}' \subset \mathcal{L}(f) \text{ and } \cap_{L \in \mathcal{L}'} L = \emptyset\}.$$

In words, the Nakamura number associated with a noncollegial simple rule f is the number of coalitions in the smallest noncollegial subfamily, $\mathcal{L}$, of $\mathcal{L}(f)$. For example, if f is simple majority rule (and $n \neq 4$), then its Nakamura number is $s(f) = 3$; and if f is the Pareto extension rule, then $s(f) = \infty$. An important result is that a simple rule f defined on the unrestricted domain $\mathcal{R}^n$ over a finite set of alternatives X is acyclic on X if and only if $s(f) > |X|$ [PPTI, Theorem 3.2].

Simple rules comprise an important subset of the more general class of *voting rules*. Although, like all preference aggregation rules, voting rules induce (possibly empty) collections of decisive sets, if a voting rule f is not simple then it cannot be completely characterized by the family $\mathcal{L}(f)$. To define voting rules, therefore, we need to extend the idea of a family of decisive coalitions to that of a decisive structure. The *decisive structure* for an aggregation rule f, denoted $\mathcal{D}(f)$, is a family of ordered pairs of coalitions $(S, W) \subseteq N \times N$ such that

$$(S, W) \in \mathcal{D}(f) \Leftrightarrow S \subseteq W \text{ and } \forall x, y \in X, \forall \rho \in \mathcal{R}^n,$$

$$[xP_i y, \forall i \in S \text{ and } xR_j y, \forall j \in W] \Rightarrow xPy.$$

Individuals in S (respectively, W) strictly (respectively, weakly) prefer one alternative to another. Thus the decisive structure of f is a set of pairs of coalitions, with one coalition a subset of the other, such that when all individuals in the smaller coalition strictly prefer alternative x to alternative y and all individuals in the larger coalition weakly prefer x to y, then society strictly prefers x to y. Note that $\mathcal{L}(f)$ is the family of coalitions $L \subseteq N$ such that $(L, L) \in \mathcal{D}(f)$: as long as the members in L strictly prefer (say) x to y, then society strictly prefers x to y irrespective of the preferences of the remaining individuals. Thus simple rules are also voting rules but the converse is not true; plurality rule, for instance, is a voting rule. To check this, recall

$$\mathcal{L}(f_p) = \{L \subseteq N : |L| > n/2\}$$

and derive

$$\mathcal{D}(f_p) = \{(S, W) \subseteq N \times N : S \subseteq W \ \& \ |S| > |N \backslash W|\}.$$

Clearly, $|L| > n/2$ if and only if $|L| > |N \backslash L|$. Hence $L \in \mathcal{L}(f_p)$ if and only if $(L, L) \in \mathcal{D}(f_p)$; but $(S, W) \in \mathcal{D}(f_p)$ does not imply $S \in \mathcal{L}(f_p)$. On the other hand, if f_m is majority rule, we have $\mathcal{L}(f_m) \equiv \mathcal{L}(f_p)$ and

$$\mathcal{D}(f_m) = \{(L, L') \subseteq N \times N : L \in \mathcal{L}(f_m), \ L \subseteq L'\}.$$

Now for any set $\mathcal{D} \subseteq 2^N \times 2^N$ such that $(S, W) \in \mathcal{D}$ implies $S \subseteq W$, define the aggregation rule $f_\mathcal{D}$ induced by $\mathcal{D}$ as

$$\forall x, y \in X, xPy \Leftrightarrow [\exists (S, W) \in \mathcal{D} : \forall i \in S, \ xP_i y \text{ and } \forall i \in W, \ xR_i y].$$

Definition 1.5 *An aggregation rule f is a voting rule if $f = f_{\mathcal{D}(f)}$.*

A focus of *Positive Political Theory I* is on the existence of the *core*. Given any binary preference relation $R \in \mathcal{B}$ and nonempty subset of alternatives $S \subseteq X$, define the maximal set of alternatives in S under R by

$$M(R, S) = \{x \in S : \forall y \in S \backslash \{x\}, \ xRy\}.$$

1.1. REVIEW

The *core of f at ρ* is then given by

$$C_f(\rho) = M(f(\rho), X).$$

In the case that $X \subset \Re^k$ is convex and compact it can be proved that, if f is a voting rule and ρ is a profile of strictly convex preference orders, then $C_f(\rho) = C_{f_{\mathcal{L}(f)}}(\rho)$ [PPTI, Theorem 5.2]. In words, the core of a voting rule $f : \mathcal{R}_{cs}^n \to \mathcal{B}$ is exactly the core of the simple rule induced by the decisive coalitions of $f_{\mathcal{L}(f)}$. Moreover, if $X \subset \Re^k$ is convex, compact and has dimension $k \geq 1$, any simple rule $f : \mathcal{R}_{cs}^n \to \mathcal{B}$, with Nakamura number $s(f)$, has a nonempty core for all profiles $\rho \in \mathcal{R}_{cs}^n$ if and only if $s(f) > k+1$ [PPTI, Theorems 5.3 and 5.4].

Suppose $X \subset \Re^k$, $f : \mathcal{R}_{cs}^n \to \mathcal{B}$ is a simple rule and, for all $i \in N$, let u_i denote the (strictly) quasi-concave utility function representing $R_i \in \mathcal{R}_{cs}$. Let ℓ be any straight line through $\Re^k$ and, for any $i \in N$, let

$$b_i(\ell) = \arg\max[u_i(z) : z \in \ell \cap X]$$

be i's *induced ideal point* on ℓ. For any $y \in \ell \cap X$, partition ℓ into $\{y\}$ and the two open half-lines, $h^-(y)$ and $h^+(y)$, originating from y; let

$$L^+(y) = \{i \in N : b_i(\ell) \in h^+(y)\}$$

and

$$L^-(y) = \{i \in N : b_i(\ell) \in h^-(y)\}.$$

Then, for all $\rho \in \mathcal{R}_{cs}^n$, the set of *induced f-medians* in X on ℓ is defined by

$$\mu_f(\rho|\ell) = \{z \in \ell \cap X : L^+(z) \notin \mathcal{L}(f) \ \& \ L^-(z) \notin \mathcal{L}(f)\}.$$

If an aggregation rule f is weakly Paretian, then the core $C_f(\rho)$ for $\rho \in \mathcal{R}^n$ is necessarily a subset of the *Pareto set at ρ*, $PS_N(\rho)$

$$PS_N(\rho) = \{x \in X : \forall y \neq x, \ P(y, x; \rho) \neq \emptyset \Rightarrow P(x, y; \rho) \neq \emptyset\}.$$

An alternative x is in the Pareto set, or is *Pareto efficient*, at ρ if, whenever some individual strictly prefers an alternative y to x, there is a distinct individual who strictly prefers x to y. In other words, an alternative y is *not* in the Pareto set if there exists a feasible alternative x such that, for all $i \in N$, xR_iy and, for some $j \in N$, xP_jy. Unlike the core, however, the Pareto set is never empty (at least on compact sets of alternatives).

Oftentimes, the interest is in selecting particular alternatives directly from X rather than worrying about deriving some sort of collective preference relation over X as a whole. In these circumstances, the relevant notion is that of a collective choice rule. A *collective choice rule* on a preference domain $\mathfrak{D}$ is a map, $\varphi : \mathfrak{D} \times \mathcal{X} \to \mathcal{X}$, such that $\varphi(\rho, S) \subseteq S$ for all $(\rho, S) \in \mathfrak{D} \times \mathcal{X}$ [PPTI, sect.2.5]. A rule φ is *anonymous* if and only if, for all $S \in \mathcal{X}$ and all $\rho, \rho' \in \mathfrak{D}$ such that ρ' differs from ρ only in the assignment of preference orderings to individuals, $\varphi(\rho, S) = \varphi(\rho', S)$; thus anonymous rules treat individuals' names or labels as irrelevant for collective choice [PPTI, sect.3.5]. A collective choice rule φ is *resolute* if $\varphi(\rho, S)$ is singleton at every point; resolute collective choice rules are *collective choice functions*. In effect, if the core of a preference aggregation rule f on $\mathfrak{D}$ is nonempty, it is a collective choice rule on the domain $\mathfrak{D} \times \{X\}$. Unless explicitly noted otherwise, the subset of alternatives $S \in \mathcal{X}$ to which a choice rule φ is applied is assumed to be X; in this case, we simply write $\varphi : \mathfrak{D} \to \mathcal{X}$ or $\varphi : \mathfrak{D} \rightrightarrows X$ when φ is a possibly multivalued choice rule and write $\varphi : \mathfrak{D} \to X$ if φ is resolute.

1.2 Decision theory

Rational choice theory, broadly understood to refer to the assumption that individuals choose only actions and alternatives from among those available that rank highest in their preference orderings, imposes no constraints at all upon how individuals might or might not evaluate uncertainty. For this book we assume individuals make decisions under uncertainty according to *expected utility theory*. For an individual faced with making a decision under uncertainty, the consequences of any action or choice are known only up to a (typically subjective) specification of their probabilities of occurrence, conditional on that action or choice. Choosing between acts under uncertainty is equivalent, therefore, to choosing between lotteries. For example, choosing between driving within, and driving faster than, the speed limit may or may not result in a speeding ticket. The probability of getting a ticket when driving within the speed limit is zero and it is some number $p \in (0, 1)$ if you speed. Thus in choosing between keeping to or exceeding the speed limit, you are in effect choosing between the (degenerate) lottery in which the probability of a speeding ticket is zero and the (nondegenerate) lottery in which it is $p > 0$.

In general there are several (possibly a continuum of) feasible consequences, any of which may or may not occur with positive probability conditional on any one available act being chosen. In the trivial example above, although the consequence "get speeding ticket" exists whichever act is chosen, it carries positive probability only if the act chosen is "exceed the speed limit". Assume, for convenience, that there is only a finite set of possible

1.2. DECISION THEORY

outcomes.

Definition 1.6 *A lottery on (finite) X is a function $p : X \to \Re$ such that: (1) for all $x \in X$, $p(x) \in [0, 1]$, and (2) $\sum_{x \in X} p(x) = 1$.*

Let $\mathbf{P}(X)$ be the set of lotteries over X. Then we can identify choosing an act with choosing a lottery $p \in \mathbf{P}(X)$. (For more general sets X, the definition replaces summations with integrals of appropriate probability distribution functions, or probability measures, on X.) Observe that $\mathbf{P}(X)$ is a compact and convex subset of $\Re^{|X|}$; in particular, X finite does not imply $\mathbf{P}(X)$ finite.

Expected utility theory postulates a set of axioms on individual preferences over lotteries, and shows that a person can satisfy these axioms if and only if there exists a utility function u defined over X, a *von Neumann-Morgenstern utility*, such that lottery p is considered at least as good as lottery p' by the individual if and only if

$$\sum_{x \in X} p(x)u(x) \geq \sum_{x \in X} p'(x)u(x).$$

Furthermore, if u is a von Neumann-Morgenstern utility and $\alpha \in \Re$, $\beta > 0$ then the function $v = \alpha + \beta u$ is also a von Neumann-Morgenstern utility. In other words, von Neumann-Morgenstern utility functions are unique up to positive affine transformations. For this reason, von Neumann-Morgenstern utilities are cardinal although not comparable, since there is no presumption that the parameters α, β are common across individuals.

Formally, let $\tilde{R}$ denote a binary preference relation on $\mathbf{P}(X)$, with asymmetric and symmetric parts $\tilde{P}$ and $\tilde{I}$, respectively.

Definition 1.7 *A binary relation $\tilde{R}$ on $\mathbf{P}(X)$ satisfies*
(1) continuity if, for all $p, p', p'' \in \mathbf{P}(X)$, $p\tilde{P}p'\tilde{P}p''$ implies there exists a number $t \in [0, 1]$ such that $[tp + (1-t)p'']\tilde{I}p'$;
(2) independence if, for all $p, p', p'' \in \mathbf{P}(X)$ and all $t \in (0, 1)$, $p\tilde{R}p'$ implies

$$[tp + (1-t)p'']\tilde{R}[tp' + (1-t)p''].$$

Continuity means that if an individual can strictly order three distinct lotteries, then there is always another lottery, defined by a particular convex combination of the best- and worst-ranked lotteries, that is indifferent to the middle-ranked lottery. Figure 1.1 illustrates the idea for a two-outcome set X. All lotteries over two outcomes can be summarized by the probability p that the most preferred of the two alternatives occurs, so $\mathbf{P}(X) = [0, 1]$ and lotteries $[t'p + (1-t')p'']$, $t' \in [0, 1]$, are described by the upward-sloping line.

$p\tilde{P}p'\tilde{P}p''$

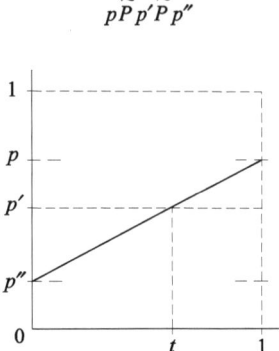

Figure 1.1: The continuity property

Independence is a less transparent property. It says that if an individual (at least weakly) prefers one lottery p to another p', then that individual should always prefer a compound lottery defined by any convex combination of p and some arbitrary third lottery p'' to the compound lottery defined by the same convex combination of p' and p''. Figure 1.2 gives a diagrammatic representation of independence: the upper panel illustrates the lotteries p and p'; the lower panel describes the compound lotteries $[tp + (1-t)p'']$ and $[tp' + (1-t)p'']$.

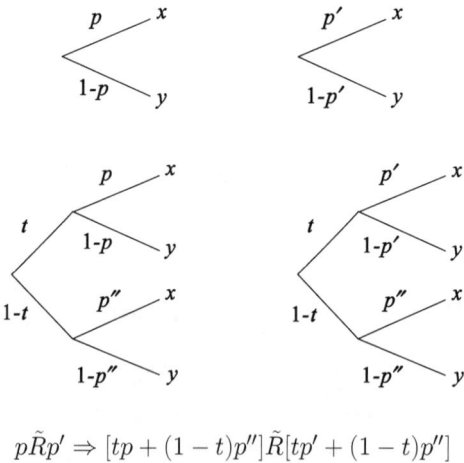

$p\tilde{R}p' \Rightarrow [tp + (1-t)p'']\tilde{R}[tp' + (1-t)p'']$

Figure 1.2: The independence property

1.2. DECISION THEORY

Substantively, independence means that an individual decomposes lotteries into components as far as possible and ranks the lotteries only on the basis of the distinctive components of each gamble. In the example of Figure 1.2, the lottery p'' appears identically in both of the illustrated compound lotteries and, therefore, is deemed irrelevant to the individual's ranking of these gambles.

Example 1.2 Consider the two-stage gamble in which, first, a biased coin is flipped and then, conditional on the outcome of the coin-flip, payoffs are allocated according to a second randomization device. Specifically, with probability 1/3 the coin comes up Heads and with probability 2/3 the coin comes up Tails; if Heads is the outcome, there is a payoff u with probability 1/5, a payoff u' with probability 2/5, and a payoff u'' with probability 2/5; on the other hand, if Tails is the outcome, there is a payoff v with probability 1/6, a payoff v' with probability 1/2, and a payoff v'' with probability 1/3.

Now consider a single-stage gamble in which there is a payoff u with probability 1/15, a payoff u' with probability 2/15, and a payoff u'' with probability 2/15, a payoff v with probability 1/9, a payoff v' with probability 1/3, and a payoff v'' with probability 2/9.

Under the independence axiom, these two gambles are, as is easily confirmed, identical. □

Assuming an individual's preferences over lotteries can be described by a continuous and independent weak preference ordering yields some useful properties of that ordering. A degenerate lottery is a lottery p for which $p(x) = 1$ for some $x \in X$.

Lemma 1.1 Assume $\tilde{R}$ is a weak order on $\mathbf{P}(X)$ satisfying continuity and independence and let $p, p', p'' \in \mathbf{P}(X)$. Then:

(1) $p\tilde{P}p'$ and $0 \leq s < t \leq 1$ imply

$$[tp + (1-t)p']\tilde{P}[sp + (1-s)p'];$$

(2) $p\tilde{R}p'\tilde{R}p''$ and $p\tilde{P}p''$ imply there exists a unique $t^* \in [0,1]$ such that

$$[t^*p + (1-t^*)p'']\tilde{I}p';$$

(3) There exist degenerate lotteries $\bar{p}, \underline{p} \in \mathbf{P}(X)$ such that, for all $p \in \mathbf{P}(X)$,

$$\bar{p}\tilde{R}p\tilde{R}\underline{p}.$$

Proof (1) Suppose $s = 0$. Then $p\tilde{P}p'$, independence and $0 < t \leq 1$ imply

$$[tp + (1-t)p']\tilde{P}[tp' + (1-t)p'] = p' = [sp + (1-s)p'].$$

Now suppose $s > 0$; let $r = s/t$ and write $p'' = [tp + (1-t)p']$. By independence and $r < 1$,

$$p'' = [(1-r)p'' + rp'']\tilde{P}[(1-r)p' + rp''];$$

and by definition

$$\begin{aligned}(1-r)p' + rp'' &= (1-r)p' + r[tp + (1-t)p']\\ &= sp + (1-s)p'.\end{aligned}$$

Therefore,

$$p'' = [tp + (1-t)p']\tilde{P}[sp + (1-s)p']$$

as required.

(2) Continuity implies existence and uniqueness follows from claim (1) and $p\tilde{P}p''$.

(3) Let $\mathbf{L} \subset \mathbf{P}(X)$ be the set of degenerate lotteries; by definition, $|\mathbf{L}| = |X|$. By assumption, $\tilde{R}$ is a weak order on $\mathbf{P}(X)$ and, therefore, $\tilde{R}|_\mathbf{L}$ is a weak order on $\mathbf{L}$. Hence there exist degenerate lotteries $\bar{p}, \underline{p} \in \mathbf{L}$ such that, for all $q \in \mathbf{L}$, $\bar{p}\tilde{R}q\tilde{R}\underline{p}$. The claim therefore holds on $\mathbf{L}$. We now argue by induction on the cardinality of the support of lotteries to show the claim holds on $\mathbf{P}(X)$. So suppose that, for any (nondegenerate) lottery $p \in \mathbf{P}(X)$ with support of cardinality $1 \leq m < |X|$, we have $\bar{p}\tilde{R}p\tilde{R}\underline{p}$ (the support of p is the set, $\{x \in X : p(x) > 0\}$). By independence, for all $t \in (0,1)$ and any degenerate lottery $q \in \mathbf{L}$,

$$[t\bar{p} + (1-t)q]\tilde{R}[tp + (1-t)q]\tilde{R}[t\underline{p} + (1-t)q].$$

But since $\bar{p}\tilde{R}q\tilde{R}\underline{p}$ for all $q \in \mathbf{L}$, independence also yields

$$\bar{p} = [t\bar{p} + (1-t)\bar{p}]\tilde{R}[t\bar{p} + (1-t)q]$$

and

$$[t\underline{p} + (1-t)q]\tilde{R}[t\underline{p} + (1-t)\underline{p}] = \underline{p}.$$

Hence, by transitivity of $\tilde{R}$, $\bar{p}\tilde{R}[tp+(1-t)q]\tilde{R}\underline{p}$. But the support of the lottery $[tp + (1-t)q]$ is $m+1$ and, because both p and q are chosen arbitrarily (up to p having support of cardinality m, and $q \in \mathbf{L}$), we have that the claim holds for all $p' \in \mathbf{P}(X)$ with support $m+1$; that is, $\bar{p}\tilde{R}p'\tilde{R}\underline{p}$. Since the claim

1.2. DECISION THEORY

surely holds on **L** and therefore for all lotteries with support of cardinality one, the result follows from induction. □

We can now prove the existence of a von Neumann-Morgenstern utility function. The proof is constructive. The basic idea of the construction is to note, by part (3) of the lemma, that there is a best-ranked, $\bar{p}$, and a worst-ranked lottery, $\underline{p}$, and these are degenerate, putting probability one on, say, $\bar{x}$ and $\underline{x}$ respectively; set $u(\bar{x}) = 1$ and $u(\underline{x}) = 0$. Now, for every other alternative $x' \in X$ there is a degenerate lottery p' with $p'(x') = 1$; moreover, $\bar{p}\tilde{R}p'\tilde{R}\underline{p}$ by definition of $\bar{p}$ and $\underline{p}$. Therefore, part (2) of the lemma can be used to find a unique number $t' \in [0,1]$ such that $[t'\bar{p} + (1-t')\underline{p}]\tilde{I}p'$; set $u(x') = t'$. The complications in the proof come from dealing with nondegenerate lotteries and checking that the construction indeed admits the expected utility representation for the ordering $\tilde{R}$.

Theorem 1.1 *If $\tilde{R}$ is a weak order on $\mathbf{P}(X)$ satisfying continuity and independence, then there exists a utility function $u : X \to \Re$ such that $\sum_{x \in X} p(x)u(x)$ represents $\tilde{R}$; that is, for all $p, p' \in \mathbf{P}(X)$,*

$$p\tilde{R}p' \Leftrightarrow \sum_{x \in X} p(x)u(x) \geq \sum_{x \in X} p'(x)u(x).$$

Proof Let $\tilde{R}$ satisfy the hypotheses of the theorem and define $\bar{p}, \underline{p} \in \mathbf{L}$ as in Lemma 1.1(3). If $\bar{p}\tilde{I}\underline{p}$ then Lemma 1.1(3) implies $p\tilde{I}p'$ for all $p, p' \in \mathbf{P}(X)$, in which case choosing $u(x) = a$ for some constant a and all $x \in X$, suffices. So assume hereafter that $\bar{p}\tilde{P}\underline{p}$.

For any $p \in \mathbf{P}(X)$, define the function $f(p) = t$ where $t \in [0,1]$ is such that $[t\bar{p} + (1-t)\underline{p}]\tilde{I}p$; by Lemma 1.1(2), t exists and is unique. By Lemma 1.1(1) and $\tilde{R}$ a weak order,

$$f(p) > f(p') \Leftrightarrow [f(p)\bar{p} + (1-f(p))\underline{p}]\tilde{P}[f(p')\bar{p} + (1-f(p'))\underline{p}] \Leftrightarrow p\tilde{P}p'.$$

Thus f represents $\tilde{R}$. It remains to show f must be the expectation claimed in the statement of the theorem. To do this, first note that repeated use of independence implies that, for all $p, p' \in \mathbf{P}(X)$ and $t \in [0,1]$,

$$[tp + (1-t)p']\tilde{I}\left(t[f(p)\bar{p} + (1-f(p))\underline{p}] + (1-t)[f(p')\bar{p} + (1-f(p'))\underline{p}]\right).$$

By definition of f, therefore,

$$f(tp + (1-t)p') = tf(p) + (1-t)f(p') \qquad (*)$$

For any $x \in X$, let $q_x \in \mathbf{L}$ denote the degenerate lottery with $q(x) = 1$. Then, for all $x \in X$, choose $u(x) = f(q_x)$. By $(*)$, the result is proved if $f(p) = \sum_{x \in X} p(x)u(x)$ for all $p \in \mathbf{P}(X)$. This is obviously true if $p \in \mathbf{L}$, since then $p(x) = 1$ for some $x \in X$ and $p(x') = 0$ for all $x' \neq x$. Given this fact, the argument proceeds by induction. Assume the equality is true for any lottery with support of cardinality $m - 1 \geq 1$, $|X| > m - 1$, and consider any lottery p with support of cardinality $m > 1$. Take any $x' \in X$ with $p(x') > 0$ and define $p' \in \mathbf{P}(X)$ by

$$p'(x) = \begin{cases} 0 & \text{if } x = x' \\ p(x)/[1 - p(x')] & \text{if } x \neq x' \end{cases}.$$

Then p' has support of cardinality $m - 1$ and

$$p = p(x')q_{x'} + (1 - p(x'))p'.$$

Using $(*)$ and an induction hypothesis on p', we obtain

$$\begin{aligned} f(p) &= p(x')f(q_{x'}) + (1 - p(x'))f(p') \\ &= p(x')u(x') + (1 - p(x')) \sum_{x \in X \setminus \{x'\}} \frac{p(x)}{1 - p(x')} u(x) \\ &= \sum_{x \in X} p(x)u(x). \end{aligned}$$

Because the support of any lottery is finite, the theorem now follows by induction. □

It is worth emphasizing that the theorem applies equally to lotteries over infinite sets of alternatives (with general probability distributions or measures replacing the finite lotteries, $p \in \mathbf{P}(X)$); the formal arguments for this case, however, are more intricate and add little to the intuition.

Expected utility theory is a powerful tool. It is not, however, unassailable and there are many examples to suggest that individual behavior is not always consistent with the underlying axioms. Perhaps the most famous example in this regard is the Allais Paradox, described in Example 1.3. The "paradox" in the example derives from individuals making what seem to be perfectly sensible decisions that turn out to violate the independence axiom; such individuals, therefore, cannot be acting as expected utility maximizers.

Example 1.3 There are three possible monetary payoffs consequent on some gamble:

$$x = \$2.5m; \ y = \$0.5m; \ z = \$0.$$

1.2. DECISION THEORY

Here are four lotteries over these payoffs, $p_i \in \mathbf{P}(\{x,y,z\})$, $i = 1, \ldots, 4$:

$$(p_1(x), p_1(y), p_1(z)) = (0, 1, 0),$$
$$(p_2(x), p_2(y), p_2(z)) = (.10, .89, .01),$$
$$(p_3(x), p_3(y), p_3(z)) = (0, .11, .89),$$
$$(p_4(x), p_4(y), p_4(z)) = (.10, 0, .90).$$

In many applications, when offered the two pairwise choices, people rank p_1 strictly preferred to p_2 *and* rank p_4 strictly preferred to p_3. This is inconsistent with expected utility theory. To see why, suppose the contrary and let u be a von Neumann-Morgenstern utility function. Then

$$p_1 \tilde{P} p_2 \Rightarrow u(y) > (.10)u(x) + (.89)u(y) + (.01)u(z).$$

Adding $[(.89)u(z) - (.89)u(y)]$ to both sides yields

$$(.11)u(y) + (.89)u(z) > (.10)u(x) + (.90)u(z)$$

which implies $p_3 \tilde{P} p_4$: contradiction. And it is clear that the "culprit" here is the independence axiom. Specifically, let $\hat{p} = (\frac{10}{11}, 0, \frac{1}{11})$ and note that $p_2 = [.11\hat{p} + .89p_1]$. By independence,

$$[p_1 \tilde{P} p_2] \Leftrightarrow [.11p_1 + .89p_1]\tilde{P}[.11\hat{p} + .89p_1]$$
$$\Rightarrow p_1 \tilde{P} \hat{p}.$$

But since $p_3 = [.11p_1 + .89(0, 0, 1)]$ and $p_4 = [.11\hat{p} + .89(0, 0, 1)]$, a second application of independence yields

$$p_1 \tilde{P} \hat{p} \Rightarrow p_3 \tilde{P} p_4,$$

confirming that the observed behavior is inconsistent with the independence axiom. □

The Allais Paradox notwithstanding, throughout this book individuals are assumed to make decisions under uncertainty in accordance with expected utility theory. And in this framework, an individual's attitude to risk can easily be captured in terms of the shape of his or her von Neumann-Morgenstern utility function, u. Intuitively, an individual dislikes taking risks if he or she prefers to receive the expected value of a lottery for sure, rather than accept the gamble over all possible outcomes. Conversely, if an individual exhibits the opposite preference, that is, for the lottery rather than the expected value of that lottery, then the individual shows a preference for taking risks.

Definition 1.8 *An individual with von Neumann-Morgenstern utility function u is risk-averse if, for any lottery p with expected value $\bar{x} = \sum_{x \in X} p(x)x$,*

$$u(\bar{x}) \geq \sum_{x \in X} p(x)u(x)$$

and strictly risk-averse if the inequality is strict. Similarly, the individual is risk-acceptant if, for any lottery p with expected value $\bar{x} = \sum_{x \in X} p(x)x$,

$$u(\bar{x}) \leq \sum_{x \in X} p(x)u(x)$$

and strictly risk-acceptant if the inequality is strict. If the individual is both risk-averse and risk-acceptant, then he or she is risk-neutral.

Geometrically, u exhibits risk-aversion (respectively, risk-acceptance) if u is a concave (respectively, convex) function; risk-neutrality therefore means u is linear. Although an individual might be risk-averse over all lotteries, it is quite possible for a person to be risk-averse over some lotteries but risk-acceptant over others. Figure 1.3 illustrates such a function; all three lotteries in the diagram are assumed to be nondegenerate.

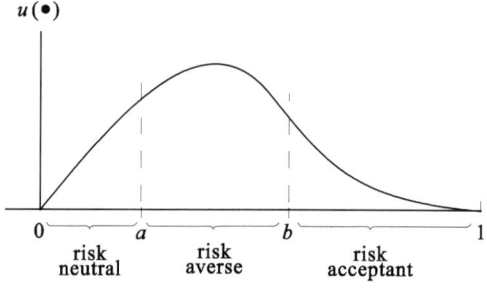

$u(p \cdot 0 + (1-p) \cdot a) = pu(0) + (1-p)u(a)$

$u(p' \cdot a + (1-p') \cdot b) > p'u(a) + (1-p')u(b)$

$u(p'' \cdot b + (1-p'') \cdot 1) < p''u(b) + (1-p'')u(1)$

Figure 1.3: Attitudes to risk

1.3 Discussion

The text to follow uses the preceding material throughout. In addition, the tools needed for the theory (especially those of noncooperative game theory)

1.4. EXERCISES

are, for the most part, introduced and developed as necessary. There is no presumption, therefore, that the notes above are sufficient for the arguments to follow; they are, however, necessary.

The following chapter motivates the focus of this book on strategic behavior: we prove there exist no reasonable collective choice rules immune to individuals having both opportunity and incentive for misrepresenting their preferences. As a result, simply asking people to report their preferences and applying a suitable aggregation rule to the revealed preference profile cannot be guaranteed to yield those collective choices that would be chosen were preferences known for sure.

1.4 Exercises

1.1 A preference aggregation rule $f : \mathfrak{D} \to \mathcal{B}$, is *quasitransitive* if, for all $\rho \in \mathfrak{D}$ and all triples $x, y, z \in X$, $xP_{f(\rho)}y$ and $yP_{f(\rho)}z$ imply $xP_{f(\rho)}z$.

(a) *Prove*: f transitive implies f quasitransitive, and f quasitransitive implies f acyclic.

(b) Provide a counterexample that simultaneously shows that the converse of each implication in (a) is false.

1.2 Suppose f is a preference aggregation rule. Prove $\mathcal{L}(f)$ is *proper* ($L, L' \in \mathcal{L}(f)$ implies $L \cap L' \neq \emptyset$) and *monotonic* ($L \subset L'$ and $L \in \mathcal{L}(f)$ imply $L' \in \mathcal{L}(f)$).

1.3 Prove the converse of Theorem 1.1. That is, if there exists a utility function u such that $p\tilde{R}p' \Leftrightarrow \sum_{x \in X} p(x)u(x) \geq \sum_{x \in X} p'(x)u(x)$, then $\tilde{R}$ must be a weak ordering of $\mathbf{P}(X)$ satisfying continuity and independence.

1.4 Prove the claim in the text that if u is a von Neumann-Morgenstern utility then $u' = \alpha + \beta u$ is an equivalent function for all $\alpha \in \Re$ and $\beta > 0$. Give an example to show that if u' is not a linear (strictly speaking, affine) transformation of u, then it cannot be equivalent to u: there exist lotteries p, p' such that p is strictly preferred to p' given u but p' is strictly preferred to p given u'.

1.5 Let u be a strictly increasing and thrice-differentiable von Neumann-Morgenstern utility defined on $\Re$. Letting primes denote derivatives as usual, define the following functions for any $w \in \Re$:

$$a(w) = -\frac{u''(w)}{u'(w)}; \quad r(w) = -\frac{wu''(w)}{u'(w)}.$$

These are, respectively, the absolute and the relative measures of (local) risk-aversion. Interpret what each function means in terms of the changing attitudes toward risk exhibited by u as w varies. How are they related? What is implied about the third derivative (if anything) by $a'(w) < 0$? Answer the same question if $r'(w) < 0$.

1.5 Further reading

The material of section 1.1 is from Austen-Smith and Banks [13], where references to the relevant literature can be found. von Neumann and Morgenstern [200] and Savage [181] are the fundamental references for expected utility theory; the main conceptual difference between these two is that Savage treats probabilities as subjective evaluations rather than some sort of objective (e.g. frequency) measure. The development of the theory here closely follows Kreps [110], which contains a great deal more on the subject. Useful surveys of decision theory include Epstein [69] and Camerer and Weber [41]. The theory of risk-aversion is explored in Arrow [5] and Pratt [167]; see also Rothschild and Stiglitz [177].

Chapter 2

Strategy-Proof Collective Choice

Positive Political Theory I is concerned with aggregating various profiles of individual preferences. However, as we emphasized in that book, there is no logical necessity for choice and preference to coincide; individuals might abstain or might choose strategically. Of course, given that individuals have preferences, we expect any such strategic behavior to be directed toward promoting these preferences. For instance, consider Example 2.1.

Example 2.1 Let $N = \{1,2,3\}$, $X = \{w,x,y,z\}$, and assume preferences are aggregated with the Borda rule under which, for all $a,b \in X$, aPb if and only if $\sum_N r_i(a) < \sum_N r_i(b)$, where $r_i(a)$ is the ordinal rank of a in i's preference ordering (assumed strict here for convenience). Let the profile $\rho \in \mathcal{R}^n$ be given by

$$xP_1yP_1wP_1z$$
$$xP_2yP_2wP_2z$$
$$yP_3xP_3wP_3z.$$

Given ρ, the Borda rule ranks $xPyPwPz$. Now suppose individual 3 strategically reports the preference ordering, $yP_3'wP_3'zP_3'x$. Under the profile (R_1, R_2, R_3'), the Borda rule yields $yP'xP'wP'z$. So given true preferences ρ, we might expect individual 3 to dissemble, report preferences R_3', and secure y. □

From a normative perspective, the possibility of strategic misrepresentation of preferences is troublesome. For instance, a fundamental premise common in arguments for proportional representation schemes for elections is that proportional representation generates legislatures with a distribution of representatives' preferences that reflects that of the electorate at large. But if individuals misrepresent their true preferences by voting strategically then the validity of this premise is suspect. More generally, individuals' preferences are typically private information to the individuals themselves. Consequently, if a collective choice rule is subject to the sort of incentives to dissemble illustrated in the preceding example, then we cannot expect individuals to report their preferences honestly when simply asked to do so. In which case, there is no guarantee that the output of the collective choice process truly reflects the extant preference profile in the relevant society (committee, electorate, or whatever).

There are two approaches to the problem of strategic preference manipulation. The first is to look for collective choice rules that give no incentive to dissemble in the reporting of preferences; such rules are said to be *strategy-proof*. Unfortunately, the class of strategy-proof rules is known to be very small in general and, from a normative perspective, not very attractive. This chapter is concerned with characterizing this class of rules, both for the discrete case (X finite) and for the spatial model (X some compact convex subset of $\Re^k$). The second approach is to look for ways to internalize the strategic behavior of individuals. That is, given a collective choice rule, can we design an institution or mechanism with the property that strategic behavior nevertheless leads to outcomes that would have been chosen if the preferences were known? This latter question is known as the *implementation problem* and it is the subject of the next chapter.

2.1 Strategy-proofness on finite sets

Assume that the set of alternatives, X, is fixed, finite and contains at least three alternatives, and consider a collective choice function defined on an unrestricted domain, $\varphi : \mathcal{R}^n \to X$ (section 1.1). When considering collective choice functions, we abuse notation somewhat and write $\varphi(\rho) = x$, for instance, rather than $\varphi(\rho) = \{x\}$.

For any profile $\rho = (R_1, ..., R_n) \in \mathcal{R}^n$ and any subset $L \subseteq N$, let ρ_L denote the restriction of the profile ρ to individuals of L and define $\rho_{-L} \equiv \rho_{N \setminus L}$. For example, suppose $\rho = (R_1, \ldots, R_5)$ and $L = \{1, 3, 5\} \subset N$; then ρ can be written (ρ_L, ρ_{-L}) with $\rho_L = (R_1, R_3, R_5)$ and $\rho_{-L} = (R_2, R_4)$. A particularly important case is when $L = \{i\}$ for some individual $i \in N$; then we write $\rho_{-i} = (R_1, R_2, ..., R_{i-1}, R_{i+1}, ..., R_n)$ and $\rho = (R_i, \rho_{-i})$. The

2.1. STRATEGY-PROOFNESS ON FINITE SETS

following concept is fundamental.

Definition 2.1 *A collective choice function φ is strategy-proof if and only if, for all $\rho \in \mathcal{R}^n$ and any $i \in N$, $\varphi(R_i, \rho_{-i}) R_i \varphi(R'_i, \rho_{-i})$ for all $R'_i \in \mathcal{R}$.*

Thus a collective choice function is strategy-proof if, for any i, given every individual other than i reports their true preferences, i can do no better than likewise report his or her true preferences. An equivalent and useful way of defining strategy-proofness is in terms of manipulability:

Definition 2.2 *A collective choice function φ is manipulable at profile $\rho = (R_1, ..., R_n)$ if and only if there exists some $i \in N$ and some $R'_i \neq R_i$ such that $\varphi(R'_i, \rho_{-i}) P_i \varphi(R_i, \rho_{-i})$. Then φ is strategy-proof if it is not manipulable at any profile.*

In other words, strategy-proof collective choice functions provide no opportunities for any individual to manipulate the outcome profitably by misrepresenting his or her preferences, given all others tell the truth.

Notice that if φ were not assumed to be resolute, then the definitions of manipulability and strategy-proofness would not be well-defined. The difficulty is that, in general, there is no unequivocal way of inducing individual preferences over $\mathcal{X}$, the family of nonempty subsets of X, from information only on preferences over X. However, given that we are interested in collective choice functions, the concept of stategy-proofness is really quite appealing. In particular, if φ is strategy-proof, then it is irrelevant whether or not any individual even knows the preferences of others because whatever they might happen to be, reporting one's own preferences truthfully is always a best thing to do. Unfortunately, the only strategy-proof collective choice functions capable of distinguishing between at least three alternatives are dictatorial. Let Π_φ denote the range of φ, $\Pi_\varphi \equiv \cup_{\rho \in \mathcal{R}^n} \varphi(\rho) \subseteq X$.

Definition 2.3 *A collective choice function φ is dictatorial if and only if there exists some $i \in N$ such that, for all $\rho \in \mathcal{R}^n$ and all $y \in \Pi_\varphi$, $\varphi(\rho) R_i y$.*

So a dictatorial collective choice function invariably respects the preferences of exactly one individual in the society.

Theorem 2.1 (Gibbard-Satterthwaite) *If the range of a strategy-proof collective choice function contains at least three alternatives, then it is dictatorial.*

The classical argument supporting this result uses Arrow's Possibility Theorem [PPTI, Theorem 2.1]:

Theorem 2.2 (Arrow) *Suppose there are at least three alternatives. If an aggregation rule with unrestricted domain is transitive, weakly Paretian and independent of irrelevant alternatives, then it is dictatorial.*

Where, we recall (Definition 1.2), a transitive preference aggregation rule with unrestricted domain, $f : \mathcal{R}^n \to \mathcal{R}$, is *weakly Paretian* if, for any distinct alternatives $x, y \in X$, if $P(x, y; \rho) = N$ then xPy; and it is *independent of irrelevant alternatives* if, for every $\rho, \rho' \in \mathcal{R}^n$ and for any $x, y \in X$, $\rho|_{\{x,y\}} = \rho'|_{\{x,y\}}$ implies $f(\rho)|_{\{x,y\}} = f(\rho')|_{\{x,y\}}$.

The idea of the proof for the Gibbard-Satterthwaite Theorem below is to show that if, contrary to the claim, there exists a nondictatorial strategy-proof collective choice function, then there must also exist a nondictatorial, weakly Paretian and transitive preference aggregation rule $f : \mathcal{R}^n \to \mathcal{R}$ that is independent of irrelevant alternatives. But, by Arrow's Theorem, no such preference aggregation rule exists. Therefore, there can exist no nondictatorial strategy-proof collective choice function (with a range of cardinality at least three). If there are only two alternatives ($|X| = 2$) then the majority preference rule satisfies Arrow's conditions and it is not hard to see that in this case the collective choice function (with ties broken arbitrarily) is likewise strategy-proof.

Before presenting the formal argument, we illustrate the theorem using an extended two-person, three-alternative example under a mild unanimity assumption on the collective choice function.

Definition 2.4 *Fix a collective choice function $\varphi : \mathcal{R}^n \to X$ with range Π_φ. Say that φ respects unanimity if and only if, for all $\rho \in \mathcal{R}^n$ and all sets $X_\rho^* \subseteq \Pi_\varphi$ such that $(x, y) \in X_\rho^* \times \Pi_\varphi \setminus X_\rho^*$ implies $P(x, y; \rho) = N$, $\varphi(\rho) \in X_\rho^*$.*

In words, φ respects unanimity if, at any profile for which it is possible to partition the range of φ into two subsets such that every alternative in one subset is strictly preferred by all individuals to every alternative in the other subset, then φ surely selects an alternative from the universally more-preferred-to set. It is easy to see that if there are multiple such sets for any profile, then they must be ordered by set-inclusion. Although similar in spirit to the Pareto criterion, respecting unanimity and weak Pareto are not equivalent (where a choice function φ is *weakly Paretian* if, for all $x, y \in X$ and all $\rho \in \mathcal{R}^n$, $P(x, y; \rho) = N$ implies $\varphi(\rho) \neq y$).

2.1. STRATEGY-PROOFNESS ON FINITE SETS

Example 2.2 Let $N = \{1, 2\}$, $X = \Pi_\varphi = \{x, y, z\}$, and suppose no individual is ever indifferent between any two alternatives: for all $a, b \in X$, either aP_ib or bP_ia, $i \in N$. Then there are 36 possible profiles $\rho = (R_1, R_2)$ on X, and all of the possible scenarios can be summarized in a 6×6 table:

	xyz	xzy	yxz	yzx	zxy	zyx
xyz						
xzy						
yxz				$\varphi(\rho_{34})$		
yzx						
zxy						
zyx						

Table 2.1: Domain of the collective choice function, φ

The rows of Table 2.1 describe the possible preferences individual 1 could have, and similarly the columns describe the possible preferences individual 2 could have. In every case, **xyz** denotes xP_iyP_iz, etc. Thus each of the 36 cells of the table corresponds to a possible profile; for instance, (row 3, column 4) gives the profile $\rho_{34} = (\mathbf{yxz}, \mathbf{yzx})$. An entry in the table then describes the associated collective choice on X generated by φ; e.g. $\varphi(\rho_{34})$.

Since φ is a collective choice function, $\varphi(\rho_{ij}) \in \{x, y, z\}$ for each of the 36 possible profiles, ρ_{ij}. Note that, given any true profile ρ_{ij}, the set of outcomes individual 1 can obtain by manipulating φ at ρ_{ij} is given by $\cup_{k=1}^{k=6} \varphi(\rho_{kj})$; and the set of outcomes individual 2 can obtain by manipulating φ at ρ_{ij} is given by $\cup_{k=1}^{k=6} \varphi(\rho_{ik})$.

Assume that φ respects unanimity. Then we must have

	xyz	xzy	yxz	yzx	zxy	zyx
xyz	x	x	x or y			
xzy	x	x			x or z	
yxz	x or y		y	y		
yzx			y	y		y or z
zxy		x or z			z	z
zyx				y or z	z	z

Table 2.2: φ respects unanimity

Assume φ is strategy-proof. Then:

$\varphi(\rho_{23}) \in \{x, y\}$ else 2 can manipulate φ at ρ_{23} by reporting $R'_2 = \mathbf{xzy}$;
$\varphi(\rho_{14}) \in \{x, y\}$ else 1 can manipulate φ at ρ_{14} by reporting $R'_1 = \mathbf{yxz}$;

$\varphi(\rho_{41}) \in \{x,y\}$ else 2 can manipulate φ at ρ_{41} by reporting $R'_2 = $ **yxz**;
$\varphi(\rho_{32}) \in \{x,y\}$ else 1 can manipulate φ at ρ_{32} by reporting $R'_1 = $ **xzy**;

$\varphi(\rho_{62}) \in \{x,z\}$ else 2 can manipulate φ at ρ_{62} by reporting $R'_2 = $ **zxy**;
$\varphi(\rho_{51}) \in \{x,z\}$ else 1 can manipulate φ at ρ_{51} by reporting $R'_1 = $ **xzy**;
$\varphi(\rho_{15}) \in \{x,z\}$ else 2 can manipulate φ at ρ_{15} by reporting $R'_2 = $ **xzy**;
$\varphi(\rho_{26}) \in \{x,z\}$ else 1 can manipulate φ at ρ_{26} by reporting $R'_1 = $ **zxy**;

$\varphi(\rho_{36}) \in \{y,z\}$ else 2 can manipulate φ at ρ_{36} by reporting $R'_2 = $ **yzx**;
$\varphi(\rho_{63}) \in \{y,z\}$ else 1 can manipulate φ at ρ_{63} by reporting $R'_1 = $ **yzx**;
$\varphi(\rho_{54}) \in \{y,z\}$ else 2 can manipulate φ at ρ_{54} by reporting $R'_2 = $ **zxy**;
$\varphi(\rho_{45}) \in \{y,z\}$ else 1 can manipulate φ at ρ_{45} by reporting $R'_1 = $ **zxy**.

Summarizing, we obtain Table 2.3.

	xyz	xzy	yxz	yzx	zxy	zyx
xyz	x	x	x or y	x or y	x or z	
xzy	x	x	x or y		x or z	x or z
yxz	x or y	x or y	y	y		y or z
yzx	x or y		y	y	y or z	y or z
zxy	x or z	x or z		y or z	z	z
zyx		x or z	y or z	y or z	z	z

Table 2.3: φ strategy-proof

Now, either $\varphi(\rho_{15}) = x$ or $\varphi(\rho_{15}) = z$; suppose $\varphi(\rho_{15}) = z$. Then, using Table 2.3:

(1) $\varphi(\rho_{16}) = z$, else 2 can manipulate φ at ρ_{16} by reporting $R'_2 = $ **zxy**; therefore, for all $i = 2, \ldots, 6$, $\varphi(\rho_{i6}) = \varphi(\rho_{i5}) = z$ else 1 can manipulate φ at ρ_{i6} (respectively, ρ_{i5}) by reporting his or her preferences at the profile ρ_{i6} (respectively, ρ_{i5}) such that $\varphi(\rho_{i6}) \neq z$ (respectively, $\varphi(\rho_{i5}) \neq z$);

$\Rightarrow$ (2) $\varphi(\rho_{14}) = y$, else 2 can manipulate φ at ρ_{14} by reporting $R'_2 = $ **zxy**; therefore, $\varphi(\rho_{13}) = y$, else 2 can manipulate φ at ρ_{13} by reporting $R'_2 = $ **yzx**. Hence, $\varphi(\rho_{23}) = y$, else 1 can manipulate φ at ρ_{13} by reporting $R'_1 = $ **xzy**, and this in turn implies $\varphi(\rho_{24}) = y$ to insure 2 cannot manipulate φ at ρ_{24} by reporting $R'_2 = $ **yxz**. But then we must have $\varphi(\rho_{i4}) = \varphi(\rho_{i3}) = y$ at every $i = 3, 4, 5, 6$, else 1 can manipulate φ at ρ_{24} (respectively, ρ_{23}) by reporting his or her preferences at the profile ρ_{i4} (respectively, ρ_{i3}) such that $\varphi(\rho_{i4}) \neq y$ (respectively, $\varphi(\rho_{i3}) \neq y$);

$\Rightarrow$ (3) $\varphi(\rho_{32}) = x$, else 2 can manipulate φ at ρ_{32} by reporting $R'_2 = $ **zxy**; and this implies $\varphi(\rho_{31}) = x$ to insure 2 cannot manipulate φ at ρ_{31} by

2.1. STRATEGY-PROOFNESS ON FINITE SETS

reporting $R'_2 = \mathbf{xzy}$. But then $\varphi(\rho_{41}) = x$, else 1 can manipulate φ at ρ_{31} by reporting $R'_1 = \mathbf{yzx}$, in which case $\varphi(\rho_{42}) = x$ also, else 2 can manipulate φ at ρ_{42} by reporting $R'_2 = \mathbf{xyz}$. Now arguing as in (2), conclude $\varphi(\rho_{i1}) = \varphi(\rho_{i2}) = x$ at $i = 5, 6$.

Together, (1), (2) and (3) yield Table 2.4.

	xyz	**xzy**	**yxz**	**yzx**	**zxy**	**zyx**
xyz	x	x	y	y	z	z
xzy	x	x	y	y	z	z
yxz	x	x	y	y	z	z
yzx	x	x	y	y	z	z
zxy	x	x	y	y	z	z
zyx	x	x	y	y	z	z

Table 2.4: The consequence of assuming $\varphi(\rho_{15}) = z$

In words, if φ respects unanimity and is strategy-proof, then $\varphi(\rho_{15}) = z$ implies individual 2 must be a dictator. And by symmetry, had we specified the remaining possibility, $\varphi(\rho_{15}) = x$, then individual 1 would turn out to be a dictator. $\square$

We begin the formal argument with a lemma, showing that strategy-proof collective choice functions must respect unanimity. The basic idea for the proof of Lemma 2.1 is illustrated in Figure 2.1 and is used repeatedly in the formal arguments to follow.

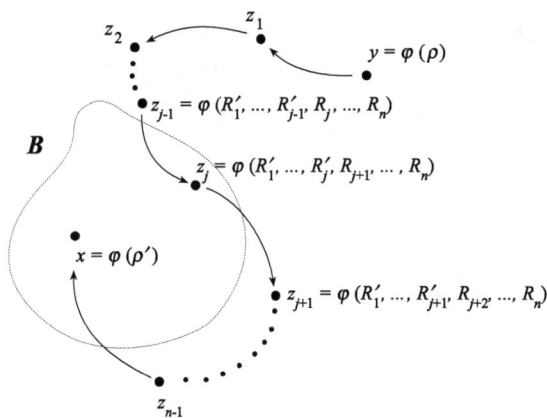

Figure 2.1: Argument for Lemma 2.1

Lemma 2.1 *If a collective choice function $\varphi : \mathcal{R}^n \to X$ is strategy-proof, then φ respects unanimity.*

Proof Suppose the lemma is false. Then $|\Pi_\varphi| \geq 2$ and, for some $\rho \in \mathcal{R}^n$, there is a nonempty set $X_\rho^* \subseteq \Pi_\varphi$ such that $x \in X_\rho^*$ and $y \in \Pi_\varphi \backslash X_\rho^*$ implies xP_iy for all $i \in N$, but $\varphi(\rho) = y \notin X_\rho^*$. Since $X_\rho^* \subseteq \Pi_\varphi$, there is a distinct profile ρ' under which $\varphi(\rho') = x \in X_\rho^*$. For $i = 0, 1, ..., n$, let

$$z_i = \varphi(R_1', R_2', ..., R_i', R_{i+1}, ..., R_n).$$

Then, $z_0 = y$ and $z_n = x$. Define $j \equiv \min[i \in \{0, ..., n\} : z_i \in X_\rho^*]$; since $x \in X_\rho^*$ and $y \notin X_\rho^*$, j exists and $j > 0$. Then $z_{j-1} \notin X_\rho^*$, $z_j \in X_\rho^*$ and, by hypothesis,

$$\varphi(\rho_{L_j}', \rho_{-L_j}) = z_j P_j z_{j-1} = \varphi(\rho_{L_{j-1}}', \rho_{-L_{j-1}})$$

where, for each $i \in N$, $L_i = \{1, ..., i\}$. But then φ is manipulable at $(\rho_{L_{j-1}}', \rho_{-L_{j-1}})$: contradiction.$\square$

The next result connects strategy-proofness to the existence of Arrovian preference aggregation rules [PPTI, sect.2.1] when there is no indifference, either among individuals over alternatives or in the collective preference relation.

Lemma 2.2 *Assume $\varphi : \mathcal{P}^n \to X$ and $|\Pi_\varphi| \geq 3$. If φ is strategy-proof then there exists a weakly Paretian preference aggregation rule $f : \mathcal{P}^n \to \mathcal{P}$ that is independent of irrelevant alternatives.*

Proof Consider the profile (of strict preferences) $\rho = (P_1, ..., P_n) \in \mathcal{P}^n$ and any $x, y \in X$. Define a new profile $\rho(xy) = (P_1(xy), ..., P_n(xy))$ from ρ by, for each $i \in N$, moving x and y to the top of i's ordering and keeping all other relative rankings the same as under P_i; i.e. for all individuals $i \in N$,

(1) $\forall w \notin \{x, y\}$, $xP_i(xy)w$ & $yP_i(xy)w$;
(2) $xP_i(xy)y \Leftrightarrow xP_iy$;
(3) $\forall w, z \in X \backslash \{x, y\}$, $wP_i(xy)z \Leftrightarrow wP_iz$.

Now define the preference aggregation rule f_φ by

$$\forall x, y \in X, \ xPy \Leftrightarrow x = \varphi(\rho(xy)).$$

f_φ is weakly Paretian by Lemma 2.1. f_φ is also independent of irrelevant alternatives. To see this, suppose the contrary. Then there are profiles $\rho, \rho' \in \mathcal{P}^n$ and alternatives $x, y \in X$ such that $\rho|_{\{xy\}} = \rho'|_{\{xy\}}$, xPy and

2.1. STRATEGY-PROOFNESS ON FINITE SETS 27

$yP'x$. Then by definition of f_φ, $\varphi(\rho(xy)) = x$ and $\varphi(\rho'(xy)) = y$. For $i = 0, 1, ..., n$, let

$$z_i = \varphi(P'_1(xy), ..., P'_i(xy), P_{i+1}(xy), ..., P_n(xy)).$$

So $z_0 = x$ and $z_n = y$. Define $j \equiv \min[i \in \{0, ..., n\} : z_i \neq x]$; clearly j exists and $j > 0$. Since, by hypothesis, $\rho(xy)|_{\{xy\}} \equiv \rho'(xy)|_{\{xy\}}$, there are two cases.

(1) If $z_j P_j(xy) x$ then $z_j \equiv y$ by construction of $P_j(xy)$. Therefore, since $z_{j-1} \equiv x$ by definition of j, $z_j P_j(xy) z_{j-1}$. Hence φ is manipulable at $(P'_1(xy), ..., P'_{j-1}(xy), P_j(xy), ..., P_n(xy))$: contradiction.

(2) If $x P'_j(xy) z_j$, then (since $x \equiv z_{j-1}$) $z_{j-1} P'_j(xy) z_j$. So φ is manipulable at $(P'_1(xy), ..., P'_j(xy), P_{j+1}(xy), ..., P_n(xy))$: contradiction.

Therefore, f_φ must be independent of irrelevant alternatives. It remains to check that P is a (strict) ordering on X. Completeness and asymmetry are immediate from the definition of φ, so all we have to show is that P is transitive. Suppose not. Then there is a profile ρ and a triple $\{a, b, c\}$ such that aPb, bPc and cPa; that is,

$$a = \varphi(\rho(ab)); \ b = \varphi(\rho(bc)); \ \text{and} \ c = \varphi(\rho(ca)).$$

Define the profile $\rho(abc)$ by moving $\{a, b, c\}$ to the top of everyone's ordering under ρ, leaving all other relative rankings unchanged. By Lemma 2.1, $\varphi(\rho(abc)) \in \{a, b, c\}$; without loss of generality, assume $\varphi(\rho(abc)) = a$. Now define the profile $\hat{\rho}(abc)$ by placing b third in each individual's ranking under $\rho(abc)$: for all $i \in N$,

(1) $\forall w \notin \{a, b, c\}, \ a\hat{P}_i(xy)w, \ b\hat{P}_i(xy)w \ \& \ c\hat{P}_i(xy)w;$
(2) $a\hat{P}_i(xy)b, \ c\hat{P}_i(xy)b \ \& \ [a\hat{P}_i(xy)c \Leftrightarrow aP_ic];$
(3) $\forall w, z \in X \backslash \{a, b, c\}, \ w\hat{P}_i(xy)z \Leftrightarrow wP_iz.$

Then $\hat{\rho}(abc)|_{\{ac\}} \equiv \rho|_{\{ac\}}$. Therefore, since $\varphi(\rho(ac)) = c$ if and only if cPa by supposition, f_φ independent of irrelevant alternatives implies $\varphi(\hat{\rho}(abc)) = c$. For $i = 0, 1, ..., n$, let

$$z_i = \varphi(\hat{P}_1(abc), ..., \hat{P}_i(abc), P_{i+1}(abc), ..., P_n(abc)).$$

So $z_0 = a$ and $z_n = c$. Define $j \equiv \min[i \in \{0, ..., n\}| z_i \neq a]$; clearly j exists and $j > 0$. By Lemma 2.1, $z_j \in \{c, b\}$ and, since $\hat{\rho}(abc)|_{\{ac\}} \equiv \rho(abc)|_{\{ac\}}$, either $cP_j(abc)a$ or $a\hat{P}_j(abc)c$. If $cP_j(abc)a$ and $z_j = c$ then (because $z_{j-1} = a$), $z_j P_j(abc) z_{j-1}$ and so φ is manipulable by j at

$$(\hat{P}_1(abc), ..., \hat{P}_{j-1}(abc), P_j(abc), ..., P_n(abc)).$$

If $a\hat{P}_j(abc)c$ and $z_j = c$, or if $z_j = b$, then $z_{j-1}\hat{P}_j(abc)z_j$ and φ is manipulable by j at

$$(\hat{P}_1(abc), ..., \hat{P}_j(abc), P_{j+1}(abc), ..., P_n(abc)).$$

Therefore φ is not strategy-proof, which contradiction establishes f_φ transitive and completes the proof. $\square$

Arrow's Theorem states that if any transitive preference aggregation rule satisfies weak Pareto and independence of irrelevant alternatives, then it is dictatorial. Consequently, extending Lemma 2.2 to the full domain proves Theorem 2.1, the Gibbard-Satterthwaite Theorem.

Proof of Theorem 2.1 If φ is strategy-proof on $\mathcal{R}^n$, then necessarily φ is strategy-proof on $\mathcal{P}^n \subset \mathcal{R}^n$. And since Lemma 2.1 does not require strict preferences, the range of φ, Π_φ, cannot be any smaller when the domain of φ is $\mathcal{R}^n$ than when the domain of φ is $\mathcal{P}^n$. Therefore, Lemma 2.1, Lemma 2.2 and Arrow's Theorem together imply that φ is dictatorial on the restricted domain, $\mathcal{P}^n \subset \mathcal{R}^n$. Let h be the dictator on this subdomain and suppose, contrary to the claim, that h is not a dictator over the full domain, $\mathcal{R}^n$. Then there must exist a profile $\hat{\rho} \in \mathcal{R}^n$ such that $\varphi(\hat{\rho}) \notin A$, where

$$A = \{x \in \Pi_\varphi : \forall y \in \Pi_\varphi, x\hat{R}_h y\}.$$

Choose the profile of strict preferences $\rho' = (P'_1, ..., P'_n) \in \mathcal{P}^n$ such that, for all $x \in A$ and all $y \in X \setminus A$, both $xP'_h y$ and, for all $i \neq h$, $yP'_i x$. For $i = 0, 1, ..., n$, let

$$z_i = \varphi(P'_1, ..., P'_i, \hat{R}_{i+1}, ..., \hat{R}_n),$$

and define $j \equiv \min[i \in \{0, ..., n\} : z_i \in A]$. Since $z_0 = \varphi(\hat{\rho}) \notin A$, $j > 0$. Since h is dictatorial on $\mathcal{P}^n$, $z_n = \varphi(\rho') \in A$ and, therefore, $j \leq n$. There are two cases.

(1) If $j = h$, then

$$\varphi(P'_1, ..., P'_h, \hat{R}_{h+1}, ..., \hat{R}_n)\hat{P}_h \varphi(P'_1, ..., P'_{h-1}, \hat{R}_h, ..., \hat{R}_n),$$

and φ is manipulable by h at $(P'_1, ..., P'_{h-1}, \hat{R}_h, ..., \hat{R}_n)$.

2.2. APPLICATION: THE AMENDMENT RULE

(2) If $j \neq h$, then

$$\varphi(P'_1, ..., P'_{j-1}, \hat{R}_j, ..., \hat{R}_n) P'_j \varphi(P'_1, ..., P'_j, \hat{R}_{j+1}, ..., \hat{R}_n),$$

and φ is manipulable by j at $(P'_1, ..., P'_j, \hat{R}_{j+1}, ..., \hat{R}_n)$.

Therefore, if φ is strategy-proof then $\varphi(\hat{\rho}) \in A$, which completes the proof. $\square$

2.2 Application: The amendment rule

A common procedure for making collective choices in parliamentary systems is the amendment rule. For convenience here, assume individuals have strict preferences over alternatives and that there is an odd number of individuals. Then the amendment rule works by fixing an ordering of the alternatives and then proceeds as follows: consider the first two alternatives under the ordering and eliminate the alternative less preferred by a majority; compare the surviving alternative with the third alternative listed and eliminate whichever of the two is less preferred by a majority; repeat this step through the entire ordering until we are left with a single surviving alternative; choose this alternative. In principle, faced with any set of alternatives, a parliament or committee is free to consider them in any order it wishes. The alternatives themselves, however, are often given by proposals and amended proposals for changing a status quo policy and, in this case, the ordering of alternatives is often given by convention as the reverse of the proposal sequence (indeed, the name "amendment rule" derives from this convention). Thus, a proposal (y) to change the status quo (z) that induces an amendment to that proposal (x), reflects a *proposal sequence* (z, y, x) and induces a *voting sequence* (x, y, z); the collective choice is then found by first using majority voting to select x or y, the winner then being paired against z to yield the final outcome.

Assuming preferences are strict, amendment rules define a family of collective choice functions, one for each strict ordering α of the alternatives, $\varphi_\alpha : \mathcal{P}^n \to X$. To fix ideas and keep the notation minimal, suppose $X = \{x, y, z\}$, $\alpha = (x, y, z)$ and, for any alternatives $a, b \in X$ and profile ρ, $P(a, b; \rho)$ is the set of individuals who strictly prefer a to b at ρ. Then, for all profiles $\rho \in \mathcal{P}^n$,

$$\varphi_\alpha(\rho) = \begin{cases} x \Leftrightarrow \min\{|P(x, y; \rho)|, |P(x, z; \rho)|\} > \frac{n}{2} \\ y \Leftrightarrow \min\{|P(y, x; \rho)|, |P(y, z; \rho)|\} > \frac{n}{2} \end{cases}$$

and

$$\varphi_\alpha(\rho) = z \Leftrightarrow \begin{cases} \textit{either} \ [\min\{|P(y,x;\rho)|, |P(z,y;\rho)|\} > \frac{n}{2}] \\ \textit{or} \ [\min\{|P(x,y;\rho)|, |P(z,x;\rho)|\} > \frac{n}{2}] \end{cases}.$$

Theorem 2.1 implies φ_α must be subject to manipulation at some profile $\rho \in \mathcal{P}^n$. Let $n = 3$ and consider $\rho \in \mathcal{P}^n$ such that

$$xP_1yP_1z$$
$$zP_2xP_2y$$
$$yP_3zP_3x.$$

Hence, $\varphi_\alpha(\rho) = z$. Now suppose individual $i = 1$ reports R'_i under which $yP'_1xP'_1z$; then $\varphi_\alpha(R'_1, \rho_{-1}) = y$ and yP_1z. Therefore, φ_α is manipulable at ρ and so not strategy-proof. In fact, by symmetry, φ_α is manipulable at some profile for every strict ordering α of X. It follows that an observation of some legislator apparently voting against her constituents' interests on a particular vote when decision-making is by the amendment rule does not by itself justify an inference that in fact that legislator was behaving inappropriately as a representative; she may well have been voting strategically to avoid a worse outcome from her constituents' perspective.

2.3 Strategy-proofness and Arrovian aggregation

There is, as the proof of Lemma 2.2 reveals, an intimate relationship between strategy-proof collective choice functions and Arrovian preference aggregation rules; i.e. weakly Paretian and transitive preference aggregation rules satisfying independence of irrelevant alternatives. Specifically, the proof shows that if there exists a nondictatorial strategy-proof collective choice function, there exists a nondictatorial Arrovian aggregation rule; in fact, when preferences over X are strict, the relationship is deeper.

For any preference aggregation rule f and profile $\rho \in \mathcal{R}^n$, the maximal set for $f(\rho)$ is given by

$$M(f(\rho), X) = \{x \in X : \forall y \in X \backslash \{x\}, \ xf(\rho)y\}.$$

Let f be a preference aggregation rule. Say that f is a *strict Arrovian preference aggregation rule* if and only if $f : \mathcal{P}^n \to \mathcal{P}$ and f is weakly Paretian and independent of irrelevant alternatives. For any transitive strict rule f (whether or not it is an Arrovian aggregation rule) and all $\rho \in \mathcal{P}^n$,

2.3. STRATEGY-PROOFNESS AND ARROVIAN AGGREGATION 31

the maximal set $M(f(\rho), X)$ is necessarily singleton; in this case, therefore, we can define a resolute collective choice function φ_f by setting $\varphi_f(\rho) = M(f(\rho), X)$ for all $\rho \in \mathcal{P}^n$. Say that φ_f is *derived from* f. A collective choice function $\varphi : \mathcal{P}^n \to X$ has *full range* if $\cup_{\mathcal{P}^n} \varphi(\rho) = X$.

Lemma 2.3 *Let f be a strict Arrovian preference aggregation rule. Then φ_f is a strategy-proof collective choice function with full range.*

The proof of this Lemma uses the following property of preference aggregation rules: a preference aggregation rule f is *weakly monotonic* if, for all $x, y \in X$ and all $\rho, \rho' \in \mathcal{R}^n$ such that $\rho|_{X \setminus \{x\}} = \rho'|_{X \setminus \{x\}}$,

$$[P(x, y; \rho) \subseteq P(x, y; \rho'), \ R(x, y; \rho) \subseteq R(x, y; \rho') \ \& \ xPy] \Rightarrow xP'y.$$

Proof of Lemma 2.3 Since $f : \mathcal{P}^n \to \mathcal{P}$, φ_f is a collective choice function by definition. And by f weakly Paretian, for all x in X there exists a strict profile $\rho_x \in \mathcal{P}^n$ such that, for any $y \neq x$, $xf(\rho_x)y$; hence, φ_f has full range. Moreover, by Arrow's Theorem, f is dictatorial and therefore weakly monotonic. Now suppose φ_f is manipulable at $\rho \in \mathcal{P}^n$. Then there is some individual j such that $\varphi_f(P'_j, \rho_{-j}) P_j \varphi_f(P_j, \rho_{-j})$. Let $\rho' = (P'_j, \rho_{-j})$, $\varphi_f(P'_j, \rho_{-j}) = x$ and $\varphi_f(P_j, \rho_{-j}) = y$. Then xP_jy and, by definition of φ_f, $xP'y$ and yPx. If xP'_jy, then $\rho|_{\{xy\}} = \rho'|_{\{xy\}}$ and therefore, by f independent of irrelevant alternatives, $P|_{\{xy\}} = P'|_{\{xy\}}$: contradiction. So assume yP'_jx and define $\rho'' \in \mathcal{P}^n$ such that (1) $P''_i = P_i \ (= P'_i)$, all $i \neq j$; (2) yP''_jx; and (3) $P''_j|_{X \setminus \{xy\}} = P_j|_{X \setminus \{xy\}}$. Then $\rho''|_{\{xy\}} = \rho'|_{\{xy\}}$; hence $xP'y$ and f independent of irrelevant alternatives imply $xP''y$. But since yPx, f weakly monotonic implies $yP''x$: contradiction. Therefore φ_f must be strategy-proof. $\square$

Recall from the proof of Lemma 2.2 that for any $\rho \in \mathcal{P}^n$ and $x, y \in X$, $\rho(xy)$ is the profile derived from ρ by moving $\{x, y\}$ to the top of each individual i's ranking, P_i, leaving the relative positions of $\{x, y\}$ and of $X \setminus \{x, y\}$ unaltered. With this construction, define f_φ by: for all $\rho \in \mathcal{P}^n$ and all distinct alternatives $x, y \in X$,

$$xf_\varphi(\rho)y \Leftrightarrow x = \varphi(\rho(xy)).$$

This is only one way in which a preference aggregation rule might be derived from a given collective choice function. A strict (not necessarily Arrovian) preference aggregation rule f is said to be *derivable* from a collective choice rule φ if, for all ρ in $\mathcal{P}^n$, $M(f(\rho), X) = \varphi(\rho)$.

We are now in a position to elucidate the connection between Arrow's Theorem and the Gibbard-Satterthwaite Theorem. Let

$$\Psi = \{\varphi : \mathcal{P}^n \to X : \varphi \text{ is strategy-proof with full range}\};$$

and

$$\mathcal{F} = \{f : \mathcal{P}^n \to \mathcal{P} : f \text{ is weakly Paretian and}$$
$$\text{independent of irrelevant alternatives}\}.$$

Theorem 2.3 *There exists a one-to-one map* $\lambda : \Psi \to \mathcal{F}$. *Moreover, if* $f = \lambda(\varphi)$ *then* $f = f_\varphi$ *and* $\varphi = \varphi_f$.

Proof By Lemmas 2.2 and 2.3, $\forall \varphi \in \Psi$, $\exists f \in \mathcal{F}$, and conversely. By definition, for any $f \in \mathcal{F}$, φ_f is the unique collective choice function in Ψ derivable from f. It remains to show that for any $\varphi \in \Psi$, f_φ is the unique preference aggregation rule in $\mathcal{F}$ derivable from φ. Suppose not. Then there exist $f, g \in \mathcal{F}$ derivable from $\varphi \in \Psi$. Since $f \neq g$ by supposition, there is a profile $\rho \in \mathcal{P}^n$ such that $f(\rho) \neq g(\rho)$. Therefore, there exist $x, y \in X$ such that $xf(\rho)y$ and $yg(\rho)x$. By independence of irrelevant alternatives, $xf(\rho(xy))y$ and $yg(\rho(xy))x$. By f and g weakly Paretian, for all $(w, z) \in \{x, y\} \times X \setminus \{x, y\}$, $wf(\rho(xy))z$ and $wg(\rho(xy))z$. Hence, $\varphi_f(\rho(xy), X) = x$ and $\varphi_g(\rho(xy), X) = y$ (since f and g are strict). But since f and g are derivable from φ, $\varphi_f(\rho(xy), X) = \varphi_g(\rho(xy), X)$: contradiction. $\square$

Assuming throughout that preferences are strict, Theorem 2.3 says that Arrow's Theorem and the Gibbard-Satterthwaite Theorem are equivalent: for each collective choice function satisfying the Gibbard-Satterthwaite conditions there exists a unique strict Arrovian preference aggregation rule, and conversely. Because the Gibbard-Satterthwaite result critically exploits resoluteness of the collective choice rule, it should not be surprising that the equivalence result cannot be generalized to the whole of class of Arrovian preference aggregation rules since this class admits non-singleton maximal sets for some profiles. For example, suppose $f : \mathcal{R}^n \to \mathcal{R}$ is such that $M(f(\rho), X) = \{x, y\}$ at some profile ρ (as would be the case if f simply reflects a fixed individual's preferences and that individual is indifferent between these two alternatives at ρ, but strictly prefers them to all others). Then $\varphi_f(\rho)$ is not singleton and φ_f cannot be resolute. Insisting on resoluteness requires φ_f to make a selection at ρ; but then there are (at least) two possible resolute collective choice functions, say φ_f and φ'_f, that can be derived from f, depending on whether $\varphi_f(\rho) = x$ or $\varphi'_f(\rho) = y$.

2.4. SINGLE-PEAKED PREFERENCES

On the other hand, the equivalence of strategy-proof choice functions and strict Arrovian aggregation rules offers an important perspective on the canonic "impossibility" results in the theory of preference aggregation: it is not the fact that nondictatorial collective preference cannot be assured acyclic that is most significant, but that the possibility of preference cycles admits the opportunity for strategic manipulation. In other words, preference aggregation is either dictatorial or subject to manipulation.

2.4 Single-peaked preferences

Theorem 2.3 establishes the equivalence of strategy-proof collective choice functions and strict preference aggregation rules satisfying Arrow's conditions of transitivity, independence of irrelevant alternatives and weak Pareto. The result therefore says that restrictions on the admissible preference domain insuring the existence of *nondictatorial* strict Arrovian aggregation rules also insure the existence of nondictatorial strategy-proof collective choice functions. And although the equivalence does not extend to preference domains admitting indifference, it is a reasonable conjecture that at least some restricted domains supporting nondictatorial Arrovian aggregation rules more generally, also support nondictatorial strategy-proof collective choice functions. This conjecture turns out to be correct for a particularly important class of preference profiles, that of single-peaked preferences [PPTI, sect.4.1].

Definition 2.5 *Let $X = \{a_1, \ldots, a_r\}$, $r \geq 2$; let Q be a strict ordering of X and label X so that $a_{t+1} Q a_t$ for all $t = 1, \ldots, r-1$. $R_i \in \mathcal{R}$ is single-peaked on X with respect to Q if and only if there exists $t \in \{1, \ldots, r\}$ such that*

$$a_t P_i a_{t+1} P_i a_{t+2} P_i \ldots P_i a_r \ \& \ a_t P_i a_{t-1} P_i a_{t-2} \ldots P_i a_1.$$

Single-peaked preferences have the property that we can assign each of the r outcomes uniquely to one of the first r natural numbers and then moves away from the individual's most preferred outcome are associated with moves down the individual's preference ordering.

Assuming an individual's preferences are single-peaked means that the individual cannot exhibit too much indifference over the feasible set of alternatives; that is, if $x I_i y$ and R_i is single-peaked, then necessarily x and y are on opposite sides of i's most preferred alternative, or *ideal point*. Assuming that all individuals have single-peaked preferences relative to a given ordering of alternatives, however, imposes an important degree of homogeneity across society.

Definition 2.6 *A profile $\rho \in \mathcal{R}^n$ is single-peaked on X if and only if there is a strict ordering Q of X such that, for all $i \in N$, R_i is single-peaked on X with respect to Q.*

Let $\mathcal{S} \subset \mathcal{R}^n$ denote the set of single-peaked preference profiles.

If the domain is restricted to that of single-peaked profiles, we can find strategy-proof collective choice functions. Before doing this, however, it is important to emphasize two things, both of which arise because the set $\mathcal{S}$ is not in general rectangular: profiles of single-peaked individual preferences are not necessarily single-peaked profiles. The first thing is that, when considering choice functions defined on single-peaked domains, the only deviations an individual can consider to manipulate a collective choice at some profile $\rho \in \mathcal{S}$ are deviations R'_i such that the profile (R'_i, ρ_{-i}) is also single-peaked. It is typically not enough to permit any deviation R'_i such that R'_i is single-peaked, as Example 2.3 illustrates.

Example 2.3 Let $N = \{1, 2, 3\}$ and $X = \{x, y, z\}$. Consider the profile ρ such that

$$xP_1yP_1z$$
$$zP_2yP_2x$$
$$yP_3zP_3x$$

ρ is single-peaked with respect to the strict order $zQyQx$ (and, by symmetry, $xQyQz$). Now consider the profile (R'_2, ρ_{-2}) where R'_2 is zP_2xP_2y. Because R'_2 is linear it is surely a single-peaked ordering on X; the profile (R'_2, ρ_{-2}), however, is not single-peaked. □

Say that a unilateral deviation R'_i from a single-peaked profile ρ is *admissible* if and only if (R'_i, ρ_{-i}) is single-peaked; where there is no ambiguity, the qualification "admissible" is often left implicit.

The second, and perhaps less apparent but related, thing to emphasize is that any results concerning strategy-proof collective choice functions on single-peaked profiles are results on domains that are single-peaked with respect to a *fixed* ordering Q of X. In this respect, therefore, the domain restriction here is stronger than it is for preference aggregation rules in the absence of manipulation. Specifically, for any such ordering Q, let $\mathcal{S}_Q \subset \mathcal{S}$ denote the family of preference profiles on X that are single-peaked with respect to Q. Then results for single-peaked profiles are results assuming a given subdomain $\mathcal{S}_Q \subset \mathcal{S}$ and not for the entire domain $\mathcal{S} \equiv \cup \{\mathcal{S}_Q \subset \mathcal{S} : Q$ is

2.4. SINGLE-PEAKED PREFERENCES

a strict ordering of X}. It is simply not possible to find sequences of single-peaked profiles that take a profile $\rho \in S_Q$ into a distinct profile $\rho' \in S_{Q'}$ unless $Q = Q'$ or its inverse. Example 2.4 illustrates the point.

Example 2.4 Let $X = \{a, b, c\}$ and $N = \{1, 2, 3\}$. Consider the profiles ρ and ρ', where

$$\rho = \left\{ \begin{array}{c} aP_1bP_1c \\ bP_2cP_2a \\ cP_3bP_3a \end{array} \right. ; \rho' = \left\{ \begin{array}{c} aP_1'bP_1'c \\ cP_2'aP_2'b \\ aP_3'cP_3'b \end{array} \right. .$$

It is easy to check $\rho, \rho' \in S$. However, because $\rho \in S_{\{aQbQc\}} = S_{\{cQbQa\}}$ and $\rho' \in S_{\{cQaQb\}} = S_{\{bQaQc\}}$, there is no sequence of profiles $(\rho_k) \to \rho'$ with $\rho_0 = \rho$ and $\rho_k \in S$ for every k involving, at each step ρ_k to ρ_{k+1}, an admissible deviation in exactly one individual's preference ordering. Consequently, statements on strategy-proofness (as defined here) that apply to a single-peaked subdomain S_Q for any strict ordering Q of X, are not well-defined when applied to the entire single-peaked domain, S. □

Although the preceding remarks are important when dealing with arbitrary sets of alternatives, they are less of a concern for at least one substantively important setting, that is, when X is a subset of the real line. In this case, alternatives are naturally ordered by the strict inequality ">" and any family of preference orderings on $X \subseteq \Re$, each member of which is single-peaked with respect to ">", induces a single-peaked profile on X [PPTI, sect.4.3].

Keeping the two caveats discussed above in mind, consider the following example.

Example 2.5 Let $N = \{1, \ldots, n\}$ and $X = \{a_1, \ldots, a_r\}$; assume $r \geq 3$ and n odd. For each individual $i \in N$ and all $\rho \in S$, let $x_i \in X$ denote the individual's most preferred alternative at profile ρ. For any strict ordering Q of X, define a collective choice function $\varphi : S_Q \to X$ by

$$\forall \rho \in S_Q, \ \varphi(\rho) = med_Q\{x_i : i \in N\}$$

where, for any set $T \subseteq X$, $med_Q T$ is the median alternative in T with respect to Q. Because n is odd by assumption, $\varphi(\rho)$ is singleton for every $\rho \in S_Q$. And φ clearly has full range with $|\Pi_\varphi| = |X| \geq 3$. Now fix $\rho \in S_Q$ and consider any $i \in N$. If $x_i = med_Q\{x_i : i \in N\}$, then $\varphi(\rho) R_i \varphi(R_i', \rho_{-i})$ for all admissible R_i' and i has no incentive to report anything other than his or her true preferences. So suppose $\varphi(\rho) Q x_i$ and consider any admissible R_i' with most preferred alternative x'_i. If $\sim [x'_i Q\varphi(\rho)]$ then $\varphi(R'_i, \rho_{-i}) = \varphi(\rho)$ and $\varphi(R_i, \rho_{-i}) I_i \varphi(R'_i, \rho_{-i})$; if $x'_i Q\varphi(\rho)$ then $\varphi(R'_i, \rho_{-i}) Q\varphi(\rho)$ and, by R_i single-peaked, $\varphi(R_i, \rho_{-i}) P_i \varphi(R'_i, \rho_{-i})$. Since the remaining possibility, $x_i Q\varphi(\rho)$, is symmetric and i was chosen arbitrarily, we have φ strategy-proof on $\mathcal{S}_Q$. □

The key features admitting strategy-proofness in Example 2.5 are that any individual increasingly dislikes alternatives as they move away from his or her most preferred alternative and that the collective choice function selects on the basis of an order-statistic, here the median of the revealed most preferred alternatives. If any individual i can change the alternative defined by the median through reporting some preference ordering R'_i other than the true one R_i, then the change can only be away from i's ideal point x_i. Evidently, the same reasoning holds if the collective choice function exploits some other order statistic; for instance, at any single-peaked profile ρ, choose the minimal alternative with respect to Q from the set $\{x_i : i \in N\}$. This observation raises the questions of whether there exist any other sorts of non-dictatorial strategy-proof collective choice function on a domain of single-peaked preferences $\mathcal{S}_Q$ and, if so, what they might look like.

Let $\varphi : \mathcal{S}_Q \to X$ be any collective choice function on $\mathcal{S}_Q$, where Q is any given strict ordering of X. Trivially, φ is strategy-proof if φ is a constant function: $\varphi(\rho) = x$ for all profiles $\rho \in \mathcal{S}_Q$. Constant functions are ruled out in the Gibbard-Satterthwaite Theorem (Theorem 2.1) by the requirement that the range of φ contain at least three distinct alternatives. A technically stronger, but normatively more appealing, requirement that also excludes constant collective choice functions is citizen sovereignty.

Definition 2.7 *A collective choice function $\varphi : \mathcal{S}_Q \to X$ satisfies citizen sovereignty if, for all $x \in X$, there exists some profile $\rho \in \mathcal{S}_Q$ such that $\varphi(\rho) = x$.*

Thus citizen sovereignty insures that for every alternative, there exists some single-peaked (with respect to Q) profile on X at which that alternative is chosen. This is clearly stronger than requiring that there is simply some single-peaked profile on X at which the alternative is chosen and it is trivially satisfied by dictatorial collective choice functions. It turns out that all strategy-proof collective choice functions satisfying citizens' sovereignty are based essentially on order-statistics.

Given the discussion to follow concerns collective choice functions defined on a domain of single-peaked profiles for fixed Q, $\mathcal{S}_Q$, it is notationally convenient to associate alternatives in X with real numbers so that, for all

2.4. SINGLE-PEAKED PREFERENCES

$x, y \in X$, xQy if and only if $x > y$, and $\sim [xQy]$ if and only if $x \leq y$. Unless otherwise stated, therefore, assume throughout this section that Q is the relation ">" and define alternatives a_1 and a_r, respectively, to be the minimal and maximal alternatives in X with respect to Q.

Given any profile $\rho \in \mathcal{S}_Q$ with associated set of ideal points $\{x_i\}_{i \in N}$, let $\{i_1, i_2, \ldots, i_n\}$ be a labeling of N such that $x_{i_1} \leq x_{i_2} \leq \ldots \leq x_{i_n}$.

Definition 2.8 *A collective choice function $\varphi : \mathcal{S}_Q \to X$ is an augmented median voter rule if and only if, for all $L, M \subseteq N$, there exist alternatives $y_L, y_M \in X$ such that $L \subseteq M$ implies $y_L \geq y_M$ and, for all $\rho \in \mathcal{S}_Q$,*

$$\varphi(\rho) = med_Q\{x_1, \ldots, x_n, y_\emptyset, y_{\{i_1\}}, y_{\{i_1, i_2\}}, \ldots, y_N\}.$$

Thus an augmented median voter rule is a rule that, for each profile $\rho \in \mathcal{S}_Q$, chooses the median alternative from a list consisting of the n individuals' ideal points and $n+1$ other alternatives from a given set $\{y_L : L \subseteq N\}$, with the selection depending upon the rank-ordering of the ideal points under ρ. This class of rules is quite broad, as Example 2.6 illustrates.

Example 2.6 Fix $N = \{1, \ldots, n\}$, $X = \{a_1, \ldots, a_r\}$ and suppose φ is an augmented median voter rule.

(1) *Simple median voter rule.* The usual median voter rule used in Example 2.5 for n odd is defined by setting

$$y_\emptyset = y_{\{i_1\}} = y_{\{i_1, i_2\}} = \ldots = y_{\{i_1, \ldots, i_{(n-1)/2}\}} = a_r$$

and

$$y_{\{i_1, \ldots, i_{(n+1)/2}, i_{(n+3)/2}\}} = y_{\{i_1, \ldots, i_{(n+1)/2}, i_{(n+3)/2}, i_{(n+5)/2}\}} = \ldots = y_N = a_1;$$

then for all $\rho \in \mathcal{S}_Q$,

$$\begin{aligned}\varphi(\rho) &= med_Q\{x_1, \ldots, x_n, y_\emptyset, y_{\{i_1\}}, y_{\{i_1, i_2\}}, \ldots, y_N\} \\ &= med_Q\{x_i : i \in N\}.\end{aligned}$$

(2) *Dictatorial rules.* Fix an individual $j \in N$ and define the augmented median voter rule φ_j as follows. For all profiles $\rho \in \mathcal{S}_Q$, choose alternatives y_L such that

(1) $\forall L \subseteq N : j \in L$, $y_L = a_1$;
(2) $\forall L \subseteq N : j \notin L$, $y_L = a_r$.

Let ρ be any profile and suppose $j = i_k$; then

$$j \in L \Leftrightarrow L = \{i_1, \ldots, i_l\} \text{ and } l \geq k.$$

Hence,

$$\begin{aligned}
\varphi_j(\rho) &= med_Q\{x_{i_1}, \ldots, x_{i_k}, \ldots, x_{i_n}, y_\emptyset, y_{\{i_1\}}, y_{\{i_1,i_2\}}, \ldots, y_N\} \\
&= med_Q\{x_{i_1}, \ldots, x_{i_k}, \ldots, x_{i_n}, \underbrace{a_r, \ldots, a_r}_{k \text{ times}}, \underbrace{a_1, \ldots, a_1}_{n-k+1 \text{ times}}\} \\
&= x_{i_k} = x_j.
\end{aligned}$$

(3) *Nonanonymous and nondictatorial rules.* Let $n = 3$ and consider $\rho \in \mathcal{S}_Q$ such that $x_2 < x_1 < x_3$; then $(i_1, i_2, i_3) = (2, 1, 3)$ and

$$\begin{aligned}
\varphi(\rho) &= med_Q\{x_1, x_2, x_3, y_\emptyset, y_{\{i_1\}}, y_{\{i_1,i_2\}}, y_N\} \\
&= med_Q\{x_1, x_2, x_3, y_\emptyset, y_{\{2\}}, y_{\{2,1\}}, y_N\}.
\end{aligned}$$

Now let $\rho' \in \mathcal{S}_Q$ be such that $x_1' = x_1$, $x_2' = x_3$ and $x_3' = x_2$. Then the set of ideal points under ρ' is identical to that under ρ, $\{x_i'\}_{i=1,2,3} = \{x_i\}_{i=1,2,3}$, but the respective orderings of individuals by ideal point are distinct: $(i_1', i_2', i_3') = (3, 1, 2) \neq (i_1, i_2, i_3)$. Hence,

$$\begin{aligned}
\varphi(\rho') &= med_Q\{x_1', x_2', x_3', y_\emptyset, y_{\{i_1'\}}, y_{\{i_1',i_2'\}}, y_N\} \\
&= med_Q\{x_1, x_2, x_3, y_\emptyset, y_{\{3\}}, y_{\{3,1\}}, y_N\}.
\end{aligned}$$

Suppose

$$y_\emptyset = y_{\{2\}} = y_{\{3\}} = y_{\{2,1\}} = a_r > y_{\{3,1\}} = y_N = a_1.$$

Then $\varphi(\rho) = x_3 > \varphi(\rho') = x_1' = x_1$. Consequently, although φ is not dictatorial, it is the case that exactly *who* holds a given preference ordering is important for collective choice.

(4) *Non-Paretian rules.* Let $PS_N(\rho)$ denote the *Pareto set* at ρ (section 1.1); that is, the subset of X with the property that no alternative in the subset is unanimously less preferred to some other available alternative ($x, y \in X$ and xP_iy for all $i \in N$ implies $y \notin PS_N(\rho)$). A collective choice function φ is *weakly Paretian* if and only if, for all profiles ρ in its domain, $\varphi(\rho) \in PS_N(\rho)$. For any single-peaked profile $\rho \in \mathcal{S}_Q$,

$$PS_N(\rho) = \{a \in X : \min\{x_i\}_{i \in N} \leq a \leq \max\{x_i\}_{i \in N}\},$$

where the min and max operators are with respect to Q. Then the augmented median voter rule such that $y_L = a_1$ for every subset $L \subseteq N$ is not

2.4. SINGLE-PEAKED PREFERENCES

weakly Paretian. To see this, consider any profile $\rho \in \mathcal{S}_Q$ such that $x_i > a_1$ for all $i \in N$. Then

$$\begin{aligned}\varphi(\rho) &= med_Q\{x_{i_1},\ldots,x_{i_k},\ldots,x_{i_n},y_\emptyset,y_{\{i_1\}},y_{\{i_1,i_2\}},\ldots,y_N\} \\ &= med_Q\{x_{i_1},\ldots,x_{i_k},\ldots,x_{i_n},\underbrace{a_1,\ldots,a_1}_{n+1 \text{ times}}\} \\ &= a_1.\end{aligned}$$

Therefore, $\varphi(\rho) < \min\{x_i\}_{i \in N}$ and so $\varphi(\rho) \notin PS_N(\rho)$. □

The last possibility considered in Example 2.6 shows that augmented median voter rules need not be weakly Paretian. They can also fail to satisfy citizen sovereignty unless $y_\emptyset = a_r$ and $y_N = a_1$: suppose $y_\emptyset < a_r$; then $y_L < a_r$ for all sets $L \subseteq N$ in which case, by definition of an augmented median voter rule, $\varphi(\rho) < a_r \in X$ for every profile $\rho \in \mathcal{S}_Q$. A similar conclusion follows if $y_N > a_1$. Consequently, if we insist on collective choice functions satisfying citizen sovereignty, we can ignore $y_\emptyset$ and y_N, and write a typical augmented median voter rule as

$$\varphi(\rho) = med_Q\{x_1,\ldots,x_n,y_{\{i_1\}},y_{\{i_1,i_2\}},\ldots,y_{\{i_1,\ldots,i_{n-1}\}}\}.$$

It follows immediately that although, as observed above, citizen sovereignty does not by itself imply weak Pareto, if an augmented median voter rule satisfies citizen sovereignty then the rule is necessarily weakly Paretian since, for all $\rho \in \mathcal{S}_Q$,

$$\min\{x_i\}_{i \in N} \leq med_Q\{x_1,\ldots,x_n,y_{\{i_1\}},y_{\{i_1,i_2\}},\ldots,y_{\{i_1,\ldots,i_{n-1}\}}\} \leq \max\{x_i\}_{i \in N}.$$

The importance of augmented median voter rules in the present context is suggested by the following result.

Lemma 2.4 *Let $\varphi : \mathcal{S}_Q \to X$ be an augmented median voter rule with $y_\emptyset = a_r$ and $y_N = a_1$. Then φ is strategy-proof and satisfies citizen sovereignty.*

Proof (Citizen sovereignty) Let φ be an augmented median voter rule with $y_\emptyset = a_r$ and $y_N = a_1$. Let $\rho \in \mathcal{S}_Q$ be such that $x_i = z$ for some $z \in X$ and all $i \in N$. By definition, $a_1 \leq z \leq a_r$ and, therefore,

$$\begin{aligned}\varphi(\rho) &= med_Q\{x_1,\ldots,x_n,y_\emptyset,y_{\{1\}},y_{\{1,2\}},\ldots,y_N\} \\ &= med_Q\{z,\ldots,z,y_{\{1\}},y_{\{1,2\}},\ldots,y_{\{1,\ldots,n-1\}}\} \\ &= z.\end{aligned}$$

Hence φ satisfies citizen sovereignty.

(Strategy-proofness) To establish φ strategy-proof, consider any $\rho \in \mathcal{S}_Q$ and, without loss of generality, relabel N if necessary so that $x_1 \leq x_2 \leq \ldots \leq x_n$; then $(i_1, i_2, \ldots, i_n) = (1, \ldots, n)$. Clearly, if $\varphi(\rho) = x_i$ for some i, individual i has no incentive to manipulate φ; so assume $x_i < \varphi(\rho)$ for some i (the argument for the remaining possibility is symmetric). There are two cases.

(1) $\varphi(\rho) = x_j$ for some $j \in N$. Then

$$x_1 \leq \ldots \leq x_i \leq \ldots \leq x_j = \varphi(\rho) \leq x_{j+1} \leq \ldots \leq x_n.$$

By definition of φ, there must be exactly n alternatives from the set

$$\{x_1, \ldots, x_n, y_\emptyset, y_{\{1\}}, y_{\{1,2\}}, \ldots, y_N\}$$

lying (weakly) to the left of x_j, and n alternatives from the set lying (weakly) to the right of x_j. Therefore, by definition of y_L, $L \subseteq N$,

$$y_N \leq \ldots \leq y_{\{1,\ldots,j\}} \leq x_j = \varphi(\rho) \leq y_{\{1,\ldots,j-1\}} \leq \ldots \leq y_\emptyset.$$

(1a) Consider any admissible R'_i with $x'_i \leq x_j$; write $\rho' = (R'_i, \rho_{-i})$. At ρ', as at ρ, all individuals $k < j$ have ideal points weakly to the left of x_j and all individuals $k > j$ have ideal points weakly to the right of x_j. Further, $x'_i \leq x_j$ implies individual i is a member of every set $L \in \{\{i'_1, \ldots, i'_k\} : k = j-1, \ldots, n\}$. Therefore, for all $k = j-1, \ldots, n$, $y_{\{i'_1,\ldots,i'_k\}} = y_{\{i_1,\ldots,i_k\}}$ implying

$$y_N \leq \ldots \leq y_{\{i'_1,\ldots,i'_j\}} \leq x_j = \varphi(\rho) \leq y_{\{i'_1,\ldots,i'_{j-1}\}}.$$

And since $L \subseteq M$ implies $y_L \geq y_M$, we have $y_{\{i'_1,\ldots,i'_{j-1}\}} \leq y_L$ for all $L \subset \{i'_1, \ldots, i'_{j-1}\}$. Hence,

$$\begin{aligned}\varphi(\rho') &= med_Q\{x_1, \ldots, x'_i, \ldots, x_n, y_\emptyset, y_{\{i'_1\}}, y_{\{i'_1,i'_2\}}, \ldots, y_N\} \\ &= med_Q\{x_1, \ldots, x_i, \ldots, x_n, y_\emptyset, y_{\{1\}}, y_{\{1,2\}}, \ldots, y_N\} \\ &= \varphi(\rho),\end{aligned}$$

in which case $\varphi(\rho) I_i \varphi(R'_i, \rho_{-i})$ for all admissible R'_i with $x'_i \leq x_j = \varphi(\rho)$.

(1b) Consider any admissible R''_i with $x''_i > x_j$; write $\rho'' = (R''_i, \rho_{-i})$. At ρ'', $j-2$ individuals (all $k < j$, $k \neq i$) have ideal points weakly to the left of x_j and $(n-j+1)$ individuals (all $k > j$ along with individual i) have ideal points weakly to the right of x_j. Suppose $\varphi(\rho) > \varphi(\rho'')$; by definition of φ and $x_j = \varphi(\rho)$,

$$y_N \leq \ldots \leq y_{\{i''_1,\ldots,i''_{j-2}\}} < x_j = \varphi(\rho).$$

2.4. SINGLE-PEAKED PREFERENCES

Further, because ρ and ρ'' essentially differ only in the location of i's ideal point and $x_i'' > x_j$,

$$\{i_1'', \ldots, i_{j-2}''\} = \{1, \ldots, i-1, i+1, \ldots, j-1\}$$

and

$$\{i_1, \ldots, i_{j-1}\} = \{1, \ldots, j-1\}.$$

Therefore, because $\varphi(\rho) \leq y_{\{1,\ldots,j-1\}}$ at profile ρ, $y_{\{1,\ldots,i-1,i+1,\ldots,j-1\}} < y_{\{1,\ldots,j-1\}}$. But, by definition of the alternatives y_L, $\{1, \ldots, i-1, i+1, \ldots, j-1\} \subset \{1, \ldots, j-1\}$ implies $y_{\{1,\ldots,i-1,i+1,\ldots,j-1\}} \geq y_{\{1,\ldots,j-1\}}$: contradiction. Hence, $\varphi(\rho'') \geq \varphi(\rho)$ in which case $\varphi(\rho) R_i \varphi(R_i'', \rho_{-i})$ for all admissible R_i'' with $x_i'' > x_j = \varphi(\rho)$.

Together, (1a) and (1b) yield φ strategy-proof here, as required.

(2) $\varphi(\rho) = y_{\{1,\ldots,j\}}$ for some $j \in N$. The proof is similar to that for Case (1): details are left as an Exercise. □

While Lemma 2.4 shows that augmented median voter rules appropriately generalize Example 2.5, it leaves open the possibility that other sorts of strategy-proof collective choice functions can be found on single-peaked domains. But, in fact, no such functions exist.

Theorem 2.4 *A collective choice function* $\varphi : \mathcal{S}_Q \to X$ *is strategy-proof and satisfies citizen sovereignty if and only if* φ *is an augmented median voter rule with* $y_\emptyset = a_r$ *and* $y_N = a_1$.

Lemma 2.4 already establishes sufficiency; the argument for necessity is rather long and involves three intermediate steps. These steps, however, are of some interest in their own right as they expose a variety of properties implied by strategy-proofness and citizen sovereignty. The first claim (Lemma 2.5) is that, under citizen sovereignty on $\mathcal{S}_Q$, if φ is strategy-proof then the function must ignore all preference information save for the location of individuals' ideal points in X; given this fact, it then turns out (Lemma 2.6) that φ strategy-proof requires an individually-specific median property to hold simultaneously for every individual $i \in N$; finally, the last step is an observation that the median property identified in Lemma 2.6 means strategy-proof collective choice functions satisfying citizen sovereignty must also exhibit a monotonicity property and be insensitive to individuals revealing ever more extreme ideal points (Lemma 2.7). Together, Lemmas 2.5, 2.6 and 2.7 permit a proof for the claim that strategy-proofness and citizen sovereignty imply a collective choice function must be an augmented median voter rule.

Definition 2.9 *A collective choice function $\varphi : S_Q \to X$ satisfies,*

(1) peak only if for all $\rho, \rho' \in S_Q$ such that $x_i = x'_i$ for all $i \in N$, $\varphi(\rho) = \varphi(\rho')$;

(2) unanimity if for all $\rho \in S_Q$ such that $x_i = x_j$ all $i, j \in N$, $\varphi(\rho) = x_i$.

From an information processing perspective, having collective decision-making in single-peaked environments depends only on the list of individuals' ideal points (peak only) is welcome; but from a normative perspective, save for the case in which all individuals share the same most preferred alternative (unanimity), it is less appealing ignoring as it does information about how individuals rank other alternatives. This is perhaps most starkly illustrated by observing that, if applied to the entire domain S rather than to each separate subdomain S_Q, "peak only" rejects the *Condorcet criterion*, whereby an alternative strictly preferred by some majority over every other alternative in a pairwise comparison should, if one exists, be chosen: Example 2.7 demonstrates the point and further illustrates how results on strategy-proofness with single-peaked preferences are more limited than those on rational preference aggregation rules [PPTI, ch.1].

Example 2.7 Let $X = \{a, b, c\}$ and $N = \{1, 2, 3\}$. Consider the profiles ρ and ρ', where

$$\rho = \begin{cases} aP_1bP_1c \\ bP_2cP_2a \\ cP_3bP_3a \end{cases} ; \rho' = \begin{cases} aP_1cP_1b \\ bP_2cP_2a \\ cP_3aP_3b \end{cases} .$$

It is easy to check $\rho, \rho' \in S$ and $x_i = x'_i$ for all $i \in N$. Then peak only, applied to full domain S, insists $\varphi(\rho) = \varphi(\rho')$. But this is inconsistent with application of the Condorcet criterion: at ρ there are strict majorities preferring b to a and to c; at ρ' there are strict majorities preferring c to a and to b. $\square$

Example 2.7 notwithstanding, if we are committed to strategy-proofness and to citizens' sovereignty separately on all domains S_Q, then we are likewise committed to peak only and weak Paretianism (and therefore unanimity) on these domains. Let Q be a strict ordering of X with respect to which preferences are single-peaked and $a_t Q a_{t-1}$ for all $t = 2, ..., r$, $r \equiv |X|$; let $i \in N$ have ideal point $x_i = a_t$ and let $y \in X \setminus \{x_i\}$. Recalling that $R_i^{-1}(y)$ is the set of alternatives ranked no better than y by individual i, it is useful to define the alternative $\iota_i(y) \in X$ by

$$\iota_i(y) = \begin{cases} \max_{s<t}\{a_s \in R_i^{-1}(y) \cup \{a_1\}\} \text{ if } yQx_i, \\ \min_{s>t}\{a_s \in R_i^{-1}(y) \cup \{a_r\}\} \text{ if } x_iQy \end{cases} .$$

2.4. SINGLE-PEAKED PREFERENCES

Thus, with respect to Q, x_i lies between $\iota_i(y)$ and y. To understand the definition, suppose (without loss of generality) that yQx_i and $x_i = a_t$. Consider Figure 2.2, below, illustrating a single-peaked preference order. If, as shown in the top panel of the figure, $\{a_1,...,a_{t-1}\} \cap R_i^{-1}(y)$ is empty, then $a_s P_i y$ for all $s \leq t-1$ and $\iota_i(y) = a_1$. If, on the other hand, $\{a_1,...,a_{t-1}\} \cap R_i^{-1}(y)$ is nonempty, then $\iota_i(y) = a_s$ for some $s \leq t-1$. In this case, either $yP_i\iota_i(y)$ and $a_{s+1}P_iy$, as shown in the middle panel of Figure 2.2, or, as shown in the lower panel of the figure, $\iota_i(y)I_iy$.

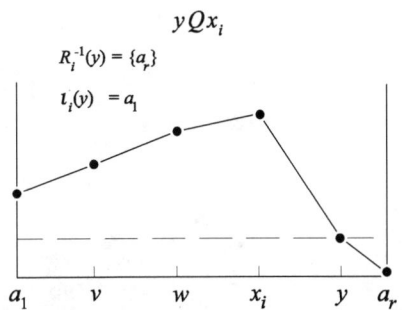

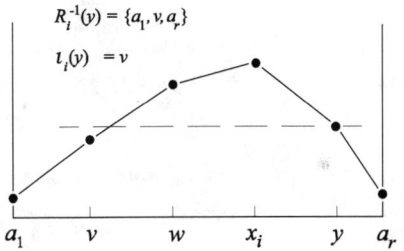

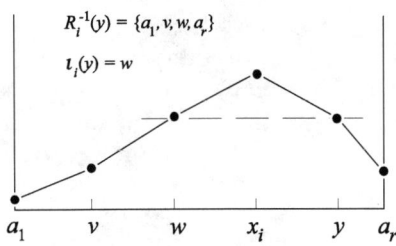

Figure 2.2: The function $\iota_i(y)$

Lemma 2.5 Let $\varphi : S_Q \to X$ be strategy-proof and satisfy citizen sovereignty. Then φ is weakly Paretian and satisfies peak only.

Proof (Weakly Paretian) To show $\min\{x_i\}_{i \in N} \leq \varphi(\rho) \leq \max\{x_i\}_{i \in N}$ for all $\rho \in S_Q$, we first show that strategy-proofness and voter sovereignty imply unanimity. To this end, let $\rho \in S_Q$ be any profile such that, for all $i \in N$, $x_i = x$; we want to show $\varphi(\rho) = x$. By citizen sovereignty there exists a profile $\rho' \in S_Q$ such that $\varphi(\rho') = x$. By strategy-proofness, for all admissible single-peaked R'_1, $\varphi(R_1, \rho'_{-1}) R_1 \varphi(R'_1, \rho'_{-1})$; in particular, since $\varphi(R'_1, \rho'_{-1}) \equiv \varphi(\rho') = x_1$ by hypothesis and ideal points are uniquely defined, we must have $\varphi(\rho') = \varphi(R_1, \rho'_{-1})$. But $\varphi(R_1, \rho'_{-1}) = x$ and $x = x_2$; hence, by strategy-proofness, it must also be that $\varphi(R_1, \rho'_{-1}) = \varphi(R_1, R_2, \rho'_{-\{1,2\}})$. Repeating the argument for $j = 3, .., n$ yields $\varphi(\rho) = x$. Thus φ satisfies unanimity.

Now consider any profile $\rho^\circ \in S_Q$ such that $x_1 \leq x_2 \leq \ldots \leq x_n$ and $x_1 < x_n$ and suppose, contrary to φ weakly Paretian, $\varphi(\rho^\circ) > x_n$. For $k = 1, 2, \ldots, n-1$, fix an admissible profile $\rho^k = (\rho'_{\{1,\ldots,k\}}, \rho^\circ_{-\{1,\ldots,k\}}) \in S_Q$ such that, for all $j \leq k$, $x'_j = x_n$ and $\varphi(\rho^\circ) P'_j a_t$ for all $a_t < x_n$. By φ strategy-proof, $\varphi(\rho^\circ) R_1 \varphi(\rho^1)$. By R_1 single-peaked, therefore, either $\varphi(\rho^1) \geq \varphi(\rho^\circ) > x_n$ or $\varphi(\rho^1) \leq \iota_1(\varphi(\rho^\circ)) < x_1$. Suppose the latter case holds, so $\varphi(\rho^1) < x_1 < x_n$ and, by definition of P'_1, $\varphi(\rho^\circ) P'_1 \varphi(\rho^1)$. But then $j = 1$ can profitably manipulate φ by reporting R_1 instead of R'_1 at ρ^1. So, $\varphi(\rho^1) \geq \varphi(\rho^\circ)$. Moreover, since φ strategy-proof requires $\varphi(\rho^1) R'_1 \varphi(\rho^\circ)$ which, by R'_1 single-peaked, implies $\varphi(\rho^1) \leq \varphi(\rho^\circ)$, we must have $\varphi(\rho^\circ) = \varphi(\rho^1)$. Now applying this argument iteratively, we find $\varphi(\rho^{n-1}) = \ldots = \varphi(\rho^1) = \varphi(\rho^\circ) > x_n$. But by construction, ρ^{n-1} is such that $x'_j = x_n$ for all $j \in N$, in which case, φ unanimous implies $\varphi(\rho^{n-1}) = x_n$: contradiction. A symmetric argument accounts for the case $\varphi(\rho^\circ) < x_1$. Hence, φ must be weakly Paretian.

(Peak only) Now fix $\rho \in S_Q$, arbitrary $i \in N$ and any single-peaked preference ordering R'_i with $x_i = x'_i$. To prove the lemma, it suffices to show $\varphi(\rho) = \varphi(R'_i, \rho_{-i})$. If $\varphi(\rho) = x'_i$, then the result is trivial. So, without loss of generality, assume $x'_i = x_i > \varphi(\rho)$. There are two cases (in what follows, the alternative $\iota'_i(y)$ is defined in exactly the same way as the alternative $\iota_i(y)$, above, but with respect to the preference ordering R'_i rather than to the ordering R_i).

(1) $\iota'_i(\varphi(\rho)) < \iota_i(\varphi(\rho))$. Suppose $\varphi(\rho) \neq \varphi(R'_i, \rho_{-i})$. Then, depending on the relative position of the alternative $\varphi(R'_i, \rho_{-i})$, there are three possibilities, each of which (given single-peakedness) contradicts strategy-proofness:

2.4. SINGLE-PEAKED PREFERENCES

see Figure 2.3.

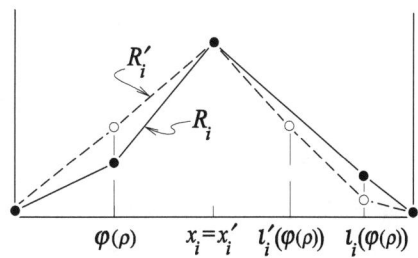

Figure 2.3: Lemma 2.5, case (1)

(1a):

$$\varphi(R'_i, \rho_{-i}) < \varphi(\rho) \Rightarrow \varphi(R'_i, \rho_{-i}) < \varphi(\rho) < x'_i$$
$$\Rightarrow \varphi(\rho) P'_i \varphi(R'_i, \rho_{-i})$$
$$\Rightarrow \varphi \text{ manipulable at } (R'_i, \rho_{-i}).$$

(1b):

$$\varphi(\rho) < \varphi(R'_i, \rho_{-i}) \leq \iota'_i(\varphi(\rho))$$
$$\Rightarrow \varphi(\rho) < \varphi(R'_i, \rho_{-i}) < \iota_i(\varphi(\rho))$$
$$\Rightarrow \varphi(R'_i, \rho_{-i}) P_i \varphi(\rho)$$
$$\Rightarrow \varphi \text{ manipulable at } \rho.$$

(1c):

$$\iota'_i(\varphi(\rho)) < \varphi(R'_i, \rho_{-i}) \Rightarrow x'_i < \iota'_i(\varphi(\rho)) < \varphi(R'_i, \rho_{-i})$$
$$\Rightarrow \varphi(\rho) P'_i \varphi(R'_i, \rho_{-i})$$
$$\Rightarrow \varphi \text{ manipulable at } (R'_i, \rho_{-i}).$$

Therefore, if, contrary to the claim, $\varphi(\rho) \neq \varphi(R'_i, \rho_{-i})$, we must have $\varphi(R'_i, \rho_{-i}) \geq \iota_i(\varphi(\rho)) > x'_i$ and $\iota_i(\varphi(\rho)) \leq \iota'_i(\varphi(\rho))$, the second case.

(2) $\iota_i(\varphi(\rho)) \leq \iota'_i(\varphi(\rho))$. In this case, we need to take a more indirect approach than in case (1) to proving the claim. To this end, let $L = \{j \in N : x_j > x'_i\}$. If $L = \emptyset$ then $x'_i = x_i \geq x_k$ for all $k \in N$. But since, $\varphi(\rho) \neq \varphi(R'_i, \rho_{-i})$ implies $\varphi(R'_i, \rho_{-i}) > x'_i$ from Case (1), this contradicts φ weakly Paretian. So assume $L \neq \emptyset$. By relabeling if necessary, let $L = \{1, ..., \ell\}$ and $x_1 \leq x_2 \leq ... \leq x_\ell$. For all $j \in L$, let R'_j be such that $x'_j = x'_i$ and $x_j \leq \iota'_j(\varphi(\rho)) \leq \iota_j(\varphi(\rho))$: see Figure 2.4 for the situation in which all of the inequalities are strict for i and some $j \in L$.

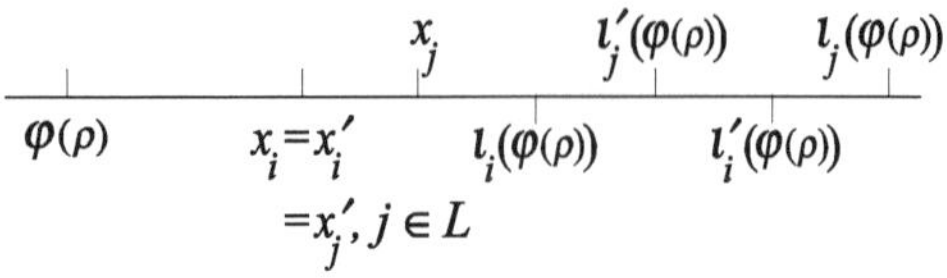

46   CHAPTER 2. STRATEGY-PROOF COLLECTIVE CHOICE

```
                        x_j        ι'_j(φ(ρ))     ι_j(φ(ρ))
    |——————|———————————|—————————————|————————————|————
    φ(ρ)   x_i=x'_i     ι_i(φ(ρ))     ι'_i(φ(ρ))
           =x'_j, j ∈ L
```

Figure 2.4: Lemma 2.5, case (2)

Consider $\ell \in L$ and the choice $\varphi(R'_\ell, \rho_{-\ell})$. Suppose $\varphi(R'_\ell, \rho_{-\ell}) \neq \varphi(\rho)$. Arguing similarly to Case (1), single-peaked preferences implies that φ is manipulable by ℓ unless $\varphi(R'_\ell, \rho_{-\ell}) \geq \iota_\ell(\varphi(\rho)) > x_\ell$. But since, by definition, $x_\ell \geq x_k$ for all $k \in N$, $\varphi(R'_\ell, \rho_{-\ell}) > x_\ell$ contradicts φ weakly Paretian. Hence $\varphi(R'_\ell, \rho_{-\ell}) = \varphi(\rho)$. Applying the same argument, *mutatis mutandis*, to $\ell - 1$ then yields $\varphi(R'_\ell, R'_{\ell-1}, \rho_{-\{\ell,\ell-1\}}) = \varphi(R'_\ell, \rho_{-\ell}) = \varphi(\rho)$. And continuing in this way iteratively for $\ell - 2, \ell - 3, \ldots, 1$, conclude $\varphi(\rho) = \varphi(\rho'_L, \rho_{-L})$. Now consider the profile $\rho' = (\rho'_{L \cup \{i\}}, \rho_{-L \cup \{i\}})$. There are five possibilities for the relative location of $\varphi(\rho')$. In four of these, $\varphi(\rho') \neq \varphi(\rho)$ and we show that i has opportunity to manipulate the outcome profitably; thus we must have $\varphi(\rho') = \varphi(\rho)$ and, in this case we show $\varphi(\rho') = \varphi(R'_i, \rho_{-i})$ as claimed.

(2a): $\varphi(\rho') < \varphi(\rho)$. Referring to Figure 2.4, observe

$$\begin{aligned}
\varphi(\rho') &< \varphi(\rho) \Rightarrow \varphi(\rho') < \varphi(\rho) < x'_i \\
&\Rightarrow \varphi(\rho) P'_i \varphi(\rho') \\
&\Rightarrow \varphi \text{ manipulable at } \rho'.
\end{aligned}$$

(2b): $\varphi(\rho') = \varphi(\rho)$. In this subcase, we need to show: $\varphi(\rho') = \varphi(R'_i, \rho_{-i})$. We first show $\varphi(\rho') = \varphi(R_1, \rho'_{-1})$; to do this, suppose the contrary, $\varphi(\rho') \neq \varphi(R_1, \rho'_{-1})$. Then arguing as for Case (1), φ strategy-proof implies $\iota'_1(\varphi(\rho')) \leq \varphi(R_1, \rho'_{-1}) \leq \iota_1(\varphi(\rho'))$ with $x_1 < \varphi(R_1, \rho'_{-1})$. Now, for all $j \neq 1$, let R''_j be an admissible single-peaked ordering such that $x''_j = x_1$ and

$$\begin{aligned}
j &\in L \setminus \{1\} \Rightarrow \iota'_j(\varphi(R_1, \rho'_{-1})) < \iota''_j(\varphi(R_1, \rho'_{-1})), \\
j &\notin L \Rightarrow \iota_j(\varphi(R_1, \rho'_{-1})) < \iota''_j(\varphi(R_1, \rho'_{-1})).
\end{aligned}$$

Figure 2.5 illustrates the construction.

2.4. SINGLE-PEAKED PREFERENCES

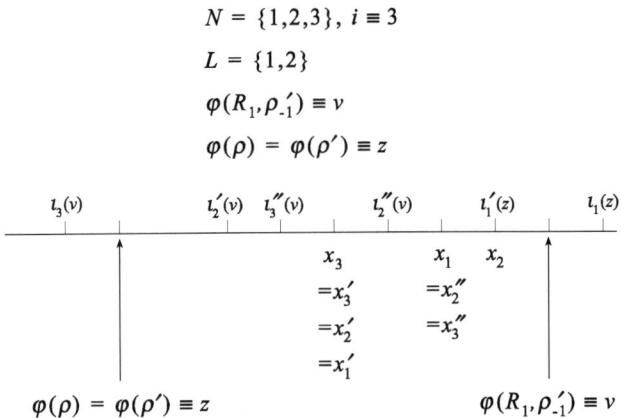

Figure 2.5: Lemma 2.5, case (2b)

Using a similar argument to that above for $\varphi(\rho) = \varphi(\rho'_L, \rho_{-L})$, conclude $\varphi(R_1, \rho'_{-1}) = \varphi(R_1, \rho''_{-1})$. But then $x_1 = x''_2 = \ldots = x''_n < \varphi(R_1, \rho'_{-1})$, contradicting φ unanimous; therefore, $\varphi(\rho') = \varphi(R_1, \rho'_{-1})$ necessarily. Serially repeating the preceding argument for each $j \in L$ yields

$$\varphi(\rho') = \varphi(R_1, \rho'_{-1}) = \varphi(R_1, R_2, \rho'_{-\{1,2\}}) = \ldots = \varphi(\rho_L, \rho'_{-L}) = \varphi(R'_i, \rho_{-i})$$

as required.

(2c): $\varphi(\rho) < \varphi(\rho') < \iota_i(\varphi(\rho))$. But then $\varphi(\rho) = \varphi(\rho'_L, \rho_{-L})$ implies

$$\begin{aligned}\varphi(\rho'_L, \rho_{-L}) &< \varphi(\rho'_{L\cup\{i\}}, \rho_{-L\cup\{i\}}) < \iota_i(\varphi(\rho)) \\ &\Rightarrow \varphi(\rho') P_i \varphi(\rho) \\ &\Rightarrow \varphi \text{ manipulable at } \rho.\end{aligned}$$

(2d): $\iota_i(\varphi(\rho)) \leq \varphi(\rho') \leq \iota'_i(\varphi(\rho))$. In this case, a similar argument as that for (2b) yields a contradiction of φ unanimous [Exercise].

(2e): $\varphi(\rho') > \iota'_i(\varphi(\rho))$. Referring to Figure 2.4, observe

$$\begin{aligned}\varphi(\rho') &> \iota'_i(\varphi(\rho)) \Rightarrow x'_i < \iota'_i(\varphi(\rho)) = \iota'_i(\varphi(\rho'_L, \rho_{-L})) < \varphi(\rho') \\ &\Rightarrow \varphi(\rho'_L, \rho_{-L}) P'_i \varphi(\rho') \\ &\Rightarrow \varphi \text{ manipulable at } \rho'.\end{aligned}$$

Because the situation where $\varphi(\rho) > x'_i$ is completely symmetric, the lemma is proved. □

Because unanimity clearly implies citizen sovereignty, Lemma 2.5 implies that, in the presence of strategy-proofness, citizen sovereignty and unanimity are equivalent on the domains $\mathcal{S}_Q$. The next step is to show similarly that, in the presence of strategy-proofness, peak only is equivalent to collective choice functions having a particular median property. Let $\underline{R}_i$ (respectively, $\bar{R}_i$) denote any admissible single-peaked preference ordering with $\underline{x}_i = a_1$ (respectively, $\bar{x}_i = a_r$).

Lemma 2.6 *A collective choice function $\varphi : \mathcal{S}_Q \to X$ is strategy-proof and satisfies peak only if and only if, for all $\rho \in \mathcal{S}_Q$ and all $i \in N$,*

$$\varphi(\rho) = med_Q\{x_i, \varphi(\underline{R}_i, \rho_{-i}), \varphi(\bar{R}_i, \rho_{-i})\}.$$

Proof (Necessity) Let φ be strategy-proof and satisfy peak only. Fix $\rho \in \mathcal{S}_Q$ and $i \in N$. If $\varphi(\bar{R}_i, \rho_{-i}) < \varphi(\underline{R}_i, \rho_{-i})$ then $\varphi(\bar{R}_i, \rho_{-i}) < \varphi(\underline{R}_i, \rho_{-i}) \leq \bar{x}_i = a_r$, implying $\varphi(\underline{R}_i, \rho_{-i})\bar{P}_i\varphi(\bar{R}_i, \rho_{-i})$. But this contradicts φ strategy-proof at $(\bar{R}_i, \rho_{-i})$. Hence, $\varphi(\underline{R}_i, \rho_{-i}) \leq \varphi(\bar{R}_i, \rho_{-i})$. Consider two cases.

(1) If $\varphi(\underline{R}_i, \rho_{-i}) < x_i < \varphi(\bar{R}_i, \rho_{-i})$, $med_Q\{x_i, \varphi(\underline{R}_i, \rho_{-i}), \varphi(\bar{R}_i, \rho_{-i})\} = x_i$. Now suppose that $\varphi(\rho) \neq x_i$. Without loss of generality, assume $\varphi(\rho) < x_i$. Let R'_i be an admissible single-peaked ordering such that $x'_i = x_i$ and $\varphi(\bar{R}_i, \rho_{-i})P'_i\varphi(\rho)$. By peak only, $\varphi(R'_i, \rho_{-i}) = \varphi(\rho)$, so $\varphi(\bar{R}_i, \rho_{-i})P'_i\varphi(R'_i, \rho_{-i})$ contradicting φ strategy-proof at (R'_i, ρ_{-i}).

(2) If $x_i \leq \varphi(\underline{R}_i, \rho_{-i})$, $med_Q\{x_i, \varphi(\underline{R}_i, \rho_{-i}), \varphi(\bar{R}_i, \rho_{-i})\} = \varphi(\underline{R}_i, \rho_{-i})$. Suppose, again without loss of generality, $\varphi(\rho) < \varphi(\underline{R}_i, \rho_{-i})$. Then $\underline{x}_i \leq \varphi(\rho) < \varphi(\underline{R}_i, \rho_{-i})$, in which case $\varphi(\rho)\underline{P}_i\varphi(\underline{R}_i, \rho_{-i})$ contradicting φ strategy-proof at $(\underline{R}_i, \rho_{-i})$. The remaining possibility, $x_i \geq \varphi(\bar{R}_i, \rho_{-i})$, similarly leads to a contradiction.

(Sufficiency) [Exercise]. □

In words, Lemma 2.6 says that if φ is strategy-proof and peak only, then no individual must be able to profit by reporting an extreme ideal point (unless, of course, such an extreme preference is that individual's true preference). In view of single-peakedness, therefore, the collective choice at any profile must either be the individual's ideal point itself or an outcome that the individual could induce by pretending to be extreme, given all others report the truth. Moreover, this must be so for *every* individual at the same time.

We now use the median property of Lemma 2.6 to connect strategy-proofness to two other useful properties a collective choice function might exhibit.

2.4. SINGLE-PEAKED PREFERENCES

Definition 2.10 *A collective choice function $\varphi : \mathcal{S}_Q \to X$ is,*
(1) peak monotonic if for all $\rho \in \mathcal{S}_Q$, all $i \in N$, and all admissible R_i' such that $x_i' \geq x_i$, $\varphi(R_i', \rho_{-i}) \geq \varphi(\rho)$;
(2) uncompromising if for all $\rho \in \mathcal{S}_Q$, all $i \in N$, and all admissible R_i' such that either $[\varphi(\rho) < x_i$ and $\varphi(\rho) \leq x_i']$ or $[\varphi(\rho) > x_i$ and $\varphi(\rho) \geq x_i']$, $\varphi(\rho) = \varphi(R_i', \rho_{-i})$.

In words, "peak monotonicity" requires collective decisions not to respond perversely in changes in individuals' ideal points; "uncompromising" collective choice functions preclude individuals shifting collective decisions by revealing ever more extreme ideal points. It is straightforward to check that peak monotonicity implies (but is not implied by) peak only [Exercise]. And by definition of φ specified in Lemma 2.6, the following claim is true.

Lemma 2.7 *If, for all $\rho \in \mathcal{S}_Q$ and all $i \in N$,*

$$\varphi(\rho) = med_Q\{x_i, \varphi(\underline{R}_i, \rho_{-i}), \varphi(\bar{R}_i, \rho_{-i})\},$$

then φ is peak monotonic and uncompromising.

Proof [Exercise]. □

We are now ready to prove Theorem 2.4.

Proof of Theorem 2.4 Sufficiency follows from Lemma 2.4. To prove necessity, let φ be strategy-proof and satisfy citizen sovereignty. By Lemmas 2.5, 2.6 and 2.7, φ satisfies unanimity, peak monotonicity and is uncompromising. Let $\underline{\rho} = (\underline{R}_1, \ldots, \underline{R}_n)$ and $\bar{\rho} = (\bar{R}_1, \ldots, \bar{R}_n)$. For all $L \subseteq N$, define $y_L = \varphi(\underline{\rho}_L, \bar{\rho}_{-L})$. By unanimity, $y_N = \varphi(\underline{\rho}) = a_1 < y_\emptyset = \varphi(\bar{\rho}) = a_r$. Now consider any profile $\rho \in \mathcal{S}_Q$ and, without loss of generality, relabel N if necessary so $x_1 \leq x_2 \leq \ldots \leq x_n$; then $(i_1, \ldots, i_n) = (1, \ldots, n)$. We wish to show

$$\varphi(\rho) = med_Q\{x_1, \ldots, x_n, y_\emptyset, y_{\{1\}}, y_{\{1,2\}}, \ldots, y_N\}.$$

By repeated applications of peak monotonicity, $L \subseteq M \subseteq N$ implies $y_L \geq y_M$; in particular,

$$y_\emptyset \geq y_{\{1\}} \geq y_{\{1,2\}} \geq \ldots \geq y_N$$

or, equivalently,

$$\varphi(\bar{\rho}) \geq \varphi(\underline{R}_1, \bar{\rho}_{-1}) \geq \varphi(\underline{R}_1, \underline{R}_2, \bar{\rho}_{-\{1,2\}}) \geq \ldots \geq \varphi(\underline{\rho}).$$

Then exactly one of the following must obtain:

$$
\begin{array}{rcccc}
a_r & = & \varphi(\bar{\rho}) & \leq & x_1 \\
\varphi(\underline{R}_1, \bar{\rho}_{-1}) & < & x_1 & < & \varphi(\bar{\rho}) \\
x_1 & \leq & \varphi(\underline{R}_1, \bar{\rho}_{-1}) & \leq & x_2 \\
\varphi(\underline{R}_1, \underline{R}_2, \bar{\rho}_{-\{1,2\}}) & < & x_2 & < & \varphi(\underline{R}_1, \bar{\rho}_{-1}) \\
x_2 & \leq & \varphi(\underline{R}_1, \underline{R}_2, \bar{\rho}_{-\{1,2\}}) & \leq & x_3 \\
& & \cdots & & \\
x_{n-1} & \leq & \varphi(\underline{\rho}_{N\setminus\{n\}}, \bar{R}_n) & \leq & x_n \\
\varphi(\underline{\rho}) & < & x_n & < & \varphi(\underline{\rho}_{N\setminus\{n\}}, \bar{R}_n) \\
x_n & \leq & \varphi(\underline{\rho}) & = & a_1
\end{array}
$$

There are three cases to consider.

(1) $\varphi(\bar{\rho}) \leq x_1$ or $x_n \leq \varphi(\underline{\rho})$. Without loss of generality, suppose $\varphi(\bar{\rho}) \leq x_1$. Because $\varphi(\bar{\rho}) = a_r$, therefore, $x_i = a_r$ for all $i \in N$. So, by unanimity,

$$\varphi(\bar{\rho}) = \varphi(\rho) = med_Q\{x_1, \ldots, x_n, y_\emptyset, y_{\{1\}}, y_{\{1,2\}}, \ldots, y_N\}$$

as required.

(2) $\varphi(\underline{\rho}_{\{1,\ldots,i\}}, \bar{\rho}_{-\{1,\ldots,i\}}) < x_i < \varphi(\underline{\rho}_{\{1,\ldots,i-1\}}, \bar{\rho}_{-\{1,\ldots,i-1\}})$ for some $i \in N$. For any $j \in N$, let $L_j = \{1, \ldots, j\}$. We first show $x_i = \varphi(\underline{\rho}_{L_{i-1}}, R_i, \bar{\rho}_{-L_i})$. To do this, assume the contrary and, without loss of generality, let $x_i > \varphi(\underline{\rho}_{L_{i-1}}, R_i, \bar{\rho}_{-L_i})$. Because $\bar{x}_i = a_r > \varphi(\underline{\rho}_{L_{i-1}}, R_i, \bar{\rho}_{-L_i})$, φ uncompromising implies

$$\varphi(\underline{\rho}_{L_{i-1}}, \bar{\rho}_{-L_{i-1}}) = \varphi(\underline{\rho}_{L_{i-1}}, R_i, \bar{\rho}_{-L_i}) < x_i,$$

which contradicts $x_i < \varphi(\underline{\rho}_{\{1,\ldots,i-1\}}, \bar{\rho}_{-\{1,\ldots,i-1\}})$. So $x_i = \varphi(\underline{\rho}_{L_{i-1}}, R_i, \bar{\rho}_{-L_i})$ as required. We now show

$$\varphi(\underline{\rho}_{L_{i-1}}, R_i, \bar{\rho}_{-L_i}) = med_Q\{x_1, \ldots, x_n, y_\emptyset, y_{\{1\}}, y_{\{1,2\}}, \ldots, y_N\}.$$

Since, for all $j < i$, $x_j \leq x_i = \varphi(\underline{\rho}_{L_{i-1}}, R_i, \bar{\rho}_{-L_i})$,

$$a_1 \leq x_j \leq \varphi(\underline{\rho}_{L_{i-1}}, R_i, \bar{\rho}_{-L_i}).$$

Similarly, for all $j > i$,

$$\varphi(\underline{\rho}_{L_{i-1}}, R_i, \bar{\rho}_{-L_i}) \leq x_j \leq a_r.$$

2.4. SINGLE-PEAKED PREFERENCES

Therefore, by $x_i = \varphi(\underline{\rho}_{L_{i-1}}, R_i, \bar{\rho}_{-L_i})$ and the hypothesis $\varphi(\underline{\rho}_{L_i}, \bar{\rho}_{-L_i}) < x_i < \varphi(\underline{\rho}_{L_{i-1}}, \bar{\rho}_{-L_{i-1}})$,

$$\varphi(\underline{\rho}_{L_{i-1}}, R_i, \bar{\rho}_{-L_i}) = med_Q\{x_1, \ldots, x_n, y_\emptyset, y_{\{1\}}, y_{\{1,2\}}, \ldots, y_N\}.$$

It remains to show $\varphi(\rho) = x_i$ here. Suppose to the contrary that $x_i > \varphi(\rho)$. By φ uncompromising and $x_i \leq a_r$, $\varphi(\rho) = \varphi(\bar{R}_i, \rho_{-i})$. Therefore, $x_{i+1} \geq x_i$ and φ uncompromising imply $\varphi(\rho) = \varphi(\bar{R}_i, \rho_{-i}) = \varphi(\bar{R}_i, \bar{R}_{i+1}, \rho_{-\{i,i+1\}})$. Repeating the step for all $j \geq i+2$ eventually yields $\varphi(\rho) = \varphi(\underline{\rho}_{L_{i-1}}, \bar{\rho}_{-L_{i-1}})$. By peak monotonicity, $\varphi(\underline{\rho}_{L_{i-1}}, \bar{\rho}_{-L_{i-1}}) \leq \varphi(\underline{\rho}_{L_{i-1}}, \bar{\rho}_{-L_{i-1}})$. But the hypothesis for case (2) includes $x_i < \varphi(\underline{\rho}_{L_{i-1}}, \bar{\rho}_{-L_{i-1}})$ in which case $x_i < \varphi(\underline{\rho}_{L_{i-1}}, \bar{\rho}_{-L_{i-1}})$ also, contradicting $x_i > \varphi(\rho) = \varphi(\underline{\rho}_{L_{i-1}}, \bar{\rho}_{-L_{i-1}})$. Hence,

$$\varphi(\rho) = med_Q\{x_1, \ldots, x_n, y_\emptyset, y_{\{1\}}, y_{\{1,2\}}, \ldots, y_N\}$$

as required.

(3) $x_i \leq \varphi(\underline{\rho}_{L_i}, \bar{\rho}_{-L_i}) \leq x_{i+1}$ for some $i \leq n-1$. In this case,

$$\forall j \leq i, \; a_1 \leq x_j \leq \varphi(\underline{\rho}_{L_i}, \bar{\rho}_{-L_i})$$

and

$$\forall j > i, \; \varphi(\underline{\rho}_{L_i}, \bar{\rho}_{-L_i}) \leq x_j \leq a_r.$$

Therefore,

$$\varphi(\underline{\rho}_{L_i}, \bar{\rho}_{-L_i}) = med_Q\{x_1, \ldots, x_n, y_\emptyset, y_{\{1\}}, y_{\{1,2\}}, \ldots, y_N\}.$$

We have to show $\varphi(\rho) = \varphi(\underline{\rho}_{L_i}, \bar{\rho}_{-L_i})$. Without loss of generality, suppose $\varphi(\rho) > \varphi(\underline{\rho}_{L_i}, \bar{\rho}_{-L_i})$. Then, by the hypothesis for case (3), $x_i < \varphi(\rho)$. By φ uncompromising and $x_j \leq x_i$ for all $j < i$, $\varphi(\rho) = \varphi(\underline{\rho}_{L_i}, \rho_{-L_i})$; and by peak monotonicity and $x_j \geq x_i$ for all $j > i$, $\varphi(\underline{\rho}_{L_i}, \rho_{-L_i}) \leq \varphi(\underline{\rho}_{L_i}, \bar{\rho}_{-L_i})$. But then the supposition entails

$$\varphi(\rho) = \varphi(\underline{\rho}_{L_i}, \rho_{-L_i}) \leq \varphi(\underline{\rho}_{L_i}, \bar{\rho}_{-L_i}) < \varphi(\rho)$$

which is absurd. Therefore $\varphi(\rho) = \varphi(\underline{\rho}_{L_i}, \bar{\rho}_{-L_i})$, implying

$$\varphi(\rho) = med_Q\{x_1, \ldots, x_n, y_\emptyset, y_{\{1\}}, y_{\{1,2\}}, \ldots, y_N\}$$

as required and completing the proof of necessity. $\square$

Given that citizen sovereignty is required of any collective choice process, Theorem 2.4 characterizes all strategy-proof collective choice functions on single-peaked domains. However, augmented median voter rules can be dictatorial as Example 2.6(2) shows. On the other hand, there are clearly many nondictatorial collective choice functions within the class.

Dictatorship is an extreme violation of the normative requirement of anonymity: recall that a collective choice function $\varphi : \mathcal{R}^n_{cs} \to X$ is anonymous if and only if $\varphi(\rho) = \varphi(\rho')$ for all profiles $\rho, \rho' \in \mathcal{R}^n$ that differ only in the assignment of preference orderings to individuals. Thus anonymous collective choice functions completely ignore information about which particular preference ordering is held by which particular individual at any profile; only the unordered list of preference orderings itself matters. And as Example 2.6(3) indicates, an augmented median voter rule is anonymous if and only if, for all $L \subseteq N$, y_S depends exclusively on $|L|$. With this in mind, we have

Corollary 2.1 *A collective choice function $\varphi : S_Q \to X$ is strategy-proof, anonymous and satisfies citizen sovereignty if and only if there exist $n - 1$ alternatives $\{y_1, \ldots, y_{n-1}\} \subseteq X$ such that, for all $\rho \in S_Q$,*

$$\varphi(\rho) = med_Q\{x_1, \ldots, x_n, y_1, \ldots, y_{n-1}\}.$$

Proof (Necessity) By Theorem 2.4, φ is strategy-proof and satisfies citizen sovereignty only if it is an augmented median voter rule with $y_\emptyset = a_r$ and $y_N = a_1$. And φ is anonymous only if, for all $L, M \subseteq N$, $|L| = |M|$ implies $y_L = y_M$. The claim now follows because, for all proper subsets $L \subset N$, $|L| \in \{1, \ldots, n - 1\}$.

(Sufficiency) [Exercise]. □

2.5 Application: The amendment rule revisited

In general, the amendment rule φ_α described in section 2.2 is subject to manipulation. On single-peaked domains this is no longer the case. To see this, recall that for any single-peaked profile $\rho \in S_Q$ for some ordering Q of alternatives, there exists a *Condorcet winner*: an alternative $x \in X$ such that $|P(x, y; \rho)| > n/2$ for every $y \in X \backslash \{x\}$ (where n is assumed odd for convenience). It follows, therefore, that for all $\rho \in S_Q$ and any sequence of alternatives α, $\varphi_\alpha(\rho)$ must be the Condorcet winner at ρ. Consequently, φ_α is manipulable at a profile $\rho \in S_Q$ if and only if there is an individual i and

2.6. STRATEGY-PROOFNESS IN THE SPATIAL MODEL

an admissible ordering R'_i such that $\varphi_\alpha(R'_i, \rho_{-i})$ is strictly preferred by i to the Condorcet winner at ρ. But since (with n odd) the Condorcet winner at any profile is defined by the median ideal point [PPTI, Theorem 4.4], $x_{i_{(n+1)/2}}$, the amendment rule on a single-peaked domain $\mathcal{S}_Q$ is equivalent to the (anonymous) augmented median voter rule

$$\varphi(\rho) = med_Q\{x_1, \ldots, x_n, \underbrace{a_r, \ldots, a_r}_{(n+1)/2 \text{ times}}, \underbrace{a_1, \ldots, a_1}_{(n+1)/2 \text{ times}}\}.$$

Therefore, by Theorem 2.4, no such individual i or admissible ordering R'_i exists.

2.6 Strategy-proofness in the spatial model

The argument for the Gibbard-Satterthwaite Theorem (Theorem 2.1) used the unrestricted domain assumption in critical ways. In particular, when constructing sequences of profiles, individual preferences could in principle vary discontinuously. But in the spatial model [PPTI, ch.5], where X is a compact subset of $\Re^k$, natural assumptions on preferences include continuity and convexity. Consequently, not all of the arguments for the Gibbard-Satterthwaite Theorem are applicable in the spatial model, and hence the validity of the theorem in this setting becomes unclear. Thus, at this point, it is an open question whether there exist nondictatorial strategy-proof collective choice functions on X when X is a compact convex subset of $\Re^k$ and $\rho \in \mathcal{R}_{cs}^n$, the set of continuous and strictly convex preferences on X. This section is devoted to answering this question; specifically, if the dimensionality of the range of a collective choice function φ on X is at least two, then in fact Theorem 2.1 goes through.

Theorem 2.5 *Let X be a compact convex set in $\Re^k$ and let $\varphi : \mathcal{R}_{cs}^n \to X$ be a strategy-proof collective choice function. If the range of φ is at least two-dimensional, then it is dictatorial.*

Just as for the proof to Theorem 2.1, the theorem is first proved under a more restrictive domain assumption and then extended to the full domain of continuous and convex preferences. Before introducing the restricted domain, however, it is useful to establish a preliminary result demonstrating the existence of a best element in the range of φ for any weak preference ordering.

Lemma 2.8 Let φ be strategy-proof and let $R \in \mathcal{R}$. Then there exists an alternative $x \in \Pi_\varphi$ such that, for all $y \in \Pi_\varphi$, xRy.

Proof If φ is strategy-proof then for all $\rho, \rho' \in \mathcal{R}^n$

$$\begin{array}{ccc} \varphi(R_1, \rho'_{-1}) & R_1 & \varphi(\rho') \\ \varphi(R_1, R_2, \rho'_{-\{1,2\}}) & R_2 & \varphi(R_1, \rho'_{-1}) \\ & \cdots & \\ \varphi(\rho_{-n}, R'_n) & R_{n-1} & \varphi(\rho_{\{1,\ldots,n-2\}}, R'_{n-1}, R'_n) \\ \varphi(\rho) & R_n & \varphi(\rho_{-n}, R'_n) \end{array}$$

Suppose that, for all $i \in N$, $R_i = R$; then $\rho = (R, \ldots, R)$. Let $\varphi(\rho) = x$ and $\varphi(\rho') = y$. Then the sequence of binary comparisons above and R transitive imply $\varphi(\rho) R \varphi(\rho')$ or, equivalently, xRy. And since ρ', and thereby $y \in \Pi_\varphi$, is chosen arbitrarily, this proves the lemma. $\square$

When X is finite, as in the previous sections, Lemma 2.8 is trivial. But in the current case there is no guarantee that the range of φ is closed, in which case the existence of a best element in Π_φ has to be proven. On the other hand, because the preference domain $\mathcal{R}_{cs}^n$ is rectangular, Lemma 2.1 applies directly to the spatial model (subject to the obvious qualification that the profiles ρ, ρ' exploited in the argument be chosen from $\mathcal{R}_{cs}^n$).

The more restrictive domain used in the proof of Theorem 2.5 is one in which each individual's preferences can be represented by a weighted Euclidean utility function with ideal point in the range of φ [PPTI, sect.6.3]. Specifically, individual i's preference ordering $R_i \in \mathcal{R}_{cs}$ is *weighted Euclidean* on X if there exists a point $x_i \in X$ and a symmetric positive definite $k \times k$ matrix A_i such that

$$\forall y, z \in X, \ yR_iz \Leftrightarrow -(x_i - y)'A_i(x_i - y) \geq -(x_i - z)'A_i(x_i - z).$$

The indifference surfaces of a weighted Euclidean preference ordering in X are ellipsoids. A special case is when A_i is the identity matrix, implying R_i simple Euclidean with spherical indifference surfaces. Say a profile $\rho \in \mathcal{R}_{cs}^n$ is weighted Euclidean if every component R_i, $i \in N$ is weighted Euclidean. Let $\mathcal{W} \subset \mathcal{R}_{cs}$ denote the set of weighted Euclidean preference orderings such that, for all $i \in N$, $x_i \in \Pi_\varphi$ (the dependency of $\mathcal{W}$ on φ is left implicit without ambiguity).

The initial domain restriction, then, is to profiles $\rho \in \mathcal{W}^n$. Let φ^* denote the restriction of φ to $\mathcal{W}^n$. The first step in the argument is to show that strategy-proofness of φ on the full domain $\mathcal{R}_{cs}^n$ implies strategy-proofness

2.6. STRATEGY-PROOFNESS IN THE SPATIAL MODEL 55

of φ^* on the more limited domain $\mathcal{W}^n$ and, furthermore, that the range of φ and of φ^* coincide. It follows that if φ^* is manipulable at some profile $\rho \in \mathcal{W}^n$, then φ cannot be strategy-proof on $\mathcal{R}_{cs}^n$.

Lemma 2.9 *Suppose φ is strategy-proof on $\mathcal{R}_{cs}^n$. Then*
(1) φ^* is strategy-proof on $\mathcal{W}^n$;
(2) $\Pi_\varphi = \Pi_{\varphi^*}$.

Proof (1) Since $\mathcal{W}^n \subset \mathcal{R}_{cs}^n$ and $\varphi^* \equiv \varphi|_{\mathcal{W}^n}$, if φ^* is manipulable at $\rho \in \mathcal{W}^n$ then φ is manipulable at $\rho \in \mathcal{R}_{cs}^n$.

(2) By definition, $\Pi_{\varphi^*} \subseteq \Pi_\varphi$; so it suffices to show $\Pi_{\varphi^*} \supseteq \Pi_\varphi$. Let $x \in \Pi_\varphi$ and choose $R \in \mathcal{R}_{cs}$ with $R|_{\Pi_\varphi}$ representable by the utility function $u(y) = -\|y - x\|^2$, $y \in \Pi_\varphi$; clearly, $R|_{\Pi_\varphi}$ is weighted Euclidean with A equal to the identity matrix. By Lemma 2.1, therefore, $\varphi^*(R, \ldots, R) = x \in \Pi_{\varphi^*}$.
□

Note that Lemma 2.9(2) and definition of $\mathcal{W}$ imply that if $R_i \in \mathcal{W}$ and u_i represents R_i, then

$$\arg\max_{y \in \Pi_\varphi} u_i(y) = \{x_i\} \in \Pi_{\varphi^*}.$$

This fact is taken as given and used repeatedly in what follows (where we also abuse notation somewhat and write $\arg\max_{y \in \Pi_{\varphi^*}} u_i(y) = x_i$ if there is no ambiguity).

For each individual $i \in N$ and weighted Euclidean preference ordering $R_i \in \mathcal{W}$, let $O_{-i}(R_i)$ be the set of options available to society as a function of ρ_{-i} when R_i is fixed,

$$O_{-i}(R_i) = \{x \in X : x = \varphi^*(R_i, \rho'_{-i}) \text{ for some } \rho'_{-i} \in \mathcal{W}^{n-1}\}.$$

The set $O_{-i}(R_i)$ is the range of φ^* given i's preferences, R_i. The next result argues for the existence of an individual $j \in N$ for whom $O_{-j}(R_j)$ is exactly j's ideal point, that is $O_{-j}(R_j) = \{x_j\}$ for every weighted Euclidean ordering R_j. Such an individual j is by definition a dictator for φ on the domain $\mathcal{W}^n$. The argument is broken down into six steps. To save on notation, write $u_i \in \mathcal{R}_{cs}$ whenever u_i is a utility function representing $R_i \in \mathcal{R}_{cs}$ and recall that $R_i \in \mathcal{R}_{cs}$ implies u_i is strictly quasi-concave [PPTI, ch.4]; that is,

$$[x, y \in X \text{ and } t \in (0,1)] \Rightarrow u_i(tx + (1-t)y) > \min\{u_i(x), u_i(y)\}.$$

Similarly, denote profiles $\rho \in \mathcal{R}_{cs}^n$ by their utility representations; thus we occasionally write $O_{-i}(u_i) \equiv O_{-i}(R_i)$, $u = (u_1, \ldots, u_n) \in \mathcal{R}_{cs}^n$, and so on.

CHAPTER 2. STRATEGY-PROOF COLLECTIVE CHOICE

Lemma 2.10 *If φ^* is strategy-proof and has at least two-dimensional range, then it is dictatorial on $\mathcal{W}^n$.*

Proof For each of the six claims following, it is understood that φ^* is presumed strategy-proof and all preference orderings are weighted Euclidean with $\rho \in \mathcal{W}^n$.

Claim 1: The set $O_{-i}(u_i)$ is closed.

Proof: Let $w \in \partial \Pi_{\varphi^*}$, the boundary of Π_{φ^*}, and let $v(y) = -\|y-w\|^2$. By Lemmas 2.8 and 2.9(2), $\arg\max_{y \in \Pi_{\varphi^*}} v(y) = w \in \Pi_{\varphi^*}$. Therefore $w \in \partial\Pi_{\varphi^*}$ implies Π_{φ^*} closed. Now consider any $x \in \partial O_{-i}(u_i)$. Since Π_{φ^*} is closed, $x \in \Pi_{\varphi^*}$. By Lemma 2.9(2), therefore, $u_i(y) = -\|y - x\|^2 \in \mathcal{W}$. Given u_i fixed, φ^* strategy-proof on $\mathcal{W}^n$ implies φ^* strategy-proof on $\mathcal{W}^{n-1}$ with, by definition of $O_{-i}(\cdot)$, range $O_{-i}(u_i)$. The argument for Π_{φ^*} closed, therefore, yields $O_{-i}(u_i)$ closed.

Claim 2: For any $u_i \in \mathcal{W}$, $x_i \in O_{-i}(u_i)$.

Proof: Choose any ρ' such that $\varphi^*(\rho') = x_i$. Then φ^* strategy-proof requires $u_i(\varphi^*(u_i, \rho'_{-i})) \geq u_i(\varphi^*(\rho'))$; in which case $\varphi^*(u_i, \rho'_{-i}) = x_i \in O_{-i}(u_i)$, as required.

Claim 3: For all $y \in O_{-i}(u_i)$ and all $\lambda \in [0,1]$, $\lambda x_i + (1-\lambda)y \in O_{-i}(u_i)$.

Proof: By Claim 2, $x_i \in O_{-i}(u_i)$. Suppose the claim is false. Then Claim 1 implies there exists $y \in \partial O_{-i}(u_i) \subset O_{-i}(u_i)$ and $\lambda \in (0,1)$ such that $\lambda x_i + (1-\lambda)y \equiv w \notin O_{-i}(u_i)$. Let $\gamma_y(w)$ denote the straight line passing through y and w. By changing the basis if necessary we can, without loss of generality, assume $\gamma_y(w)$ contains the basis vector e_1:

$$\gamma_y(w) = \{a \in \Re^k : a = te_1 \text{ for some } t \in \Re\}.$$

By $O_{-i}(u_i)$ closed, there is a $p = t(w-y)$, $t > 0$, such that $(y, w+2p] \cap O_{-i}(u_i) = \emptyset$. Let $c = p + (y+w)/2$ and define the utility function

$$u^{(r)}(z) = -(z-c)'A^{(r)}(z-c) \in \mathcal{W}$$

where

$$A^{(r)} = \begin{bmatrix} 1 & 0 & 0 & \cdots & 0 \\ 0 & 1/r & 0 & \cdots & 0 \\ \vdots & \vdots & \ddots & \vdots & \vdots \\ 0 & 0 & 0 & 1/r & 0 \\ 0 & 0 & 0 & 0 & 1/r \end{bmatrix}, \; r \geq 1.$$

See Figure 2.6 which illustrates both the utility $u^{(r)}$ and the argument below.

2.6. STRATEGY-PROOFNESS IN THE SPATIAL MODEL

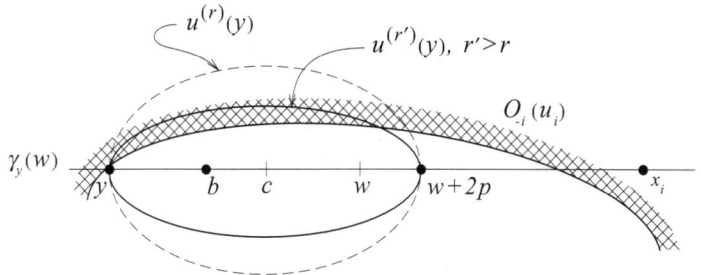

Figure 2.6: Argument for Claim 3

Consider a sequence of profiles $((u_i, u_{-i}^{(r)}))_{r\to\infty}$ and the associated sequence of choices $(\varphi^*(u_i, u_{-i}^{(r)}))_{r\to\infty}$, where $u_{-i}^{(r)} = (u_j^{(r)})_{j\neq i}$ and $u_j^{(r)} = u^{(r)}$ for all $j \neq i$. Given u_i fixed, φ^* is strategy-proof for $N\setminus\{i\}$ on $\mathcal{W}^{n-1}$; hence Lemmas 2.1 and 2.8 imply that, for all $r \geq 1$, $u^{(r)}(\varphi^*(u_i, u_{-i}^{(r)})) \geq u^{(r)}(y)$. Therefore, $(\varphi^*(u_i, u_{-i}^{(r)}))_{r\to\infty}$ is a bounded sequence, in which case it contains a subsequence converging to some point d. By construction, $d \in [y, w + 2p]$ and, by Claim 1, $d \in O_{-i}(u_i)$, the range of φ^* for fixed u_i. Hence $d = y$ since $(y, w+2p] \cap O_{-i}(u_i) = \emptyset$. Now consider the utility $v_i(x) = -\|x - w\|^2 \in \mathcal{W}$. By Claim 2, $w \in O_{-i}(v_i)$. So, arguing as above, Lemma 2.1, Lemma 2.8 and $u^{(r)}$ symmetric on $\gamma_y(w)$ about c, imply the sequence $(\varphi^*(v_i, u_{-i}^{(r)}))_{r\to\infty}$ (or some subsequence thereof) converges to a point $b \in [y + 2p, w]$. Since u_i is continuous, combining these results yields

$$\lim_{r\to\infty} u_i(\varphi^*(u_i, u_{-i}^{(r)})) = u_i(y) \text{ and } \lim_{r\to\infty} u_i(\varphi^*(v_i, u_{-i}^{(r)})) = u_i(b).$$

By φ^* strategy-proof,

$$\forall r \geq 1, \ u_i(\varphi^*(u_i, u_{-i}^{(r)})) \geq u_i(\varphi^*(v_i, u_{-i}^{(r)})).$$

Proceeding to the limit yields $u_i(y) \geq u_i(b)$. But u_i strictly quasi-concave implies

$$u_i(x_i) > u_i(b) > u_i(y),$$

a contradiction. So Claim 3 is true.

Claim 4: For all $u_i, u_i' \in \mathcal{W}$, if $x_i = x_i'$ then $O_{-i}(u_i) = O_{-i}(u_i')$.

Proof: Let $x_i = x_i'$. By Claims 1 and 3, if $O_{-i}(u_i) \neq O_{-i}(u_i')$ there must exist $w \in O_{-i}(u_i')$ and $y \in \partial O_{-i}(u_i) \subset O_{-i}(u_i)$ such that, for some $t \in (0, 1)$, $y = [tx_i' + (1-t)w]$ and, for some $\lambda \in (0, 1]$, $[\lambda w + (1-\lambda)y] \notin O_{-i}(u_i)$: see Figure 2.7.

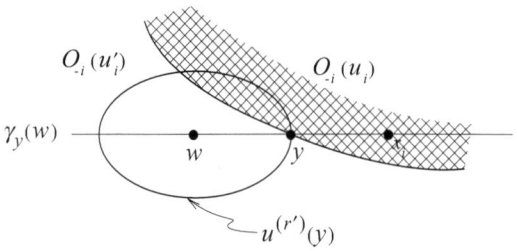

Figure 2.7: Argument for Claim 4

As above, let $\gamma_y(w)$ denote the straight line passing through y and w, assume $\gamma_y(w)$ contains the basis vector e_1 and let $u^{(r)}(x) = -(x - w)'A^{(r)}(x - w)$. Proceeding as in the argument for Claim 3, the sequence $(\varphi^*(u_i, u_{-i}^{(r)}))_{r \to \infty}$ (or some subsequence thereof) converges to y and similarly, by Lemma 2.1, u_i fixed and $w \in O_{-i}(u_i')$, the sequence $(\varphi^*(u_i', u_{-i}^{(r)}))_{r \to \infty}$ converges to w. By φ^* strategy proof,

$$\forall r \geq 1,\ u_i'(\varphi^*(u_i', u_{-i}^{(r)})) \geq u_i'(\varphi^*(u_i, u_{-i}^{(r)})).$$

In the limit, therefore, $u_i'(w) \geq u_i'(y)$. But u_i' strictly quasi-concave implies

$$u_i'(x_i') \geq u_i'(y) > u'_i(w),$$

which contradiction proves the claim.

Claim 5: For all $u_i \in \mathcal{W}$, either (i) $O_{-i}(u_i) = \{x_i\}$, or (ii) $O_{-i}(u_i) = \Pi_{\varphi^*}$.

Proof: Suppose there exists some $u_i \in \mathcal{W}$ for which the claim is false. Then there exist points $w \in \Pi_{\varphi^*} \backslash O_{-i}(u_i)$ and $y \in O_{-i}(u_i) \backslash \{x_i\}$. By assumption, $\dim \Pi_{\varphi^*} \geq 2$; hence w and y can be chosen so that x_i does not lie on the straight line through them. Consider any $v \in \mathcal{W}$ such that $\arg\max_{\Pi_{\varphi^*}} v(z) = w$ and, for all $\lambda \in [0, 1]$,

$$[\lambda w + (1 - \lambda)x_i] \notin \arg\max_{O_{-i}(u_i)} v(z).$$

Such a utility clearly exists by choice of w, y. And since $\arg\max_{O_{-i}(u_i)} v(z)$ is compact, we can find a utility $u_i' \in \mathcal{W}$ such that $x_i' = x_i$ and

$$x \in \arg\max_{O_{-i}(u_i)} v(z) \Rightarrow u_i'(w) > u_i'(x).$$

Figure 2.8 illustrates the utilities v and u_i'.

2.6. STRATEGY-PROOFNESS IN THE SPATIAL MODEL

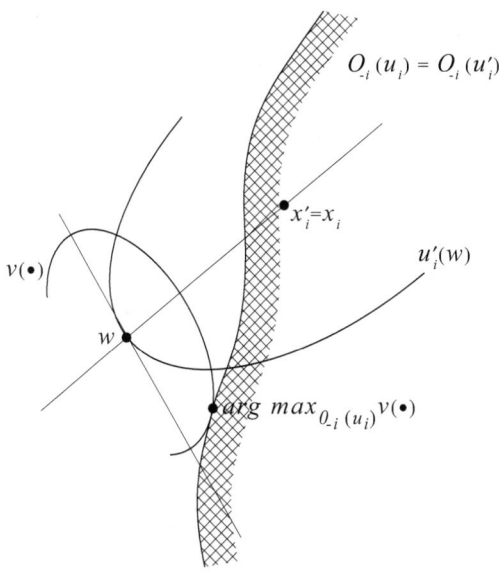

Figure 2.8: Argument for Claim 5

Now consider the profile (u'_i, v_{-i}) in which $v_j = v$, all $j \neq i$. By Lemma 2.1 and definition of $O_{-i}(u'_i)$,

$$\varphi^*(u'_i, v_{-i}) \in \arg\max_{O_{-i}(u'_i)} v(z).$$

By Claim 4, $O_{-i}(u'_i) = O_{-i}(u_i)$. Hence, $\varphi^*(u'_i, v_{-i}) \in \arg\max_{O_{-i}(u_i)} v(z)$. Let $\hat{u}_i(x) = -\|x - w\|^2$. Then Lemma 2.1 implies $\varphi^*(\hat{u}_i, v_{-i}) = w$, in which case $u'_i(\varphi^*(\hat{u}_i, v_{-i})) > u'_i(\varphi^*(u'_i, v_{-i}))$: contradiction of φ^* strategy-proof. Therefore there cannot exist any utility u_i for which the claim is false.

Claim 6: There exists $i \in N$ such that, for all $u_i \in \mathcal{W}$, $O_{-i}(u_i) = \{x_i\}$.

Proof: The proof is by induction on n. First assume $n = 2$ and suppose the claim is false. Then Claim 5 implies $O_{-1}(u_1) = O_{-2}(u_2) = \Pi_{\varphi^*}$ for all $(u_1, u_2) \in \mathcal{W}^2$. That is, whatever the true profile might be, the set of alternatives that individual $i \in \{1,2\}$ can achieve under φ^* by reporting some suitable utility u'_i given u_j is exactly the range of φ^*. Hence, since φ^* is strategy-proof, Claim 2 implies

$$\varphi^*(u_1, u_2) = x_i, \ i = 1, 2.$$

But this is impossible for any profile (u_1, u_2) with $x_1 \neq x_2$. Therefore, because profiles with $x_1 \neq x_2$ clearly exist in $\mathcal{W}^2$, the supposition must be false (and so Claim 6 true) for $n = 2$. Now suppose the claim is true for $n = m$; we show it must then be true for $n = m + 1$, which proves the result. If the claim is false for $n = m + 1$, Claim 5 implies for any profile $(u_1, ..., u_m, u_{m+1})$ and, for all $i \in N$, $O_{-i}(u_i) = \Pi_{\varphi^*}$. Consequently, if u_k is taken as fixed for any k, φ^* is strategy-proof for $N \backslash \{k\}$ on $\mathcal{W}^m$. Let $k = 1$ and fix k's preferences at u_1'; by the induction hypothesis, there exists $i \neq 1$ such that $\varphi^*(u_1', u_{-1}) = x_i$ for any $u_{-1} \in \mathcal{W}^m$. Now fix i's utility at u_i' such that $x_i' \neq x_1$. Then again the induction hypothesis yields there exists $j \neq i$ such that $\varphi^*(u_i', u_{-i}) = x_j$ for any $u_{-i} \in \mathcal{W}^m$. Finally, choose u_j' such that $x_j' \neq x_i'$ and let

$$\hat{u} = (u_1', u_i', u_j', u_{-\{1,i,j\}}).$$

Then

$$[\varphi^*(u_1', u_{-1}) = x_i, \ \forall u_{-1} \in \mathcal{W}^m] \Rightarrow \varphi^*(\hat{u}) = x_i'$$

and

$$[\varphi^*(u_i', u_{-i}) = x_j, \ \forall u_{-i} \in \mathcal{W}^m] \Rightarrow \varphi^*(\hat{u}) = x_j'$$

which is absurd. Hence the claim must be true for $m + 1$, and we are done. In particular, if $O_{-i}(u_i) = \{x_i\}$ for some fixed $i \in N$ and all profiles $\rho \in \mathcal{W}^n$ then i is by definition a dictator and the Lemma is proved. $\square$

The proof for Theorem 2.5, claiming that any strategy-proof collective choice function $\varphi : \mathcal{R}_{cs}^n \to X$ with at least a two-dimensional range is dictatorial, is completed by demonstrating that if j is a dictator for $\varphi = \varphi^*$ on $\mathcal{W}^n$, then j is a dictator on the full domain of φ, $\mathcal{R}_{cs}^n$. This we now do.

Proof of Theorem 2.5 By Lemmas 2.9 and 2.10, there exists a dictator, say $h \in N$, on the domain $\mathcal{W}^n \subset \mathcal{R}_{cs}^n$. Without loss of generality take $h = 1$ and suppose h is not dictatorial on the full domain $\mathcal{R}_{cs}^n$. Then there exists a profile $\rho \in \mathcal{R}_{cs}^n$ (with utility representation $(u_1, \ldots, u_n)$) such that

$$\varphi(u_1, u_{-1}) \notin \arg\max_{y \in \Pi_\varphi} u_1(y) \quad (*)$$

Let $\hat{x} \in \arg\max_{y \in \Pi_\varphi} u_1(y)$ and define $\hat{u}_1(y) = -\|y - \hat{x}\|^2 \in \mathcal{W}$ and consider the profile $(\hat{u}_1, u_{-1})$. By φ strategy-proof,

$$u_1(\varphi(\hat{u}_1, u_{-1})) \leq u_1(\varphi(u_1, u_{-1}))$$

which, with (*), implies $\varphi(\hat{u}_1, u_{-1}) \notin \arg\max_{y \in \Pi_\varphi} u_1(y)$. Let $u'(y) = -\|y - \varphi(\hat{u}_1, u_{-1})\|^2 \in \mathcal{W}$ and, for $j = 2, ..., n$, define the profile

$$v^j = (\hat{u}_1, u_2', \ldots, u_j', u_{j+1}, \ldots, u_n)$$

2.7. APPLICATION: THE ISSUE-BY-ISSUE RULE

where, for all $j > 1$, $u'_j = u'$. Suppose there is some $j > 1$ such that $\varphi(v^j) \neq \varphi(\hat{u}_1, u_{-1})$. By definition of u'_j, therefore,

$$u'_j(\varphi(\hat{u}_1, u_{-1})) \equiv u'_j(\varphi(\hat{u}_1, u_j, u_{-\{1,j\}})) > u'_j(\varphi(\hat{u}_1, u'_j, u_{-\{1,j\}})) \equiv u'_j(\varphi(v^j)),$$

contradicting φ strategy-proof. Hence, φ strategy-proof implies that, for all $j > 1$, $\varphi(v^j) = \varphi(\hat{u}_1, u_{-1})$; in particular, $\varphi(v^n) = \varphi(\hat{u}_1, u_{-1})$. But $v^n \in \mathcal{W}^n$ and individual 1 is a dictator on $\mathcal{W}^n$. Therefore,

$$\varphi(\hat{u}_1, v^n_{-1}) \equiv \varphi(v^n) = \arg\max_{y \in \Pi_\varphi} u_1(y),$$

a contradiction. $\square$

2.7 Application: The issue-by-issue rule

When policies are multidimensional, as is the case, for example, with budget allocations, a common approach for reaching collective choices is to consider changes in the status quo policy, one dimension or issue at a time. For instance, if a committee is to choose how to allocate a given tax-revenue between public education, health and defense then it may well vote over the share to be given to education and then over the share to health, leaving the residual for defense. In each case, decisions on items appearing later in the sequence take earlier decisions as fixed. Although there is no logical necessity for a committee or legislature to use a common choice rule for each issue, in practice it is fairly typical to find simple majority preference being used at each step. In this case the underlying collective choice function is defined as follows.

Let the set of feasible alternatives be a compact and convex set $X \subset \Re^k$ and, for any profile $\rho \in \mathcal{R}^n_{cs}$ and individual $i \in N$, recall $x_i = (x_{i1}, \ldots, x_{ik}) \in X$ is i's most preferred alternative in X; since X is assumed compact and convex, x_i is uniquely defined. Assume n odd for convenience. For any $x \in X$ and each issue $j = 1, \ldots, k$, let $\gamma_x(e_j)$ be the set of points having j^{th} coordinate equal to y_j,

$$\gamma_x(e_j) = \{y \in \Re^k : y = x + te_j \text{ for some } t \in \Re\}$$

(where e_j is the usual basis vector with j^{th} coordinate 1 and all other coordinates zero); evidently, $\gamma_x(e_j)$ is simply a line through x parallel to the jth axis. Now, for each $i \in N$ and $j = 1, \ldots, k$, let $b_i(\gamma_x(e_j))$ be i's *induced ideal point* in $\gamma_x(e_j)$ [PPTI, sect.5.4]:

$$b_i(\gamma_x(e_j)) = \{z \in \gamma_x(e_j) \cap X : \forall w \in \gamma_x(e_j) \cap X, \ zR_iw\}.$$

Because preferences are strictly convex, individuals' induced ideal points along any line in the issue space are single-peaked and, therefore, $b_i(\gamma_x(e_j))$ is unique for all i, j, x. Then for any profile $\rho \in \mathcal{R}_{cs}^n$ and status quo $z \in X$, the majority rule issue-by-issue collective choice function

$$\varphi(\rho; z) = (\varphi_1(\rho; z), \ldots, \varphi_k(\rho; z))$$

is such that

$$\varphi_1(\rho; z) = med_Q\{b_1(\gamma_z(e_1)), \ldots, b_n(\gamma_z(e_1))\}$$

and, for all $j > 1$,

$$\varphi_j(\rho; z) = med_Q\{b_1(\gamma_{(\overleftarrow{\varphi_{j-1}}, \overrightarrow{z_j})}(e_j)), \ldots, b_n(\gamma_{(\overleftarrow{\varphi_{j-1}}, \overrightarrow{z_j})}(e_j))\},$$

where Q is the natural ordering " $>$ " in each dimension j and, by an abuse of notation,

$$(\overleftarrow{\varphi_{j-1}}, \overrightarrow{z_j}) \equiv (\varphi_1(\rho; z), \ldots, \varphi_{j-1}(\rho; z), z_j, \ldots, z_k).$$

Clearly, $\varphi_j(\rho; z)$ is an augmented median voter rule for each dimension j.

Figure 2.9 illustrates the rule for a three-person committee and two-dimensional issue space. In the figure, individuals 1 and 3 have simple Euclidean preferences, $u_i(y) = -\|y - x_i\|^2$, $i = 1, 3$, and individual 2 has weighted Euclidean preferences,

$$u_2(y) = -(y - x_2)' \begin{bmatrix} a & -b \\ -b & a \end{bmatrix} (y - x_2)$$

with $a > b > 0$. Note that there is no majority core [PPTI, Definition 4.5] at the profile $\rho = (u_1, u_2, u_3)$, so majority preference is cyclic [PPTI, ch.5].

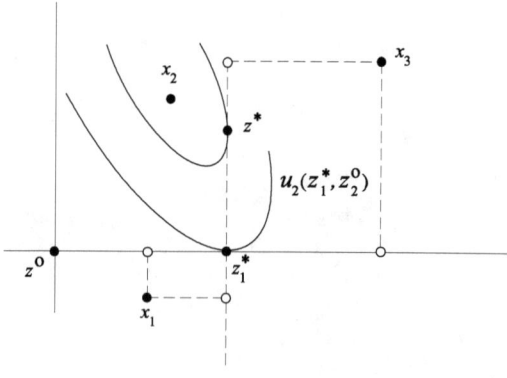

Figure 2.9: The issue-by-issue rule

2.8. SEPARABLE PREFERENCES

The status quo is z^0 and the collective choice $\varphi(\rho; z^0) = (z_1^*, z_2^*)$ is the induced median under ρ as shown. But Theorem 2.5 says that the rule $\varphi(\rho; z)$ is not assured to be strategy-proof on $\mathcal{W}^n$ for any status quo z or profile ρ in its domain and, indeed, this is the situation here. Suppose individual 2 reports the preference ordering $u_2' = -\|y - x_2\|^2$, yielding the profile $\rho' = (u_1, u_2', u_3) \in \mathcal{W}^n$. Applying the issue-by-issue choice function gives $\varphi(\rho'; z^0) = (z_1', z_2')$ as illustrated in Figure 2.10: clearly, $\varphi(\rho'; z^0) P_2 \varphi(\rho; z^0)$ so, given z^0, the rule is manipulable at ρ.

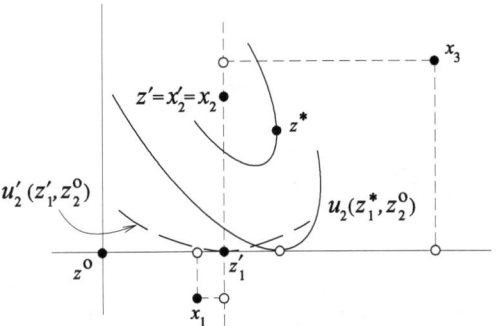

Figure 2.10: Manipulability of the issue-by-issue rule

2.8 Separable preferences

First note that no use is made of the finiteness of X in the proof of Theorem 2.4. Consequently, we have the following result for the spatial model.

Theorem 2.6 *Suppose $X \subset \Re$ is compact. A collective choice function $\varphi : \mathcal{R}_{cs}^n \to X$ is strategy-proof and satisfies citizen sovereignty if and only if φ is an augmented median voter rule with $y_0 = a_r$ and $y_N = a_1$.*

Proof Because the set of alternatives X is compact and one-dimensional, $X \subset \Re$, any profile ρ of continuous and strictly convex preferences, $\rho \in \mathcal{R}_{cs}^n$, is necessarily single-peaked on X [PPTI, sect.4.3]. The result is therefore immediate from Theorem 2.4. □

However, when X is multidimensional virtually no profile $\rho \in \mathcal{R}_{cs}^n$ is single-peaked on X [PPTI, Example 5.1]. On the other hand, because the restriction of a profile $\rho \in \mathcal{R}_{cs}^n$ to any one-dimensional subspace of $\Re^k$ is single-peaked, Theorem 2.6 suggests that some sort of issue-by-issue collective choice scheme might be immune to manipulation. This turns out to be true, subject to one further restriction on the preference domain.

The key feature of augmented median voter rules for eliminating manipulation on single-peaked preference domains is that, if any individual can move the collective choice at all by dissembling, then such a move must be away from the individual's true ideal point and, by single-peakedness, such moves necessarily make the individual worse off. In a multidimensional setting, however, induced preferences over one issue are in general contingent on what is happening on other issues: what would be a bad move on one issue were decisions on the remaining issues fixed, might well be a good thing if it induces compensating changes in these other issues. And this is precisely what is happening in the example of manipulation illustrated in Figures 2.9 and 2.10 above. By dissembling and shifting the decision on the first issue away from his true induced ideal point on that issue (relative to the status quo z^0), individual 2 induces a compensating change on the second issue, resulting in a final outcome under issue-by-issue collective choice that she strictly prefers.

When induced preferences over any given dimension are independent of what happens on other dimensions, the possibility of inducing appropriately compensating changes under the issue-by-issue choice function disappears. To see this, suppose in the example above, the true profile is $\rho' = (u_1, u_2', u_3)$ under which all individuals have simple Euclidean preferences. Then any individual's induced preferences over either dimension are independent of the remaining issue, in which case changes in one dimension affect overall utility only through that dimension. In the example, there is no preference ordering u_i' for $i \in \{1, 3\}$ that can lead to a better outcome for i than the truthful outcome $\varphi(\rho'; z^0) = (z_1', z_2')$. Furthermore, for all status quo policies $z \in X$, $\varphi(\rho'; z) = (z_1', z_2')$. The relevant domain restriction, then, is to preference profiles exhibiting some sort of independence across issues. For any $z \in \Re^k$ and (possibly empty) subset $J \subseteq \{1, 2, \ldots, k\}$, let $z^J \in \Re^k$ be defined by: $z_r^J = z_r$ if $r \in J$ and $z_r^J = 0$ otherwise.

Definition 2.11 *A preference ordering R is separable on $\Re^k$ if, for all distinct $x, y \in X$, all $J \subseteq \{1, 2, \ldots, k\}$ and $j \in J$,*

$$[x + (y-x)^J]R[x + (y-x)^{J\setminus\{j\}}] \Leftrightarrow [x + (y-x)^{\{j\}}]Rx.$$

In the case that R has utility representation $u(y) = -(y-x)'A(y-x)$ with A positive definite, R is separable if and only if the off-diagonal entries in A are

2.8. SEPARABLE PREFERENCES

all zero. More generally, if an individual i has preferences $R_i \in \mathcal{R}_{cs}$ with ideal point $x_i \in X \subseteq \Re^k$, separability of R_i means that i's most preferred level on any dimension $j = 1, \ldots, k$ is independent of the remaining $k-1$ dimensions: for all $y \in X$ and all $j = 1, \ldots, k$, $b_i(\gamma_y(e_j)) = x_{ij}$. Let $\mathcal{R}_{sep} \subset \mathcal{R}_{cs}$ be the set of separable, continuous and strictly convex preference orderings on $\Re^k$.

For any ordering $R \in \mathcal{R}_{sep}$, denote the restriction of R to the jth dimension by $R|_j$ and, for any profile $\rho \in \mathcal{R}_{sep}^n$, write $\rho|_j = (R_1|_j, \ldots, R_n|_j)$. It is worth emphasizing that the profile of most preferred values for the jth issue under $\rho|_j$ is independent of values on issues $l \neq j$: for all $y \in X$ and $j = 1, \ldots, k$,

$$(b_1(\gamma_y(e_j)), \ldots, b_n(\gamma_y(e_j))) = (x_{1j}, \ldots, x_{nj}).$$

Theorem 2.7 *Suppose $X = \Re^k$, $k > 1$. Then $\varphi : \mathcal{R}_{sep}^n \to X$ is strategy-proof and satisfies citizen sovereignty if and only if, for all $\rho \in \mathcal{R}_{sep}^n$,*

$$\varphi(\rho) = (\varphi_1(\rho|_1), \ldots, \varphi_k(\rho|_k))$$

and, for all $j = 1, \ldots, k$, φ_j is an augmented median voter rule.

Given preferences are separable, sufficiency follows immediately from Lemma 2.4. Similarly, conditional on the function φ being decomposable into k choice functions φ_j, one for each dimension or issue, separability and Theorem 2.6 imply the necessity statement. So what remains to be shown is that strategy-proofness and citizen sovereignty imply the choice function φ must be decomposable. This is not easy.

The formal argument for decomposability is lengthy, somewhat technical, and we omit it here. The steps of the argument are easy to describe, however. First note that the argument of Lemma 2.5 to show strategy-proofness and citizen sovereignty imply unanimity applies directly here. Now fix a profile $\rho \in \mathcal{R}_{sep}^n$ and consider the jth coordinate of the outcome $\varphi(\rho)$, say $\varphi_j(\rho)$. Then strategy-proofness and unanimity can be shown to imply that $\varphi_j(\rho)$ must lie between the minimal and the maximal ideal points on the jth dimension:

$$\min_{i \in N}\{x_{ij}\} \leq \varphi_j(\rho) \leq \max_{i \in N}\{x_{ij}\}.$$

This fact, along with strategy-proofness and unanimity, then yields φ_j invariant to changes in individuals' preferences that leave the profile of ideal points on the jth dimension unaffected:

$$[x_{ij} = x'_{ij} \; \forall i \in N] \Rightarrow [\varphi_j(\rho) = \varphi_j(\rho')].$$

It follows that we can write $\varphi_j(\rho) = \varphi_j(x_{1j}, \ldots, x_{nj})$ and the remaining step for the proof is to argue, for any strategy-proof collective choice function φ respecting unanimity and any profile $\rho \in \mathcal{R}^n_{sep}$,

$$\varphi(\rho) = (z_1, \ldots, z_k) \Rightarrow [\forall j = 1, \ldots, k, \ z_j = \varphi_j(x_{1j}, \ldots, x_{nj})].$$

In view of Theorem 2.7, any issue-by-issue collective choice function characterized by a family of augmented median voter rules is surely strategy-proof when preferences are separable. But separability is not a very natural property to expect of preferences over a multidimensional issue space. For example, an individual's assessment of the appropriate budget allocation to the army is presumably contingent on the allocation to the air force; similarly, a legislator's position on foreign aid to a country often depends on the legislator's perception of that country's record on human rights. So while single-peakedness along any one of several spatial issues is a plausible assumption on individual preferences, the added restriction of separability is less appealing. However, as Theorem 2.5 makes clear, admitting interdependence between issues, even if we restrict attention to weighted Euclidean preference profiles (Lemma 2.10), essentially leaves us with only dictatorial strategy-proof collective choice functions on multidimensional spaces.

2.9 Discussion

When preferences are private information they have to be elicited before any collective choice rule can be applied. The Gibbard-Satterthwaite Theorem (Theorem 2.1) tells us that simply asking people to state or otherwise reveal their preferences will not in general lead to the true preference profile. Indeed, when the set of alternatives is finite, if there is any rule that offers no incentive for any individual to dissemble then there is a transitive and weakly Paretian preference aggregation rule satisfying independence of irrelevant alternatives; but the only such rules are dictatorial by Arrow's Theorem. This result does not depend on the finiteness of the alternative set (Theorem 2.5). Thus the only resolute strategy-proof collective choice rules on an unrestricted domain are dictatorial. As with the existence of acyclic preference aggregation rules, however, the existence of non-dictatorial and strategy-proof rules can be assured if the number of alternatives is constrained [PPTI, ch.3]. In particular, if the choice is between exactly two alternatives then majority rule is strategy-proof. Similarly, it is possible to identify nondictatorial strategy-proof choice functions on restricted preference domains.

2.10. EXERCISES

One such restricted domain is important for political science, that of single-peaked domains. Indeed, looking for strategy-proof functions on this domain is suggested by the equivalence of strategy-proof choice functions and strict Arrovian preference aggregation rules (Theorem 2.3): because single-peaked preferences admit nondictatorial Arrovian preference aggregation, it is a reasonable conjecture that nondictatorial strategy-proof choice is also possible on these domains. In fact, not only do strategy-proof functions exist for single-peaked profiles but all such functions satisfying citizen sovereignty on these domains are augmented median voter rules (Theorems 2.4 and 2.6). Consequently, strategy-proof functions under single-peakedness have an appealing voting structure under which individuals simply report their most preferred alternative from any set.

The equivalence relation between strategy-proof choice functions and strict Arrovian aggregation rules is also important for interpreting the classical preference aggregation theorems: what matters in the latter is less the possibility of cycles *per se* and more that the possibility of cycles is equivalent to the opportunity for manipulation of collective choice.

The general import of the results on strategy-proofness is that strategic behavior is endemic in any nondictatorial (in the Arrovian sense) procedure for arriving at collective decisions. Thus, even if agreement could be found on what procedure is the "best" of those available, it would typically be impossible to use this procedure directly to arrive at those collective choices that would have been chosen were preferences known. One creative way around the apparent impasse is to exploit the strategic incentives facing individuals explicitly. That is, rather than hope that people will report their preferences honestly in all circumstances, design an institution such that strategic behavior within the institution leads to precisely those outcomes deemed acceptable by the collective choice procedure given the true profile of preferences. The problem of solving for such institutions is the "implementation problem" to which we turn in the next chapter.

2.10 Exercises

2.1 Prove claim (2) of Lemma 2.4.

2.2 Prove claim (2d) of Lemma 2.5.

2.3 Prove the sufficiency part of Lemma 2.6.

2.4 Show that peak monotonicity (Definition 2.10) implies (but is not implied by) peak only (Definition 2.9).

2.5 Prove Lemma 2.7 and the sufficiency part of Corollary 2.1.

2.6 A similar argument to that for Lemma 2.6 shows that a collective choice function satisfies the median property identified in Lemma 2.5 if and only if it is uncompromising. Use this to give a somewhat different proof for the sufficiency part of Theorem 2.4 (i.e. Lemma 2.4).

2.7 (a) Show that augmented median voter rules are anonymous if and only if $|S| = |T|$ implies $y_S = y_T$.

(b) A collective choice rule is *neutral* if, for all $w, x, y, z \in X$ and all profiles $\rho, \rho' \in \mathcal{R}^n$ such that, for all $i \in N$, $wR_ix \Leftrightarrow yR'_iz$, $\varphi(\rho) = w$ if and only if $\varphi(\rho') = y$ [see also, I, Definition 2.10]. Show that augmented median voter rules violate neutrality.

2.11 Further reading

Arrow [4] and Black [35] are responsible for modern social choice theory. Gibbard [83] and Satterthwaite [180] are the seminal papers on strategy-proof collective choice, independently proving Theorem 2.1. The proof to Theorem 2.1 here is due to Schmeidler and Sonnenschein [182]. The subsequent literature is enormous. Muller and Satterthwaite [141] prove an important result for the domain of strict preferences, showing the equivalence of a monotonicity property [PPTI, Definition 3.17] and strategy-proofness of collective choice functions; more broadly, Muller and Satterthwaite [142] review the literature on strategy-proofness, focusing on the role of domain restrictions. Theorem 2.3 is due to Satterthwaite [180]; Zhou [205] proved the spatial version of Gibbard-Satterthwaite (Theorem 2.5). Efforts to extend the Gibbard-Satterthwaite Theorem to non-resolute collective choice rules include Pattanaik [164], Barbera [27] and Peleg [165]. Moulin [138] first characterized strategy-proof rules on single-peaked domains. The (more general) version of Moulin's result proved here (Theorem 2.4 and Theorem 2.6) and the formal arguments supporting them are due to Ching [42]. Theorem 2.7 is due to Border and Jordan [38]; see also Barbera, Gul and Stacchetti [28].

Chapter 3

Implementable Collective Choice

The Gibbard-Satterthwaite Theorem (Theorem 2.1) says that if we ask people to tell us their preferences to arrive at some social choice, we cannot be sure that they will tell us the truth. But this result does not say that it is generally impossible to elicit the truthful revelation of preferences. Indeed, given a (possibly set-valued) collective choice rule φ, the primary concern is in selecting the "right" outcomes $\varphi(\rho) \subseteq X$ for any preference profile, ρ. Consequently, if it is possible to insure an outcome in $\varphi(\rho)$ for any truthful profile ρ, then whether or not we can identify the details of the profile itself is immaterial. Exploring this possibility is known as the *implementation problem*.

Suppose a society has agreed upon some collective choice rule to be used for making compromises among the constituent individuals' preferences and suppose, further, that application of the rule in any particular choice is the responsibility of a distinct agent, a "planner"; for example, a government agency or a judge. Although the concerned individuals know the true preference profile over the set of alternatives, it is assumed the planner does not. This is reasonable if the application is, for instance, to a small group of signatories to a contract and the planner is a judge; it is somewhat less plausible if the application is to a large and disparate electorate where the planner is an election board. Nevertheless, when individuals are presumed to know at most their own preferences, the problem is more subtle but qualitatively similar which, at least in part, legitimates a working assumption that the preference profile is known to all but the planner. Given the assumption, the problem confronting a planner faced with such limited knowledge and an interest in respecting the collective choice rule is to design an institution or a set of rules with the property that, when acting under these rules, strategically rational individuals induce outcomes that would be chosen under the collective choice rule were the true preference profile known to the planner.

Whether institutions with the requisite properties exist for any collective choice rule turns out to depend in general on the assumed strategic theory of individual choice. The concept of strategy-proofness reflects a particularly appealing hypothesis: if an individual can never do better than report his or her true preferences, then we expect the individual to reveal these preferences. But when reporting true preferences is not the best an individual could do, the minimal behavioral assumption of strategy-proofness makes no prediction and a stronger model of strategic decision-making is necessary. Although there are several possibilities, the most important such model and the central concept for much of this and subsequent chapters is Nash equilibrium. Loosely speaking, the idea here is to look for institutions under which every individual does the best they can by revealing their true preferences, given that everyone else is likewise revealing their true preferences. Thus, Nash behavior generalizes strategy-proof behavior in that, if telling the truth is the best anyone can do whatever others are doing (strategy-proof), then it is also the best anyone can do when others are telling the truth (Nash); the converse, however, is not true. So Nash equilibrium exists and yields predictions in cases where strategy-proofness is silent; the price of such general existence, however, is that there typically exist many Nash equilibria in any given setting, not all of which involve mutual truth-telling.

3.1 Mechanisms and equilibria

The idea of implementation is to design a mechanism, or set of rules, with the property that strategic individuals making choices under these rules end up with outcomes that would be chosen were we to apply the relevant collective choice rule to their true preference profile directly. If we can do this, then the fact that a given collective choice rule is not strategy-proof becomes unimportant because individuals' efforts to manipulate the mechanism turn out to be mutually offsetting. The first thing to do, therefore, is make precise what is meant by a "mechanism" and by "mutually offsetting" strategic behavior. This we now do.

Assume the set of alternatives, X, is finite. For any individual $i \in N$, let $\mathcal{M}_i$ denote a set of *messages* or, more generally, *actions* that an individual has available. For example, a message could be a preference ordering over

3.1. MECHANISMS AND EQUILIBRIA

the set of alternatives ($\mathcal{M}_i = \mathcal{R}$), an alternative ($\mathcal{M}_i = X$), or a real number ($\mathcal{M}_i = \Re$). More complicated messages are possible. For instance, individuals might be required to submit a triple consisting, say, of a profile, an alternative and a number: $\mathcal{M}_i = \mathcal{R}^n \times X \times \Re$. Given any list of messages $m = (m_1, ..., m_n) \in \prod_{i \in N} \mathcal{M}_i$, an *outcome function* g identifies a unique alternative in X with m; thus, $g : \prod_{i \in N} \mathcal{M}_i \to X$. Let $\mathcal{M} = \prod_{i \in N} \mathcal{M}_i$. Then the pair $(\mathcal{M}, g)$ is called a *mechanism* or *game form*. If, in addition, $\mathcal{M}_i = \mathcal{R}$ for every $i \in N$, the mechanism $(\mathcal{R}^n, g)$ is said to be *direct*.

Theorem 2.1 gives substance to questions of strategy-proofness and implementation: goal-oriented individuals cannot be expected to reveal their true preferences under all circumstances. Consequently, we need some theory or model of how individuals with particular preferences make decisions to promote those preferences. Here, the relevant individual decision concerns which message to send and the rule describing any individual's decision is a strategy. Formally, given a mechanism $(\mathcal{M}, g)$, a *pure strategy* for individual i is a function σ_i that maps preference profiles over X into the set of possible messages that the individual could send: for all $i \in N$ and all $\rho \in \mathcal{R}^n$, $\sigma_i(\rho) = m_i \in \mathcal{M}_i$. Where there is no ambiguity, we identify the message chosen under a pure strategy with the strategy itself, writing m_i for $\sigma_i(\rho)$ and, similarly, we refer to the message profile $m = (m_1, \ldots, m_n)$ rather than to the pure strategy profile $\sigma(\rho) = (\sigma_1(\rho), \ldots, \sigma_n(\rho)) \in \mathcal{M}$. A pure strategy, therefore, is a formal description of what message or action an individual chooses as a function of the preference profile over the set of final alternatives. The idea of a *mixed* strategy, that is, a probability distribution over pure strategies, is introduced in a later chapter; until then, we use the terms "strategy" and "pure strategy" interchangeably.

In general, there are many strategies available to an individual. Which of these are predicted to be chosen is the content of various concepts of equilibrium. A pair (γ, ρ), where $\gamma = (\mathcal{M}, g)$ is a mechanism and $\rho \in \mathcal{R}^n$ is a preference profile, is called a *game*. Given a game $G = (\gamma, \rho)$, an *equilibrium* for G is a strategy profile $\sigma(\rho) \in \mathcal{M}$ that satisfies a specified set of properties. We consider three particular equilibrium concepts in the chapter, details of which are deferred until necessary. For now, we simply refer generically to β-equilibria, with β being understood to describe the defining properties of a particular sort of equilibrium.

If individuals choose strategies according to criteria reflected in the properties β, then, under equilibrium theory, only profiles of mutually consistent strategies relative to β support robust predictions of decisions within a society of strategically interacting individuals. The extent to which conclusions concerning equilibrium behavior have any substantive relevance, therefore, rests in large part on the extent to which β captures salient features of individual decision-making under the mechanism. Similarly, the weaker are assumptions on behavior underlying an equilibrium concept, the stronger are positive conclusions predicated on that concept.

Fix a mechanism $\gamma = (\mathcal{M}, g)$. For any profile $\rho \in \mathcal{R}^n$ and any defining property β, let

$$\beta(\rho, \gamma) = \{m \in \mathcal{M} : m = \sigma(\rho) \text{ is a } \beta\text{-equilibrium}\}$$

and

$$g(\beta(\rho, \gamma)) = \{x \in X : x = g(m^*) \text{ for some } m^* \in \beta(\rho, g)\}.$$

Thus, $g(\beta(\rho, \gamma))$ is the set of outcomes that are generated by individuals playing β-equilibrium strategies when the game is $((\mathcal{M}, g), \rho)$. For any mechanism and many definitions β, there exist multiple equilibria and, therefore, multiple equilibrium outcomes. It turns out that such multiplicity complicates the implementation problem.

Definition 3.1 *A collective choice rule $\varphi : \mathcal{R}^n \to \mathcal{X}$ is:*
(1) implementable in β-equilibrium if and only if there exists a mechanism γ such that, for all $\rho \in \mathcal{R}^n$, $\varphi(\rho) = g(\beta(\rho, \gamma))$;
(2) truthfully implementable in β-equilibrium if and only if there exists a direct mechanism γ such that, for all $\rho \in \mathcal{R}^n$, $\rho \in \beta(\rho, \gamma)$ and $g(\rho) \in \varphi(\rho)$.

In words, a collective choice rule φ is implementable in β-equilibrium if there is a mechanism γ such that every alternative chosen under φ given the profile ρ is an outcome generated by some β-equilibrium list of strategies. The reason why equilibrium outcomes other than those chosen under φ are precluded is apparent: the object of implementation theory is to achieve desirable outcomes with respect to the collective choice rule and not simply to obtain some outcomes. On the other hand, assuming $g(\beta(\cdot, \gamma))$ is not empty and g is not constant, it is not so apparent why $g(\beta(\rho, \gamma)) \subset \varphi(\rho)$ is deemed unsatisfactory. Indeed, some conclusions to follow hold for this weaker criterion. Yet there is an important normative reason for insisting on the equivalence, $\varphi(\rho) = g(\beta(\rho, \gamma))$.

If the collective choice $\varphi(\cdot)$ describes the maximal elements of some more-or-less implicit rational collective preference relation R, then the statement "$x, y \in \varphi(\cdot)$" means x and y are considered indifferent relative to R; in this case, demanding only $g(\beta(\rho, \gamma)) \subset \varphi(\rho)$ is legitimate since, under the collective preference relation at ρ, there is truly no relevant normative difference between the two. But the existence of such a rational collective preference

3.1. MECHANISMS AND EQUILIBRIA

relation is rare [PPTI, ch.7] in which case the statement "$x, y \in \varphi(\cdot)$" need not imply that x and y are (normatively) indifferent. For instance, suppose individual preferences are aggregated under the plurality preference relation f_p and ρ is such that

$$xPy, yPz, zPx$$

and, for all $b \notin \{x, y, z\}$ and all $a \in \{x, y, z\}$, aPb. Now suppose the choice rule φ is defined by the top cycle set for f_p [PPTI, sect.6.3; see also Definition 4.2, below]; then

$$\varphi(\rho) \equiv T_{f_p}(\rho) = \{x, y, z\}$$

but it is clearly not the case here that, say, x is considered socially indifferent to y. Consequently, if $g(\beta(\rho, \gamma)) \subset \varphi(\rho)$ is justified in such circumstances, there must be some rationale for excluding at least one of the alternatives $a \in \varphi(\rho)$ in favor of implementing a distinct alternative $b \in \varphi(\rho)$. But then the same rationale can be applied to the choice rule directly to conclude that a should not be chosen in the presence of b, in which case, $a \notin \varphi(\rho)$ after all.

In sum, if φ is implementable in β-equilibrium and if individuals' behavior is consistent with the choice of such strategies, then using the mechanism $(\mathcal{M}, g)$ leads to an outcome in $\varphi(\rho)$; i.e. individuals' behavior, strategic or otherwise, results in a collective choice that could be made if individuals were simply asked to reveal their preferences and responded truthfully. Figure 3.1 illustrates these ideas.

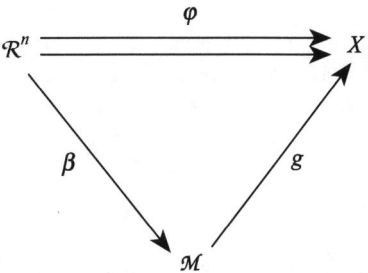

Figure 3.1: $(\mathcal{M}, g)$ implements φ in β-equilibrium

Similarly, φ is truthfully implementable if, when individuals are asked to state their preferences, telling the truth is invariably an equilibrium strategy (but possibly not the only one) and the outcome function yields an alternative in $\varphi(\rho)$. Example 3.2 in the next section, illustrates the distinction between implementability and truthful implementability for a particular specification of β.

Finally, say that a collective choice function (that is, a resolute collective choice rule) $\varphi : \mathcal{R}^n \to X$ is *self-implementable* in β-equilibrium if the direct mechanism $(\mathcal{R}^n, \varphi)$ implements φ in β-equilibrium. If φ is self-implementable it is necessarily truthfully self-implementable.

3.2 The Revelation Principle

Perhaps the mildest claim regarding how a rational individual chooses is that if an individual has a strategy, or decision, that is always the best for them, then the individual can be expected to choose that strategy. Such strategies are called *dominant*. Formally, fix a game $G = ((\mathcal{M}, g), \rho)$.

Definition 3.2 *For any individual $i \in N$, a message $m_i \in \mathcal{M}_i$ is dominated in G if there exists a distinct message $m'_i \in \mathcal{M}_i$ such that, for all possible $m_{-i} \in \mathcal{M}_{-i}$, $g(m'_i, m_{-i}) R_i g(m_i, m_{-i})$ and, for some $m'_{-i} \in \mathcal{M}_{-i}$, $g(m'_i, m'_{-i}) P_i g(m_i, m'_{-i})$. A message m_i is undominated if it is not dominated.*

There is no presumption in Definition 3.2 that dominant strategies are always unique or are necessarily strictly better than any other strategy in every circumstance. Among other possibilities, an individual may have multiple dominant strategies, all of which yield equivalent outcomes whatever others are doing, or have a unique dominant strategy which is only strictly better in some circumstances; in such cases, dominant strategies are often qualified as being weakly dominant. On the other hand, if an individual has a (necessarily unique) dominant strategy which is strictly better than all others whatever other individuals choose, the strategy is said to be strictly dominant. The following simple example illustrates the distinction.

Example 3.1 Assume $N = \{1, 2\}$ and $X = \{x, y, z\}$. Let ρ be

$$xP_1yP_1z$$
$$zP_2yP_2x.$$

Consider the mechanism $(\mathcal{M}, g)$ such that $\mathcal{M}_1 = \mathcal{M}_2 = \{a, b\}$. The outcome function $g(m_1, m_2)$ is described by the following table, in which the rows

3.2. THE REVELATION PRINCIPLE

correspond to individual 1's message, $m_1 \in \mathcal{M}_1$, and the columns correspond to individual 2's message, $m_2 \in \mathcal{M}_2$.

$$g: \begin{array}{c|cc} & a & b \\ \hline a & x & y \\ b & z & y \end{array}$$

Then $m_1 = a$ weakly dominates $m'_1 = b$ for individual 1: either $m_2 = a$ in which case $g(a,a)P_1g(b,a)$ or $m_2 = b$ and $g(a,b)I_1g(b,b)$. On the other hand, both of individual 2's messages are undominated: if $m_1 = a$ then 2 strictly prefers to send $m_2 = b$; if $m_1 = b$ then 2 strictly prefers to send $m_2 = a$. Now suppose we change g to g' by replacing the outcome y in the first row with the outcome x, leaving the remaining three entries the same. Then the message $m_1 = a$ strictly dominates $m'_1 = b$ for individual 1: $g'(a,a)P_1g'(b,a)$ and $g'(a,b)P_1g'(b,b)$. □

The idea that rational individuals never choose dominated strategies gives rise to the following equilibrium concept.

Definition 3.3 *Fix a game $G = ((\mathcal{M},g),\rho)$. Then $\sigma^*(\rho) \in \mathcal{M}$ is a dominant strategy equilibrium for G if and only if, for all $i \in N$, all messages $m_i \in \mathcal{M}_i$ and all $m_{-i} \in \prod_{j \neq i} \mathcal{M}_j$, $g(\sigma_i^*(\rho), m_{-i})R_i g(m_i, m_{-i})$.*

In words, given a profile ρ, a list of messages $\sigma^*(\rho)$ is a dominant strategy equilibrium if, for each individual $i \in N$, the message i sends, $\sigma_i^*(\rho)$, gives i the best outcome i can obtain under the outcome function g *irrespective* of the messages sent by other individuals, $m_{-i} = (m_1, \ldots, m_{i-1}, m_{i+1}, \ldots, m_n)$.

Dominant strategy equilibrium is a very appealing concept; in effect, individuals have an unequivocally best decision independent of any information about what other individuals' decisions might be. And comparing the definition of dominant strategy equilibrium with that of manipulability, Definition 2.2, note that a collective choice function φ is not manipulable at a profile ρ if and only if every individual i reporting his or her true preferences at ρ is a dominant strategy for i in the direct mechanism $(\mathcal{R}^n, \varphi)$.

Define

$$\delta(\rho, \gamma) = \{m \in \mathcal{M} : m = \sigma(\rho) \text{ is a dominant strategy equilibrium}\},$$

so $\beta = \delta$ describes the defining equilibrium property that message strategies are dominant, and

$$g(\delta(\rho, \gamma)) = \{x \in X : x = g(m^*) \text{ for some } m^* \in \delta(\rho, g)\}.$$

Although φ being truthfully implementable in δ-equilibrium does not imply φ is implementable in δ-equilibrium (see Example 3.2 below), there is an important connection between the two concepts. This connection is known as the Revelation Principle.

Theorem 3.1 *(The Revelation Principle) Suppose $\varphi : \mathcal{R}^n \to \mathcal{X}$ is implementable in dominant strategy equilibrium. Then there exists a direct mechanism that truthfully implements φ in dominant strategy equilibrium.*

Proof Let $\gamma = (\mathcal{M}, g)$ implement φ, and define the direct mechanism $\gamma^* = (\mathcal{R}^n, h)$ such that
$$\forall \rho \in \mathcal{R}^n, \ h(\rho) \equiv g(\sigma(\rho)).$$
By assumption, $\forall \rho \in \mathcal{R}^n$ and $\forall \sigma^*(\rho) \in \delta(\rho, \gamma)$, $g(\sigma^*(\rho)) \in \varphi(\rho)$. By definition of dominant strategy implementation, $\forall R_i \in \mathcal{R}$, $\forall m'_i \in \mathcal{M}_i$, $\forall \rho_{-i} \in \mathcal{R}^{n-1}$,
$$g(\sigma_i^*(\rho), \sigma_{-i}^*(\rho)) R_i g(m'_i, \sigma_{-i}^*(\rho)).$$
Hence, $\forall R'_i \in \mathcal{R}$, $h(R_i, \rho_{-i}) R_i h(R'_i, \rho_{-i})$. Therefore, $\rho \in \delta(\rho, \gamma^*)$ and $h(\rho) \in \varphi(\rho)$. $\square$

The Revelation Principle is a useful result: if there exists no direct mechanism capable of truthfully implementing a given choice rule in dominant strategy equilibrium, then there exists no mechanism of any sort capable of implementing the rule in dominant strategy equilibrium. To identify choice rules that are implementable in dominant strategy equilibrium, therefore, it is enough to identify those rules that are truthfully implementable in dominant strategy equilibrium. And since the space of direct mechanisms is considerably smaller than that of all mechanisms, searching for particular direct mechanisms for truthful implementation is easier than searching for an arbitrary mechanism for implementation.

The following example illustrates the Revelation Principle and shows that truthful implementation does not imply implementation.

Example 3.2 Let $N = \{1, 2\}$ and $X = \{a, b, c, d\}$. Suppose the domain of the collective choice function φ is the set of four profiles,
$$\{(R_1, R_2), (R'_1, R_2), (R_1, R'_2), (R'_1, R'_2)\},$$
where
$$\begin{aligned} R_1 &: \quad bI_1 dP_1 a I_1 c \\ R'_1 &: \quad dP'_1 c P'_1 a P'_1 b \\ R_2 &: \quad cI_2 dP_2 a I_2 b \\ R'_2 &: \quad dP'_2 b P'_2 a P'_2 c \end{aligned}$$

3.2. THE REVELATION PRINCIPLE

Using the same tabular representation as for Example 2.2, assume φ is described by

	R_2	R'_2
R_1	a	b
R'_1	c	d

Consider the indirect mechanism $\gamma = (\mathcal{M}, g)$, where $\mathcal{M}_i = \{p_i, q_i, r_i\}$, $i = 1, 2$, and the outcome function $g : \mathcal{M}_1 \times \mathcal{M}_2 \to X$ is

	p_2	q_2	r_2
p_1	a	b	b
q_1	c	d	c
r_1	c	b	a

The mechanism γ implements φ in dominant strategy equilibrium: for all $i \in N$, if i's true preferences are R_i (respectively, R'_i) then p_i (respectively, q_i) is a dominant strategy in γ. Now define the direct mechanism $\gamma^* = (\mathcal{M}', h)$ where $\mathcal{M}'_i = \{R_i, R'_i\}$, $i = 1, 2$, and $h \equiv \varphi$. Then γ^* truthfully implements φ in dominant strategy equilibrium since, for any profile ρ in the domain of φ, $\rho \in \delta(\rho, \gamma^*)$. But γ^* does *not* implement φ because choosing the message R'_i when i's true preferences are R_i, $i \in N$, is also a dominant strategy. Hence, $(R'_1, R'_2) \in \delta((R_1, R_2), \gamma^*)$ but $h(R'_1, R'_2) = d \notin \varphi(R_1, R_2) = a$. And notice, moreover, that both individuals have $dP_i a$, so the outcome induced by truthful revelation under γ^* is Pareto dominated here. □

The next result exploits the Revelation Principle to relate the notion of implementability to that of strategy-proof collective choice.

Corollary 3.1 *Let $\varphi : \mathcal{R}^n \to X$ be a collective choice function with at least three alternatives in its range. Then φ is implementable in dominant strategy equilibrium only if φ is dictatorial.*

Proof Given the definition of a strategy-proof collective choice rule, the result is immediate from Theorem 2.1 and the Revelation Principle. □

Despite its appeal, then, the possibility of implementing nondictatorial collective choice rules in dominant strategy equilibrium is necessarily going to be limited. Unfortunately, the same is true of implementation in Nash equilibrium, a less demanding standard.

3.3 Nash implementation

It is rarely the case that individuals have dominant strategies in that their best decision is independent of others. Moreover, as the results of the previous section suggest, at least on unrestricted domains the use of mechanisms insuring the existence of dominant strategies is extremely limited. In such circumstances, then, it is plausible to think of individuals doing the best they can given the circumstances in which they find themselves; specifically, individuals might reasonably choose to adopt the best strategy contingent on the decisions of others. The concept of Nash equilibrium captures this intuition.

Definition 3.4 *Fix a game* $G = ((\mathcal{M}, g), \rho)$. *A profile* $\sigma^*(\rho) \in \mathcal{M}$ *is a Nash equilibrium for* G *if and only if, for all* $i \in N$ *and all* $m_i \in \mathcal{M}_i$,

$$g(\sigma_i^*(\rho), \sigma_{-i}^*(\rho)) R_i g(m_i, \sigma_{-i}^*(\rho)).$$

Thus a list of message strategies $\sigma^*(\rho)$ is a Nash equilibrium if no individual i, *given* the messages sent by others, $\sigma_{-i}^*(\rho)$, can send a different message and make himself or herself strictly better off. Dominant strategy equilibria are also Nash equilibria but the converse is not true: in general, the best strategy for an individual under Nash varies with the strategies of others. Let $\beta = \eta$ denote the Nash property and define

$$\eta(\rho, \gamma) = \{m \in \mathcal{M} : m = \sigma(\rho) \text{ is a Nash equilibrium}\},$$

and

$$g(\eta(\rho, \gamma)) = \{x \in X : x = g(m^*) \text{ for some } m^* \in \eta(\rho, g)\}.$$

Theorem 3.2 *A collective choice rule* $\varphi : \mathcal{R}^n \to \mathcal{X}$ *is truthfully implementable in Nash equilibrium if and only if* φ *is truthfully implementable in dominant strategy equilibrium.*

Proof Sufficiency is immediate since for any mechanism γ and any profile ρ, $\delta(\rho, \gamma) \subseteq \eta(\rho, \gamma)$. To check necessity, let γ^* be a direct mechanism that truthfully implements φ in Nash equilibrium and suppose $h(\rho) \in \varphi(\rho)$. By truthful Nash implementation, $\forall i \in N$, $\forall R_i' \in \mathcal{R}$, $h(R_i, \rho_{-i}) R_i h(R_i', \rho_{-i})$. But since $\rho_{-i} \in \mathcal{R}^{n-1}$ is arbitrary, this statement implies that reporting R_i is a dominant strategy for i; hence, $\rho \in \delta(\rho, \gamma^*)$ as required. □

With respect to truthful implementation, therefore, there is no gain from moving from dominant strategy equilibrium to Nash equilibrium.

3.3. NASH IMPLEMENTATION

The normative intuition that a winning candidate should not be harmed when it accrues more support is widespread and often fundamental to any notion of a fair or just collective choice process. It also turns out to be fundamental to the positive possibility of implementing any such collective choice.

Definition 3.5 *A collective choice rule* $\varphi : \mathcal{R}^n \to \mathcal{X}$ *is Maskin monotonic if, for all profiles* $\rho, \rho' \in \mathcal{R}^n$ *and all alternatives* $x \in X$, *if* $x \in \varphi(\rho)$ *and, for all* $w \in X$, $R(x, w; \rho) \subseteq R(x, w; \rho')$ *then* $x \in \varphi(\rho')$.

That is, if x is chosen under some preference profile ρ and if, in another preference profile ρ', x is at least as highly ranked in ρ' by all individuals as in ρ, then x should be chosen under ρ'.

Maskin monotonicity is one of a variety of axioms reflecting the idea that adding support for a winning alternative should not be a handicap to that alternative. Where the axioms differ is principally in their characterization of what constitutes "adding support". In this regard, Maskin monotonicity expresses one of the least demanding conceptions: so long as the set of individuals who at least weakly prefer x to any other alternative w does not shrink, then x should continue to be chosen if it was so in the first place. Toward the other end of the spectrum is "weak monotonicity", used instrumentally in section 2.3 above: to insist that x should continue to be chosen if it was so in the first place, weak monotonicity requires not only what is required by Maskin monotonicity, but also that the set of those strictly preferring x to any other alternative w does not shrink *and* that all individuals' preferences over all alternatives other than x remain unchanged [PPTI, Exercise 2.2]. And between these two conditions lies, *inter alia*, "monotonicity" [PPTI, sect.3.1] which coincides with weak monotonicity except that changes in individuals' orderings over alternatives other than x are deemed irrelevant. Formally, Maskin monotonicity implies monotonicity which in turn implies weak monotonicity. Of the three conditions, therefore, Maskin monotonicity imposes the most severe restriction on collective choice. Example 3.3 illustrates this fact.

Example 3.3 Let $N = \{1, 2\}$ and $X = \{w, x, y, z\}$. Consider the following four profiles:

$$\begin{aligned} \rho &= (w I_1 x P_1 y P_1 z;\ x P_2 z P_2 w P_2 y) \\ \rho' &= (w I_1' x P_1' y P_1' z;\ x I_2' z P_2' w P_2' y) \\ \rho'' &= (x P_1'' w P_1'' z P_1'' y;\ x P_2'' z P_2'' y P_2'' w) \\ \rho''' &= (x P_1''' w P_1''' y P_1''' z;\ x P_2''' z P_2''' w P_2''' y) \end{aligned}$$

Assume $\varphi(\rho) = \{x\}$. Then,

1. *Maskin Monotonicity* implies $\varphi(\rho') = \varphi(\rho'') = \varphi(\rho''') = x$;
2. *Monotonicity* implies $\varphi(\rho'') = \varphi(\rho''') = x$;
3. *Weak Monotonicity* implies $\varphi(\rho''') = x$.

Fix any $a \in \{w, y, z\}$. Then Claim 1 follows because the set of individuals who consider x at least as good as a under each profile ρ', ρ'', ρ''' is unchanged. Claim 2 follows because in moving from ρ to ρ'' or ρ''', the set of individuals who consider x weakly preferred to a does not shrink and the set of individuals who strictly prefer x to a gets bigger. However, when moving from ρ to ρ', individual 2 moves from having a strict preference for x over z to being indifferent between the two and, therefore, monotonicity permits the collective choice at ρ' to differ from that at ρ. Finally, Claim 3 follows because weak monotonicity requires the same of profile changes as monotonicity and, in addition, that individuals' orderings of alternatives other than x remain unaffected. While this latter requirement is satisfied when comparing ρ with ρ''', it fails when comparing ρ with either ρ' or ρ''.
□

Theorems 2.1 and 2.5 showed that strategy-proof collective choice functions on sufficiently rich preference domains are essentially dictatorial. If we continue to focus on collective choice functions, that is, on resolute collective choice rules then even dictatorships become impossible in the presence of Maskin monotonicity.

Definition 3.6 *A collective choice function $\varphi : \mathcal{R}^n \to X$ is constant if, for all profiles $\rho, \rho' \in \mathcal{R}^n$, $\varphi(\rho) = \varphi(\rho')$.*

Thus a constant collective choice function selects the same alternative whatever individual preferences happen to be. If anything, constant collective choice functions are less appealing than dictatorial rules. Unfortunately, the following is true.

Theorem 3.3 *A collective choice function φ with domain $\mathcal{R}^n$ is Maskin monotonic if and only if it is constant.*

Proof That constant rules are Maskin monotonic is trivial. To prove necessity, let $\varphi : \mathcal{R}^n \to X$ be Maskin monotonic and let ρ, ρ' be any pair of distinct profiles in $\mathcal{R}^n$. Let $\hat{\rho}$ denote the profile under which every individual $i \in N$ is indifferent between every pair of alternatives in X: $\forall i \in N, \forall x, y \in X$,

3.3. NASH IMPLEMENTATION

$x\hat{I}_i y$. Then Maskin monotonicity requires $\varphi(\hat{\rho}) = \varphi(\rho)$ and $\varphi(\hat{\rho}) = \varphi(\rho')$. Hence $\varphi(\rho) = \varphi(\rho')$. □

Although Theorem 3.3 is striking, it rests on the possibility of universal indifference. This is unlikely to occur in any interesting application, so it is important to know what can happen if such an extreme preference configuration is ruled out as irrelevant. As in the proof to Theorem 3.3, let $\hat{\rho}$ denote the profile under which every individual is indifferent between every pair of alternatives in X.

Theorem 3.4 *If $\varphi : \mathcal{R}^n \backslash \{\hat{\rho}\} \to X$ is a Maskin monotonic collective choice function with at least three alternatives in its range, then φ is dictatorial.*

Proof Assume φ Maskin monotonic and $|\prod_\varphi| \geq 3$. Suppose φ is not strategy-proof. Then $\exists \rho \in \mathcal{R}^n \backslash \{\hat{\rho}\}$ and $\exists i \in N$ such that $\varphi(R'_i, \rho_{-i}) P_i \varphi(\rho)$ for some $R'_i \in \mathcal{R}$, $R'_i \neq R_i$. Let $\varphi(\rho) = y$ and $\varphi(R'_i, \rho_{-i}) = x$, so $xP_i y$. Now construct the profile $\rho(xy)$ as before, by moving alternatives x, y to the top of all individuals' orderings at ρ, leaving their relative rankings of x and y and of all other pairs of alternatives unchanged. Similarly, define $\rho'(xy)$ by setting $\rho'_{-i}(xy) \equiv \rho_{-i}(xy)$ and moving x, y to the top of individual i's ordering R'_i, leaving his relative rankings elsewhere the same as under R'_i. Then Maskin monotonicity implies $\varphi(\rho(xy)) = y$ and $\varphi(\rho'(xy)) = x$. But since, $\forall w \neq x$, $xP_i y$ implies $xP_i(xy)w$, we have: $\forall w \neq x$, $R(x, w; \rho'(xy)) \subseteq R(x, w; \rho(xy))$. Therefore, φ Maskin monotonic implies $\varphi(\rho(xy)) = x$, a contradiction. Hence, φ must be strategy-proof. The desired result now follows from Corollary 3.1 and $\mathcal{R}^n \backslash \{\hat{\rho}\} \subset \mathcal{R}^n$. □

Together, Theorems 3.3 and 3.4 constitute an argument against insisting on collective choice functions with unrestricted domains (and it is easy to check that the argument for Theorem 3.4 applies even if the domain of the choice function is further limited to the set of all strict preference profiles on X). Alternatively, Maskin monotonicity is a reasonable property to require of collective choice rules only if the domain is suitably restricted or if the rule itself is not resolute. On the other hand, if we reject Maskin monotonicity for a collective choice rule, it turns out that we reject any possibility of that rule being Nash implementable on an unrestricted domain.

The importance of Maskin monotonicity for Nash implementation theory is easily seen. If a profile m^* is a Nash equilibrium under some mechanism γ, then for any individual $i \in N$, the outcome induced by m^*, say x, must represent the best outcome that i can obtain given all others' messages,

m^*_{-i}. Consequently, if i changes her preferences in such a way that x moves higher up her preference ordering, i can still do no better than play m^*_i against m^*_{-i}; the message profile m^*, that is, remains a Nash equilibrium at the new preference profile. Therefore, if γ Nash implements the collective choice rule, it had better be the case that x continues to be chosen. Lemma 3.1 is a formal statement of this observation.

Lemma 3.1 *If $\varphi : \mathcal{R}^n \to \mathcal{X}$ is implementable in Nash equilibrium then φ is Maskin monotonic.*

Proof Let $x \in \varphi(\rho)$ and consider any $\rho' \in \mathcal{R}^n$ such that, $\forall i \in N$, $\forall w \in X$, $xR_iw \Rightarrow xR'_iw$. Since φ is implementable in Nash equilibrium, there is a mechanism γ such that $\varphi(\rho) = g(\eta(\rho, \gamma))$. Hence, $\exists m^* = \sigma^*(\rho) \in \mathcal{M}$ such that $\forall i \in N$, $\forall m_i \in \mathcal{M}_i$, $g(\sigma^*_i, \sigma^*_{-i}) R_i g(m_i, \sigma^*_{-i})$ and $g(\sigma^*) = x$. By choice of ρ', we have that for all $i \in N$ and all $m_i \in \mathcal{M}_i$, $xR'_i g(m_i, \sigma^*_{-i})$. Hence, $m^* \in \eta(\rho', \gamma)$ and, therefore, $x \in g(\eta(\rho', \gamma))$. Finally, by definition of implementation in Nash equilibrium, $\varphi(\rho') = g(\eta(\rho', \gamma))$; in which case $x \in \varphi(\rho')$ as required. $\square$

It is worth emphasizing here that Lemma 3.1 does not require φ to be resolute: a necessary condition for *any* collective choice rule to be implementable in Nash equilibrium is that it satisfies Maskin monotonicity. The next result says that this condition is also virtually sufficient.

Definition 3.7 *A collective choice rule $\varphi : \mathcal{R}^n \to \mathcal{X}$ satisfies no veto if and only if, for all $x \in X$ and all $\rho \in \mathcal{R}^n$, $|\cap_{y \in X} R(x, y; \rho)| \geq n - 1$ implies $x \in \varphi(\rho)$.*

In words, if there is some alternative ranked (weakly) best by a coalition of at least $n-1$ individuals, then that alternative must be among those chosen. When $n \geq 3$, this condition is weak, being satisfied by any collective choice rule φ_f derived from a noncollegial simple preference aggregation rule f [Exercise]. It is worth observing, however, that the "no veto" property can fail if the aggregation rule f is not simple and preferences admit indifference. It is easily seen, for example, that if f is plurality rule then φ_f violates "no veto".

Theorem 3.5 *Assume $n \geq 3$ and suppose $\varphi : \mathcal{R}^n \to \mathcal{X}$ satisfies no veto. Then φ is implementable in Nash equilibrium if and only if φ is Maskin monotonic.*

3.3. NASH IMPLEMENTATION

Proof Necessity follows from Lemma 3.1. The proof of sufficiency is by construction of a mechanism $\gamma = (\mathcal{M}, g)$ that implements φ in Nash equilibrium. In the mechanism, a typical message is a triple consisting of a preference profile, an alternative and a positive integer; $m_i = (\rho^i, x^i, k^i)$. The message space $\mathcal{M} \equiv \prod_{i \in N} \mathcal{M}_i$ is divided into two mutually exclusive subsets. Any list $m \in \mathcal{M}$ from the first subset is characterized by at least $n-1$ individuals choosing a common message in which the reported alternative x and the reported profile ρ are such that $x \in \varphi(\rho)$. Given such a message, the outcome function g yields x unless there is an individual i whose message includes an alternative $x^i \neq x$, in which case g selects x^i if and only if x is ranked weakly higher than x^i according to i's preferences *as reported by the remaining* $n-1$ individuals. The remaining set in the partition comprises all other possible lists of messages; and for any message in this set, the outcome function selects the reported alternative of the individual with the smallest index j whose message contains the largest integer, k^j. Formally, define γ as follows.

For each $i \in N$, let $\mathcal{M}_i = \mathcal{R}^n \times X \times \{1, 2, 3, \ldots\}$ and $\mathcal{M} \equiv \prod_{i \in N} \mathcal{M}_i$. Partition $\mathcal{M}$ into two subsets, $\{\mathcal{M}_I, \mathcal{M}_{II}\}$, such that

$$\mathcal{M}_I = \{m \in \mathcal{M} : \exists i \in N \text{ such that, } \forall j \neq i, \; m_j = (\rho, x, k) \text{ and } x \in \varphi(\rho)\},$$
$$\mathcal{M}_{II} = \mathcal{M} \setminus \mathcal{M}_I.$$

Now for any message profile $m = ((\rho^1, x^1, k^1), \ldots, (\rho^n, x^n, k^n)) \in \mathcal{M}$, define the outcome $g(m)$ by

$$m \in \mathcal{M}_I \Rightarrow g(m) = \begin{cases} x^i & \text{if } xR_i x^i \\ x & \text{otherwise} \end{cases};$$
$$m \in \mathcal{M}_{II} \Rightarrow g(m) = x^j, \; j \equiv \min[j \in N : \forall i \in N, \; k^i \leq k^j].$$

By assumption, $n > 2$ so the function g is well-defined (if $n = 2$, g is not well-defined on $\mathcal{M}_I$). We now show that for any profile ρ, $\varphi(\rho) = g(\eta(\rho, \gamma))$.

Claim 1: For all $\rho \in \mathcal{R}^n$, $\varphi(\rho) \subseteq g(\eta(\rho, \gamma))$.

Proof: Let $x \in \varphi(\rho)$ and, $\forall i \in N$, let $m_i^* = (\rho, x, 1)$. Then $m^* \in \mathcal{M}_I$ and, therefore, since ρ is the true profile, $\forall i \in N, \forall m_i \neq m_i^*$,

$$g(m_i, m_{-i}^*) \neq g(m^*) \Rightarrow g(m^*) R_i g(m_i, m_{-i}^*).$$

Hence, $m^* = ((\rho, x, 1), \ldots, (\rho, x, 1)) \in \eta(\rho, \gamma)$ and $g(m^*) = x$.

Claim 2: For all $\rho \in \mathcal{R}^n$, $\varphi(\rho) \supseteq g(\eta(\rho, \gamma))$.

Proof: Let $m^* \in \eta(\rho, \gamma)$ and $g(m^*) = x$; we need to show $x \in \varphi(\rho)$. There are three cases to consider.

(2a) For all $i \in N$, $m_i^* = (\rho', x, k)$ and $x \in \varphi(\rho')$. In this case $m^* \in \mathcal{M}_I$ and therefore, by definition of $m^* \in \eta(\rho, \gamma)$, $\forall i \in N$, $\forall m_i \neq m_i^*$,

$$\begin{aligned} g(m_i, m_{-i}^*) &\neq g(m^*) \Rightarrow g(m^*) R_i' g(m_i, m_{-i}^*) \\ &\Rightarrow g(m^*) R_i g(m_i, m_{-i}^*). \end{aligned}$$

Hence, φ Maskin monotonic yields $x \in \varphi(\rho)$.

(2b) For all $i \in N$, $m_i^* = (\rho', x, k)$ and $x \notin \varphi(\rho')$. Then $m^* \in \mathcal{M}_{II}$. Choose $j \in N$ arbitrarily and let $m_j = (\rho^j, y, k^j)$ be any message with $k^j > k$. Then $g(m_j, m_{-j}^*) = y$. But $m^* \in \eta(\rho, \gamma)$ implies $x R_j y$. Therefore, because j and y are arbitrary, we must have that for all $y \in X$, $|R(x, y; \rho)| \geq n - 1$. Hence, φ satisfies no veto yields $x \in \varphi(\rho)$.

(2c) There exist individuals $i, k \in N$ such that $m_i^* \neq m_k^*$. Without loss of generality, let $m_1^* \neq m_2^*$. Choose $j \in N \backslash \{1, 2\}$ arbitrarily and let $m_j = (\rho^j, y, k^j)$ be any message with $k^j > k^i$, all $i \neq j$. Then $m^* \in \mathcal{M}_{II}$ and $g(m_j, m_{-j}^*) = y$. But $m^* \in \eta(\rho, \gamma)$ implies $g(m^*) R_j y$. Now, either $m_j^* \neq m_1^*$ or $m_j^* \neq m_2^*$; without loss of generality, assume $m_j^* \neq m_1^*$. Then repeating the preceding argument with j and $i = 2$ interchanged yields $g(m^*) R_2 y$. Therefore, because j and y are arbitrary, we must have that for all $y \in X$, $|R(x, y; \rho)| \geq n - 1$. Hence, φ satisfies no veto yields $x \in \varphi(\rho)$. □

Theorem 3.5 is an existence result. For all practical purposes, it characterizes the class of collective choice rules that can be implemented in Nash equilibrium when $n \geq 3$. It is a small class; hardly any collective choice rules are Maskin monotonic on the full domain $\mathcal{R}^n$. Example 3.4 illustrates this for the choice rules derived, respectively, from the Pareto extension (Example 1.1(4)), plurality preference (Example 1.1(3)), and Borda aggregation rules (Example 2.1).

Example 3.4 For any preference aggregation rule f, define the choice rule $\varphi_f(\cdot) = M(f(\cdot), X)$.

(1) *The Pareto extension rule.* Let f be the Pareto extension rule,

$$\forall \rho \in \mathcal{R}^n, \; \forall x, y \in X, \; x P y \Leftrightarrow [R(x, y; \rho) = N \; \& \; P(x, y; \rho) \neq \emptyset].$$

Let $N = \{1, 2\}$ and $X = \{x, y\}$. Suppose ρ, ρ' are, respectively, given by

$$\begin{aligned} \rho &= ((x P_1 y), (y P_2 x)); \\ \rho' &= ((x I_1' y), (y P_2' x)). \end{aligned}$$

3.3. NASH IMPLEMENTATION

Then $\varphi_f(\rho) = \{x, y\}$ and $\varphi_f(\rho') = \{y\}$. But Maskin monotonicity requires $x \in \varphi_f(\rho')$.

(2) *Plurality rule.* Let f be plurality rule,

$$\forall \rho \in \mathcal{R}^n, \; \forall x, y \in X, \; xPy \Leftrightarrow |P(x,y;\rho)| > |P(y,x;\rho)|.$$

Let $N = \{1, 2, 3, 4, 5\}$ and $X = \{x, y\}$. Suppose ρ, ρ' are, respectively, given by

$$\rho = ((xP_1y), (xP_2y), (yP_3x), (yP_4x), (yP_5x));$$
$$\rho' = ((xP_1'y), (xP_2'y), (yP_3'x), (yI_4'x), (yI_5'x)).$$

Then $\varphi_f(\rho) = \{y\}$ and $\varphi_f(\rho') = \{x\}$. But Maskin monotonicity requires $y \in \varphi_f(\rho')$.

(3) *Borda rule.* Let f be the Borda rule,

$$\forall \rho \in \mathcal{R}^n, \; \forall x, y \in X, \; xPy \Leftrightarrow \sum_N r_i(x) < \sum_N r_i(y)$$

where, for all alternatives $x \in X$, let $r_i(x)$ denote the ordinal rank of x in i's preference ordering on X. Suppose $N = \{1, 2, 3\}$ and $X = \{w, x, y, z\}$. Let $\rho, \rho' \in \mathcal{R}^n$ be given by

$$\rho = \begin{cases} xP_1yP_1wP_1z \\ xP_2yP_2wP_2z \\ yP_3wP_3zP_3x \end{cases} ; \; \rho' = \begin{cases} xP_1'yP_1'wP_1'z \\ xP_2'yP_2'wP_2'z \\ yP_3'xP_3'wP_3'z \end{cases}.$$

Then $\varphi_f(\rho) = \{y\}$ and $\varphi_f(\rho') = \{x\}$. But Maskin monotonicity requires $y \in \varphi_f(\rho')$. □

The motivation behind Nash equilibrium is essentially that, if any pattern of decisions has a claim to stability in a society of rational individuals, then that pattern should at least have the so-called *best response* property: conditional on what others decide, each individual's decision is the best that he or she can make. By itself, however, this best response property is consistent with people adopting dominated strategies which, as argued in the previous section, is *prima facie* unreasonable, at least in some settings. In other words, the appropriate notion of a rational individual "doing the best that he or she can" should include a presumption that individuals never use a dominated strategy in the sense of Definition 3.2. Assuming that individuals eschew the use of dominated strategies leads to a simple but powerful refinement of Nash equilibrium.

Definition 3.8 *Fix a game $G = ((\mathcal{M}, g), \rho)$. Then $\sigma^*(\rho) \in \mathcal{M}$ is an undominated Nash equilibrium for G if and only if $\sigma^*(\rho)$ is a Nash equilibrium in which no individual uses a dominated strategy.*

The following example illustrates the value of refining the Nash equilibrium concept to exclude dominated strategies.

Example 3.5 Let $N = \{1, 2, 3\}$, $X = \{x, y\}$ and suppose N is to choose between x and y using plurality rule. The underlying collective choice rule φ is therefore defined in Example 3.4(2). Now suppose the plurality voting mechanism is used to arrive at decision. The mechanism $\gamma = (\mathcal{M}, g)$ is defined by $\mathcal{M}_i = \{x, y\}$ for all $i \in N$ and, for all $m \in \mathcal{M}$,

$$g(m) = [a \in X : |\{m_i = a\}| \geq 2].$$

Thus messages are votes, abstention is not permitted and the outcome function selects the alternative with the most votes. Consider the unanimous preference profile, $\rho = (xP_1y, xP_2y, xP_3y)$; obviously, $\varphi(\rho) = \{x\}$. However,

$$\eta(\rho, \gamma) = \{(x, x, x), (y, y, y), (x, x, y), (x, y, x), (y, x, x)\}$$

which implies $g(\eta(\rho, \gamma)) = \{x, y\}$. Therefore, γ does not implement φ in Nash equilibrium. Yet the possibility that y might be selected seems absurd. The only reason it is possible is that if two of the three individuals, say $i = 2, 3$, are sending the message, $m_i = y$ then $g(x, m_{-1}) = g(y, m_{-1}) = y$, in which case individual 1 may as well send the message $m_1 = y$ too. But such a reason is hardly compelling: given the mechanism γ is used to choose between x and y and given xP_1y, the message $m_1 = y$ is weakly dominated by the message $m'_1 = x$. Either $m_2 = m_3$ and so $g(x, m_{-1}) = g(y, m_{-1})$, or $m_2 \neq m_3$ in which case $g(x, m_{-1}) = x \neq g(y, m_{-1}) = y$. Therefore, given xP_1y, individual 1 can never lose, and can sometimes do strictly better, by sending the message "x" rather than the message "y". In particular, assuming no individual uses a weakly dominated message, the only undominated Nash equilibrium profile here is the "truthful" message strategy, $m^* = (x, x, x)$ and so γ implements φ in *undominated Nash equilibrium* at the profile ρ. □

It is not hard to check to that the argument in Example 3.5 applies quite generally: the (suitably extended) mechanism γ implements plurality rule in undominated Nash equilibrium for any binary decision and any number of (non-indifferent) individuals. In fact, much more is true.

3.3. NASH IMPLEMENTATION

Theorem 3.6 *Assume $n \geq 3$ and that no individual is ever indifferent over all alternatives in X. Then if $\varphi : \mathcal{R}^n \to \mathcal{X}$ satisfies no veto, φ is implementable in undominated Nash equilibrium.*

As with the argument for Theorem 3.5, the proof of this result is constructive; a particular mechanism is defined and shown to have the requisite properties. Unlike the mechanism in the proof to Theorem 3.5, however, the general mechanism used here is complex and we omit the details. The key idea underlying the mechanism, however, is easy to see with a two-person example.

Example 3.6 Let $N = \{1, 2\}$ and $X = \{w, x, y, z\}$. Suppose φ is a collective choice function with domain $\{\rho, \rho'\}$, where

$$\begin{aligned} \rho &= ((wP_1xP_1yP_1z), (xP_2yP_2wP_2z)); \\ \rho' &= ((wP_1'yP_1'xP_1'z), (xP_2'wP_2'yP_2'z)). \end{aligned}$$

Assume $\varphi(\rho) = w$ and $\varphi(\rho') = x$. Thus φ is not Maskin monotonic and therefore, by Lemma 3.1, not implementable in Nash equilibrium. Yet φ *is* implementable in undominated Nash equilibrium. Consider the mechanism $\gamma = ((\mathcal{M}_1, \mathcal{M}_2), g)$ with $\mathcal{M}_1 = \mathcal{M}_2 = \{\rho, \rho'\} \times \{1, 2, \ldots\}$ and g as follows. Let

$$m = ((a, k^1), (b, k^2)) \in \mathcal{M}_1 \times \mathcal{M}_2.$$

Then $g(m) = z$ if $a \neq b$; otherwise

$$g((\rho, k^1), (\rho, k^2)) = \begin{cases} w & \text{if } k^1 \leq k^2 \\ y & \text{if } k^1 > k^2 \end{cases}$$

and

$$g((\rho', k^1), (\rho', k^2)) = \begin{cases} x & \text{if } k^1 \geq k^2 \\ y & \text{if } k^1 < k^2 \end{cases}$$

Because outcome $z \in X$ is uniquely worst for both individuals at any profile in the domain, $g(m) = z$ implies m cannot possibly be a Nash equilibrium message profile. Consequently, if $m = ((a, k^1), (b, k^2))$ is a Nash equilibrium message profile under γ then $a = b$.

Suppose the true profile is $\rho = (R_1, R_2)$. Then $m_1 = (\rho, 1)$ is individual 1's only undominated strategy and evidently $m = ((\rho, 1), (\rho, 1)) \in \eta(\rho, \gamma)$ with $g(m) = \varphi(\rho) = w$. Now suppose the profile is ρ but $m' = ((\rho', k^1), (\rho', k^2))$; in particular suppose $k^1 = k^2 = 1$. Then m' is a Nash equilibrium but it is not an *undominated* Nash equilibrium: at profile ρ,

xP_1y and, therefore, any message $(\rho', k^1) \in \mathcal{M}_1$ is weakly dominated by the message $(\rho', k^1 + 1) \in \mathcal{M}_1$. Hence, $m = ((\rho, 1), (\rho, 1))$ is the only undominated Nash equilibrium at ρ. An entirely symmetric argument applies when the true profile is $\rho' = (R'_1, R'_2)$; in this case $m' = ((\rho', 1), (\rho', 1))$ is the only undominated Nash equilibrium at ρ' and $g(m') = \varphi(\rho') = x$. Therefore, γ implements φ in undominated Nash equilibrium. □

The device of having individuals report an integer $k^i \in \{1, 2, \ldots\}$ and using this component of any message to decide among an inconsistent set of messages is often referred to as "tail chasing". The idea is to insure that only consistent message profiles can arise in equilibrium; in Theorem 3.5, for instance, consistency requires (among other things) individuals to send messages of the form $m_i = (\rho, x, k)$ with $x \in \varphi(\rho)$. Because there is no largest positive integer, any message profile that triggers a decision predicated on tail chasing cannot be a Nash equilibrium profile as there is always a higher integer for an otherwise losing individual to report. In the mechanism used to prove Theorem 3.6, tail chasing is exploited even more widely to eliminate "unwanted", from the perspective of implementation, equilibria involving consistent messages. This is clear from Example 3.6 where we observed that while $m' = ((\rho', 1), (\rho', 1))$ was a perfectly consistent Nash equilibrium at the true preference profile ρ, it was not an undominated Nash equilibrium: the message $(\rho', k^1 + 1)$ weakly dominates the message (ρ', k^1) for individual 1 and all k^1, so there exists no undominated Nash equilibrium at ρ involving messages reporting ρ'.

By including a mild assumption on individuals' decisions, Theorem 3.6 overturns the negative inference drawn from Theorem 3.5, vividly illustrating the sensitivity of results in implementation theory to variations in the assumed model of strategic choice. On the other hand, as remarked above, although the mechanisms used to prove the theorems are simply technical constructs for demonstrating implementability, they are hardly very natural or intuitive. We argue in section 3.5 that more appealing mechanisms can be found in more limited environments. For general environments, however, the use of tail chasing or similarly arcane schemes appears to be essential: this is the content of Theorem 3.7, below.

Definition 3.9 *A mechanism $\gamma = (\mathcal{M}, g)$ is bounded relative to $(\mathcal{R}^n, X)$ if, whenever a message $m_i \in \mathcal{M}_i$ is dominated at some preference $R_i \in \mathcal{R}$, $i \in N$, there exists a message $m'_i \in \mathcal{M}_i$ that dominates m_i at R_i and is itself undominated at R_i.*

3.3. NASH IMPLEMENTATION

It should be clear that bounded mechanisms preclude tail chasing schemes. In particular, the deletion of dominated strategies in a bounded mechanism always leaves a well-defined decision for any individual and, consequently, seems to be a minimal restriction for more practical mechanisms.

Now generalize the idea of strategy-proofness for collective choice functions to that of strategy-resistance for collective choice rules.

Definition 3.10 *A collective choice rule $\varphi : \mathcal{R}^n \to \mathcal{X}$ is strategy-resistant if and only if, for all $\rho \in \mathcal{R}^n$, all $i \in N$, all $R'_i \in \mathcal{R}$ and each $y \in \varphi(R'_i, \rho_{-i})$, there exists an alternative $x \in \varphi(\rho)$ such that xR_iy.*

In words, if an individual i can obtain some collective choice y by unilaterally misrepresenting his or her preferences as R'_i rather than R_i, then there is a distinct alternative x that i considers at least as good as y which is selected by the choice rule under truth-telling. It is easy to check that if φ is resolute, then strategy-resistance and strategy-proofness are identical properties.

For any profile $\rho = (R_1, \ldots, R_n) \in \mathcal{R}^n$, let

$$\delta^-(\rho, \gamma) = \{m \in \mathcal{M} : \forall i \in N, \; m_i \text{ is undominated at } R_i\}$$

and say that a rule φ is *implementable in undominated strategies* (not necessarily Nash best response strategies) if there exists a mechanism $\gamma = (\mathcal{M}, g)$ such that, for all $\rho \in \mathcal{R}^n$,

$$\varphi(\rho) = g(\delta^-(\rho, \gamma)).$$

Clearly, if φ is implementable in undominated Nash equilibrium strategies then it is implementable in undominated strategies, but the converse is not necessarily true. Thus implementation in undominated strategies is a very weak requirement. Nevertheless, the following is true.

Theorem 3.7 *A collective choice rule $\varphi : \mathcal{R}^n \to \mathcal{X}$ is implementable in undominated strategies by a bounded mechanism only if φ is strategy-resistant.*

Proof Suppose φ is implementable in undominated strategies by a bounded mechanism; we need to show φ is strategy-resistant. To do this, choose any $i \in N$, $\rho \in \mathcal{R}^n$, $R'_i \in \mathcal{R}$ and $y \in \varphi(R'_i, \rho_{-i})$. Then there exists a mechanism $(\mathcal{M}, g)$ and message profile $m \in \mathcal{M}$ such that (1) m_j is undominated for all $j \neq i$ at R_j, and (2) m_i is undominated at R'_i and $g(m) = y$. If m_i is undominated at R_i then $y \in \varphi(\rho)$ and φ is strategy-resistant at ρ. If m_i is dominated at R_i then, because $(\mathcal{M}, g)$ is a bounded mechanism, there exists a message $m'_i \in \mathcal{M}_i$ which is both undominated at R'_i and which dominates m_i at R_i. Therefore, $g(m'_i, m_{-i}) \in \varphi(\rho)$ and $g(m'_i, m_{-i})R_i y$, so φ is again strategy-resistant at ρ. Since i, ρ and R'_i are chosen arbitrarily, this proves the result. $\square$

Conditional on individuals being assumed not to play dominated strategies, the implication of Theorem 3.7 is that either a mechanism capable of generally implementing an arbitrary collective choice rule must be unbounded, or the choice rule itself must be strategy-resistant. In the first case, the mechanism must exploit peculiarities such as tail chasing schemes; in the second case, there is little reason to worry about implementation at all as individuals have little or no incentive to dissemble. And since strategy-resistant collective choice functions are strategy-proof, the result immediately yields that collective choice functions implementable in undominated strategies by bounded mechanisms are strategy-proof.

3.4 Application: Monotonicity of electoral rules

There is, as remarked earlier, a strong intuition that collective choice should exhibit some sort of monotonicity: loosely speaking, if an alternative x is chosen over another alternative y, and if any individual's ranking of x at worst stays unchanged relative to y, then x should still be chosen over y. It is not surprising, therefore, that a recurrent theme in comparing electoral rules, rules that map lists of ballots over alternatives into chosen alternatives, concerns the extent to which various rules are monotonic. But an electoral rule is only one link in a representative electoral system: voters are concerned with policy outcomes and policy is chosen by elected representatives who in turn are chosen by voters through the electoral rule. Consequently, it is important to distinguish between monotonicity of the electoral rule *per se* and monotonicity of the electoral system of which the rule is a part. In other words, it is in principle consistent for an electoral rule not to be monotonic, in that more votes for some candidate could harm that candidate's chances of legislative election, but nevertheless for the representative system as a whole to be monotonic, in that increased support for a policy never harms that policy's chance of being chosen by an elected legislature.

Although distinguishing between electing legislatures and legislative policy choice is important for understanding representative systems as whole, it suffices here to suppress the distinction and assume individuals' preferences over final policies induce well-defined preference profiles over candidates for elected office. Under this assumption, an electoral system is monotonic if

3.4. APPLICATION: MONOTONICITY OF ELECTORAL RULES 91

and only if its constituent electoral rule is monotonic. On the other hand, because the domain of an electoral rule is the set of admissible ballots, it remains necessary to distinguish between monotonicity of a rule with respect to *votes* and monotonicity with respect to the underlying *preferences*.

A vote, or ballot, is a report of an individual's preferences and an electoral rule is a mapping, taking lists of ballots into the set of alternatives, or candidates. In the language developed above (and given our assumption connecting preferences over legislative policies to preferences over candidates), an electoral rule is simply a mechanism $(\mathcal{M}, g)$ where, for any individual i, $\mathcal{M}_i$ describes the admissible ballots individual i can report and $g: \mathcal{M} \to X$ maps ballots into elected candidates. And to remove any trivialities, assume throughout that if $(\mathcal{M}, g)$ is an electoral rule, then the range of g is precisely X, so every candidate is elected under some list of votes.

Example 3.7 Suppose there are three candidates $X = \{x, y, z\}$. Examples of electoral rules $(\mathcal{M}, g)$ include

(1) *Plurality voting*. For all $i \in N$,

$$\mathcal{M}_i = \{x, y, z, \emptyset\},$$

where a indicates a vote for candidate $a \in X$, the message $\emptyset$ indicates abstention and, for all $m \in \mathcal{M}$,

$$g(m) = [a \in X : \forall b \neq a, \ |\{i : m_i = a\}| \geq |\{i : m_i = b\}|]$$

with, say, ties broken lexicographically.

(2) *Borda voting*. For all $i \in N$,

$$\mathcal{M}_i = \{(x, y, z), (x, z, y), (y, x, z), (y, z, x), (z, x, y), (z, y, x)\}$$

where an alternative a in the jth coordinate of a message indicates that j is the ordinal rank assigned to a; for instance, $m_i = (y, z, x)$ indicates i reports candidate y first-ranked, candidate z second-ranked and candidate x last-ranked. For all $m \in \mathcal{M}$,

$$g(m) = [a \in X : \forall b \neq a, \ \sum_N r_i(a) \leq \sum_N r_i(b)]$$

where $r_i(a)$ is i's reported ordinal rank for candidate a and ties are broken lexicographically. □

For any electoral rule $(\mathcal{M}, g)$, any individual $i \in N$ and any pair of candidates $x, y \in X$, let $xm_i y$ indicate that i votes for (or, as appropriate, ranks) x over y.

Definition 3.11 *An electoral rule $(\mathcal{M}, g)$ is vote monotonic if and only if $g(m) = x$ and $m' \in \mathcal{M}$ is such that, for all $i \in N$ and all $y \in X$, $x m_i y$ implies $x m'_i y$, then $g(m') = x$.*

In words, if an electoral rule is vote monotonic then any winning candidate in some situation who receives (weakly) more votes relative to any other candidate in a different situation, remains winning.

Now for each individual i and mechanism $(\mathcal{M}, g)$, $\sigma_i(\rho) = m_i \in \mathcal{M}_i$ is the message i chooses. In the current context, where the mechanism is an electoral rule, a message m_i is a vote and so σ_i is appropriately interpreted as i's voting strategy under the electoral rule, with $g(\sigma(\rho))$ being the elected candidate from X given the votes cast at preference profile ρ. As before, the particular distributions of votes that arise are taken to reflect β-equilibrium decisions for some behavioral theory β. And because there is no reason in general to think that the set of β-equilibria, $\beta(\rho, \gamma)$, is singleton, the composite mapping $\beta \circ g$ can be set-valued; that is, $\beta \circ g : \mathcal{R}^n \to \mathcal{X}$. In sum, given an electoral rule $\gamma = (\mathcal{M}, g)$ and a β-equilibrium theory, the set of candidates who could be elected at ρ are, in the earlier notation, $g(\beta(\rho, \gamma))$.

Definition 3.12 *An electoral rule $(\mathcal{M}, g)$ is preference monotonic if and only if the composite map $\beta \circ g : \mathcal{R}^n \to \mathcal{X}$ is Maskin monotonic.*

Whereas vote monotonicity is exclusively a property of the electoral outcome function g on the vote domain, $\mathcal{M}$, preference monotonicity is a property of the correspondence $\beta \circ g$ induced by the electoral rule on the preference domain, $\mathcal{R}^n$. Thus preference monotonicity concerns how underlying preferences, rather than votes *per se*, are translated into outcomes.

For any $i \in N$, let $\hat{m}_i$ denote abstention, or the message ranking all candidates as equivalent. Say that an electoral rule is dictatorial if there exists an individual $i \in N$ such that, for all vote profiles $m \in \mathcal{M}$, $x m_i y$ for all y implies $g(m) = x$. Then Theorem 3.4 implies

Corollary 3.2 *Consider any electoral rule $\gamma = (\mathcal{M}, g)$ such that, for all $i \in N$, $\hat{m}_i \notin \mathcal{M}_i$ and the range of g contains at least three candidates. Then g is vote monotonic only if g is dictatorial.*

Proof By definition of γ, g is single-valued and, by assumption, has at least three candidates in its range. Hence $g : \mathcal{M} \to X$ is a collective choice function and Theorem 3.4 applies directly. $\square$

On the other hand, Lemma 3.1 yields

3.4. APPLICATION: MONOTONICITY OF ELECTORAL RULES

Corollary 3.3 *Suppose individuals choose Nash equilibrium strategies, so $\beta = \eta$. Then all electoral rules $\gamma = (\mathcal{M}, g)$ are preference monotonic.*

Proof Under the Nash assumption, $\eta \circ g : \mathcal{R}^n \to \mathcal{X}$ is a set-valued collective choice rule and is trivially implementable in Nash equilibrium. The result is now immediate from Lemma 3.1. $\square$

Comparing the two preceding corollaries, it is clear that while vote monotonicity is in general impossible for nondictatorial electoral rules, the normatively more significant preference monotonicity is invariably satisfied for any electoral rule when individuals are strategically rational according to Nash equilibrium. An example illustrates the distinction.

Example 3.8 Suppose there are four candidates $X = \{w, x, y, z\}$ and three voters $N = \{1, 2, 3\}$. Assume the electoral rule $\gamma = (\mathcal{M}, g)$ is Borda voting as described in Example 3.7(2): for all $i \in N$, m_i is an ordinal ranking of X and g selects the candidate with the highest ordinal rank, that is, $a \in X$ such that $\sum_N r_i(a)$ is minimal (ties being broken lexicographically). Let $\rho, \rho' \in \mathcal{R}^n$ be given by

$$\rho = \begin{cases} xP_1yP_1wP_1z \\ xP_2yP_2wP_2z \\ yP_3wP_3zP_3x \end{cases} ; \rho' = \begin{cases} xP_1'yP_1'wP_1'z \\ xP_2'yP_2'wP_2'z \\ yP_3'xP_3'wP_3'z \end{cases}.$$

Consider the "sincere" vote profiles, respectively $m = m(\rho)$ and $m' = m(\rho')$, such that

$$m = ((x, y, w, z), (x, y, w, z), (y, w, z, x));$$
$$m' = ((x, y, w, z), (x, y, w, z), (y, x, w, z)).$$

Under γ, Borda voting yields $g(m) = y$ and $g(m') = x$; but vote monotonicity requires $g(m') = y$. However, when preferences are ρ, the sincere vote profile $m(\rho)$ is not a Nash equilibrium. Given how the other two individuals vote at $m(\rho)$, individual $i = 1$ (or, symmetrically, $i = 2$) can instead choose the vote, $m_1'' = (x, w, z, y)$ which gives $g(m_1'', m_2, m_3) = x$ and xP_1y. Similarly, given how individuals $i = 1, 2$ vote at $m(\rho')$, individual $i = 3$ can vote m_3 rather than (sincerely) m_3' when preferences are ρ' to obtain $g(m_1', m_2', m_3) = y$ and $yP_3'x$; so the sincere vote profile $m(\rho')$ is not a Nash equilibrium at ρ'.

While there exist several Nash equilibrium vote profiles at each preference profile, it is left as an exercise to check

$$g(\eta(\rho, \gamma)) = g(\eta(\rho', \gamma)) = X.$$

Therefore, although the electoral rule γ is not vote monotonic, it is surely preference monotonic. In particular, if $g(m^*) = y$ and $m^* \in \eta(\rho, \gamma)$, then $m^* \in \eta(\rho', \gamma)$. □

That the set of Nash equilibrium outcomes in Example 3.8 should, for example, include candidate z at profile ρ' is entirely because Nash equilibrium *per se* fails to rule out dominated strategies. Because undominated Nash equilibria are nevertheless Nash equilibria, Corollary 3.3 continues to hold with undominated Nash replacing Nash equilibrium and $z \notin g(\bar{\eta}(\rho, \gamma)) \cup g(\bar{\eta}(\rho', \gamma))$, where $\bar{\eta}(\cdot, \gamma)$ is the set of undominated Nash equilibria [Exercise].

3.5 Quasi-linear preferences

In Chapter 2, we found a class of nondictatorial and strategy-proof collective choice functions on domains of single-peaked preferences, augmented median voter rules. The key feature of such rules is that if any individual reports a preference ordering other than his or her true one at some (single-peaked) profile, either the collective choice remains unaffected or it moves in a way that makes the individual strictly worse off. In other words, if an individual's report is pivotal in the decision, the best the individual can do is to report truthfully. It follows that any augmented median voter rule φ is self-implementable in dominant strategy equilibrium on single-peaked domains. The idea of exploiting a pivotal property turns out to be useful on another empirically important domain, that of *quasi-linear* preferences [PPTI, sect.4.4].

Quasi-linear preferences are especially germane when collective choice concerns costly public projects: public works, welfare programs, space exploration programs, and so forth. In such circumstances, collective decisions involve both selection of a public project (including, possibly, the project of doing nothing) and a distribution of some private good among individuals. Typically, the private good is interpreted as money with the distribution reflecting any costs associated with the chosen project. A feasible alternative, then, is a pair $(x, t) \in X \times \Re^n$ where $x \in X$ denotes the project and $t = (t_1, \ldots, t_n) \in \Re^n$ is a distribution of the private good; any such pair (x, t) is called an *allocation*. Because public projects may be fully divisible (for example, a given welfare program could in principle be initiated at any scale) or indivisible (for example, build a particular bridge or not), both possibilities are covered by assuming only that the set X is compact.

3.5. QUASI-LINEAR PREFERENCES

Definition 3.13 *An individual $i \in N$ has quasi-linear preferences on the set of allocations, $X \times \Re^n$, if and only if i's preferences can be represented by a utility function $u_i : X \times \Re^n \to \Re$ such that, for all $(x, t) \in X \times \Re^n$, $u_i(x, t) = v_i(x) + t_i$.*

Thus quasi-linear preferences are separable and linear increasing in the private good, implying preferences over allocations are independent of any initial endowments which, therefore, can be ignored. Furthermore, with the exception of admitting a utility representation, quasi-linearity places no restrictions on an individual's preferences over X (they need not, for example, be single-peaked); consequently, we abuse notation somewhat and write $v = (v_1, \ldots, v_n) \in \mathcal{R}^n$ for the restricted profile over X induced by a quasi-linear profile $u = (u_1, \ldots, u_n)$ over $X \times \Re^n$.

Example 3.9 (1) *Cost sharing for a discrete public project.* Let $N = \{1, \ldots, n\}$ and $X = \{x, y\}$. For all $i \in N$ and all allocations $(a, t) \in \{x, y\} \times \Re^n$, assume

$$u_i(a, t) = \begin{cases} v_i - t_i & \text{if } a = x \\ 0 & \text{otherwise} \end{cases}$$

where $v_i \in [\underline{v}, \bar{v}] \subset \Re$, $\underline{v} < \bar{v}$. The interpretation here is that if the discrete public project is chosen, $a = x$, then i gains a (finite) utility v_i and pays a sum $t_i \geq 0$ toward the monetary cost, say $C > 0$, of the project; if the project is not chosen, $a = y$, then all payoffs are normalized to zero. Now suppose the collective choice rule $\varphi : \mathcal{R}^n \to \{x, y\} \times \Re^n$ is defined by

$$\forall v \in \mathcal{R}^n, \ \varphi(v) = \begin{cases} (x; \frac{C}{n}, \ldots, \frac{C}{n}) & \text{if } \sum_N v_i > C \\ (y; 0, \ldots, 0) & \text{otherwise.} \end{cases}$$

Then φ is a nondictatorial collective choice function satisfying weak Pareto. Because the range of φ contains less than three alternatives, however, Theorem 2.1 does not apply. Nevertheless, consider a profile v such that

$$0 < v_1 < C/n < v_2 \leq v_3 \leq \ldots \leq v_n;$$

$$\sum_{i=2}^{i=n} v_i < C < v_1 + \sum_{i=2}^{i=n} v_i.$$

Then φ is manipulable at v by individual $i = 1$; specifically, for $v_1' = 0$,

$$u_1(\varphi(v_1', v_{-1})) = 0 > u_1(\varphi(v)) = v_1 - \frac{C}{n}.$$

Moreover, the allocation $(x; \frac{C}{n}, \ldots, \frac{C}{n}) \in PS_N(v)$, whereas $(y; 0, \ldots, 0) \notin PS_N(v)$. For instance, suppose $n = 3$, $C = 1$ and, for some small $\varepsilon > 0$, $v = (\frac{1}{3} - \varepsilon, \frac{1}{3} + \varepsilon, \frac{1}{3} + 2\varepsilon)$; then the allocation $(x; \frac{1}{3} - \frac{3}{2}\varepsilon, \frac{1}{3} + \frac{1}{2}\varepsilon, \frac{1}{3} + \varepsilon)$ is strictly preferred by all individuals to (and so Pareto dominates) the allocation $(y; 0, 0, 0)$.

(2) *Choosing a divisible public good.* Let $N = \{1, \ldots, n\}$ and $X = [0, \infty)$. For all $i \in N$ and all allocations $(x, t) \in [0, \infty) \times \Re^n$, assume $u_i(x, t) = v_i(x) - t_i(x)$ with v_i differentiable and strictly increasing concave in x. In this example, x describes the production level of a public good valued according to $v_i(x)$ by $i \in N$, and $t_i(x) \geq 0$ is that part of the total cost of x that individual i is required to pay. Let $C(x)$ be the total cost of x and assume C is differentiable and strictly increasing convex in x. Suppose the collective choice rule is

$$\forall v \in \mathcal{R}^n, \ \varphi(v) = \{(x; \frac{C(x)}{n}, \ldots, \frac{C(x)}{n}) : \sum_N \frac{\partial v_i(x)}{\partial x} = \frac{\partial C(x)}{\partial x}\}.$$

Then φ is a nondictatorial collective choice function satisfying weak Pareto; in this case, however, the range of φ certainly includes more than three alternatives and, therefore, cannot be strategy-proof by Theorem 2.1. An explicit example illustrating this fact is left as an exercise. □

When preferences are quasi-linear, there exist collective choice functions for allocations that can be implemented in dominant strategy equilibrium. To prove this claim, we use the Revelation Principle, Theorem 3.1. Let $\varphi : \mathcal{R}^n \to X \times \Re^n$ be a collective choice function; by Theorem 3.1, if φ is implementable in dominant strategy equilibrium, then there exists a direct mechanism $(\mathcal{R}^n, g)$ that truthfully implements φ in dominant strategy equilibrium. But since φ is a function and $g : \mathcal{R}^n \to X \times \Re^n$, it must be that $g \equiv \varphi$. Therefore, to identify the family of dominant strategy implementable choice functions, it suffices to consider only choice functions that are self-implementable in dominant strategy equilibrium. The following example provides some idea of what such functions look like.

Example 3.10 Consider the discrete public project problem described in Example 3.9(1). Because $X = \{x, y\}$ and, for all $i \in N$, $v_i(x) = v_i \in [\underline{v}, \bar{v}]$ and $v_i(y) = 0$, we can define a direct mechanism $\gamma^* = ([\underline{v}, \bar{v}]^n, g^*)$ such that, for all message profiles $m \in [\underline{v}, \bar{v}]^n$,

$$g^*(m) = \begin{cases} (x; t_1, \ldots, t_n) & \text{if } \sum_N m_i > C \\ (y; t_1, \ldots, t_n) & \text{otherwise} \end{cases}$$

3.5. QUASI-LINEAR PREFERENCES

where, for all $j \in N$, t_j is given by

$$t_j = \begin{cases} 0 & \text{if } \sum_N m_i \leq C \text{ and } \sum_{i \neq j} m_i \leq \frac{n-1}{n}C \\ \sum_{i \neq j} m_i - \frac{n-1}{n}C & \text{if } \sum_N m_i \leq C \text{ and } \sum_{i \neq j} m_i > \frac{n-1}{n}C \\ C - \sum_{i \neq j} m_i & \text{if } \sum_N m_i > C \text{ and } \sum_{i \neq j} m_i < \frac{n-1}{n}C \\ \frac{C}{n} & \text{if } \sum_N m_i > C \text{ and } \sum_{i \neq j} m_i \geq \frac{n-1}{n}C \end{cases}.$$

To understand how the transfer, or cost, t_j is defined, look at each row in turn. A message m_i here is simply a statement of how much an individual i values the project x relative to doing nothing, y. In the first row, then, as revealed by the message profile m, the aggregate evaluation of the project x falls short of its cost $C > 0$, both when j's message is included in the aggregate and when it is not. In other words, j's report is not "pivotal" to the outcome under g^*; hence the net transfer t_j is set equal to zero. Under the message profile described in the second row, however, individual j is pivotal: without j's message, the aggregate reported value of the project exceeds its cost; with j's message, the aggregate reported value of the project at most equals its cost. Hence, conditional on what everyone else reports, m_{-j}, j's message m_j tips the balance in favor of choosing y over x. The transfer required of j, t_j, is precisely the total surplus that the $n-1$ other individuals would have experienced had j not been included in the decision and x were chosen over y. And this is sensible since this surplus is in effect the cost to the others of j being included in the decision. The remaining two rows have symmetric interpretations: in the third row, the message profile is such that j is pivotal in favor of x over y with the transfer t_j being the net cost j's message imposes on the others; and the final row says that if j is not pivotal in a decision to undertake the project x, then j simply pays the average cost of x.

The mechanism γ^* has a remarkable property. Recall, $\delta(v, \gamma^*)$ is the set of dominant strategy equilibria under the mechanism γ^* at the (quasi-linear) profile $v \in [\underline{v}, \bar{v}]^n$.

Claim: $\delta(v, \gamma^*) = \{m \in [\underline{v}, \bar{v}]^n : m_i = v_i, \text{ all } i \in N\}$.

Proof: Fix $\sum_{i \neq j} m_i \in [(n-1)\underline{v}, (n-1)\bar{v}]$ arbitrarily and consider j's decision. There are four cases.

(1) $\sum_N m_i \leq C$ and $\sum_{i \neq j} m_i \leq \frac{n-1}{n}C$. Then $u_j(g^*(m)) = 0$. Suppose $v_j + \sum_{i \neq j} m_i \leq C$; then $u_j(g^*(v_j, m_{-j})) = u_j(g^*(m))$. On the other hand, if $v_j + \sum_{i \neq j} m_i > C$,

$$u_j(g^*(v_j, m_{-j})) = v_j - [C - \sum_{i \neq j} m_i] > 0.$$

(2) $\sum_N m_i > C$ and $\sum_{i \neq j} m_i \leq \frac{n-1}{n} C$. Then

$$u_j(g^*(m)) = v_j - [C - \sum_{i \neq j} m_i].$$

If $v_j + \sum_{i \neq j} m_i > C$, $u_j(g^*(v_j, m_{-j})) = u_j(g^*(m))$. But if $v_j + \sum_{i \neq j} m_i \leq C$,

$$u_j(g^*(v_j, m_{-j})) = 0 \geq v_j - [C - \sum_{i \neq j} m_i].$$

Consequently, whenever $\sum_{i \neq j} m_i \leq \frac{n-1}{n} C$, individual j can never do worse and may, on occasion, do strictly better by sending the message v_j rather than any message $m_j \neq v_j$. To complete the proof for the Claim, it remains to check the remaining two cases, that is, when $\sum_{i \neq j} m_i > \frac{n-1}{n} C$ [Exercise]. □

For the discrete public project problem of Example 3.9(1), therefore, the direct mechanism γ^* of Example 3.10 supports a unique dominant strategy equilibrium in which all individuals truthfully report their relative valuation of the project x. Thus the mechanism recommends going ahead with the project if and only if the aggregate valuation of doing so exceeds its cost. In other words, on the domain of quasi-linear preferences over allocations, the collective choice function $\varphi \equiv g^*$ is self-implementable (and so simultaneously implementable and truthfully implementable) in dominant strategy equilibrium.

The mechanism of Example 3.10 is a pivotal mechanism, one of the class of *Groves* mechanisms. To see why it is pivotal, suppose the project x is chosen over y. Then all individuals pay an equal share of the cost, C/n, and those individuals whose message, given the messages of all others, changed the decision from y to x are charged an additional tax that depends on the messages of others. Similarly, if the decision is y, then the only individuals who pay anything at all are those whose message, given the messages of others, changed the decision from x to y. In other words, only individuals who sent pivotal messages are taxed beyond an equal share of the total production cost of the public decision when the decision is x and zero when it is y.

Groves mechanisms insure that the necessary condition for Pareto efficiency (produce a public good or undertake a public project only if the aggregate valuation of so doing exceeds the cost) can be met: under such mechanisms, telling the truth is a dominant strategy. Groves mechanisms,

3.5. QUASI-LINEAR PREFERENCES

that is, are strategy-proof collective choice functions on the domain of quasi-linear preferences over allocations. And given the behavioral appeal of dominant strategies, this is a striking result. More striking is that, on this domain, *only* Groves mechanisms have this property. Consequently, if there exists a strategy-proof collective choice function with quasi-linear preferences, then it is a Groves mechanism. Unfortunately, it is also true that no Groves mechanism is weakly Paretian on this domain: the sufficient conditions for Pareto efficiency cannot be guaranteed. Inducing individuals to tell the truth about a public project almost always requires extracting more taxes than the total cost of the project.

Example 3.11 Consider a special case of Example 3.10. Let $N = \{1, 2, 3\}$, $v = (\frac{3}{5}, \frac{3}{5}, \frac{8}{5})$ and $C = 2$. Then $\sum_i v_i > C$ implying that, if an allocation is in the Pareto set, the project is undertaken:

$$a \in PS_N(v) \Rightarrow a = (x, t) \text{ for some } t.$$

As argued in Example 3.9(1), the collective choice rule φ defined there is not strategy-proof and the unique outcome from the mechanism $(\mathcal{R}^n, \varphi)$ is the allocation $(y; 0, 0, 0) \notin PS_N(v)$. On the other hand, under the mechanism γ^* of Example 3.10, all individuals report their true valuations: $\delta(v, \gamma^*) = \{(\frac{3}{5}, \frac{3}{5}, \frac{8}{5})\}$. Because, for each $i = 1, 2$, $v_i + v_3 > C = 2$, individual i is not pivotal. But $v_1 + v_2 < \frac{n-1}{n}C = 4/3$ and $\sum_i v_i > C$ implies that individual 3 is pivotal. Consequently, $m = v$ implies

$$\begin{aligned} g^*(v) &= (x; \frac{C}{n}, \frac{C}{n}, [\frac{C}{n} + (\frac{n-1}{n}C - v_1 - v_2)]) \\ &= (x; \frac{2}{3}, \frac{2}{3}, \frac{4}{5}). \end{aligned}$$

Therefore, $\sum_i t_i = 32/15 > C$; the mechanism γ^* elicits a surplus of $2/15$ in providing incentives for truthful preference revelation. Furthermore, the allocation $g^*(v)$ results in a realized utility profile

$$\begin{aligned} u(g^*(v)) &= (v_1 - t_1, v_2 - t_2, v_3 - t_3) \\ &= (-\frac{1}{15}, -\frac{1}{15}, \frac{4}{5}) \end{aligned}$$

and so individuals 1 and 2 are strictly worse off with the allocation $g^*(v)$ than they would have been had the public decision been y, implying $u_i(y; t) = 0$, all $i \in N$. □

We now make good on the claims above regarding Groves mechanisms. For the general quasi-linear case, where the set of alternatives X need not be finite, assume that every individual has a well-defined most preferred alternative in X: for all $i \in N$, $\arg\max_{x \in X} v_i(x) \in X$. Furthermore, to save notation, assume that the cost of realizing any alternative $x \in X$ is zero. Although some of the definitions to follow have to be modified slightly in obvious ways to accommodate non-zero costs, none of the subsequent results are affected; the assumption is therefore without any loss of generality. It is also convenient at times to write $g(v) = (x(v), t(v))$, where g is the outcome function for some direct mechanism.

Two properties a direct mechanism might satisfy are important.

Definition 3.14 *Let $(\mathcal{R}^n, g)$ be a direct mechanism. Say that g is:*
(1) independent of individual utility levels if, for any $i \in N$, $v \in \mathcal{R}^n$ and $c \in \Re$, $g(v_i, v_{-i}) = g(v_i + c, v_{-i})$;
(2) decision efficient if, for all $v \in \mathcal{R}^n$, $g(v) = (x, t)$ implies that for all $y \in X$, $\sum_N v_i(x) \geq \sum_N v_i(y)$.

In words, if the outcome function of a direct mechanism (or, simply, a direct mechanism) is independent of individual utility levels it does not depend on the origin chosen for the utility representation of any individual's preferences over X. So no individual can alter the chosen allocation under a utility level independent direct mechanism by simply adding a constant to her utility valuation of every allocation. And a direct mechanism is decision efficient if it always selects an alternative to maximize aggregate utility on X (but not necessarily on the set of all allocations, $X \times \Re^n$). Decision efficiency is necessary for a mechanism to be weakly Paretian but not, as Example 3.11 illustrates, sufficient.

Definition 3.15 *A direct mechanism $\gamma = (\mathcal{R}^n, g)$ is a Groves mechanism if g is independent of individual utility levels, decision efficient and, for all $i \in N$, there exists an arbitrary function $\tau_i : \mathcal{R}^{n-1} \to \Re$ such that, for all $v \in \mathcal{R}^n$, $t_i(v) = \sum_{j \neq i} v_j(x(v)) - \tau_i(v_{-i})$.*

The key feature of a Groves mechanism is that, for any individual i, the transfer t_i consequent on some public decision is independent of i's message regarding her own preferences over X. Thus no individual can influence their transfer, in which case truthful reporting is a strategically best decision. In the Example 3.10, for instance, the tax payment demanded of any individual i, $t_i(m)$, is independent of m_i and the resulting function g^* proved to be self-implementable in dominant strategy equilibrium.

Recall, in the current setting, that a collective choice function φ is strategy-proof if it is self-implementable in dominant strategy equilibrium;

3.5. QUASI-LINEAR PREFERENCES

that is, if the direct mechanism $(\mathcal{R}^n, \varphi)$ is such that, for all $v \in \mathcal{R}^n$, all $i \in N$ and all $v'_i \in \mathcal{R}$, $u_i(\varphi(v)) \geq u_i(\varphi(v'_i, v_{-i}))$.

Theorem 3.8 *Let all individuals have quasi-linear preferences over the set of allocations and let φ be a collective choice function on this domain. Then φ is strategy-proof and decision efficient if and only if $(\mathcal{R}^n, \varphi)$ is a Groves mechanism.*

Proof (Sufficiency) Let $(\mathcal{R}^n, \varphi)$ be a Groves mechanism and fix a profile $v \in \mathcal{R}^n$. By definition, φ is decision efficient. To show φ strategy-proof, consider any $i \in N$ and $v'_i \in \mathcal{R}$. Then

$$t_i(v) = \sum_{j \neq i} v_j(x(v)) - \tau_i(v_{-i})$$

and

$$t_i(v'_i, v_{-i}) = \sum_{j \neq i} v_j(x(v'_i, v_{-i})) - \tau_i(v_{-i}).$$

Hence, by φ decision efficient,

$$u_i(\varphi(v)) - u_i(\varphi(v'_i, v_{-i}))$$
$$= v_i(x(v)) - v_i(x(v'_i, v_{-i})) + \sum_{j \neq i} v_j(x(v)) - \sum_{j \neq i} v_j(x(v'_i, v_{-i}))$$
$$= \sum_{j \in N} v_j(x(v)) - \sum_{j \in N} v_j(x(v'_i, v_{-i})) \geq 0.$$

Therefore, φ is strategy-proof.

(Necessity) Let $(\mathcal{R}^n, \varphi)$ have φ strategy-proof and decision efficient. We need to show that φ is independent of individual utility levels. Equivalently, defining $\xi_i(v) = \sum_{j \neq i} v_j(x(v)) - t_i(v)$ for any $v \in \mathcal{R}^n$ and any $i \in N$, we need to show ξ_i independent of v_i. Fix $v_{-i} \in \mathcal{R}^{n-1}$ arbitrarily and let $v_i, v'_i \in \mathcal{R}$. At the profile (v_i, v_{-i}), φ strategy-proof implies

$$v_i(x(v)) + t_i(v) \geq v_i(x(v'_i, v_{-i})) + t_i(v'_i, v_{-i}) \qquad \Leftrightarrow$$

$$\sum_{j \in N} v_j(x(v)) - \xi_i(v) \geq \sum_{j \in N} v_j(x(v'_i, v_{-i})) - \xi_i(v'_i, v_{-i}) \qquad \Leftrightarrow$$

$$\sum_{j \in N} v_j(x(v)) - \sum_{j \in N} v_j(x(v'_i, v_{-i})) \geq \xi_i(v) - \xi_i(v'_i, v_{-i}).$$

And similarly, at the profile (v'_i, v_{-i}), φ strategy-proof implies

$$\sum_{j \in N} v_j(x(v'_i, v_{-i})) - \sum_{j \in N} v_j(x(v)) \geq \xi_i(v'_i, v_{-i}) - \xi_i(v).$$

102   CHAPTER 3. IMPLEMENTABLE COLLECTIVE CHOICE

In the case $x(v) = x(v'_i, v_{-i})$, the last two inequalities imply $\xi_i(v'_i, v_{-i}) = \xi_i(v)$. So for all $x \in X$ and $v'_i \in \mathcal{R}$, if $x(v'_i, v_{-i}) = x$ set $\xi_i(x) = \xi_i(v'_i, v_{-i})$. Now choose any distinct pair of alternatives $y, z \in X$ and let $v''_i \in \mathcal{R}$ satisfy

$$\begin{aligned} v''_i(y) + \sum_{j \neq i} v_j(y) &= v''_i(z) + \sum_{j \neq i} v_j(z) \\ &\geq v''_i(x) + \sum_{j \neq i} v_j(x), \text{ all } x \in X \backslash \{y, z\}. \end{aligned}$$

For $\varepsilon > 0$, define v_i^ε and $\bar{v}_i^\varepsilon$ by

$$\begin{aligned} v_i^\varepsilon(y) &= v''_i(y) + \varepsilon \text{ and, } \forall x \neq y, \ v_i^\varepsilon(x) = v''_i(x); \\ \bar{v}_i^\varepsilon(z) &= v''_i(z) + \varepsilon \text{ and, } \forall x \neq z, \ \bar{v}_i^\varepsilon(x) = v''_i(x). \end{aligned}$$

Hence, for all $\varepsilon > 0$,

$$\begin{aligned} v_i^\varepsilon(y) + \sum_{j \neq i} v_j(y) &> v_i^\varepsilon(x) + \sum_{j \neq i} v_j(x), \text{ all } x \neq y; \\ \bar{v}_i^\varepsilon(z) + \sum_{j \neq i} v_j(z) &> \bar{v}_i^\varepsilon(x) + \sum_{j \neq i} v_j(x), \text{ all } x \neq z. \end{aligned}$$

Therefore, by φ decision efficient, $x(v_i^\varepsilon, v_{-i}) = y$ and $x(\bar{v}_i^\varepsilon, v_{-i}) = z$. At the profile $(v_i^\varepsilon, v_{-i})$, φ strategy-proof implies

$$[v_i^\varepsilon(y) + \sum_{j \neq i} v_j(y)] - [\bar{v}_i^\varepsilon(z) + \sum_{j \neq i} v_j(z)] \geq \xi_i(y) - \xi_i(z).$$

Since $v''_i(y) + \sum_{j \neq i} v_j(y) = v''_i(z) + \sum_{j \neq i} v_j(z)$ by construction,

$$\lim_{\varepsilon \to 0} \left[[v_i^\varepsilon(y) + \sum_{j \neq i} v_j(y)] - [\bar{v}_i^\varepsilon(z) + \sum_{j \neq i} v_j(z)] \right] = 0.$$

Hence, $\xi_i(y) \leq \xi_i(z)$. And arguing in the same way at the profile $(v_i^\varepsilon, v_{-i})$ yields $\xi_i(y) \geq \xi_i(z)$, implying $\xi_i(y) = \xi_i(z)$. Therefore, because y and z were chosen arbitrarily, this equality proves ξ_i is independent of v_i as required. □

Theorem 3.8 justifies the focus on Groves mechanisms for making collective choices when preferences are quasi-linear on allocations: Groves mechanisms constitute the only strategy-proof and decision efficient collective choice rules on the domain. On the other hand, Example 3.11 illustrated a claim that Groves mechanisms need not satisfy weak Pareto; the specific mechanism used in the example, γ^*, is not peculiar.

3.5. QUASI-LINEAR PREFERENCES

Theorem 3.9 *Let all individuals have quasi-linear preferences over the set of allocations. There exists no Groves mechanism such that, for all profiles $v \in \mathcal{R}^n$, $\sum_{i \in N} t_i(v) = 0$.*

The argument for this result exploits a mathematical fact about real valued functions. Let $\theta : \Re^n \to \Re$ and let $K = \{1,2\}^n$ be the set of mappings $\kappa : N \to \{1,2\}$. For any $\kappa \in K$, let $s(\kappa) = \sum_{i=1}^{i=n} \kappa(i)$. For any two vectors $v^1, v^2 \in \Re^n$ and mapping $\kappa \in K$, define the vector $v^\kappa = (v_1^\kappa, \ldots, v_n^\kappa)$ by: for all $i \in N$, $v_i^\kappa = v_i^{\kappa(i)}$. For example, if $n = 3$ and $\kappa = (\kappa(1), \kappa(2), \kappa(3)) = (2, 1, 2)$,

$$v^\kappa = (v_1^{\kappa(1)}, v_2^{\kappa(2)}, v_3^{\kappa(3)}) = (v_1^2, v_2^1, v_3^2).$$

Then $\theta(v)$ is decomposable into a sum of n functions, $\{\tau_i\}_{i=1}^{i=n}$, each of which is a function of $n-1$ variables v_{-i}, that is $\theta(v) = \sum_{i=1}^{i=n} \tau_i(v_{-i})$, only if, for all selections $v^1, v^2 \in \Re^n$,

$$\sum_{\kappa \in K} (-1)^{s(\kappa)} \theta(v^\kappa) = 0. \qquad (*)$$

We are now ready to prove the theorem.

Proof of Theorem 3.9 Let $(\mathcal{R}^n, \varphi)$ be a Groves mechanism. Let $v \in \mathcal{R}^n$ with $\varphi(v) = (x(v), t(v))$; by Theorem 3.8, φ is strategy-proof and decision efficient. For all profiles $v \in \mathcal{R}^n$, define $\theta(v) \equiv \sum_{i=1}^{i=n} \tau_i(v_{-i})$. If φ is budget balancing for any profile $v \in \mathcal{R}^n$, $\sum_{i=1}^{i=n} t_i(v) = 0$ and, because φ is a Groves mechanism,

$$\sum_{i=1}^{i=n} t_i(v) = 0 \Leftrightarrow \theta(v) = \sum_{i=1}^{i=n} \left[\sum_{j \neq i} v_j(x(v)) \right] = (n-1) \max_{z \in X} \sum_{i=1}^{i=n} v_i(z)$$

where the second equality follows from decision efficiency. Consider alternatives $a, b \in X$ and profiles $v^1, v^2 \in \mathcal{R}^n$ such that, for all $i \in N$ and all $x \in X \backslash \{a, b\}$,

$$\begin{aligned} v_i^1(a) &= 1, \ v_i^1(b) = (1+n)/n, \ v_i^1(x) = 0; \\ v_i^2(a) &= 1, \ v_i^2(b) = v_i^2(x) = 0. \end{aligned}$$

Then, for $\kappa = (1, \ldots, 1)$,

$$\max_{z \in X} \sum_{i=1}^{i=n} v_i^\kappa(z) = \sum_{i=1}^{i=n} v_i^1(b) = 1 + n;$$

and, for all $\kappa \in K\backslash\{(1,\ldots,1)\}$,

$$\max_{z \in X} \sum_{i=1}^{i=n} v_i^\kappa(z) = \sum_{i=1}^{i=n} v_i^\kappa(a) = n.$$

Therefore,

$$\begin{aligned}
\sum_{\kappa \in K} (-1)^{s(\kappa)} \theta(v^\kappa) &= \sum_{j=0}^{j=n} (-1)^j \binom{n}{j} \max_{z \in X} \sum_{i=1}^{i=n} v_i^\kappa(z) \\
&= n \sum_{j=0}^{j=n-1} (-1)^j \binom{n}{j} + (-1)^n (n+1) \\
&= (-1)^n.
\end{aligned}$$

Since $(-1)^n \in \{-1, 1\}$, we have a contradiction of $(*)$. Consequently, if φ satisfies $\sum_{i \in N} t_i(v) = 0$ for all profiles v, φ cannot be a Groves mechanism. □

Together, Theorems 3.8 and 3.9 say that there exist no weakly Paretian, strategy-proof and decision efficient collective choice functions on the domain of quasi-linear preferences over allocations. There is always the possibility that aggregate transfers, $\sum_{i \in N} t_i(\cdot)$, are strictly negative, in which case the price of eliciting honest preference revelation is that more taxes have to be raised than are needed to cover the cost of the public decision (even when the cost is zero). Indeed, as illustrated in Example 3.11, individuals can be left strictly worse off following application of the mechanism than they would have been had nothing been done.

3.6 Application: Collective action

Suppose a group of individuals $N = \{1, \ldots, n\}$ all share a common interest in having a particular legislative proposal b passed into law. All members of the group evaluate both b and the status quo q identically, say $v_i(b) = 1 > v_i(q) = 0$ for all $i \in N$. There are, however, several ways in which the group can try to influence the legislative outcome: direct lobbying, public advertising and education, demonstration, litigation and so on. Assume that each choice of action $a \in X$ carries a particular cost c_a, where $0 < c_a < n$ for every action a. Although they agree on the costs and actions confronting the group, group members differ widely in their assessments of the relative likelihoods of success across the various feasible actions. That is, letting $p_i^a \in [0,1]$ denote individual i's (fixed) assessment that collective action a proves successful in getting b passed, it is typically the case that, for any action a and any two individuals $i, j \in N$, $p_i^a \neq p_j^a$.

In principle, the group wishes to take an action a^* from the set

$$X^* \equiv \arg\max_{a \in X} \left[\sum_N p_i^a - c_a \right].$$

The costs of the chosen action are assumed to be borne equally by all group members. Thus the expected net payoff to $i \in N$ from adoption of action $a \in X$ is

$$u_i(a) = p_i^a - \frac{c_a}{n}.$$

Exactly as for Example 3.9(1), if the group leadership simply asks the members to report their assessments $p_i = (p_i^a)_{a \in X}$ directly, there is no guarantee that all individuals will reveal the truth and no assurance of identifying X^*. However, if the leadership asks for the assessments under a Groves mechanism then, by Theorem 3.8, they are assured of being able to implement X^* in dominant strategy equilibrium.

3.7 Discussion

Among other things, political systems aggregate preferences. Ideally, individuals truthfully report their respective evaluations of alternatives and some agent or mediator (possibly mechanical) applies a previously agreed-upon collective choice rule to the revealed profile and identifies the appropriate collective choice (or, at least, the subset of alternatives surely not to be chosen). When rational individuals both differ in their evaluations and understand how the choice rule is applied, however, there can be an incentive to dissemble and report preferences other than the ones they truly hold; in other words, the rule may not be strategy-proof. And when this is the case, there is no assurance that direct application of a rule leads to the desired outcomes under that rule. Although the possibility of individuals strategically manipulating a collective choice process has long been recognized, it took the Gibbard-Satterthwaite Theorem (Theorem 2.1) to make clear the extent to which collective choice rules induce such an incentive. One response to the ubiquity of the phenomenon is to look for strategy-proof collective choice rules on restricted domains of preferences. For some important domains, in particular single-peaked domains, there do indeed exist such rules. Unfortunately, there is no guarantee that such domains are the ones that occur, in which case the problem persists. Implementation theory is a positive response to this fact.

Preference aggregation in empirical political systems is rarely by simply asking people to record their rankings of alternatives. For example, a representative democracy (loosely speaking) is an indirect process in which collective choice over policy alternatives is determined by citizens first voting over a set of candidates for legislative and executive offices and, second, by the elected legislature subsequently choosing a policy. As such, representative democracy is a formal institution distinct from, say, a direct democracy in which policy is chosen in one stage by applying a collective choice rule to the reported policy preferences of the electorate. There are, moreover, at least as many possible variations in the design of representative, or indirect, institutions for collective decision-making as there are in the design of collective choice rules *per se*. With this in mind, the goal of implementation theory is to identify classes of choice rule for which there are institutions that induce strategically rational individuals to reveal their preferences truthfully, either directly or indirectly. To say that an institution induces strategic individuals to reveal their preferences does not imply that all individuals literally report their true preferences, although this is not excluded. Rather, it amounts to saying that the set of outcomes supported by equilibrium behavior under that institution more or less coincides with those outcomes chosen by the choice rule given the true preference profile. Of course, exactly what constitutes equilibrium behavior has to be defined, as does the acceptable degree to which the set of equilibrium outcomes coincides with the set of outcomes chosen under a fully informed application of the choice rule.

In this chapter, we consider two important theories of equilibrium behavior, dominant strategy and Nash, and two (mutually compatible) measures of how equilibrium outcomes reflect collective choices under these theories, truthful implementation and (full) implementation. The original notion of strategy-proofness is that individuals have no strict incentive to misreport their preferences under a choice rule, conditional on all others likewise reporting truthfully. Because this is required to hold at every possible preference profile $\rho \in \mathcal{R}^n$, strategy-proofness coincides with reporting true preferences being a dominant strategy for every individual in a *direct* mechanism $(\mathcal{R}^n, h)$. Where implementation theory has more leverage than strategy-proofness *per se*, at least in principle, is in not requiring the application of a direct mechanism. Consequently, we first look for mechanisms, or institutions, that implement or truthfully implement collective choice rules in dominant strategy equilibrium. Unfortunately, the additional degree of free-

3.7. DISCUSSION

dom offered by admitting any mechanism turns out not to help too much here: the Revelation Principle (Theorem 3.1) says that if we can implement a collective choice rule in dominant strategy equilibrium with some mechanism, then we can truthfully implement that rule in dominant strategy equilibrium with a direct mechanism. Consequently, if the collective choice rule is resolute then the Revelation Principle and the Gibbard-Satterthwaite Theorem imply that only dictatorial (or constant) collective choice functions can be implemented in dominant strategy equilibrium (Corollary 3.1).

One interpretation of the Revelation Principle is that restricting attention to dominant strategies is too weak a behavioral model. This is not too surprising, as the existence of dominant strategies essentially removes any problem with strategic interaction. So although any satisfactory theory of individually rational strategic behavior includes rejection of strictly dominated strategies, some specification of what people do when there are no such strategies is required. The central concept here is Nash equilibrium. But even with Nash behavior, asking only that a mechanism have truth-telling as an equilibrium is not enough: if we can insure direct truth-telling as a Nash equilibrium then we can do the same in dominant strategy equilibrium (Theorem 3.2). Similarly, only constant or dictatorial choice functions are implementable in Nash equilibrium on unrestricted preference domains (Theorems 3.3 and 3.4).

In sum, therefore, to finesse the problem of preference misrepresentation in nondictatorial collective choice on unrestricted domains, we have to focus on (full) implementation of set-valued collective choice rules in a strategic theory stronger than dominant strategy equilibrium.

If a collective choice rule is implementable in Nash equilibrium, it is Maskin monotonic (Lemma 3.1). Traditionally, some sort of monotonicity property is a normative requirement for democratic preference aggregation: no alternative should be disadvantaged as a consequence of receiving more support. Thus Lemma 3.1 shows that if the goal is to aggregate true preferences rather than simply to aggregate reported (Nash equilibrium) preferences, then at least Maskin monotonicity is a positive requirement irrespective of any independent normative argument. And when there are at least three individuals, Maskin monotonicity is almost a sufficient condition for a rule to be implementable in Nash equilibrium (Theorem 3.5). Although a positive result, there do exist nondictatorial and nonconstant rules that are implementable in Nash equilibrium, it turns out that Maskin monotonicity is very hard to satisfy on an unrestricted preference domain when there are at least three alternatives (Example 3.4). This limitation is completely removed if we strengthen the behavioral theory somewhat by assuming individuals reject not only strictly but also weakly dominated strategies. Under this revision and a trivial assumption on preferences (no universal indifference), virtually all collective choice rules are implementable in undominated Nash equilibrium whether or not they are monotonic (Theorem 3.6).

The proofs for Theorem 3.5 and Theorem 3.6 are constructive: a mechanism is exhibited and shown to have a set of equilibrium outcomes coinciding with the set of collectively chosen alternatives at every profile. The mechanisms, however, are quite unusual, bearing little resemblance to any observed real-world institutions. From the purely technical perspective, this is immaterial; they are formal proofs of existence theorems and there is no reason that such proofs should reflect any empirical phenomena. Moreover, as the application to the question of monotonicity of electoral rules illustrates (Corollaries 3.2 and 3.3), the results themselves are useful independent of the means of proving them. On the other hand, to the extent that implementation theory is a theory of institutional design, the absence of empirically plausible institutions capable of implementing choice rules attenuates its substantive relevance for political science. In this respect, the fact that peculiarities in the formal mechanisms seem to be necessary rather than analytically convenient, at least for general environments, might be problematic (Theorem 3.7). There are two ways to address such a concern. The first is to constrain the class of mechanisms available for implementation and ask what can be done within the constraints; the second is to narrow the domain of collective choice. Both approaches are manifest when concerned with collective choice in environments with a fungible resource, such as money.

When the set of alternatives is a set of "allocations", involving both public and private goods, then preferences can often be reasonably approximated as quasi-linear functions over this set. And for this important class of problem, not only is it the case that there exist collective choice functions implementable in dominant strategy equilibrium, these functions can (using the Revelation Principle) be completely characterized as direct mechanisms with a simple and quite natural structure, Groves mechanisms (Theorem 3.8). Unfortunately, no Groves mechanism can be guaranteed budget-balancing: the price of eliciting truthful preference revelation is that more taxes are typically elicited than needed to fund any project (Theorem 3.9).

The argument of the previous chapter is that incentives for individuals to manipulate collective decision-making in their favor are inherent in virtually any reasonable choice rule on an unrestricted domain. When preference profiles are single-peaked, however, there exist choice rules immune to individual manipulation. From the perspective of implementation the-

3.8. EXERCISES

ory, that is, such rules are self-implementable in dominant strategy equilibrium on the domain of single-peaked preferences. But preference profiles are not always single-peaked and in general collective choice rules are not self-implementable in any strategic theory. Insofar as collective choice rules reflect desirable properties for preference aggregation, self-implementability is unimportant (although a nice feature to have); more important is that the alternatives recommended at any profile by the choice rule are indeed the ones that arise from equilibrium strategic behavior by individuals. Less prosaically, implementation theory treats the ends of collective decision-making as more important than the means. Thus implementation theory addresses what it is in principle possible to achieve when individuals are strategically rational. In the next chapter we pursue this theme for a peculiarly important class of mechanisms, or institutions, for political science: binary voting schemes.

3.8 Exercises

3.1 (a) Let $\mathcal{P}$ denote the set of linear orders on a finite set X and let φ be a collective choice function, $\varphi : \mathcal{P}^n \to X$. Say that φ is *strongly monotonic* if, for all $x \in X$ and all $\rho, \rho' \in \mathcal{P}^n$,

(i) $P(y, z; \rho) = P(y, z; \rho')$, $y \neq x$, $z \neq x$ *and* (ii) $P(x, w; \rho) \subseteq P(x, w; \rho')$, $\forall w \in X$,

then either $\varphi(\rho) = \varphi(\rho')$ or $\varphi(\rho') = x$.

Recall that φ is *Maskin monotonic* if $\varphi(\rho) = x$ and ρ, ρ' are such that (ii) holds, then $\varphi(\rho') = x$. Prove that φ is strongly monotonic if and only if φ is Maskin monotonic.

(b) Prove or provide a counterexample to the previous result when the domain of φ is $\mathcal{R}^n$.

3.2 Let f be a noncollegial simple rule on the unrestricted domain, $\mathcal{R}^n$; let φ_f be the choice rule derived from f. Show that φ_f satisfies "no veto" [Definition 3.7].

3.3 Suppose $\varphi : \mathcal{P}^n \to X$ is a strategy-proof collective choice function with $\Pi_\varphi \geq 3$. Prove or provide a counterexample to the claim φ is weakly Paretian on its range: $\forall x, y \in \Pi_\varphi$, $\forall \rho \in \mathcal{P}^n$, $P(x, y; \rho) = N \Rightarrow y \notin \varphi(\rho)$.

3.4 A collective choice function, $\varphi : \mathcal{R}^n \to X$, is *constant* if, $\forall \rho, \rho' \in \mathcal{R}^n$, $\varphi(\rho) = \varphi(\rho')$.

(a) Discuss the implication of Theorem 3.3 for Theorem 3.5.

(c) Prove or provide a counterexample to Theorem 3.3 if the domain of φ is $\mathcal{P}^n$ (i.e. no individual indifference allowed).

3.5 Confirm in Example 3.8 that there exist several Nash equilibrium vote profiles at each preference profile ρ, ρ' but $g(\eta(\rho, \gamma)) = g(\eta(\rho', \gamma)) = X$.

3.6 Show that Corollary 3.3 continues to hold with undominated Nash replacing Nash equilibrium and $z \notin g(\bar{\eta}(\rho, \gamma)) \cup g(\bar{\eta}(\rho', \gamma))$, where $\bar{\eta}(\cdot, \gamma)$ is the set of undominated Nash equilibria.

3.7 It was remarked, in Example 3.9(2), that the range of the nondictatorial and weakly Paretian collective choice function φ includes more than three alternatives and, therefore, cannot be strategy-proof by Theorem 2.1. Construct an explicit example to justify the remark.

3.8 Complete the proof of the Claim in Example 3.10.

3.9 Further reading

An early statement of Theorem 3.1, the revelation principle for dominant strategies, can be found in Dasgupta, Hammond and Maskin [52], who also prove Theorem 3.2. Example 3.2 is due to Repullo [168]. The seminal paper on Nash equilibrium is [151]. Maskin [119] (the paper circulated as a working paper from 1977) is the original paper on Nash implementation (Theorem 3.4), giving rise to a huge literature; the proof for Theorem 3.4 here is due to Repullo [169]. Outstanding guides to the literature are Maskin [118], Moore [132] who reviews the literature on implementation in environments with complete information, and Palfrey [159] who surveys implementation results when information is incomplete. Theorem 3.3 is due to Saijo [179]. Palfrey and Srivastava [163] establish Theorem 3.6 and provide Example 3.4; Example 3.6 is adapted from an example in Moore [132]. Jackson [103] addresses some practicality problems in the theory of implementation and is responsible for Theorem 3.7. Alternative approaches to implementation theory include Abreu and Matsushima [1] who introduce the idea of "virtual implementation" to allow for approximately implementing choice rules, and Moore and Repullo [133] who initiate the study of implementation in subgame perfect equilibrium (on which, see section 5.3, below). Baliga, Corchon and Sjostrom [15] allow for the mechanism designer also to be a player with

3.9. FURTHER READING

preferences over outcomes. Section 3.4 is due to Austen-Smith and Banks [12].

The theory of implementation with quasi-linear preferences and transferable utility (money) derives largely from Clarke [43], Groves [90] and Groves and Ledyard [91], all of whom proved versions of Theorem 3.8; see also Green and Laffont [85]. The discussion of section 3.5 and several examples therein owe much to Moulin [140] and McKelvey [125, section 4.4]. Theorem 3.9, *inter alia*, is due to Green and Laffont [85]; see also Walker [201].

Chapter 4
Binary Agendas

In Chapter 2 we argued that incentives for strategic misrepresentation of preferences are inherent in nondictorial collective choice. A positive response to this fact is to design institutions for collective decision-making that internalize such strategic incentives and yield the desired outcomes irrespective of individual efforts at manipulation. Chapter 3 pursued this idea and studied the relationship between various collective choice rules and the mechanisms (in effect, institutions) that implement those rules. And it turns out that these relationships typically depend in important ways on the details of individual behavior and institutional design. In this chapter, we essentially turn the issue around: rather than beginning with a choice rule and exploring what sort of mechanism might implement it, we first specify a mechanism and explore what sort of rule it might support. Specifically, we focus on an empirically important class of institution, or mechanism, for voting over a given set of mutually exclusive alternatives when the number of individuals eligible to vote is relatively small, as is the case, for example, in legislative and judicial committees, parliamentary cabinets and so forth. With a slight abuse of conventional understanding, we refer to such small-number voting bodies generically as "committees".

For purposes of this chapter, the salient feature of voting in committees is that it is more often than not governed by fixed rules. Widely used committee voting rules include amendment agendas (section 2.2), successive elimination agendas and issue-by-issue voting (section 2.7): these are all examples of *binary agendas*, under which voting is sequential, with every decision in the sequence involving two (possibly composite) alternatives. In view of the prevalence of binary agendas, it is important to understand how they work. In particular, since voting rules themselves are at some stage subject to collective choice, rational individuals' preferences over rules are, at least in part, induced by their expectations on the likely consequences for committee decision-making of adopting one set of rules rather than another. So, to develop any understanding of why the decision-making institutions we observe are in place, we first need to understand how they might be expected to connect policy preferences to policy choices and this, at least for the class of binary agendas, is the subject of the chapter.

There are three principal sorts of question that can be asked of any class of voting institution: the first concerns the structure of voting behavior; the second concerns how institutional details affect the set of achievable outcomes from any given set of feasible alternatives; and the third concerns how, under any institution, the set of feasible alternatives is determined. In this chapter we consider only the first two of these for the class of binary agendas, deferring the third to Chapter 5. Specifically, given a fixed and finite set of feasible alternatives, we examine the structure of Nash equilibrium (that is, mutual best response) voting behavior on arbitrary binary agendas and subsequently characterize the set of equilibrium outcomes for particular sub-classes of binary agenda. In part, this second issue concerns the extent to which those in control of the agenda are able to influence the outcome through the exercise of such control. It turns out that both the extent of agenda-setting power and the qualitative properties of equilibrium outcomes vary with the form of the agenda. Thus the purely procedural details of voting rules are consequential.

4.1 Binary agendas and sophisticated voting

Consider a committee of n individuals. Unless explicitly stated otherwise, we assume throughout this and the following two sections that the set of alternatives X is finite, that the committee uses simple majority rule to make decisions and, to avoid complications with ties, that n is odd with no individual indifferent over any pair of alternatives in X. The set of preference profiles is therefore $\mathcal{P}^n$ with typical element $\rho = (P_1, ..., P_n)$. Although we have not presumed a total absence of indifference hitherto (save as an intermediate step in proving various theorems), when the set of alternatives is exogenously given and finite, the assumption, although certainly a limitation, is not too demanding. One way to think about this is to consider the finite set X as coming from some underlying continuous space; for example, when X is a finite set of budget allocations. Then individuals' preferences can be assumed continuous on the underlying space,

4.1. BINARY AGENDAS AND SOPHISTICATED VOTING

in which case any indifference between two alternatives included in X will not survive an arbitrarily small perturbation in the individual's preference ordering that leaves the relative preferences over the rest of X unaffected. In any event, given the preceding assumptions, the majority preference relation P is a complete and asymmetric (although not necessarily acyclic) relation on X.

We consider sequential voting methods for selecting a unique outcome from X. An important example of such a rule is the amendment rule introduced in section 2.2 above. More generally, the voting procedures we examine are characterized by binary voting trees. Before giving a formal description of a binary voting tree, it is useful to fix ideas with a geometric representation. Figure 4.1 gives one such representation for the amendment rule example (informally) described in section 2.2, where $X = \{x, y, z\}$ and the ordering is (x, y, z).

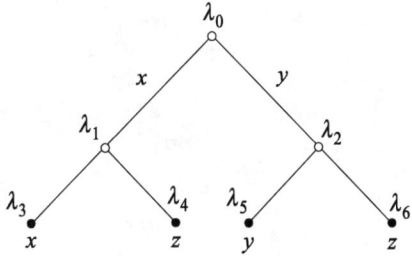

Figure 4.1: A binary voting tree

In the diagram, the set of elements $\{\lambda_t : t = 0, 1, \ldots, 6\}$ is a set of nodes: λ_0 is the initial node, $\{\lambda_0, \lambda_1, \lambda_2\}$ are decision nodes and the remaining nodes, $\{\lambda_3, \lambda_4, \lambda_5, \lambda_6\}$, are terminal nodes. In view of the diagram, these terms are self-explanatory. And notice that each terminal node is associated with exactly one alternative in X and every alternative in X is associated with at least one terminal node. As discussed in section 2.2, the procedure represented by the tree is that the committee first votes over x and y, subsequently choosing between the majority winner and z; the majority winner of this final ballot is the committee choice.

Formally, given X, let Λ be a finite set of *nodes* and let $\succ$ be a *precedence relation* on Λ; that is, a transitive and asymmetric relation on Λ such that, for any pair of nodes $\lambda, \lambda' \in \Lambda$, $\lambda \succ \lambda'$ if and only if λ "follows" λ' and

(1) there exists a unique element $\lambda_0 \in \Lambda$, the *initial node*, such that $\lambda_0 \succ \lambda$ for no $\lambda \in \Lambda$;

(2) for all $\lambda, \lambda' \in \Lambda$ such that $\lambda \succ \lambda'$, there exists a unique subset $L = \{\lambda_1, \ldots, \lambda_m\} \subset \Lambda$ such that

$$\lambda \succ \lambda_1 \succ \lambda_2 \succ \ldots \succ \lambda_m \succ \lambda';$$

that is, if λ follows λ' then there is exactly one path beginning at λ' and arriving at λ. Given a pair $(\Lambda, \succ)$, $\succ$ partitions Λ into a subset of *terminal nodes* and a subset of *decision nodes* defined, respectively, by

$$\begin{aligned} \Lambda^t &= \{\lambda \in \Lambda : \lambda' \succ \lambda \text{ for no } \lambda' \in \Lambda\}; \\ \Lambda^d &= \Lambda \backslash \Lambda^t. \end{aligned}$$

Now let $\theta : \Lambda^t \to X$ be an *onto* function assigning each terminal node of the tree to exactly one alternative in X. By definition of onto, every alternative $x \in X$ is associated with at least one terminal node. Consequently, the requirement that θ is onto insures that each alternative in X is the selected outcome for some sequence of committee decisions.

A *binary voting tree*, or *binary agenda*, is a triple, $\Gamma = (\Lambda, \succ, \theta)$, such that each decision node has precisely two nodes immediately following it:

$$\forall \lambda \in \Lambda^d, \ |\{\lambda' \in \Lambda : \lambda' \succ \lambda \ \& \ \sim [\exists \hat{\lambda} : \lambda' \succ \hat{\lambda} \succ \lambda]\}| = 2.$$

Because we always have our voting trees move "down" the page, it is convenient to label the nodes immediately following some $\lambda \in \Lambda^d$ as $l(\lambda)$ ("left") and $r(\lambda)$ ("right"), and label the (unique) node immediately preceding $\lambda \in \Lambda \backslash \{\lambda_0\}$ as $a(\lambda)$ ("above"). With this convention, define a *final decision node* to be a node $\lambda \in \Lambda^d$ such that $\{l(\lambda), r(\lambda)\} \subseteq \Lambda^t$. In Figure 4.1, for example, the set of final decision nodes is $\{\lambda_1, \lambda_2\}$ with $\{l(\lambda_1), r(\lambda_1)\} = \{\lambda_3, \lambda_4\}$, $\{l(\lambda_2), r(\lambda_2)\} = \{\lambda_5, \lambda_6\}$ and $a(\lambda_1) = a(\lambda_2) = \lambda_0$.

In a binary voting tree, each decision node characterizes an instance in which the individuals in N simultaneously vote between two alternatives. For example, suppose $X = \{x, y, z\}$ and the voting procedure is of the form "vote on x vs. y first, and then pit the winner of this vote against z"; then we have the voting tree shown in Figure 4.1. Alternatively, consider the procedure "vote either to accept x as the outcome or not; if not, vote to accept y as the outcome or not; and if y is not so approved, z is the outcome"; then we have the voting tree shown in Figure 4.2.

4.1. BINARY AGENDAS AND SOPHISTICATED VOTING

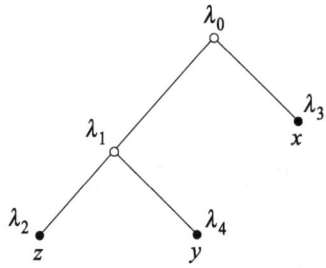

Figure 4.2: Another voting tree

We argue below that the labels attached to the choices at each decision node are immaterial; rather, we can simply think of the decision to be made as being whether to choose the "left" or the "right" branch at each node.

A sequential binary voting procedure, or more succinctly the resulting voting tree $\Gamma = (\Lambda, \succ, \theta)$, defines a mechanism, or game form, $\gamma_\Gamma = (\mathcal{M}, g)$ in the sense of Chapter 3. Specifically, for any $i \in N$, an action m_i under γ_Γ is a list of votes, one vote for each and every decision node. The set of actions for i is therefore the set $\mathcal{M}_i = \{l, r\}^{|\Lambda^d|}$ and a *strategy* for i is a function $\sigma_i : \mathcal{P} \to \mathcal{M}_i$ where, for each strict ordering P_i of X, $\sigma_i(P_i) \in \mathcal{M}_i$ describes how i votes at each decision node. A profile of strategies $\sigma = (\sigma_1, ..., \sigma_n) \in \mathcal{M}$ then determines a unique path of majority rule decisions through the voting tree, ultimately leading to a particular terminal node, denoted $\lambda(\sigma) \in \Lambda^t$ and a final alternative $\theta(\lambda(\sigma)) \in X$; hence the outcome function g for γ_Γ is such that, for all $\sigma \in \mathcal{M}$, $g(\sigma) = \theta(\lambda(\sigma))$.

The mechanism γ_Γ with a profile $\rho \in \mathcal{P}^n$ of committee members' preferences then defines a *binary voting game* (γ_Γ, ρ). As before, some model of strategic individual choice has to be defined and we consider only Nash equilibrium theory here. And because, as illustrated in Example 3.5, all individuals voting identically irrespective of their preferences is both a Nash equilibrium and an absurdity, we further restrict attention to a class of undominated Nash equilibria. Before describing this class, however, we first make a useful observation regarding undominated strategies in binary voting procedures.

An important consequence of insisting on individuals using only undominated strategies in a binary voting game (γ_Γ, ρ) is that, at any final decision node λ, an individual $i \in N$ votes for outcome $\theta(l(\lambda))$ if and only if $\theta(l(\lambda)) P_i \theta(r(\lambda))$. In other words, all individuals *vote sincerely* at all final decision nodes. Given majority rule, strict preferences and an odd number of individuals, we have, therefore, that at any final decision node λ (that is, a node immediately followed by a pair of terminal nodes)

$$\theta(l(\lambda))P\theta(r(\lambda)) \Leftrightarrow |P(\theta(l(\lambda)), \theta(r(\lambda)); \rho)| > n/2.$$

Denote the majority winner here by $s(\lambda)$. Because the preference profile ρ is known to all committee members, the outcome $s(\lambda)$ conditional on arriving at the decision node λ is understood by every individual. In other words, arriving at the final decision node λ is equivalent to choosing the outcome $s(\lambda) \in \{\theta(l(\lambda)), \theta(r(\lambda))\}$; call $s(\lambda)$ the *sophisticated equivalent* of λ. Applying the same reasoning to every final decision node λ, we can delete the set of terminal nodes by associating each final decision node with its sophisticated equivalent, in effect converting the final decision nodes into the strategically relevant terminal nodes with associated outcomes $\{s(\lambda) : \lambda$ is a final decision node$\}$. And there is no reason to stop at this point. Once the original set of terminal nodes for any binary tree at a given profile is replaced by the sophisticated equivalents of the final decision nodes, the same argument can be applied to the new set of terminal nodes, and so on back up the tree until we are left with a unique alternative, the *sophisticated outcome* $s(\lambda_0)$, of (γ_Γ, ρ). Formally, the algorithm is defined inductively on any binary voting game (γ_Γ, ρ) by

(a) for all $\lambda \in \Lambda^t$, $s(\lambda) = \theta(\lambda)$ and

(b) for all $\lambda \in \Lambda^d$, $s(\lambda) = \begin{cases} s(l(\lambda)) & \text{if } s(l(\lambda))Ps(r(\lambda)) \\ s(r(\lambda)) & \text{otherwise} \end{cases}$.

The strategy profile induced by this procedure is for each individual, at every decision node $\lambda \in \Lambda^d$, to vote sincerely over the sophisticated equivalents $\{s(l(\lambda)), s(r(\lambda))\}$; call this the *sophisticated voting profile*. As we shall argue below, the sophisticated outcome supported by this profile is the unique undominated Nash equilibrium outcome; first, however, it is useful to illustrate the procedure with an example.

Example 4.1 Let $N = \{1, 2, 3\}$, $X = \{w, x, y, z\}$ and suppose $\rho \in \mathcal{P}^3$ is

$$wP_1xP_1yP_1z$$
$$yP_2wP_2zP_2x$$
$$zP_3xP_3yP_3w$$

The majority preference under ρ is cyclic on two of the four triples, specifically

$$[wPxPy, \; yPw] \text{ and } [xPyPz, \; zPx];$$

4.1. BINARY AGENDAS AND SOPHISTICATED VOTING

and transitive on the remaining two triples,

$$[yPwPz,\ yPz] \text{ and } [wPzPx,\ wPx].$$

We consider two sorts of agenda under which the committee might select an alternative from X.

(1) *Amendment agenda.* The voting tree Γ^a in Figure 4.3 (where only the initial decision node is explicitly labeled) describes an amendment agenda with voting sequence (w, x, y, z).

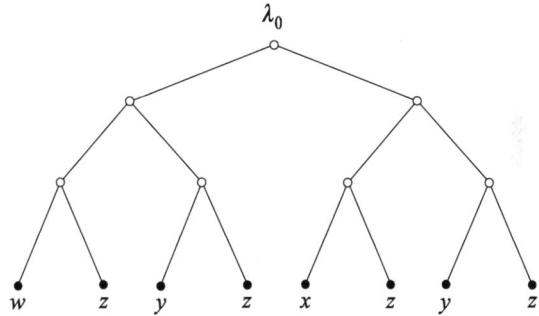

Figure 4.3: Amendment agenda tree

There are four final decision nodes in the tree; should a voting strategy profile σ lead the committee to the left-most final decision node and a choice between w and z, each individual's unique undominated choice is to vote sincerely for their most preferred alternative of the two. By majority decision, therefore, w is the final outcome. Hence, the sophisticated equivalent of this node is w. Similarly, since y is majority preferred to z, the sophisticated equivalent for the two final decision nodes involving $\{y, z\}$ is y; and the remaining final decision node has sophisticated equivalent z since zPx. Deleting the original terminal nodes and replacing the final decision nodes by their sophisticated equivalents yields the tree in Figure 4.4(a) with two final decision nodes. Applying the same reasoning to this pruned tree, the sophisticated equivalent of both nodes $l(\lambda_0)$ and $r(\lambda_0)$ is y. Deleting the terminal nodes of the tree in Figure 4.4(a) and replacing the two final decision nodes with their sophisticated equivalents yields the binary decision of Figure 4.4(b).

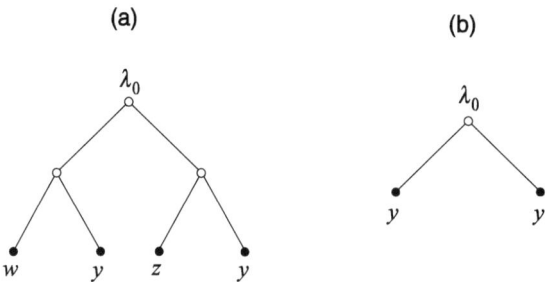

Figure 4.4: Substituting sophisticated equivalents

Given the use of undominated strategies at subsequent stages of the original tree, a vote for either branch at the initial node λ_0 yields a final committee decision of y. Therefore, individuals can rationally cast any vote at this stage, including voting sincerely over the nominal choice over $\{w, x\}$.

In sum, the undominated Nash strategy profile for the game $(\gamma_{\Gamma^a}, \rho)$ illustrated in Figure 4.3 is for each committee member to adopt the strategy: "At every decision node $\lambda \in \Lambda^d$, vote sincerely over the sophisticated equivalents $\{s(l(\lambda)), s(r(\lambda))\}$". There are three things to note about this strategy in the example. First, it is unique (although sincere voting over two identical sophisticated equivalents is consistent with voting for either of branches stemming from the decision node); second, it does not imply individuals always vote sincerely over branches (for example, at the node $r(\lambda_0)$ in Figure 4.3, individual $i = 1$ strictly prefers y to z, yet is observed to vote for z because she understands that a sincere vote for y at this node is in effect a vote for z, her least preferred alternative); and third, computing the sophisticated outcome (equivalently, the final choice of a committee in which no individual uses a dominated strategy) requires information only about the majority preference relation and not the distribution of preferences within the committee.

(2) *Successive elimination agenda.* Now consider the binary voting tree Γ^s illustrated in Figure 4.5; assume the preference profile ρ is the same as is the sequence, (w, x, y, z). This tree represents a successive, or sequential, elimination agenda under which the first alternative in the sequence is offered as the final choice; if a majority votes in favor of the alternative, it is accepted and the remaining possibilities rejected; if a majority votes against the alternative, it is rejected and the second alternative in the sequence is considered; and so on.

4.1. BINARY AGENDAS AND SOPHISTICATED VOTING

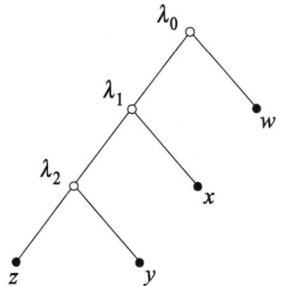

Figure 4.5: Successive elimination agenda

Unlike in an amendment agenda, therefore, at all but the very last decision node of the tree, the vote is between a single alternative and a subset of alternatives. In this case, exactly what is meant by a "sincere" vote is obscure. On the other hand, the very last decision node (λ_2 in the figure) is between the penultimate and the last alternatives in the sequence, and thus sincere voting is well-defined. In particular, we can identify the sophisticated equivalent of this node exactly as before: under ρ, a majority strictly prefers y to z so, conditional on w and x being rejected earlier in the voting, the final alternative when individuals use only undominated strategies is $s(\lambda_2) = y$. Deleting the two left-most terminal decision nodes and replacing λ_2 with the outcome $s(\lambda_2) = y$ gives a pruned tree in which the original nominal choice between x and $\{y, z\}$ is replaced by a choice between x and y: see Figure 4.6(a).

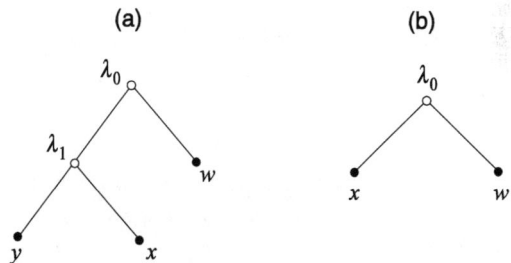

Figure 4.6: Substituting sophisticated equivalents

The sophisticated equivalent here, therefore, is x as a majority strictly prefers x to y; all individuals understand that rejecting x at this stage leads to a final vote between y and z, a vote that y surely wins under undominated voting behavior. Backing up the tree one last time (Figure 4.6(b)), the effective choice confronting committee members at λ_0 is between w and x as opposed to the nominal choice between w and $\{x, y, z\}$. Since undominated voting means voting sincerely over sophisticated equivalents and wPx, the alternative w is the sophisticated outcome of the game $(\gamma_{\Gamma^s}, \rho)$. Observe that this is distinct from the sophisticated outcome under the amendment agenda: institutional details affect collective choice. □

The algorithm above for finding the outcome of the voting game under undominated strategies produced a unique prediction for the profile ρ in each case. This is not an accident: given individuals have strict preferences over finite sets of alternatives, all binary voting trees are members of a wider class of game forms, or mechanisms, for which uniqueness is a defining property. Fix an arbitrary game form $(\mathcal{M}, g)$ and a profile $\rho \in \mathcal{P}^n$. For any individual $i \in N$ and subset of messages, or strategies, $\mathcal{M}'_i \subseteq \mathcal{M}_i$, let $D_i(P_i; \mathcal{M}'_i) \subseteq \mathcal{M}_i$ denote the set of undominated strategies for i when i's available strategy set is restricted to $\mathcal{M}'_i$. For example, suppose $\mathcal{M}_i = \{m, m', m''\}$ and m dominates both m' and m'' for i, but m' neither dominates nor is dominated by m''; then $D_i(P_i; \mathcal{M}_i) = \{m\}$ and $D_i(P_i; \{m', m''\}) = \{m', m''\}$.

Definition 4.1 Let $(\mathcal{M}, g)$ be a game form and $\rho \in \mathcal{P}^n$; for any integer $t \geq 0$, let $M^t = (M^t_1, \ldots, M^t_n) \subseteq \mathcal{M}$. The iterated elimination of dominated strategies is a decreasing sequence $(M^t)_{t=0}^{t=\infty}$ such that, for all $i \in N$ and, for all $t = 0, 1, \ldots$

$$M_i^0 = \mathcal{M}_i \text{ and } M_i^{t+1} = D_i(P_i; M_i^t).$$

$(\mathcal{M}, g)$ is dominance solvable at ρ if there exists an integer T such that M_i^T is singleton for all $i \in N$; $(\mathcal{M}, g)$ is dominance solvable if it is dominance solvable at every profile $\rho \in \mathcal{P}^n$.

If a mechanism or game form is dominance solvable, it yields a unique prediction identifiable by successively eliminating dominated strategies until every individual has but a single undominated strategy remaining. The sophisticated voting profile illustrated above is an example of such an iterated elimination. Note, however, that the definition is agnostic about the order in which dominated strategies are eliminated (it does not matter) and about the details of the game form (it does not matter if it involves sequences of messages, as in binary voting trees, or a single one-shot message, as in the mechanism used to prove Theorem 3.5).

4.1. BINARY AGENDAS AND SOPHISTICATED VOTING

Example 4.2 To illustrate the idea of a dominant solvable game form, consider the following mechanism $(\mathcal{M}, g)$ and payoffs.

	m_{21}	m_{22}	m_{23}
m_{11}	4, 5	3, 2	1, 1
m_{12}	0, 3	2, 4	5, 0

Here, $\mathcal{M}_1 = \{m_{11}, m_{12}\}$, and $\mathcal{M}_2 = \{m_{21}, m_{22}, m_{23}\}$. In each cell, the first number is the payoff to player $i = 1$ conditional on the strategy pair defining that cell being played: for instance, $g(m_{11}, m_{22})$ yields a value 3 to individual $i = 1$ and a value 2 to individual $i = 2$. By inspection, individual 1 has no dominated strategies but m_{23} is dominated for individual 2. Hence the sets of individual strategies surviving one round of deletion of dominated strategies are

$$M_1^1 = D_1(P_1; M_1^0) = \mathcal{M}_1 \text{ and } M_2^1 = D_2(P_2; M_2^0) = \{m_{21}, m_{22}\}.$$

Given 2 deletes her dominated strategy m_{23}, individual 1 finds m_{12} strictly dominated by m_{11}; therefore

$$M_1^2 = D_1(P_1; M_1^1) = \{m_{11}\} \text{ and } M_2^2 = D_2(P_2; M_2^1) = \{m_{21}, m_{22}\}.$$

Finally, given 1 deletes m_{12}, the strategy m_{22} becomes strictly dominated for individual 2. Consequently,

$$M_1^3 = D_1(P_1; M_1^2) = \{m_{11}\} \text{ and } M_2^3 = D_2(P_2; M_2^2) = \{m_{21}\}.$$

Therefore, we have found an iteration $T = 3$ for which M_i^T is singleton for $i = 1, 2$ and $(\mathcal{M}, g)$ is dominance solvable at the given profile with predicted outcome $g(m_{11}, m_{21})$. □

Example 4.2 shows that there can, in general, be a difference in any given game between profiles of undominated strategies (for instance, any profile $m \in M_1^1 \times M_2^1$) and profiles of strategies that have survived the iterated elimination of dominated strategies (that is, the profile $m \in M_1^3 \times M_2^3$): being undominated in the full game does not imply surviving the iterated deletion of dominated strategies within that game. Insofar as the latter procedure results in a unique prediction for equilibrium behavior (that is, insofar as a game is dominance solvable), the refinement to such equilibria is compelling. Of course, it is quite possible for multiple strategy profiles to survive the iterated elimination of dominated strategies, in which case the game is not dominance solvable. Nevertheless, restricting attention to such surviving profiles is a natural strengthening of the restriction to equilibria in undominated strategies. Hereafter, we require any undominated Nash equilibrium profile to survive the iterated elimination of dominated strategies. And to avoid repeatedly having to include the relevant qualification, we leave it as understood that any reference to equilibria in undominated strategies is to equilibria consistent with the iterated elimination of dominated strategies. With these comments in mind, then, Theorem 4.1 is of considerable interest.

Theorem 4.1 *Every binary voting tree* $\Gamma = (\Lambda, \succ, \theta)$ *on a finite set of alternatives induces a dominance solvable game form* $\gamma_\Gamma = (\mathcal{M}, g)$.

Proof Let Γ be an arbitrary binary voting tree and $\rho \in \mathcal{P}^n$; consider the sophisticated voting profile induced by the algorithm above. As we argued when defining the algorithm, the sophisticated outcome supported by this profile is unique. What has to be proved, therefore, is that the game form $\gamma_\Gamma = (\mathcal{M}, g)$ is dominance solvable and selects the sophisticated outcome. To do this, first let Γ' denote the pruned tree derived from Γ by replacing the final decision nodes of Γ with their respective sophisticated equivalents. Now, given n odd, a simple majority vote between two alternatives defines a trivial binary voting tree with an associated game form that is likewise trivially dominance solvable (given any $\rho \in \mathcal{P}^n$, voting sincerely is every individual's unique undominated strategy) and yields the sophisticated outcome; to prove γ_Γ is dominance solvable for an arbitrary finite set of alternatives X, therefore, it suffices to prove the induction step: $\gamma_{\Gamma'}$ dominance solvable implies γ_Γ dominance solvable.

Fix $\rho \in \mathcal{P}^n$ arbitrarily and let $H_i(P_i) \subset \mathcal{M}_i = \{l,r\}^{|\Lambda^d|}$ denote the set of i's strategies where i votes sincerely at every final decision node of the tree Γ. From construction of the sophisticated voting profile on Γ, for all individuals $i \in N$, the set of undominated strategies for i on $\mathcal{M}_i$ is a subset of the set of i's sincere voting strategies: $D_i(P_i; \mathcal{M}_i) \subseteq H_i(P_i) \subset \mathcal{M}_i$. Define the mechanism, $\gamma' = (\Pi_{i \in N} H_i(P_i), g)$; then γ' and $\gamma_{\Gamma'}$ are clearly isomorphic so $\gamma_{\Gamma'}$ is dominance solvable if and only if γ' is dominance solvable. Consequently, we argue that γ' dominance solvable implies γ_Γ dominance solvable; in fact, the converse is also true. Let $A = \Pi_{i \in N} A_i \subseteq \mathcal{M}$ and $B = \Pi_{i \in N} B_i \subseteq \mathcal{M}$ be arbitrary subsets of strategy profiles (where $A_i, B_i \subseteq \mathcal{M}_i$ for all $i \in N$) and, for $C = A, B$, let $G(C) = (C, g, \rho)$ be the game defined by the mechanism (C, g) with the profile $\rho \in \mathcal{P}^n$; similarly define $G(C^t)$ to be the game derived from $G(C)$ following t iterations of successive elimination of dominated strategies. Write $A \to B$ if, for all

4.1. BINARY AGENDAS AND SOPHISTICATED VOTING

$i \in N$, $A_i \subseteq B_i$ and, for every strategy σ_i in B_i, there exists a strategy σ'_i in A_i such that, whatever strategies others choose, any outcome that i can obtain using σ_i, i can also obtain using σ'_i; formally,

$$\forall \sigma_i \in B_i, \ \exists \sigma'_i \in A_i : \forall \sigma_{-i} \in B_{-i}, \ g(\sigma_i, \sigma_{-i}) = g(\sigma'_i, \sigma_{-i}).$$

In words, if $A \to B$ then, for every individual i, if the strategy profile σ_{-i} used by all others lies in some subset $\Pi_{j \neq i} B_j \subseteq \mathcal{M}_{-i}$, then i is indifferent between being restricted to choosing a strategy from $A_i \subseteq \mathcal{M}_i$ and being restricted to choosing a strategy from a larger set $B_i \supseteq A_i$. We now make a useful claim.

Claim: Suppose $A \to B$. Then $G(B)$ is dominance solvable if and only if $G(A)$ is dominance solvable, in which case their sophisticated outcomes are identical.

Proof: Let $\sigma_i \in A_i$ survive the first round of deletion of dominated strategies from A_i but fail to survive the first round of deletion of dominated strategies from B_i: that is, $\sigma_i \in A_i^1$ but $\sigma_i \notin B_i^1$. Then there exists some $s_i \in B_i$ such that s_i dominates σ_i in $G(B)$. We show that this means σ_i must be dominated in $G(A)$, contradicting $\sigma_i \in A_i^1$. By $A \to B$, there exists a strategy $\sigma'_i \in A_i$ such that $g(s_i, \sigma_{-i}) = g(\sigma'_i, \sigma_{-i})$ for every $\sigma_{-i} \in B_{-i}$. And since s_i dominates σ_i by supposition, there is a profile $\sigma_{-i} \in B_{-i}$ such that $g(\sigma'_i, \sigma_{-i}) P_i g(\sigma_i, \sigma_{-i})$. By definition of $A \to B$, for each individual $j \in N \setminus \{i\}$ and each strategy $\sigma_j \in B_j$, there is a strategy $s'_j \in A_j$ such that $g(\sigma_i, s'_{-i}) = g(\sigma_i, \sigma_{-i})$ and $g(\sigma'_i, s'_{-i}) = g(\sigma'_i, \sigma_{-i})$. Hence, $g(\sigma'_i, \sigma_{-i}) P_i g(\sigma_i, \sigma_{-i})$ implies $g(\sigma'_i, s'_{-i}) P_i g(\sigma_i, s'_{-i})$ and, therefore, σ'_i dominates σ_i in $G(A)$, contradicting $\sigma_i \in A_i^1$. Consequently, $A \to B$ and $\sigma_i \in A_i^1$ imply $\sigma_i \in B_i^1$ in which case, by i arbitrary, $A^1 \subseteq B^1$.

Now choose any strategy $\sigma_i \in B_i^1$; we look for a strategy $\sigma'_i \in A_i^1$ such that, $\forall \sigma_{-i} \in B_{-i}, \ g(\sigma_i, \sigma_{-i}) = g(\sigma'_i, \sigma_{-i})$. To do this, note that $A \to B$ and $B_i^1 \subseteq B_i$ implies there is a strategy $\sigma'_i \in A_i$ such that $g(\sigma_i, \sigma_{-i}) = g(\sigma'_i, \sigma_{-i})$, all $\sigma_{-i} \in B_{-i}$. Suppose $\sigma'_i \notin A_i^1$; then there is some $s_i \in A_i$ such that s_i dominates σ'_i in $G(A)$. Following the same reasoning as that showing $A^1 \subseteq B^1$, we conclude σ_i must be dominated in $G(B)$, contradicting $\sigma_i \in B_i^1$ [Exercise]. Hence, $A \to B$ implies $A^1 \to B^1$ and therefore, by induction, $A \to B$ implies $A^t \to B^t$ for all positive integers t. It follows that if $G(B)$ is dominance solvable then $G(A)$ is dominance solvable and their sophisticated outcomes must coincide. And if $G(A)$ is dominance solvable then for some t, $|g(A^t)| = 1$ in which case, $A^t \to B^t$ implies that for every $\sigma \in B^t$ there exists a strategy profile $\sigma' \in A^t$ with $g(\sigma') = g(\sigma)$; thus $g(A^t) = g(B^t)$ and the claim is proved.

Now suppose the lemma is true for $|\mathcal{M}| \leq r-1$, where r is some integer, and consider γ_Γ with $|\mathcal{M}| = r$; then for all $i \in N$,

$$D_i(P_i; \mathcal{M}_i) = M_i^1 \subseteq H_i(P_i) \subset \mathcal{M}_i.$$

Let $H = \Pi_{i \in N} H_i(P_i)$. If $|H| = |\mathcal{M}|$, γ' and γ_Γ coincide and there is nothing to prove. So assume $|H| \leq r - 1$. Set $B = H^1 \cup M^2$ and note $H^1 \subseteq B \subseteq H$. By the induction assumption, therefore,

(∗) $G(B)$ is dominance solvable if and only if $G(H) = (\gamma', \rho)$ is dominance solvable and their sophisticated outcomes are identical.

Define $A = (H^1 \cap M^1) \cup M^2$; we show $A \to B$. By definition of A and B, $A \subseteq B$. Choose $i \in N$ arbitrarily and let $\sigma_i \in B_i \backslash A_i$, where

$$B_i = (H_i^1 \cup M_i^2) \text{ and } A_i = (H_i^1 \cap M_i^1) \cup M_i^2;$$

then $\sigma_i \in H_i^1$ but $\sigma_i \notin M_i^1$. Since $\mathcal{M}$ is finite, therefore, there exists some strategy $s_i \in M_i^1$ such that s_i dominates σ_i. But $M_i^1 \subseteq H_i$ so $s_i \in H_i$, in which case $\sigma_i \in H_i^1$ implies $g(\sigma_i, \sigma_{-i}) = g(s_i, \sigma_{-i})$ for all $\sigma_{-i} \in H_{-i}$. Hence $s_i \in H_i^1$ so $s_i \in (H_i^1 \cap M_i^1) \subseteq A_i$, proving $A \to B$. By the Claim and (∗), it now follows that $G(H)$ is dominance solvable if and only if $G(A)$ is dominance solvable and they share the same sophisticated outcomes. Finally, note $M^2 \subseteq A \subseteq M^1$; by the induction hypothesis, $G(A)$ is dominance solvable if and only if $G(M^1)$ is dominance solvable with identical sophisticated outcomes. And by definition of dominance solvability, $G(M^1)$ is dominance solvable if and only if $G(\mathcal{M})$ is dominance solvable and we are done. □

An important analytical implication of Theorem 4.1 is that to identify the outcome, or committee choice, from any binary voting game satisfying the assumptions of the result, it suffices to know the majority preference relation rather than any details about the distribution of individuals' preferences supporting that relation. And if the theory is agnostic about committee size, then any preference relation over a finite set of alternatives is a majority preference relation for some profile $\rho \in \mathcal{P}^n$ and integer $n \geq 2$.

Theorem 4.2 *Let $R \in \mathcal{R}$ be any complete preference relation over a finite set of alternatives, X. There exists an integer $n \geq 2$ and a profile $\rho \in \mathcal{P}^n$ such that, for all distinct $x, y \in X$, xPy if and only if $|P(x, y; \rho)| > n/2$.*

4.1. BINARY AGENDAS AND SOPHISTICATED VOTING

Proof Fix a complete relation R on X, $|X| = r$, and consider any pair of distinct alternatives $x, y \in X$. Suppose xPy. Then, for some $i(xy) \in N$, choose $P_{i(xy)} \in \mathcal{P}$ such that

$$xP_{i(xy)}yP_{i(xy)}a_1P_{i(xy)}a_2P_{i(xy)}\ldots P_{i(xy)}a_{r-2},$$

where $\{a_1, \ldots, a_{r-2}, x, y\} = X$. Let $j(xy) \in N \backslash \{i(xy)\}$ and choose $P_{j(xy)} \in \mathcal{P}$ such that

$$a_{r-2}P_{j(xy)}a_{r-1}P_{j(xy)}\ldots P_{j(xy)}a_1P_{j(xy)}xP_{j(xy)}y.$$

If xIy then choose $P_{i(xy)} \in \mathcal{P}$ as before but now choose $P'_{j(xy)} \in \mathcal{P}$ such that

$$a_{r-2}P'_{j(xy)}a_{r-1}P'_{j(xy)}\ldots P'_{j(xy)}a_1P'_{j(xy)}yP'_{j(xy)}x.$$

In both cases, individuals $i(xy)$ and $j(xy)$ have opposing preferences over all pairs save at most $\{x,y\}$, where they have opposing preferences only in the case xIy. Now for each pair of alternatives $\{v,w\}$ in X, assign preferences to a distinct pair of individuals $i(vw)$ and $j(vw)$ in a similar way as for $i(xy)$ and $j(xy)$. Doing this defines a group of $n = 2\binom{r}{2}$ individuals and a profile $\rho \in \mathcal{P}^n$ under which, for all pairs of alternatives,

$$xPy \Leftrightarrow |P(x,y;\rho)| > n/2$$

and xIy otherwise. In particular, for any pair of alternatives in X, all but at most two individuals' preferences under ρ are strictly opposed. $\square$

It is worth remarking here that the construction used to prove Theorem 4.2 does not provide the smallest group of individuals for which any given preference relation can be justified as that group's majority preference at some profile. For instance, if $|X| = 3$ and P is cyclic, the construction yields a group of six individuals, twice as many as are in fact necessary. Specifically, suppose $X = \{x, y, z\}$ and xPy, yPz and zPx; applying the construction, we obtain $n = 6$ and the profile

$$xP_1yP_1z; \quad zP_2xP_2y;$$
$$yP_3zP_3x; \quad xP_4yP_4z;$$
$$zP_5xP_5y; \quad yP_6zP_6x;$$

where $i(xy) = 1$, $j(xy) = 2$, and so on. But a committee of three persons with preferences

$$xP_1yP_1z; \quad zP_2xP_2y; \quad yP_3zP_3x$$

likewise justifies P as a majority preference relation. Moreover, Theorem 4.2 does not say that any preference relation can be so justified for any group; only that for any preference relation P, there exists a group and a profile justifying P as the group's majority preference at that profile. This qualification notwithstanding, Theorems 4.1 and 4.2 jointly provide a method for computing outcomes from binary voting mechanisms for arbitrary committees when individuals all play undominated Nash equilibrium strategies. As such, they are powerful analytical tools, tools that we now apply.

4.2 Equilibrium outcomes of binary agendas

Example 4.1 shows that institutional details can matter: for a fixed profile, the collective decision under an amendment agenda in the example differs from that under a successive elimination agenda. Consequently, if individual 1 in the example has control over the committee's decision rules, we expect her to choose the amendment agenda Γ^a; on the other hand, if either individual 2 or 3 were to control the agenda, we expect the successive elimination tree Γ^s to govern the committee's choice process. More generally, Example 4.1 raises questions about how the structure of an agenda influences the sorts of alternatives that can arise as (undominated Nash) equilibrium collective decisions under that agenda. To address the questions, fix an arbitrary finite binary voting tree Γ and let P be any majority preference relation on the set of alternatives X. By Theorems 4.1 and 4.2, the pair (Γ, P) suffices for any analysis of the set undominated Nash equilibrium outcomes and details of committee preference profiles can typically be ignored without loss of generality (when it is necessary to be explicit about the profile ρ underlying some particular majority relation P, we write P_ρ). With a slight abuse of terminology, we call (Γ, P) a voting game.

By Theorem 4.1, when the majority preference relation is P and the agenda is $\Gamma = (\Lambda, \succ, \theta)$, the sophisticated outcome $s(\lambda_0)$ is uniquely defined. Let $S(\Gamma, P) = s(\lambda_0) \in X$ denote this outcome and define

$$V(P) = \{x \in X : x = S(\Gamma, P) \text{ for some binary agenda } \Gamma\}$$

to be the set of alternatives that are sophisticated outcomes for some binary agenda under the majority relation P. Now recall that the top cycle set for majority preference consists of all those alternatives reachable from every other feasible alternative by a finite sequence of binary comparisons under majority preference; formally

4.2. EQUILIBRIUM OUTCOMES OF BINARY AGENDAS

Definition 4.2 *For any set X and complete majority relation P, the top cycle set of P on X is*

$$T(P) = \{x \in X : \forall y \in X\setminus\{x\}, \exists\{a_0,\ldots,a_r\} \subseteq X \text{ such that} \\ a_0 = x, a_r = y, r < \infty \text{ and, } \forall t \leq r-1, a_t P a_{t+1}\}.$$

So x is in the top cycle set if, for any distinct alternative y, we can get from y to x in a finite number of majority preference steps of the form, $a_t P a_{t+1}$ [PPTI, sect.6.3]. In particular, if both x and y are in the top cycle set, then there is a majority path from y to x and also from x back to y. Lemma 4.1 claims more is true: for every complete majority relation P, every element in the top cycle set $T(P)$ can be linked in a single majority cycle under P.

Lemma 4.1 *Let $|T(P)| = t$. There exists an ordering $\alpha : \{1,\ldots,t\} \to T(P)$ such that*

$$\alpha(1)P\alpha(2)P\ldots P\alpha(t)P\alpha(1).$$

Furthermore, $x \in T(P)$ and $z \in X\setminus T(P)$ implies xPz.

Proof [Exercise]. □

The lemma identifies two useful properties of top cycle sets and helps prove the following characterization theorem.

Theorem 4.3 *For all majority preference relations P, $V(P) = T(P)$.*

Proof (1) $V(P) \subseteq T(P)$. Fix a binary voting game $(\Gamma, P) = ((\Lambda, \succ, \theta), P)$. By definition of a sophisticated equivalent and the second statement of Lemma 4.1, for any node $\lambda \in \Lambda\setminus\{\lambda_0\}$, if the sophisticated equivalent of λ is an alternative in the top-cycle set then the sophisticated equivalent of the node above λ must also lie in the top-cycle set: $s(\lambda) \in T(P)$ implies $s(a(\lambda)) \in T(P)$. Moreover, since θ maps Λ^t onto X, there exists some $\lambda \in \Lambda$ such that $s(\lambda) \in T(P)$. Hence, $s(\lambda_0) = S(\Gamma, P) \in T(P)$.

(2) $T(P) \subseteq V(P)$. By Lemma 4.1, for any alternative $x \in T(P)$ there exists a labeling of $T(P)$ such that $x \equiv a_1$, $T(P) = \{a_1,\ldots,a_t\}$ and $a_1 P a_2 P \ldots P a_t$. Label $X\setminus T(P) = \{a_{t+1},\ldots,a_r\}$ arbitrarily. Now consider a successive elimination agenda Γ^s defined by the voting sequence $(a_{t+1},\ldots,a_r,a_1,\ldots,a_t)$: see Figure 4.7.

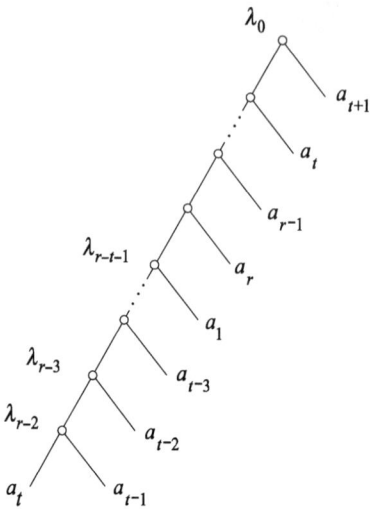

Figure 4.7: The successive elimination agenda

Given P: $s(\lambda_{r-2}) = a_{t-1}$, $s(\lambda_{r-3}) = a_{t-2}, \ldots, s(\lambda_{r-t-1}) = a_1$ and, by Lemma 4.1, $a_1 P a_s$ for all $s \geq t+1$. Therefore, $s(\lambda_0) = a_1 \equiv x = S(\Gamma^s, P)$. Since x was chosen arbitrarily from $T(P)$, this completes the proof. □

The theorem says that sophisticated outcomes must necessarily be elements of the top cycle set and, conversely, any element of the top cycle set is the sophisticated outcome for some binary voting game.

There is an immediate corollary to Theorem 4.3.

Corollary 4.1 *If xPy for all $y \in X\backslash\{x\}$, then $V(P) = \{x\}$; otherwise $|V(P)| \geq 3$.*

Proof [Exercise]. □

If there is a Condorcet winner under P in X, then any binary voting game yields this alternative as the sophisticated outcome; in other words, the outcome is independent of the binary voting procedure used in committee. On the other hand, if no Condorcet winner exists, then there must be at least three alternatives, each of which is the sophisticated outcome for some agenda.

Theorem 4.3 tells us that using binary voting games to make collective decisions implies that only alternatives in the top cycle set are chosen.

4.2. EQUILIBRIUM OUTCOMES OF BINARY AGENDAS

Unfortunately, the top cycle set can include Pareto dominated alternatives and, in the spatial model, typically includes almost every alternative [PPTI, Theorem 6.3]. Example 4.3 illustrates the first remark.

Example 4.3 Let $N = \{1,2,3\}$, $X = \{w,x,y,z\}$ and suppose $\rho \in \mathcal{P}^3$ is

$$wP_1xP_1yP_1z$$
$$zP_2wP_2xP_2y$$
$$yP_3zP_3wP_3x$$

Then $x \in T(P)$, since xPy, $xPyPz$ and $xPyPzPw$, and hence a successive elimination agenda with voting sequence (x,y,z,w) yields x as the sophisticated outcome. On the other hand, wP_ix for all $i \in N$ so $x \notin PS_N(\rho)$. □

Furthermore, if we consider the sophisticated outcome mapping $S(\Gamma, \cdot)$ as a collective choice function on the domain of all complete majority preference relations for a fixed binary agenda Γ then, as shown by Example 4.4, $S(\Gamma, \cdot)$ violates weak monotonicity.

Example 4.4 Let $N = \{1,2,3\}$, $X = \{w,x,y,z\}$ and suppose the agenda Γ is described by Figure 4.8.

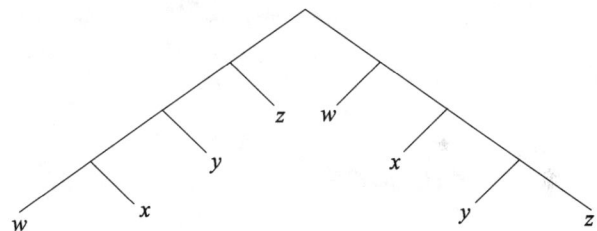

Figure 4.8: Agenda for Example 4.4

Consider the profile $\rho \in \mathcal{P}^3$:

$$yP_1zP_1xP_1w$$
$$xP_2wP_2yP_2z$$
$$zP_3wP_3yP_3x$$

Then majority preference has wPy, yPz, zPx, xPw, yPx and zPw. Hence $S(\Gamma, P) = w$. Now consider $\rho' = (P'_1, P_2, P_3) \in \mathcal{P}^3$ where

$$yP'_1zP'_1wP'_1x$$

So the only difference between ρ and ρ' is that individual 1 has reversed his preference between w and x. In this case, the only change in the majority preference relation is $wP'x$ rather than the reverse, all other pairwise majority rankings being unaffected. Consequently, weak monotonicity requires $S(\Gamma, P') = w$; but applying the sophisticated voting algorithm yields $S(\Gamma, P') = z$. □

Examples 4.3 and 4.4 suggest that collective decision-making with arbitrary binary voting games can be quite badly behaved. This need not be true, however, for some well-defined classes of such games. One especially important class with nicer properties is the family of amendment agendas. Although the idea of an amendment agenda has already been introduced more-or-less informally, it is now useful to be a little more precise.

Definition 4.3 *Let $|X| = r$. A binary voting tree on X is an amendment agenda if there exists an ordering $\alpha : \{1, \ldots, r\} \to X$ such that the majority voting sequence is $(\alpha(1), \alpha(2), \ldots, \alpha(r))$, where $\alpha(1)$ is first voted against $\alpha(2)$, the winner voted against $\alpha(3)$, etc. Let Γ_α denote the amendment agenda with ordering α and let $\mathcal{A}(X)$ denote the family of all amendment agendas on X.*

Figure 4.3 in Example 4.1 shows a typical amendment agenda Γ_α, $\alpha = (w, x, y, z)$, and illustrates a general feature of the mapping θ of terminal nodes into alternatives for amendment agendas: all final decision nodes involve $\alpha(r)$ and every alternative $\alpha(t)$, $t < r$, is associated with at least one terminal node. Therefore, a necessary condition for any alternative other than $\alpha(r)$ to be the sophisticated outcome of an agenda Γ_α is that this alternative be majority preferred to $\alpha(r)$; alternatively, if $\alpha(r)$ is majority preferred to each $\alpha(t)$, $t < r$, then $\alpha(r)$ must be the sophisticated outcome, exactly as Corollary 4.1 claims.

Consider an amendment agenda Γ_α and majority preference relation P. There are two possibilities; first suppose that $\alpha(r-1)P\alpha(r)$. Then $\alpha(r)$ cannot be the sophisticated outcome since, in the tree derived from Γ_α by replacing the final decision nodes of Γ_α by their sophisticated equivalents, we find that either $\alpha(r)$ is not a sophisticated equivalent of any such node or, if $\alpha(r)P\alpha(t)$ for some $t < r - 1$, $\alpha(r)$ must be paired against $\alpha(r-1)$ at some of the final nodes of the pruned tree, and so on. Therefore, when $\alpha(r-1)P\alpha(r)$ we can delete $\alpha(r)$ to obtain a reduced amendment agenda $\Gamma'_\alpha = (\alpha(1), \ldots, \alpha(r-1))$. The second possibility is $\alpha(r)P\alpha(r-1)$; then every final decision node involving $\alpha(r-1)$ has the sophisticated equivalent $\alpha(r)$ in which case the reduced agenda is $\Gamma''_\alpha = (\alpha(1), \ldots, \alpha(r-2), \alpha(r))$.

4.2. EQUILIBRIUM OUTCOMES OF BINARY AGENDAS

Now consider the alternative $\alpha(r-2)$ and suppose, first, the pruned agenda is Γ'_α; then one of the following cases must obtain:

(1) $\alpha(r)P\alpha(r-2)$;
(2) $\alpha(r-1)P\alpha(r-2)$;
(3) $\alpha(r-2)P\alpha(r-1)$ and $\alpha(r-2)P\alpha(r)$.

If case (1) holds then $\alpha(r-2)$ cannot be the sophisticated equivalent of any decision node, since $\alpha(r) \in \{l(\lambda), r(\lambda)\}$ for every final decision node $\lambda \in \Lambda^d$. If case (2) holds then $\alpha(r-2)$ cannot be the sophisticated outcome since it must come against $\alpha(r-1)$ at some decision node in the tree at which point it is eliminated. Finally, suppose case (3) obtains. Then $\alpha(r-2)$ is not eliminated at any final decision node involving $\alpha(r)$ and we can repeat the argument above for the full agenda Γ_α, replacing $\alpha(r-1)$ with $\alpha(r-2)$ and replacing $\alpha(r)$ with $\alpha(r-1)$.

An entirely symmetric argument holds if we begin with the pruned tree Γ''_α derived from the supposition $\alpha(r)P\alpha(r-1)$, rather than with the tree Γ'_α. That is, in either case Γ'_α or Γ''_α, the same logic can be applied to yield a further reduced agenda: if Γ'_α is derived from Γ_α, then (following the argument of the preceding paragraph) a second pruning yields $(\alpha(1), \ldots, \alpha(r-2))$ or $(\alpha(1), \ldots, \alpha(r-3), \alpha(r-1))$; and if Γ''_α is derived from Γ_α, then we obtain $(\alpha(1), \alpha(2), \ldots, \alpha(r-2))$ or $(\alpha(1), \alpha(2), \ldots, \alpha(r-3), \alpha(r))$.

Generalizing the preceding logic suggests the following definition.

Definition 4.4 *The sophisticated agenda of an amendment agenda game* (Γ_α, P), $\varsigma(\alpha) = (\varsigma_1(\alpha), \ldots, \varsigma_r(\alpha))$, *is given by fixing* $\varsigma_r(\alpha) = \alpha(r)$ *and, for all* $1 \leq t < r$,

$$\varsigma_t(\alpha) = \begin{cases} \alpha(t) & \text{if } \alpha(t)P\varsigma_s(\alpha) \text{ for all } s > t \\ \varsigma_{t+1}(\alpha) & \text{otherwise} \end{cases}.$$

Example 4.5 illustrates the idea and shows that sophisticated agendas typically involve some redundancy.

Example 4.5 Let $X = \{v, w, x, y, z\}$ and zPv, zPx, yPz, yPv, xPy, wPy, wPz, vPw. Suppose $\alpha = (v, w, x, y, z)$ and apply the definition to obtain the sophisticated agenda of the game (Γ_α, P):

$$\varsigma_5(\alpha) = z;$$
$$\varsigma_4(\alpha) = y \text{ because } yPz;$$
$$\varsigma_3(\alpha) = y \text{ because, although } xPy, zPx;$$
$$\varsigma_2(\alpha) = w \text{ because } wPy \text{ and } wPz;$$
$$\varsigma_1(\alpha) = w \text{ because, although } vPw, yPv.$$

Therefore, $\varsigma(\alpha) = (w, w, y, y, z)$. On the other hand, if $\alpha' = (y, x, w, z, v)$ then applying the definition gives the sophisticated agenda of $(\Gamma_{\alpha'}, P)$ as $\varsigma(\alpha') = (y, z, z, z, v)$. $\square$

Lemma 4.2 summarizes the rationale for constructing sophisticated agendas.

Lemma 4.2 *For all $\Gamma_\alpha \in \mathcal{A}(X)$ and any strict majority preference relation P, $S(\Gamma_\alpha, P) = \varsigma_1(\alpha)$.*

Proof [Exercise]. $\square$

An immediate implication of the lemma is that, as a collective choice function on strict majority preference relations, $S(\Gamma_\alpha, \cdot)$ must be weakly monotonic: $S(\Gamma_\alpha, P) = \varsigma_1(\alpha)$ implies $\varsigma_1(\alpha) P \varsigma_s(\alpha)$ for all $\varsigma_s(\alpha) \neq \varsigma_1(\alpha)$ in which case, if the only change in preferences is that $\varsigma_1(\alpha)$ is now preferred to more alternatives, it must still be the case that $\varsigma_1(\alpha) P \varsigma_s(\alpha)$ for all $\varsigma_s(\alpha) \neq \varsigma_1(\alpha)$. So while $S(\Gamma, \cdot)$ need not be monotonic for an arbitrary binary agenda Γ (Example 4.4), the sophisticated outcome mapping for an amendment agenda, $S(\Gamma_\alpha, \cdot)$, is surely monotonic. Similarly, it turns out that, in contrast to an arbitrary agenda Γ (Example 4.3), the sophisticated outcome of any amendment agenda game, $S(\Gamma_\alpha, P)$, is in the Pareto set.

Let P be any strict majority preference relation. Let

$$A(P) = \{x \in X : x = S(\Gamma_\alpha, P) \text{ for some } \Gamma_\alpha \in \mathcal{A}(X)\}$$

denote the set of alternatives that are sophisticated outcomes of some amendment agenda game (Γ_α, P). By Theorem 4.3, the set of alternatives that could arise as sophisticated outcomes from suitably chosen binary agendas, $V(P)$, is fully characterized by the top cycle set, $T(P)$; that is, $V(P) \subseteq T(P)$ and $T(P) \subseteq V(P)$. And since amendment agendas are a proper subset of all binary agendas, therefore, the set of sophisticated outcomes from suitably chosen amendment agendas, $A(P)$, must likewise satisfy $A(P) \subseteq T(P)$. In fact, this inclusion can be strict. The following concept proves useful as a first step to demonstrating this fact and to justifying the claim that the sophisticated outcomes of amendment agendas are Pareto efficient.

Definition 4.5 *For any $x, y \in X$ and strict majority preference relation P, say that x covers y, xCy, if both xPy and $P(x) \subset P(y)$. The uncovered set for P is*

$$U(P) = \{x \in X : yCx \text{ for no } y \in X\}$$

where, for all $z \in X$, $P(z) = \{y \in X : yPz\}$.

4.2. EQUILIBRIUM OUTCOMES OF BINARY AGENDAS

In words, x covers y if it is majority preferred to y and anything that is majority preferred to x is also majority preferred to y. This latter property is equivalent to saying that if, for any $z \in X$, yPz then xPz too. So if there is a Condorcet winner under P, then the uncovered set is precisely this alternative.

It is easily seen that the covering relation is an asymmetric and irreflexive, but not necessarily complete, binary relation. Covering is also transitive: suppose xCy and yCz; then

$$[xPy \ \& \ P(y) \subset P(z)] \Rightarrow xPz$$

and

$$[P(x) \subset P(y) \ \& \ P(y) \subset P(z)] \Rightarrow P(x) \subset P(z).$$

Hence xCz, proving C transitive in which case, if $y \notin U(P)$ then xCy for some $x \in U(P)$. Moreover, Corollary 4.1 holds if we replace $V(P)$ by $U(P)$ [Exercise].

Although the uncovered set is naturally defined in terms of the covering relation, it has a simple characterization in terms of the underlying majority preference that immediately connects it to the top cycle set.

Lemma 4.3 *For any strict majority preference relation P, $x \in U(P)$ if and only if, for all $y \in X\setminus\{x\}$, either xPy or there exists some $z \in X$ such that xPz and zPy.*

Proof (Sufficiency) If xPy then certainly $\sim [yCx]$ and if, for some $z \in X$, xPz and zPy then again $\sim [yCx]$. Since, by hypothesis, one of these possibilities obtains for every $y \in X$, $x \in U(P)$.

(Necessity) Let $x \in U(P)$ and $y \neq x$. By definition, $\sim [yCx]$. Therefore, by P complete, either xPy or

$$\begin{aligned}[yPx \ \& \ \sim [yCx]] &\Rightarrow \ \sim [P(y) \subset P(x)] \\ &\Rightarrow \exists z \in P(y)\setminus P(x) \\ &\Rightarrow xPz \ \& \ zPy. \ \square\end{aligned}$$

Lemma 4.3 is often called the "two-step principle": any alternative in the uncovered set can be reached from any other alternative via the majority preference relation in at most two steps. Because, by definition, any alternative in the top cycle set can be similarly reached from any other alternative in some finite sequence of steps, it is necessarily the case that the uncovered set is a subset of the top cycle set and therefore, by Theorem 4.3, also a subset of the set of alternatives implementable as the sophisticated outcomes of some binary agenda: $U(P) \subseteq T(P) = V(P)$. Furthermore, unlike alternatives in the top cycle set, uncovered alternatives must be Pareto efficient.

Lemma 4.4 *For all $\rho \in \mathcal{P}^n$, $U(P_\rho) \subseteq PS_N(\rho)$.*

Proof Choose $x \notin PS_N(\rho)$. By definition, therefore, there exist an alternative $z \in X$ such that $P(z, x; \rho) = N$; hence, zPx. Now let $y \in X$ be such that xPy. Therefore, by transitivity of individual preferences and $P(z, x; \rho) = N$, zPy. Hence, zCx implying $x \notin U(P_\rho)$. □

The final step in the argument that sophisticated outcomes of amendment agendas are necessarily Pareto efficient is to show that the set of such outcomes, $A(P)$, is contained in the uncovered set for any strict majority preference relation.

Theorem 4.4 *For all $\rho \in \mathcal{P}^n$, $A(P_\rho) \subseteq PS_N(\rho)$.*

Proof Given Lemma 4.4, it suffices to show that, for any strict majority preference relation P, $A(P) \subseteq U(P)$. So let $x = S(\Gamma_\alpha, P)$ and suppose to the contrary that $x \notin U(P)$. Let y cover x. By Lemma 4.2, $x = \varsigma_1(\alpha)$ in which case $xP\varsigma_s(\alpha)$ for all $\varsigma_s(\alpha) \neq x$. But since yCx, $yP\varsigma_s(\alpha)$ for all $s = 1, \ldots, r$ and, therefore, $y = \varsigma_t(\alpha)$ for some t. But then $\varsigma_t(\alpha)Px$ contradicting $x = S(\Gamma_\alpha, P)$. □

The argument for Theorem 4.4 shows $A(P) \subseteq U(P)$. Were the converse also true, then the uncovered set would completely characterize the set $A(P)$. For some preference relations P and sufficiently large sets of alternatives X, however, the inclusion is strict.

For any strict majority preference relation P on a set X, let

$$T(P) = \{Y \subseteq X : P \text{ is transitive on } Y\}$$

denote those subsets of alternatives on which the majority preference relation is transitive. Since X is finite, for every $Y \in T(P)$ there exists a top-ranked alternative in Y relative to P; let $m(Y)$ denote this maximal alternative. Now define

$$\mathcal{E}(P) = \{Y \subseteq X : \forall z \notin Y, \exists y \in Y \text{ such that } yPz\}$$

to be those subsets of alternatives such that, for every alternative not in the set, there exists some alternative in the set that is strictly preferred

4.2. EQUILIBRIUM OUTCOMES OF BINARY AGENDAS

by a majority; thus $\mathcal{E}(P)$ is the family of "externally stable" subsets of X, conditional on the majority preference relation P. By Lemma 4.1, the top cycle set is an element of $\mathcal{E}(P)$. Finally, let

$$B(P) = \{x \in X : x = m(Y) \text{ for some } Y \in \mathcal{T}(P) \cap \mathcal{E}(P)\}.$$

Clearly, the top cycle set is not in $\mathcal{T}(P)$ and, if $Y', Y \in \mathcal{T}(P)$ are such that $Y \subset Y'$ and $m(Y')Pm(Y)$, then $Y \notin \mathcal{E}(P)$. Thus the set $\mathcal{T}(P) \cap \mathcal{E}(P)$ contains only maximal subsets (by set-inclusion) of X on which P is transitive.

Theorem 4.5 *For all strict majority preference relations P, $A(P) = B(P)$.*

Proof Choose any amendment agenda game (Γ_α, P) and consider its sophisticated agenda $\varsigma(\alpha)$. Let $Z \equiv \cup_{t=1}^{t=r} \varsigma_t(\alpha)$; by construction of $\varsigma(\alpha)$, $Z \in \mathcal{T}(P)$. Similarly, $w \in X$ and $wP\varsigma_t(\alpha)$ for all $\varsigma_t(\alpha) \neq w$ implies $w \in Z$; hence $Z \in \mathcal{E}(P)$ and $m(Z) \in B(P)$. By Lemma 4.2, $\varsigma_1(\alpha) \in A(P)$. By construction of $\varsigma(\alpha)$, $m(Z) = \varsigma_1(\alpha)$. Therefore, $A(P) \subseteq B(P)$.

To prove the converse, choose any $y \in B(P)$. Let $y = m(Y)$ label X so that $X \backslash Y = \{x_1, \ldots, x_s\}$ and $Y \backslash \{y\} = \{x_{s+2}, \ldots, x_r\}$. Consider the amendment agenda $\alpha = (x_1, \ldots, x_s, y, x_{s+2}, \ldots, x_r)$. By definition, $y = m(Y) \in B(P)$ if and only if $Y \in \mathcal{T}(P) \cap \mathcal{E}(P)$; hence, $\varsigma_1(\alpha) = y$ and, by Lemma 4.2, $y \in A(P)$. Therefore, $B(P) \subseteq A(P)$. □

Theorem 4.5 describes the set of undominated Nash equilibrium outcomes to amendment agenda games. Again, it is easy to check that Corollary 4.1 holds if we replace $V(P)$ by $B(P)$ [Exercise]. Therefore, if $A(P)$ is, as is generally the case, a proper subset of the uncovered set, there must be at least four alternatives in X; Example 4.6 assumes $|X| = 9$.

Example 4.6 Let $X = \{x_1, \ldots, x_9\}$. It is easiest in this case to represent the majority preference relation P on X with a dominance matrix, $\mathbf{D} = [d_{st}]$, where $d_{st} = 1$ if $x_s P x_t$ and $d_{st} = 0$ otherwise. A useful property of the representation $\mathbf{D}$ is that the matrix $\mathbf{D}^2$ describes which alternatives can be reached from which via P in exactly two steps. For instance, suppose there are three alternatives and $x_1 P x_2$, $x_2 P x_3$ and $x_3 P x_1$; then

$$\mathbf{D} = \begin{bmatrix} 0 & 1 & 0 \\ 0 & 0 & 1 \\ 1 & 0 & 0 \end{bmatrix} \text{ and } \mathbf{D}^2 = \begin{bmatrix} 0 & 0 & 1 \\ 1 & 0 & 0 \\ 0 & 1 & 0 \end{bmatrix}.$$

It follows by the two-step principle, Lemma 4.3, that we can compute the uncovered set from the matrix $[\delta_{st}] = \mathbf{D} + \mathbf{D}^2$; specifically, $x_s \in U(P)$ if and only if $\delta_{st} \in \{1,2\}$ for every $t \neq s$. So for the preceding three-alternative example,

$$\mathbf{D} + \mathbf{D}^2 = \begin{bmatrix} 0 & 1 & 1 \\ 1 & 0 & 1 \\ 1 & 1 & 0 \end{bmatrix}$$

and $U(P) = \{x_1, x_2, x_3\}$.

With these observations in mind, suppose P is given by

$$\mathbf{D} = \begin{bmatrix} 0 & 1 & 0 & 0 & 0 & 0 & 1 & 1 & 1 \\ 0 & 0 & 1 & 0 & 0 & 0 & 1 & 1 & 1 \\ 1 & 0 & 0 & 1 & 1 & 1 & 1 & 1 & 1 \\ 1 & 1 & 0 & 0 & 1 & 0 & 1 & 1 & 0 \\ 1 & 1 & 0 & 0 & 0 & 1 & 1 & 0 & 1 \\ 1 & 1 & 0 & 1 & 0 & 0 & 0 & 1 & 1 \\ 0 & 0 & 0 & 0 & 0 & 1 & 0 & 1 & 0 \\ 0 & 0 & 0 & 0 & 1 & 0 & 0 & 0 & 1 \\ 0 & 0 & 0 & 1 & 0 & 0 & 1 & 0 & 0 \end{bmatrix}$$

Computing $\mathbf{D} + \mathbf{D}^2$ for this case yields $U(P) = \{x_1, \ldots, x_6\}$. On the other hand, it is left as an exercise to check $B(P) = \{x_2, \ldots, x_6\}$. Therefore, by Theorem 4.5, $x_1 \in U(P) \backslash A(P)$ and there is no amendment agenda Γ_α for which $S(\Gamma_\alpha, P) = x_1$. $\square$

4.3 Application: Agenda independence

For the preceding analysis, the set of alternatives X is taken as fixed and any possible ordering of X is considered an admissible voting sequence. Not all possible orderings, however, are always admissible. For example, a common procedural rule in committee decision-making is that the status quo policy is necessarily considered last in any voting sequence. The idea, as the term amendment procedure suggests, is that the agenda is built up from a list of potential amendments to the status quo policy; the proposed changes are then either accepted or rejected until the committee arrives at a perfected proposal chosen to go against the status quo, with the majority winner being the committee decision.

Suppose $x^0 \in X$ is a status quo policy and assume admissible amendment agendas $\Gamma_\alpha \in \mathcal{A}(X)$ are defined by $\alpha(r) = x^0$, where $|X| = r$. Let $\mathcal{A}(x^0) \subset \mathcal{A}(X)$ be the set of admissible agendas and let

$$A(P; x^0) = \{x \in X : x = S(\Gamma_\alpha, P) \text{ for some } \Gamma_\alpha \in \mathcal{A}(x^0)\}.$$

4.3. APPLICATION: AGENDA INDEPENDENCE

Let $y \in X$ and $y \neq x^0$. Applying Lemma 4.2, a necessary condition for y to replace the status quo x^0 is that a majority strictly prefers y to the status quo x^0 in a pairwise vote; furthermore, since any element of $A(P; x^0)$ must also be an element of $A(P)$, Theorem 4.5 implies that $y \in B(P)$ is a necessary condition for y to be a sophisticated outcome. On the other hand, a sufficient condition for an alternative $y \in X \backslash \{x_0\}$ to be the sophisticated outcome irrespective of the agenda $\Gamma_\alpha \in \mathcal{A}(x_0)$, is that

$$y \in P(x_0) \text{ and, } \forall z \in P(x_0)\backslash\{y\}, \ y \in P(z). \qquad (*)$$

That is, if y satisfies (*) then, for all $\Gamma_\alpha \in \mathcal{A}(x_0)$, $S(\Gamma_\alpha, P) = y$. To see this, recall that every terminal node of an amendment agenda pairs the status quo x_0 against an alternative from the agenda, with every such alternative appearing on at least one terminal node. By the first property of (*), that $y \in P(x_0)$, and the earlier logic for solving binary voting games, y must be the sophisticated equivalent of every terminal node at which y is compared with x_0. Now consider any alternative $z \neq y$. If z is the sophisticated equivalent of some terminal node, then either $z = x_0$ or $z \in P(x_0)$. In either case, (*) implies that y must be the sophisticated equivalent of any pairwise comparison between y and z at the next stage; and so on back up the voting tree, thus establishing the claim. In other words, the outcome y is *independent* of the order in which alternatives are considered (save for $\alpha(r) = x^0$). Agenda independence can be defined for procedures other than amendment agendas.

Definition 4.6 *Let P be any strict majority preference relation and assume $\mathcal{G}$ describes the set of admissible binary agendas. An alternative $x \in X$ is an agenda-independent outcome for $\mathcal{G}$ if and only if $x = S(\Gamma, P)$ for all $\Gamma \in \mathcal{G}$.*

It is worth noting here that if there exists an agenda-independent outcome for some committee decision problem, there are no grounds for any procedural conflicts in committee regarding which of the admissible agendas to adopt.

To illustrate the idea of agenda-independence, suppose N is a set of n legislators, n odd. Each legislator $i \in N$ represents electoral district i and is seeking federal funding of a project that yields benefit $b_i > 0$ to the district at a cost $c_i > 0$. Assume no two projects cost the same and label districts so $c_1 < c_2 < \ldots < c_n$. Since projects are given, they are either approved or not; thus the set of possible legislative alternatives is $X = \{0, 1\}^n$ where, for any $x = (x_1, \ldots, x_n) \in X$ and any $i \in N$, $x_i = 1$ if and only if the ith project is approved. And given a project is implemented only if approved by the legislature, the status quo policy $x^0 \in X$ is naturally defined by the vector of no funded projects, that is $x^0 = (0, \ldots, 0)$.

For any $x \in X$, let $Z(x) \subseteq N$ denote the set of funded projects. Although the benefits of any project approved by the legislature accrue exclusively to the district, the costs are shared equally among districts through general taxation. The payoff to legislator i from outcome x, therefore, is

$$u_i(x) = b_i x_i - \frac{1}{n} \sum_{j=1}^{j=n} c_j x_j.$$

Let x^α be a least expensive set of at least $(n+1)/2$ projects: then $Z(x^\alpha) = \{i \in N : i \leq (n+1)/2\}$ and we suppose $i \in Z(x^\alpha)$ implies $u_i(x^\alpha) > 0$. We claim that x^α is an agenda-independent outcome for $\mathcal{A}(x^0)$. To prove this, it suffices to check the two conditions of $(*)$ above. First, because $u_i(x^0) = 0$ for every legislator but, by assumption, $u_i(x^\alpha) > 0$ for all $i \in Z(x^\alpha)$, $x^\alpha \in P(x^0)$. Second, choose any alternative $x \in P(x^0) \setminus \{x^\alpha\}$; for all $i \in Z(x^\alpha)$,

$$u_i(x^\alpha) - u_i(x) = b_i(1 - x_i) + \frac{1}{n}\left[\sum_{j \in Z(x)} c_j x_j - \sum_{j \in Z(x^\alpha)} c_j x_j^\alpha\right] > 0$$

by definition of x^α. Therefore, $(*)$ holds and x^α is an agenda-independent outcome for $\mathcal{A}(x^0)$.

A superficially similar agenda to an amendment agenda arises when legislators treat independent policy issues sequentially to arrive at a final policy outcome. For the discrete setting, suppose there are a set of independent issues $K = \{1, \ldots, k\}$, each of which may be accepted or rejected by the legislature; then the set of alternatives is $X = \{0,1\}^k$ and, for any $x = (x_1, \ldots, x_n) \in X$ and $i \in K$, $x_i = 1$ if and only if the ith issue is approved. Analogous to an amendment agenda, an issue-by-issue agenda is an ordering of the issues $\iota : K \to K$ such that $\iota(1)$ is first voted up or down, respectively, $\iota(1) = 1$ or $\iota(1) = 0$, following which the second listed issue $\iota(2)$ is voted up or down, and so on. Thus for all $j = 1, \ldots, k$, the final outcome x satisfies $x_j = 1$ if and only if the jth issue is approved when it comes up for consideration, $\iota^{-1}(j) = 1$. Let $\mathcal{I}_K$ denote the family of issue-by-issue agendas on the set of issues K.

To see that issue-by-issue agendas can support final outcomes distinct from amendment agendas, set $k = n = 3$ and interpret each project of the example above as an issue. Suppose the agenda has the three issues being considered in reverse order; that is,

$$\Gamma_\iota = (\iota(1), \iota(2), \iota(3)) = (3, 2, 1).$$

4.3. APPLICATION: AGENDA INDEPENDENCE

Given the payoffs $\{u_i(x)\}_{i=1,2,3}$ specified earlier and applying the algorithm for sophisticated voting, we find the sophisticated outcome to be the status quo alternative $x^0 = (0,0,0)$ rather than the outcome x^α. It is straightforward to confirm that this must be true for any (odd) number of legislators with preferences $\{u_i(x)\}_{i \in N}$ and for any issue-by-issue agenda. In other words, for this distributive example, the status quo $x^0 = (0, \ldots, 0)$ is an agenda-independent outcome for $\mathcal{I}_N$. Figure 4.9 describes the voting tree for $\Gamma_\iota = (3,2,1)$.

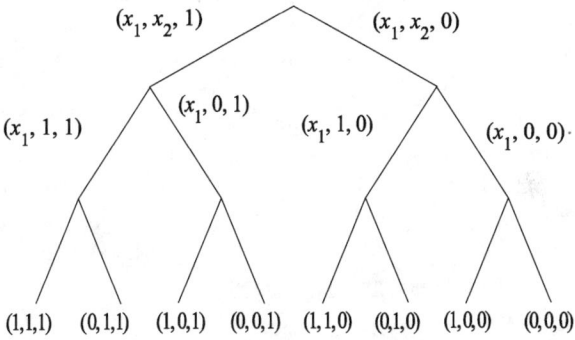

Figure 4.9: The voting tree Γ_ι

A more general agenda-independence result for issue-by-issue voting is available. Let $J \subseteq K$ be an arbitrary set of accepted issues and suppose the majority preference relation satisfies the following property:

$$\forall J \subseteq K \,\&\, \forall j \in J, \ J \backslash \{j\} P J. \tag{**}$$

In words, removing any issue from a subset of accepted issues is majority preferred to including that issue. If majority preference satisfies (**), as it surely does under the preferences $\{u_i(x)\}_{i \in N}$ above, then the alternative whereby no issues are accepted, $x^0 = (0, \ldots, 0)$, is an agenda-independent outcome for $\mathcal{I}_K$. To check this, note that all of the final decision nodes of an agenda $\Gamma_\iota \in \mathcal{I}_K$ involve a choice between some non-empty set of accepted issues J and a set $J \backslash \{j\}$, where $\iota(j) = k$; by (**), $J \backslash \{j\} P J$ so the smaller set of accepted issues is the sophisticated equivalent of the final decision nodes. Repeating this step back up the tree eventually gives the sophisticated outcome x^0 as claimed.

4.4 Discussion

A great deal of collective decision-making is by voting under more-or-less well-defined rules. Until this chapter, such rules or institutional details have been left largely unspecified. Instead, we focussed on characterizing those collective choice rules that are either immune from strategic misrepresentation of preferences (Chapter 2) or capable in principle of being implemented by suitably constraining the strategic environment (Chapter 3). And although the design of institutional rules is an explicit concern for implementation, the principal question addressed in Chapter 3 is posed at a high level of abstraction: "Given any choice rule satisfying a given list of properties, does there exist *any* sort of institutional arrangement (mechanism) that implements the rule?" In particular, we paid virtually no attention to whether or not, when such an institution does exist for some class of choice rule, it is practical, let alone in use. In contrast, this chapter takes a more pragmatic approach, beginning with describing some empirically relevant and substantively important classes of institution and then exploring the implications of strategic behavior under these institutions for collective choice.

When a relatively small group of people has to make a choice of one among several competing alternatives, it is both feasible and commonplace to make the choice by, typically, simple majority rule under some sequential pairwise choice procedure, or binary agenda. Yet even with few people and few alternatives, the set of possible sequential pairwise procedures is very large: with three people and three alternatives, for instance, there are three amendment and three successive elimination agendas; there are composite agendas of the form "use an amendment agenda to choose between the three successive elimination agendas, then use the winning agenda to choose the final alternative", and so on. As the number of alternatives grows, so too does the number of different sequential pairwise choice procedures. Despite the plethora of possible procedures, it turns out that if all individuals' preferences are strict and no individual uses a dominated voting strategy, then rational voting over any binary agenda has a relatively simple structure. In effect, given any binary agenda and any strict majority preference relation over the relevant alternatives, there exists a practical algorithm for computing the equilibrium outcome from strategically rational voting. Along with the order of voting, this algorithm depends only on knowing the strict majority preference relation for the committee, rather than on any details of the profile itself, and the undominated equilibrium outcome (that is, the sophisticated outcome) is unique (Theorem 4.1). Furthermore, *any* strict and complete binary relation over a finite set of alternatives is the strict

4.4. DISCUSSION

majority preference relation for some set of individuals and some preference profile (Theorem 4.2).

Together, Theorems 4.1 and 4.2 make possible a fairly general understanding of majoritarian committee voting over binary agendas. In particular, if a committee is unconstrained in the sort of binary agenda it uses for decision-making, then the set of achievable sophisticated outcomes is the (majority) top cycle set for the underlying preference profile (Theorem 4.3). As a collective choice rule, therefore, the sophisticated outcome mapping for an arbitrary binary agenda is not very attractive. Although it necessarily selects the Condorcet winner when one exists (because in this case the top cycle set is exactly the Condorcet winner), it can violate weak monotonicity (Example 4.4) and, absent a Condorcet winner, it can yield Pareto dominated alternatives (Example 4.3). But not every sort of binary agenda is widely used. Although examples of many agenda-forms can be found in various circumstances, the set of empirically important agenda-forms is relatively small and, within this set, amendment and issue-by-issue agendas have particular significance.

Permitting only amendment agendas considerably limits the set of alternatives achievable as equilibrium outcomes (Theorem 4.5), illustrating the commonplace that institutional details are consequential for collective choice. Moreover, the set of equilibrium (sophisticated) outcomes under amendment agendas exhibits some desirable properties, partly accounting for its prominence in parliamentary procedure. Such properties include, first, that the sophisticated outcome mapping for any amendment agenda is necessarily monotonic (Lemma 4.2): if preferences change to give a winning alternative under one profile additional support, then that alternative remains winning after the change. Second, amendment agendas yield only Pareto efficient alternatives (Theorem 4.4) and, third, choose the Condorcet winner when it exists.

Insofar as responsibility for choosing the committee's voting procedure rests with an interested individual (the committee chair, for example), limiting the responsibility to selecting a voting sequence for an amendment rather for an arbitrary binary agenda effectively constrains that individual's ability to manipulate the committee decision. An agenda-setter's influence over committee choice by judicious selection of a voting sequence is further limited when there is a status quo alternative. Here it is common practice to insist on considering the status quo last in any voting sequence (indeed, this is largely what gives the amendment agenda its name: first a proposal to replace the status quo is offered followed by an amended proposal and so on; second, voting is used to choose between the proposal and the amended proposal, with the winner being put against the status quo). Applying the results characterizing amendment agenda outcomes, the only alternatives capable of upsetting the status quo in such agendas are those alternatives that cover the status quo, that is, alternatives which are majority preferred to the status quo and to any alternative to which the status quo itself is majority preferred (Definition 4.5). In the case that this set is empty, therefore, agenda-setters have no influence at all and the status quo is, loosely speaking, a stable committee choice.

The example of agenda-independence for issue-by-issue voting in the preceding section (section 4.3) involves a given finite set of alternatives. But the idea of issue-by-issue voting is, as suggested earlier (section 2.7), perhaps most natural for the spatial model. Furthermore, when the set of competing alternatives is fixed the only real issue for an agenda-setter concerns the form of the agenda (amendment, successive, and so on) and the voting sequence; as such, the fixed alternative model is ill-suited for understanding why the particular set of alternatives appearing on an agenda are the ones they are and not some others. We consider these issues in Chapter 5.

4.5 Exercises

4.1 Complete the (second paragraph) argument for the Claim in the proof of Theorem 4.1 to conclude that σ_i must be dominated in $G(B)$.

4.2 Let X be a finite set of alternatives and suppose the strict majority preference relation on X for some committee is $P \in \mathcal{P}$. Assume the committee has to choose a single alternative from X and uses the following *two-stage amendment process*: X is partitioned into two subsets X_1, X_2 ($X_1 \cap X_2 = \emptyset$, $X_1 \cup X_2 = X$), and alternatives in X_1 and X_2 are ordered by, respectively, α_1 and α_2; then a single alternative, say z_1, is selected from X_1 using the amendment agenda defined by α_1 (Definition 4.3); given z_1, a single alternative, z_2, is selected from X_2 using the amendment agenda defined by α_2; finally, z_1 and z_2 are paired and a majority vote is decides which of the two is the final committee decision.

(a) Draw the voting tree for $X = \{a, b, c, x, y, z\}$, $X_1 = \{a, b, c\}$, $\alpha_1 = (a, b, c)$ and $\alpha_2 = (x, y, z)$.

(b) Assume P is such that

$$P(a) = \{x\}; P(b) = \{a, c, z\}; P(c) = \{a, y\};$$
$$P(x) = \{b, c, y\}; P(y) = \{a, b, z\}; P(z) = \{a, c, x\}.$$

Find the sophisticated outcome of the two-stage amendment process defined in part (a). Compare your answer to the sophisticated outcome under a single-stage amendment agenda on X defined by $\alpha = (a, b, c, x, y, z)$.

(c) Derive the sophisticated agenda ς (Definition 4.4) for the two-stage amendment process defined in part (a) and check whether your answer to part (b) is the same as the first alternative of this sophisticated agenda ς.

4.3 Let $P \in \mathcal{P}$ be a strict majority preference relation on (finite) X. For any two nonempty subsets $S, T \subseteq X$, define the dominance relation $\Vdash$ by: $S \Vdash T$ if and only if, for all $t \in T$, there exists an $s \in S$ such that sPt. For any $x \in X$, let $\bar{P}(x) = P^{-1}(x) \cup \{x\}$ be the union of set of alternatives that x defeats with x itself.

(a) For any $x, y \in X$, explain the connection between the statements, "xCy" and "$\{x\} \Vdash \bar{P}(y)$".

(b) Suppose a committee with majority preferences P uses a two-stage amendment process (defined in question **4.2**) to choose an alternative from X. Let $S^*(X_2)$ be the set of sophisticated voting outcomes for any orderings α_1, α_2 of the sets $X_2 \subset X$, $X_1 = X \backslash X_2$.

Prove: For all $X_2 \subset X$, $x \in X_1 \cap S^*(X_2)$ only if (i) $\{x\} \Vdash X_2$ and (ii) $x \in U(P)$.

Prove: For all $X_2 \subset X$, $x \in X_2 \cap S^*(X_2)$ only if (i) $X_2 \Vdash X_1$, (ii) yCx for no $y \in X_2$ and (iii) xPz, some $z \in X_1$.

4.4 Prove Lemma 4.1 and Corollary 4.1.

4.5 Prove Lemma 4.2.

4.6 (a) Construct an example to confirm the covering relation is asymmetric, irreflexive and incomplete.

(b) Prove Corollary 4.1 is true if $V(P)$ is replaced with either $U(P)$ or $B(P)$.

4.7 The mapping $B(\cdot)$ in Theorem 4.5 can be considered as a (non-resolute) collective choice rule, $B : \mathcal{P} \times \mathcal{X} \rightrightarrows X$, where $\mathcal{X}$ is the family of all nonempty subsets of X. Three properties that such a rule might satisfy are

Set contraction property, α: $\forall P \in \mathcal{P}$, $\forall S, V \in \mathcal{X}$,

$$S \subseteq V \Rightarrow B(P, V) \cap S \subseteq B(P, S);$$

Set contraction property ϵ: $\forall P \in \mathcal{P}$, $\forall S, V \in \mathcal{X}$,

$$S \subset V \Rightarrow \sim [B(P,V) \subset B(P,S)];$$

Path Independence, PI: $\forall P \in \mathcal{P}$, $\forall S, V \in \mathcal{X}$,

$$B(P, B(P,V)) \cup B(P, B(P,S)) = B(P, S \cup V).$$

(a) Briefly interpret each property, being careful to describe what each means for collective decision-making.

(b) For each property, prove or provide a counterexample to the claim that $B(\cdot)$ satisfies that property.

4.8 Confirm $B(P) = \{x_2, \ldots, x_6\}$ in Example 4.6.

4.9 Provide a necessary and sufficient condition for the status quo x^0 to be the agenda independent outcome for any amendment agenda $\Gamma_\alpha \in \mathcal{A}(x^0)$.

4.10 Confirm the voting behavior is as claimed for Figure 4.9.

4.6 Further reading

The seminal contribution to the strategic theory of voting over sequential binary agendas is due to Farquharson [71]. Theorem 4.1 is due to Moulin [137]. The proof here is due to Gretlein [88]; see also McKelvey and Niemi [126]. McGarvey [121] established Theorem 4.2. McKelvey and Niemi prove Theorem 4.3; see too, Miller [129]. The idea of sophisticated agendas and Lemma 4.2 is due to Shepsle and Weingast [193]. Miller [130] first defined the uncovered set for finite agendas and, *inter alia*, proved the two-step principle (Lemma 4.3) and Theorem 4.4. Banks [17] characterized the sophisticated outcomes for amendment agendas, Theorem 4.5, and supplied Example 4.6. Subsequently, the set $B(P)$ has come to be called the "Banks set". See also Moulin [139] and Banks and Bordes [19] for axiomatic analyses of the Banks set and related solution concepts. Laslier [112] and Miller [131] provide comprehensive surveys of the theory of voting in committees. In section 4.3, the application to amendment agenda independence is based on Ferejohn, Fiorina and McKelvey [78] and that to issue-by-issue agenda independence is based on Kramer [104]. The analysis of two-stage amendment agendas introduced in Exercises 4.2 and 4.3 is due to Banks [18].

Chapter 5

Spatial Voting in Committees

More often than not, a committee is a relatively small subset of individuals from a larger group, charged with making some decision on behalf of that larger group. Canonical examples include representative legislatures and legislative committees, parliamentary *ad hoc* committees, judicial committees, and so on. And while Chapter 4 concerns the structure and implications of voting over given finite sets of alternatives, a great deal of policy-making in committee is perhaps more naturally addressed with the spatial voting model, where the set of alternatives over which an agenda is defined is typically a finite selection from a (multidimensional) continuum. In this setting, a principal problem is to account for how that selection is determined given that the final collective choice from the selection is decided by application of some voting procedure. Although there are many such procedures, we restrict attention to binary agendas, so building on the results derived in Chapter 4.

As observed earlier, issue-by-issue voting is a fairly natural institution for the spatial model: there are multiple policy issues, or dimensions, each being a continuum of feasible alternatives and a reasonable way to arrive at a policy choice is to make a series of partial decisions, fixing one issue at a time, that jointly describe the final policy outcome. Indeed, a plausible (albeit somewhat coarse) description of many legislative bodies is as a collection of more-or-less autonomous committees with jurisdiction over particular policy issues. From this perspective, legislative policy outcomes are simply the composite of the various committee decisions within their respective jurisdictions and, as such, approximate legislative policy choice under issue-by-issue voting. We begin, therefore, by developing the theory of issue-by-issue agenda-formation and voting for the spatial model in some detail, subsequently going on to consider agenda-formation when committee members are unconstrained to offer only single-dimensional proposal or vote over only one policy issue at a time.

5.1 Issue-by-issue voting in the spatial model

Suppose that the set of feasible alternatives is given by a nonempty, compact and strictly convex set $X \subset \Re^k$ and that any individual i's preferences are continuous and strictly convex, $R_i \in \mathcal{R}_{cs}$, hence representable by continuous and strictly quasi-concave utility functions, $u_i : X \to \Re$ [PPTI, sect.4.3]. Thus our earlier assumption that individuals' preferences are strict on X must be relaxed. To avoid trivialities, assume X has full dimension and let $K = \{1, \ldots, k\}$ denote the set of issue dimensions.

Although the focus of this section is on issue-by-issue agendas under majority rule in the spatial model, the analysis hinges on a more widely relevant result that does not depend on majority rule; it is with this result that we begin.

Recall that for all $x \in X$ and $j \in K$, $\gamma_x(e_j)$ is a line through x parallel to the jth axis:

$$\gamma_x(e_j) = \{y \in \Re^k : y = x + te_j \text{ for some } t \in \Re\}$$

where e_j is the usual basis vector with j^{th} coordinate one and all other coordinates zero. For each issue dimension $j \in K$, let f_j denote a simple preference aggregation rule associated with dimension j [PPTI, ch.3]. Majority preference is a simple rule but not all simple rules are majoritarian, so we admit a richer class of aggregation procedures than hitherto in this chapter (in particular, the strict collective preference relation P need not be the majority preference relation). Permitting different issues to be evaluated under different rules admits the possibility that the legislature is not neutral with respect to issues. For instance, issues dealing with constitutional change are often subject to supramajority rules, whereas issues dealing with farm subsidies are decided by simple majorities.

For any $x \in X$ and $j \in K$, let $\bar{\gamma}_x(e_j) = \gamma_x(e_j) \cap X$. Any simple rule f_j is characterized by a family of decisive coalitions, $\mathcal{L}(f_j)$ (Definition 1.3). Consequently, for all distinct alternatives $y, z \in X$,

$$yPz \Leftrightarrow [\exists x \in X, \exists j \in K, \exists L \in \mathcal{L}(f_j) : y, z \in \bar{\gamma}_x(e_j) \ \&\ \forall i \in L, yP_iz].$$

5.1. ISSUE-BY-ISSUE VOTING IN THE SPATIAL MODEL

It follows that social preference may be strict if y and z differ in only one dimension, but y and z can be judged socially indifferent should they differ in more than one dimension.

Definition 5.1 *Let $\mathcal{F} = \{f_j\}_{j \in K}$ denote the family of simple rules governing changes in the k issue dimensions. An alternative $x^* \in X$ is an issue-by-issue core with respect to $\mathcal{F}$ if $x^* R y$ for all $y \in X$.*

By assumption, X is compact and convex; hence, for all $x \in X$ and $j \in K$, the set $\bar{\gamma}_x(e_j)$ is likewise compact and convex. Furthermore, since R_i is continuous and strictly quasi-concave on X, all $i \in N$, the restriction of R_i to any set $\bar{\gamma}_x(e_j)$, $R_i|_{\bar{\gamma}_x(e_j)}$, must be continuous and single-peaked. Therefore, given a profile $\rho \in \mathcal{R}_{cs}^n$, the set of core outcomes on any $\bar{\gamma}_x(e_j)$ is nonempty, convex and characterized by the set of induced f_j-medians on $\bar{\gamma}_x(e_j)$, $\mu_{f_j}(\rho|_{\bar{\gamma}_x}) \subseteq \bar{\gamma}_x(e_j)$ [PPTI, Theorems 4.5 and 5.5]. An issue-by-issue core is thus an alternative $x^* \in \cap_{j=1}^{j=k}\mu_{f_j}(\rho|_{\bar{\gamma}_{x^*}})$. Example 5.1 illustrates these ideas.

Example 5.1 Let $N = \{1, 2, 3\}$ and $X \subset \Re^2$. Assume $\rho \in \mathcal{R}_{cs}^3$ and consider Figure 5.1: individuals 1 and 3 have Euclidean preferences with ideal points as indicated and individual 2's preferences, represented by u_2, are as drawn.

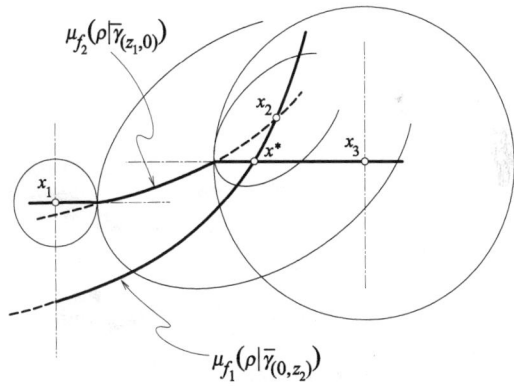

Figure 5.1: Preferences and outcomes for Example 5.1

Both f_1 and f_2 are majority rule. In this case, the induced median $\mu_{f_j}(\rho|_{\bar{\gamma}_z})$ for each j and any $z \in X$ is singleton. The graph of $\mu_{f_1}(\rho|_{\bar{\gamma}_{(0,z_2)}})$ as a function of z_2, and of $\mu_{f_2}(\rho|_{\bar{\gamma}_{(z_1,0)}})$ as a function of z_1, are illustrated in

Figure 5.1 by, respectively, the curves labeled μ_{f_1} and μ_{f_2}. It is easy to see for this example that x^* is the issue-by-issue core point: individual 2's indifference curve through x^* is tangential to the horizontal line through x^* and, therefore, there is no deviation in issue 1 alone that is preferred by any majority to x_1^*; similarly, individual 3's indifference curve through x^* is tangential to the vertical line through x^* and, therefore, there is no deviation in issue 2 alone that is preferred by any majority to x_2^*. □

Establishing the general existence of issue-by-issue core points for the spatial model requires checking a technical property of the sets $\mu_{f_j}(\rho|_{\bar{\gamma}_x})$. In Example 5.1 each set $\mu_{f_j}(\rho|_{\bar{\gamma}_z})$ is singleton for every interval $\bar{\gamma}_z(e_j)$; consequently, because $\bar{\gamma}_z(e_j)$ is completely defined by z, μ_{f_j} can be viewed as a function from X into X. In general, however, there is no reason to expect the set of induced medians to be singleton on any line through X (for instance, with $n = 4$ and distinct induced ideal points on some $\bar{\gamma}_x$, $x \in X$, the set of induced majority preference medians is a nondegenerate interval in $\bar{\gamma}_x$). Thus, the induced median mapping, μ_{f_j} is better treated as a correspondence that takes points from X into nonempty (and not necessarily singleton) subsets of X. Then the technical property we need is that such correspondences exhibit a particular form of continuity.

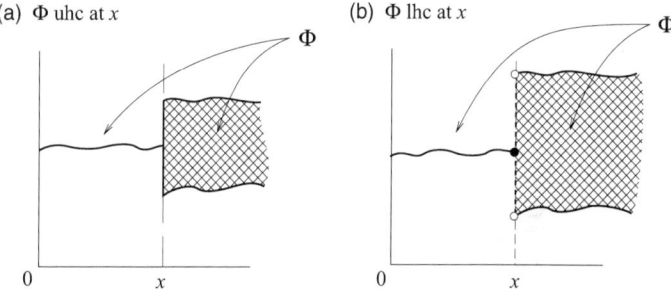

Figure 5.2: Hemicontinuity of a correspondence

Let $\Phi : Y \rightrightarrows Z$ be an arbitrary correspondence. Say that Φ is *upper hemicontinuous (uhc)* at $y \in Y$ if, for all open sets $T \subseteq Z$ such that $\Phi(y) \subset T$, there exists an open set U such that $y \in U$ and, for all $y' \in U \cap Y$, $\Phi(y') \subset T$; the correspondence Φ is *uhc* if it is uhc at every $y \in Y$. Similarly, say that Φ is *lower hemicontinuous (lhc)* at $y \in Y$ if, for all open sets $T \subseteq Z$ such that $\Phi(y) \cap T \neq \emptyset$, there exists an open set U such that $y \in U$ and, for all $y' \in U \cap Y$, $\Phi(y') \cap T \neq \emptyset$; the correspondence Φ is *lhc* if it is lhc at

5.1. ISSUE-BY-ISSUE VOTING IN THE SPATIAL MODEL 151

every $y \in Y$. Figure 5.2 above illustrates these definitions (and confirming so is left as an exercise). Finally, say Φ is *continuous* if it is both uhc and lhc. Note that if Φ is in fact single-valued, then it is a function from Y to Z and both uhc and lhc are equivalent to the usual concept of continuity of a function.

Lemma 5.1 *For all $\rho \in \mathcal{R}_{cs}^n$ and all $j \in K$, the correspondence $\mu_{f_j} : X \rightrightarrows X$ is uhc.*

Proof To save on notation, leave the profile $\rho \in \mathcal{R}_{cs}^n$ as understood and write $S_j(x) \equiv \mu_{f_j}(\rho|\bar{\gamma}_x)$. We first prove $\mu_{f_j} : X \rightrightarrows X$ has a closed graph: that is, $(x^m) \to x$, $(y^m) \to y$ and $y^m \in \mu_{f_j}(\rho|\bar{\gamma}_{x^m})$ for all m imply $y \in \mu_{f_j}(\rho|\bar{\gamma}_x)$. To see this, consider any sequences (x^m) and (y^m) from X such that $(x^m) \to x$, $(y^m) \to y$ and $y^m \in S_j(x^m)$. Suppose, contrary to the claim, $y \notin S_j(x)$. Then by definition of S_j, there exists some alternative $z \in \bar{\gamma}_x(e_j)$ such that zPy. The idea is now to show that if indeed such an alternative z can be found then, by continuity of individual preferences, we can also find an alternative $w \in \bar{\gamma}_{x^M}(e_j)$, M finite, such that wPy^M, contradicting the assumption that $y^M \in S_j(x^M)$.

Let $L \in \mathcal{L}(f_j)$ be the decisive coalition supporting the social preference zPy and, for $\lambda \in (0,1)$, let $v = \lambda z + (1-\lambda)y$. By strict convexity of preferences, vP_iy for all $i \in L$; by strict convexity of X, v is in the interior of X. Suppose there is an individual $i \in L$ for whom, for any $\delta > 0$, there exists a point y^r of the sequence (y^m) such that $|y^r - y| < \delta$ and

$$u_i(y^r) \geq u_i(y^r + v - y).$$

Then there exists a subsequence (y^l) of (y^m) such that $(y^l) \to y$ and $u_i(y^l) \geq u_i(y^l + v - y)$. By continuity of u_i, therefore,

$$u_i(y) = \lim_{l \to \infty} u_i(y^l) \geq \lim_{l \to \infty} u_i(y^l + v - y) = u_i(v).$$

But then yR_iv, contradicting $i \in L$. Hence there can exist no such individuals and, for every $i \in L$, there exists $\delta_i > 0$ such that $|y^r - y| < \delta_i$ implies $u_i(y^r + v - y) > u_i(y^r)$. Further, by L decisive under f_j,

$$\left[|y^r - y| < \delta^* \equiv \min_{i \in L} \delta_i \right] \Rightarrow [u_i(y^r + v - y) > u_i(y^r), \forall i \in L]$$
$$\Rightarrow (y^r + v - y)Py^r.$$

Figure 5.3 illustrates the situation.

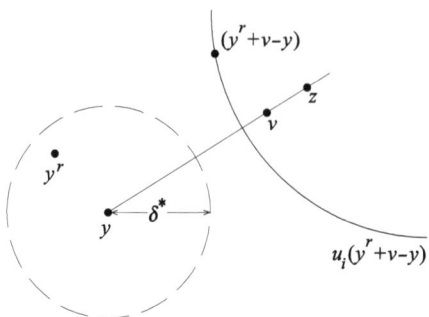

Figure 5.3: Argument for Lemma 5.1

Evidently, $\lim_{m\to\infty}(y^m + v - y) = v$ and, since v is an interior point,

$$\exists \epsilon > 0 : [\epsilon > |(y^m + v - y) - v| = |y^m - y|] \Rightarrow (y^m + v - y) \in X.$$

Moreover, we can write $y = x + te_j$, $v = x + t'e_j$ and $y^m = x^m + t''e_j$; therefore,

$$(y^m + v - y) = x^m + (t' + t'' - t)e_j$$

in which case

$$[\epsilon > |y^m - y|] \Rightarrow (y^m + v - y) \in \bar{\gamma}_{x^m}(e_j).$$

Since $(y^m) \to y$ there must be some finite M such that $|y^M - y| < \min\{\epsilon, \delta^*\}$; that is, $(y^M + v - y) \in \bar{\gamma}_{x^M}(e_j)$ and $(y^M + v - y)Py^M$. But these implications directly contradict the assumption, $y^M \in S_j(x^M)$. Hence we must have $y \in S_j(x)$ as required. Moreover, since $S_j(x) \subset X$ and X is compact, S_j having a closed graph implies $S_j(x)$ is compact.

Now suppose S_j is not uhc. Then there exists a policy x and an open set T containing $S_j(x)$ such that, for all open sets U with $x \in U$, there is an alternative $y \in U$ with $S_j(y) \not\subseteq T$. Hence there are sequences $(y^m) \to x$, $z^m \in S_j(y^m)$ with $z^m \notin T$ all m. By assumption, X is compact; therefore (z^m) has a convergent subsequence, $(z^{m_k}) \to z$. But by the preceding argument, S_j has a closed graph, so $z \in S_j(x) \subseteq T$: contradiction. □

As we vary $x \in X$ the feasible set of alternatives to x that differ only in the jth component x_j, $\bar{\gamma}_x(e_j)$, also varies and, therefore, so in principle does the set of changes from x_j sanctioned by the aggregation rule f_j, $\mu_{f_j}(\rho|\bar{\gamma}_x)$. Thus the content of the lemma is essentially that such variations in the core alternatives $\mu_{f_j}(\rho|\bar{\gamma}_x)$ on any issue dimension j exhibit at least a minimal

5.1. ISSUE-BY-ISSUE VOTING IN THE SPATIAL MODEL

amount of continuity in variations of the reference policy, x. Being so nicely behaved allows us to prove the required existence theorem.

Theorem 5.1 *For all $\rho \in \mathcal{R}_{cs}^n$ and any family of simple rules $\mathcal{F}$, there exists an issue-by-issue core relative to $\mathcal{F}$.*

Proof To prove the result, we need to show there exists an alternative x^* such that $x^* \in \cap_{j=1}^{j=k} \mu_{f_j}(\rho|\bar{\gamma}_{x^*})$. The relevant mathematical tool for the task in this case is Kakutani's Fixed Point Theorem (a proof of which can be found in Border [37, ch.15]).

(Kakutani's Fixed Point Theorem) Let $Y \subset \Re^k$ be compact and convex and suppose $\Phi : Y \rightrightarrows Y$ is an uhc correspondence such that, for all $y \in Y$, $\Phi(y) \subset Y$ is nonempty, compact and convex. Then Φ has a fixed point; that is, for some $y \in Y$, $y \in \Phi(y)$.

Again using the notation $S_j(x) \equiv \mu_{f_j}(\rho|\bar{\gamma}_x)$, define the correspondence $S : X \rightrightarrows X$ by

$$\forall x \in X, \ S(x) = \frac{1}{k}\sum_{j=1}^{j=k} S_j(x).$$

By definition, for any $x \in X$, $S(x)$ is a convex combination of nonempty convex subsets of X and, therefore, is itself nonempty and convex. By Lemma 5.1, $S_j(\cdot)$ is uhc for all $j \in K$ and, therefore, so is $S(\cdot)$. Hence, by Kakutani's Fixed Point Theorem, there exists an alternative $x^* \in S(x^*)$. We now confirm $x^* \in S_j(x^*)$ for every $j \in K$, so completing the proof. By definition of $S(\cdot)$, we can write

$$x^* = \frac{1}{k}\sum_{j=1}^{j=k} y^j$$

where, for all $j \in K$, $y^j \in S_j(x^*)$. And since $y^j \in \bar{\gamma}_{x^*}(e_j)$ each j, we have

$$y^j = x^* + t^j e_j$$

for some $t^j \in \Re$. Therefore,

$$x^* = \frac{1}{k}\sum_{j=1}^{j=k} y^j = \frac{1}{k}\sum_{j=1}^{j=k}[x^* + t^j e_j] = x^* + \frac{1}{k}\sum_{j=1}^{j=k} t^j e_j,$$

implying $\sum_{j=1}^{j=k} t^j e_j = 0$. But since the basis vectors $\{e_j\}_{j \in K}$ are linearly independent, $\sum_{j=1}^{j=k} t^j e_j = 0$ only if $t^j = 0$ for all $j \in K$. Hence, $x^* = y^j \in S_j(x^*)$ for every $j \in K$ as required. $\square$

Given the existence result, assume (unless explicitly stated otherwise) that f_j is majority rule for every dimension $j \in K$ and consider issue-by-issue agendas. Intuitively, issue-by-issue agendas in the k-dimensional spatial model work in much the same way as those in the finite setting: beginning with some status quo policy, changes in each dimension are decided serially without any possibility within the agenda of revising earlier decisions in light of later decisions; the final outcome is then defined by the composite of the k decisions. Figure 4.9 above illustrates a typical voting tree for such agendas. Unlike the finite example of section 4.3, however, the underlying set of alternatives X need not be rectangular (that is, of the form $[\underline{z}_1, \bar{z}_1] \times \ldots \times [\underline{z}_k, \bar{z}_k]$), so there is no guarantee in general that every issue-by-issue sequence connecting two arbitrary alternatives in X leads to a feasible alternative X. The definition of issue-by-issue agendas for the spatial model is complicated by this fact. An example illustrates the problem and helps motivate the definition to follow.

Example 5.2 Suppose $X \subset \Re^2$ with status quo x^0 and alternative $y \in X$ as drawn in Figure 5.4(a). Clearly x^0 and y differ on both issue dimensions.

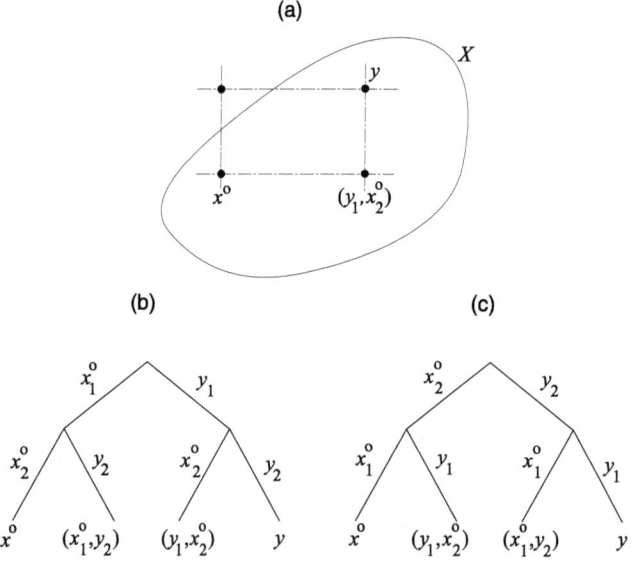

Figure 5.4: Agendas for Example 5.2

There are two possible issue-by-issue sequences to get from x^0 to y, each

5.1. ISSUE-BY-ISSUE VOTING IN THE SPATIAL MODEL 155

of which gives rise to an issue-by-issue amendment tree; these are illustrated in Figures 5.4(b) and (c). Neither of the possible binary trees constitute a legitimate binary agenda since, in each case, there is a terminal node associated with an alternative not in X: $(x_1^0, y_2) \notin X$, an inconsistency with one of the defining characteristics of binary agendas *viz.* that every terminal node must be associated with an available alternative. Of course, since X is convex and both x^0 and y are in X, there exist legitimate binary agendas connecting x^0 and y such that each decision node involves a comparison of alternatives differing in exactly one dimension; for example, vote x^0 against (y_1, x_2^0) and the winner against y. While such an agenda is well-defined, it is not an issue-by-issue agenda as understood here. □

Let $x, y \in X$ be any two policies and let

$$I(x,y) = \{j \in \{1, \ldots, k\} : x_j \neq y_j\}$$

denote the set of issue dimensions on which x and y differ. For any vector $z \in \Re^k$ and (possibly empty) subset $J \subseteq \{1, \ldots, k\} \equiv K$, define $z^J \in \Re^k$ by setting $z_j^J = z_j$ if $j \in J$ and $z_j^J = 0$ otherwise. Then given $x \in X$, an outcome of a sequential issue-by-issue procedure must be an alternative of the form $[x + (y - x)^J] \in X$ for some $y \in X$ and subset of accepted changes $J \subseteq I(x, y)$.

Definition 5.2 *An outcome $y \in X$ is a feasible alternative to $x \in X$ if, for all $J \subseteq K$, $[x + (y - x)^J] \in X$. Let $F(x)$ be the set of feasible alternatives to x.*

In Figure 5.4(a) of Example 5.2, $(y_1, x_2^0) \in F(x^0)$ but $y \notin F(x^0)$ because $[x^0 + (y - x^0)^{\{2\}}] = (x_1^0, y_2) \notin X$. And note that if X is of full dimension, as assumed throughout this section, $F(x)$ is nonempty for every $x \in X$.

Definition 5.3 *Let $X \subset \Re^k$ be compact and strictly convex. An issue-by-issue agenda relative to $x \in X$ consists of an alternative $y \in F(x)$ and a finite binary voting tree such that there exists an ordering of the issues, $\iota : \{1, \ldots, |I(x,y)|\} \to I(x,y)$, under which $y_{\iota(1)}$ is first voted against $x_{\iota(1)}$ following which $y_{\iota(2)}$ is voted against $x_{\iota(2)}$, and so on. Let $\Gamma_\iota(x, y)$ denote the issue-by-issue agenda with ordering ι and alternative $y \in F(x)$ and let $\mathcal{I}(x, y)$ denote the family of all agendas $\Gamma_\iota(x, y)$.*

Sophisticated voting over any issue-by-issue agenda $\Gamma_\iota(x, y)$ is no different from sophisticated voting over any other sort of binary agenda: given

$x \in X$ and any $y \in F(x)$, the agenda $\Gamma_\iota(x, y)$ is finite and the preceding analysis applies directly. The interesting variation admitted by the spatial model is that for any status quo policy x^0 there exists a continuum of potential alternatives $y \in F(x^0)$, each of which induces a family of possible changes from x^0 given by the set

$$\{z \in F(x^0) : z = [x^0 + (y - x^0)^J] \text{ for some } J \subseteq I(x^0, y)\}.$$

What is of particular interest here, therefore, is the alternative $y \in F(x^0)$ defining the agenda $\Gamma_\iota(x^0, y)$. In general, we might imagine the selection of such an alternative depends both on the status quo itself and on the detailed preferences of the agenda setter and the committee. Rather than make any special assumptions concerning these parameters, we instead pursue the idea of agenda-independence and look for status quo policies x^0 that are immune to change under any agenda $\Gamma_\iota(x^0, y)$.

Definition 5.4 Let $\rho \in \mathcal{R}_{cs}^n$. An alternative $x^0 \in X$ is an issue-by-issue sophisticated voting equilibrium for P_ρ if, for all $y \in F(x)$ and all $\Gamma_\iota(x^0, y) \in \mathcal{I}(x^0, y)$, $S(\Gamma_\iota(x^0, y), P_\rho) = x^0$.

Unlike for much of the fixed alternative analysis, details of the committee preference profile $\rho \in \mathcal{R}_{cs}^n$ underlying the majority preference relation P_ρ can matter in the spatial model. Before illustrating exactly how, it is useful first to establish a simple preliminary result.

Lemma 5.2 An alternative $x^0 \in X$ is an issue-by-issue sophisticated voting equilibrium for P_ρ only if x^0 is an issue-by-issue core.

Proof By Theorem 5.1, there exists an issue-by-issue core $x^* \in X$. Suppose $x^0 \in X$ is an issue-by-issue sophisticated voting equilibrium but $x^0 \neq x^*$. Then $I(x^0, x^*) \neq \emptyset$. Recall that for any $j \in I(x^0, x^*)$, $z^{(j)} = [x^0 + (x^* - x^0)^{\{j\}}]$; for any $t \in (0, 1)$, define $z^{\{j\}}(t) = [tx^0 + (1-t)z^{(j)}]$. By X strictly convex, $z^{\{j'\}}(t') \in F(x^0)$ for some $j' \in I(x^0, x^*)$ and $t' \in (0, 1)$. By definition of an issue-by-issue core, $\exists L \in \mathcal{L}(f_{j'})$ such that, $\forall i \in L$, $z^{\{j'\}}(t') P_i x^0$. But then, $\forall \Gamma_\iota(x^0, z^{\{j'\}}(t')) \in \mathcal{I}(x^0, z^{\{j'\}}(t'))$, $S(\Gamma_\iota(x^0, z^{\{j'\}}(t')), P_\rho) = z^{\{j'\}}(t')$ contradicting the supposition. □

Although the lemma does not hinge on any properties of the preference profile other than continuity and strict convexity, it establishes only a necessary condition for the existence of issue-by-issue sophisticated voting equilibria; additional properties prove salient for identifying sufficient conditions.

5.1. ISSUE-BY-ISSUE VOTING IN THE SPATIAL MODEL 157

Example 5.3 Suppose $X \subset \Re^2$ and $N = \{1, 2, 3\}$ with preferences as illustrated in Figure 5.5(a). It is easy to check that the unique issue-by-issue core alternative here is x^*. By Lemma 5.2, x^* is the only candidate for a sophisticated voting equilibrium here. Now consider $y \in F(x^*)$ as indicated in Figure 5.5(a). Let $\iota = (\iota(1), \iota(2)) = (2, 1)$ and choose $\Gamma_\iota(x^*, y) \in \mathcal{I}(x^*, y)$; Figure 5.5(b) describes the voting tree for $\Gamma_\iota(x^*, y)$.

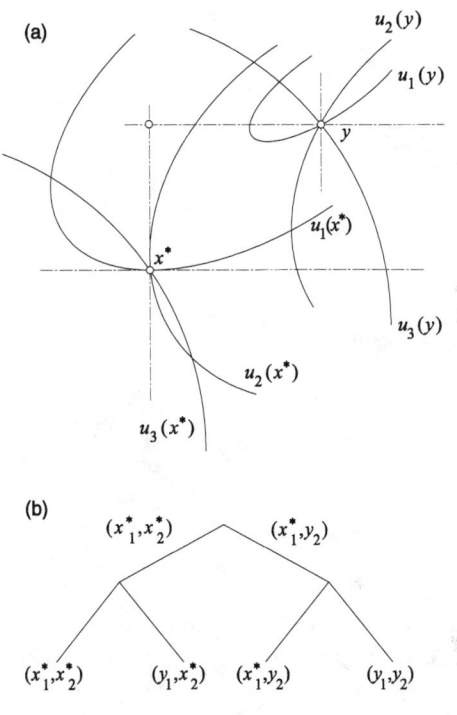

Figure 5.5: Preferences and agenda for Example 5.3

Applying the sophisticated voting algorithm for the preferences in Figure 5.5(a) yields $S(\Gamma_\iota(x^*, y), P_\rho) = y$. Hence there exists no issue-by-issue sophisticated voting equilibrium. □

The absence of a sophisticated voting equilibrium in Example 5.3 is due entirely to an individual's most preferred alternative on one issue being sensitive to decisions on the other issue; that is, individuals have nonseparable preferences (Definition 2.11). If all individuals' preferences are separable in the sense of Definition 2.11, then any individual's most preferred value for any one dimension is independent of decisions on the others. Such preferences insure that issue-by-issue core points are immune to change under issue-by-issue voting. Recall $\mathcal{R}_{sep}^n \subset \mathcal{R}_{cs}^n$ denotes the set of separable preference profiles on X.

Theorem 5.2 *Assume $\rho \in \mathcal{R}_{sep}^n$. Then there exists an issue-by-issue sophisticated voting equilibrium for P_ρ.*

Proof By Theorem 5.1, there exists an issue-by-issue core alternative $x^* \in X$ and, by Lemma 5.2, if there exists an issue-by-issue sophisticated voting equilibrium for P_ρ, say x^0, then x^0 must be such a core alternative; without loss of generality, set $x^0 = x^*$. Choose any issue-by-issue agenda $\Gamma_\iota(x^*, y) \in \mathcal{I}(x^*, y)$. By Definition 2.11, $\rho \in \mathcal{R}_{sep}^n$ implies the majority preference relation P_ρ satisfies property (**), defined in section 4.3 above, on $\Gamma_\iota(x^*, y)$. Therefore, the agenda-independence argument for the fixed alternative example of section 4.3 applies to $\Gamma_\iota(x^*, y)$ and we have $S(\Gamma_\iota(x^*, y), P_\rho) = x^*$. Hence, $x^0 = x^*$ is an issue-by-issue sophisticated voting equilibrium as required. □

Theorem 5.2 is the main result for issue-by-issue voting: so long as individual preferences are separable, there exists an alternative immune to change through issue-by-issue voting; moreover, such an alternative must be an issue-by-issue core alternative or, equivalently, an issue-by-issue median. Unfortunately, the separability restriction on spatial preference profiles is demanding and seems unlikely to obtain in many empirical settings. With the results on the existence of strategy-proof collective choice rules for the spatial model (Theorems 2.5 and 2.7), the theorem suggests that preference interdependencies across issue dimensions greatly expand the opportunity for manipulation of collective decisions, leaving any status quo policy vulnerable to change even under restrictive rules governing committee decision-making.

5.2 Application: Committees and cabinets

Decision-making in legislatures is rarely by the direct application of majority preference to the entire multidimensional policy space. In the US Congress, for example, legislative choice is decentralized to committees, each of which has some responsibility for decision-making on a subset of issues. Similarly, in parliamentary systems, coalition governments are made up of a subset of represented parties, each of which is allocated a set of issue portfolios,

5.2. APPLICATION: COMMITTEES AND CABINETS

or ministries, over which they exercise control. Legislative outcomes are then the composite of committee or ministry decisions. In other words, policy choice is built up on an essentially issue-by-issue basis with different issues being determined (at least in part) by different subsets of legislators or representatives.

Although both of these sorts of institutional arrangement have some things in common, there are differences. One of the more important differences is that any given committee tends to comprise a relatively disparate set individuals from different parties and electoral districts, whereas a parliamentary ministry tends to be monopolistically held by a more-or-less cohesive political party. So while one might imagine strategic behavior between committees to be similar to that between ministries, intra-committee and intra-ministry decision-making are likely to look rather different. Such a substantive distinction between committee and parliamentary institutions suggests differences in how each might best be modeled. In the remainder of this section, then, we apply the theoretical results for issue-by-issue voting separately to the two institutions, beginning with a committee system for a majoritarian legislature.

Assume the policy space is $X \subset \Re^k$, where X is a compact and strictly convex set with dimension k, and that legislative choice is decentralized to committees, each of which has some responsibility for decision-making on a subset of issues from $K = \{1, \ldots, k\}$. Because the existence of a nonempty core in two and higher dimensions is unlikely [PPTI, ch.5], suppose that no legislative committee has responsibility over more than one issue dimension. So assume $n \geq k$ and define a *committee system* to be a pair $(\{N_j\}_{j \in K}, \mathcal{F})$, where $\{N_j\}_{j \in K}$ is a family of k disjoint subsets of N such that N_j is nonempty for all $j \in K$ and $\mathcal{F} = \{f_j\}_{j \in K}$ is a family of simple rules. Because N_j is nonempty for all $j \in K$, every issue is assigned to at least one individual and, because $N_j \cap N_l = \emptyset$ for all distinct $j, l \in K$, no individual is assigned to more than a single issue; it may be, however, that $\cup_{j \in K} N_j \subset N$ in which case there are individuals in N who are members of no subset N_j. The set N_j is the *committee*, assigned to issue j and the family of subsets $\{N_j\}_{j \in K}$ is the *committee assignment*. For convenience, suppose $|N_j|$ is odd for all $j \in K$ and say that issue j is the *jurisdiction* of committee N_j.

Because the committee assignment insures no legislator is a member of more than one committee, an assumption that any given committee makes its decisions taking the decisions of all other committees as given is well-defined. So assume that for each $j \in K$, committee N_j takes the decisions of other committees as given and determines the policy decision within its jurisdiction using the simple rule $f_j \in \mathcal{F}$ (where it is understood that f_j is defined with respect to N_j). More precisely, let $\rho \in \mathcal{R}_{cs}^n$ be the preference profile of all legislators and, for any $j \in K$, let x_{-j} denote a vector of issue decisions by committees other than N_j. The set of feasible alternatives for N_j at x_{-j} is given by $F_j(x_{-j}) = \{y \in X : y_{-j} = x_{-j}\}$. Given x_{-j}, let $C_{f_j}(\rho_{N_j}; x_{-j}) \subseteq F_j(x_{-j})$ denote the core of f_j at ρ_{N_j} [PPTI, Definition 4.5]: $y \in C_{f_j}(\cdot)$ implies there is no feasible alternative strictly preferred by a decisive coalition $L \in \mathcal{L}(f_j)$.

Definition 5.5 *An outcome $x^* \in X$ is a committee equilibrium for the system $(\{N_j\}_{j \in K}, \mathcal{F})$ at ρ if $x^* \in \cap_{j=1}^{j=k} C_{f_j}(\rho_{N_j}; x_{-j}^*)$.*

In other words, a committee equilibrium is an alternative such that no decisive coalition of any committee can implement a preferred outcome.

Corollary 5.1 *For all $\rho \in \mathcal{R}_{cs}^n$ and all committee systems $(\{N_j\}_{j \in K}, \mathcal{F})$, there exists a committee equilibrium for $(\{N_j\}_{j \in K}, \mathcal{F})$ at ρ.*

Proof Consider any $j \in K$ and x_{-j}. Because $\rho \in \mathcal{R}_{cs}^n$, the restriction of ρ_{N_j} to $F_j(x_{-j})$ is single-peaked and, therefore, $C_{f_j}(\rho_{N_j}; x_{-j})$ is the set of induced f_j-medians for N_j on $\bar{\gamma}_x(e_j)$. Hence, $x^* \in X$ is a committee equilibrium for $(\{N_j\}_{j \in K}, \mathcal{F})$ at ρ if and only if x^* is an issue-by-issue core alternative with respect to $\mathcal{F}$. Applying Theorem 5.1, therefore, yields the result. $\square$

A key feature of the decision-making procedure supporting Corollary 5.1 is that, at least strategically, committees make their respective decisions simultaneously. Although there are certainly circumstances under which such an assumption is justified, they are not typical. More often than not, at least some legislative committees are required to report decisions to the legislature as a whole before others, in which case rational members of such committees can be expected to condition any decision within their jurisdictions on the best responses of committees reporting later. The existence result assured by Corollary 5.1 does not generally extend to this institutional variation, as the next example shows.

Example 5.4 Let $X \subset \Re^2$, $\rho \in \mathcal{R}_{cs}^n$ and assume f_j is simple majority rule, each $j \in \{1, 2\}$ (and to avoid irrelevant complications, let n be even for this example). Assume the committee system $(\{N_j\}_{j \in K}, \{f_1, f_2\})$ has $N_1 = \{1, 2, 3\}$ and $N_2 = N \backslash N_1$. The preferences of individuals in N_1 are illustrated in Figure 5.6 below: individuals 1 and 3 have Euclidean preferences and individual 2 has nonseparable preferences over X. Suppose further that the profile $\rho \in \mathcal{R}_{cs}^n$ implies the locus of core allocations for N_2 as a function

5.2. APPLICATION: COMMITTEES AND CABINETS   161

of x_1, $C_{f_2}(\rho_{N_2}; z_1)$, is illustrated by $\mu_{f_2}(z_1)$ in Figure 5.6 (that such preferences exist should be clear from Example 5.1). Then x^* is the committee equilibrium.

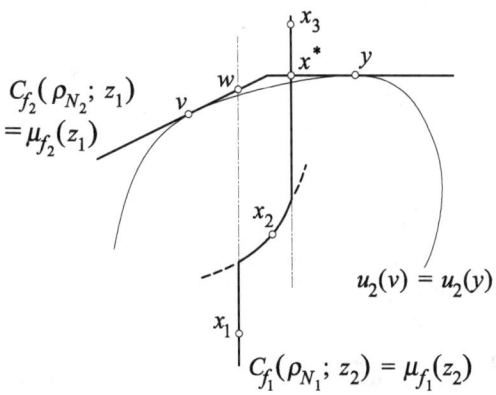

Figure 5.6: Committee equilibrium for Example 5.6

Now suppose the legislative decision-making rules have N_1 first fix the policy component, x_1, following which N_2 chooses the remaining component, x_2, to determine the legislative outcome $x \in X$. It is no longer reasonable to presume N_1 treats the subsequent policy choice of N_2 as fixed; instead, rational N_1-committee members recognize the dependency of $C_{f_2}(\rho_{N_2}; z_1)$, and thereby the final legislative policy outcome, on their initial decision. In other words, the relevant prediction for the decisions of rational N_1-committee members over their jurisdiction is not, as under simultaneous committee decision-making, the set $C_{f_1}(\rho_{N_1}; z_2)$, but rather the set $C_{f_1}(\rho_{N_1}; \mu_{f_2}(z_1))$. Because $\mu_{f_2}(z_1) \equiv C_{f_2}(\rho_{N_2}; z_1)$ unequivocally characterizes the N_2-committee decision once N_1 has fixed x_1, a *sequential committee equilibrium* can be defined here as an alternative $x^{**} = (x_1^{**}, x_2^{**}) \in X$ such that $x_2^{**} = \mu_{f_2}(x_1^{**})$ and $x_1^{**} = C_{f_1}(\rho_{N_1}; \mu_{f_2}(x_1^{**}))$.

We claim there is no sequential committee equilibrium in the example. To see this, consider Figure 5.7, below. In this diagram, we graph the induced preferences of N_1-committee members over the set $\mu_{f_2}(z_1)$. Referring to Figure 5.6, we find that while the induced issue-1 preferences for individuals 1 and 3 are single-peaked, those for individual 2 are not. As shown in Figure 5.6, individual 2 has an indifference curve tangential to the induced issue-1 median line at two distinct points, v and y, such that $v_1 < x_2 < y_1$, so 2's induced preferences over the first issue have two maxima. On the other hand, individuals 1 and 3 have single-peaked induced preferences over the issue, with peaks w_1 and x_3^* respectively, lying between v_1 and y_1.

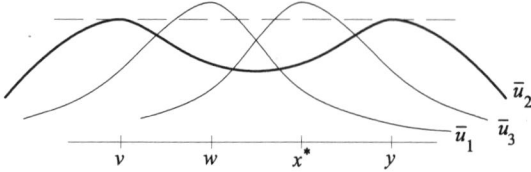

Figure 5.7: Induced preferences over $\mu_{f_2}(z_1)$

It is not hard, then, to confirm that there is no Condorcet winner in $\mu_{f_2}(z_1)$ for N_1 [Exercise]; in other words, since f_1 is majority rule for N_1, there exists no sequential committee equilibrium. □

In common with establishing the existence of sophisticated voting equilibria, the difficulty with insuring existence for a sequential committee equilibrium in the example is due to nonseparable preferences. With separability (that is, $\rho \in \mathcal{R}_{sep}^n$), all individuals' most preferred positions for any dimension are independent of those for any other dimension and, therefore, core allocations $C_{f_j}(\rho_{N_j}; x_{-j})$ are independent of x_{-j} for all $j \in K$ and all committee systems $(\{N_j\}_{j \in K}, \mathcal{F})$. Consequently, irrespective of whether committees choose within their jurisdictions simultaneously or sequentially, there exists a (sequential) committee equilibrium. Unlike for sophisticated voting equilibria, however, committee equilibria need not be Condorcet consistent despite separable preferences; that is, a profile $\rho \in \mathcal{R}_{sep}^n$ can support a majority (not simply an issue-by-issue) core alternative, yet this alternative need not be the committee equilibrium.

Example 5.5 Let $X \subset \Re^3$ be rectangular; let $n = 9$ and let f be simple majority rule. Assume all individuals have Euclidean preferences, so $\rho \in \mathcal{R}_{sep}^n$, with ideal points in X: $x^1 = (0,0,0)$, $x^2 = x^3 = (1,0,0)$, $x^4 = x^5 = (-1,0,0)$, $x^6 = (0,1,0)$, $x^7 = (0,-1,0)$, $x^8 = (0,0,1)$ and $x^9 = (0,0,-1)$. Then the majority core for the entire legislature is $C_f(\rho) = \{(0,0,0)\}$. Now suppose the committee system $(\{N_j\}_{j \in K}, \{f, f, f\})$ has $N_1 = \{1,2,3\}$; then whatever the composition of the remaining two committees, the committee equilibrium x^* must have first component $x_1^* = 1$ insuring $x^* \notin C_f(\rho)$. On the other hand, suppose the committee system is $(\{N_j'\}_{j \in K}, \{f, f, f\})$ with $N_1' = \{1,2,4\}$, $N_2' = \{3,6,7\}$, and $N_3' = \{5,8,9\}$. Then the committee equilibrium is the core alternative, $x^{**} = (0,0,0)$. The reason why the

5.2. APPLICATION: COMMITTEES AND CABINETS

committee system ($\{N_j\}_{j\in K}, \{f,f,f\}$) fails to support the underlying core alternative is that the individual with ideal point equal to this alternative, that is $i = 1$, is not the median member of N_1 with respect to the committee's jurisdiction; under ($\{N'_j\}_{j\in K}, \{f,f,f\}$), however, individual 1 is the median member of N'_1. $\square$

As observed above, committee systems are not the only legislative organizations in which decision-making is decentralized among legislators by issue. Parliamentary democracies typically exhibit similar institutions although, in parliaments, the locus of control is more at the party, as opposed to the individual, level. In common with the committee system, each dimension of the policy space in a parliamentary system is associated with a different "ministry", or portfolio. Unlike a committee system, however, in a parliamentary system a single party, rather than a collection of independent legislators, controls any given ministry. Consequently, assuming parties can be treated as unitary actors, this concentration of decision-making power at the portfolio level allows a party to control more than one ministry, thereby having a multidimensional jurisdiction.

We finesse questions of intraparty behavior and imagine a parliament N of n fully coordinated parties, with each party $i \in N$ having preferences representable by a strictly quasi-concave utility u_i on the policy space X. Define an *issue allocation* as a mapping $\omega : N \to 2^K$ such that

$$\cup_{i \in N} \omega(i) = K \text{ and, for all } i, j \in N, \ \omega(i) \cap \omega(j) = \emptyset.$$

So every issue is allocated to at most one party and $\omega(i) \subseteq K$ is the set of issues allocated to party $i \in N$. Let Ω denote the set of issue allocations and, for each $\omega \in \Omega$, define the *governing coalition* N_ω to be the set of parties holding at least one issue portfolio,

$$N_\omega = \{i \in N : \omega(i) \neq \emptyset\}.$$

Assume that each party of the governing coalition only uses Nash equilibrium strategies, monopolistically selecting issue positions within their portfolios while taking the choices of other coalition members as given. Formally, for any $i \in N_\omega$ and $x \in X$ let

$$F_i^\omega(x) = \{y \in X : \text{for some } \{t^j\}_{j \in \omega(i)} \subset \Re, \ y = x + \sum_{j \in \omega(i)} t^j e_j\}$$

describe the set of feasible changes in x under the control of party i with issue allocation $\omega(i)$.

164   CHAPTER 5. SPATIAL VOTING IN COMMITTEES

Definition 5.6 *An outcome $x^* \in X$ is an ω-monopoly equilibrium for the issue allocation ω at ρ if x^* is such that, for all $i \in N_\omega$ and all $y \in F_i^\omega(x^*)$, $u_i(x^*) \geq u_i(y)$.*

The key distinction between this definition and that of a committee equilibrium is that the latter exploits the (cooperative) structure of intra-committee decision-making by a preference aggregation rule, whereas the former is entirely in terms of (noncooperative) strategic Nash behavior by parties. So the assumptions that no individual belongs to more than one committee and no committee has jurisdiction over more than one issue dimension, results in committee equilibria being issue-by-issue core alternatives. But when a heterogenous collection of unitary actors each make decisions on several dimensions, there is no assurance that the resulting Nash equilibrium outcome, an ω-monopoly equilibrium, is any sort of core alternative. In particular, although unitary parties hold monopoly decision-making power over their respective portfolios, the existence of an ω-monopoly equilibrium is complicated by the possibility that X is not a rectangular set; this implies that not only is a party's set of best response decisions conditioned on the decisions of others, but also that the set of *feasible* decisions over issues within its control can itself depend on the decisions of others. For example, suppose $n = k = 2$ and X is a disc in $\Re^2$ centered at the origin with radius one, as in Figure 5.8.

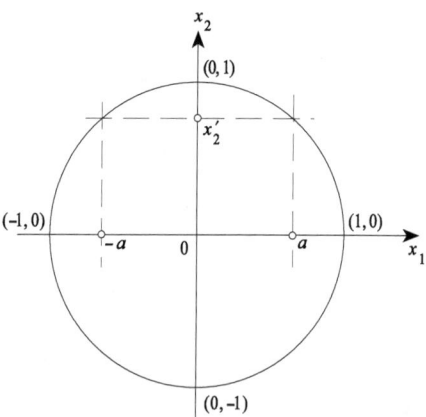

Figure 5.8: Interdependency of feasible decisions

Assume $N_\omega = \{1, 2\}$ and $\omega(i) = i$, $i \in N_\omega$; then the set of all possible decisions by, say, party 1 is given by $[-1, 1]$. But not all of these decisions

5.2. APPLICATION: COMMITTEES AND CABINETS

are available to 1 for some choices of party 2; for instance, if, as illustrated in the figure, 2 chooses x'_2, the feasible set for party 1 is $[-a, a]$.

The setting illustrated in Figure 5.8 is of course possible for the committee system model. Indeed, the heart of the proof for Theorem 5.1, which underlies the existence result for committee equilibria, is to insure that the core on any one issue is suitably continuous in the decisions on other issues and the argument nowhere used any assumption that X is rectangular. On the other hand, the argument certainly used the assumption that issue dimensions could be treated separately with decisions for each being core alternatives; thus there was no consideration of individuals' strategic behavior to justify selection of one-dimensional core alternatives. Sidestepping the individual (party) level strategic behavior in the case of ω-monopoly equilibria is not possible: by definition, an ω-monopoly equilibrium is the consequence of a set of mutually consistent, strategically rational best responses by parties exerting monopoly control over portfolios within their respective jurisdictions. However, a simple modification of the argument for Theorem 5.1 serves to prove existence here too.

Theorem 5.3 *There exists an ω-monopoly equilibrium for all $\rho \in \mathcal{R}_{cs}^n$ and all issue allocations $\omega \in \Omega$.*

Proof For any $x \in X$ and any $i \in N_\omega$, the set $F_i^\omega(x)$ is the intersection of X with the dimensions of the policy space $\omega(i)$ through x and, by assumption, X is nonempty, convex and compact. Therefore, $F_i^\omega(x)$ is similarly nonempty, convex and compact. Now for each $i \in N_\omega$ and $x \in X$, define the set of utility-maximizing choices of i at x

$$S_i^\omega(x) = \arg\max[u_i(y) : y \in F_i^\omega(x)].$$

Weierstrass' Theorem [197, Theorem 3.1] states that any continuous real-valued function on a compact set achieves a maximum and a minimum on that set. Since u_i is continuous and $F_i^\omega(x)$ compact, therefore, $S_i^\omega(x)$ is nonempty for all $x \in X$. Furthermore, by u_i strictly quasi-concave and $F_i^\omega(x)$ convex, $S_i^\omega(x)$ is convex. Finally, since the correspondence $F_i^\omega : X \rightrightarrows X$ is evidently continuous, the Maximum Theorem [197, Theorem 9.14] implies $S_i^\omega : X \rightrightarrows X$ is uhc. Define the correspondence

$$\forall x \in X, \ S^\omega(x) = \frac{1}{|N_\omega|} \sum_{i \in N_\omega} S_i^\omega(x).$$

By definition, for any $x \in X$, $S^\omega(x)$ is a convex combination of nonempty convex subsets of X and, therefore, is itself nonempty and convex. Because, for all $i \in K$, the correspondence $S_i^\omega(\cdot)$ is uhc, so is $S^\omega(\cdot)$. Hence, by Kakutani's Fixed Point Theorem, there exists an alternative $x^* \in S^\omega(x^*)$. We now confirm $x^* \in S_i^\omega(x^*)$ for every $i \in N_\omega$, completing the proof. By definition of $S^\omega(\cdot)$, we can write

$$x^* = \frac{1}{|N_\omega|} \sum_{i \in N_\omega} y_i$$

where, for all $i \in N_\omega$, $y_i \in S_i^\omega(x^*)$. And since $S_i^\omega(x^*) \subseteq F_i^\omega(x^*)$ each i, we have

$$y_i = x^* + \sum_{j \in \omega(i)} t^j e_j$$

for some $\{t^j\}_{j \in \omega(i)} \subset \Re$. Therefore,

$$\begin{aligned} x^* &= \frac{1}{|N_\omega|} \sum_{i \in N_\omega} \left[x^* + \sum_{j \in \omega(i)} t^j e_j \right] \\ &= x^* + \frac{1}{|N_\omega|} \sum_{i \in N_\omega} \sum_{j \in \omega(i)} t^j e_j \\ &= x^* + \frac{1}{|N_\omega|} \sum_{j=1}^{j=k} t^j e_j \end{aligned}$$

implying $\sum_{j=1}^{j=k} t^j e_j = 0$. But since the basis vectors $\{e_j\}_{j \in K}$ are linearly independent, $\sum_{j=1}^{j=k} t^j e_j = 0$ only if $t^j = 0$ for all $j \in K$. Hence, for every $i \in N_\omega$, $x^* = y_i \in S_i^\omega(x^*)$. □

Example 5.6 Let $X \subset \Re^7$ be rectangular. Assume $\rho \in \mathcal{R}_{sep}^n$ with $n \geq 3$ and let $\omega(1) = \{1,3,4\}$, $\omega(2) = \{2,5\}$ and $\omega(3) = \{6,7\}$. Then $N_\omega = \{1,2,3\}$ and, by separable preferences, each party $i \in N_\omega$ has a dominant strategy to choose its most preferred position within its feasible set, $F_i^\omega(\cdot)$. Let x^i be party i's ideal point; by X rectangular, any admixture of party ideal points is an alternative in X and, therefore, the ω-monopoly equilibrium here is simply $x^* = (x_1^1, x_2^2, x_3^1, x_4^1, x_5^2, x_6^3, x_7^3)$. Evidently, there is no reason to suppose x^* is an issue-by-issue median for the parliament as a whole. □

5.3 Endogenous agendas

The analysis of issue-by-issue voting in the spatial model introduced some degree of endogenous agenda formation. In Theorem 5.2 for example, the

5.3. ENDOGENOUS AGENDAS

status quo x^0 is given and anchors one end of a voting sequence, but the alternatives comprising any given issue-by-issue agenda $\Gamma_\iota(x^0, y)$ depend on the choice of some alternative $y \in F(x^0)$; variations in y induce variations in the qualitative and quantitative character of the set of possible final outcomes. And under the committee system, each component of a final legislative choice is chosen according to some (possibly) issue-specific preference aggregation rule by subsets of voters. Indeed, although we assume committee-level decisions on given issues are determined by direct preference aggregation, the associated assumption of single-dimensional jurisdictions admits a more strategic model of intra-committee decision-making. Specifically, given any feasible set of changes $F_j(x_{-j})$ for committee N_j, we could imagine an open proposal procedure within the committee whereby each committee member $i \in N_j$ offers an alternative $y_j^i \in F_j(x_{-j})$ for consideration as the committee's decision; the committee choice from among the $|N_j|$ proposals $\{y_j^i\}$ is then decided by voting over these proposals under some binary agenda. Because individuals' induced preferences are single-peaked over $F_j(x_{-j})$ there is necessarily a Condorcet winner $y^* \in \{y_j^i\}$; by Corollary 4.1, therefore, y^* is surely the sophisticated outcome of any such agenda. Moreover, if preferences are separable the Condorcet winner in any committee is the median committee member's ideal position over the relevant jurisdiction, implying Corollary 5.1 extends to this setting [Exercise].

The suggestion that committee decisions are themselves voting outcomes of some binary agenda over a set of endogenous proposals from committee members, raises a more general question: What if anything can be said about the pattern of endogenous proposals and subsequent voting behavior when the set of conceivable alternatives for committee consideration is the full k-dimensional set $X \subset \Re^k$ rather than some one-dimensional subset of X? To address this question it is useful first to introduce another refinement of the underlying Nash equilibrium concept. An example motivates why.

Example 5.7 Consider a committee of at least five individuals, two of whom have the right to suggest an agenda to decide from the finite set of alternatives $X = \{w, x, y, z\}$. Let individuals 1 and 2 be the agenda-setters and suppose the committee procedure is as follows. *First*, individual 1 proposes an alternative $a \in \{w, x\}$; *second*, given a, individual 2 proposes an alternative $b \in \{y, z\}$; and *third*, the committee majority votes over $\{a, b\}$. Assume the majority preference relation has wPy, zPw, yPx and xPz, and let the agenda-setters' preferences be

$$[wP_1 y P_1 x P_1 z] \text{ and } [x P_2 y P_2 w P_2 z].$$

Assume all individuals vote sincerely, the unique undominated voting strategy here, and consider the proposal strategy-pair

$$(\pi_1, \pi_2) = ([propose\ x],\ [\forall a \in \{w, x\},\ propose\ z]).$$

These strategies are Nash equilibrium behavior. To check this, first note that given individual 1 proposes x, then proposing z is the best 2 can do since it results in the agenda $\{x, z\}$ and, under sincere voting, 2's best outcome x; and given individual 2 proposes z whatever 1 does, proposing x to induce final outcome x is strictly better for individual 1 than proposing w which results in 1's worst outcome z.

A little reflection suggests the equilibrium strategy-pair (π_1, π_2) is not very compelling. Suppose individual 1 knows 2 to be rational and also knows her preferences; then he might reason that if in fact 1 proposes alternative w at the first stage then 2 would not do what she claims (propose z) here because, if she did follow through and propose z, then z would win resulting in 2's worst outcome. Rather, 1 might sensibly conjecture that if confronted with an effective choice between final outcomes w or z, 2 would propose y to induce w. In other words, the strategy π_2, while surely a Nash best response to π_1, is not credible. □

Assuming the argument above is persuasive, it says that "satisfactory" Nash equilibrium predictions for sequential games should not, in contrast to the strategy-pair (π_1, π_2) of Example 5.7 for instance, involve incredible threats. In Example 5.7, there is another Nash equilibrium strategy-pair; that is

$$(\pi_1', \pi_2') = ([propose\ w],\ [(propose\ y\ if\ a = w), (propose\ z\ if\ a = x)]).$$

The equilibrium outcome here is w and, unlike the equilibrium pair (π_1, π_2), the second ($i = 2$) proposer's best response π_2' specifies using an optimal decision (best response) for 2 at *each* of her decision nodes; under (π_1, π_2), 2 only uses a best response "along the equilibrium path", that is, only at 2's decision node "$a = x$" as specified by π_1.

The equilibrium refinement that serves to exclude incredible threats is that of *subgame perfection*. To make the refinement a little more precise, we need to introduce the important idea of a mechanism in *extensive form*. The main distinguishing feature of a mechanism in extensive form is that not all individuals' choices are strategically simultaneous. That is, a mechanism $(\mathcal{M}, g)$ is in extensive form if at least one individual $i \in N$ makes at least some choice having observed a choice of at least one distinct individual $j \in N$. The proposal sequence of Example 5.7 is an example of

5.3. ENDOGENOUS AGENDAS

such an extensive form mechanism; individual 2 makes her decision having seen individual 1's choice. Other examples include binary voting agendas and sequential public roll-call votes over a pair of alternatives: the former are extensive form mechanisms in which everyone votes simultaneously at any decision node having observed all the previous votes (including their own), while the latter permit those casting their vote later in the roll-call sequence to observe the earlier votes. On the other hand, a binary committee vote in which individuals simply write down their choice on a piece of paper and serially hand this ballot to a committee chair for counting is not an extensive form mechanism: all strategically relevant choices are made simultaneously. When a preference profile ρ over final outcomes is specified, the pair $((\mathcal{M}, g), \rho)$ is an *extensive form game*; thus binary voting games (γ_Γ, ρ) are extensive form games.

Just as binary agendas can be usefully illustrated with voting trees, extensive form mechanisms can be depicted figuratively with *game trees*. A game tree shows the sequence of possible decisions, identifies which individuals are to make what choices at any and all decision nodes, and so on. For example, the game tree for the procedure of Example 5.7 is illustrated in Figure 5.9: individual $i = 1$ makes the initial move (or chooses the first action), proposing either w or x, following which individual $i = 2$ proposes either y or z with, as indicated in the diagram, 2's choice possibly contingent on 1's opening move.

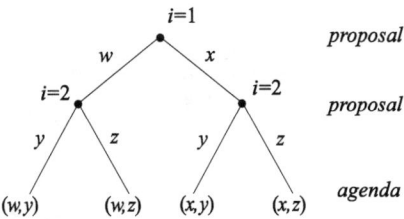

Figure 5.9: Game tree for Example 5.7

And if the procedure illustrated in Figure 5.9 is augmented by having a committee chairperson first choose which of individuals 1 and 2 is to offer the initial proposal, we obtain the game tree of Figure 5.10. This tree essentially differs from Figure 5.9 only in the inclusion of the Chair's move, identifying the first proposer.

170   CHAPTER 5. SPATIAL VOTING IN COMMITTEES

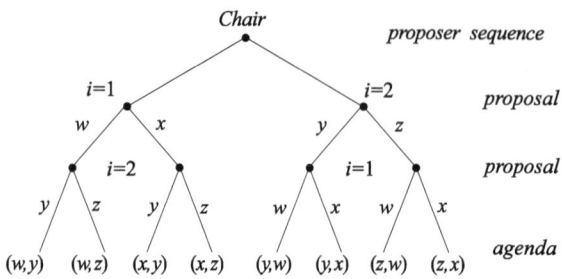

Figure 5.10: Augmenting Example 5.7

As a final illustration, we note that a binary voting tree is simply a particular sort of game tree in which each decision node is associated with all committee members (typically left understood) "moving", that is, voting simultaneously over the alternatives associated with each branch from the node, and each terminal node identifies the final committee decision under the sequence of votes leading to that node.

When decisions are made sequentially, it is particularly important to be clear about what exactly the decision maker knows at the time of his or her choice. Here we maintain the assumption of full and complete information about preferences, the history of past decisions and so on. In particular, in an extensive form game with full information there is never any ambiguity about which decision node has been reached: in Example 5.7 individual 2 knows for sure which alternative 1 chose and what is to happen following her own decision; similarly, in a full information amendment agenda game every individual knows exactly the node at which the committee is voting and the final outcomes that can emerge following the committee's current vote. Consequently, once any particular decision node λ of a full information extensive form game $G = ((\mathcal{M}, g), \rho)$ has been reached, the situation from that point on is itself a self-contained extensive form game G_λ with initial node λ and, for each individual $i \in N$, an action set $\mathcal{M}_i^\lambda$ defined by the restriction of $\mathcal{M}_i$ to the decision nodes of G_λ; the game G_λ is a *subgame* of G. Indeed, every decision node λ of any full and complete information extensive form game G defines a subgame G_λ of G with initial decision node λ. Because the initial node of any extensive form game is a decision node, it follows that the whole game is a subgame of itself; subgames associated with decision nodes following the initial node are *proper* subgames. In Figure 5.11(a), for instance, an arbitrary extensive form game is drawn and the three proper subgames are described in Figures 5.11(b), (c) and (d).

5.3. ENDOGENOUS AGENDAS

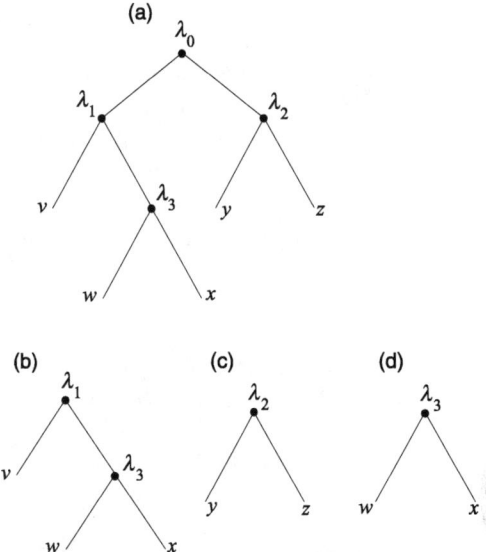

Figure 5.11: A game and its subgames

Finally, recall from section 4.1 above that a strategy for any individual in a voting game is a mapping that describes how that individual votes at each and every decision node. We make the same requirement for individual strategies in more general extensive form games. Specifically, a strategy for an individual in any extensive form game is a complete description of the choices the individual makes at every decision node where the individual has any choice to make. Insisting on strategies being explicit about decisions under all circumstances (that is, at every logically possible decision node) is not an unnecessary formalism; equilibrium behavior is contingent on what happens out of equilibrium. For instance, individual 1's choice of $a = x$ (the strategy π_1) in Example 5.7 is a best response to σ_2 precisely because of what 2 does when $a = w$, an unreached decision node in the equilibrium (π_1, π_2).

Definition 5.7 *Let $G = ((\mathcal{M}, g), \rho)$ be an extensive form game, $\rho \in \mathcal{R}^n$, and let $\sigma^*(\rho)$ be a Nash equilibrium for G. Then $\sigma^*(\rho)$ is (undominated) subgame perfect if the restriction of $\sigma^*(\rho)$ to every subgame of G constitutes a (undominated) Nash equilibrium for that subgame.*

In words, a Nash equilibrium σ^* for an extensive form game is a strategy profile specifying all individual actions at every decision node with the property that, for each individual $i \in N$, i's strategy σ_i^* is a best response to the profile of others' strategies, σ_{-i}^*; for the profile to be subgame perfect, it is further required that the restriction of σ_i^* to every subgame is likewise a best response to the similarly restricted profile σ_{-i}^*. Thus the equilibrium profile (π_1, π_2) of Example 5.7 is not subgame perfect: the restriction of π_2 to the (trivial) subgame beginning at the node "$a = w$" requires 2 to propose z, which is evidently not a best response for 2 conditional on finding herself at this node. A more abstract example is the following.

Example 5.8 Consider the extensive form game G summarized in Figure 5.12, where the outcome associated with each terminal node of the game tree is defined in terms of the payoffs (u_1, u_2) to individuals 1 and 2 respectively.

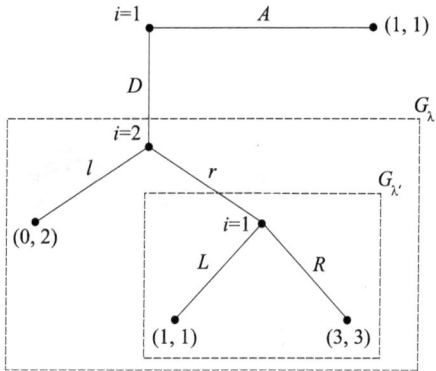

Figure 5.12: The game G

The feasible strategy sets for the two individuals are

$$\mathcal{M}_1 = \{(D, L), (D, R), (A, L), (A, R)\},$$
$$\mathcal{M}_2 = \{l, r\}.$$

There are three Nash equilibria $\sigma = (\sigma_1, \sigma_2) \in \mathcal{M}_1 \times \mathcal{M}_2$ to G:

$$\sigma^* = ((A, L), l); \ \sigma^{**} = ((A, R), l); \text{ and } \sigma^{***} = ((D, R), r).$$

To check σ^* and σ^{**} are both Nash equilibria note that, given $\sigma_2^* = l$, the best 1 can do is play A at his first decision node to obtain a payoff of one rather than zero and, given 1 chooses A, no subsequent decision nodes are

5.3. ENDOGENOUS AGENDAS

reached, so specifying 2 plays l is as good as anything else since 2 receives payoff one in any case; similarly, given 2 plays l, 1 is indifferent between L or R at the final decision node. That σ^{***} is also a Nash equilibrium follows easily from the observation that it yields the unique best payoff for each individual. Moreover, we claim σ^{***} is the only subgame perfect Nash equilibrium to G.

To see that σ^* and σ^{**} are not subgame perfect, consider the two proper subgames, G_λ and $G_{\lambda'}$, in turn. The restriction of σ^* to G_λ is the strategy pair (L, l) which is easily checked to be a Nash equilibrium for G_λ. On the other hand, the restriction of σ^* to $G_{\lambda'}$ is the decision "L" for individual 1, which is clearly not a best response at this decision node. Thus σ^* is not a subgame perfect equilibrium strategy profile for G. Similar reasoning shows σ^{**} is not subgame perfect: here, the restriction of σ^{**} to the (trivial) subgame $G_{\lambda'}$ has individual 1 choosing a best response, but then the restriction of σ^{**} to the subgame G_λ is not a Nash equilibrium for G_λ. This is because individual 2 choosing l is not a best response in G_λ to 1's choice of R, despite the fact that $\sigma_2^{**} = l$ is a best response in G to $\sigma_1^{**} = (A, R)$. Finally, it is easy to check that σ^{***} is a subgame perfect Nash equilibrium to G as claimed. □

We now return to the problem of endogenous agenda-setting. A committee has to select an alternative from the (compact and strictly convex) feasible set $X \subset \Re^k$; for the moment, assume there is no status quo policy. Let $\rho \in \mathcal{R}_{cs}^n$ be the committee preference profile over X. The alternatives on the committee's agenda are proposed by members of the committee, with each member suggesting exactly one distinct alternative for consideration. Suppose committee rules require "proposing forward and voting backwards". Specifically, there is a fixed ordering of individuals $\alpha^{-1} : N \to \{1, \ldots, n\}$ (by seniority, for instance) in which individuals may propose alternatives and, once every individual has added an alternative to the agenda, the committee's final choice is determined by applying the amendment agenda Γ_α to the resulting set of proposals. Thus the voting sequence is given by the reverse of the proposal sequence: $\Gamma_\alpha = \Gamma_{(\alpha^{-1})^{-1}}$.

Example 5.9 Suppose $N = \{1, 2, 3\}$ and α^{-1} such that

$$\alpha^{-1}(1) = 2; \ \alpha^{-1}(2) = 3; \ \alpha^{-1}(3) = 1.$$

In words, under the ordering α^{-1}, $i = 3$ offers the first proposal, $i = 1$ makes the next proposal and $i = 2$ offers the final proposal. Let $y_{\alpha^{-1}(j)} \in X$ be individual j's proposal, $j \in N$. Then α^{-1} yields a proposal sequence

$$(y_{\alpha^{-1}(3)}, y_{\alpha^{-1}(1)}, y_{\alpha^{-1}(2)}) = (y_3, y_1, y_2).$$

The voting sequence for Γ_α is therefore (y_2, y_1, y_3); that is, "y_2 vs. y_1, the winner against y_3". □

Hereon, label N to insure that for all $j \in \{1, \ldots, n\}$, $\alpha^{-1}(j) = j$ so $\alpha(j) = [n+1-j]$. Reintroducing the possibility of a status quo policy x^0 and adopting the notational convention $x^0 \equiv y_0$, the sequence of proposals under α^{-1} is therefore $(y_0, y_1, \ldots, y_n)$ implying an agenda $\Gamma_\alpha \in \mathcal{A}(x^0)$ with voting sequence $(y_n, \ldots, y_1, y_0)$. Individuals are not obliged to offer alternatives when given the opportunity to do so, instead they can "pass". If $i \in N$ passes at the proposal stage, set $y_i = \emptyset$ and say that i offers the null proposal. Similarly, we write $x^0 = \emptyset$ to denote the absence of a status quo policy.

For each individual i, i's strategy σ_i is a pair (π_i, v_i). The first component, π_i, is i's *proposal strategy* and specifies an alternative y_i to add to the agenda as a function of those proposals already made, including the status quo, $x^0 \in [X \cup \{\emptyset\}]$. Specifically, for all individuals $i \in N$, i's proposal strategy is a map

$$\pi_i : [X \cup \{\emptyset\}]^i \to [X \cup \{\emptyset\}] \setminus \{y_j : j < i \text{ and } y_j \neq \emptyset\}.$$

So, reflecting the usual rules governing construction of amendment agendas, no individual is permitted to propose an alternative already placed on the agenda. In the event that some proposals are null, the effective amendment agenda over which the committee votes is defined by deleting the null proposals from the sequence and keeping the relative ordering of the non-null proposals the same. For instance, if the proposal stage yields $(y_0, y_1, y_2, y_3, y_4) = (\emptyset, y_1, \emptyset, y_3, y_4)$, the amendment agenda becomes (y_4, y_3, y_1). To avoid unnecessarily cluttering the notation, however, we leave this procedure as understood and write amendment agendas as if there are no null proposals. The second component, v_i, of i's strategy is a *voting strategy*, specifying how i votes at any decision node of any agenda resulting from individuals' proposal decisions.

An equilibrium $\sigma = (\pi, v)$ to the agenda-setting game is a subgame perfect profile of proposal strategies $\pi = (\pi_1, \ldots, \pi_n)$ and a profile of undominated voting strategies $v = (v_1, \ldots, v_n)$. Unlike the finite case with strict preferences, however, the possibility of indifference at any decision node in the spatial model can cause difficulties for proving the existence of subgame perfect Nash equilibria. Example 5.10 illustrates the problem.

5.3. ENDOGENOUS AGENDAS

Example 5.10 Let $N = \{1, 2, 3\}$ and individuals have preferences as indicated in Figure 5.13; assume there is no status quo alternative and y_1 is as shown. Consider individual 2's best response, $\pi_2(y_1)$.

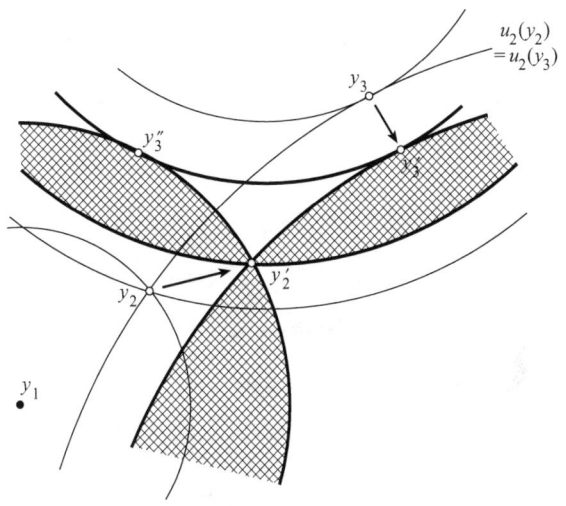

Figure 5.13: Preferences and proposals

Suppose 2 chooses the alternative y_2. Then 3's best response is $\pi_3(y_1, y_2) = y_3$; although individual 2 is indifferent between y_2 and y_3, subgame perfection requires 2 to vote surely for y_3 here. To see why, suppose 2 votes for y_3 with some probability strictly less than one; then 3 can improve his payoff by proposing an alternative w arbitrarily close to y_3 but strictly interior to the set $P(y_2) = \{x \in X : xPy_2\}$, in which case 2's best response is to vote surely for w. But then 3 cannot be optimizing: $P(y_2)$ is an open set implying that there is always something better for 3 than any alternative strictly interior to $P(y_2)$. In other words, a voting strategy in which 2 fails to vote surely for 3's proposal when indifferent cannot be part of a subgame perfect equilibrium. On the other hand, since 2 voting surely for y_3 against y_2 when indifferent is an optimal decision for 2, the only pair of mutually consistent (subgame perfect) best response decisions by 2 and 3 here has 3 proposing y_3 on the boundary of $P(y_2)$ and 2 voting surely for y_3 against y_2.

Given the proposal sequence (y_1, y_2, y_3), the voting sequence is (y_3, y_2, y_1) and the preceding argument (along with inspection of Figure 5.13) yields the final outcome y_3. Now consider a sequence of proposals $(y_2^t) \to y_2'$ with $y_2^0 = y_2$ as indicated in the figure. The associated sequence of best response proposals by 3 is then $(y_3^t) \to y_3'$ and the final committee choice for each t is y_3^t. Clearly, individual 2's payoff from the eventual committee decision is strictly improving as $t \to \infty$. However, whereas 3's best response proposal is uniquely defined at every finite step t, the nonconvexity in the sets $P(y_2^t)$ results in 3 indifferent between proposing y_3' and proposing y_3'' when we proceed to the limit. And if 3 in fact proposes y_3'' rather than y_3' in response to y_2', then 2's payoff is discontinuous at y_2', taking a downwards jump. But then, for similar reasons as discussed earlier regarding voting behavior when indifferent, if there is any chance that 3 responds to y_2' with y_3'', 2 improves her payoff by proposing some y_2^t arbitrarily close to y_2'; thus there is no well defined best response for 2 in this case. Again, the difficulty can be fixed by requiring 3 to propose the alternative most favored by 2 whenever 3 is indifferent over several possible best response proposals to the alternatives already offered by 1 and 2.

If we now ask how individual 1 should respond to the postulated strategies for 2 and 3, we again run into similar indifference possibilities at both the proposal and voting stages but the same resolutions may not be available. In particular, having 3 break a tie at the proposal stage in favor of 2 can result in 1, who has to take explicit account of the subsequent behavior of *both* individuals 2 and 3, having no consistent best-response proposal. □

Establishing existence of (undominated) subgame perfect Nash equilibria for the endogenous agenda-setting game amounts to checking there is always some suitable combination of mutually consistent and best response tie-breaking decisions of the sort discussed in Example 5.10. For individuals 2 and 3 in that example, the tie-breaking decisions involved 2 always voting for 3's proposal against her own whenever indifferent, and having 3 always propose 2's most preferred alternative from among 3's best responses to (y_1, y_2'). With more than two individuals, however, more combinations of tie-breaking decision at both proposal and voting stages are necessary. That they are also feasible is the content of Theorem 5.4, the argument for which is constructive and rather long. The underlying idea, however, is straightforward.

To prove the theorem, we have to find a sequence of proposals starting with the status quo y_0 for which there exists a voting equilibrium such that, given expectations regarding this voting equilibrium, every proposal is indeed optimal for the relevant proposer. Along with the technical complication of insuring all individuals have well-defined best-response strategies,

5.3. ENDOGENOUS AGENDAS

the principal difficulty in the construction is to specify what happens off the equilibrium path; that is, the profile of strategies has to insure that if any individual deviates from the prescribed path, either by making an unexpected proposal or by casting an unexpected vote, then subsequent decisions by others must be both (credible) best responses and, relative to the equilibrium outcome, induce a worse final committee decision for the deviant. To do this, we begin with the final proposer and, given the other proposals and a specified pattern of voting, we can identify the set of alternatives that that individual ($i = n$) can induce as final committee decisions by a suitable proposal. Once this set is described, we can then go back a stage and similarly identify those proposals that the penultimate proposer can induce as final choices by suitably choosing an alternative to affect the final proposer's decision. And so on.

Theorem 5.4 *Assume all individuals have continuous preferences over X. Then there exists an undominated subgame perfect equilibrium to the endogenous amendment agenda game.*

Proof Given a profile of continuous preferences, $\rho \in \mathcal{R}^n$, let P denote the associated strict majority preference relation on X. For any $i \leq n - 1$, let $(y_0, y_1, \ldots, y_i)$ be any list of $i + 1$ proposals, including the status quo y_0. Given $\{y_0, y_1, \ldots, y_i\}$ is finite, there surely exists an undominated voting equilibrium to the partial agenda $y^i = (y_i, \ldots, y_1, y_0)$. However, because individuals can be indifferent over alternatives, the restriction of P to $\{y_0, y_1, \ldots, y_i\}$ can be incomplete. The sophisticated agenda for y^i is thus not well-defined and, therefore, the set of possible undominated voting equilibrium outcomes need not be singleton, the multiplicity arising from various tie-breaking assumptions.

Let $\zeta_i = \zeta(y^i)$ be a possible equilibrium voting outcome for the partial agenda y^i (in Example 5.10, for instance, $\zeta_3 = \zeta((y'_3, y'_2, y_1))$ is either y'_3 or y'_2 depending on the way 2 breaks her indifference between y'_3 and y'_2); call ζ_i the *provisional choice* for y^i. Now set $i = n - 1$ and consider individual n's proposal decision, y_n. Given proposals $(y_0, y_1, \ldots, y_{n-1})$, assume $z^{n-1} = (\zeta_{n-1}, \zeta_{n-2}, \ldots, \zeta_0)$ describes the equilibrium voting outcomes from each partial agenda y^j, $j = 0, \ldots, n - 1$. Then given undominated voting behavior and Lemma 4.2, y_n is surely the final committee choice if $y_n \in \cap_{j=0}^{j=n-1} P(\zeta_j)$ and ζ_{n-1} is surely the committee choice if $y_n = \emptyset$. Thus, given z^{n-1}, individual n can guarantee a final payoff of at least

$$\underline{u}_n(z^{n-1}) = \sup\{u_n(x) : x \in \cap_{j=0}^{j=n-1} P(\zeta_j) \text{ or } x = \zeta_{n-1}\}.$$

Because $\cap_{j=0}^{j=n-1} P(\zeta_j)$ is open, $\underline{u}_n$ is lower semi-continuous (where $\underline{u}_n$ is lower semi-continuous at x if, for any sequence $(x^m) \to x$, $\liminf_{m\to\infty} \underline{u}_n(x^m) \geq \underline{u}_n(x)$; loosely speaking, any discontinuity in $\underline{u}_n$ must be a jump down to $\underline{u}_n(\zeta_{n-1})$). Now define the set of outcomes giving at least $\underline{u}_n(z^{n-1})$ to $i = n$:

$$B_n(z^{n-1}) = \{x \in [\cap_{j=0}^{j=n-1} R(\zeta_j)] \cup \{\zeta_{n-1}\} : u_n(x) \geq \underline{u}_n(z^{n-1})\}$$

where $R(x) = \{y \in X : yRx\}$. By assumption, X is compact and u_n continuous; so, by $\cap_{j=0}^{j=n-1} R(\zeta_j)$ closed and $\underline{u}_n$ lower semi-continuous, B_n is nonempty, compact and has a closed graph. Thus, given the preceding proposals and the expected voting behavior on each voting subgame defined by the $n - 1$ partial agendas y^i, $i = 1, \ldots, n - 1$, B_n describes the set of alternatives achievable by n as equilibrium outcomes.

For every $x \in B_n(z^{n-1})$, define

$$s_n^x(y_n | z^{n-1}) = \begin{cases} y_n & \text{if } y_n \in [\cap_{j=0}^{j=n-1} P(\zeta_j)] \cup \{x\} \\ \zeta_{n-1} & \text{otherwise} \end{cases}.$$

In words, the alternative s_n^x is the nth individual's proposal y_n if either y_n is strictly majority preferred to all previous provisional choices or if $y_n = x$ (note that $x \in \cap_{j=0}^{j=n-1} P(\zeta_j)$ is possible), otherwise s_n^x is the provisional choice for y^{n-1}. The idea here is that in the case x is indifferent (under majority preferences) to at least one preceding provisional choice from the historically given sequence of proposals, the relevant indifferent voters are assigned to support n's proposal when x is proposed by n. Thus choosing s_n^x is consistent with all individuals using undominated voting strategies over the agenda $y^n = (y^{n-1}, y_n)$ and, furthermore, s_n^x is an optimal outcome for n given y^{n-1} and the postulated voting behavior. (Note that if the strict majority preference relation P is complete on $\{y_0, \ldots, y_n\}$, then s_n^x is simply the sophisticated outcome of the final agenda y^n.)

Now we proceed inductively, considering each individual $i = n - 1, n - 2, \ldots, 1$ in sequence. Given an agenda y^{i-1}, define

$$\underline{u}_i(z^{i-1}) = \sup_w \min_x \{u_i(x) : x \in B_{i+1}(z^{i-1}, w) \ \& \ w \in [\cap_{j=0}^{j=i-1} P(\zeta_j)] \cup \{\zeta_{i-1}\}\};$$

then

$$\begin{aligned} B_i(z^{i-1}) &= \{x \in X : \exists w \in [\cap_{j=0}^{j=i-1} R(\zeta_j)] \cup \{\zeta_{i-1}\} \text{ with} \\ x &\in B_{i+1}(z^{i-1}, w) \ \& \ u_i(x) \geq \underline{u}_i(z^{i-1})\} \end{aligned}$$

5.3. ENDOGENOUS AGENDAS

is the set of optimal final outcomes achievable by i. We assume for the moment that the min operation for $\underline{u}_i$ is well-defined and that B_i is nonempty. By construction, for all $x \in B_i(z^{i-1})$ there is an alternative $p_i^x \in [\cap_{j=0}^{j=i-1} R(\zeta_j)] \cup \{\zeta_{i-1}\}$ with $x \in B_n(z^{i-1}, p_i^x)$; that is, an alternative x is available as a final outcome for i only if there is some alternative p_i^x that is at least as good as all of the preceding $i-1$ provisional choices which, if proposed by i, renders x an optimal achievable outcome for the final proposer, n. Thus define the ith provisional choice,

$$s_i^x(y_i|z^{i-1}) = \begin{cases} y_i & \text{if } y_i \in [\cap_{j=0}^{j=i-1} P(\zeta_j)] \cup \{p_i^x\} \\ \zeta_{i-1} & \text{otherwise} \end{cases}$$

As with individual n's proposal the provisional choice for $y^i = (y^{i-1}, y_i)$ is ζ_{i-1} unless i either offers an alternative that is strictly preferred to all preceding provisional choices, or offers the alternative p_i^x (an alternative at least as good as all preceding provisional choices), in which case the provisional choice is y_i. (Again, if P is complete on the agenda y^i then s_i^x is the sophisticated outcome of the partial agenda y^i.)

For any alternative $w \in [\cap_{j=0}^{j=i-1} P(\zeta_j)] \cup \{\zeta_{i-1}\}$, let $w' \in B_n(z^{i-1}, w)$ be such that $u_i(w') \leq u_i(x)$, where x is the alternative intended (in this construction) as the final committee choice; that such alternatives w' exist follows from $[\cap_{j=0}^{j=n-1} P(\zeta_j)]$ open. Define

$$o_i^x(y_i|z^{i-1}) = \begin{cases} x & \text{if } y_i = p_i^x \\ y_i' & \text{if } y_i \in [\cap_{j=0}^{j=i-1} P(\zeta_j)] \setminus \{p_i^x\} \\ \zeta_{i-1}' & \text{otherwise} \end{cases}$$

Thus $o_i^x(y_i|z^{i-1})$ describes the final outcome of the agenda process conditional on i's proposal, given all preceding provisional choices and the subsequent proposal decisions of individuals $i+1$ through n. For instance, if $i = n-1$ then, other things equal, n is taken to propose $y_n = x$ in response to a proposal $y_{n-1} = p_{n-1}^x$ but otherwise propose $y_n = y'_{n-1}$ or (as appropriate) some alternative ζ'_{n-2} no better for individual $n-1$ than ζ_{n-2}; in each case, the alternative that n is expected to propose is in fact optimal for n, that is, an element of $B_n(z^{n-2}, y_{n-1})$. Given the anticipated voting behavior on the voting subgame, therefore, proposing $y_i = p_i^x$ is an optimal response for all $i \leq n-1$.

Let $x \in B_1(y^0)$; that is, given subsequent proposal and (implicitly) voting behavior as described above, x is an optimal alternative for the first proposer given the initial "agenda" $y^0 = (y_0)$. To obtain x as a subgame perfect equilibrium outcome, first specify undominated equilibrium voting behavior for an arbitrary list of proposals, $(y_1, \ldots, y_n)$. The agenda $\Gamma_\alpha(y_0)$ is given by the voting sequence $(y_n, \ldots, y_1, y_0)$; either $x \in \{y_0, y_1, \ldots, y_n\}$ or not. Set $\hat{\zeta}_0 = y_0$ and define the desired outcome and provisional choice consequent on 1's proposal y_1 to be, respectively,

$$\hat{y}_1 = o_1^x(y_1|\hat{z}^0)$$

and

$$\hat{\zeta}_1 = s_1^x(y_1|\hat{z}^0).$$

By definition of the functions $o_1^x(y_1|\hat{z}^0)$ and $s_1^x(y_1|\hat{z}^0)$, $\hat{y}_1 = \hat{\zeta}_1 = x$ if y_1 was chosen appropriately but, should individual 1 have offered any alternative other than that supporting a final outcome x, then $o_1^x(y_1|\hat{z}^0)$ yields a committee choice that is at most as good as the outcome x for individual 1. Moreover, s_1^x is such that all individuals are using undominated best response voting strategies at the final decision nodes of $\Gamma_\alpha(y_0)$. Similarly, for each individual $i = 2, \ldots, n$, the desired outcome and provisional choice consequent on i's proposal y_i are, respectively,

$$\hat{y}_i = o_i^{x_{i-1}}(y_i|\hat{z}^{i-1})$$

and

$$\hat{\zeta}_i = s_i^{x_{i-1}}(y_i|\hat{z}^{i-1})$$

where x_{i-1} is the desired outcome after the proposal y_{i-1}, and we set $x_1 = x$. Note that if, at each proposal y_i, individual i has indeed proposed as required to support x as the final outcome, then $x_{i-1} = x$ for all i. And irrespective of whether or not the proposal sequence does support x, the voting strategies implicit in the definitions of $o_i^{x_{i-1}}$ and $s_i^{x_{i-1}}$ constitute undominated equilibrium profiles on each voting subgame of $\Gamma_\alpha(y_0)$. Furthermore, identification of $\hat{y}_i$ at each step depends only on the proposals $(y_0, \ldots, y_i)$.

Now for each $i \in N$, consider $\hat{z}^{i-1} = (\hat{\zeta}_0, \ldots, \hat{\zeta}_{i-1})$ as defined and have individual i propose the alternative $y_i = p_i^{x_{i-1}}$, where x_{i-1} is the desired outcome after the proposal y_{i-1} and $p_i^{x_{i-1}}$ is as defined above. By construction of the mappings B_i, the resulting sequence of proposals,

$$(y_0, y_1, \ldots, y_n) = (y_0, p_1^x, p_2^x, \ldots, p_n^x = x),$$

is optimal given expectations that the voting behavior is as described above. And under this voting behavior, the associated sequence of provisional choices for the agenda $(y_0, y_1, \ldots, y_n)$ is indeed

$$(\hat{\zeta}_0, \hat{\zeta}_1, \ldots, \hat{\zeta}_n) = (y_0, \hat{y}_1, \hat{y}_2, \ldots, \hat{y}_n = x)$$

5.3. ENDOGENOUS AGENDAS

with final committee outcome x.

To complete the proof we have to justify the technical working assumption, for each $i \in N$, that the min operation for $\underline{u}_i$ is well-defined and that B_i is nonempty. The first assumption follows if B_i has a closed graph and it has already been shown that B_n is nonempty and has a closed graph. Exploiting this fact, the argument for $i < n$ is by induction. Accordingly, assume that, for some $i \geq 2$, B_i is nonempty and has a closed graph; we check this implies B_{i-1} is likewise nonempty and has a closed graph. To see $B_{i-1}(z^{i-2}) \neq \emptyset$, consider sequences (x^m) and (w^m) such that, for all m, $w^m \in [\cap_{j=0}^{j=i-2} P(\zeta_j)] \cup \{\zeta_{i-2}\}$ and

$$x^m \in \arg\min\{u_{i-1}(x) : x \in B_i(z^{i-2}, w^m)\}$$

with $\underline{u}_{i-1}(z^{i-2}) = \lim_{m \to \infty} u_{i-1}(x^m)$. Because B_i is compact by hypothesis, the min operator here is well-defined. By X compact, we can find alternatives $\bar{x}, \bar{w} \in X$ such that $(x^m) \to \bar{x}$ and $(w^m) \to \bar{w}$ (taking subsequences as required). Since $R(\cdot)$ is closed, $\bar{w} \in [\cap_{j=0}^{j=i-2} R(\zeta_j)] \cup \{\zeta_{i-2}\}$ and, since B_i has a closed graph by hypothesis, $\bar{x} \in B_i(z^{i-2}, \bar{w})$. Since u_{i-1} is continuous, $u_{i-1}(\bar{x}) = \underline{u}_{i-1}(z^{i-2})$; that is, $\bar{x} \in B_{i-1}(z^{i-2})$ so $B_{i-1}(z^{i-2}) \neq \emptyset$.

To show B_{i-1} has a closed graph, take any sequences $((\zeta_0^m, \ldots, \zeta_{i-2}^m))$ and (x^m) such that $x^m \in B_{i-1}(\zeta_0^m, \ldots, \zeta_{i-2}^m)$ for all m, $((\zeta_0^m, \ldots, \zeta_{i-2}^m)) \to z^{i-2}$ and $(x^m) \to \bar{x}$. For each m there exists $w^m \in [\cap_{j=0}^{j=i-2} R(\zeta_j^m)] \cup \{\zeta_{i-2}^m\}$ such that $x^m \in B_i(\zeta_0^m, \ldots, \zeta_{i-2}^m, w^m)$. By X compact, there is no loss in generality in assuming $(w^m) \to \bar{w} \in X$. Since $R(\cdot)$ is closed, $\bar{w} \in [\cap_{j=0}^{j=i-2} R(\zeta_j)] \cup \{\zeta_{i-2}\}$ and, since B_i has a closed graph by hypothesis, $\bar{x} \in B_i(z^{i-2}, \bar{w})$. We now need to show $u_{i-1}(\bar{x}) \geq \underline{u}_{i-1}(z^{i-2})$. Since $u_{i-1}(x^m) \geq \underline{u}_{i-1}(\zeta_0^m, \ldots, \zeta_{i-2}^m)$ for all m (by definition of B_{i-1}) and u_{i-1} is continuous, the inequality obtains if $\underline{u}_{i-1}$ is lower semi-continuous. By u_{i-1} continuous and X compact, B_i closed implies

$$u_{i-1}^*(z^{i-2}, w) = \min_x \{u_{i-1}(x) : x \in B_i(z^{i-2}, w)\}$$

is lower semi-continuous [2, Lemma 16.30]. And with $P(\cdot)$ open, u_{i-1}^* lower semi-continuous implies

$$\underline{u}_{i-1}(z^{i-2}) = \sup_w \{u_{i-1}^*(z^{i-2}, w) : w \in [\cap_{j=0}^{j=i-2} P(\zeta_j)] \cup \{\zeta_{i-2}\}\}$$

is lower semi-continuous [2, Lemma 16.29]. Hence, B_{i-1} has a closed graph.

Thus B_i nonempty and closed implies B_{i-1} nonempty and closed, $i \geq 2$. Because B_n is already shown nonempty and closed, this completes the proof. □

It is worth emphasizing that the argument for Theorem 5.4 exploits only the continuity assumption on individual preferences and does not depend at all on preferences being convex. Hence the result can be applied to committee decisions in which the set of alternatives, X, is not a set of final outcomes but a set of intermediate decisions. For example, committee members might ultimately be concerned and have preferences defined over some measures of collective "security" and "health"; their decision problem, however, is to choose among policies such as defense and vaccination programs intended to promote "security" and "health". In such cases, individuals' decision-relevant preferences are induced from their preferences over final outcomes and their understandings of how various policies contribute to promoting those outcomes. And while preferences over levels of "security" and "health" may well be strictly convex, individuals' induced preferences over defense and vaccination programs may exhibit nonconvexities (because, for instance, sharing limited resources between the two programs results in both being ineffective whereas a focus on only one program results in progress on at least that issue).

Theorem 5.4 insures the existence of undominated subgame perfect equilibrium outcomes to the endogenous amendment agenda-setting process. It does not, however, identify what those outcomes might be. Although a complete characterization is unavailable, it is not hard to see that if there exist a unique majority core policy then this is implementable with an endogenous amendment agenda mechanism. Specifically, recall that the majority core for a profile $\rho \in \mathcal{R}^n$ is the set of alternatives $x \in X$ for which there exist no distinct alternatives $y \in X$ such that $yP_\rho x$ [PPTI, Definition 4.5]. Then the following is true.

Theorem 5.5 *If x is the unique majority core alternative for $\rho \in \mathcal{R}^n$, then x is the unique undominated subgame perfect equilibrium outcome to the endogenous amendment agenda game.*

Proof [Exercise.] □

The intuition for the result is easy to see. Suppose, to the contrary, that some policy y not in the core is the collective choice. By definition, a core alternative cannot be beaten in any pairwise majority choice. Hence there must be an individual i who at least weakly prefers a core policy, say x, to y; but then i would do better by proposing x rather than the proposal consisting with y being the eventual choice. And this contradicts i using an optimal strategy given others' behavior.

5.3. ENDOGENOUS AGENDAS

When n is odd and all individuals' preferences are strictly convex, then the majority core is necessarily singleton. But this is not generally the case and Theorem 5.5 leaves open the possibility that, when there are several core policies, there exist subgame perfect equilibria to the agenda-setting game with outcomes outside of the core; Example 5.11 shows that this can in fact occur.

Example 5.11 Let the set of alternatives be an interval, $X = [w, v]$ and suppose $N = \{1, 2, 3\}$. Assume individual 1 is indifferent over all alternatives, so $u_1(a) = 0$ for every $a \in X$; individuals 2 and 3, however, have single-peaked preferences over the interval as illustrated in Figure 5.14.

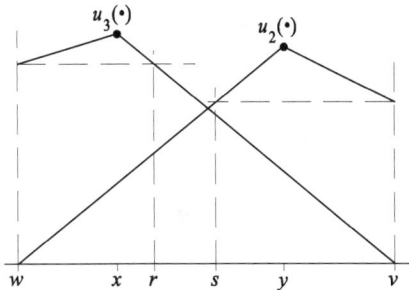

Figure 5.14: Preferences for Example 5.11

This profile is weakly single-peaked and the majority core is the interval $[x, y]$. Assume v is the status quo policy and that individual 1 proposes y; since 1 is indifferent over all outcomes, her proposal is necessarily a best response to any subsequent decisions of individuals 2 and 3. Now consider any proposal sequence (v, y, a, b), where a and b are, respectively, 2's and 3's proposals. By assumption, no individual can propose a non-null alternative that is already on the agenda. In particular, neither a nor b can be v or y and $a \neq \emptyset$ implies $b \neq a$. Let voting behavior over the agenda (b, a, y, v) yield provisional choices (v, y, ζ_2, ζ_3) where

$$\zeta_2 = \begin{cases} w & \text{if } a = w \\ y & \text{otherwise} \end{cases}$$

and

$$\zeta_3 = \begin{cases} w & \text{if } b = \emptyset \text{ and } a = w \\ w & \text{if } b = w \text{ and } a \neq w \\ y & \text{otherwise} \end{cases}.$$

Because individual 1 is indifferent over all pairs of alternatives, the voting behavior implicit in the specification of the list of provisional choices constitutes an undominated voting equilibrium on all of the possible voting subgames (confirming this fact is left as an exercise). Given this voting behavior and $u_3(w) > u_3(y)$, choosing $b = w$ is evidently 3's best response for all proposals $a \neq w$ and, if $a = w$, choosing $b = \emptyset$ is a best response. Consequently, individual 2 can have no influence on the final outcome in which case proposing $a = x$ or passing, $a = \emptyset$ is a best response for 2. The subgame perfect equilibrium outcome for these strategies, therefore, is w, an alternative not in the core. Finally, observe that allowing repeated proposals (for example, admitting $a = b$ and so on) makes no difference here. □

The equilibrium outcome, w, in Example 5.11 is not in the Pareto set, either for the alternatives comprising the equilibrium agenda $\{v, y, x, w\}$ or for the policy space as a whole X: both individuals 2 and 3 strictly prefer x to w and individual 1 is indifferent. Thus the example is in apparent contradiction to Theorem 4.4, above, which claims that all equilibrium outcomes from a finite amendment agenda must be Pareto efficient. The difference is that not all individuals' preferences in Example 5.11 are strict; thus the assumption of strict preference profiles is essential for Theorem 4.4. In the case of an exogenously given agenda, such an assumption reflects the typical situation. When the agenda is chosen endogenously from a continuum, however, indifference is intrinsic and can be consequential.

5.4 Application: Sophisticated sincerity

Insofar as sophisticated voting behavior reflects rational calculation on the part of elected legislators, it is of some interest to identify circumstances under which sincere and sophisticated voting offer different predictions regarding legislators' vote records. Were it the case that agendas are given exogenously to legislators for consideration, such circumstances would in principle be relatively straightforward to find. However, such exogeneity is rarely the case: legislative alternatives typically arise through legislative discussion in which case rational individuals take account of the likely consequences at any vote of adding one rather than another alternative to the agenda. And what this implies for observed voting patterns is not immediately apparent.

Confining attention to amendment agendas, let $\sigma = (\pi, v)$ be an equilibrium strategy profile for the endogenous amendment agenda game with preferences $\rho \in \mathcal{R}_{cs}^n$; assume no two individuals have identical preferences and

5.4. APPLICATION: SOPHISTICATED SINCERITY 185

denote the amendment agenda associated with π by $y^n(\pi) = (y_n, \ldots, y_1, y_0)$. Recall that an individual $i \in N$ is said to vote sincerely over a pair of alternatives $\{a, b\}$ at any decision node if $aP_i b$ implies i votes for a against b at that node.

Theorem 5.6 *Assume $\rho \in \mathcal{R}_{cs}^n$ and suppose there is no Condorcet winner in X. Let $\sigma^* = (\pi^*, v^*)$ be any subgame perfect equilibrium to the endogenous amendment agenda game. Then all individuals vote sincerely on $y^n(\pi^*)$.*

Proof The sequence of equilibrium proposals under σ^* is $(y_0^*, y_1^*, \ldots, y_n^*)$, yielding an amendment agenda $y^n(\pi^*) = (y_n^*, \ldots, y_1^*, y_0^*)$. Without loss of generality, assume y_i^* non-null for all i (otherwise, consider the reduced agenda with null proposals removed). By the proof to Theorem 5.4, for all $i = 1, \ldots, n$,

$$y_i^* \in \cap_{j=0}^{j=i-1} R(y_j^*). \tag{$\dagger$}$$

Consider the amendment agenda voting tree for $y^n(\pi^*)$ and let λ be any final decision node of the tree; that is, a node involving a vote between y_0^* and y_i^* for $i > 0$. Because individual voting strategies must be undominated in equilibrium, any individual with a strict preference between y_0^* and y_i^* votes sincerely at λ under v^*. And in the event that there is no strict majority preference over the alternatives $\{y_0^*, y_i^*\}$, v^* specifies an appropriate tie-breaking decision for the indifferent individuals. Thus v^* induces a strict preference relation P^* for every final decision node of the agenda $y^n(\pi^*)$, where P^* is more resolute than the strict majority preference relation, P, induced by $\rho \in \mathcal{R}_{cs}^n$; that is, for any final decision over a pair (y_0^*, y_i^*), $y_i^* P y_0^*$ implies $y_i^* P^* y_0^*$ and $y_0^* P y_i^*$ implies $y_0^* P^* y_i^*$. Define the P^*-sophisticated equivalent of λ to be the preferred alternative from $\{y_0^*, y_i^*\}$ under P^*. Deleting the terminal nodes of the voting tree and replacing the final decision nodes with their respective P^*-sophisticated equivalents defines a pruned tree that coincides with the original tree up to the specification of the terminal nodes (now given by the relevant P^*-sophisticated equivalents); repeating the same argument, we can replace the final decision nodes of the pruned tree with their P^*-sophisticated equivalents, where P^* is induced by v^* and P to any decisions not involving y_0^* as before; and so on. Substituting P^* for P in Definition 4.4 above, define the P^*-sophisticated agenda for $y^n(\pi^*)$ in the same way. Let $\varsigma(y^n(\pi^*)) = (\varsigma_0^*, \ldots, \varsigma_n^*)$ be the P^*-sophisticated agenda for $y^n(\pi^*)$. By ($\dagger$), $\varsigma_j^* = y_{n-j}^*$ for all $j = 0, 1, \ldots, n$. Therefore, undominated voting along the equilibrium voting path under v^* implies $y_i^* P^* y_{i-1}^*$ for all $i = 1, \ldots, n$; in particular, since $P \subseteq P^*$, every individual with a strict preference between any consecutive pair of alternatives (y^*_{i-1}, y^*_i) votes sincerely over this pair. □

Theorem 5.6 says that sophisticated voting behavior along the equilibrium path of an endogenous amendment agenda is observationally equivalent to sincere voting along that path; in other words, observed voting satisfies "sophisticated sincerity". It follows that finding evidence of sincere voting over amendment agendas is insufficient to reject a hypothesis of strategically rational individuals: if the amendment agendas under scrutiny are set endogenously, then strategically rational proposal strategies internalize any anticipated strategic voting in such a way that observed strategic voting is sincere. In other words, the incidence of strategic decision-making in committees lies more in the agenda-setting stages than in any voting stage.

Although the theorem is proved for the typical case of no Condorcet winner in the feasible set X, it is not hard to check that there always exist subgame perfect equilibria to the endogenous amendment agenda game that exhibit the same voting behavior even when such a winner exists. The difference is that not all such equilibria need involve sophisticated sincerity: if there exists a Condorcet winner then it is surely placed on the agenda by some individual $i \in N$ and, once included, it is assured of being the sophisticated outcome of the eventual voting subgame, irrespective of any other alternative on the agenda (Corollary 4.1). Consequently, subsequent proposers are indifferent over a wide variety of alternatives to add to the agenda, in which case the argument for Theorem 5.6 insures only that equilibrium path voting is sophisticatedly sincere following the first decision node at which the Condorcet winner is considered. So while sincere voting along the entire equilibrium path constitutes one equilibrium profile, it is not the only one.

5.5 Discussion

Issue-by-issue voting is a key feature of a variety of institutions ranging from the legislative committee systems of presidential polities such as the USA, to the coalitional governments typical of parliamentary polities common in Europe. Although, as with amendment agendas, the occurrence of agenda independent outcomes under issue-by-issue voting is possible, it is unlikely for an arbitrary and exogenously given set of alternatives. Indeed, for issue-by-issue voting on a finite set (where an issue is either adopted or not), agenda independence requires a further assumption on the majority

5.5. DISCUSSION

preference relation that removing an issue from any accepted bundle of issues is always strictly majority preferred (section 4.3). This seems a very demanding property for the underlying committee preference profile to satisfy. On the other hand, as a choice process, issue-by-issue voting is most naturally suited to spatial problems in which alternatives are representable as points in some multidimensional space. And here we are able to show two main results. The first both characterizes and insures the existence of an issue-by-issue core alternative (Theorem 5.1), while the second identifies sufficient (and essentially necessary) conditions for the existence of an agenda independent outcome for the spatial model (Theorem 5.2). Applications of these results provided (admittedly spare and abstract) models of both legislative committee systems and parliamentary governments. In particular, the restriction supporting the existence of agenda independent outcomes, that preferences be separable over the space of alternatives, implies that equilibrium outcomes in a committee system with rational legislators are not assured when legislators' most preferred position on some issue is contingent on the adopted positions on other issues. In such circumstances, further institutional restrictions (for example, making any legislatively-approved policy subject to presidential veto) can be necessary to support well-defined outcomes.

With the partial exception of the applications to legislatures and parliaments, the theory developed so far is exclusively an equilibrium theory of voting. Although voting over a set of possible alternatives is the last stage in a committee's collective choice process, it is rarely the only stage in the process: committees often generate those alternatives that comprise the agenda and, when proposing alternatives for committee consideration, rational individuals take account of the consequences for the final decision of one proposal rather than another. Identifying equilibrium voting behavior for an arbitrarily given feasible set, therefore, is a prerequisite for identifying equilibrium proposal behavior when the feasible set is endogenous.

Addressing questions of endogenous agenda formation, even within the relatively limited confines of amendment agendas, raises some new technical complexities. Voting over binary trees is inherently a sequential procedure; nevertheless, conditional on individuals having strict preferences, Theorem 4.1 demonstrates that the assumption that individuals use only undominated strategies is sufficient to solve for equilibrium behavior and outcomes. Unfortunately, the same is not true when we go back a stage to consider strategic agenda-setting. Just as the restriction to undominated Nash equilibria is in part justified by a desire to exclude the absurdity of allowing all individuals, irrespective of their preferences, to vote for the same alternative as logically possible equilibrium behavior with non-unanimous voting rules (Example 3.5), the restriction to subgame perfect Nash equilibria is in part justified by a desire to exclude the absurdity of allowing rational individuals to threaten to do patently irrational things conditional on the realization of particular counterfactual circumstances (Example 5.7). By definition, the use of such incredible threats to support otherwise equilibrium decisions is ruled out by subgame perfection, making the refinement an intuitively sensible limitation on the class of Nash equilibrium predictions for extensive form games.

The existence of undominated subgame perfect equilibria for an endogenous amendment agenda procedure is confirmed with Theorem 5.4. And Theorem 5.5 shows that, so long as every individual is given the opportunity to propose an alternative, the earlier claim (Corollary 4.1) that sophisticated voting invariably selects the Condorcet winner when exactly one exists is robust to endogenous agenda setting. When there exist multiple Condorcet winners, however, endogenous agenda setting in the spatial context can result in an equilibrium outcome that is not a Condorcet winner (Example 5.11). In any case, unlike with sophisticated voting over an exogenous amendment agenda, equilibrium voting with endogenous amendment agendas is observationally equivalent to sincere voting (Theorem 5.6). This fact is evidently relevant to any empirical search for sophisticated voting in committees and, more generally, points to the strategic importance of agenda-setting, a theme we pursue more thoroughly in Chapter 6.

5.6 Exercises

5.1 Confirm the correspondences illustrated in Figure 5.2 satisfy the hemicontinuity properties as claimed.

5.2 Comment on relationship between Theorem 2.7 and Theorem 5.2.

5.3 Suppose *intra*-committee j decision-making, all $j \in K$, is by having all N_j-committee members propose some alternative within the committee's jurisdiction and selecting the f_j-median proposal as the committee's decision. Prove that if preferences are separable, all of the undominated Nash equilibrium outcomes here are precisely committee equilibria. Prove or provide a counterexample to the claim that the same result goes through with nonseparable preferences.

5.4 Assume the preferences of all members of a committee (with an odd

5.6. EXERCISES

number of members) are separable over a multidimensional policy space and that committee jurisdictions are single-dimensional. Show that Corollary 5.1 extends to the setting in which intra-committee proposals are determined by each member offering a single alternative and the final proposal determined by an arbitrary (simple majority rule) binary agenda over the suggested alternatives.

5.5 Check there exists no Condorcet winner as claimed in Example 5.4.

5.6 Suppose the individuals of a three-person committee have single-peaked preferences over $X = [-1, 1]$ with ideal points $-1 < x_1 < x_2 = 0 < x_3 < 1$. Suppose there is a status quo policy x^0 and that individual 3 has the right to propose an alternative policy y under a *closed rule*: given any proposal by 3, the committee uses simple majority rule to accept or to reject the proposal; if the proposal is rejected or if 3 makes no proposal, the status quo remains in place; if a majority accepts the proposal, the alternative replaces the status quo.

(a) Describe this situation formally as a game.

(b) Draw a diagram to illustrate the undominated Nash equilibrium outcome of the game as a function of the status quo $x^0 \in X$.

(c) What happens if 3 makes proposals under an *open rule*: if 3 makes no proposal the status quo remains in place; if 3 makes a proposal y then either or both other committee members can offer a counter-proposal and the final outcome is decided using a majority rule amendment agenda over the set of proposals in which the status quo is considered last, 3's proposal is considered next-to-last and the order of the (at most two) remaining alternatives is chosen randomly.

(d) Comment on the implications for your answers to (b) and (c) of the policy space being two-dimensional and the preference distribution supporting no majority core.

5.7 A three person committee has to choose both the level and distribution of a budget over a two-dimensional issue space, $X = \Re^2_+$. Assume each person $i = 1, 2, 3$ has Euclidean preferences over X with a finite ideal point, x_i. The horizontal axis measures dollars allocated to issue x and the vertical axis measures dollars allocated to issue y. Consider two schemes for reaching a decision. In the *budget process*, the committee first uses majority rule to decide the total budget, $b_B \geq 0$ and then, having fixed b, chooses the distribution of b between the two issues, $x + y \leq b_B$. In the *appropriations process*, the committee first uses majority rule to decide the level of expenditure on issue x and then, having fixed x, chooses the level of expenditure on issue y. The total budget b is then defined by summing the two allocation decisions, $b_A = x + y$. All legislators are strategically rational.

(a) Illustrate examples of distributions of ideal points under which there are undominated subgame perfect Nash equilibrium outcomes such that $b_B > b_A$; $b_B < b_A$; and $b_B = b_A$.

(b) Identify conditions on the distribution of ideal points that characterize when $b_B \leq b_A$.

5.8 Let $Q(\omega) \subseteq X$, denote the set of ω-monopoly equilibrium outcomes for an issue allocation $\omega \in \Omega$ (see Definition 5.6) and let $Q = \cup_{\omega \in \Omega} Q(\omega)$. Given a profile $u \in \mathcal{R}_{cs}^n$ of party preferences, define the *portfolio allocation core* to be the set

$$C_Q(u) = \{x \in Q : y \in P_L(x) \text{ for no } y \in Q, \ |L| > n/2\}$$

where, as usual, $P_L(x)$ is the set of alternatives strictly preferred to x by all $i \in L$, $L \subseteq N$. Recall that $C_{f_m}(u) \subset X$ is the simple majority core at a profile u.

(a) Interpret $C_Q(u)$ in the context of coalition government formation.

(b) *Prove*: If u is a profile of Euclidean preferences over X, then $C_{f_m}(u) \neq \emptyset$ implies $C_Q(u) \neq \emptyset$, but the converse is false.

(c) *Prove*: If u is a profile of Euclidean preferences over X and $n = 3$, then $C_Q(u) \neq \emptyset$.

(d) Use an example to comment on the role of Euclidean preferences in (a) and (b). Is the assumption necessary or simply a convenience?

5.9 Prove Theorem 5.5.

5.10 Find the Nash and subgame perfect Nash equilibria for the example illustrated in Figure 5.9. For Example 5.11, write down all of the voting trees consistent with any admissible proposal sequence (v, y, a, b) and confirm that all individuals are using undominated best response strategies.

5.7 Further reading

Kramer [104] proves Theorems 5.1 and 5.2. Shepsle [191] developed a theory of committee delegation and equilibrium under sincere voting, establishing Corollary 5.1 in so doing. See also Black and Newing [36]. Complications of the sort illustrated by Example 5.4 are identified and studied in Denzau and MacKay [59] and Krehbiel [109]. Austen-Smith and Banks [11] and

5.7. FURTHER READING

Laver and Shepsle [114] explore taking Shepsle's [191] approach to coalition formation in parliamentary governments, proving versions of Theorem 5.3. Both papers explore a great deal more of the subject than is discussed here. See Laver and Shepsle [115] for an extended discussion. The proof to Theorem 5.3 exploits an argument due to Banks and Duggan [21]. Endogenous agenda selection in voting games is explored for three-person committees in Banks and Gasmi [26]. Examples 5.10 and 5.11, and Theorems 5.4 and 5.5 are due to Duggan [62]. Selten [189], [190] introduced the idea of subgame perfect equilibrium and proved its existence for finite games; existence proofs for subgame perfect equilibria in general continuous games can be found in Harris [92] and in Hellwig, Leininger, Reny and Robson [94]. Section 5.4 is based on Austen-Smith [6]. Groseclose and Krehbiel [89] offer an extensive discussion of sophisticated sincerity. The theory of monopolistic agenda setting suggested in Exercise 5.6 is due to Romer and Rosenthal [176]; see also Krehbiel [108]. Ferejohn and Krehbiel [79] provide a formal comparison of the appropriations and the budget processes of Exercise 5.7.

Chapter 6

Legislative Bargaining

Binary voting agendas are well-defined mechanisms, describing how a committee arrives at a collective choice from a given set of alternatives. And it is clear from Chapter 4, where we study the strategic implications of these mechanisms, that institutional details matter: even with a fixed preference profile, distinct collective choices can arise from small variations in the choice procedure. Not all committee decision-making, however, is governed by such well-defined procedures and it is implausible to look for an exhaustive description of how institutional variation maps into policy variation. While there are almost always rules and regulations covering some dimensions of any choice problem, for instance concerning who has the right to speak at any time or when final votes of legislative approval are required, there is much that is only loosely governed by formal procedure. Bargaining theory offers a quite general framework that plausibly captures at least some important aspects common to informal committee procedures. To the extent that this is the case, therefore, results derived from political bargaining models provide relatively institution-free insights into a wide class of collective choice processes.

The chapter is concerned with developing a particular noncooperative theory of legislative bargaining. Although others can readily be imagined, the underlying structure of the theory below has a claim to being canonical: it is predicated on an intuitive and natural abstraction for any sort of noncooperative model of bargaining; it reflects fundamental tradeoffs across both time and participants; and it is extremely flexible, permitting considerable latitude in applying the basic framework to many distinct problems and environments. The key idea for the theory is perhaps most easily appreciated by first considering two-person bargaining, say between a buyer and a seller of some indivisible good such as a car. A plausible approximation for how the bargaining might evolve is that the buyer first makes an offer of a purchase price to the seller who then either accepts or rejects the offer; if she accepts then the transaction is completed and the bargaining over; on the other hand, should she reject the opening offer, the seller has the opportunity to make a counter-offer which the buyer in turn is free to accept or reject, making a second offer, and so on until such time that a mutually agreeable price is reached. In general, individuals are impatient and so the later the bargaining reaches closure, the less the participants value the outcome; there is then a premium on obtaining an agreement earlier and such impatience endows the more patient individual with some strategic advantage. The objective of the theory is to explain the bargainers' optimal sequences of proposals, counter-proposals, acceptance criteria and so forth, so predicting the price at which the transaction is completed as a function of the parameters of the model (e.g. the seller's willingness to sell, the buyer's willingness to buy, the individuals' discount factors, etc).

The legislative bargaining theory developed below amounts to an extension of the two-person sequential bargaining model to more general n-person bargaining over political decisions. The complication in making the extension is that typically not all n people are needed for a proposal to be accepted; under majority rule with n odd, for instance, a proposer needs only $(n-1)/2$ others to have his proposal accepted. The implications of this fact for legislative policy making are far-reaching and the subject of the chapter.

6.1 A basic framework

In this section we sketch the abstract *sequential bargaining procedure* for committee decision-making, common to the various environments considered in the remainder of the chapter.

A committee $N = \{1, \ldots, n\}$ has to reach a collective choice from a nonempty compact, convex set of feasible alternatives, $X \subset \Re^k$, with status quo alternative $x^0 \in X$. Every committee member $i \in N$ is assumed to have preferences over X, representable by a continuous concave utility function $u_i : X \to \Re$; that is, the underlying preference profile ρ lies in $\mathcal{R}_{cs}^n$ (section 1.1). Decision making takes place as follows. There is an infinite number of discrete periods, indexed $t = 1, 2, \ldots$, each of which in principle includes a proposal stage and voting stage. At the start of the first period, some committee member is chosen randomly to offer a proposal $x \in X$; once the proposal is made all committee members simultaneously vote over whether

6.1. A BASIC FRAMEWORK

to accept it. If the committee vote is to accept the proposal x, it becomes the committee choice, x is implemented and payoffs accrue; if the vote is to reject the proposal then the status quo x^0 remains as the provisional outcome, the process moves to the second period and the sequence repeats until such time as the committee accepts a proposal (note that a proposal in any period might be to retain the status quo, $x = x^0$, which, if passed, then constitutes the committee choice). Thus a typical sequence of (provisional) decisions to the (final) committee choice is of the form $(x^0, \ldots, x^0, x^t, \ldots)$, where $x^t \neq x^0$ is the first accepted proposal distinct from the status quo. Figure 6.1 describes the game tree.

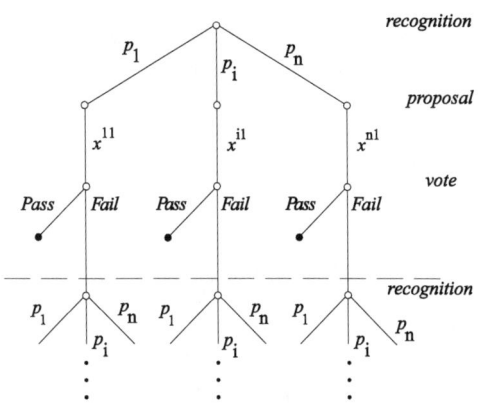

Figure 6.1: Game tree for a sequential bargaining process

Suppose the proposal offered in period t, say $x^t \in X$, is the alternative eventually accepted by the committee. For each $i \in N$, $\delta_i \in (0, 1)$ is i's discount factor. It is technically convenient, although substantively irrelevant, to normalize individual payoffs from the process by the discounted value of time, $[\sum_{t=1}^{\infty} \delta_i^{t-1}]^{-1} = (1 - \delta_i)$; then for any $t = 1, 2, \ldots$, individual i's payoff from the bargaining sequence $(x^0, \ldots, x^0, x^t, \ldots)$ is

$$\frac{1}{[\sum_{t=1}^{\infty} \delta_i^{t-1}]} \left[\sum_{s=1}^{t-1} \delta_i^{s-1} u_i(x^0) + \sum_{s=t}^{\infty} \delta_i^{s-1} u_i(x^t) \right] = (1 - \delta_i^{t-1}) u_i(x^0) + \delta_i^{t-1} u_i(x^t).$$

Note that if the status quo payoff is set at zero, i's final payoff is simply $\delta_i^{t-1} u_i(x^t)$.

Conditional on no proposal being accepted before period t, let $p_i \in [0, 1]$ denote the probability that $i \in N$ is selected to make the period-t proposal (that is, i is the period-t agenda-setter). Assume the distribution

$p = (p_1, \ldots, p_n)$ is independent of t and, whenever i is the randomly chosen agenda-setter for t, say that i is *recognized* in t. The outcomes from committee voting are described by any fixed simple rule f (Definition 1.3); as usual, let P be the strict preference relation on X given the committee preference profile.

The assumption that bargaining may continue indefinitely is not intended to be taken literally; legislative sessions have finite terms, legislators leave office and so on. Rather, the assumption captures the ideas that no individual is assured the "last word" in any decision and the committee can entertain as many proposals as members wish to offer before reaching closure, subject to the price of delay reflected in the discount factors δ_i. The lower is δ_i, the more impatient is individual i or, equivalently, the higher the utility cost to the individual of reaching decisions later in the process; conversely, as δ_i goes to one, i's relative evaluation of the future with respect to the present increases, with i becoming indifferent in the limit over when exactly a proposal is accepted. And in the case where $\delta_i = \delta$ for all $i \in N$, the common discount factor can also be interpreted as a measure of how swiftly the decision-making process takes place. The closer is δ to one, the less real time it takes to go through any given proposal and vote stage; in the limit, each such stage requires only infinitesimal time to complete. Although literally absurd, the abstraction of imagining each separate decision stage taking an infinitesimal amount of time is not an unreasonable model of a deliberative process in which committee members offer proposals and reach tentative decisions continually in the course of conversation.

A *history* at any period t describes the sequence of agenda-setters, their respective proposals and the associated pattern of votes in the preceding $t - 1$ periods. In general, individuals' strategies in sequential bargaining games are mappings from all conceivable histories of all finite t into the relevant decision sets of proposals and votes. Strictly speaking, then, a formal description of the full set of strategy profiles requires a similarly formal description of the set of such histories. Although we shall argue shortly that doing this is not very productive for the sequential bargaining procedure, it is first useful to provide some intuition for how the process evolves with a finite horizon example. This example further motivates an important extension of what is to be understood as a strategy for any individual.

Example 6.1 A three person committee $N = \{1, 2, 3\}$ is required to allocate one unit of a homogenous good. The feasible set is

$$X = \{x^t = (x_1^t, x_2^t, x_3^t) : x_1^t + x_2^t + x_3^t \leq 1 \text{ and}, \forall i \in N, x_i^t \geq 0\}.$$

6.1. A BASIC FRAMEWORK

For all $i \in N$ and all $x^t \in X$, $u_i(x^t) = x_i^t$. Assume further that the status quo alternative is $x^0 = (0,0,0)$, that voting is under simple majority rule, and that there are only three possible periods, $t = 1, 2, 3$. Finally, suppose all individuals share a common discount factor $\delta_i = \delta$ and, in each period t, the probability that any individual $i \in N$ is recognized is $p_i = 1/3$. If no majority agreement is reached over a distribution of the good in any of the three periods, the allocation $(0,0,0)$ is implemented. A strategy for any individual is then a proposal and a voting decision rule that describe what the individual does, conditional on the particular decision node reached and on the history of the game to that node. Formally, let $x^{it} \in X$ denote individual i's proposal in period t, given i is recognized for that period, and let $v(x^{it}) = (v_1^t, v_2^t, v_3^t) \in \{0,1\}^3$ describe the consequent vote profile in t; here, a vote $v_j^t = 0$ (respectively, 1) means individual j voted against (respectively, for) the proposal x^{it}. The history of the game at the start of period $t = 2, 3$ is $h^t = ((x^{i(t-s)}, v(x^{i(t-s)}))_{s=1}^{s=t-1}$. Let H^t be the set of possible histories to the start of period $t = 2, 3$ and write H^0 for the empty history at the start of $t = 1$. Then for each $i \in N$, i's proposal strategy for period t conditional on i being the agenda-setter for t is a map

$$\pi_i^t : H^t \to X;$$

and i's voting strategy for period t is a map

$$v_i^t : H^t \times X \to \{0, 1\}.$$

A strategy for i is a sequence of proposal and voting strategies, one pair for each t:

$$\sigma_i = ((\pi_i^1, v_i^1), (\pi_i^2, v_i^2), (\pi_i^3, v_i^3)).$$

We look for a subgame perfect Nash equilibrium $\sigma^* = (\sigma_1^*, \sigma_2^*, \sigma_3^*)$ to the game.

Suppose no proposal is accepted by a majority in the first two periods and let individual k be recognized in the final period, $t = 3$. If k's proposal is rejected then all individuals receive zero payoff. Consequently k's unique best proposal is $x^{k3} = e_k$, where k receives all of the available good ($x_k^{k3} = 1$) and the other committee members receive nothing ($x_l^{k3} = 0$, $l \neq k$), and this proposal is then accepted by a majority. The argument for why individuals $l \neq k$ vote surely for k's proposal despite being offered nothing by k is exactly that spelled out in Example 4.16: k has no best response proposal if $l \neq k$ fails to vote surely for x^{k3} when indifferent between k's proposal and the default outcome, $(0,0,0)$; but by definition, equilibrium decisions must constitute a profile of mutual best responses and, in this case, the only such profile is for k to propose e_k and a majority to vote surely for that proposal.

Now let individual j be recognized to make a proposal in the second period, $t = 2$, and let x^{j2} be j's proposal. If x^{j2} is rejected the process moves to the final period and, for every $l \in N$, the period three proposal e_k yields a discounted payoff δ to l if $l = k$, which occurs with probability $p_l = 1/3$, and a payoff zero to l otherwise. Thus, l's expected payoff at $t = 2$ conditional on x^{j2} being rejected is

$$E[u_l(x)|x^{j2} \text{ rejected}] = \delta/3,$$

where E is the expectation operator with respect to the distribution $p = (1/3, 1/3, 1/3)$. And following the same logic as before, any individual $l \neq j$ votes surely in equilibrium for a proposal x^{j2} that yields l at least a payoff $\delta/3$. A best response proposal x^{j2}, therefore, is a division of the good that gives nothing to one committee member, a sure payoff $\delta/3$ to the other and the residual, $1 - (\delta/3)$, to j. Because $p_l = 1/3$ for all $l \in N$, j is indifferent over the person to whom he or she offers nothing and we assume j chooses between them with probability $1/2$ (on the other hand, if the probabilities p_l are distinct, j surely offers nothing to the individual with the highest probability of being the final proposer).

Finally, suppose individual i is recognized in the first period, $t = 1$, and let x^{i1} be i's proposal. If x^{i1} is rejected the process moves to the second period where the period two proposal x^{j2} is accepted by the committee. In this case, the probability any individual l is chosen as the period two proposer is $p_l = 1/3$ in which case l obtains a discounted payoff $\delta[1 - (\delta/3)]$. If, however, l is not the period two proposer then, with probability $1/2$, l obtains a discounted payoff $\delta/3$ from x^{j2} and, with probability $1/2$, receives nothing. Hence l's expected payoff at $t = 1$ conditional on x^{i1} being rejected in favor of x^{j2} is

$$E[u_l(x)|x^{i1} \text{ rejected}] = \delta \frac{1}{3}[1 - (\delta/3)] + \delta \frac{2}{3}\left[\frac{1}{2}(\delta/3)\right]$$
$$= \delta/3.$$

Because i is indifferent over which other individual to include in her coalition, we assume as before that i chooses according to a fair coin flip; in any event, i's best response proposal x^{i1} is to offer $\delta/3$ to one other committee member and keep the residual $1-(\delta/3)$ for herself. This proposal is accepted, following the earlier arguments.

In sum, there is (up to the tie-breaking assumption over proposals) a unique symmetric (in that the names of individuals are irrelevant) subgame

6.1. A BASIC FRAMEWORK

perfect equilibrium σ^* to the division game here: for each $i \in N$, if i is the proposer in period $t = 3$ then i proposes allocating the entire amount of the good to herself and nothing to the others; if i is the proposer in either period $t = 1, 2$ then i proposes allocating an amount $1 - (\delta/3)$ to herself and, with no loss of generality, offers $\delta/3$ to each of the other committee members with probability $1/2$; whenever i is not a proposer, i votes to accept any proposal that offers i at least her expected payoff from rejecting the proposal and moving to the next period. Thus, there is no delay in equilibrium. The very first proposal is accepted and every individual's expected payoff evaluated prior to the start of period one is therefore

$$E[u_i|\sigma^*] = \frac{1}{3}\left[1 - (\delta/3)\right] + \frac{2}{3}\left[\frac{1}{2}(\delta/3)\right] = 1/3.$$

In view of the symmetry of the committee in the example, this expected value is quite intuitive. Although there is a premium from being the *de facto* period one agenda-setter, because $[1 - (\delta/3)] > (\delta/6)$, the likelihood of this event is the same for all committee members. □

There are two things to note about the best-response strategies described in Example 6.1. The first thing is that the individual recognized to make a proposal in any period selects an allocation that takes explicit account of the expected evolution of the process consequent on this proposal and conditional on the best-response decisions of subsequent decision makers; similarly, every individual votes taking account of the expected consequences of their decision for possible outcomes later in the process. This farsightedness property of equilibrium strategies is called *sequential rationality*. The second thing to note in the example is that the agenda-setters for periods $t = 1, 2$ propose allocations that give strictly positive payoffs only to themselves and one other committee member, thus forming a *minimum winning* coalition, that is, a decisive coalition such that removal of any one member makes the coalition not decisive. But since the agenda-setters in each case are absolutely indifferent over who they select as a coalition partner, we assume they made the choice by flipping a fair coin. Such a decision rule is an example of a *mixed strategy* in contrast to a determinate decision rule, or *pure strategy*. If an individual uses a mixed strategy at any decision node, his or her *de facto* choice at that node depends on the realization of some random variable.

Formally, a mixed strategy for an individual is a probability distribution over the set of feasible actions for the individual at the relevant decision node. Note that a pure strategy is simply a special sort of mixed strategy under which 100% of the probability mass is on a given action. It is not hard to see that if an individual's strategy is both mixed and a best response, then the individual must be indifferent over those actions given a positive probability of being played: if two feasible actions yield distinct payoffs to the individual, then he or she is clearly better off by insuring that the least profitable action is never used when the other is available.

Mixed strategies play an increasingly important role in what follows and, indeed, are at times essential to insure the existence of equilibria in some settings. The substantive interpretation of a mixed strategy, however, is not always apparent. Although a literal interpretation in terms of "flipping a fair coin" can be sensible, as is the case for Example 6.2 below, this is far from always being the case. For instance, it is difficult to imagine a candidate for electoral office using an explicit randomization device to choose the policy platforms on which to campaign, even if such randomizations are necessary to identify equilibria. A more subtle interpretation is to presume that each individual in fact chooses a deterministic action, a pure strategy, but others in the game are not sure of this action; then these others attach probabilities to the individual's possible decisions and behave *as if* he or she were using a mixed strategy given by the probabilities. A mixed strategy equilibrium can then be understood as a mutual consistency property on individuals' expectations about the (pure) decisions of others. A formal justification and elaboration of this approach to understanding mixed strategies, known as the *purification* of mixed strategies, is possible but leads us too far astray. Instead, we simply remark that while substantive interpretations of mixed strategy equilibria are rarely immediate and occasionally unconvincing, mixed strategies nevertheless admit a coherent formal analysis of strategic settings in which an insistence on pure strategy equilibria yields no solution. The following abstract examples illustrate the point.

Example 6.2 Suppose two individuals, $i = 1, 2$, must each choose an action simultaneously; the feasible set of actions for each i is $A_i = \{a, b\}$ and payoffs are as follows (the rows indicate individual 1's actions and the first number in each cell is 1's payoff given the associated action profile).

	a	b
a	1, −1	−1, 1
b	−1, 1	1, −1

The set of pure strategies for i is A_i and the set of mixed strategies for i is, in this case, the interval $[0, 1]$, where a choice $r_i \in [0, 1]$ is the probability that i chooses action (pure strategy) $a \in A_i$. A little thought shows there is

6.1. A BASIC FRAMEWORK

no equilibrium to the game (called "matching pennies") in pure strategies: $i = 1$'s best response to any action $c \in A_2$ is to choose $c \in A_1$ but, at the same time, $i = 2$'s best response to any action $c \in A_1$ is to choose $d \in A_2$, $d \neq c$. On the other hand, assume that individual 2 chooses action a with probability r_2; then 1's expected payoff from choosing a with probability r_1 is given by

$$E[u_1|r_1, r_2]$$
$$= r_1[r_2 u_1(a,a) + (1-r_2) u_1(a,b)] + (1-r_1)[r_2 u_1(b,a) + (1-r_2) u_1(b,b)]$$
$$= [2r_1 - 1][2r_2 - 1].$$

Given r_2, a best response strategy for individual 1 is any value of r_1 that maximizes $E[u_1|r_1, r_2]$. Doing the maximization yields the best response mapping $r_1^*(r_2)$ for individual 1: if 2 chooses a with any probability greater than 1/2 then 1's unique best response is to use the pure strategy a ($r_2 > 1/2$ implies $E[u_1|1, r_2] > E[u_1|0, r_2]$); similarly, if 2 chooses a with any probability less than 1/2 then 1's unique best response is to use the pure strategy b ($r_2 < 1/2$ implies $E[u_1|1, r_2] < E[u_1|0, r_2]$). However, should 2 choose a with probability exactly 1/2, then 1 is indifferent *ex ante* between her two actions ($E[u_1|1, \frac{1}{2}] = E[u_1|0, \frac{1}{2}]$) and is therefore willing in principle to adopt any mixed strategy at all, that is, any value of r_1. This best response mapping is illustrated in Figure 6.2.

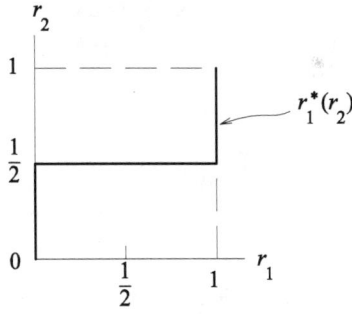

Figure 6.2: The best response mapping $r_1^*(r_2)$

Reversing the roles of the two individuals in the preceding argument, we find

$$E[u_2|r_1, r_2] = [2r_2 - 1][1 - 2r_1].$$

Maximizing $E[u_2|r_1, r_2]$ with respect to r_2 yields 2's best response mapping $r_2^*(r_1)$: if $r_1 > 1/2$, then 2's unique best response is to use the pure strategy

b as $E[u_2|r_1, 0] > E[u_2|r_1, 1]$; if $r_1 < 1/2$, then 2's unique best response is to use the pure strategy a as $E[u_2|r_1, 1] > E[u_2|r_1, 0]$; and if $r_1 = 1/2$, then $E[u_2|\frac{1}{2}, 1] = E[u_2|\frac{1}{2}, 0]$ so any strategy $r_2 \in [0, 1]$ is a best response. Combining $r_2^*(r_1)$ with $r_1^*(r_2)$ yields Figure 6.3.

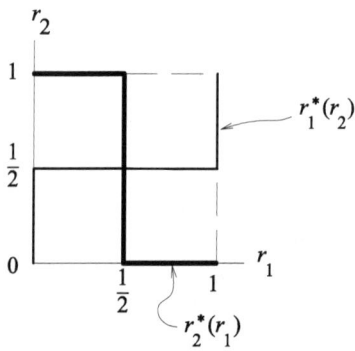

Figure 6.3: Mixed strategy equilibrium for "matching pennies"

Inspection of Figure 6.3 shows that the only pair of mutually consistent best response strategies are mixed and, intuitively, prescribe that each individual chooses a with probability $1/2$. Thus the unique Nash equilibrium to the game is $(r_1^*, r_2^*) = (1/2, 1/2)$.

As a second illustration (historically labeled "battle of the sexes"), consider the coordination problem given by changing the payoffs in "matching pennies" to

	a	b
a	2, 1	0, 0
b	0, 0	1, 2

In this case, both individuals prefer to choose the same action rather than not, but they disagree over the action on which to coordinate. For this strategic problem, there are three Nash equilibria: two in pure strategies, $\{(a, a), (b, b)\}$, and the third in mixed strategies, $(r_1^*, r_2^*) = (1/3, 2/3)$. (And note that because pure strategies are simply degenerate mixed strategies, the set of Nash equilibria here can be written $\{(1, 1), (0, 0), (1/3, 2/3)\}$.) We leave it as an exercise to rehearse similar calculations as those for "matching pennies" and derive the best response mappings $(r_1^*(r_2), r_2^*(r_1))$ illustrated in Figure 6.4.

6.1. A BASIC FRAMEWORK

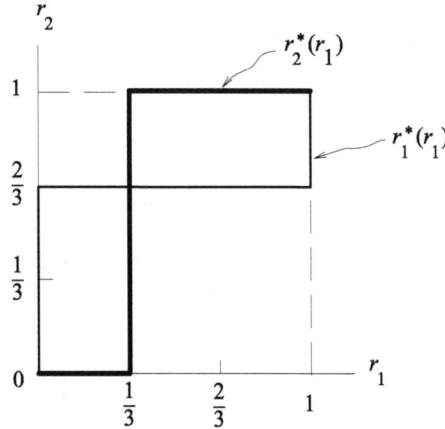

Figure 6.4: Equilibria for "battle of the sexes"

Inspection of Figure 6.4 justifies the three equilibrium strategy profiles. □

Unless explicitly stated otherwise, the word "strategy" is herein understood to cover both mixed and pure strategies.

The description of an individual's strategy in Example 6.1, although manageable because of there being only three periods, is notationally cumbersome and becomes increasingly more so as the number of possible periods goes to infinity. However, as suggested earlier, describing histories formally for the infinite horizon game is largely unnecessary. For the sort of bargaining problems of interest in this chapter, that is, we can exploit a symmetry property of the underlying extensive form game tree illustrated in Figure 6.1 and focus for the most part (although not exclusively) on an important subset of strategies called *stationary strategies*. Stationary strategies are history-independent. For example, if a given individual is chosen to be the proposer in distinct periods t and t', $t > t'$, where no proposal is accepted up through period $t-1$, then that individual's set of optimal proposals is the same in t as it was in t'; similarly, individuals' best response voting strategies in any t are not conditioned on any previous voting or proposal decisions other than the period t proposal. To generate predictions for committee behavior and decisions under the sequential bargaining procedure (with an infinite number of periods), therefore, we look for undominated subgame perfect equilibria in stationary strategies (defined formally below).

Although we offer a justification for concentrating on (undominated subgame perfect) equilibria supported by stationary strategies in the next section, their principal advantage is tractability: the full set of strategies available in the sort of infinite horizon game being considered is immense and characterizing the full set of equilibrium profiles is a daunting task. On the other hand, stationary strategies rule out substantively important considerations such a legislative reciprocity and retribution. Under stationarity, for example, a committee member who is excluded from some proposal which subsequently fails ignores this fact when constructing his or her own proposal later in the process; conversely, an individual i cannot induce some other individual j to include i in j's proposal by promising to reciprocate should j's proposal fail and i is chosen as the agenda-setter.

6.2 Bargaining over distributions

Much of politics concerns the allocation of benefits and costs across individuals, groups and districts. Exactly how any given amount of a limited and divisible resource is distributed through the political system is obscure. In this section we apply the abstract bargaining model sketched above to ask how a fixed total of a divisible resource is allocated, or distributed, among the bargainers, that is the members of a legislative committee, $N = \{1, \ldots, n\}$. Assume there is one unit of a divisible resource to be allocated among the $n \geq 3$ individual committee members. The set of feasible allocations for the committee is thus

$$X = \{(x_1, \ldots, x_n) : \sum_{i=1}^{i=n} x_i \leq 1 \text{ and, } \forall i \in N, \ x_i \geq 0\}.$$

Each individual is assumed selfish and risk-neutral; that is, for all $i \in N$ and all $x^t \in X$, $u_i(x^t) = x_i^t$. Assume further that the status quo alternative is $x^0 = (0, \ldots, 0)$ and that the decision rule used at every vote, f, is a given q-rule with $n/2 < q < n$: specifically, given any period t proposal $x^t \in X$, if at least q individuals vote for x^t then this proposal is implemented as the committee decision, otherwise it is rejected and the decision-making sequence moves on to period $t + 1$.

The approach to finding an undominated subgame perfect equilibrium in Example 6.1 is much the same as that for identifying equilibria to the agenda games of Chapter 4: starting with the final decision nodes of the tree, solve for the undominated Nash equilibrium strategies conditional on reaching the relevant node and then work back up the tree, using these strategies to fix expectations about how the sequence of decisions unfolds from any non-final decision node on. For extensive form games with finite horizons and no

6.2. BARGAINING OVER DISTRIBUTIONS

uncertainty regarding which particular decision node is reached when, this procedure is known as "backwards induction". But backwards induction is not possible when the game might go on indefinitely as there is no final decision node with which to anchor the induction. This is not a difficulty for finding subgame perfect equilibria in general, however, as the argument for the following result illustrates; and the result itself provides a substantive, rather than simply technical, motivation for looking only for equilibria in stationary strategies.

Theorem 6.1 *Assume $n \geq q+2 \geq 5$, $\min_{i \in N} \delta_i \in (q/(n-1), 1)$ and let $x \in X$ be arbitrary. There exists an undominated subgame perfect equilibrium for which x is the equilibrium outcome.*

Proof Fix a strategy profile with the following properties.

(1) For all $i \in N$ and $t = 1, \ldots$, if i is recognized in t, i proposes $x^{it} = x$ and all individuals vote for x.

(2) If x is rejected under the q-rule in t, the individual $j \in N$ chosen to propose in $t+1$ proposes $x^{j(t+1)} = x$.

(3) If, in any period t, the chosen agenda-setter $i \in N$ proposes an alternative other than x, say $x^{it} = y \in X \backslash \{x\}$, then:

(3.1) a set $M(y)$ of at least q individuals rejects y;

(3.2) the period $t+1$ proposer, say j, offers an allocation $z(y)$ such that $z_i(y) = 0$ and all individuals in $M(y)$ vote for $z(y)$ against y.

(4) If, in (3.2), the period $t+1$ the proposer j offers some alternative $y' \neq z(y)$, repeat (3) with y' replacing y and j replacing i.

Statement (1) specifies what is supposed to happen along the equilibrium path; statements (2), (3) and (4) jointly specify the consequences of any deviation from the behavior recommended in (1). That is, (2), (3) and (4) describe off-equilibrium path behavior. To prove the theorem, therefore, we need to show that the specified strategy profile does indeed constitute equilibrium behavior.

Suppose, without loss of generality, that $i = n \in N$ is the period t agenda-setter and assume $x^{nt} = y \neq x$. By relabeling $N \backslash \{n\}$ if necessary, suppose $y_j \leq y_{j+1}$ for all $j = 1, \ldots, n-2$. Under (3.1) and (3.2), a q-majority $M(y)$ is to reject y and the next proposer is to offer some distribution $z(y)$ with $z_n(y) = 0$ that $M(y)$ approves. We have to check there exists such a distribution $z(y) \in X$ for which (3.1) and (3.2) describe best response behavior to y. Assume first that the proposer conditional on y being rejected is some individual $j \neq n$. Let $M^*(y) = \{1, \ldots, q\}$, let

$$Y^* = \sum_{i \in M^*(y)} y_i$$

and let $m^* = |\{i \in M^*(y) : y_i = 0\}|$. Now define the allocation $z(y)$ as follows: for all $i \notin M^*(y)$ set $z_i(y) = 0$ and, for all $i \in M^*(y)$, set

$$z_i(y) = \begin{cases} \frac{y_i}{Y^*} - \eta\varepsilon & \text{if } y_i > 0 \\ \varepsilon & \text{if } y_i = 0 \end{cases},$$

where $\varepsilon > 0$ is small and $\eta \equiv \frac{m^*}{q-m^*}$; by definition of $M^*(y)$, if $y_i > 0$ for some $i \in M^*(y)$ then $Y^* > 0$ and $m^* < q$. By construction, $z_i(y) > y_i$ for all $i \in M^*(y)$. If $z(y)$ is rejected then, under (4), it will simply become the next proposal and so on; consequently, if $\delta_i z_i(y) > y_i$ for any $i \in M^*(y)$, i's unique undominated best voting decision is to vote in favor of $z(y)$. It remains to identify those discount factors $\delta_i \in (0,1)$ and committee sizes n for which the inequality $\delta_i z_i(y) > y_i$ holds for all $i \in M^*(y)$. Since the inequality evidently holds for all $\delta_i > 0$ if $y_i = 0$, suppose $y_i > 0$ for some $i \in M^*(y)$. Then $\delta_i z_i(y) > y_i$ if and only if

$$\delta_i > \frac{y_i}{z_i(y)} = \frac{Y^*}{1 - [\eta\varepsilon Y^*/y_i]}.$$

The least upper bound on Y^* is given by the most costly allocation y to defeat. This particular allocation is uniquely given by $y = (1/(n-1), \ldots, 1/(n-1), 0)$; that is, the deviating agenda-setter, individual n, gives herself nothing and shares the remainder of the resource evenly among all other committee members. In this case, $Y^* = q/(n-1)$. Consequently, letting ε approach zero, an arbitrary allocation $x \in X$ can be supported in equilibrium only if

$$\min_{i \in M^*(y)} \delta_i > \max Y^* = q/(n-1).$$

Since $n \geq q + 2 \geq 5$ by assumption, $\max Y^* < 1$. It follows that if $\min_{i \in N} \delta_i \in (q/(n-1), 1)$ and no individual is recognized in consecutive periods, then an agenda-setter cannot benefit from proposing any allocation $y \neq x$, any $x \in X$.

To complete the proof, we have check that if the same individual (here, individual n) is recognized in two consecutive periods, she still cannot profit

6.2. BARGAINING OVER DISTRIBUTIONS

from proposing any allocation other than x. So suppose individual n's first deviation to some $y \neq x$ is rejected in period t and n is again recognized in period $t+1$. In this case, (3.2) demands that n herself propose the allocation $z(y)$, thus "punishing" herself for her initial deviation. Should she fail to do this and instead propose some $y' \neq z(y)$, (4) requires a q-majority to reject y' and the period $t+2$ agenda-setter to offer $z(y)$, which then passes. Therefore, the only circumstance under which the period t agenda-setter ($i = n$) can avoid having $z(y)$ proposed and accepted in response to an initial deviation to $y \neq x$, is when n is chosen in every period as the agenda-setter. But since no q-majority ever approves any deviation under the specified strategy profile and $\delta_n < 1$, we have $\lim_{s \to \infty} \delta_n^s y_n = 0$, in which case the agenda-setter n is again no better off deviating than she is proposing x as required. □

Theorem 6.1 is an example of a class of results collectively known as "folk theorems": given a sufficiently long time horizon (here, infinite) and sufficiently patient individuals (for example, if n is odd and q is majority rule, "sufficiently patient" means $\delta_i > (n+2)/[2(n-1)]$ for every committee member i), virtually any distribution of feasible payoffs can be supported in (subgame perfect) equilibria. Although the particular construction of the equilibrium strategy profile supporting any given payoff distribution is oftentimes subtle and complex, the underlying intuition for such results is very straightforward: if individuals value the future enough and there is enough future to value, then we can find an appropriate stream of punishment, or relatively bad, payoffs to impose on individuals should they ever deviate from the required equilibrium behavior. Observationally, the result here says that undominated subgame perfect behavior is consistent with absolutely any division of the resource among committee members using a sequential bargaining process. Substantively, such a result may not be very appealing if only because it is impossible to refute empirically. Moreover, a result that says a self-interested agenda-setter is willing to abide by a committee process in which he or she is expected to support proposals in which she gets absolutely nothing is empirically suspect. Consequently, we look for a further refinement of the class of equilibria for infinite horizon extensive form games.

It is apparent from Figure 6.1 above that the game form or mechanism describing the sequential bargaining process exhibits a great deal of symmetry. In particular, the subgame beginning with the random selection of an agenda-setter for any period $t \geq 1$ is (up to the period index) identical to the subgame beginning with the random selection of an agenda-setter for any period $t' > t$: the likelihood of any given committee member $i \in N$ being selected, p_i, and the number of remaining periods available in the future, infinite, are identical in each case. And while the realized histories to t and to t' must be distinct, the set of achievable payoffs to any individual as evaluated at the start of any period is independent of how exactly the process evolved to that point. In other words, the decision problem facing any committee member at the start of any period t is independent of t: if a given individual $i \in N$ is chosen as the agenda-setter in periods t and $t' > t$ and a proposal x is optimal for i at t, then x must be optimal for i at t'. Consequently, a natural restriction on the class of subgame perfect equilibria is stationarity. So if, in the immediately preceding example, i proposes $x^{it} = x$ at t then, conditional on x being rejected at t, i similarly proposes $x^{it'} = x$ at t'; likewise, if indeed x is rejected at t then, under stationarity, x is also rejected at t'.

For any set Y, let ΔY denote the family of probability distributions over Y. Then a *stationary strategy* σ_i for any individual $i \in N$ consists of a mixed proposal $\pi_i \in \Delta X$ to be used at every period in which i is the selected agenda-setter and a voting strategy $v_i : X \to [0, 1]$, where $v_i(x)$ is the probability i votes to accept a proposal x. (In case an individual uses a pure strategy, we occasionally identify the action with the degenerate mixed strategy: for example, write $\pi_i = x^i$ rather than "π_i puts probability one on the allocation x^i".) Thus stationary strategies are independent of t and, consequently, of any history $h^t \in H^t$. If all individuals' strategies in a profile $\sigma = (\sigma_1, \ldots, \sigma_n)$ are stationary, say that the profile σ is stationary. Evidently, the strategy profile constructed in the argument for Theorem 6.1 is not stationary.

If a stationary profile σ^* is an undominated subgame perfect equilibrium in the space of all stationary strategy profiles, then σ^* is also an undominated subgame perfect equilibrium in the space of all strategy profiles. To see this, fix σ^*_{-i} and permit individual i to choose any (not only a stationary) strategy in response. Can i do any better by choosing a nonstationary strategy $\sigma_i \neq \sigma^*_i$? If so, then there must be two distinct histories h^t and $h^{t'}$ following each of which i is confronted with the identical decision problem but makes distinct decisions. There are two possibilities: i is either the agenda-setter at t and t' or is required to vote on the same proposal in each period. Because σ^*_{-i} is stationary, the set of proposals any individual other than i votes to accept is history independent. Therefore the set of optimal proposals for i consequent on h^t is precisely the same as it is consequent on $h^{t'}$. Hence, given all others use stationary voting strategies, i cannot improve on a stationary best response proposal strategy. Similarly, if i can

6.2. BARGAINING OVER DISTRIBUTIONS

improve her payoff by voting differently between accepting and rejecting a given alternative at two distinct histories, then i must be pivotal in both cases: if i is pivotal in neither case then i can clearly do no better by voting differently at the two histories whereas, by σ_{-i}^* stationary, i is pivotal with respect to accepting x at h^t if and only if i is pivotal with respect to accepting x at $h^{t'}$. But since σ^* is a subgame perfect equilibrium by assumption, σ_i^* must prescribe a best response vote for i at h^t and $h^{t'}$. Therefore, if voting (say) in favor of x at h^t is a best response conditional on i pivotal at this decision node, then likewise voting in favor of x at $h^{t'}$ is a best response. In sum, if σ^* is a subgame perfect equilibrium in stationary strategies, then it is a subgame perfect equilibrium in the space of all strategies. In other words, although equilibria in stationary strategies do not describe the full set of equilibria in a typical infinite horizon extensive form game, they are a subset of the full set of equilibria.

Hereon, we refer to an undominated subgame perfect equilibrium in stationary strategies more succinctly as a *stationary equilibrium*.

Let $\sigma = (\sigma_1, \ldots, \sigma_n)$ be any stationary strategy profile and, for any $i \in N$, let $V_i(\sigma)$ be i's expected payoff from this profile as evaluated prior to the random selection of the initial agenda-setter at $t = 1$. By definition of stationarity, $V_i(\sigma)$ is also i's expected payoff from this profile conditional on any period $t \geq 0$ proposal being rejected by some majority. That is, conditional on σ and on any period t proposal being rejected, $V_i(\sigma)$ is i's *continuation value* from moving to period $t+1$. Because i's continuation value is the most that i can expect to get from continuing the decision-making process beyond period t, the requirement that voting decisions be subgame perfect best responses in equilibrium implies that i votes for (respectively, against) any period t proposal that insures i a payoff worth at least (respectively, less than) $\delta_i V_i(\sigma)$. With this in mind, suppose $i \in N$ is recognized in period t and let $\mathcal{L}_i(\sigma) \in 2^{N \setminus \{i\}}$ denote the family of cheapest coalitions for i to attract and have her proposal accepted conditional on being recognized. Specifically,

$$\mathcal{L}_i(\sigma) = \{M \subset N \setminus \{i\} : |M| = q - 1 \text{ and,}$$

$$\forall j \in M, \forall l \notin M \cup \{i\}, \; \delta_j V_j(\sigma) \leq \delta_l V_l(\sigma)\}.$$

Note that if all committee members are equally impatient and have the same recognition probabilities so that $\delta_j V_j(\sigma) = \delta_l V_l(\sigma)$ for all $j, l \in N$, then $\mathcal{L}_i(\sigma)$ is the family of all coalitions from $N \setminus \{i\}$ of size $q - 1$; on the other hand if, for all $j, l \in N$, $\delta_j V_j(\sigma) \neq \delta_l V_l(\sigma)$, then $\mathcal{L}_i(\sigma) = \{M\}$ where M comprises the $q - 1$ individuals with the smallest discounted continuation values. It is also useful to define, for each $i, j \in N$, the family of cheapest coalitions for i to attract that include j; viz.

$$\mathcal{L}_i^j(\sigma) = \{M \in \mathcal{L}_i(\sigma) : j \in M\}.$$

Evidently, it is quite possible for this set to be empty for some i, j, σ.

The following result claims existence of stationary equilibria and characterizes stationary equilibrium behavior. In effect, if recognized in any period, an individual allocates just enough to $q-1$ other individuals to induce them to vote for the proposal and allocates the residual to herself, leaving the other $n-q$ committee members with nothing. Not surprisingly, therefore, the agenda-setter always chooses to offer a positive amount to a least expensive coalition of $q-1$ individuals; because there may exist several such coalitions (i.e. $|\mathcal{L}_i(\sigma)| > 1$), the agenda-setter randomizes over which particular least expensive coalition to form.

Theorem 6.2 *(1) There exists a stationary equilibrium. (2) Let σ be a stationary equilibrium and suppose $i \in N$ is recognized in some period. Then i randomly chooses a coalition $M \in \mathcal{L}_i(\sigma)$ according to a probability distribution $\gamma_i = (\gamma_{iM})_{M \in \mathcal{L}_i(\sigma)}$ and proposes an alternative $x^i \in X$ such that:*
(2.1) $x_i^i = 1 - \sum_{j \in M} \delta_j V_j(\sigma)$;
(2.2) $x_j^i = \delta_j V_j(\sigma)$ if $j \in M$ and $x_j^i = 0$ otherwise;
(2.3) for all $l \in N$

$$V_l(\sigma) = p_l(1 - \sum_{J \in \mathcal{L}_l(\sigma)} \gamma_{lJ} \sum_{j \in J} \delta_j V_j(\sigma)) + \delta_l V_l(\sigma) \sum_{j \neq l} p_j \sum_{L \in \mathcal{L}_j^l(\sigma)} \gamma_{jL},$$

where $\gamma_{lJ} \geq 0$ and $\sum_{J \in \mathcal{L}_l(\sigma)} \gamma_{lJ} = 1$.
Furthermore, for all $i, j \in N$, all $x^i \in X$, $v_j(x^i) = 1$ if and only if $x_j^i \geq \delta_j V_j(\sigma)$.

Proof (1) The existence claim is more conveniently proved as a corollary to a general existence result (Theorem 6.4) established later: a formal proof for the claim is therefore deferred.

(2) By earlier arguments, in any subgame perfect equilibrium, any $j \in N$ must vote for (respectively, against) any proposal $x^i \in X$ such that $x_j^i \geq \delta_j V_j(\sigma)$ (respectively, $x_j^i < \delta_j V_j(\sigma)$), where $\delta_j V_j(\sigma)$ is j's discounted continuation value under the equilibrium strategy profile σ. By $u_i(\cdot)$ strictly increasing in x_i^i therefore, $x_j^i \leq \delta_j V_j(\sigma)$ for all $j \in N$, with equality only if j is included in i's chosen coalition. And since i needs at least $q-1$ other committee members to constitute a winning coalition in favor of i's

6.2. BARGAINING OVER DISTRIBUTIONS

proposal, similar reasoning yields $\{j \in N\backslash\{i\} : x_j^i = \delta_j V_j(\sigma)\} \in \mathcal{L}_i(\sigma)$. By definition, i's payoff is constant with respect to the coalitions in $\mathcal{L}_i(\sigma)$ and i is therefore willing to choose $M \in \mathcal{L}_i(\sigma)$ randomly. In equilibrium, however, the probability vector used by i, $\gamma_i = (\gamma_{iM})_{M \in \mathcal{L}_i(\sigma)}$, must induce the stationary payoff vector, $V(\sigma) = (V_1(\sigma), \ldots, V_n(\sigma))$. To check that this is indeed the case, set $l = i$ in (2.3). With probability p_i, i is recognized at the start of period t, in which case i's payoff is $[1 - \sum_{j \in M} \delta_j V_j(\sigma)]$ for some $M \in \mathcal{L}_i(\sigma)$. With probability p_j, a distinct individual $j \neq i$ is recognized in which case, given σ, $x_i^j = 0$ if i is "too expensive", that is, if $\mathcal{L}_j^i(\sigma) = \emptyset$ and $x_i^j = \delta_i V_i(\sigma)$ with probability $\sum_{L \in \mathcal{L}_j^i(\sigma)} \gamma_{jL}$ otherwise. Because this holds for all $j \neq i$, the right side of (2.3) defines i's continuation value at the start of t, prior to the selection of the period t agenda-setter. In other words, all individuals i randomizing over $\mathcal{L}_i(\sigma)$ as described, conditional on being recognized in any period, induces the stationary payoff profile $V(\sigma)$ as required. And since σ is stationary by hypothesis, no unilateral deviation by any individual in any period t can affect the continuation values. □

Comparing Theorem 6.2 with Theorem 6.1 makes clear just how powerful a restriction is the refinement to stationary equilibria. Without stationarity any outcome, that is, any payoff distribution $(V_1, \ldots, V_n)$ and list of probability vectors $(\gamma_1, \ldots, \gamma_n)$, is supportable as an undominated subgame perfect equilibrium outcome; imposing stationarity reduces the set of possible equilibrium outcomes to a small and qualitatively similar class. In particular, all equilibrium committee decisions involve only a minimal winning coalition receiving a positive allocation with the agenda-setter receiving the largest share. Furthermore, all stationary equilibria are *no-delay* equilibria in that the very first individual recognized makes a passing proposal; equilibria are therefore efficient with all realized gains being immediately realized.

It is intuitive that the recognized individual can extract some monopoly rent from having agenda-setting power in the current period. Moreover, the differential does not vanish as committee members become increasingly patient. Although impatient individuals ($\delta_i < 1$) are indeed willing to pay a premium for an earlier decision, the ability to make a proposal confers a gain to the setter even if no individual discounts the future at all ($\delta_i = 1$). The reason for this is that when the voting rule falls short of unanimity, no individual is assured being included in a winning coalition. So the risk of being excluded and receiving zero in any future period makes those currently offered a strictly positive share willing to accept less than the proportion they would accept otherwise.

Example 6.3 Assume that for all $i \in N$, $\delta_i = \delta$, $p_i = 1/n$ and $q = (n+1)/2$, where n is odd. Then for all stationary profiles σ and all $i \in N$,

$$\mathcal{L}_i(\sigma) = \{M \subset N\backslash\{i\} : |M| = (n-1)/2\}.$$

Any stationary equilibria to the sequential bargaining process are such that, whenever an individual $i \in N$ is recognized to make a proposal, i proposes giving herself an amount $x_i^i = 1 - [(n-1)\delta]/2n$, giving an amount $x_j^i = \delta/n$ to each member of a coalition $M \in \mathcal{L}_i(\sigma)$, chosen randomly with probability $\gamma_{iM} = \binom{(n-1)/2}{(n-1)}$, and giving $x_l^i = 0$ to all remaining individuals. Since, for all $j \in N\backslash\{i\}$, $|\mathcal{L}_i^j(\sigma)| = \frac{1}{2}|\mathcal{L}_i(\sigma)|$, the probability that an arbitrary individual $j \in N\backslash\{i\}$ is included in i's coalition under σ is $1/2$ and, therefore, for all $j \in N$,

$$\begin{aligned} V_j(\sigma) &= \frac{1}{n}[1 - \frac{(n-1)\delta}{2n}] + \frac{n-1}{n}[\frac{1}{2}\frac{\delta}{n}] \\ &= \frac{1}{n}. \end{aligned}$$

All committee members vote for any proposal that gives them at least an amount δ/n and vote against any proposal yielding strictly less than δ/n. The period $t = 1$ proposal is accepted and, relative to others in the winning coalition, the individual recognized in this period realizes a gain of

$$[x_i^i - x_j^i] = 1 - \frac{(n+1)\delta}{2n} \geq \frac{n-1}{2n}$$

where the minimum is achieved at $\delta = 1$. Thus the premium conferred on the agenda-setter by virtue of majority rule alone is $[n-1]/2n$; the residual surplus is due to any impatience among committee members. □

It is useful to decompose the probability any individual $i \in N$ offers strictly positive amounts to any winning coalition into the implied probabilities that i offers a strictly positive allocation to any individual $j \in N\backslash\{i\}$. For any $i \in N$, $j \in N\backslash\{i\}$ and stationary strategy profile σ, let $r_{ij}(\sigma) \geq 0$ be the probability that i offers j a strictly positive allocation conditional on i being recognized in any period. By Theorem 6.2, if σ is an equilibrium profile,

$$r_{ij}(\sigma) = \begin{cases} \sum_{M \in \mathcal{L}_i^j} \gamma_{iM} & \text{if } \mathcal{L}_i^j(\sigma) \neq \emptyset \\ 0 & \text{otherwise} \end{cases}$$

for all $i \in N$ and $j \neq i$. Suppressing the dependency on σ, write $r_i = (r_{ij})_{j\neq i}$ and $r = (r_1, \ldots, r_n)$. Then for all $i \in N$, i's continuation value at the very

6.2. BARGAINING OVER DISTRIBUTIONS

start of a period is

$$V_i = p_i(1 - \sum_{j \in N \setminus \{i\}} r_{ij}\delta_j V_j) + \delta_i V_i \sum_{j \in N \setminus \{i\}} p_j r_{ji}$$

and $\sum_i V_i = 1$. The stationary equilibrium outcome induced by σ is now the pair (V, r) where $V = (V_1, \ldots, V_n)$ and $r = (r_1, \ldots, r_n)$.

Although existence of stationary equilibria is assured, this not true of uniqueness: there can, as the next example shows, easily be multiple stationary equilibria.

Example 6.4 Let $N = \{1, 2, 3\}$, $\delta_i = \delta$ all i and $q = 2$. By Theorem 6.2, any individual $i \in N$ recognized in the first period proposes an allocation giving a strictly positive amount δV_j to exactly one other committee member $j \neq i$ and nothing to the remaining individual. Consequently, the following three equations must hold in any stationary equilibrium:

$$V_1 = p_1[1 - r_{12}\delta V_2 - r_{13}\delta V_3] + \delta V_1[p_2 r_{21} + p_3 r_{31}];$$
$$V_2 = p_2[1 - r_{21}\delta V_1 - r_{23}\delta V_3] + \delta V_2[p_1 r_{12} + p_3 r_{32}];$$
$$V_3 = p_3[1 - r_{31}\delta V_1 - r_{32}\delta V_2] + \delta V_3[p_1 r_{13} + p_2 r_{23}].$$

Noting $r_{21} = 1 - r_{12}$ etc, this system can be written in matrix notation,

$$H(V)r = p \qquad (*)$$

where

$$H(V) = \begin{bmatrix} p_1\delta(V_2 - V_3) & p_2\delta V_1 & -p_3\delta V_1 \\ -p_1\delta V_2 & p_2\delta(V_3 - V_1) & p_3\delta V_2 \\ p_1\delta V_3 & -p_2\delta V_3 & p_3\delta(V_1 - V_2) \end{bmatrix}$$

and, by a slight abuse of notation, $r = [r_{12}, r_{23}, r_{31}]'$ and $p = [p_1, p_2, p_3]'$ are column vectors. No individual i uses a nondegenerate probability r_{ij} in equilibrium unless indifferent over which of the other two committee members to attract. Suppose $r_{12} \in (0, 1)$ and $r_{23} \in (0, 1)$; then indifference requires $V_i = 1/3$ for all i and the matrix $H(V)$ has rank two. Therefore, there can be a continuum of randomization choices r satisfying $(*)$, that is, there can be a continuum of equilibria differing only in the relative likelihoods of any particular minimal winning majority forming. If $\delta = 0.8$ and $p = (0.45, 0.35, 0.2)$, for instance, any r such that

$$r_{12} = 0.19 + 0.44 r_{31}; \quad r_{23} = 0.96 + 0.57 r_{31}; \quad r_{31} \in [0, 0.0625]$$

constitutes stationary equilibrium behavior. □

The multiplicity of equilibria exhibited in Example 6.4 is not apparent in the *ex ante* equilibrium payoffs that the strategy profiles support; specifically, $V = (1/3, 1/3, 1/3)$ for every stationary equilibrium with $r_{12} \in (0,1)$ and $r_{23} \in (0,1)$. This is not an accident. In fact a stronger statement can be made: for the sequential bargaining procedure on distributions with risk-neutral individuals having arbitrary (nondegenerate) discount factors and recognition probabilities, there is a unique (*ex ante*) vector of stationary equilibrium payoffs. At the start of the decision-making process, that is, individuals' expected payoffs are invariant across stationary equilibria and, therefore, all committee members are indifferent over which particular equilibrium is played.

Before stating and proving the uniqueness claim formally, it is convenient to record some simple properties of any stationary equilibrium, σ. For any $i \in N$, let

$$c_i = \sum_{j \in M} \delta_j V_j, \ M \in \mathcal{L}_i,$$

and

$$\omega_i = \sum_{j \neq i} p_j r_{ji} \in [0, 1 - p_i]$$

(where the dependency of these values on the strategy profile σ is suppressed). In words, c_i is the total payment individual i needs to make to others to construct a winning coalition for i's proposal whenever i is recognized as the agenda-setter; and ω_i is the probability that i is included in the winning coalition whenever i is not recognized as the agenda-setter. Using these notations, we can rewrite an individual's equilibrium continuation value from condition (2.3) of Theorem 6.2 as

$$V_i = p_i(1 - c_i) + \delta_i \omega_i V_i$$

or, equivalently,

$$V_i = \frac{p_i(1 - c_i)}{1 - \delta_i \omega_i}. \tag{e1}$$

Let $\{i_1, \ldots, i_n\}$ be a labeling of N such that, for all $k = 1, \ldots, n-1$, $\delta_{i_k} V_{i_k} \leq \delta_{i_{k+1}} V_{i_{k+1}}$. Then in equilibrium, for all $i \in N$,

$$\omega_i = \left\{ \begin{array}{l} 1 - p_i \text{ if } \delta_i V_i < \delta_{i_q} V_{i_q} \\ 0 \text{ if } \delta_i V_i > \delta_{i_q} V_{i_q} \end{array} \right\} \text{ and } \omega_i \leq 1 - p_i \text{ otherwise;} \tag{e2}$$

6.2. BARGAINING OVER DISTRIBUTIONS

and

$$c_i = \begin{cases} c_{i_q} = \sum_{j=i_1}^{j=i_q-1} \delta_j V_j & \text{if } \delta_i V_i \geq \delta_{i_q} V_{i_q} \\ c_{i_q} + \delta_{i_q} V_{i_q} - \delta_i V_i & \text{if } \delta_i V_i \leq \delta_{i_q} V_{i_q} \end{cases} \quad (e3)$$

Assuming the cost of securing i's vote is distinct from that of all other committee members, property (e2) says that the likelihood any individual i is included in someone else's winning coalition is zero if i is not one of the q cheapest committee members to attract and is exactly i's probability of not being the next period agenda-setter otherwise. Similarly, property (e3) says that the necessary cost to i of forming a winning coalition to support i's equilibrium proposal is given by the cost of the cheapest $q-1$ individuals whenever i is not one of these people and is otherwise given by the cost of securing the cheapest q individuals less the price of i's own vote.

Using (e2) and (e3), expression (e1) can be rewritten

$$V_i = \begin{cases} p_i(1 - c_{i_q}) & \text{if } \delta_i V_i > \delta_{i_q} V_{i_q} \\ \frac{p_i}{1-\delta_i}(1 - c_{i_q} - \delta_{i_q} V_{i_q}) & \text{if } \delta_i V_i < \delta_{i_q} V_{i_q} \end{cases} \quad (e4)$$

and, because $1 - p_i \geq \sum_{j \neq i} p_j r_{ji} \geq 0$, if $\delta_i V_i \geq \delta_{i_q} V_{i_q}$ then

$$p_i \delta_i (1 - c_{i_q}) \leq \delta_i V_i \leq \frac{p_i \delta_i}{1 - \delta_i + p_i \delta_i}(1 - c_{i_q}). \quad (e5)$$

Finally, note that if $\delta_k V_k \geq \delta_{i_q} V_{i_q} > \delta_i V_i$ then (e4) implies

$$\delta_k V_k > \delta_i V_i \geq \frac{p_i}{1-\delta_i}(1 - c_{i_q} - \delta_k V_k)$$

so

$$\delta_k V_k > \frac{p_i \delta_i}{1 - \delta_i + p_i \delta_i}(1 - c_{i_q}). \quad (e6)$$

The next result uses (e1) through (e6) to expose several less immediate monotonicity properties of stationary equilibrium behavior, providing the key to establishing the uniqueness of equilibrium payoffs.

Lemma 6.1 *Fix a stationary equilibrium profile σ and assume $\delta_{i_k} V_{i_k} \leq \delta_{i_{k+1}} V_{i_{k+1}}$, all $k = 1, \ldots, n-1$. Then*
(1) $\delta_k V_k > \delta_{i_q} V_{i_q} \geq \delta_i V_i$ implies $p_k \delta_k > p_i \delta_i$;
(2) $\delta_{i_q} V_{i_q} \geq \delta_k V_k > \delta_i V_i$ implies $p_k \delta_k/(1 - \delta_k) > p_i \delta_i/(1 - \delta_i)$;
(3) $\delta_k V_k \geq \delta_{i_q} V_{i_q}$ and $p_k \delta_k \geq p_i \delta_i$ implies $\delta_k V_k \geq \delta_i V_i$;
(4) $\delta_{i_q} V_{i_q} > \delta_k V_k$ and $p_k \delta_k/(1 - \delta_k) \geq p_i \delta_i/(1 - \delta_i)$ implies $\delta_k V_k \geq \delta_i V_i$.

Proof *(1)* If $\delta_{i_q} V_{i_q} > \delta_i V_i$ then (e4) and (e6) imply

$$p_k \delta_k (1 - c_{i_q}) > \frac{p_i \delta_i}{1 - \delta_i + p_i \delta_i}(1 - c_{i_q})$$

so the claim follows from $1 - \delta_i + p_i \delta_i < 1$. If $\delta_{i_q} V_{i_q} = \delta_i V_i$ then (e4) and (e5) immediately give the result since

$$\delta_k V_k = p_k \delta_k (1 - c_{i_q}) > \delta_i V_i \geq p_i \delta_i (1 - c_{i_q}).$$

(2) If $\delta_{i_q} V_{i_q} > \delta_k V_k$ then (e4) implies

$$\frac{p_i \delta_i}{1 - \delta_i}(1 - c_{i_q} - \delta_{i_q} V_{i_q}) = \delta_i V_i < \delta_k V_k = \frac{p_k \delta_k}{1 - \delta_k}(1 - c_{i_q} - \delta_{i_q} V_{i_q})$$

and, if $\delta_{i_q} V_{i_q} = \delta_k V_k$, (e5) and (e6) imply

$$\frac{p_i \delta_i}{1 - \delta_i + p_i \delta_i}(1 - c_{i_q}) < \delta_k V_k \leq \frac{p_k \delta_k}{1 - \delta_k + p_k \delta_k}(1 - c_{i_q}).$$

Together, these inequalities directly yield the claim and complete the proof.

(3) Let $p_k \delta_k \geq p_i \delta_i$ and suppose $\delta_k V_k < \delta_i V_i$. Since $\delta_k V_k \geq \delta_{i_q} V_{i_q}$, $\delta_i V_i > \delta_{i_q} V_{i_q}$. Hence, (e4) and (e5) imply

$$\delta_i V_i = p_i \delta_i (1 - c_{i_q}) > \delta_k V_k \geq p_k \delta_k (1 - c_{i_q})$$

which gives $p_i \delta_i > p_k \delta_k$, a contradiction.

(4) Let $p_k \delta_k / (1 - \delta_k) \geq p_i \delta_i / (1 - \delta_i)$ and suppose $\delta_i V_i > \delta_k V_k$. If $\delta_i V_i \leq \delta_{i_q} V_{i_q}$ then *(2)* implies $p_i \delta_i / (1 - \delta_i) > p_k \delta_k / (1 - \delta_k)$, a contradiction. On the other hand, if $\delta_i V_i > \delta_{i_q} V_{i_q}$ then (e5) and (e6) imply

$$\frac{p_i \delta_i}{1 - \delta_i + p_i \delta_i}(1 - c_{i_q}) \geq \delta_i V_i > \frac{p_k \delta_k}{1 - \delta_k + p_k \delta_k}(1 - c_{i_q}).$$

Hence,

$$\frac{p_i \delta_i}{1 - \delta_i + p_i \delta_i} > \frac{p_k \delta_k}{1 - \delta_k + p_k \delta_k}$$

which implies $p_i \delta_i / (1 - \delta_i) > p_k \delta_k / (1 - \delta_k)$, a contradiction. □

Although Lemma 6.1 is of most value here as a step in proving Theorem 6.3 below, it is worth observing that parts (3) and (4) of the lemma imply two intuitive properties of stationary equilibrium payoffs in more symmetric environments. Specifically, if all committee members are equally patient,

6.2. BARGAINING OVER DISTRIBUTIONS

then individuals' equilibrium payoffs are nonnegatively correlated with their probabilities of being the agenda-setter in any period:

$$\delta_i = \delta \text{ for all } i \in N \text{ implies } [p_i \leq p_j \Rightarrow V_i \leq V_j];$$

and if all committee members are equally likely to be recognized as agenda-setter in any period, then individuals' equilibrium payoffs are nonnegatively correlated with their discount factors:

$$p_i = 1/n \text{ for all } i \in N \text{ implies } [\delta_i \leq \delta_j \Rightarrow V_i \leq V_j].$$

Let (V, r) and $(\bar{V}, \bar{r})$ be any two stationary equilibrium outcomes. The next result connects the rank-orderings of individuals' discounted payoffs across the two equilibria and justifies a useful notational simplification.

Lemma 6.2 *Let* $\{i_1, \ldots, i_n\}$ *and* $\{j_1, \ldots, j_n\}$ *be labelings of N such that, for all* $k = 1, \ldots, n-1$, $\delta_{i_k} V_{i_k} \leq \delta_{i_{k+1}} V_{i_{k+1}}$ *and* $\delta_{j_k} \bar{V}_{j_k} \leq \delta_{j_{k+1}} \bar{V}_{j_{k+1}}$.
(1) Either

$$[\delta_k V_k \leq \delta_{i_q} V_{i_q} \Rightarrow \delta_k \bar{V}_k \leq \delta_{j_q} \bar{V}_{j_q}, \ \forall k \in N]$$

or

$$[\delta_k \bar{V}_k \leq \delta_{j_q} \bar{V}_{j_q} \Rightarrow \delta_k V_k \leq \delta_{i_q} V_{i_q}, \ \forall k \in N].$$

(2) There exists $k \in N$ such that $\delta_k V_k = \delta_{i_q} V_{i_q}$ and $\delta_k \bar{V}_k = \delta_{j_q} \bar{V}_{j_q}$.

Proof *(1)* Suppose the claim is false. Then there exist individuals k, k' for which

$$\delta_k V_k \leq \delta_{i_q} V_{i_q} \text{ and } \delta_k \bar{V}_k > \delta_{j_q} \bar{V}_{j_q}$$

and

$$\delta_{k'} \bar{V}_{k'} \leq \delta_{j_q} \bar{V}_{j_q} \text{ and } \delta_{k'} V_{k'} > \delta_{i_q} V_{i_q}.$$

Hence $\delta_k V_k \leq \delta_{i_q} V_{i_q} < \delta_{k'} V_{k'}$ and $\delta_{k'} \bar{V}_{k'} \leq \delta_{j_q} \bar{V}_{j_q} < \delta_k \bar{V}_k$. But by Lemma 6.1(1), the first string of inequalities implies $p_{k'} \delta_{k'} > p_k \delta_k$ and the second string implies $p_{k'} \delta_{k'} < p_k \delta_k$: contradiction.

(2) Given (V, r), partition N into three subgroups:

$$\begin{aligned} N_1 &= \{k \in N : \delta_k V_k < \delta_{i_q} V_{i_q}\}; \\ N_2 &= \{k \in N : \delta_k V_k = \delta_{i_q} V_{i_q}\}; \\ N_3 &= \{k \in N : \delta_k V_k > \delta_{i_q} V_{i_q}\}. \end{aligned}$$

Similarly define the partition $(\bar{N}_1, \bar{N}_2, \bar{N}_3)$ for the equilibrium outcome $(\bar{V}, \bar{r})$. By *(1)*, we can assume, without loss of generality, that $N_1 \cup N_2 \subseteq \bar{N}_1 \cup \bar{N}_2$.

Suppose the claim *(2)* is false, so $N_2 \cap \bar{N}_2 = \emptyset$. Then $N_2 \subseteq \bar{N}_1$ and, in particular, $\delta_{i_q} \bar{V}_{i_q} < \delta_{j_q} \bar{V}_{j_q}$. Now, if $N_1 \cap \bar{N}_2 \neq \emptyset$ there must exist some individual k for whom $\delta_k V_k < \delta_{i_q} V_{i_q}$ and $\delta_k \bar{V}_k = \delta_{j_q} \bar{V}_{j_q} > \delta_{i_q} \bar{V}_{i_q}$; but, by Lemma 6.1(2), the first inequality implies $p_k \delta_k / (1 - \delta_k) < p_{i_q} \delta_{i_q} / (1 - \delta_{i_q})$ and the second inequality implies $p_k \delta_k / (1 - \delta_k) > p_{i_q} \delta_{i_q} / (1 - \delta_{i_q})$. Hence, $N_1 \cap \bar{N}_2 = \emptyset$ and, therefore, $(N_1 \cup N_2) \cap \bar{N}_2 = \emptyset$. But by part *(1)*, $N_1 \cup N_2 \subseteq \bar{N}_1 \cup \bar{N}_2$. Therefore, $N_1 \cup N_2 \subseteq \bar{N}_1$ which is absurd because, by definition, $|N_1 \cup N_2| \geq q$ and $|\bar{N}_1| \leq q - 1$. □

Hereafter, suppose that under any equilibrium outcomes (V, r) and $(\bar{V}, \bar{r})$, for all $i \leq q$, $\delta_i V_i \leq \delta_q V_q$ and $\delta_i \bar{V}_i \leq \delta_q \bar{V}_q$ and, for all $i \geq q$, $\delta_i V_i \geq \delta_q V_q$ and $\delta_i \bar{V}_i \geq \delta_q \bar{V}_q$.

Theorem 6.3 *Let (V, r) and $(\bar{V}, \bar{r})$ be two stationary equilibrium outcomes. Then $V = \bar{V}$.*

Proof We begin by first proving a series of claims.

Claim 1: If $c_i \geq \bar{c}_i$ and $\omega_i \leq \bar{\omega}_i$ then $V_i \leq \bar{V}_i$, with strict inequality if $c_i \neq \bar{c}_i$ or $\omega_i \neq \bar{\omega}_i$.

Proof: Immediate from (e1) which implies,

$$V_i = \frac{p_i(1 - c_i)}{1 - \delta_i \omega_i} \leq \frac{p_i(1 - \bar{c}_i)}{1 - \delta_i \bar{\omega}_i} = \bar{V}_i.$$

Claim 2: If $c_i \geq \bar{c}_i$ and $\omega_i \geq \bar{\omega}_i$ then $\bar{V}_i - V_i \leq c_i - \bar{c}_i$, with strict inequality if $c_i \neq \bar{c}_i$ or $\omega_i \neq \bar{\omega}_i$.

Proof: The claim is trivial if $\bar{V}_i < V_i$, so assume $\bar{V}_i \geq V_i$. Then by (e1),

$$\begin{aligned}
\bar{V}_i - V_i &= \frac{p_i(1 - \bar{c}_i)}{1 - \delta_i \bar{\omega}_i} - \frac{p_i(1 - c_i)}{1 - \delta_i \omega_i} \\
&\leq \frac{p_i(1 - \bar{c}_i)}{1 - \delta_i \omega_i} - \frac{p_i(1 - c_i)}{1 - \delta_i \omega_i} \\
&= \frac{p_i(c_i - \bar{c}_i)}{1 - \delta_i \omega_i} \\
&\leq c_i - \bar{c}_i
\end{aligned}$$

where the last inequality follows from $\omega_i \in [0, 1 - p_i]$ and $\delta_i < 1$ which imply $0 < p_i / [1 - \delta_i \omega_i] < 1$.

Claim 3: If $\omega_i > \bar{\omega}_i$ then there exists some $j \in N$ with $\omega_j < \bar{\omega}_j$ such that (a) $\delta_j V_j \geq \delta_q V_q \geq \delta_i V_i$ and (b) $\delta_i \bar{V}_i \geq \delta_q \bar{V}_q \geq \delta_j \bar{V}_j$. Further, if either

6.2. BARGAINING OVER DISTRIBUTIONS

inequality in (a) (respectively, (b)) is strict, both the inequalities in (b) (respectively, (a)) hold with equality.

Proof: Fix $i \in N$ with $\omega_i > \bar{\omega}_i$. Then there must exist some $j \in N$ with $\omega_j < \bar{\omega}_j$, else at least one individual $k \in N$ cannot be making a proposal to a cost-minimizing coalition conditional on k being agenda-setter. If $\delta_q V_q < \delta_i V_i$, then (e2) implies $\omega_i = 0$, contradicting $\omega_i > \bar{\omega}_i \geq 0$; so $\delta_q V_q \geq \delta_i V_i$. And since $1 - p_i \geq \omega_i > \bar{\omega}_i$, (e2) further implies $\delta_i \bar{V}_i \geq \delta_q \bar{V}_q$. Similar reasoning yields $\delta_j V_j \geq \delta_q V_q$ and $\delta_q \bar{V}_q \geq \delta_j \bar{V}_j$.

To prove the last statement, assume $\delta_j V_j > \delta_q V_q \geq \delta_i V_i$; then, by Lemma 6.1(1), $p_j \delta_j > p_i \delta_i$. Moreover, by Lemma 6.2 and the maintained labeling convention for N, $\delta_j V_j > \delta_q V_q$ implies $j > q$ and hence $\delta_j \bar{V}_j \geq \delta_q \bar{V}_q$; therefore (b), implies $\delta_j \bar{V}_j = \delta_q \bar{V}_q$. Finally, if $\delta_i \bar{V}_i > \delta_q \bar{V}_q = \delta_j \bar{V}_j$, then Lemma 6.1(1) implies $p_j \delta_j < p_i \delta_i$, a contradiction. Hence, $\delta_j V_j > \delta_q V_q$ implies $\delta_i \bar{V}_i = \delta_q \bar{V}_q = \delta_j \bar{V}_j$, as required. Now assume $\delta_q V_q > \delta_i V_i$ and apply similar reasoning (in this case, using Lemma 6.1(2)) to conclude that here too it must be $\delta_i \bar{V}_i = \delta_q \bar{V}_q = \delta_j \bar{V}_j$. The proof follows.

Claim 4: If $\omega_i > \bar{\omega}_i$ and $c_i \geq \bar{c}_i$, then $V_i \leq \bar{V}_i$ with strict inequality if $c_i > \bar{c}_i$.

Proof: Claim 3 insures that there exists some $j \in N$ with $\omega_j < \bar{\omega}_j$ and implies that there are two cases to consider.

(1) $\delta_i \bar{V}_i \geq \delta_q \bar{V}_q \geq \delta_j \bar{V}_j$ and $\delta_j V_j = \delta_q V_q = \delta_i V_i$. If $V_j < \bar{V}_j$ then $\delta_i V_i = \delta_j V_j < \delta_j \bar{V}_j \leq \delta_i \bar{V}_i$, so the claim obtains. Suppose $V_j \geq \bar{V}_j$. Then, by Claim 1, $c_j \leq \bar{c}_j$. By (e3),

$$(\bar{c}_j - c_j) = (\bar{c}_q - c_q) + \delta_q(\bar{V}_q - V_q) - \delta_j(\bar{V}_j - V_j)$$

so

$$\delta_q(\bar{V}_q - V_q) = [(\bar{c}_j - c_j) + \delta_j(\bar{V}_j - V_j)] + (c_q - \bar{c}_q).$$

By Claim 2, the term in square brackets is nonnegative and $(c_q - \bar{c}_q) \geq 0$ since, again by (e3), $c_q = c_i \geq \bar{c}_i = \bar{c}_q$. The claim now follows from $\delta_i \bar{V}_i \geq \delta_q \bar{V}_q$ and $\delta_i V_i = \delta_q V_q$.

(2) $\delta_i \bar{V}_i = \delta_q \bar{V}_q = \delta_j \bar{V}_j$ and $\delta_j V_j \geq \delta_q V_q \geq \delta_i V_i$. If $V_j < \bar{V}_j$ then $\delta_i V_i \leq \delta_j V_j < \delta_j \bar{V}_j = \delta_i \bar{V}_i$, so the claim obtains. Suppose $V_j \geq \bar{V}_j$. Then, by Claim 1, $c_j \leq \bar{c}_j$. Now, since $\omega_i > \bar{\omega}_i$, $c_i \geq \bar{c}_i$ and $V_j \geq \bar{V}_j$, Claim 2 implies

$$0 \leq V_j - \bar{V}_j < \bar{c}_j - c_j = \bar{c}_q - c_q.$$

And by (e3), $c_i = c_q + \delta_q V_q - \delta_i V_i$ and $\bar{c}_i = \bar{c}_q = \bar{c}_q + \delta_q \bar{V}_q - \delta_i \bar{V}_i$. Further, since $c_i \geq \bar{c}_i$,

$$\delta_i(\bar{V}_i - V_i) \geq (\bar{c}_q - c_q) - \delta_q(V_q - \bar{V}_q).$$

By $(\bar{c}_q - c_q) > \delta_j(V_j - \bar{V}_j) \geq \delta_q(V_q - \bar{V}_q)$, $\delta_i(\bar{V}_i - V_i) > 0$; the claim follows.

Claim 5: For all $i \in N$, $V_i = \bar{V}_i$ if and only if $\bar{c}_i = c_i$.
Proof: Apply Claims 1, 2 and 4.

Claim 6: If $c_i \geq \bar{c}_i$, then $0 \leq \delta_i(\bar{V}_i - V_i) \leq c_i - \bar{c}_i$ with inequalities strict if and only if $c_i > \bar{c}_i$.

Proof: By Claims 1 and 4, $0 \leq \bar{V}_i - V_i$. We need to show $\delta(\bar{V}_i - V_i) \leq c_i - \bar{c}_i$. If $\omega_i \geq \bar{\omega}_i$, the inequality holds by Claims 2 and 4. Suppose $\omega_i < \bar{\omega}_i$. By Claim 3, there exists some $j \in N$ with $\omega_j > \bar{\omega}_j$ and there are two possible cases.

(1) $\delta_j \bar{V}_j \geq \delta_q \bar{V}_q \geq \delta_i \bar{V}_i$ and $\delta_i V_i = \delta_q V_q = \delta_j V_j$. By (e3), $c_j = c_q = c_i$ and $\bar{c}_i \geq \bar{c}_q = \bar{c}_j$; hence $c_j \geq \bar{c}_j$. And by Claims 2 and 4, $\omega_j > \bar{\omega}_j$ implies $0 \leq \bar{V}_j - V_j \leq c_j - \bar{c}_j$. Now, $c_j - \bar{c}_j = c_q - \bar{c}_q$ and

$$\bar{V}_j - V_j \geq \delta_j(\bar{V}_j - V_j) \geq \delta_q(\bar{V}_q - V_q).$$

Therefore, $c_q - \bar{c}_q \geq \delta_q(\bar{V}_q - V_q)$. Further, by (e3),

$$c_i - \bar{c}_i = [(c_q - \bar{c}_q) - \delta_q(\bar{V}_q - V_q)] + \delta_i(\bar{V}_i - V_i).$$

By hypothesis, $c_i \geq \bar{c}_i$, and we have just shown the term in square brackets to be nonnegative; the claim follows.

(2) $\delta_j \bar{V}_j = \delta_q \bar{V}_q = \delta_i \bar{V}_i$ and $\delta_i V_i \geq \delta_q V_q \geq \delta_j V_j$. By (e3), $c_j \geq c_q = c_i$ and $\bar{c}_i = \bar{c}_q = \bar{c}_j$; hence $c_j \geq \bar{c}_j$. And by Claims 2 and 4, $\omega_j > \bar{\omega}_j$ implies $0 \leq \bar{V}_j - V_j \leq c_j - \bar{c}_j$. From (e3) too, we have

$$c_j = c_q + \delta_q V_q - \delta_j V_j \leq c_i + \delta_i V_i - \delta_j V_j$$

and

$$\bar{c}_j = \bar{c}_q + \delta_q \bar{V}_q - \delta_j \bar{V}_j = \bar{c}_i + \delta_i \bar{V}_i - \delta_j \bar{V}_j.$$

Therefore,

$$c_i - \bar{c}_i \geq [(c_j - \bar{c}_j) - \delta_j(\bar{V}_j - V_j)] + \delta_i(\bar{V}_i - V_i)$$

and the claim follows as before.

Finally, to see the inequalities are strict only if $c_i > \bar{c}_i$, suppose $c_i = \bar{c}_i$. Then $0 \leq \delta_i(\bar{V}_i - V_i) \leq c_i - \bar{c}_i = 0$, which is possible only if both inequalities are in fact equalities.

Claim 7: $c_q \geq \bar{c}_q$ implies $c_i \geq \bar{c}_i$, all $i \in N$, with inequality strict if and only if $c_q > \bar{c}_q$.

Proof: The claim follows directly from (e3) for $i \geq q$. Suppose $i < q$; by (e3)
$$c_i - \bar{c}_i \geq [(c_q - \bar{c}_q) - \delta_q(\bar{V}_q - V_q)] + \delta_i(\bar{V}_i - V_i) \quad (*)$$
By Claim 6, therefore, $c_i - \bar{c}_i \geq \delta_i(\bar{V}_i - V_i)$ with strict inequality only if $c_q > \bar{c}_q$. Suppose $c_i < \bar{c}_i$. Then Claim 6 gives $0 < \delta_i(V_i - \bar{V}_i) < \bar{c}_i - c_i$ but, by $(*)$, $\bar{c}_i - c_i \leq \delta_i(V_i - \bar{V}_i)$: contradiction. Hence $c_i \geq \bar{c}_i$ and, by $(*)$, the inequality is strict if $c_q > \bar{c}_q$. Finally, if $c_q = \bar{c}_q$ then $\bar{V}_q = V_q$ and, therefore, $(*)$ implies $c_i - \bar{c}_i = \delta_i(\bar{V}_i - V_i) \geq \bar{V}_i - V_i$, which is possible only if $c_i = \bar{c}_i$.

We now complete the proof for the theorem. By Claims 5 and 7, it suffices to show $c_q = \bar{c}_q$. Suppose the contrary and, without loss of generality, let $c_q > \bar{c}_q$. By Claim 7, $c_i > \bar{c}_i$ for all $i \in N$ and, therefore, by Claim 6, $\bar{V}_i > V_i$ for all $i = 1, \ldots, q-1$. But then (e3) implies

$$\bar{c}_q = \sum_{i=1}^{i=q-1} \delta_i \bar{V}_i > \sum_{i=1}^{i=q-1} \delta_i V_i = c_q,$$

a contradiction. □

6.3 Application: Pork barrel politics

Among the things on which legislatures decide is the allocation of collectively funded but particularistic benefits among legislative districts. There is more than one way to think about this sort of allocative decision. One possibility is as a more-or-less disparate collection of regional projects, each of which is approved or not separately with the resulting aggregate cost being diffused nationally; examples include decisions on independent projects such as local road networks, dams and flood controls proposed by the various district representatives. Another way is as a division of a given sum of general revenues among a set of possible regional projects as, for instance, when there is an excess of tax-revenues beyond those earmarked for specific programmes. And a third possibility is as the allocation of pieces of a given national project with fixed aggregate benefits as well as fixed aggregate costs. For example, successful implementation of large-scale multifaceted projects like the development of a new generation of fighter planes can be associated (albeit not precisely) with given total benefit-cost ratios and it is the distribution of the component benefits and costs, rather than choice of the project itself, that is determined in committee. But whichever way we think of the decision, the jointly key features of the allocation are that benefits are enjoyed by few while costs are borne by many.

Because we wish to exploit theoretical insights from the general model of bargaining over distributions to shed some light on pork barrel politics, it is most useful to assume that a project defined by a given aggregate benefit-cost ratio is given to the committee. We also suppose that the costs of the project are shared evenly across all legislative districts and the committee consists of exactly one representative per legislative district. The committee's task is thus to distribute the total benefits among their respective districts. In this context, the main questions concern how various features of the decision-making environment (for instance, the decision rule used at any voting stage of the bargaining process or legislators' degree of patience) affect the extent to which economically efficient projects (that is, projects whose aggregate benefits exceed their costs) are adopted. To address these issues, consider the following model.

A committee of n individuals, n odd, is charged to allocate the benefits of a given aggregate project defined by a finite benefit-cost ratio, $B/C > 0$. The total cost accruing to each district is fixed at C/n and it is the distribution of benefits B which is to be determined. The committee uses the sequential bargaining process as described in the previous section, with a common recognition probability, $p_i = 1/n$ all $i \in N$, and a q-rule, $(n+1)/2 \leq q \leq n$. Each committee member i's preferences are linear in net benefits to his or her district. For each $i \in N$, let $x_i^t = b_i^t - (C/n)$ denote the net benefit from any committee decision $x^t = (x_1^t, \ldots, x_n^t)$, let

$$X^1 = \{(x_1^t, \ldots, x_n^t) : \forall i \in N, \ x_i^t \geq -(C/n) \text{ and } \sum_{i \in N} x_i^t = B - C\},$$

and let $X = X^1 \cup \{x^0\}$ denote the set of possible committee decisions, where x^0 is the default outcome "reject the project". Assuming $x^0 = (0, \ldots, 0)$ as usual, i's payoff from a decision $x^t \in X$ made in legislative period t is $u_i(x^t) = \delta^{t-1} x_i^t$, where $\delta \in (0,1)$ is the common discount factor among committee members.

By sequential rationality, individual i votes in favor of proposal $x^j \in X$ in any stationary equilibrium if and only if

$$x_i^j = b_i^j - \frac{C}{n} \geq \delta V_i \Leftrightarrow b_i^j \geq \frac{C}{n} + \delta V_i,$$

where V_i is i's undiscounted continuation value from the proposal being voted down. By symmetry, $V_i = V_j = V$ for all $i, j \in N$ in any stationary equilibrium. Applying conditions (2.1) and (2.2) of Theorem 6.2, therefore, an agenda-setter i's best proposal is to offer $q - 1$ individuals a benefit level

6.3. APPLICATION: PORK BARREL POLITICS

$b_j^i = (C/n) + \delta V$, offer nothing to $n - q$ individuals, and propose

$$b_i^i = B - (q-1)(\frac{C}{n} + \delta V)$$

for herself; the first such proposal offered (in $t = 1$) is accepted.

Assuming any agenda-setter i uses a fair lottery to decide to which particular $q-1$ individuals $j \in N\setminus\{i\}$ to offer a benefit $b_j^i = (C/n)+\delta V$, and noting that being excluded from a winning coalition implies a cost $(-C/n) < 0$, condition (2.3) of Theorem 6.2 requires

$$V = p_i \left[B - (q-1)(\frac{C}{n} + \delta V) - \frac{C}{n}\right] + (1-p_i)\left[\frac{q-1}{n-1}\delta V - \frac{n-q}{n-1}\frac{C}{n}\right].$$

Substituting $p_i = 1/n$ and solving for V yields

$$V = \frac{B-C}{n}.$$

Therefore, the value of the decision-making process to any committee member is simply $(1/n)^{\text{th}}$ of the net difference between the aggregate benefits and costs, which is evidently positive only if the project is economically efficient, $B/C \geq 1$; by Theorem 6.3, this is the only stationary equilibrium value.

Whether a project B/C is adopted – that is, whether any agenda-setter chooses to make an acceptable proposal $x \in X^1$ in equilibrium – depends on whether the net payoff to that individual from any acceptable proposal is positive. And the condition for acceptability is not economic efficiency, $B/C \geq 1$, but rather

$$B - (q-1)(\frac{C}{n} + \delta V) - \frac{C}{n} \geq 0.$$

For if this inequality fails to obtain for some project B/C, then no committee member recognized to offer a proposal would find it profitable to do so; the only proposals that provide sufficient incentive for an agenda-setter to make them are those that would surely be rejected in equilibrium. In effect, the committee would never wish to see such a project implemented. Substituting for V and solving, the acceptability condition is equivalent to

$$\frac{B}{C} \geq \frac{1 + (1-\delta)(q-1)}{n - \delta(q-1)}.$$

The set of projects adopted by the committee is given by those for which this inequality obtains and, therefore, economically *inefficient* projects are surely rejected under the committee bargaining process if and only if

$$\frac{1+(1-\delta)(q-1)}{n-\delta(q-1)} \geq 1 \Leftrightarrow n \leq q.$$

Hence there exist acceptable but inefficient projects for all q-rules shy of unanimity, $q = n$. On the other hand, although there is no assurance the committee rejects all inefficient projects for $q < n$, the committee certainly adopts every efficient project within its jurisdiction (since $B/C \geq 1$ and $q < n$ imply B/C satisfies the acceptability condition).

Writing $q \equiv kn$, where $k \in (1/2, 1)$ is constant, define the critical acceptability ratio

$$\beta(k, \delta, n) \equiv \frac{1+(1-\delta)(kn-1)}{n-\delta(kn-1)}.$$

For any $k < 1$, $q < n$ and $\beta(k, \delta, n) < 1$. It is straightforward to confirm that $\beta(k, \delta, n)$ is strictly increasing in k and in n, but strictly decreasing (respectively, increasing) in δ for $k < (n-1)/n$ (respectively, $k > (n-1)/n$). In other words, the proportion of inefficient projects accepted by a committee is decreasing in size of the coalition required for passage of a proposal and in the size of the committee itself; but, at least for relatively low q, the proportion is increasing in the extent to which committee members are patient. Insofar as the discount factor can be interpreted as a probability of legislative reelection, therefore, this result says that the more secure are incumbents, the larger the set of inefficient projects they approve. This incentive is offset by requiring supermajorities to implement any proposal.

6.4 Bargaining over policy

Theorems 6.2 and 6.3 characterize the substantively most important features of stationary equilibria in a model of committee bargaining over the distribution of some benefit. An important characteristic of the pure distribution setting is the ability of agenda-setters to transfer utility freely between committee members. For instance, a proposer might allocate 50% of the total benefit to himself and share the remaining 50% in any number of ways between two or three others. Such freedom to adjust utility allocations is unavailable in more general environments involving public policy rather than purely distributive decisions. The constraint is that policy is technically a public good: if the committee agrees to some policy position then all individuals' utilities are defined with respect to this policy. Except in relatively rare circumstances, it is not feasible to change a policy to affect

6.4. BARGAINING OVER POLICY

only some individuals' payoffs and not others. In this section, therefore, we generalize the sequential legislative bargaining model to include policy as well as purely distributional decisions.

The underlying sequential bargaining process is unchanged from section 6.2 above, save the decision rule f is permitted to be any simple rule characterized by a nonempty set of decisive coalitions, $\mathcal{L}$. The feasible set of alternatives, however, is now taken to be any nonempty convex and compact subset $X \subset \Re^k$. Let $x^0 \in X$ be the status quo policy and assume all n committee members have a common discount factor, $\delta \in (0,1)$. The implications of allowing discount factors to vary across individuals are discussed later. The final modification to the distributional model is to permit spatial preferences: for all $i \in N$, i's preferences are assumed representable by a continuous and concave von Neumann-Morgenstern utility function, $u_i : X \to \Re$ with ideal point $x_i \in X$. In the pure distribution case, we assume any individual's payoff from maintaining the status quo x^0 is zero. When x^0 is a policy rather than a distribution of a homogenous good, however, such a common normalization for status quo utilities is typically inappropriate: x^0 might be one person's most preferred alternative but a terrible outcome for some other individual. In this case therefore, payoffs from any bargaining sequence $(x^0, \ldots, x^0, x^t, \ldots)$ depend essentially on the status quo and are given by

$$(1 - \delta^{t-1})u_i(x^0) + \delta^{t-1}u_i(x^t).$$

Because linear preferences are concave, the pure distribution model is a special case of these assumptions: let X be defined as for section 6.2 above, let $x^0 = (0, \ldots, 0)$ and note $x_i = e_i \in X$ for all $i \in N$.

Proving that stationary equilibria generally exist in the sequential legislative bargaining game requires dealing with essentially the same difficulty as that encountered in proving the existence of subgame perfect equilibria for the endogenous agenda-setting game (Theorem 5.9). Because there are typically multiple winning coalitions under any admissible rule f, the set of acceptable proposals an individual might offer at any stage is rarely convex: Figure 5.12 is an illustration for majority rule with $n = 3$ and $X \subset \Re^2$. To accommodate complications induced through nonconvexities of the social acceptance sets, we have to allow for nondegenerate mixed proposal strategies (as is true of Example 6.4, for instance).

Recall that for any set Y, ΔY is the family of probability distributions over Y and that a stationary proposal strategy for any $i \in N$ is a mixed proposal $\pi_i \in \Delta X$ to be used at every period in which i is the selected agenda-setter; write $Supp[\pi_i]$ for the support of π_i. Let $\sigma = (\pi, v)$ be a profile of undominated stationary strategies. Given that all voting strategies under σ are required to be undominated, for any $j \in N$ let

$$A_j(\sigma) = \{x \in X : u_j(x) \geq (1-\delta)u_j(x^0) + \delta V_j(\sigma)\}$$

denote the set of proposals j is willing to accept under σ; that is, $v_j(x) = 1$ if and only if $x \in A_j(\sigma)$. For any coalition $L \subseteq N$ let $A_L(\sigma) = \cap_{j \in L} A_j(\sigma)$ and let $A(\sigma) = \cup_{\mathcal{L}} A_L(\sigma)$, where $\mathcal{L}$ is the set of decisive coalitions characterizing f. Then, by sequential rationality and undominated choices, any individual recognized to make a proposal must either offer a passing alternative that defeats the status quo and makes him or her better off when such a proposal exists or, in the case that such a proposal does not exist, must offer an alternative surely rejected in favor of maintaining the status quo. That is (leaving the strategy profile σ implicit), for any $i \in N$ with continuation value V_i, if

$$\sup\{u_i(y) : y \in A\} > (1-\delta)u_i(x^0) + \delta V_i$$

then

$$Supp[\pi_i] \subseteq \arg\max\{u_i(y) : y \in A\};$$

if there exists no such alternative $y \in A$ then $Supp[\pi_i] \subseteq X \backslash A$ and, in the case of indifference,

$$Supp[\pi_i] \subseteq \arg\max\{u_i(y) : y \in A\} \cup [X \backslash A].$$

For example, if δ is very small and $i = 3$ then, conditional on $y_2 = y_2'$ in Figure 5.12 (where the status quo x^0 is presumed extreme),

$$\arg\max\{u_3(y) : y \in A\} = \{y_3', y_3''\}$$

and $Supp[\pi_3] \subseteq \{y_3', y_3''\}$. On the other hand, if we set $x^0 = x_3$ then, for almost every sequence of prior proposals by other committee members, $\sup\{u_3(y) : y \in A\} < (1-\delta)u_3(x^0) + \delta V_3$ and $Supp[\pi_3] \subseteq X \backslash A$.

Following the same logic as for the pure distribution case, individual i's continuation value given a profile of stationary strategies σ satisfying the optimality properties above, is constructed as follows. At the start of any period there is a probability p_j that individual $j \in N$ is recognized to make a proposal; given j is recognized, i's total expected payoff from j's proposal is given by the weighted sum of two terms. The first term is i's expected payoff conditional on j offering a proposal $z \in A$, in which case, by definition of $A \subseteq X$, z is immediately accepted and the decision process ends. The second term is i's expected payoff conditional on j offering a

6.4. BARGAINING OVER POLICY

proposal $z \in X \backslash A$ which, again by definition of A, is rejected; in this event, i's payoff is given by the sum of a one period return from retaining the status quo x^0 and i's discounted continuation value from the process moving to the next period. Therefore, summing over all $j \in N$,

$$V_i = \sum_{j \in N} p_j \left[\int_A u_i(z) d\pi_j(z) + \int_{X \backslash A} [(1-\delta) u_i(x^0) + \delta V_i] d\pi_j(z) \right].$$

Solving for V_i:

$$V_i = \frac{\sum_{j \in N} p_j [\int_A u_i(z) d\pi_j(z) + (1-\delta) \int_{X \backslash A} d\pi_j(z) u_i(x^0)]}{1 - \delta \sum_{j \in N} p_j \int_{X \backslash A} d\pi_j(z)}.$$

It is possible to simplify the notation a little at this point and rewrite the acceptance set A_j for any individual j in a more convenient form. To do this, for any set $Y \subseteq X$ and $z \in X$ let $I_Y(z)$ be an indicator function that takes the value $I_Y(z) = 1$ if $z \in Y$ and $I_Y(z) = 0$ otherwise; now define a distribution ξ on X such that, for all $Y \subseteq X$,

$$\int_Y d\xi(y) = \frac{\sum_{j \in N} p_j [\int_{Y \cap A} d\pi_j(z) + I_Y(x^0)(1-\delta) \int_{X \backslash A} d\pi_j(z)]}{1 - \delta \sum_{j \in N} p_j \int_{X \backslash A} d\pi_j(z)}.$$

Then

$$\int_X u_i(z) d\xi(z)$$

$$= \int_X u_i(z) d \frac{\left[\sum_{j \in N} p_j [I_{X \cap A}(z) \pi_j(z) + I_X(x^0)(1-\delta) \int_{X \backslash A} d\pi_j(z)] \right]}{1 - \delta \sum_{j \in N} p_j \int_{X \backslash A} d\pi_j(z)}$$

$$= \frac{\sum_{j \in N} p_j [\int_A u_i(z) d\pi_j(z) + (1-\delta) \int_{X \backslash A} d\pi_j(z) u_i(x^0)]}{1 - \delta \sum_{j \in N} p_j \int_{X \backslash A} d\pi_j(z)}$$

$$= V_i.$$

Finally, let $\beta \in \Delta X$ be the probability distribution such that, for all $Y \subseteq X$,

$$\int_Y d\beta(y) = (1-\delta) I_Y(x^0) + \delta \int_Y d\xi(y)$$

so, for all individuals $j \in N$,

$$\int_X u_j(z) d\beta(z) = \int_X u_j(z) d[(1-\delta) I_X(x^0) + \delta \xi(z)]$$

$$= (1-\delta) u_j(x^0) + \delta \int_X u_j(z) d\xi(z)$$

$$= (1-\delta) u_j(x^0) + \delta V_j$$

and we can write

$$A_j(\sigma) = \{x \in X : u_j(x) \geq \int_X u_j(z)d\beta(z)\}.$$

A common feature of the stationary equilibria identified for the pure distribution case is that all such equilibria imply the proposal of the first person recognized is surely accepted by the committee; that is, $\int_{X\setminus A} d\pi_j(z) = 0$ for all $j \in N$ and the equilibria satisfy *no-delay*. At least in part, this is because the status quo alternative, $x^0 = (0,\ldots,0)$, is unanimously agreed to be a worst alternative. When bargaining over policy, however, the first proposer could be someone for whom the status quo is the best possible outcome, in which case delay is in principle possible. Nevertheless, the existence theorem establishes that even in such cases there also exists a no-delay equilibrium. To prove the theorem, we first need a technical lemma. The required lemma involves establishing continuity of the correspondence $A(\cdot)$ that maps strategies into sets of collectively acceptable alternatives. In turn, this requires a more general notion of continuity for a function than we have used hitherto.

To see why a more general notion of continuity is needed, recall the familiar idea of continuity of a function defined on subsets of Euclidean space, say $h : X \to Z$ where $X \subseteq \Re^k$ and $Z \subseteq \Re^l$. Let $d(a,b) \equiv \|a - b\|$ denote the Euclidean distance between any two points a,b in a Euclidean space; then h is continuous on X if, for all $x \in X$ and every convergent sequence (x^m) in X with $d(x^m, x) \to 0$, we have $d(h(x^m), h(x)) \to 0$ as $m \to \infty$. But the functions of concern below are individuals' continuation value functions, V_i, $i \in N$. Specifically, given undominated voting behavior, v, each individual i's strategy involves choice of a probability distribution π_i from ΔX and consequently, as described explicitly above, i's continuation value V_i is a function that takes "points" $\pi = (\pi_1, \ldots, \pi_n)$ from $[\Delta X]^n$ into the real line $\Re$ and $[\Delta X]^n$ is clearly not a subset of some Euclidean space. So while the idea of convergence in terms of Euclidean distance is well-defined on the range $\Re$ of V_i, to talk about continuity of V_i on the domain of probability distributions $[\Delta X]^n$, we have to specify what it means for a sequence of probability distributions $\pi^m = (\pi_1^m, \ldots, \pi_n^m)$ to converge to a profile $\pi = (\pi_1, \ldots, \pi_n)$.

Intuitively, two probability distributions from ΔX are "close" if, for any subset $S \subset X$, the probability mass assigned to S under one distribution is "close" to that assigned under the other. Formally, for any nonempty subset $S \subset X$ and any $\eta > 0$, let $S^\eta \subset X$ denote the set of points whose Euclidean distance from S is less than η; that is

$$S^\eta = \{y \in X : \inf_{z \in S} d(y,z) < \eta\}.$$

6.4. BARGAINING OVER POLICY

Let $\pi_i, \hat{\pi}_i \in \Delta X$ and define the Prohorov distance between π_i and $\hat{\pi}_i$ by

$$d_P(\hat{\pi}_i, \pi_i) = \inf\{\eta \geq 0 : \int_S d\pi_i \leq \int_{S^\eta} d\hat{\pi}_i + \eta, \text{ all } S \subset X\}.$$

A sequence of probability distributions (π_i^m) in ΔX *converges weakly* to $\pi_i \in \Delta X$ if and only if $d_P(\pi_i^m, \pi_i) \to 0$ as m goes to infinity. A sequence (π^m) in $[\Delta X]^n$ converges weakly to a profile $\pi \in [\Delta X]^n$ if every component π_i^m of π^m converges weakly to π_i. Then a function $g : [\Delta X]^n \to \Re$ is continuous on $[\Delta X]^n$ if, for all $\pi \in [\Delta X]^n$ and every weakly convergent sequence (π^m) in $[\Delta X]^n$ with $d_P(\pi^m, \pi) \to 0$, we have $d(g(\pi^m), g(\pi)) \to 0$ as $m \to \infty$.

Lemma 6.3 *Let $\sum_0$ denote the set of undominated stationary strategy profiles σ such that, for all $j \in N$, $\int_{X \setminus A(\sigma)} d\pi_j(z) = 0$. Then for all $\sigma \in \sum_0$, $A(\sigma)$ is nonempty, compact and the correspondence $A : \sum_0 \rightrightarrows X$ is continuous.*

Proof Given $\sigma = (\pi, v) \in \sum_0$ there is no delay in accepting any proposal under π and we can abuse notation slightly, writing i's continuation value as

$$V_i(\pi) = \sum_{j \in N} p_j \int u_i(z) d\pi_j(z),$$

where the undominated voting strategies are understood (similarly, we also write $\pi \in \sum_0$ and so on). By u_i continuous on X and X compact, $V_i : [\Delta X]^n \to \Re$ is continuous on $[\Delta X]^n$. Following the same notational convenience define, for all $i \in N$, the acceptance sets $A_i(\pi)$ and, for all $L \in \mathcal{L}$, the sets $A_L(\pi) = \cap_{i \in L} A_i(\pi)$ and $A(\pi) = \cup_\mathcal{L} A_L(\pi)$. Recalling the distribution β let $\hat{x}(\beta)$ denote the expected committee decision under σ at the start of any proposal period. By u_i concave,

$$u_i(\hat{x}(\beta)) \geq \int_X u_i(z) d\beta(z)$$

so $\hat{x}(\beta) \in A_i(\pi)$ all i. Moreover, X compact and u_i continuous imply $A_i(\pi)$ compact and, therefore, $A_L(\pi)$ is also nonempty and compact, all $L \in \mathcal{L}$. It remains to check continuity. If, for all $L \in \mathcal{L}$, A_L continuous, then A is the finite union of continuous correspondences and thereby continuous [2, Theorem 16.27]. It suffices, therefore, to prove A_L continuous, all $L \in \mathcal{L}$. Fix a coalition $L \in \mathcal{L}$ arbitrarily; continuity of A_L follows from the following three claims.

Claim 1: A_L is uhc.

Proof: Let $i \in L$, $\pi \in \sum_0$ and suppose $A_i(\pi)$ is not uhc at π. Then there is an open set $T \subset X$ with $A_i(\pi) \subseteq T$ and a sequence $(\pi_m) \to \pi$ such that, for all m, $\pi_m \in \sum_0$ and $A_i(\pi_m) \setminus T \neq \emptyset$. For all m, let $x_m \in A_i(\pi) \setminus T$; then the sequence (x_m) lies in $X \cap T^c$ which, by T open and X compact, is a compact set. Without loss of generality, therefore, assume $(x_m) \to x \in X \cap T^c$. Now the difference

$$\psi_i(\pi_m, x_m) = u_i(x_m) - \delta V_i(\pi_m)$$

is jointly continuous in (π_m, x_m) [34, Theorem 5.5], so $(\pi_m, x_m) \to (x, \pi)$ implies $\psi_i(\pi_m, x_m) \to \psi_i(\pi, x)$. By construction, $x_m \in A_i(\pi_m)$ for all m and so, by definition of $A_i(\pi_m)$, $\psi_i(\pi_m, x_m) \geq 0$ for all m; but then continuity implies $\psi_i(\pi, x) \geq 0$ which means $x \in A_i(\pi) \subseteq T$: contradiction. Hence $A_i(\pi)$ is uhc. Because $i \in L$ is arbitrary and, by definition, $A_L(\pi)$ is the finite intersection of compact-valued uhc correspondences, $A_L(\pi)$ is also uhc [2, Theorem 16.25].

For each $i \in L$, define the correspondence $A_i^s : \sum_0 \rightrightarrows X$ by

$$A_i^s(\pi) = \{x \in X : \psi_i(\pi, x) > 0\}$$

and let $A_L^s(\pi) = \cap_{i \in L} A_i^s(\pi)$.

Claim 2: A_L^s is nonempty and has open graph.

Proof: By assumption, $\delta \in (0, 1)$. Let $u_i(x) > 0$ for some $x \in X$ and all $i \in L$. Then by u_i concave, nonnegative and continuous, $\delta < 1$ implies that, for sufficiently small $\lambda \in (0, 1)$,

$$u_i(\lambda x + (1 - \lambda)\hat{x}(\beta)) > \delta V_i(\pi).$$

In particular, there exists a sufficiently small $\lambda' > 0$ for which this inequality holds for all $i \in L$. Hence, $(\lambda' x + (1 - \lambda')\hat{x}(\beta)) \in A_L^s$. Now let $i \in L$ and consider (π, x) such that $\psi_i(\pi, x) > 0$. By ψ_i continuous on $\sum_0 \times X$, there exists an open set $T \subseteq \sum_0 \times X$ such that $(\pi, x) \in T$ and $\psi_i(\pi', x') > 0$ for all $(\pi', x') \in T$; but then A_i^s is open. And since A_L^s is the finite intersection of open sets, it too is open by $i \in L$ arbitrary.

Claim 3: A_L is lhc.

Proof: By assumption, $\delta \in (0, 1)$. Consider any $x \in A_L(\pi)$, $\pi \in \sum_0$. By Claim 2, there exists some $y \in A_L^s(\pi)$ and, by u_i concave for all $i \in L$,

$$\frac{1}{m}[y + (m-1)x] \in A_L^s(\pi)$$

6.4. BARGAINING OVER POLICY

for all integers, $m = 1, 2, \ldots$. Taking m to infinity then yields $x \in \overline{A_L^s(\pi)}$. But $\overline{A_L^s(\pi)} = A_L(\pi)$ and, by Claim 2, $A_L^s(\pi)$ is open. Therefore, $A_L(\pi)$ differs from an open subcorrespondence only at points of closure. Since $\pi \in \sum_0$ was chosen arbitrarily, lower hemicontinuity of A_L follows from Aliprantis and Border [2, Lemma 16.22]. □

We are now in a position to establish the general existence theorem for legislative bargaining games. And because the pure distribution setting with a common discount factor is a special case of the current model, proving this theorem also yields Theorem 6.2(1). Recall that in general a set Y is said to be compact if every open cover of Y contains a finite subcover [PPTI, sect.5.1]. If $Y \subset \Re^k$, openness is defined here with respect to the Euclidean metric d: $T \subset \Re^k$ is open if, for all $x \in T$, there is $\epsilon > 0$ such that $B_d(x, \epsilon) \subset T$. Similarly, when $Y \subset [\Delta X]^n$ we define openness with respect to the Prohorov metric d_P: $T \subset [\Delta X]^n$ is open if, for all $\pi \in T$, there is $\epsilon > 0$ such that $B_{d_P}(\pi, \epsilon) \subset T$.

Theorem 6.4 *There exists a no-delay stationary equilibrium.*

Proof The argument to follow uses a generalization of Kakutani's Fixed Point Theorem to any metric (rather than just a Euclidean) space due to Glicksberg [84].

(Glicksberg's Fixed Point Theorem) Let $Y \subseteq Z$ be a compact and convex subset of a metric space Z (that is, a distance function is defined on Z); suppose $\Phi : Y \rightrightarrows Y$ is an uhc correspondence such that, for all $y \in Y$, $\Phi(y) \subset Y$ is nonempty, compact and convex. Then Φ has a fixed point; that is, for some $y \in Y$, $y \in \Phi(y)$.

The theorem claims there exists a stationary equilibrium strategy profile $\sigma = (\pi, v) \in \sum_0$. As in the proof of Lemma 6.3, it is convenient to leave the voting strategy understood and simply write $\pi \in \sum_0$. For all $i \in N$, define

$$B_i(\pi) = \arg\max\{u_i(x) : x \in A(\pi)\}$$

as the set optimal proposals for i at $\pi \in \sum_0$. By Lemma 6.3 and the Maximum Theorem [197, ch.9], B_i has nonempty and compact values and is uhc in π. Then for all $i \in N$, $\Delta B_i(\pi)$ is nonempty, compact and convex-valued uhc correspondence [2, Theorem 16.14]. Define

$$\Delta B(\pi) = \Delta B_1(\pi) \times \Delta B_2(\pi) \times \ldots \times \Delta B_n(\pi).$$

Then $\Delta B : [\Delta X]^n \rightrightarrows [\Delta X]^n$ inherits the properties of each $\Delta B_i(\pi)$ [2, Theorem 16.14]. Because $[\Delta X]^n$ is convex and compact and the Prohorov metric is well-defined on $[\Delta X]^n$, Glicksberg's Theorem implies there exists a fixed point $\pi^* \in \sum_0$; in particular $\sigma^* = (\pi^*, v^*) \in \sum_0$ where v^* is such that $v_i^*(x) = 1$ if and only if $x \in A_i(\pi^*)$, all $i \in N$. It remains to check that the restriction of strategies $\sigma \in \sum_0$ is not binding; that is, no individual i can improve her payoff relative to π^* by deviating to a proposal $x_i \in X \setminus A(\pi^*)$. By definition of $X \setminus A(\pi^*)$, the payoff to such a deviation is $(1-\delta)u_i(x^0) + \delta V_i(\sigma^*)$. Recalling $\hat{x}(\beta^*)$ is the expected outcome under σ^*, u_i concave implies

$$u_i(\hat{x}(\beta^*)) \geq \int_X u_i(x) d\beta^*(x) = (1-\delta)u_i(x^0) + \delta V_i(\sigma^*)$$

and, by Lemma 6.3, $\hat{x}(\beta^*) \in A_i(\pi^*)$. So i cannot improve her payoff by such a deviation and the proof is complete. □

A key step for the preceding proof is to insure the nonemptiness of the acceptance set $A(\pi)$. The argument for nonemptiness here rests on the concavity of individual preferences along with the common assessment of the induced equilibrium probability distribution β. If preferences are not concave then it is in principle possible for risk-acceptant individuals always to prefer the lottery triggered by rejecting any proposal to the payoff implied by accepting some offer. In problems with more structure on the alternative set, the voting rule and so forth, concavity might well prove unnecessary: here, it is simply a (substantively reasonable) sufficient condition. On the other hand, allowing variations across individuals in the probability distribution over final outcomes, although likewise possible in principle, seems much harder to relax and continue to derive the existence of (at least) no-delay equilibria. The assumption that supports a common assessment is that all individuals share a common discount factor, δ. Were individually-specific discount factors permitted, the probability distributions over final outcomes determining individual continuation values would also vary by individual (as inspection of the definition for β makes apparent). The reason this does not cause difficulties in the pure distribution model is that the status quo outcome in that environment is unanimously considered a worst outcome and, therefore, no individual has any incentive to retain it indefinitely by rejecting all other proposals or proposing anything better when recognized.

Corollary 6.1 *Suppose, for all $i \in N$ and all $x \in X$, that $u_i(x) \geq u_i(x^0)$. Suppose further that individual discount factors can vary across N. Then there exists a no-delay stationary equilibrium.*

6.4. BARGAINING OVER POLICY

Proof To apply the argument for Theorem 6.4, it suffices to show the social acceptance set is nonempty. Specifically, we wish to show

$$A(\sigma) = \cup_{L \in \mathcal{L}} [\cap_{i \in L} A_j(\sigma)]$$
$$= \cup_{L \in \mathcal{L}} \left[\cap_{i \in L} \{x \in X : u_i(x) \geq (1 - \delta_i) u_i(x^0) + \delta_i V_i(\sigma)\} \right]$$
$$\neq \emptyset$$

at every no-delay stationary equilibrium, $\sigma = (\pi, v)$. Let

$$\hat{x}(\pi) = \sum_{i \in N} p_i \int_X z d\pi_i(z)$$

denote the expected outcome under σ. By assumption, u_i is concave for all $i \in N$ and $u_i(x) \geq u_i(x^0)$ for all $x \in X$. Hence, for all $i \in N$, $\delta_i \in (0,1)$ implies $u_i(\hat{x}(\pi)) \geq (1 - \delta_i) u_i(x^0) + \delta_i V_i(\sigma)$, yielding the result and proving Theorem 6.2(1). □

That the status quo is unanimously considered a worst outcome is not necessarily true for more general policy spaces. Technically, therefore, there is a tradeoff: either the model can assume a universally bad status quo and permit various discount factors across committee members, or it can assume unconstrained evaluations of the status quo across members but must insist on a common discount factor. Which constitutes the best modeling choice depends on the problem at hand.

Theorem 6.4 establishes existence of at least one equilibrium profile by showing the existence of a no-delay equilibrium. This does not imply that only no-delay stationary equilibria exist.

Example 6.5 Let $N = \{1, 2, 3\}$, $X = [0, 1]$, $x^0 = 0$ and assume f is majority rule. Let $u_1(x) = 1 - x$ and suppose $u_j(x) = x$, $j = 2, 3$. Finally, for all $i \in N$, let $p_i = 1/3$ and $\delta_i = \delta \in (0, 1)$. Then there is an equilibrium with delay: consider the pure strategy proposal profile $\sigma = (\pi, v)$, where

$$\pi = (\pi_1, \pi_2, \pi_3) = (0, 1, 1)$$

and the voting profile $v = (v_1, v_2, v_3)$ is defined by acceptance sets

$$A_1(\sigma) = [0, x^*] \text{ and, for each } j = 2, 3, A_j(\sigma) = [x^*, 1].$$

If σ does indeed describe equilibrium behavior for some x^*, then it is an equilibrium with delay: with positive probability, individual $i = 1$ makes the first offer of zero and it is rejected; only individuals $j = 2, 3$ make accepted offers. To show σ is an equilibrium, therefore, first requires finding a strictly interior value for x^* consistent with best response behavior by all individuals to the proposal profile π. To do this, fix π and consider $j \in \{2, 3\}$. By definition

$$\begin{aligned} V_j(\sigma) &= p_1[(1-\delta)u_j(x^0) + \delta V_j(\sigma)] + [p_2 + p_3]u_j(1) \\ &= \frac{1}{3}[\delta V_j(\sigma) + 2] \end{aligned}$$

so $V_j(\sigma) = 2/[3 - \delta]$. Hence,

$$\begin{aligned} A_j(\sigma) &= \{x \in X : u_j(x) \geq (1-\delta)u_j(x^0) + \delta V_j(\sigma)\} \\ &= \{x \in X : x \geq 2\delta/[3-\delta]\} \\ &= [\frac{2\delta}{3-\delta}, 1]. \end{aligned}$$

Setting $x^* = 2\delta/[3 - \delta]$, therefore, yields $x^* \in (0, 1)$ as required. It remains to check $A_1(\sigma) = [0, x^*]$ similarly describes an undominated voting strategy for $i = 1$. But

$$\begin{aligned} V_1(\sigma) &= p_1[(1-\delta)u_1(x^0) + \delta V_1(\sigma)] + [p_2 + p_3]u_1(1) \\ &= \frac{1}{3}[(1-\delta) + \delta V_1(\sigma)] \end{aligned}$$

so $V_1(\sigma) = [1 - \delta]/[3 - \delta]$ and, therefore,

$$\begin{aligned} A_1(\sigma) &= \{x \in X : u_1(x) \geq (1-\delta)u_1(x^0) + \delta V_1(\sigma)\} \\ &= \{x \in X : 1 - x \geq (1-\delta) + \delta \left[\frac{1-\delta}{3-\delta}\right]\} \\ &= [0, \frac{2\delta}{3-\delta}]. \end{aligned}$$

And since it is evident that π is a best response to v as described, σ is shown to constitute equilibrium behavior.

Finally, it is worth noting that the threshold $x^* \to 1$ as $\delta \to 1$. In other words, as all committee members become increasingly patient, the minority member, $i = 1$, becomes increasingly willing to accept any change while those in the majority, $j = 2, 3$, become increasingly unwilling to accept anything but their common ideal point, the majority core outcome. □

With respect to applications and empirical content, existence theorems are rather dry. It is the characterization of equilibria that yield the substantive insights, intuition and empirical predictions on how collective decisions

6.4. BARGAINING OVER POLICY

and decision-making might be expected to evolve; Theorem 6.2(2) is a case in point. However, such insights and intuition are vacuous if there is no assurance that the equilibria being described could exist and, for this reason, it is essential to confirm that a particular formal abstraction is sufficiently well-defined to admit a solution. Theorem 6.4 insures that at least the general legislative bargaining model for committee decision-making possesses a solution.

In general there can exist many stationary equilibria to a legislative policy bargaining process. At least with respect to identifying equilibrium outcomes, the next result helps to narrow down where to look. Call a stationary equilibrium *static* if the induced equilibrium committee decision is the status quo, x^0. Static equilibria may or may not involve delay, depending on the realized sequence of agenda-setters and so on. Given a concave preference profile $u = (u_1, \ldots, u_n)$ and a simple aggregation rule f, $C_f(u) \subseteq X$ is the core of f at u [PPTI, sect.4.2].

Theorem 6.5 *Let u be the utility profile describing committee members' preferences over X and assume $p_j > 0$ for all $j \in N$.*
(1) There exists a static stationary equilibrium if and only if $x^0 \in C_f(u)$.
(2) If in addition u is a strictly concave utility profile on X, then every stationary equilibrium is either static or involves no-delay.

Proof (1) Let σ be a static equilibrium. By definition of σ static, $V_i(\sigma) = u_i(x^0)$ for all $i \in N$. Assume $x^0 \notin C_f(u)$; then there exists some decisive coalition $L \in \mathcal{L}$ and a distinct alternative $y \in X$ such that, for all $j \in L$, $u_j(y) > V_j(\sigma)$. By the restriction to undominated strategies, therefore, $y \in A_L \subseteq A$. By sequential rationality, for all $j \in L$, $x^0 \notin Supp[\pi_j]$. But then $p_j > 0$ implies σ is not static: if any individual $j \in L$ is recognized and proposes y, then y is accepted as the final decision. Now let $x^0 \in C_f(u)$. Define $\sigma = (\pi, v)$ by, for every $i \in N$, having $Supp[\pi_i] = \{x^0\}$ and

$$A_i(\sigma) = \{x \in X : u_i(x) \geq u_i(x^0)\}.$$

Then v is an undominated voting profile. To check π is sequentially rational, suppose not. Then for some $j \in N$, there exists an alternative $y \in A$ with $u_j(y) > u_j(x^0)$. But $y \in A$ and f simple imply there is a coalition $L \in \mathcal{L}$ with $u_i(y) \geq u_i(x^0)$ for all $i \in L$. But concavity implies strict quasi-concavity, so u_i concave gives

$$u_i(\frac{1}{2}y + \frac{1}{2}x^0) > u_i(x^0)$$

for all $i \in L$, contradicting $x^0 \in C_f(u)$.

(2) Let u be a strictly concave profile and suppose, to the contrary, that σ is a stationary equilibrium with delay. Then there must exist some $j \in N$ whose equilibrium proposal strategy puts weight on collectively unacceptable alternatives; i.e. $Supp[\pi_j] \cap X \backslash A \neq \emptyset$. By assumption, $\delta < 1$ and $p_i > 0$, all $i \in N$; consequently there exists positive probability on the status quo x^0 being the de facto policy in some periods. But $\delta > 0$ and σ an equilibrium profile imply there must also be strictly positive weight under σ on some alternative $x \neq x^0$ being a committee decision. Hence, strict concavity yields

$$u_i(\hat{x}(\beta)) > (1-\delta)u_i(x^0) + \delta V_i(\sigma),$$

where $\hat{x}(\beta)$ is the expected outcome under σ. By sequential rationality and $\hat{x}(\beta) \in A$, therefore, $Supp[\pi_j] \cap X \backslash A = \emptyset$: contradiction. $\square$

Note that strict concavity is essential for Theorem 6.5(2): in Example 6.5, for instance, all individuals' preferences are only weakly concave and there exists a stationary equilibrium with delay that is not static.

An important motivation for developing theories of legislative bargaining is that in general the core of the relevant preference aggregation rule for the legislature is typically empty; that is, f noncollegial implies $C_f(u) = \emptyset$ for almost all profiles u [PPTI, ch.6]. Direct preference aggregation, therefore, offers little guidance in such cases about what to expect of legislative decisions. On the other hand, when it exists, the core is a compelling solution concept: an alternative x is in the core if and only if there exists no available alternative y that is strictly more preferred under the rule. Consequently, it is reasonable to look for conditions under which legislative bargaining outcomes lie in the core when the latter is nonempty. That there is a general equivalence between bargaining outcomes and the core, however, is too much to expect even given the latter is nonempty.

Example 6.6 Assume the committee decision problem is exactly that described in Example 6.5; then f majority rule implies $C_f(u) = \{1\}$. Now, however, we consider a stationary equilibrium with no-delay. Let $y \in X = [0, 1]$ and define the pure strategy profile $\sigma = (\pi, v)$ by

$$\pi = (\pi_1, \pi_2, \pi_3) = (y, 1, 1)$$

and $v = (v_1, v_2, v_3)$ with acceptance sets

$$A_1(\sigma) = [0, x_1(\delta)] \text{ and, for each } j = 2, 3, A_j(\sigma) = [x_2(\delta), 1].$$

6.4. BARGAINING OVER POLICY

For σ to be a no-delay equilibrium requires $y \in [x_2(\delta), x_1(\delta)]$. To find this interval, fix a (stationary) proposal y by individual 1 and note that, for σ no-delay, $j \in \{2, 3\}$ has continuation value

$$V_j(\sigma) = p_1 u_j(y) + [p_2 + p_3] u_j(1)$$
$$= \frac{1}{3}[y + 2]$$

so $A_j(\sigma) = [\delta(y+2)/3, 1]$. Similarly,

$$V_1(\sigma) = p_1 u_1(y) + [p_2 + p_3] u_1(1)$$
$$= \frac{1}{3}[1 - y]$$

and $A_1(\sigma) = [0, 1 - \delta(1-y)/3]$. Therefore, any proposal

$$y \in [\frac{2\delta}{3 - \delta}, 1]$$

supports a no-delay stationary equilibrium. Moreover, for $\delta < 1$, $i = 1$'s optimal proposal is uniquely given by $y^* = 2\delta/(3 - \delta) < 1$. Hence, with probability $p_1 = 1/3$, individual 1 is recognized in the first period, proposes $y^* \notin C_f(u)$ and this proposal is surely accepted. $\square$

The reason why the equilibrium committee decision in Example 6.6 is not necessarily in the core is because committee members are impatient. If necessary, individuals 2 and 3 are willing to sacrifice some payoff to secure a relatively early decision, thus permitting individual 1 to offer an acceptable proposal that she prefers to the core outcome offered by either of the others should they be recognized before any decision is reached. However, exactly as in Example 6.5, as $\delta \to 1$ and individuals discount the future less, the minimally acceptable proposal, y^*, converges to one, the core outcome. At least for the one-dimensional policy case, this is quite general; that is, as committee members become increasingly patient, the equilibrium outcome converges to a core outcome. The following intuitive lemma is useful in proving the claim.

Lemma 6.4 *Let $X \subset \Re$ and suppose σ is a no-delay stationary equilibrium. Then the social acceptance set $A(\sigma)$ is convex and σ is a profile of pure strategies.*

Proof Let $a = \min A(\sigma)$ and $b = \max A(\sigma)$. Since $A(\sigma)$ is compact, a and b are well-defined. We wish to show that for any $y \in (a, b)$, $y \in A(\sigma)$. To do this, let $L(a) \in \mathcal{L}$ and $L(b) \in \mathcal{L}$ be decisive coalitions such that $a \in A_{L(a)}$ and $b \in A_{L(b)}$ (where the dependency on σ is understood). Evidently, the expected equilibrium committee decision induced by σ, $\hat{x}(\beta)$, lies in the convex hull of all equilibrium proposals: $\hat{x}(\beta) \in ConA$. Furthermore, by u_i concave all $i \in N$, $\hat{x}(\beta) \in A_{L(a)} \cap A_{L(b)}$. Let $y \in ConA$ and assume $y \in [a, \hat{x}(\beta)]$. By $A_{L(a)}$ convex and concave utilities, $y \in A_{L(a)} \subseteq A$. Similarly, for $y \in [\hat{x}(\beta), b]$ we have $y \in A_{L(b)} \subseteq A$. Thus $A(\sigma)$ is convex. By assumption, u_i is concave and so strictly quasi-concave. Hence, $A(\sigma)$ convex implies u_i has a unique maximizer on $A(\sigma)$. And because $\sigma = (\pi, v)$ is a no-delay equilibrium, it must be the case that π_i puts probability mass one on this maximizer. □

Theorem 6.6 *Let $X \subset \Re$ and suppose $(\delta^m) \to 1$; let (σ^m) be an associated sequence of no-delay stationary equilibria with social acceptance sets (A^m). Then there exists an alternative $x^* \in C_f(u)$ such that $(A^m) \to \{x^*\}$.*

Proof By Lemma 6.4, $A^m \equiv A(\sigma^m)$ is convex. Let $A^m = [a^m, b^m]$ and $d^m = [b^m - a^m]$ for all m; the first step is to show $(d^m) \to 0$, implying the sets A^m shrink to a point as $m \to \infty$. Suppose, contrary to the claim, that d^m does not converge to zero. Then there exists $\epsilon > 0$ and a monotone subsequence (without ambiguity, also indexed by m) such that $\liminf d^m \geq \epsilon$. Let $L(a^m) \in \mathcal{L}$ and $L(b^m) \in \mathcal{L}$ be decisive coalitions such that $a^m \in A^m_{L(a^m)}$ and $b^m \in A^m_{L(b^m)}$. Noting that simple voting rules are proper [PPTI, ch.3], there must exist some $i^m \in L(a^m) \cap L(b^m)$. Because there is a finite number of committee members and (σ^m) is an infinite sequence, there is a subsequence $(\sigma^{m'})$ for which $i^{m'} = i$ at every index m'; hereafter we consider such a subsequence (again abusing notation slightly, by indexing the sequence by m). Then $d^m \geq \epsilon$ implies $b^m \geq a^m + \epsilon$ and for all m,

$$\min\{u_i(a^m), u_i(b^m)\} \geq (1-\delta^m)u_i(x^0) + \delta^m V_i(\sigma^m) \quad (*)$$

Since X is compact by assumption, both (a^m) and (b^m) have convergent subsequences (without ambiguity, indexed also by m) with limits a and b, respectively. So $d = b - a \geq \epsilon$. Then $a < a + \epsilon \leq b$. Let (β^m) be the sequence of probability distributions induced by (σ^m). By ΔX compact, there exists a distribution $\beta \in \Delta X$ and a subsequence (again indexed by m) such that (β^m) converges weakly to β. Let $\bar{V}_i = \int u_i d\beta$. By u_i continuous and $(\beta^m) \to \beta$ weakly, $V_i(\sigma^m) \to \bar{V}_i$ and, therefore, by $(*)$ and u_i continuous,

$$\min\{u_i(a), u_i(b)\} \geq \bar{V}_i. \quad (i)$$

6.4. BARGAINING OVER POLICY

Since $\int_{a^m}^{b^m} d\beta^m = 1$ for all m, $\int_a^b d\beta = 1$. Therefore,

$$\bar{V}_i \geq \min\{u_i(x) : x \in [a,b]\}. \qquad (ii)$$

By u_i concave and continuous,

$$\min\{u_i(x) : x \in [a,b]\} = \min\{u_i(a), u_i(b)\}. \qquad (iii)$$

So combining (i), (ii) and (iii) gives

$$\bar{V}_i = \min\{u_i(x) : x \in [a,b]\}. \qquad (**)$$

Now, because $a < b$ and u_i is strictly quasi-concave, there exists $\eta > 0$ such that

$$u_i(\frac{1}{2}a + \frac{1}{2}b) = \min\{u_i(x) : x \in [a,b]\} + 2\eta.$$

By A^m convex, $[\frac{1}{2}a^m + \frac{1}{2}b^m] \in A^m$. By Lemma 6.4 also, all individuals' equilibrium proposal strategies are pure. Let $x^{im} \in A^m$ denote i's equilibrium proposal at σ^m. Then

$$u_i(x^{im}) \geq u_i(\frac{1}{2}a^m + \frac{1}{2}b^m).$$

By u_i continuous,

$$\liminf u_i(x^{im}) \geq u_i(\frac{1}{2}a + \frac{1}{2}b) = \min\{u_i(x) : x \in [a,b]\} + 2\eta.$$

Therefore, for sufficiently high m, β^m places probability at least $\delta^m p_i$ on a set of alternatives $Y \subset X$ such that for any $x \in Y$,

$$u_i(x) \geq \min\{u_i(x) : x \in [a,b]\} + \eta.$$

Since $(\delta^m) \to 1$ and $(\beta^m) \to \beta$ weakly, in the limit the distribution β must place probability at least p_i on outcomes in Y. But then

$$\begin{aligned}\bar{V}_i &\geq p_i[\min\{u_i(x) : x \in [a,b]\} + \eta] + (1-p_i)\min\{u_i(x) : x \in [a,b]\} \\ &> \min\{u_i(x) : x \in [a,b]\}\end{aligned}$$

which contradicts $(**)$. Hence, ϵ must equal zero and $(d^m) \to 0$. Thus, as $(\delta^m) \to 1$, $(A^m) \to \{x\} \in X$.

The remaining step is to show $x \in C_f(u)$; that is, x is a core point for u under the simple rule f on $X \subset \Re$. By u concave and $X \subset \Re$, $C_f(u) \neq \emptyset$ [PPTI, ch.4]. It suffices to show there must exist an individual

$i \in N$ with a no-delay equilibrium proposal $x^i \in C_f(u)$. By X compact and u_i strictly quasi-concave for all i, each individual has a unique most preferred alternative $x_i \in X$. By relabeling N if necessary, suppose $x_i \leq x_{i+1}$ for all $i = 1, \ldots, n-1$. Then there exist individuals $j, k \in N$ such that $C_f(u) = [x_j, x_k]$ [PPTI, Theorem 4.5]. Moreover, there are decisive coalitions $L_j, L_k \in \mathcal{L}$ such that

$$L_j = \{i \in N : x_i \geq x_j\} \text{ and } L_k = \{i \in N : x_i \leq x_k\}.$$

Therefore, if $\hat{x}(\beta) > x_k$, then for any $\delta \in (0,1]$ and all $i \in L_k$,

$$u_i(x_k) \geq u_i(\hat{x}(\beta)) \geq (1-\delta)u_i(x^0) + \delta V_i(\sigma)$$

so $x_k \in A_{L_k}$. Hence, $L_k \in \mathcal{L}$ implies $x_k \in A$ and, by sequential rationality, $x^k = x_k$. A symmetric argument shows $x^j = x_j$ in the case $\hat{x}(\beta) < x_j$. And finally, if $x_j \leq \hat{x}(\beta) \leq x_k$ then $\hat{x}(\beta) \in A$ implies $A \cap C_f(u) \neq \emptyset$. In this case, sequential rationality yields $x^j = x_j$ if $x_j \in A$ and yields $x^j = \min x \in A \cap C_f(u)$. Under every possibility, therefore, there must exist an individual whose no-delay equilibrium proposal is a core alternative. The theorem follows. □

When there is a unique core alternative, Theorem 6.6 is a core-equivalence result: in the limit as the discount factor goes to one, the unique no-delay stationary equilibrium outcome for the legislative bargaining process over a one-dimensional policy space is exactly the core outcome. In particular, when f is simple majority rule, the theorem provides a noncooperative bargaining rationalization for the Median Voter Theorem [PPTI, Theorem 4.4]. When the core contains multiple alternatives, however, Theorem 6.6 only claims that all bargaining outcomes are core outcomes, but not necessarily the converse. If the committee has an even number of members, for instance, then the core can be an interval bounded by two individuals' ideal points; in this case it is fairly easy to see that not all core outcomes need be stationary equilibrium outcomes [Exercise].

One-dimensional policy spaces are often reasonable models for many problems, most evidently those dealing with single issues under separable preferences. On the other hand, the one-dimensional model is relatively special [PPTI, ch.5] and much of politics involves multidimensional policy making. As a result, it is disappointing, if not perhaps unexpected, to find that the one-dimensional core equivalence result does not extend to higher dimensional policy spaces. Indeed, even for perfectly patient committee members with separable and symmetric preferences, if the policy space is

6.4. BARGAINING OVER POLICY

multidimensional it is possible to have a unique core outcome that is a single individual's ideal point and yet there can exist stationary equilibrium outcomes outside the core. An example makes the point.

Example 6.7 Let $N = \{1, 2, 3, 4, 5\}$, $\delta = 1$ and $p_i = 1/5$ all $i \in N$. Suppose each individual has strictly concave preferences over the two-dimensional policy space $X = [-1, 1] \times [-1, 1]$ such that, for each $i \in N$ and $y \in X$,

$$u_i(y) = -||y - x_i||^4.$$

Let individuals' ideal points be: $x_1 = (1, 0)$; $x_2 = (0, 1)$; $x_3 = (-1, 0)$; $x_4 = (0, -1)$; and $x_5 = (0, 0)$. Then there is a unique core allocation under majority rule at $x^* = x_5 = (0, 0)$ [PPTI, Theorem 5.8]. However, there is a no-delay equilibrium with pure strategy proposals $x^i = x_i$ for all $i \in N$, and each proposal is acceptable to some majority; that is, all individuals propose their ideal points and the first person recognized is able to have her ideal point be the equilibrium outcome. It follows that with probability 4/5 the committee outcome is not the core alternative, despite this alternative being offered by one committee member.

To check that the strategies supporting the claim are an equilibrium profile note that, if every individual's proposal is accepted by a majority, the proposals are surely best responses. And to see any individual's ideal point is acceptable to some majority, fix the proposal strategy profile and note that $V_j = [\sum_{i \in N} u_j(x_i)]/5$, all $j \in N$; hence, for all $j \neq 5$, $V_j = -5$ and $V_5 = -4/5$. If individual $j = 1$ is recognized and proposes x_1 as prescribed, individuals $i = 2, 4$ each achieve a payoff $u_i((1, 0)) = -4$ if x_1 is accepted; therefore, voting for 1's proposal is a best response for these committee members and x_1 is accepted: $\{1, 2, 4\} \in \mathcal{L}$. Individuals 2 and 4 similarly vote for x_3 if $j = 3$ is recognized and individuals 1 and 3 find proposals of x_2 and x_4 acceptable; x_5, the core proposal, is acceptable to all committee members. □

An important feature of the one-dimensional spatial model is that there is always at least one individual whose ideal point is also a core alternative [PPTI, Theorem 4.4]. In turn, the existence of such an individual implies the best response proposal strategy for at least one committee member in the bargaining process always includes proposing a core alternative, an important step in the proof to Theorem 6.6. Example 6.7, however, demonstrates that in multidimensional settings, the willingness of an individual to offer a core alternative is not sufficient for that alternative to be chosen in a no-delay stationary equilibrium. Just as is true for results on core existence for the multidimensional spatial model, details of individual preferences over the set of alternatives matter. Indeed, if every committee member i's preferences in Example 6.7 are changed (fairly significantly) from $u_i(y) = -||y - x_i||^4$ to $\hat{u}_i(y) = -||y - x_i||^2$, with everything else being left unaltered, it can be checked that the only no-delay stationary equilibrium outcome is the core outcome, $x^* = x_5 = (0,0)$ [Exercise]. It is important, therefore, to understand the extent to which equilibrium predictions drawn from some specification of the general bargaining model are robust to perturbations in this specification. For if all specifications are highly sensitive to details of individual preferences and other parameters of the model, then any conclusions derived are essentially fragile.

Assume, for all $i \in N$, that i's preferences can be parameterized by some real vector $\theta \in \mathcal{H}$ such that $u_i(x, \theta)$ is jointly continuous in (x, θ) and, for all $\theta \in \mathcal{H}$, concave in x with ideal point $x_i(\theta) \in X \subset \Re^k$. A common example in applied models is to assume u_i is quadratic on X with individual preferences differing only in their ideal points, x_i, $i \in N$; in this case, we have $\mathcal{H} = \Re^{nk}$ and $\theta = (\theta_1, \ldots, \theta_n) = (x_1, \ldots, x_n)$ is the vector of ideal points. The final theorem of this section proves that the set of no-delay stationary equilibrium outcomes is suitably continuous in the underlying parameters of the legislative bargaining model. In other words, such equilibrium predictions are robust to small perturbations in model specification; in particular if, for some profile $u(\cdot, \theta)$, there is core equivalence and preferences are perturbed slightly to a profile $u(\cdot, \theta')$ for which the core is empty, the theorem implies the set of no-delay stationary equilibrium outcomes at $u(\cdot, \theta')$ under legislative bargaining is located in the neighborhood of the core under $u(\cdot, \theta)$.

Theorem 6.7 *Let $\eta^s(p, \delta, \theta) \subseteq X \subset \Re^k$ denote the set of no-delay stationary equilibrium outcomes, given recognition probabilities p, common discount factor δ and preference parameter θ. The correspondence η^s is upper hemicontinuous.*

Proof Assume individuals use only no-delay stationary equilibrium strategies. Using obvious notation, define for all $i \in N$,

$$V_i(\pi, p, \theta) = \sum_{j \in N} p_j \int u_i(z, \theta) d\pi_j(z);$$

$$A_i(\pi, p, \delta, \theta) = \{x \in X : u_i(x, \theta) \geq (1-\delta)u_i(x^0, \theta) + \delta V_i(\pi, p, \theta)\};$$

and

$$B_i(\pi, p, \delta, \theta) = \arg\max\{u_i(x, \theta) : x \in A(\pi, p, \delta, \theta)\}.$$

6.4. BARGAINING OVER POLICY

An identical argument as that for Theorem 6.4 yields the correspondence $\Delta B_i(\pi,p,\delta,\theta)$ nonempty, compact and uhc. By Aliprantis and Border [2, Theorem 16.11], ΔB_i also has closed graph. Now consider sequences $(\pi^m) \to \pi^\circ$ and $(p^m,\delta^m,\theta^m) \to (p^\circ,\delta^\circ,\theta^\circ)$ with $\pi^m \in \eta^s(p^m,\delta^m,\theta^m)$ for all finite m; then (by definition of an equilibrium) $\pi^m \in \Delta B_i(\pi^m,p^m,\delta^m,\theta^m)$ for all $i \in N$ and all finite m. By ΔB_i having closed graph, therefore, $\pi^\circ \in \Delta B_i(\pi^\circ,p^\circ,\delta^\circ,\theta^\circ)$ all i. We need to show $\sigma_i^\circ = (\pi_i^\circ, A_i(\pi^\circ,p^\circ,\delta^\circ,\theta^\circ))$ for all $i \in N$ constitutes a no-delay stationary equilibrium. By definition, the acceptance sets $A_i(\pi^\circ,p^\circ,\delta^\circ,\theta^\circ)$ include only undominated voting decisions. Suppose π_i° is not sequentially rational for some individual i then i's expected payoff from proposing some socially unacceptable proposal must be higher than that from proposing any available socially acceptable alternative; that is

$$\int u_i(z,\theta)d\pi_i^\circ(z) < (1-\delta^\circ)u_i(x^0,\theta^\circ) + \delta^\circ V_i(\pi^\circ,p^\circ,\theta^\circ).$$

By joint continuity of payoffs, therefore, the strict inequality must obtain for sufficiently high m. But this contradicts $\pi^m \in \eta^s(p^m,\delta^m,\theta^m)$ so in fact π_i° must be sequentially rational for all $i \in N$ and $\sigma^\circ = (\sigma_1^\circ,\ldots,\sigma_n^\circ)$ is an equilibrium as required. Hence, η^s has closed graph; and since the range of η^s is compact, η^s is also upper hemicontinuous [2, Theorem 16.12]. □

It is worth remarking that the argument for Theorem 6.7 easily extends to the pure distribution model with various discount factors $\delta_1,\ldots,\delta_n$, linear preferences (that is, $u_i(x) = x_i$ for all i and all distributions x in the simplex) and the status quo being the least-valued outcome for all committee members. An implication of Theorems 6.3 and 6.7 is therefore the following corollary.

Corollary 6.2 *Let $\pi(p,\delta_1,\ldots,\delta_n,\theta)$ be any stationary equilibrium to the pure distribution legislative bargaining model with linear preferences and let $V^*(\pi(p,\delta_1,\ldots,\delta_n,\theta))$ denote the associated vector of equilibrium payoffs at $(p,\delta_1,\ldots,\delta_n,\theta)$. Then V^* is continuous in $(p,\delta_1,\ldots,\delta_n,\theta)$.*

Proof By definition, V_i^* is a maximum value function on $\eta^s(p,\delta_1,\ldots,\delta_n,\theta)$, all $i \in N$ and, by Theorem 6.3, for all $i \in N$ and all stationary equilibria π,π',

$$V_i^*(\pi(p,\delta_1,\ldots,\delta_n,\theta)) = V_i^*(\pi'(p,\delta_1,\ldots,\delta_n,\theta)).$$

Hence, $V^*(\pi(p,\delta_1,\ldots,\delta_n,\theta))$ is constant on $\eta^s(p,\delta_1,\ldots,\delta_n,\theta)$. By Theorem 6.7 and the Maximum Theorem, therefore, $V^*(\pi(p,\delta_1,\ldots,\delta_n,\theta))$ is continuous in the underlying parameters of the model. □

6.5 Application: Coalition government formation

Although the discussion so far has been in terms of legislative committee decision-making, there are other contexts in which the general bargaining model is a fairly natural approximation to the choice process. One of these is government coalition building in parliamentary democracies. Parliamentary systems are overwhelmingly associated with some form or other of proportional representation that typically fails to yield any party with a clear legislative majority. As a result, the first order of business for a newly elected legislature is to form a coalition government. Although the rules and conventions under which coalition governments are chosen vary considerably across legislatures and circumstances, the process of coalition formation is intrinsically a bargaining process between various parties.

Suppose the post-election legislature is shared between at least three distinct (but internally homogenous) political parties, none of which holds a strict majority of seats. The government must therefore be supported by at least a majority coalition consisting of a subset of the represented parties. Let N be the set of parties with legislative representation and, for each $i \in N$, let $p_i = p_i(v_1, \ldots, v_n; \theta)$ be the probability that party i is given the opportunity to (try to) form a coalition government in any period $t = 1, 2, \ldots$. Here, v_i is i's electoral vote total and θ is a vector of other arguments on which the probability p_i might depend; for example, θ might include whether party i was a member of the government in the previous electoral cycle or, in the case there is a separate vote for a prime minister, the elected prime minister's party is obliged to be included in any governing coalition, and so on. No specific assumptions are imposed on the mapping p_i save that it is a function, or single-valued. Then different institutional rules for coalitional bargaining are captured (if only in part) by different descriptions for $p = (p_1, \ldots, p_n)$.

Among other things, elected parties might have preferences over public policy outcomes, private perks of office, or the ideological character of potential coalition partners. Assuming parties are instrumentally rational, a reasonable first approximation is that they care only about policy outcomes and perks, both of which are subject to negotiation through the bargaining process. Assume there is a finite amount $B > 0$ of divisible private benefit to allocate among legislative parties; each party's allocation $b_i \in [0, B]$ is (the monetary equivalent of) its perks from office and we require $\sum_{i \in N} b_i \leq B$. Then, for each $i \in N$, $u_i(y, b) \in \Re$ denotes i's payoff from policy $y \in X \subset \Re^k$ and distribution of private perks $b = (b_1, \ldots, b_n) \in [0, B]^n$. The utility u_i is assumed concave in y and b_i with ideal point $(x_i, b_i) \in X \times [0, B]$: for

6.5. APPLICATION: COALITION GOVERNMENT FORMATION

instance, the quasi-linear preferences (with $b_i = B$ for every party i) introduced in section 3.5 above satisfy this assumption. Then Theorem 6.4 says that a legislative bargaining process over policy and the distribution of perks has at least one no-delay stationary equilibrium with the resulting government being implicitly defined by the parties voting to accept the equilibrium proposal. Furthermore, Theorem 6.7 insures that small perturbations in some set of parameters do not induce discrete shifts in the set of equilibrium government policy outcomes. On the other hand, Theorem 6.7 does not say that an observed sequence of policy choices consistent with a sequence of parametric perturbations, say in vote shares across elections, is necessarily incremental: since there typically exist multiple no-delay stationary equilibria involving mixed strategies, the realization of these strategies can induce discrete policy jumps along any sequence of small parameter changes.

To illustrate the application, suppose the post-election (majoritarian) legislature is shared between three distinct (but internally homogenous) political parties, none of which holds a strict majority of seats. Then any two parties can in principle form a majority coalition government. Assume each party has quasi-linear preferences defined over a one-dimensional issue space and perks. Then bargaining involves alternatives in $X = \Re \times [0, B]^3$ such that $\sum_{i \in N} b_i = B$ and, for each party $i \in N = \{1, 2, 3\}$ and any $(y, (b_1, b_2, b_3)) \in X$,

$$u_i(y, (b_1, b_2, b_3)) = -(x_i - y)^2 + b_i$$

where x_i is i's ideal point (perhaps the party's electoral platform). Without loss of generality, let $x_1 < x_2 = 0 < x_3$ with $|x_3| \geq |x_1|$ and status quo $(x^0, 0) = (a, 0)$, $a \in (x_1, x_2]$.

The three parties have legislative representation defined by a pure proportional representation system such that

$$p_i = \frac{v_i}{[v_1 + v_2 + v_3]}$$

is party i's recognition probability for the bargaining game. Since no party has an electoral majority, $p_i < 1/2$ all i. Consequently, because the division of perks given any policy choice is a pure distribution problem, there is no majority core alternative in this environment for any $B > 0$; at $B = 0$ the unique core alternative is $x_2 = 0$, the median party's ideal policy. Assume $p_1 \geq p_3$.

We look for a pure strategy no-delay stationary equilibrium $\sigma = (\pi, v)$ in which $\pi_1 = (y, (B - b, b, 0))$, $\pi_2 = (0, (0, B - b', b'))$ and $\pi_3 = (z, (0, b'', B -$

b'')). In words, when recognized, party 1 seeks to form a governing coalition with 2, suggesting a policy y and a division of perks that excludes the third party; similarly, party 3 seeks to include 2 in a coalition that excludes 1 and, finally, if recognized the median party insists on implementing its ideal policy and induces party 3 to support it by dividing the perks between itself and 3. If such an equilibrium exists for suitably chosen y, z and b^i_j, then

$$\begin{aligned} V_1(\pi) &= p_1[B - b - (x_1 - y)^2] - p_2 x_1^2 - p_3(x_1 - z)^2; \\ V_2(\pi) &= p_1[b - y^2] + p_2[B - b'] + p_3[b'' - z^2]; \\ V_3(\pi) &= -p_1(x_3 - y)^2 + p_2[b' - x_3^2] + p_3[B - b'' - (x_3 - z)^2]. \end{aligned}$$

Now given (π_2, π_3), party 1 solves the programme

$$\max_{(y,b)\in \Re \times [0,B]} B - b - (x_1 - y)^2$$

subject to the constraint

$$u_2(y, b) \geq (1 - \delta)u_2(a, 0) + \delta V_2(\pi).$$

Since $a < x_2$ by assumption, the solution to this programme, assuming for convenience that B is sufficiently large, has

$$y^* = \frac{1}{2}x_1$$

and $b = b(z, b', b''; p, \delta, B, a)$ chosen just to make party 2 indifferent between accepting and rejecting 1's proposal:

$$\begin{aligned} b &= y^2 + \delta V_2 - (1 - \delta)a^2 \\ &= \frac{x_1^2}{4} + \left[\frac{\delta\left[p_2(B - b') + p_3(b'' - z^2)\right] - (1 - \delta)a^2}{1 - p_1 \delta} \right]. \end{aligned}$$

Similarly, calculate

$$z^* = \frac{1}{2}x_3$$

and $b'' = b''(y, b, b'; p, \delta, B, a)$ such that

$$\begin{aligned} b'' &= z^2 + \delta V_2 - (1 - \delta)a^2 \\ &= \frac{x_3^2}{4} + \left[\frac{\delta\left[p_2(B - b') + p_1(b - y^2)\right] - (1 - \delta)a^2}{1 - p_3 \delta} \right]. \end{aligned}$$

6.5. APPLICATION: COALITION GOVERNMENT FORMATION

Finally, the solution to party 3's optimization programme given (π_1, π_3) involves offering $x_2 = 0$ and attracting the support of the least expensive of the other two parties. That is, $b' = \min_{j \in \{1,2\}} b'_j$ where

$$b'_j = x_j^2 + \delta \tilde{V}_j - (1-\delta)(x_j - a)^2$$

and $\tilde{V}_j$ is j's continuation value conditional on $b' = b'_j$. For the illustration, we have presumed $b' = b'_3$ which, given $a < x_2$, is certainly justified for p_3 sufficiently small relative to p_1 and $|x_3 - x_2|$ sufficiently large relative to $|x_1 - x_2|$.

There are three equations in the three remaining unknowns, $\{b, b', b''\}$, which, for B sufficiently large as presumed, have a solution. With policies $\{y^*, 0, z^*\}$ respectively, the strategy profile σ constitutes a no-delay stationary equilibrium as required. There are several things to note about the equilibrium. First, the equilibrium coalition is "connected" in that parties 1 and 3 never form a government; in particular, the core party with respect to the policy space is always included in any government. Second, even if the status quo policy, $a \in \Re$, is identical to party 2's ideal policy, $a = x_2 = 0$, party 2 can be induced to join a governing coalition that implements a discrete change in policy away from x_2 by either of the other parties, should they be recognized first, by a suitable allocation of perks. And third, the policy components of all parties' proposals are constant (given B sufficiently large) and so continuous in the parameters, as asserted in Theorem 6.7. The equilibrium perq distributions, however, are not constant although they are continuous in (p, δ, B, a). For example, the perks offered by 1 and 3 to 2 are increasing in the discount factor and decreasing in the distance $|a - x_2|$.

It is worth noting here that constancy of the equilibrium policy proposals implies that, even as δ approaches one, the policy component of the proposals by parties' 1 and 3 stay bounded away from, and asymmetrically distributed about, the median policy. On the other hand, this is not the case when perks are either nonexistent or not at all valued by any party. Specifically, if $B = 0$ then, conditional on being recognized, party 1 offers a policy $x_2 - \bar{x} = -\bar{x}$ and party 3 offers a policy $x_2 + \bar{x} = \bar{x}$; party 2 continues to propose its ideal policy, x_2. All proposals are collectively acceptable and, by Theorem 6.6, $\bar{x}$ converges to the core alternative, $x_2 = 0$, as δ goes to one. It is left as an exercise to confirm that these strategies are indeed a no-delay equilibrium with

$$\bar{x} = \sqrt{\frac{(1-\delta)a^2}{1 - \delta(1-p_2)}}$$

where it is evident that Theorem 6.6 applies. It is also evident that, in contrast to the situation with $B > 0$, as $a \to 0$, the unique equilibrium policy outcome converges to the core. The independent evaluation of perks (perhaps through ministerial assignments, legislative staff and so on) by political parties, therefore, has a substantively significant impact on location of public policy. Insofar as voters in the electorate at large value only policy, such an impact may not be benign.

6.6 Discussion

For some legislative decision problems, the set of policies comprising the viable alternatives to a status quo are more or less fixed and the theoretical challenge is to provide a general understanding of committee voting over these alternatives. But not all legislative decision problems involve fixed sets of alternatives. A great deal of legislative effort is devoted to the creation, design and perfection of policies for consideration, with alternatives being proposed and considered by committee members in the course of more-or-less structured discussion regarding the relevant issues. Trying to model the richness, subtlety and variety of all possible sorts of discussion in a sufficiently rigorous way to provide a useful understanding of the procedures is optimistic in the extreme and we make no attempt to do this here. Instead, the current chapter describes a fairly abstract and general analytical framework which, it is hoped, captures an empirically important class of incentives facing committee members in many collective decision-making settings. The framework, legislative bargaining theory, derives from an intuitive perspective on how any more or less formal negotiation between equals proceeds. At any stage in the negotiation, a single individual is given the right to suggest a proposal which is then voted up or down by the committee; if voted up, the proposal becomes the committee decision and the procedure stops; if voted down, the procedure moves into the next stage and another individual is recognized to offer an alternative for collective consideration; the sequence repeats until a decision is reached. The legislative bargaining model is very flexible. By specifying the individual recognition probabilities and the committee decision rule appropriately, a wide variety of institutional forms are covered, admitting individuals with veto power, precluding some legislators from offering proposals, and so on.

As is often the case for infinite horizon dynamic models, restricting attention only to sequentially rational and undominated equilibrium strategy profiles allowed virtually any committee decision to be supported by some equilibrium behavior and parameter values (Theorem 6.1). The plethora of

6.6. DISCUSSION

equilibria occurs when individuals value future payoffs sufficiently highly. In this case, equilibrium behavior can be assured by imposing a sufficiently severe long-run punishment on those who deviate from the prescribed strategies and, so long as the committee does not require unanimity to approve a proposal, there is always such a punishment available by simply excluding the deviators from any winning coalition. To refine the set of equilibria, therefore, only those equilibria supported by stationary strategies are considered. Being history-independent, such strategies are tractable and considerably sharpen the predictive power of the theory (Theorems 6.2 and 6.5). Against these significant technical advantages, however, is the fact that stationary strategies rule out much of interest in many political interactions: reciprocity, both positive and negative, is impossible without strategies being sensitive to the realized decision history.

It is convenient to distinguish two sorts of decision problem: the pure distribution model where a fixed amount of a divisible good has to be shared among committee members (or the legislative districts they represent); and the more general model where the committee decision concerns public policy. The key difference between the two settings is that utility, or payoffs more generally, are fully transferable among people in the pure distribution case but not otherwise. So, for example, despite the multiplicity of stationary equilibria in the pure distribution model, all these equilibria induce identical payoffs across the committee (Theorem 6.3). But the uniqueness result does not extend to the general policy model: Examples 6.5 and 6.6 exhibit distinct stationary equilibria to the same model and the payoffs are similarly distinct. On the other hand, the fundamental incentives induced by the legislative bargaining process are sufficiently common across both settings to permit a general existence theorem for no-delay stationary equilibria (Theorem 6.4); that is, stationary equilibria with the property that the first proposal is immediately accepted. With purely distributional policies, this may not be so striking since there is a natural "worst" alternative, nobody receives any payoff at all, from everyone's perspective; but when there is status quo public policy, it is unreasonable to assume all individuals consider this the worst outcome and the existence of no-delay equilibria is perhaps unexpected. Insofar as committee policy making rarely appears to be resolved at the first attempt, no-delay equilibria are not very appealing predictions. Stationary equilibria exhibiting delay also exist, however, so the existence theorem should not be interpreted as a point-prediction on how legislative bargaining must evolve.

One motivation for exploring models with somewhat more structure than that imposed by a preference aggregation rule alone is that the latter often fail to yield any sort of prediction; the cores of noncollegial aggregation rules, that is, are typically empty. The sequential bargaining procedure, by contrast, typically offers multiple predictions in almost all environments. An important question, then, concerns the extent to which the equilibrium predictions of legislative bargaining reflect core predictions when the latter exist. Although a complete core-equivalence theorem is not generally available, some results can be stated, particularly for the one-dimensional spatial policy model (Theorem 6.6). Moreover, irrespective of the dimensionality of the policy space, the set of stationary equilibrium decisions is suitably continuous in the underlying parameters of the model (Theorem 6.7); in particular, if some parameterization is consistent with a nonempty core for the aggregation rule used in the bargaining process, and bargaining decisions are core decisions, then perturbing the parameters to eliminate the core leaves the equilibrium bargaining decisions in the neighborhood of where the core was initially located.

Legislative bargaining theory is a useful tool for developing an understanding of how relatively open committee decision-making can result in well-defined outcomes, even when the underlying core of the aggregation rule is empty. Moreover, the predictions they support are highly, if not perfectly, correlated with those supported by preference aggregation theory alone in the case that a core exists. Having said this, legislative bargaining theory does not provide a very compelling framework for understanding collective decisions by large societies. Such an understanding requires a theory of elections, to which we now turn.

6.7 Exercises

6.1 What happens in Theorem 6.2(2) as q approaches n?

6.2 Rehearse similar calculations as those for "matching pennies" and derive the best response mappings $(r_1^*(r_2), r_2^*(r_1))$ illustrated in Figure 6.4, Example 6.2.

6.3 What is the intuition for the claim in section 6.3, that more patient committees pass more inefficient projects at relatively low q?

6.4 (a) Find the whole set of stationary equilibria with delay in Example 6.6.

(b) Provide an intuition for the equilibrium behavior as $\delta \to 1$ in the equilibrium described in Example 6.5.

6.8. FURTHER READING

6.5 Construct an example with n even and X one-dimensional with a majority core outcome that is never an equilibrium outcome to the bargaining game with $\delta = 1$. [Hint: insure the status quo is sufficiently extreme to be irrelevant.]

6.6 Prove the claim in the text following Example 6.7: if preferences are $\hat{u}_i(y) = -||y - x_i||^2$ for all i, then the only equilibrium outcome is the core alternative.

6.7 Confirm that the strategies described at the end of section 6.5 are indeed a no-delay equilibrium with $\bar{x} = \sqrt{(1-\delta)a^2/[1-\delta(1-p_2)]}$. What happens in the example if B is positive but relatively small?

6.8 Suppose, in the application of section 6.5 with three parties, that the bargaining protocol is changed to have a single stage in which party $i \in \{1, 2, 3\}$ is recognized with probability p_i and offers a proposal. If a majority accepts the proposal then it is implemented; otherwise the status quo platform $(x^0, 0)$ is implemented. Derive the undominated subgame perfect equilibrium to this game and compare the results with those of the protocol assumed in the text.

6.9 Prove or provide a counterexample to the claim that if: (1) $\delta = 1$; (2) the policy space is one-dimensional; (3) all individuals have single-peaked preferences; and (3) the preference aggregation rule f is collegial (see section 1.1), then all undominated stationary equilibrium outcomes to the bargaining game are core alternatives.

6.8 Further reading

Rubinstein [178] is the seminal paper for two-person sequential bargaining theory; excellent discussions of the basic theory and subsequent literature can be found in Osborne and Rubinstein [154] and Muthoo [143]. Harsanyi [93] is responsible for the purification argument for mixed strategy equilibria. Baron and Ferejohn [32] extend the Rubinstein model to majority rule, so initiating the literature on legislative bargaining; Theorem 6.1, Theorem 6.2 and Example 6.4 are from this paper. Theorem 6.3 is due to Eraslan [70]. The application of section 6.3 is based on Baron [29]. The material in section 6.4 on bargaining over policy relies heavily on Banks and Duggan [20] and [22], who prove Theorems 6.4 through 6.7 and the associated corollaries; Example 6.8 and Exercise 6.9 are adapted from Banks and Duggan

[20]. Section 6.5 is based on Baron [30] and Banks and Duggan [20]. An alternative model of "demand bargaining" in which legislators sequentially make demands for joining a coalition is developed by Morelli [134]; see also Winter [202]. Calvert [40] develops a theory of legislative reciprocity. The axiomatic theory of bargaining predates the noncooperative approach developed in this chapter. The key reference here is Nash [150]; Osborne and Rubinstein [154] give a useful overview.

Chapter 7
Two-Candidate Elections

Defining exactly what it is that makes a political system democratic is peculiarly difficult. A common feature of those systems typically labeled democratic, however, is the prevalence of elected officials. There are many different electoral systems in use and many more can be imagined. The institutions differ in who can vote and how often they can vote; in the number of votes any individual can cast; in the way votes are aggregated to arrive at an outcome; in the number of candidates or political parties seeking office; in the number of elected officials associated with any given geographic district or electoral constituency; and so on. In this chapter, we look at one particular sort of election: two-candidate competition for a single office under a given electoral rule. The introduction of more than two candidates and multiple offices is left for the next chapter.

In Chapter 3 (section 3.4), an electoral rule is described abstractly as a mechanism consisting of a set of admissible vote profiles on a set of possible outcomes, and an outcome function mapping vote profiles into outcomes. In what follows the focus is on two-candidate electoral competition and it is useful to be more explicit about such mechanisms. Given two candidates, an individual typically decides either to vote for one or other candidate, or to abstain. An admissible vote profile, therefore, is a list of such decisions, one for each member of the electorate, and the election is decided according to a rule for aggregating the votes. And because individuals can in general abstain or vote "strategically" for a candidate other than the one they most prefer, there is no presumption that an individual's vote invariably reflects the individual's underlying preferences over candidates.

Example 7.1 Suppose there are five individuals and two alternatives, a, b. The preference profile over a, b has individuals 1, 2 and 3 strictly prefer a

to b, and individuals 4 and 5 strictly prefer b to a. If a collective choice is made under plurality *preference* aggregation, then a is chosen. However, if individuals have to record their preferences by voting and individuals 1 and 2 abstain, plurality *vote* aggregation results in b defeating a. □

Despite the fact that recorded preferences, votes, need not coincide with individuals' true preferences, Example 7.1 indicates that, at least from a formal perspective, vote aggregation procedures are equivalent to collective choice rules, associating electoral winners with realized vote profiles. In particular, with only two candidates for an office, a vote for one of them is treated exactly as a strict preference for that candidate and abstention is treated as indifference. In this chapter, therefore, we assume for the most part that votes cast in a two-candidate election are aggregated by a simple rule (Definition 1.3). Although, among others, the class of simple rules includes majority rule and the q-rules, it excludes plurality rule and weighted q-rules. However, as we argue later, at least when individuals have continuous and strictly convex preferences over policy alternatives, the existence and characterization results for two-candidate electoral equilibria under a simple rule generalize easily to a broader class of rules ("voting rules") that includes these latter aggregation procedures along with many others.

7.1 Electoral equilibrium and the core

The benchmark model of electoral competition is a spatial voting model in which two candidates seek a single office by offering policy platforms freely chosen from some given set of alternatives. Eligible voters have given preferences over the set of alternatives and vote on the basis of the platforms offered by candidates. Let the set of candidates be $\{\alpha, \beta\}$ and let $N = \{1, \ldots, n\}$ be the electorate. The policy space is a (typically, convex and compact) set $X \subset \Re^k$. Each voter $i \in N$ has policy preferences on X representable by a strictly quasi-concave utility function $u_i : X \to \Re$. As in earlier chapters, we abuse notation slightly and occasionally write the utility profile $u \in \mathcal{R}_{cs}^n$ when $u = (u_1, \ldots, u_n)$ represents the profile $\rho \in \mathcal{R}_{cs}^n$. Candidates too have preferences although they need not be defined directly on the policy space, X; candidates, for example, might plausibly be more interested in winning office than in policy *per se*, or in some combination of winning and the policy eventually implemented, irrespective of who wins. Although the implications of adopting various assumptions for candidates' objectives are explored in this and the following chapter, it is convenient

7.1. ELECTORAL EQUILIBRIUM AND THE CORE

to begin by assuming that each candidate $c \in \{\alpha, \beta\}$ is solely motivated by winning office. There are two main reasons for supporting the assumption as a plausible starting point. First, the assumption insures a symmetry between candidates in that no electoral policy bias is introduced through any channel other than voter preferences; so while there surely exist asymmetries in real elections (if only because one candidate is often an incumbent), such asymmetries are things ultimately to be explained by the theory rather than assumed at the outset. The second, more substantive, reason is that while candidates may well have policy preferences, winning office at all is instrumental in being able to implement any policy goal.

By assumption, any winning candidate implements his or her electoral platform once in office. So a pure policy strategy for candidate $c \in \{\alpha, \beta\}$ is simply a selection of a policy, $x \in X$. Voters care about policy. Faced with a choice between policies a and b, any voter $i \in N$ can choose to vote for one or other of the two candidates or to abstain; voting for both candidates is ruled out by assumption. A permissible vote profile, therefore, consists of a list of n votes describing each individual's decision from the set {vote for α, vote for β, abstain}. The winning candidate is decided according to a simple electoral rule for aggregating votes. To define these rules, let f be a simple preference aggregation rule and let $\mathcal{L}(f)$ denote the set of decisive coalitions characterizing f (section 1.1).

Example 7.2 Important examples of simple rules include majority rule, where $\mathcal{L}(f) = \{L \subseteq N : |L| > n/2\}$; and all supra-majority q-rules, where $q \in (n/2, n]$ and $\mathcal{L}(f) = \{L \subseteq N : |L| \geq q\}$. □

A simple rule f is *collegial* if the intersection of all decisive coalitions is nonempty and is *noncollegial* otherwise; collegial simple rules are rules under which at least one individual has a veto over all outcomes. Now let $V_c \subseteq N$ denote the set of individuals who cast votes for candidate $c \in \{\alpha, \beta\}$; under the assumption that individuals can vote for at most one candidate, $V_\alpha \cup V_\beta \subseteq N$ and $V_\alpha \cap V_\beta = \emptyset$ for any permissible vote profile.

Definition 7.1 *A simple electoral rule is a noncollegial simple preference aggregation rule f defined on the domain of permissible vote profiles such that, for candidates $c, c' \in \{\alpha, \beta\}$, $c \neq c'$,*

$$cPc' \Leftrightarrow V_c \in \mathcal{L}(f),$$

where $\beta R \alpha$ if $\sim [\alpha P \beta]$ and $\alpha R \beta$ if $\sim [\beta P \alpha]$. In the case that both $\alpha R \beta$ and $\beta R \alpha$, we suppose the winner is determined by the flip of a fair coin.

Suppose the vote aggregation procedure is collegial and that individual $i \in N$ has a veto. Then it is possible for i to vote for one candidate and for all other individuals to vote for the other candidate. By definition of a veto, the election is tied in this case and so determined by a coin flip. The restriction to noncollegial vote aggregation procedures is to exclude this sort of pathology.

Assume (for now) that the cost of voting is negligible and consequently, as justified momentarily, that no person abstains. A mixed vote strategy for i is a function

$$v_i : X \times X \to [0,1]$$

where $v_i(a,b)$ is the probability that voter i votes for candidate α conditional on electoral platforms (a,b). Given a profile of vote strategies $v = (v_1, \ldots, v_n)$, $EV(a,b) \equiv \sum_{i \in N} v_i(a,b) \in [0,n]$ is the expected number of votes cast for α; then no abstention implies $n - EV(a,b)$ is the expected votes for β.

Let $W_c : X \times X \to \Re$ describe candidate c's payoff and fix f; then

$$\forall (a,b) \in X^2, \ W_\alpha(a,b) = \begin{cases} 1 & \text{if } \alpha P \beta \\ -1 & \text{if } \beta P \alpha \\ 0 & \text{otherwise} \end{cases}$$

and

$$W_\beta(a,b) = -W_\alpha(a,b).$$

Taking account of voters' behavior, candidates simultaneously make electoral policy decisions, following which voters simultaneously vote for one or other candidate under the (by assumption, correct) expectation that the winning candidate implements her electoral platform. The appropriate solution concept to this electoral game is therefore some form of undominated subgame perfect Nash equilibrium. Because voting costs are presumed negligible and the agenda is binary, the assumption that individuals use only undominated strategies implies they surely vote and do so for their most preferred candidate, irrespective of others' decisions: assuming an individual strictly prefers one candidate to the other, he or she should surely vote sincerely if pivotal and can do no worse by voting sincerely otherwise. That is, given $(a,b) \in X^2$, a profile of voting strategies v is an undominated strategy in the two candidate election game with no voting costs, if,

$$\forall i \in N, \ v_i(a,b) \in \arg\max_{p \in [0,1]} p u_i(a) + (1-p) u_i(b).$$

In the case that an individual is indifferent between the two candidates, any vote at all constitutes a best response. To close the model, assume in this

7.1. ELECTORAL EQUILIBRIUM AND THE CORE

case that the individual votes for α with probability $1/2$. Although an *ad hoc* restriction, the assumption is plausible given the model is of a single election and voters are purely policy-oriented and presumed not to abstain. It is, however, stronger than requiring only that voters treat candidates symmetrically: an individual can be indifferent between candidates at wildly different pairs of platforms and assuming the individual *always* votes for a candidate with probability $1/2$ when indifferent is to assume more than that he or she treats candidates in the same way. Some implications of assuming a weaker symmetry condition on the decisions of indifferent voters are considered later (section 7.3).

Taking the simple electoral rule, the voters' strategic behavior and the candidates' preferences as described, an undominated Nash equilibrium to the election game is defined by the candidates' policy choices. Specifically, say that a pair of electoral platforms $(a,b) \in X^2$ is a (pure strategy) *two-candidate electoral equilibrium* if, for all $y \in X$,

$$EW_\alpha(a,b) \geq EW_\alpha(y,b) \text{ and } EW_\beta(a,b) \geq EW_\beta(a,y)$$

where EW_c is candidate c's expected payoff conditional on the specified platforms and voter decisions. Because all voters surely vote sincerely over any pair of platforms, there is no ambiguity in writing $C_f(u) \subseteq X$ to denote the set of core alternatives at the preference profile u under the rule f:

$$C_f(u) = \{x \in X : \forall y \in X, \, xRy\}.$$

Theorem 7.1 *A pair of platforms (a^*, b^*) is a two-candidate electoral equilibrium if and only if $x^* \in C_f(u)$, $x^* = a^*, b^*$.*

Proof (Necessity) Let $a^* \notin C_f(u)$. Then there exists some $y \in X$ such that yPa^* and so, by individuals using weakly undominated strategies, $W_\beta(a^*, y) > 0$. Also, by definition of an equilibrium, $W_\beta(a^*, b^*) \geq W_\beta(a^*, y)$; therefore, $W_\beta(a^*, b^*) > 0$ and $W_\alpha(a^*, b^*) < 0$. But $W_\alpha(b^*, b^*) = 0$ because indifferent voters vote for each candidate with probability $1/2$. Hence, $W_\alpha(b^*, b^*) > W_\alpha(a^*, b^*)$ contradicting (a^*, b^*) an equilibrium. Therefore, $(a^*, b^*) \in C_f(u)$.

(Sufficiency) Suppose $(a^*, b^*) \in C_f(u)$. By definition of the core, x^*Ry for all $y \in X\backslash\{x^*\}$, $x^* = a^*, b^*$. By the assumption of weakly undominated strategies and the symmetry assumption on tie-breaking, therefore, $W_\alpha(a^*, b^*) + W_\beta(a^*, b^*) = 0$ implies $W_c(a^*, b^*) = 0$. Moreover, for all $y \neq a^*$, $W_\alpha(y, b^*) \leq 0$ and for all $y \neq b^*$, $W_\beta(a^*, y) \leq 0$. Hence, (a^*, b^*) a two-candidate electoral equilibrium. □

Although quite intuitive, Theorem 7.1 is useful: the result identifies the set of (noncooperative) Nash equilibrium outcomes when the election is decided by a vote aggregation rule, with the set of (cooperative) core outcomes under the equivalent preference aggregation rule.

Given a strictly convex preference profile $\rho \in \mathcal{R}_{cs}^n$ and an aggregation rule f, recall $\mu_f(\rho|_{\gamma_x}) \subseteq \gamma_x$ denotes the set of induced f-medians on the line γ_x through $x \in X$.

Corollary 7.1 *Let $\rho \in \mathcal{R}_{cs}^n$. A pair of platforms $(a^*, b^*) \in X^2$ is a two-candidate electoral equilibrium if and only if, for each $c = \alpha, \beta$ and for all lines γ_{x^*} through each $x^* \in \{a^*, b^*\}$, $x^* \in \mu_f(\rho|_{\gamma_{x^*}})$.*

Proof Apply Theorem 7.1 and [PPTI, Theorem 5.5]. □

Indirectly, therefore, Theorem 7.1 provides a characterization result for two-candidate electoral competition: in the absence of any intrinsic asymmetries or voter abstention, the incentives of office-seeking candidates under a simple rule f induce those candidates to offer only f-median policies in any electoral equilibrium. And if the set of medians is singleton, as is the case for instance, when f is majority rule and n is odd, Corollary 7.1 implies the candidates must converge in equilibrium. Unfortunately, the existence of electoral equilibria in pure strategies is far from assured.

Define the *Nakamura number*, $s(f)$, for a noncollegial simple rule f to be the cardinality of the smallest family decisive coalitions with empty intersection (Definition 1.4),

$$s(f) \equiv \min\{|\mathcal{L}'| : \mathcal{L}' \subset \mathcal{L}(f) \text{ and } \cap_{L \in \mathcal{L}'} L = \emptyset\}.$$

Applying this concept to rules in Example 7.2 (see [PPTI, Lemma 3.2]), we find $s(f) = 3$ for majority rule with $n \neq 4$ and, for any q-rule with $q < n$, $s(f) = \lceil n/(n-q) \rceil$ (where $\lceil t \rceil$ is the smallest integer greater than or equal to t). As suggested by the next result, the higher the Nakamura number, the better behaved is the aggregation rule.

Corollary 7.2 *There exists a two-candidate electoral equilibrium for all $\rho \in \mathcal{R}_{cs}^n$ if and only if $k \leq s(f) - 2$.*

Proof Apply Theorem 7.1 and [PPTI, Theorems 5.3 and 5.4]. □

If f is simple majority rule and n is odd, then Corollary 7.2 implies that two-candidate electoral equilibria exist for all strictly convex preference profiles only if the policy space is one-dimensional. Given majority rule, then, the preceding results in effect provide an application of the Median Voter Theorem [PPTI, Theorem 4.4] to electoral competition. Although the Median Voter Theorem is an abstract result about top-ranked majority preference alternatives under single-peaked preferences, rational voting over a one-dimensional issue space by policy-oriented voters yields incentives that, in equilibrium, induce office-seeking candidates to implement the median electoral policy. The same incentives apply in multidimensional spaces too but, in these settings, there are typically no "medians on all lines"; the majority core is empty and so, by Theorem 7.1, there are no pure strategy equilibria to the electoral game.

As observed earlier (and discussed extensively in [PPTI, ch.3]), simple rules are a subset of the class of voting rules (Definition 1.5); this latter class includes rules like plurality rule, weighted q-rules and extended q-rules. Then given voters have strictly convex preferences over the set of feasible policies, [PPTI, Theorem 7.2] implies that Theorem 7.1 and Corollaries 7.1 and 7.2 generalize directly to this more inclusive class of aggregation procedures. In other words, the implications for two-candidate electoral equilibria under simple electoral rules are not confined only to these rules.

Before going on to consider what in general can be said about electoral competition over multiple issues, we first illustrate the results so far for single-issue politics.

7.2 Application: Ideological convergence

A striking feature of plurality rule electoral systems in particular is the frequent dominance of two ideologically similar political parties. Indeed, a common complaint of such systems is the apparent absence of any "real" choice for the electorate. And while the existence of only two parties or candidates is simply assumed in this chapter, ideological convergence and 'the absence of a real choice' remain to be understood.

Elected legislators and governments make policy and almost all policy is multidimensional. Legislative and governmental elections, however, are often perceived more directly in terms of ideological competition. Ideological labels such as "left wing", "right wing" or "centrist" are typically associated with attitudes to policy, permitting voters to use ideological labels as predictors of how candidates can be expected to behave with respect to policy conditional on being elected to office. In turn, this induces candidates for office, at least in part, to campaign on ideology rather than on the details of policy proposals.

Assume all voters and candidates share a common interpretation of any ideological label and that any voter's ideology can be represented as a point along some Left-Right continuum. In this context, a presumption of single-peaked preferences is fairly natural: an individual has a most preferred ideological position and the more left or right wing is a candidate relative to that position the less appealing is the candidate to the individual. Assume further that the two candidates for electoral office are free to adopt any ideological label they choose. Unlike single-peaked voter preferences, this assumption on candidates' sets of feasible electoral platforms is, at least in the short term, rather less natural. Then if all voters vote and the election is decided by plurality or majority voting, Corollaries 7.1 and 7.2 predict ideological convergence by office-seeking candidates to the relative moderates in the electorate: in effect, the incentives to win office under plurality rule drive candidates to the electoral middle ground at the expense of any significant distinction between their respective platforms. It is useful to spell out the logic of the argument more fully with the following heuristic.

For convenience here, we make the technical assumption that every voter has symmetric single-peaked preferences over the ideological dimension. In this case, it is enough to know the relative distance between the two candidates' platforms and a voter's ideal point to know that voter's preferences over the candidates: for voter with ideal point x_i and any policies $y, z \in X$,

$$yP_i z \Leftrightarrow |y - x_i| < |z - x_i|.$$

Moreover, under this technical assumption, a sufficiently large finite electorate can be adequately summarized by a continuous preference distribution F over the ideological dimension $X \subset \Re$ describing for any platform $x \in X$ the proportion $F(x)$ of voters with ideal points to the left of x.

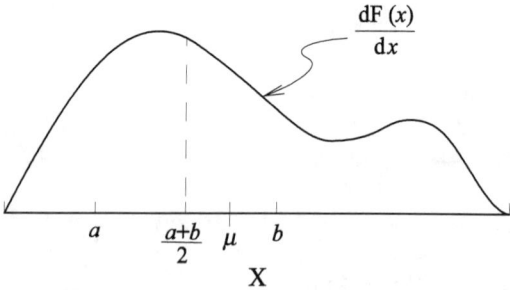

Figure 7.1: Preference distribution and candidate platforms

7.2. APPLICATION: IDEOLOGICAL CONVERGENCE

Let $\mu \in X$ denote the median ideal point, $F(\mu) = 1/2$, and suppose, for instance, that candidates have ideological platforms $a < \mu < b$, as illustrated in Figure 7.1 above. The configuration $\{a, b\}$ is not an electoral equilibrium. By the assumptions of no abstention and preference symmetry, a fraction of the electorate $F(\frac{a+b}{2}) < 1/2$ votes for candidate α and a fraction $1 - F(\frac{a+b}{2}) > 1/2$ votes for candidate β. Given b, α can improve her vote share by adopting a platform closer to b, say $a' \in (a, b)$: by no abstention, a move from a to a' does not induce any loss of votes from α's extremist voters but induces some relative moderates to switch from supporting β at b to supporting α at a'. In particular, α can insure winning by choosing any platform strictly between μ and b. This is illustrated in Figure 7.2(a) assuming $X = [0, 1]$; in both panels (a) and (b) of Figure 7.2, β's platform b is held fixed and we plot α's vote share as a function of her platform a.

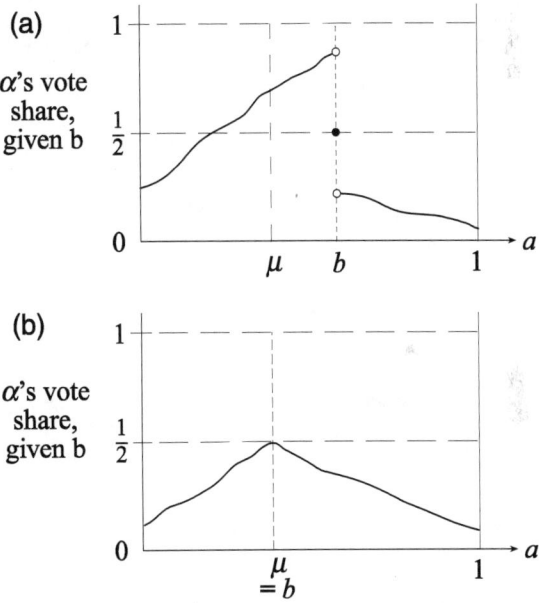

Figure 7.2: Candidate α's vote share

Because a similar logic obtains for β given a and, further, obtains for any pair of distinct platforms, it follows that any electoral equilibrium must involve ideological convergence. And it is easy to see that the only possibility for an equilibrium is at the median: if, without loss of generality, $a = b > \mu$

then, given b, candidate α could move slightly to the left and secure a strict majority rather than (by the symmetry assumption on how indifferent voters choose their votes) an expected 50% of the total vote. The only common platform where such a unilateral deviation by one of the candidates could never be profitable is the median: in this case, as shown by Figure 7.2(b), a unilateral deviation by, say, α leaves β at the median with a strict majority rather than simply 50% of the vote. In other words, if we imagine starting in Figure 7.2(a) with $b > \mu$ and moving b continuously toward μ, the left and right limit values of α's vote share function at $a = b$ converge continuously, becoming equal at $b = \mu$, as in Figure 7.2(b).

It is important to emphasize that the argument for ideological convergence here is independent of the particular distribution of voter preferences F; as long as all voters vote, the incentives induced by plurality or majority rule lead plurality-maximizing candidates to converge on the median.

7.3 Equilibrium in multidimensional spaces

Corollary 7.2 asserts that a two-candidate electoral equilibrium, at least as defined in terms of pure strategies, is not assured to exist for multidimensional policy spaces. A natural starting point to obtain a general existence theorem is to assume that the feasible set of policies is an (arbitrarily large) finite set from, rather than some convex subset of, $\Re^k$. Although there is still no guarantee of a pure strategy equilibrium with a finite set of feasible platforms, the Kakutani Fixed Point Theorem can be applied to yield existence of mixed strategy electoral equilibria in which the candidates' strategies are probability distributions over the set of platforms. By itself, however, existence *per se* is simply a check on mutual strategic consistency in candidates' behavior. To use the model for predictive or evaluative purposes requires being able to say something about the support of equilibrium mixed strategies; that is, about the policies that can be observed in equilibrium.

Let $\hat{X}$ be a finite set of feasible platforms and recall that $\Delta \hat{X}$ is the family of probability distributions over $\hat{X}$; then for each candidate $c \in \{\alpha, \beta\}$, let $\pi_c \in \Delta \hat{X}$ denote c's mixed strategy over $\hat{X}$ and, for each $x \in \hat{X}$, let $\pi_c(x) \in [0, 1]$ be the probability that c offers the platform x to the electorate. At the time the election takes place, voters are confronted with exactly two platforms between which to choose; consequently their behavior at the voting stage is unaffected by whether or not the platforms are generated through (nondegenerate) mixed or pure candidate strategies. Thus a two-candidate electoral equilibrium here is defined by a pair of mixed strategies

7.3. EQUILIBRIUM IN MULTIDIMENSIONAL SPACES

$(\pi_\alpha, \pi_\beta) \in \Delta\hat{X} \times \Delta\hat{X}$ such that, for all $x \in \hat{X}$,

$$\pi_\alpha(x) > 0 \Rightarrow x \in \arg\max_{x \in \hat{X}} \sum_{y \in \hat{X}} \pi_\beta(y) W_\alpha(x, y)$$

and

$$\pi_\beta(x) > 0 \Rightarrow x \in \arg\max_{x \in \hat{X}} \sum_{y \in \hat{X}} \pi_\alpha(y) W_\beta(y, x).$$

If both candidates are restricted to pure strategies, this definition is equivalent to that used in the previous section.

Existence of a mixed strategy electoral equilibrium on $[\Delta\hat{X}]^2$ is an immediate consequence of the Nash equilibrium existence theorem for finite games.

Theorem 7.2 (Nash) *Let $G = ((\mathcal{M}, g), u_1, \ldots, u_n)$ be a game with n agents and finite pure strategy sets $\mathcal{M}_i$, $i = 1, \ldots, n$. Then G has a mixed strategy Nash equilibrium.*

Proof It is convenient to suppress the outcome function g and define payoffs directly over strategy profiles: for any $i \in N$, define a payoff function $\hat{u}_i$ on $\mathcal{M} \equiv \prod_j \mathcal{M}_j$ by $\hat{u}_i(\mathbf{s}) \equiv u_i(g(\mathbf{s}))$, all $\mathbf{s} \in \mathcal{M}$. For any $i \in N$, let $\sigma_i \in \Delta\mathcal{M}_i$ denote i's mixed strategy and let $\sigma_i(s) \in [0,1]$ denote the probability i chooses the pure strategy $s \in \mathcal{M}_i$. For all $\sigma \in \Delta\mathcal{M}$ define

$$B_i(\sigma) = \arg\max_{\sigma_i \in \Delta\mathcal{M}_i} \sum_{\mathbf{s} \in \mathcal{M}} \hat{u}_i(\mathbf{s}) \sigma_1(s_1) \ldots \sigma_i(s_i) \ldots \sigma_n(s_n)$$

to be i's best response mixed strategy to the mixed strategies of others, σ_{-i}. For any $\sigma \in \Delta\mathcal{M}$ define

$$B(\sigma) = B_1(\sigma) \times B_2(\sigma) \times \ldots \times B_n(\sigma).$$

Then $B : [\Delta\mathcal{M}]^n \rightrightarrows [\Delta\mathcal{M}]^n$ is a correspondence mapping the set of mixed strategy profiles into itself. By definition of $B_i(\sigma)$, all $i \in N$, any fixed point of this mapping $\sigma^* \in B(\sigma^*)$ is a Nash equilibrium to G. To prove equilibrium existence, therefore, it suffices to show that the hypotheses of the Kakutani Fixed Point theorem apply (see Theorem 5.1, above). To do this, first observe that, because $\Delta\mathcal{M}$ is the set of probability distributions over a finite set, $[\Delta\mathcal{M}]^n$ is surely convex and compact. Now, for any $i \in N$, write

$$E\hat{u}_i(\sigma_i, \sigma_{-i}) \equiv \sum_{\mathbf{s} \in \mathcal{M}} \hat{u}_i(\mathbf{s}) \sigma_1(s_1) \ldots \sigma_i(s_i) \ldots \sigma_n(s_n)$$

and note that $E\hat{u}_i$ is continuous in $\sigma \in \Delta\mathcal{M}$. Moreover, since $\Delta\mathcal{M}_i$ is compact, convex and nonempty, the Maximum Theorem yields that $B_i : [\Delta\mathcal{M}]^n \rightrightarrows [\Delta\mathcal{M}]^n$ is a nonempty and compact valued uhc correspondence. Moreover, $B_i(\sigma)$ is convex for all $\sigma \in \Delta\mathcal{M}$: for all $s_i \in \mathcal{M}_i$, all $\sigma_{-i} \in \prod_{j \neq i} \mathcal{M}_j$, define

$$E\hat{u}_i(s, \sigma_{-i}) = \sum_{\mathbf{s}_{-i} \in \mathcal{M}_{-i}} \hat{u}_i(s, \mathbf{s}_{-i}) \prod_{j \neq i} \sigma_j(s_j)$$

in which case, for all $\sigma_i \in \Delta\mathcal{M}_i$,

$$E\hat{u}_i(\sigma_i, \sigma_{-i}) = \sum_{s \in \mathcal{M}_i} E\hat{u}_i(s, \sigma_{-i})\sigma_i(s);$$

hence, for all $\sigma_i, \sigma'_i \in \Delta\mathcal{M}_i$ and all $t \in [0,1]$,

$$E\hat{u}_i(t\sigma_i + (1-t)\sigma'_i, \sigma_{-i}) = tE\hat{u}_i(\sigma_i, \sigma_{-i}) + (1-t)E\hat{u}_i(\sigma'_i, \sigma_{-i})$$

so $B_i(\sigma)$ is convex. Since i is chosen arbitrarily in the preceding argument, it follows that $B : [\Delta\mathcal{M}]^n \rightrightarrows [\Delta\mathcal{M}]^n$ is a nonempty, compact and convex valued uhc correspondence. Applying Kakutani's theorem completes the proof. □

Given that $\hat{X}$ is finite and we are considering electoral competition in which the number of voters is presumed large, there is negligible loss in generality in assuming that the collective preference relation on $\hat{X}$ for any realized preference profile is strict; that is, if $x, y \in \hat{X}$ are distinct then either x is strictly preferred (under the rule f) to y or y is strictly preferred to x. Adopting this assumption yields a surprising uniqueness result, the proof of which exploits some useful properties of (finite or infinite) two-person zero-sum games; that is, for games $G = ((\mathcal{M}_1, \mathcal{M}_2, g), u_1, u_2)$ such that $\mathcal{M}_i$ is i's set of actions (finite or infinite) and, for all $\mathbf{s} \in \mathcal{M} \equiv \mathcal{M}_1 \times \mathcal{M}_2$, $u_1(g(\mathbf{s})) + u_2(g(\mathbf{s})) = 0$. Given a game G, it is convenient to adopt notation introduced in the proof to Theorem 7.2 and write $\hat{u}_i(\mathbf{s}) \equiv u_i(g(\mathbf{s}))$, all $i \in N$ and all $\mathbf{s} \in \mathcal{M}$; then the game is described more succinctly by $G = (\mathcal{M}, \hat{u}_1, \hat{u}_2)$ and, for any mixed strategy profile $\sigma \in \Delta\mathcal{M}$, let $E\hat{u}_i(\sigma) \equiv E\hat{u}_i(\sigma_i, \sigma_{-i})$ be i's expected payoff from using strategy σ_i given i's opponent uses the strategy σ_{-i}.

Lemma 7.1 *Let $G = (\mathcal{M}, \hat{u}_1, \hat{u}_2)$ be a (finite or infinite) two-person zero-sum game. If $(\sigma_1, \sigma_2), (\sigma'_1, \sigma'_2) \in \Delta\mathcal{M}$ are Nash equilibrium profiles then*

7.3. EQUILIBRIUM IN MULTIDIMENSIONAL SPACES

(1) (σ_1, σ_2') and (σ_1', σ_2) are equilibrium profiles;
(2) $E\hat{u}_i(\sigma_1, \sigma_2) = E\hat{u}_i(\sigma_1', \sigma_2') = E\hat{u}_i(\sigma_1, \sigma_2') = E\hat{u}_i(\sigma_1', \sigma_2)$, $i = 1, 2$.
Moreover,
(3) The set of Nash equilibria to G is convex;
(4) If G is symmetric ($\mathcal{M}_1 = \mathcal{M}_2 = \mathcal{M}$ and $u_i(s, s') = -u_i(s', s)$ for every $s, s' \in \mathcal{M}$ and $i = 1, 2$), there exists a symmetric equilibrium σ, $\sigma_1 = \sigma_2$.

Proof Let (σ_1, σ_2) and (σ_1', σ_2') be Nash equilibria. Then by definition of equilibrium,
$$E\hat{u}_1(\sigma_1, \sigma_2) \geq E\hat{u}_1(\sigma_1', \sigma_2) \geq E\hat{u}_1(\sigma_1', \sigma_2')$$
and
$$E\hat{u}_1(\sigma_1', \sigma_2') \geq E\hat{u}_1(\sigma_1, \sigma_2') \geq E\hat{u}_1(\sigma_1, \sigma_2).$$
And since G zero-sum means $\hat{u}_1(\mathbf{s}) = -\hat{u}_2(\mathbf{s})$, these inequalities prove claim (2). Now applying the definition of equilibrium once again for any $\sigma_i'' \in \Delta\mathcal{M}_i$, $i = 1, 2$, yields
$$E\hat{u}_1(\sigma_1, \sigma_2) = E\hat{u}_1(\sigma_1', \sigma_2) \geq E\hat{u}_1(\sigma_1'', \sigma_2)$$
and
$$E\hat{u}_1(\sigma_1', \sigma_2') = E\hat{u}_1(\sigma_1', \sigma_2) \leq E\hat{u}_1(\sigma_1', \sigma_2'').$$
Hence, (σ_1', σ_2) is an equilibrium. Similarly, (σ_1, σ_2') is an equilibrium and this proves claim (1). Claims (3) and (4) follow easily from claims (1) and (2): details are left as an exercise. □

We can now prove the uniqueness result for electoral equilibria in finite policy spaces.

Theorem 7.3 *If the feasible set of candidate platforms $\hat{X}$ is finite and the collective preference on $\hat{X}$ is strict, there exists a unique two-candidate electoral equilibrium, $(\pi, \pi) \in \Delta\hat{X} \times \Delta\hat{X}$.*

Proof Existence of an equilibrium is assured by Theorem 7.2; and if the collective preference relation on $\hat{X}$ admits a Condorcet winner, then Corollary 7.1 implies that both candidates choose this alternative with probability one. So assume the equilibrium is in nondegenerate mixed strategies (π_α, π_β). By assumption,
$$W_\alpha(a, b) + W_\beta(a, b) = 0$$
in which case the game is symmetric and Lemma 7.1(4) implies there must be a symmetric equilibrium, (π, π). And if (π, π) and (π', π') are distinct

symmetric equilibria then, by Lemma 7.1(1), (π, π') and (π', π) are distinct asymmetric equilibria. To prove uniqueness, therefore, it suffices to show there can be only one symmetric equilibrium. Suppose to the contrary that both (π, π) and (π', π') are symmetric electoral equilibria. There are two cases.

(1) $Supp[\pi] = Supp[\pi'] = Y$. For any $x \in \hat{X}$, recall $P(x)$ is the set of alternatives in $\hat{X}$ that are strictly preferred to x, and $P^{-1}(x)$ is the set of alternatives in $\hat{X}$ to which x is strictly preferred. Because the game is symmetric, Lemma 7.1(2) implies that candidates' expected payoffs in equilibrium must be equal; in particular, $W_c(x,y) \in \{-1,0,1\}$ for all $c \in \{\alpha, \beta\}$ and $x, y \in X$ implies

$$E[W_\alpha|\pi_\alpha, \pi_\beta] = E[W_\beta|\pi_\alpha, \pi_\beta] = 0$$

in any equilibrium (π_α, π_β). Therefore, since

$$E[W_\alpha|x, \pi] = (-1) \sum_{y \in P(x)} \pi(y) + (0)\pi(x) + (1) \sum_{y \in P^{-1}(x)} \pi(y)$$

and (π, π) is an equilibrium,

$$\forall x \in Y, \quad \sum_{y \in P(x)} \pi(y) = \sum_{y \in P^{-1}(x)} \pi(y)$$

and

$$\forall x \in \hat{X} \backslash Y, \quad \sum_{y \in P(x)} \pi(y) \geq \sum_{y \in P^{-1}(x)} \pi(y).$$

Let $h(y) = \pi(y) - \pi'(y)$. By the supposition, therefore, for all $x \in Y$

$$\sum_{y \in P(x)} h(y) = \sum_{y \in P^{-1}(x)} h(y) \tag{*}$$

And because both π and π' are probability distributions with common support,

$$\sum_{y \in Y} h(y) = \sum_{y \in P(x)} h(y) + h(x) + \sum_{y \in P^{-1}(x)} h(y) = 0 \tag{**}$$

The system of linear equations $\{(*), (**)\}$ involves only rational coefficients so has a rational solution h^*; multiplying through by the lowest common denominator of the components of h^* gives a solution in the integers and, therefore, by dividing through by 2 as often as needed, has a solution in

7.3. EQUILIBRIUM IN MULTIDIMENSIONAL SPACES

the integers with at least one component $h^*(\bar{y})$ odd. But combining (*) and (**), h^* must satisfy

$$h^*(\bar{y}) + 2 \sum_{y \in P^{-1}(x)} h^*(y) = 0,$$

which is impossible if $h^*(\bar{y})$ odd.

(2) $Supp[\pi] = Y \neq Y' = Supp[\pi']$. By Lemma 7.1(3), the set of mixed strategy equilibria is convex. Hence, for all $t \in (0,1)$,

$$(\pi'', \pi'') = (t\pi + (1-t)\pi', t\pi + (1-t)\pi')$$

is a symmetric electoral equilibrium with $Supp[\pi''] = Y \cup Y'$. By case (1), however, there exists a unique equilibrium with support $Y \cup Y'$. Hence, $t\pi + (1-t)\pi'$ is constant in t which contradicts $Y \neq Y'$. □

Theorem 7.3 is quite surprising. It states that if the two candidates for office care only about winning and the set of feasible policies is finite, then there exists at most one electoral equilibrium: in the case electorate preferences admit a unique maximal alternative under the electoral rule (for example, a Condorcet winner under majority rule), both candidates converge on offering only this policy; in the case there is no such maximal alternative, candidates "converge" on a specific mixed strategy. To say anything about the possible equilibrium platforms under two-candidate competition, therefore, it is necessary only to focus on those platforms that have a positive probability of being played in equilibrium by one of the candidates; that is, on the support of the equilibrium strategy, $Supp[\pi]$.

It is left as a straightforward exercise to check that any Nash equilibrium strategy must survive the iterated deletion of strictly dominated strategies (Definition 4.1); hence, $Supp[\pi]$ is a subset of those alternatives $x \in \hat{X}$ that remain after the iterated deletion of strictly dominated strategies by candidates. Now recall (Definition 4.5) that, given a majority preference P on $\hat{X}$, an alternative $x \in \hat{X}$ covers an alternative $y \in \hat{X}$ if and only if $x \in P(y)$ and $P(x) \subset P(y)$. Clearly, nothing in the definition of covering hinges on the strict preference relation P being strict majority preference; exactly the same definition applies to any aggregation rule that induces a strict binary social preference relation P on $\hat{X}$. With this generalization of covering and the uncovered set in mind, it follows that an alternative x survives the iterated deletion of strictly dominated strategies in the two-candidate electoral game under P only if x is not covered by any other alternative y. Thus the support of the equilibrium mixed strategy necessarily lies within the uncovered set for P.

Theorem 7.4 Let $(\pi, \pi) \in \Delta \hat{X} \times \Delta \hat{X}$ be the unique two-candidate electoral equilibrium under a collective preference relation P on (finite) $\hat{X}$. Then $Supp[\pi] \subseteq U(P)$.

Just as the uncovered set is important for the theory of voting in committees, therefore, it is also important for the theory of two-candidate electoral competition, a quite different institutional setting. Example 7.3 illustrates the result.

Example 7.3 Let $\hat{X} = \{v, w, x, y, z\}$ and assume preferences are aggregated by majority rule. By Theorem 4.2, there exists a preference profile ρ such that the associated majority preference relation P on $\hat{X}$ is defined by

$$\begin{aligned} P(v) &= \{w, x, y\}; P^{-1}(v) = \{z\} \\ P(w) &= \{x, z\}; P^{-1}(w) = \{y, v\} \\ P(x) &= \{z\}; P^{-1}(x) = \{v, w, y\} \\ P(y) &= \{w, x\}; P^{-1}(y) = \{v, z\} \\ P(z) &= \{v, y\}; P^{-1}(z) = \{w, x\}. \end{aligned}$$

Applying Definition 4.5, the uncovered set here is $U(P) = \{x, y, z\}$: y covers v and x covers w. And it is easily checked that the unique mixed strategy equilibrium for the two-candidate electoral competition on $\hat{X}$, (π, π), is such that

$$\pi(x) = \pi(y) = \pi(z) = 1/3$$

in which case $Supp[\pi] = U(P)$. Now suppose a majority preference relation P' is defined on $\hat{X}$ by

$$\begin{aligned} P'(v) &= \{x, y, z\}; P'^{-1}(v) = \{w\} \\ P'(w) &= \{x, v\}; P'^{-1}(w) = \{y, z\} \\ P'(x) &= \{y\}; P'^{-1}(x) = \{v, w, z\} \\ P'(y) &= \{w, z\}; P'^{-1}(y) = \{v, x\} \\ P'(z) &= \{w, x\}; P'^{-1}(z) = \{y, v\}; \end{aligned}$$

then only v is covered (by x) and $U(P') = \{w, x, y, z\}$. In this case, however, the support of the unique mixed strategy equilibrium (π', π') assured by Theorem 7.3 is a proper subset of $U(P')$, $Supp[\pi'] \subset U(P')$ [Exercise]. □

For the general spatial model, the feasible set of alternatives is assumed here to be a convex and compact subset $X \subset \Re^k$ and the preceding two

7.3. EQUILIBRIUM IN MULTIDIMENSIONAL SPACES

theorems do not apply. However, compactness of X insures the uniform probability distribution with support X is well-defined. Consequently, if we take the set of alternatives $\hat{X}$ as a finite random sample from the uniform distribution with full support on X, then we can approximate X by letting the sample size $|\hat{X}|$ go to infinity. Although this observation suggests a two-candidate equilibrium existence theorem in mixed strategies might be readily available for the multidimensional spatial model in which individuals use undominated voting strategies and randomize fairly between candidates when indifferent, no such general result yet exists (at least, as of the time of writing). The principal technical difficulty is the discontinuity inherent in the candidates' payoff functions, $W_c(\cdot)$. If both converge on a policy $x \in X$, the respective payoffs are equal at $W_\alpha(x,x) = W_\beta(x,x) = 0$; but in general there is no suitable median policy in which case, for all x in the interior of X, X°, and for *all* neighborhoods $B(x,\epsilon)$, $\epsilon > 0$, there is a deviation by, say, candidate α to a policy $y \in B(x,\epsilon)$ such that $W_\alpha(y,x) = 1 > W_\alpha(x,x)$. In turn, this discontinuity is induced by the presumed behavior of indifferent voters, who vote with probability $1/2$ for each candidate when indifferent but jump to voting surely when they have a strict preference. On the other hand, Theorem 7.4 does extend to the spatial model and, as argued later, an existence result is available for two-candidate electoral equilibria in the multidimensional model when indifferent voters are not assumed necessarily to vote with probability $1/2$ for either candidate.

We first extend Theorem 7.4 to the general spatial model and then go on to develop the equilibrium existence claim for this setting. For both issues, it is useful to begin by defining the uncovered set for the spatial model and an arbitrary preference aggregation rule, and connecting this definition to the earlier one for the finite model.

Fix a preference profile $\rho \in \mathcal{R}^n$ and, as usual, let R denote the weak collective preference relation induced by an aggregation rule on X with asymmetric part, P. Definition 7.2 extends the definitions of covering and the uncovered set for the finite alternative setting (Definition 4.5) to the spatial setting. As argued below, the essential difference between the two definitions lies in the necessity of allowing for social indifference in the spatial setting.

Definition 7.2 *For any $x, y \in X \subset \Re^k$ and collective preference relation R with asymmetric part P, say that x covers y, xCy, if (i) xPy and (ii) $R(x) \subseteq R(y)$ and $P(x) \subset P(y)$. The uncovered set for R is*

$$U(R) = \{x \in X : yCx \text{ for no } y \in X\}$$

In words, alternative x covers alternative y if x is strictly preferred to y, if the set of policies ranked at least as good as (respectively, strictly better than) x by the rule is contained in the set of those similarly ranked at least as good as (respectively, strictly better than) y. The uncovered set is the set of alternatives in X that are not covered. Figure 7.3 illustrates the definition of covering for a spatial model with three persons and two policy dimensions under majority rule.

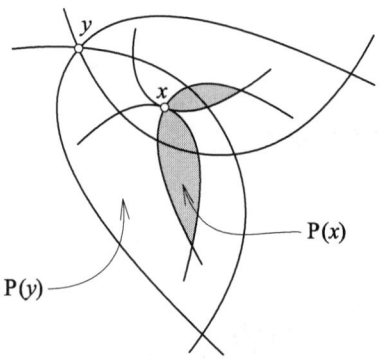

Figure 7.3: x covers y

In Figure 7.3, x covers y: x is strictly majority preferred to y and the set of policies ranked at least as good as (respectively, strictly better than) x by majority preference is contained in the set of those similarly ranked at least as good as (respectively, strictly better than) y, and at least one of these containments is strict.

Recall that the Pareto set at ρ is the subset $PS_N(\rho) \subseteq X$ with the property that no alternative in the subset is unanimously less preferred to some other available alternative [PPTI, sect.4.5]:

$$PS_N(\rho) = \{x \in X : \forall y \neq x,\ P(y,x;\rho) \neq \emptyset \Rightarrow P(x,y;\rho) \neq \emptyset\}.$$

Then, by definition of the Pareto set and the core, for any weakly Paretian collective preference $f(\rho)$ on X, $\rho \in \mathcal{R}^n$, we have

$$C_f(\rho) \subseteq U(f(\rho)) \subseteq PS_N(\rho).$$

Furthermore, if $f(\rho)$ is strict at some profile ρ then the core and the uncovered set surely coincide: $f(\rho) \in \mathcal{P}$ implies $C_f(\rho) = U(f(\rho))$ [Exercise].

In case the collective preference relation is strict everywhere on X, the definition of covering given here coincides exactly with that of Definition

7.3. EQUILIBRIUM IN MULTIDIMENSIONAL SPACES

4.5 [Exercise]. Thus Definition 7.2 differs only insofar as it takes account of indifference in the social preference relation. The relevance of being explicit with regard to social indifference is perhaps best illustrated by an example. Consider Figure 7.4 in which the preferences of four individuals over a two-dimensional policy space are described.

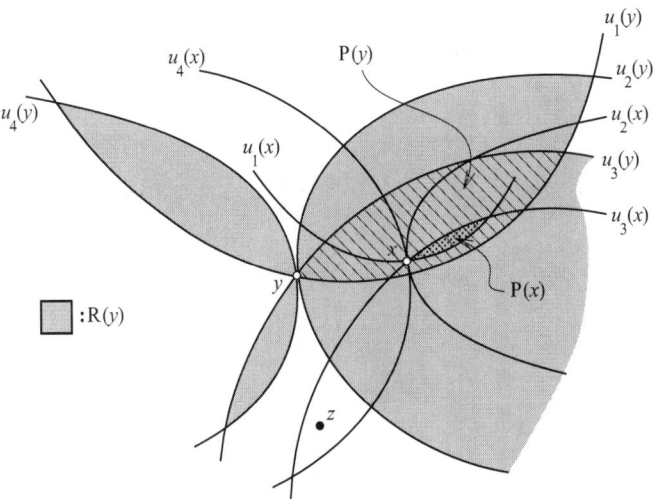

Figure 7.4: Covering and social indifference

Suppose the social preference relation R is defined by simple majority rule. Then it can be seen from the diagram that xPy and $P(x) \subset P(y)$ but $R(x) \not\subseteq R(y)$; in particular, $z \in R(x)$, $z \notin P(x)$ but $z \notin R(y)$, so x fails to cover y according to Definition 7.2. And since, in the example, there exists a distinct alternative z at least as good as x but not at least as good as y, x is not so clearly a more compelling platform than y with respect to majority preference.

Theorem 7.5 *Let* $X \subset \Re^k$ *be convex and compact, and let* $u \in \mathcal{R}_{cs}^n$. *If* $(\pi_\alpha, \pi_\beta) \in \Delta X \times \Delta X$ *is a two-candidate electoral equilibrium, then* $Supp[\pi_\alpha] = Supp[\pi_\beta]$ *is contained in the closure of the uncovered set,* $U(R)$.

A proof of Theorem 7.5 can be found in Banks, Duggan and Le Breton [24]. It is greatly complicated by difficulties involving the structure of the graph of the covering relation on $X \times X$ due to discontinuities in the candidate payoff functions. The essential intuition for Theorem 7.4 on finite sets of alternatives, however, continues to hold for Theorem 7.5: equilibrium mixed strategies do not put weight on strictly dominated strategies and the uncovered set is close to being the set of such undominated strategies.

The existence of uncovered alternatives in finite sets of alternatives is not a problem. As argued in Chapter 4, the covering relation is asymmetric and transitive although not complete; consequently it must possess maximal elements in any finite set and, by definition, it is the collection of these maximal elements that constitute the uncovered set. When the set of feasible alternatives is not finite, however, asymmetry and transitivity of a relation are insufficient to insure the existence of maximals [PPTI, sect.5.1]. And in view of Theorem 7.5, existence of mixed strategy electoral equilibria for the spatial model is possible only if the uncovered set is nonempty. Showing that the uncovered set under a simple rule is indeed nonempty in the spatial model uses the following facts.

Lemma 7.2 *(1) If $u \in \mathcal{R}_{cs}^n$ then $R(z)$ is closed, all $z \in X$. (2) Let (y_m) be an infinite sequence with $(y_m) \to y^* \in X$ and, for all m, $P(y_m) \subseteq P(x)$; then $u \in \mathcal{R}_{cs}^n$ implies $P(y^*) \subseteq P(x)$.*

Proof (1) By definition of a simple rule, any coalition whose complement is not a decisive coalition is a blocking coalition for the rule; that is, for all $z \in X$,

$$R(z) = [\cup_{\{L^c \subseteq N: L \notin \mathcal{L}\}} \cap_{i \in L^c} R_i(z)]$$

where $\mathcal{L}$ is the family of decisive coalitions defining the rule. Hence, $u \in \mathcal{R}_{cs}^n$ and n finite imply $R(z)$ closed all z.

(2) Let $(y_m) \to y^*$ be the sequence described in the lemma and suppose, by way of contradiction, that $P(y^*) \nsubseteq P(x)$. Define $A = X \backslash \overline{P(x)}$. Given $u \in \mathcal{R}_{cs}^n$, $P_i(z)$ is open for all $i \in N$ and all $z \in X$. By definition of a simple rule,

$$P(z) = \cup_{\mathcal{L}} \cap_{i \in L} P_i(z).$$

Since n is finite $P(x)$ is open, implying A is open. Therefore, $P(y^*) \cap A$ is both open and nonempty, in which case there exists a neighborhood $B(y^*, \epsilon)$, $\epsilon > 0$, such that, for all $y \in B(y^*, \epsilon)$, $P(y) \cap A \neq \emptyset$. In particular, since $(y_m) \to y^*$ there exists some m such that $y_m \in B(y^*, \epsilon)$; but this contradicts $P(y_m) \subseteq P(x)$ for all m. Therefore, $P(y^*) \subseteq P(x)$. □

Nonemptiness of the uncovered set in the spatial setting is assured by the next result.

7.3. EQUILIBRIUM IN MULTIDIMENSIONAL SPACES

Theorem 7.6 *If $u \in \mathcal{R}_{cs}^n$ and $X \subset \Re^k$ is compact then the uncovered set $U(R)$ is nonempty for any simple rule.*

Proof Define a binary relation Q on X as follows: for any $x, y \in X$,

$$xQy \Leftrightarrow [x \in R(y) \text{ and } P(x) \subseteq P(y)].$$

By definition of the covering relation, if there exist Q-maximal alternatives in X (that is, alternatives $x \in X$ such that, for all $y \in X$, yQx implies xQy), then such alternatives are necessarily uncovered in X. To see this, suppose x is Q-maximal but, for some $y \in X$, y covers x. By Definition 7.2, $y \in P(x) \subseteq R(x)$, $P(y) \subset P(x)$ and $R(y) \subseteq R(x)$; hence, yQx but not xQy: contradiction. To prove the theorem, therefore, it suffices to prove the existence of Q-maximal alternatives. First observe that although Q is not complete on X, Q is transitive: certainly $P(x) \subseteq P(y)$ and $P(y) \subseteq P(z)$ implies $P(x) \subseteq P(z)$; therefore, xQy, yQz and $\sim [xQz]$ implies $\sim [x \in R(z)]$, in which case R complete and $P(x) \subseteq P(z)$ implies $z \in P(z)$, which is absurd by P irreflexive. By X compact and Lemma 7.2, for all $x \in X$ the set

$$Q(x) = \{y \in X : yQx\}$$

is compact. Now let $S \subseteq X$ be linearly ordered by Q; that is, Q is complete and transitive on S. Let

$$T = \cap_{x \in S} Q(x).$$

Then either $T \neq \emptyset$ or $T = \emptyset$. In the first case there exists an alternative $x^* \in T$ such that, for all $y \in T \backslash \{x^*\}$, x^*Qy and x^* is an upper bound for S. Consider the second case. By Lemma 7.2, $Q(x)^c$ is open and, therefore, the family $\{Q(x)^c : x \in S\}$ is an open cover for X. By assumption, X is compact and so, by definition of compactness, there exists a finite subset $S' \subseteq S$ such that the family $\{Q(y)^c : y \in S'\}$ is an open cover for X. Because $S' \subseteq S$, S' is a finite set, linearly ordered by Q. Hence there exists an alternative $x^* \in S'$ such that x^*Qy for all $y \in S' \backslash \{x^*\}$. So, by Q transitive, $Q(x^*) \subseteq Q(y)$ for all $y \in S' \backslash \{x^*\}$. Therefore,

$$\begin{aligned}X &\subseteq Q(x^*)^c = X \backslash Q(x^*) \\ &\Rightarrow X \cap Q(x^*) = \emptyset \\ &\Rightarrow S \cap Q(x^*) = \emptyset \\ &\Rightarrow x^* \in S \text{ and, } \forall y \in S, \ \sim [yQx^*].\end{aligned}$$

But S is linearly ordered by Q, so x^*Qy all $y \in S \backslash \{x^*\}$; in other words, x^* is an upper bound for S. Because S was chosen arbitrarily among the set of linearly ordered (by Q) subsets of X, we have that all such sets in X have upper bounds. By Zorn's Lemma (which states that if every linearly ordered subset of a partially ordered set A has an upper bound, then A has a maximal element under the ordering), therefore, X has a maximal element under Q; that is, $U(R) \neq \emptyset$. □

By Theorem 7.1, core alternatives are surely two-candidate electoral equilibrium outcomes; but cores for noncollegial simple rules rarely exist in multidimensional spaces [PPTI, Theorem 5.8] and so, by Corollary 7.2, neither do pure strategy electoral equilibria. Consequently, although Theorems 7.5 and 7.6 do not constitute an existence argument for mixed strategy electoral equilibria in the spatial model, they at least suggest the uncovered set as a good approximation to the set of policies consistent with such equilibrium behavior. And given the uncovered set coincides with the core when the latter is nonempty and singleton, this suggestion is reinforced to the extent that the uncovered set itself exhibits sufficient continuity to insure that when a preference profile is "close" to supporting a nonempty (singleton) core, the uncovered alternatives at that profile are "close" to being core alternatives. Providing such a continuity result for the uncovered set occupies much of the remainder of this section.

An appropriate continuity property for the uncovered set in the spatial model involves specifying a notion of convergence of a sequence of preference profiles to a profile at which the core is not empty. Here, we use the idea of uniform convergence: an infinite sequence of real-valued functions (h^m) from X to $\Re$ *converges uniformly* to a function h if, for all $\epsilon > 0$, there exists an M such that for all $m > M$ and all $x \in X$,

$$|h^m(x) - h(x)| < \epsilon.$$

Let $u^m = (u_1^m, \ldots, u_n^m) \in \mathcal{R}_{cs}^n$ be a preference profile on X and recall that for any preference aggregation rule f, $R_{f(u^m)}$ and $P_{f(u^m)}$, respectively, denote the weak and strict social preference relations on X under f at u^m. Similarly, for any $x \in X$, let

$$P(x|u^m) = \{y \in X : yP_{f(u^m)}x\}$$

and so on.

Lemma 7.3 *Assume (u^m) converges uniformly to a profile $u \in \mathcal{R}_{cs}^n$, with $u^m \in \mathcal{R}_{cs}^n$ for all m, and let $(x_m) \to x \in X$ and $(y_m) \to y \in X$. Then for any simple rule f:*

(1) $xP_{f(u)}y$ implies $x_m P_{f(u^m)} y_m$ for sufficiently large m;

(2) $x_m R_{f(u^m)} y_m$ for all m sufficiently large implies $xR_{f(u)}y$.

7.3. EQUILIBRIUM IN MULTIDIMENSIONAL SPACES

Proof (1) The following argument is illustrated in Figure 7.5 for $X \subset \Re$.

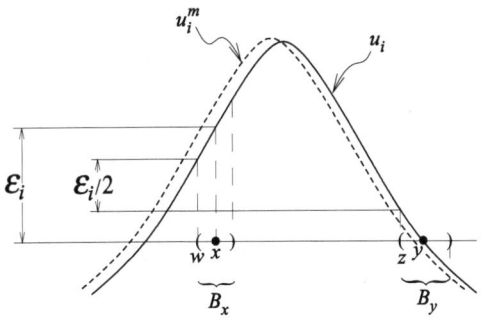

Figure 7.5: Argument for (1)

Because f is a simple rule, $xP_{f(u)}y$ implies there exists a decisive coalition $L \in \mathcal{L}$ such that $u_i(x) > u_i(y)$ for all $i \in L$. Let $u_i(x) - u_i(y) = \epsilon_i > 0$; by u_i continuous, there exist open neighborhoods B_x, B_y such that $x \in B_x$, $y \in B_y$ and, for all $(w, z) \in B_x \times B_y$, $u_i(w) - u_i(z) > \epsilon_i/2$. By uniform convergence, for m sufficiently large $|u_i^m(\cdot) - u_i(\cdot)| < \epsilon_i/4$. Hence, for all $(w, z) \in B_x \times B_y$ and m sufficiently large,

$$u_i^m(w) - u_i^m(z) > [u_i(w) - \frac{\epsilon_i}{4}] - [u_i(z) + \frac{\epsilon_i}{4}] > 0.$$

Similarly, for sufficiently large m, $x_m \in B_x$ and $y_m \in B_y$; hence, $u_i^m(x_m) > u_i^m(y_m)$. Since $i \in L$ is arbitrary and L is decisive, therefore, $x_m P_{f(u^m)} y_m$ for sufficiently large m as claimed.

(2) By (1) and R_f complete, $\sim [y_m P_{f(u^m)} x_m]$ for sufficiently large m implies $\sim [y P_{f(u)} x]$ and the claim follows. □

In words, Lemma 7.3 confirms that, at least for sequences of preference profiles that converge uniformly to some given preference profile, any strict collective preference between a pair of alternatives at the limiting profile is also a strict preference for all profiles sufficiently close to the limit. That is, collective preferences do not exhibit any sudden reversals as a sequence of preference profiles approaches a limiting profile. This fact allows a straightforward continuity argument for the uncovered set.

A simple rule f is *strong* if it can be defined by a nonempty family of decisive coalitions $\mathcal{L}$ such that, for all coalitions $L \subseteq N$, $L \notin \mathcal{L}$ implies $N \backslash L \in \mathcal{L}$ [PPTI, Definition 3.6]. The important feature of such rules is that they admit no blocking coalitions; for example, simple majority rule with n odd is strong but any q-rule other than simple majority rule is not strong. Despite this limitation, Theorem 7.6, below (with Theorem 7.5) at least in part justifies a focus on the uncovered set when the core is empty. Before stating the theorem, it is useful first to prove two properties of strong simple rules.

Lemma 7.4 *Assume $u \in \mathcal{R}_{cs}^n$ and that the collective preference relation is induced by a strong simple rule. Then: (1) for all $x \in X$, $R(x) = \{x\} \cup \overline{P(x)}$; (2) for all $x, y \in X$, $P(x) \subseteq P(y)$ implies $R(x) \subseteq R(y)$.*

Proof (1) Let $\mathcal{L} \subseteq 2^N \setminus \{\emptyset\}$ denote the set of decisive coalitions characterizing the aggregation rule. By definition of a simple rule, for all $x \in X$,

$$P(x) = \cup_\mathcal{L} P_L(x)$$
$$= \cup_\mathcal{L} \cap_{i \in L} P_i(x)$$

and, by definition of closure, for any $L \subseteq N$

$$\overline{P_L(x)} = \overline{\cap_{i \in L} P_i(x)} \subseteq \cap_{i \in L} \overline{P_i(x)}.$$

Let $y \in \cap_{i \in L} \overline{P_i(x)}$; then $y \in R_i(x)$ for all $i \in L$. By $u \in \mathcal{R}_{cs}^n$, for all $t \in (0, 1)$ and all $i \in L$,

$$z(t) = tx + (1-t)y \in P_i(x).$$

Hence $P_i(x)$ open implies $B(y, \epsilon) \cap P_i(x) \neq \emptyset$ for all sufficiently small $\epsilon > 0$, all $i \in L$. So $y \in \overline{P_L(x)}$ in which case $\cap_{i \in L} \overline{P_i(x)} \subseteq \overline{P_L(x)}$ and therefore, by the earlier inclusion, $\overline{P_L(x)} = \cap_{i \in L} \overline{P_i(x)}$. Finally, using $u \in \mathcal{R}_{cs}^n$ again, conclude that if $P(x) \neq \emptyset$ then

$$R_L(x) = \cap_{i \in L} R_i(x) = \cap_{i \in L} \overline{P_i(x)} = \overline{P_L(x)}.$$

By assumption, the aggregation rule is strong simple; thus, $R(x) = \cup_\mathcal{L} R_L(x)$. Therefore, the preceding string of equalities implies

$$R(x) = \cup_\mathcal{L} R_L(x) = \cup_\mathcal{L} \overline{P_L(x)} = \overline{\cup_\mathcal{L} P_L(x)} = \overline{P_L(x)};$$

and since $x \in R(x)$ surely, the first claim follows as required.

(2) To check the second assertion, suppose $P(x) \subseteq P(y)$; then trivially, $\{x\} \cup \overline{P(x)} \subseteq \{y\} \cup \overline{P(y)}$. Since strict preference P is not reflexive, $y \notin P(x)$; by R complete, therefore, $x \in R(y)$. Hence, by (1),

$$R(x) = \{x\} \cup \overline{P(x)} \subseteq \{x\} \cup \overline{P(y)} \subseteq R(y)$$

7.3. EQUILIBRIUM IN MULTIDIMENSIONAL SPACES

as required. □

It is worth noting that, because every blocking coalition of a strong simple rule is also a winning coalition, we have $R(y) = \cup_{\mathcal{L}} R_L(y)$ for all $y \in X$, an implication that plays a critical role in the preceding argument. When the rule is not strong, however, the equality can break down generating exactly the sort of situation illustrated in Figure 7.4, where $R(x) \neq \cup_{\mathcal{L}} R_L(x)$.

Define the distance between any two nonempty sets $Y, Z \subseteq \Re^k$ to be the least Euclidean distance between a point in Y and a point in Z; that is,

$$d(Y,Z) = \inf_{\substack{y \in Y \\ z \in Z}} \|y - z\|.$$

Let $U(f(u^m))$ denote the uncovered set at the preference profile $u^m \in \mathcal{R}^n$ under a simple rule f.

Theorem 7.7 *Assume $X \subset \Re^k$ is compact and convex. Suppose (u^m) converges uniformly to a profile $u \in \mathcal{R}_{cs}^n$, with $u^m \in \mathcal{R}_{cs}^n$ for all m, and that preference aggregation is by a strong simple rule. If $C_f(u) \neq \emptyset$ then for every $\epsilon > 0$ there exists M such that, for all $m > M$,*

$$d(C_f(u), U(f(u^m))) < \epsilon.$$

Proof Suppose f is a strong simple rule and $C_f(u) \neq \emptyset$. By X convex and $u \in \mathcal{R}_{cs}^n$, $C_f(u) = \{x^*\}$ for some $x^* \in X$ [Exercise]. Moreover, by Lemma 7.4(1), $R(x^*) = \{x^*\} \cup \overline{P(x^*)}$ and, by definition of the core, $P(x^*) = \emptyset$; therefore, $x^* P_{f(u)} y$ for all $y \in X \backslash \{x^*\}$. We need to show $d(x^*, U(f(u^m))) \to 0$ as $m \to \infty$. Suppose not. Then there is a subsequence (without ambiguity, indexed by m) and some $\epsilon > 0$ such that, for all m, there exists $x_m \in U(f(u^m))$ with $d(x^*, x^m) \geq \epsilon$. By X compact, (x_m) has a convergent subsequence (still indexed by m); say $(x_m) \to x$. To prove the theorem we show by way of contradiction that, for m sufficiently large, x^* covers x_m.

By Lemma 7.3 and $x^* P_{f(u)} y$ for all $y \in X \backslash \{x^*\}$, $x^* P_{f(u^m)} x_m$ for all m sufficiently large. Suppose $P(x^*|u^m) \not\subseteq P(x_m|u^m)$ for m large. Then there is a subsequence (indexed by m) such that, for all m, there exists $y_m \in P(x^*|u^m) \backslash P(x_m|u^m)$; that is, $y_m P_{f(u^m)} x^*$ and $x_m R_{f(u^m)} y_m$ for all m. By X compact, (y_m) has a convergent subsequence (indexed by m), $(y_m) \to y$. By Lemma 7.3, $x_m R_{f(u^m)} y_m$ implies $x R_{f(u)} y$, in which case $y \neq x^*$. But then $x^* P_{f(u)} y$ and Lemma 7.3 yields $x^* P_{f(u^m)} y_m$ for sufficiently large m, a contradiction of the supposition that $y_m P_{f(u^m)} x^*$ for all m. Hence, $P(x^*|u^m) \subseteq P(x_m|u^m)$ and, since $x^* P_{f(u^m)} x_m$, the inclusion must be strict. To complete the argument that x^* covers x_m, it remains to check $R(x^*|u^m) \subseteq R(x_m|u^m)$ for sufficiently large m. But this follows directly from Lemma 7.4(2) and the preceding argument showing $P(x^*|u^m) \subseteq P(x_m|u^m)$. Therefore, $x^* C x_m$ for sufficiently large m and, consequently, the original supposition must be false; that is, $d(x^*, U(f(u^m))) \to 0$ as $m \to \infty$. □

Considered together, Theorems 7.5 and 7.6 say that platforms in two-candidate electoral equilibria consist only of uncovered policies and, at least for strong electoral rules and voter preference profiles u' "close" to a profile u for which the core $C_f(u)$ is nonempty, Theorem 7.7 shows these platforms at u' are clustered around the core outcome $C_f(u)$. Furthermore, in such cases, Corollary 7.1 implies that the candidates' equilibrium platforms at u' do not diverge significantly.

Finally, as promised, we conclude the section by reconsidering the technical question regarding existence of mixed strategy equilibria. And in this context, it is useful first to introduce a slightly stronger notion of covering for the spatial model. Say that an alternative $x \in X$ *deeply covers* an alternative $y \in X$ if all alternatives ranked (socially) at least as good as x are considered (socially) to be strictly preferred to y; that is, if $R(x) \subseteq P(y)$. In Figure 7.3 above, for example, x deeply covers y. The *deep uncovered set* is the set of alternatives not deeply covered by any other alternative. If x deeply covers y, then clearly x covers y but the converse can be false [Exercise]; therefore, the uncovered set is a (possibly strict) subset of the deep uncovered set and Theorem 7.6 implies that the deep uncovered set is not empty. Moreover, replacing $P(x^*|u^m)$ by $R(x^*|u^m)$ and $y_m P_{f(u^m)} x^*$ by $y_m R_{f(u^m)} x^*$ in the second paragraph of the argument for Theorem 7.7, we obtain the same result for the deep uncovered set.

Two-candidate electoral equilibria are subgame perfect, but they are not obviously the only subgame perfect equilibria in undominated strategies for the spatial model. In particular, although an existence theorem is as yet unavailable for electoral equilibria in which indifferent individuals (restricted to weakly undominated voting strategies) surely vote for either candidate with probability one-half, it is possible to establish an equilibrium existence result if indifferent voters are assumed only to use symmetric (and weakly undominated) voting strategies.

A mixed voting strategy $v_i : X \times X \to [0,1]$ is *symmetric* if, for all $(a,b) \in X \times X$,

$$v_i(a,b) = 1 - v_i(b,a).$$

That is, the probability that i votes for candidate α with platform a against candidate β with platform b, is equal the probability that i votes for can-

7.3. EQUILIBRIUM IN MULTIDIMENSIONAL SPACES

didate β with platform a against candidate α with platform b. Voting with probability 1/2 for either candidate whenever indifferent is surely a symmetric strategy but, except in the case $a = b$, not all symmetric strategies involve indifferent voters necessarily voting with probability 1/2. Insisting on symmetric voting strategies does, however, preclude indifferent voters from using candidates' non-policy characteristics (for instance, the candidates' names) to decide how to vote.

A pair of electoral platforms $(a, b) \in X^2$ and a profile of mixed voting strategies $v = (v_1, \ldots, v_n)$ jointly constitute a *two-candidate electoral equilibrium in symmetric voting* if v_i is symmetric and weakly undominated for all $i \in N$ and, for all $y \in X$,

$$E[W_\alpha(a,b)|v] \geq E[W_\alpha(y,b)|v] \text{ and } E[W_\beta(a,b)|v] \geq E[W_\beta(a,y)|v]$$

where $E[W_c(a,b)|v]$ is candidate c's expected payoff conditional on the platforms (a, b) and voter strategies v.

Theorem 7.8 *Assume $X \subset \Re^k$ is compact and the election is decided by simple majority voting. There exists a two-candidate electoral equilibrium in symmetric voting. Furthermore, the supports of the mixed strategies in any such equilibrium are contained in the deep uncovered set.*

A proof of the theorem can be found in Duggan and Jackson [64]. The key step in the existence argument for Theorem 7.8 lies in a careful selection of the probability that indifferent individuals vote for one or other of the two candidates. Requiring only that voting strategies are symmetric provides sufficient flexibility to make such a selection for all pairs of candidate platforms. And by appropriately conditioning the probability for each pair of platforms on the numbers of individuals with strict preferences over the two candidates, it is possible to repair the discontinuities inherent in the candidates' payoff functions when indifferent voters are restricted to flipping a fair coin. In turn, continuous payoff functions allow construction of a mixed strategy equilibrium.

The issue of how best to specify indifferent voters' behavior in regard to establishing equilibrium existence is largely a technical issue. There is no substantively obvious way to resolve the issue when abstention is precluded and, therefore, insofar as insuring existence is a check on the internal coherence of the model, Theorem 7.8 makes evident the instrumental value of assuming symmetric voting strategies. Moreover, although there is a difference in the characterization of the support of any equilibrium mixed strategies, the substantive difference between the spatial model in which indifferent voters are restricted to vote with probability one-half for each candidate (where the support lies within the uncovered set) and that in which such voters are limited only to symmetric voting strategies (where the support lies within the deep uncovered set), is small. With these remarks in mind, we hereafter maintain the usual stronger (and analytically tractable) symmetry assumption on indifferent voters' strategies, that they invariably vote for each candidate with probability one-half.

7.4 Application: Progressive taxation

Suppose two office-seeking candidates are competing to represent a district in which constituents are divided by differential likelihoods of securing a good job. Specifically, assume the district comprises three homogenous groups of voters, $i = 1, 2, 3$, none of which is an electoral majority. Let $n_i \in (0, 1)$ be the proportion of group i voters in the district; assume $n_i < 1/2$ for all i and $n_i + n_j > 1/2$ for all i, j. The groups are distinguished from each other only by their chances of being allocated a good job (perhaps by virtue of family history, human capital endowment or racial discrimination). To make matters simple, we assume that all individuals are employed in one or other of two types of job; good jobs that pay y_h and bad jobs that pay y_l, where $y_h > y_l > 0$. Individuals freely supply one unit of labor inelastically in either job. The probability that an arbitrary member of group i is allocated a good job is p_i; assume

$$p_1 > p_2 > p_3 \geq 0$$

and let the proportion of good jobs in the economy $s \equiv \sum_i n_i p_i$. By the assumptions on group size and the likelihoods of getting good jobs, $s < 1$; assume further that there exist more good jobs than could be filled by any single group i, that is, for all $i = 1, 2, 3$, $s > n_i$.

Income from the two sorts of employment is in principle subject to taxation that funds a pure public good, g. The budget must balance so only the tax-rates on good and bad jobs, t_h and t_l respectively, are policy variables. All individuals have identical preferences over consumption and the public good: for each $i \in \{1, 2, 3\}$,

$$u_i(t_h, t_l) = p_i \ln(1 - t_h) y_h + [1 - p_i] \ln(1 - t_l) y_l + g(T)$$

where

$$g(T) \equiv g(st_h y_h + (1 - s) t_l y_l)$$

is the level of the pure public good produced given total tax revenue $T = st_h y_h + (1 - s) t_l y_l$. Assume g is increasing, twice differentiable and strictly

7.4. APPLICATION: PROGRESSIVE TAXATION

concave in T. Under the maintained assumptions, u_i is strictly quasi-concave in (t_h, t_l) on the policy space $X = [0,1]^2 \subset \Re^2$, so $u = (u_1, u_2, u_3) \in \mathcal{R}_{cs}^2$. Differentiating u_i with respect to the policy variables yields

$$\frac{\partial u_i}{\partial t_h} = g'(T)sy_h - \frac{p_i}{1-t_h};$$

$$\frac{\partial u_i}{\partial t_l} = g'(T)(1-s)y_l - \frac{1-p_i}{1-t_l}.$$

Therefore, assuming

$$\lim_{T \to 0} g'(T) > \max[\frac{p_1}{sy_h}, \frac{1-p_3}{(1-s)y_l}],$$

the first-order conditions for a maximum to u_i imply interior ideal points for individuals in group $i \in \{1,2,3\}$

$$x_i = (t_h(p_i, s, y_h), t_l(p_i, s, y_l)).$$

At such interior ideal points,

$$\frac{1 - t_l(p_i, s, y_l)}{1 - t_h(p_i, s, y_h)} = \frac{(1-p_i)sy_h}{p_i(1-s)y_l}$$

for all i, so

$$t_h(p_i, s, y_h) > t_l(p_i, s, y_l) \Leftrightarrow \frac{1-p_i}{p_i} > \frac{(1-s)y_l}{sy_h}.$$

In other words, an individual with probability of a good job p_i strictly prefers a progressive tax policy if and only if the relative likelihoods of i receiving bad and good employment exceeds the ratio of the share of national income from bad jobs to that from good jobs. Furthermore, the difference between the most preferred high and the most preferred low tax-rates is strictly decreasing in p_i. Thus, the more likely is an individual to be in low-paying employment, the more progressive a tax-schedule he or she prefers. More generally, doing the comparative statics, $t_h(p_i, \cdot)$ is strictly non-linear decreasing in p_i and $t_l(p_i, \cdot)$ is strictly non-linear increasing in p_i. Applying the core characterization result [PPTI, Theorem 5.8], therefore, $p_1 > p_2 > p_3$ implies the majority preference core $C_f(u)$ in X is empty at u.

By assumption, there are two office-seeking candidates competing for a majority vote in the district. Each candidate $c \in \{\alpha, \beta\}$ chooses a policy platform $(t_h^c, t_l^c) \in X$ to maximize their respective payoffs, W_α, W_β. By Theorem 7.1 and $C_f(u)$ empty, there is no pure strategy electoral equilibrium here. In any mixed strategy equilibrium, however, Theorem 7.6 (and, essentially, Theorem 7.8) states that equilibrium policies are uncovered. And since the uncovered set is a subset of the Pareto set, Theorem 7.6 implies that equilibrium policies must be Pareto efficient. Unfortunately, fully describing the uncovered set for any given distribution of spatial preferences is in general very hard to do; but if we assume the district contains an odd number of voters so majority rule is strong, then Theorem 7.6 allows us to say something more.

Let u^p denote the preference profile conditional on $p = (p_1, p_2, p_3)$ and consider any monotonic sequence (p^m) converging to a vector p°. Then the sequence (u^{p^m}) converges uniformly to the profile u^{p° since, for each $i \in \{1, 2, 3\}$ and any $(t_h, t_l) \in [0,1]^2$,

$$|u_i^{p^m} - u_i^{p^\circ}| = |(p_i^m - p_i^\circ) \ln \frac{(1-t_h)y_h}{(1-t_l)y_l}|;$$

so (p^m) monotonic insures that, for every $\epsilon > 0$, there exists some M for which $|u_i^{p^m} - u_i^{p^\circ}| < \epsilon$, all $m > M$. Now choose $p^\circ = (p_1^\circ, p_2^\circ, p_3^\circ)$ such that p_1° is close to one and $p_1^\circ > p_2^\circ = p_3^\circ = [1 - p_1^\circ]/2$. In this case, majority rule strong implies $C_f(u^{p^\circ}) = \{(1 - \frac{p_2^\circ}{sy_h g'(T)}, 1 - \frac{1-p_2^\circ}{(1-s)y_l g'(T)})\}$ so, by Theorem 7.7, $U(f(u^{p^m}))$ converges to the core $C_f(u^{p^\circ})$ and we can expect to observe that both candidates' equilibrium platforms increasingly reflect the interests of the relatively less advantaged groups as m gets large; in particular, the tax-system becomes more progressive as $(p^m) \to p^\circ$ with $t_h^c(p^\circ)$ strictly greater than $t_l^c(p^\circ)$.

7.5 Probabilistic voting

Until now, the basic model of electoral competition has included the technically parsimonious, but empirically extreme, assumption that candidates know every decision-relevant fact about every voter. A consequence of the assumption is that candidates' expected payoff functions exhibit critical discontinuities in policy choice and, in turn, it is these discontinuities that are largely responsible for the absence of a general existence result for two-candidate electoral equilibria in the multidimensional spatial model. Specifically, if a candidate deviates from some common platform by an arbitrarily small amount, then almost every voter is correctly expected to vote surely for one candidate or the other rather than, as is the case when candidates converge, vote for either candidate with equal probability. Although it is

7.5. PROBABILISTIC VOTING

reasonable to assume voters vote deterministically (save possibly when indifferent), it is somewhat less reasonable to assume that candidates know exactly which voter is going to vote which way for every pairwise policy choice. Relaxing the latter assumption admits the possibility that small deviations from convergent platforms need not be associated by candidates with discrete jumps in expected payoffs. Example 7.4 illustrates how this can be.

Example 7.4 Suppose a voter $i \in N$ is described not only by policy preferences over X but also by some idiosyncratic bias in favor of one candidate rather than another, perhaps on grounds of charismatic appeal or incumbency status. For any candidate $c \in \{\alpha, \beta\}$ with platform $x \in X$, let

$$\tilde{u}_i(x) = u_i(x) + \eta_{ic}$$

describe i's payoff from c winning on platform x, where $\eta_{ic} \in \Re$ is i's policy-independent bias with respect to c. Then defining $\eta_i \equiv \eta_{i\beta} - \eta_{i\alpha}$ yields that individual i votes for α over β conditional on policy platforms (a, b) if

$$\tilde{u}_i(a) - \tilde{u}_i(b) > 0 \Leftrightarrow$$
$$u_i(a) - u_i(b) > \eta_i.$$

Assume u_i is continuous in policy. Assume further that η_i is fixed and known surely to i but is known only imperfectly by the candidates. Let $F(\eta)$ be the probability that each candidate associates to the event that $\eta_i \leq \eta$ and suppose F is everywhere continuous. Then

$$\Pr[i \text{ votes for } \alpha \mid a, b] = F(u_i(a) - u_i(b))$$

and continuity of F insures continuity in the likelihood of i voting for α as a function of a conditional on b, even at points of policy convergence, $a = b$. It follows that the probability candidate c wins the election is continuous in both platforms. □

Assuming that candidates have only imperfect information about the details of individuals' decision criteria is reasonable. But exactly what it is about individuals' characteristics that gives rise to the candidate uncertainty is not clear. Example 7.4 describes one possibility, an additive policy-independent utility bias for or against a given candidate. There are other possibilities. The bias, for instance, might best be interpreted as a multiplicative factor on the policy-payoff from any platform x offered by a given candidate c, say

$$\tilde{u}_i(x) = \eta_{ic} u_i(x)$$

where $\eta_{ic} > 0$ for each candidate $c = \alpha, \beta$. The distinction between the additive and the multiplicative bias models, however, is purely one of interpretation since the logarithm of a utility is also a utility. Hence results derived for the additive model can be directly translated into results for the multiplicative model. On the other hand, some more substantive alternatives to the presumption that candidate uncertainty derives from a voter-specific and policy-independent bias can have significantly different implications.

Example 7.5 Assume the policy space is one-dimensional, $X = [0, 1]$, and that voter $i \in N$ evaluates any alternative $y \in X$ according to the quadratic utility
$$u_i(y) = -(y - x_i)^2$$
where $x_i \in X$ is i's ideal point. So given policy platforms (a, b) with $a < b$, i votes surely for α if
$$\frac{a+b}{2} > x_i,$$
votes for α with probability one half if $[a+b]/2 = x_i$ and votes surely for β otherwise. Assume, for all individuals $i \in N$, that x_i is known surely to i but is known only imperfectly to the candidates, $\{\alpha, \beta\}$. Both candidates treat an individual i's ideal point x_i as an independent random draw from a given distribution with support on X. In particular, let the smooth distribution function F describe both candidates' beliefs regarding the median voter's ideal point, x_m, where F has full support on $[0, 1]$. Then, for any pair of policy platforms $(a, b) \in X^2$, the probability each candidate assigns to the event that α wins the election under plurality rule is
$$\Pr[\alpha \text{ wins } |a, b] = \begin{cases} F(\frac{a+b}{2}) & \text{if } a < b \\ \frac{1}{2} & \text{if } a = b \\ 1 - F(\frac{a+b}{2}) & \text{if } a > b \end{cases}$$
which is clearly discontinuous at almost every point $(x, x) \in X^2$. □

The important difference between the uncertainty models of Examples 7.4 and 7.5 is that candidate uncertainty over voter policy preferences *per se* exists only in the latter; in the first example, candidate uncertainty exclusively concerns decision-relevant, but policy-independent, voter characteristics. Which model is "correct" is an empirical matter, depending on the application. The choice itself, however, is analytically consequential: the bias interpretation of candidate uncertainty is consistent with continuity of the probability of winning functions but this is not typically true of

7.5. PROBABILISTIC VOTING

the policy-preference interpretation. For the remainder of this discussion, therefore, we assume that individuals' policy preferences are not subject to uncertainty but otherwise leave details of exactly what it is that induces candidate uncertainty unspecified.

For any pair of policy platforms $(a, b) \in X^2$, any individual $i \in N$ and any candidate $c \in \{\alpha, \beta\}$, let $p_i^c(u_i(a), u_i(b)) \in [0, 1]$ denote the probability that i votes for candidate c, u_i strictly quasi-concave. Maintaining the full participation assumption that no voter abstains gives

$$p_i^\alpha(u_i(a), u_i(b)) + p_i^\beta(u_i(a), u_i(b)) = 1$$

for all $i \in N$ and $(a, b) \in X^2$. We assume throughout that, for each $c \in \{\alpha, \beta\}$, $p_i^c(\cdot)$ is jointly continuous in $(u_i(a), u_i(b))$ and non-decreasing in i's utility from c's platform. Assume also for this section that elections are determined by plurality rule with ties broken by a fair lottery. With this restriction, it is convenient to suppose candidates choose platforms to maximize their expected pluralities. Although, given some platform b, a best response platform by candidate α under plurality rule is clearly also a best response platform under the objectives specified earlier (section 7.1), the converse is not generally true: a response a to b may yield a payoff $W_\alpha(a, b) = 1$ but not maximize α's expected plurality. However, in the absence of probabilistic voting and assuming no abstention, it is straightforward to confirm that the sets of two-candidate electoral equilibria under plurality rule are independent of whether candidates $c = \alpha, \beta$ maximize the expected value $EW_c(a, b)$ as above or maximize expected plurality as assumed here [Exercise].

Given platforms (a, b), candidate α's expected plurality under probabilistic voting with no abstention is

$$\begin{aligned} \Pi(a, b) &\equiv \sum_{i \in N} [p_i^\alpha(u_i(a), u_i(b)) - p_i^\beta(u_i(a), u_i(b))] \\ &= \sum_{i \in N} [2p_i^\alpha(u_i(a), u_i(b)) - 1] \end{aligned}$$

and so β's expected plurality is simply $-\Pi(a, b)$. A pair of electoral platforms is a pure strategy probabilistic voting equilibrium if any unilateral change in platform by one candidate, given the platform of the other, reduces the deviating candidate's expected plurality. Formally, $(a, b) \in X^2$ is a (pure strategy) *two-candidate probabilistic voting equilibrium* if, for all $y \in X$,

$$\Pi(a, y) \geq \Pi(a, b) \geq \Pi(y, b).$$

As before, a mixed strategy equilibrium is a pair of probability distributions $(\pi_\alpha, \pi_\beta) \in \Delta X \times \Delta X$ such that, for all other distributions π'_α, π'_β on ΔX,

$$E_{(\pi_\alpha, \pi'_\beta)}\Pi(x,y) \geq E_{(\pi_\alpha, \pi_\beta)}\Pi(x,y) \geq E_{(\pi'_\alpha, \pi_\beta)}\Pi(x,y)$$

where $E_{(\pi_\alpha, \pi_\beta)}$ is the expectation operator with respect to (π_α, π_β); since probabilities are bounded the expectation is well-defined and given by

$$E_{(\pi_\alpha, \pi_\beta)}\Pi(x,y) = \sum_{i \in N} \left[2 \int \int p_i(u_i(x), u_i(y)) - 1 \right] d\pi_\alpha(x) d\pi_\beta(y)$$

where, to save on notation, we hereon write $p_i(\cdot) \equiv p_i^\alpha(\cdot)$ and $1 - p_i(\cdot) \equiv p_i^\beta(\cdot)$.

Theorem 7.9 *Let $X \subset \Re^k$. If X is compact, there exists a two-candidate probabilistic voting equilibrium in mixed strategies. If in addition X is convex and $\Pi(x,y)$ is strictly concave in x and strictly convex in y, all $x, y \in X$, then there exists a unique two-candidate probabilistic voting equilibrium and it is in pure strategies.*

Proof The first existence claim follows directly from Glicksberg's Fixed Point Theorem [see the proof for Theorem 6.4 above]. If X is also convex and Π is strictly concave in x, then the set of candidate α's best responses to any π_β is singleton; similarly, Π strictly convex in y implies β's best response to any π_α is a pure strategy. Thus any equilibrium must be in pure (equivalently, degenerate mixed) strategies. To check uniqueness, suppose (a,b) and (a',b') are distinct pure strategy equilibria; without loss of generality, assume $a \neq a'$. By full participation, the underlying electoral game between the candidates is zero-sum. By Lemma 7.1, therefore, (a',b) is an equilibrium and $\Pi(a,b) = \Pi(a',b)$; that is, both a and a' constitute best responses to b. But strict concavity of Π in α's strategy implies

$$\Pi(\tfrac{1}{2}a + \tfrac{1}{2}a', b) > \tfrac{1}{2}\Pi(a,b) + \tfrac{1}{2}\Pi(a',b) = \Pi(a,b)$$

contradicting the supposition that (a,b) is an equilibrium. □

Under the maintained assumptions, probabilistic voting introduces sufficient continuity in the candidates' payoff functions to insure equilibrium existence quite generally. Assuming X is convex and strengthening the assumptions on Π to strict concavity (respectively, convexity) in α's (respectively, β's) platform yields that the equilibrium is unique and necessarily in pure strategies. Sufficient conditions for the relevant concavity properties on

7.5. PROBABILISTIC VOTING

the plurality functions to obtain are that, for all $i \in N$, p_i is strictly increasing concave in $u_i(a)$, decreasing convex in $u_i(b)$ and u_i is strictly concave on X. To see this, let x, x' and y be any three platforms and let $t \in (0, 1)$; then strict monotonicity of p_i and strict concavity of u_i imply

$$p_i(u_i(tx + (1-t)x'), u_i(y)) > p_i(tu_i(x) + (1-t)u_i(x'), u_i(y))$$

while p_i concave in $u_i(a)$ implies

$$p_i(tu_i(x) + (1-t)u_i(x'), u_i(y))$$
$$\geq tp_i(u_i(x), u_i(y)) + (1-t)p_i(u_i(x'), u_i(y)).$$

Substituting into the plurality function Π gives the appropriate concavity properties. Furthermore, if these sufficient conditions in fact hold for all individuals' vote-probability and utility functions, p_i and u_i, then the unique pure strategy probabilistic voting equilibrium assured by Theorem 7.9 can be easily characterized. For all $a, b \in X$ and $i \in N$, let

$$\omega_i^\alpha(a, b) \equiv \frac{\partial}{\partial s} p_i(s, u_i(b))|_{s=u_i(a)}$$

and

$$\omega_i^\beta(a, b) \equiv \frac{\partial}{\partial t} p_i(u_i(a), t)|_{t=u_i(b)}$$

where the (almost everywhere) differentiability of p_i follows from the concavity and convexity assumptions on the function.

Theorem 7.10 *Suppose $X \subset \Re^k$ is convex and compact. Assume, for all $i \in N$, p_i^α (respectively, p_i^β) is strictly increasing concave in $u_i(a)$ (respectively, strictly decreasing convex in $u_i(b)$) with bounded partial derivatives and u_i strictly concave differentiable on X. Then there is a unique two-candidate probabilistic voting equilibrium; the equilibrium is in pure strategies (a^*, b^*) and (if interior) each candidate c adopts the policy that maximizes the weighted aggregate utility, $\sum_{i \in N} \omega_i^c(a^*, b^*) u_i(x)$.*

Proof That there exists a unique equilibrium in pure strategies, say (a^*, b^*), follows from Theorem 7.9 and the subsequent remarks. If (a^*, b^*) is interior, candidate α chooses platform $x = a$ to maximize $\Pi(x, b^*)$; by the differentiability and concavity assumptions, a^* solves

$$\frac{d}{dx} \Pi(x, b^*) = \sum_{i \in N} \frac{\partial}{\partial u_i} p_i(u_i, u_i(b^*)) \frac{\partial}{\partial x} u_i(x) = 0,$$

a system of k equations, $d\Pi(x,b^*)/dx_j = 0$, $j = 1,\ldots,k$. By $p_i \equiv p_i^\alpha$ strictly increasing in $u_i(a)$ and $\partial p_i(u_i, u_i(b))/\partial u_i$ bounded, therefore, the concavity assumptions imply a^* maximizes

$$\sum_{i \in N} \omega_i^\alpha(a^*, b^*) u_i(x).$$

But since candidate β chooses $y = b$ to maximize $-\Pi(a^*, y)$ and there is full participation, exactly the same reasoning yields that (if the equilibrium is interior) b^* maximizes

$$\sum_{i \in N} \omega_i^\beta(a^*, b^*) u_i(x)$$

which proves the theorem. □

In other words, Theorem 7.10 claims that in the case there surely exists a unique pure strategy equilibrium and it is interior to the policy space, then the electoral incentives under plurality rule with probabilistic voting lead each candidate to adopt the policy that maximizes a sum of weighted utilities, where the weights are given by the marginal contributions of individuals' votes to the candidates' equilibrium expected vote totals. An immediate implication of the theorem is the following result.

Corollary 7.3 *Assume the hypotheses of Theorem 7.10 hold. Assume further that, for all $i \in N$, $\omega_i^c(\cdot)$ is independent of i and that the unique two-candidate probabilistic voting equilibrium (a^*, b^*) is interior. Then both candidates converge on the unique policy that maximizes $\sum_{i \in N} u_i(x)$.*

Proof By assumption, $p_i(\cdot)$ is strictly increasing in $u_i(a)$ and strictly decreasing in $u_i(b)$; hence, $\omega^c(a^*, b^*) > 0$, $c = \alpha, \beta$. Therefore, x^* solves

$$\sum_{i \in N} \omega^\alpha(a^*, b^*) \frac{\partial}{\partial x} u_i(x) = \sum_{i \in N} \omega^\beta(a^*, b^*) \frac{\partial}{\partial x} u_i(x) = 0$$

if and only if x^* solves

$$\sum_{i \in N} \frac{\partial}{\partial x} u_i(x) = 0$$

which, with the concavity assumptions, implies $x^* = a^* = b^*$ maximizes $\sum_{i \in N} u_i(x)$. □

Less prosaically, the corollary says that if the vote probabilities are independent of individual labels then, under probabilistic voting, two-candidate electoral competition under plurality rule implements the Benthamite utilitarian preference aggregation rule.

On one hand, Theorems 7.9 and 7.10 stand in stark contrast to the typical nonexistence claims for electoral equilibria when candidates have perfect information regarding voters' decision criteria. Given sufficient candidate uncertainty about details of voters' decision criteria, the plurality functions exhibit enough continuity for existence of equilibria to be unproblematic and, under some plausible restrictions on voters' policy preferences and vote probabilities, there is a unique pure strategy equilibrium at the aggregate utility maximizing policy platform. On the other hand, however, the value of the results are attenuated to the extent that they are limited to candidate uncertainty only over various policy-independent influences on voters' decisions and, as such, are predicated on an *ad hoc* assumption about voter preferences. In other words, given policy decisions are the rationale for, and the final product of, electoral competition, there is every reason to assume individuals have policy preferences and act to promote them. The same is not so evident for non-policy preferences. A theory of equilibrium existence and character that hinges on details of the distribution of various idiosyncratic non-policy aspects of voter decision-making does not seem very compelling. Nevertheless, as a tool for exploring particular issues in electoral competition, rather than as a foundation for a theory of electoral competition *per se*, probabilistic voting models can be useful.

7.6 Application: Director's Law

A great deal of political decision-making involves at least some degree of resource redistribution across society, for there are almost always some who gain and some who lose. Distributional politics, however, is a high-dimensional choice problem and thus extremely difficult to resolve, in large part because the greater the dimensionality of the policy space, the easier it is to identify decisive coalitions willing to overturn any proposal [PPTI, sect.5.3 and 6.2]. Indeed, the core of all noncollegial simple rules is almost always empty on the set of purely redistributive policies. But redistributive policies are chosen in the world and it is clearly unsatisfactory to have no explanatory or predictive theory for such choices. One approach is through probabilistic voting theory.

Consider an electorate $N = \{1, \ldots n\}$ in which each individual i is endowed with finite initial wealth, $w_i > 0$. The feasible policy space from which the two plurality-maximizing candidates for office choose platforms is the set of all distributions of income across the electorate. It is convenient to work in terms of transfers, so the policy space is

$$X = \{(x_1, ..., x_n) \in \Re^n : \sum_{i \in N} x_i \leq 0 \text{ and } w_i + x_i \geq 0, \text{ all } i\}$$

which is clearly a compact and convex subset of $\Re_+^n$. Individuals care only about their wealth and the character of the candidates for elected office. The model introduced in Example 7.4 is germane. Specifically, assume voter i's payoff from a policy $x \in X$ implemented by a winning candidate $c \in \{\alpha, \beta\}$ is

$$\tilde{u}_i(x) = u_i(w_i + x_i) + \eta_{ic}$$

where $\eta_{ic} \in \Re$ describes i's bias with respect to c, independent of c's policy platform x, and u_i is strictly concave increasing in wealth: $u_i' > 0$, $u_i'' < 0$ all i. Let $\eta_i \equiv \eta_{i\beta} - \eta_{i\alpha}$ be i's view of the relative non-policy merits of the two candidates; then i votes for α over β at policy platforms (a, b) if

$$u_i(w_i + a_i) - u_i(w_i + b_i) > \eta_i.$$

Although the true value of $\eta_i \in \Re$ is known only to individual i, the two candidates agree on the distribution of this parameter. Let F_i be the smooth distribution function over η_i, with density f_i having full support. Then

$$p_i(\tilde{u}_i(a), \tilde{u}_i(b)) = F_i(u_i(w_i + a_i) - u_i(w_i + b_i)).$$

Let $z_i(a, b) = [u_i(w_i + a_i) - u_i(w_i + b_i)]$. Then doing the calculus gives that at any pair of candidate platforms (a, b),

$$\frac{\partial^2 p_i}{(\partial a_i)^2} = u_i''(w_i + a_i) f_i(z_i(a, b)) + u_i'(w_i + a_i)^2 f_i'(z_i(a, b))$$

and

$$\frac{\partial^2 p_i}{(\partial b_i)^2} = -u_i''(w_i + b_i) f_i(z_i(a, b)) + u_i'(w_i + b_i)^2 f_i'(z_i(a, b)).$$

Consequently if, for all individuals $i \in N$, the density f_i satisfies

$$\sup_z \frac{|f_i'(z)|}{f_i(z)} \leq \sup_y \frac{|u_i''(y)|}{(u_i'(y))^2}, \qquad (*)$$

then p_i is strictly concave in a_i and strictly convex in b_i. By Theorem 7.9, therefore, there exists a unique two-candidate probabilistic voting equilibrium $(a^*, b^*) \in X$ and, if this equilibrium is interior to X, then Theorem 7.10 implies a^* maximizes $\sum_{i \in N} \omega_i^\alpha(a^*, b^*) u_i(w_i + x_i)$ and b^* maximizes

7.6. APPLICATION: DIRECTOR'S LAW

$\sum_{i \in N} \omega_i^\beta(a^*, b^*) u_i(w_i + x_i)$, where

$$\omega_i^\alpha(a, b) \equiv \frac{\partial}{\partial s} p_i(s, \tilde{u}_i(b))|_{s=\tilde{u}_i(a)}$$

and

$$\omega_i^\beta(a, b) \equiv \frac{\partial}{\partial t} p_i(\tilde{u}_i(a), t)|_{t=\tilde{u}_i(b)}.$$

However, because all individuals' preferences are strictly increasing in wealth, it is easy to see that the equilibrium cannot be interior: if x maximizes c's equilibrium policy then $\sum_{i \in N} x_i = 0$. In this case, Theorem 7.10 does not directly apply. Nevertheless, the conclusion of that theorem does hold and, indeed, given that vote-probabilities depend on utility differences, a little more can be said.

First, since $p_i(\tilde{u}_i(a), \tilde{u}_i(b)) = F_i(z_i(a, b))$ for all $i \in N$,

$$\begin{aligned} \omega_i^\alpha(a, b) &= f_i(z_i(a, b)) \\ \omega_i^\beta(a, b) &= -f_i(z_i(a, b)). \end{aligned}$$

Then, since candidate α maximizes $\Pi(x, b)$ and β maximizes $-\Pi(a, x)$, the solution (a^*, b^*) to the expected plurality maximizing program implemented in the two-candidate probabilistic voting equilibrium satisfies the first-order conditions

$$\begin{aligned} f_i(z_i(a^*, b^*)) u_i'(w_i + a_i^*) - \lambda_\alpha &= 0 \\ f_i(z_i(a^*, b^*)) u_i'(w_i + b_i^*) - \lambda_\beta &= 0 \end{aligned}$$

all $i = 1, \ldots, n$ and

$$\sum_{i \in N} a_i^* = \sum_{i \in N} b_i^* = 0$$

where $\lambda_c > 0$ are the Lagrange multipliers on the candidate budget constraints. Hence

$$\frac{u_i'(w_i + a_i^*)}{u_i'(w_i + b_i^*)} = \frac{\lambda_\alpha}{\lambda_\beta}, \text{ all } i$$

in which case $u_i'' < 0$ all $i \in N$ implies equilibrium policies must converge: $a^* = b^* = x^*$. To see this, suppose $\lambda_\alpha > \lambda_b$; then $u_i'' < 0$ implies $w_i + a_i^* < w_i + b_i^*$ and $\sum_i a_i^* < \sum_i b_i^*$, a contradiction. It follows that $\lambda_\alpha = \lambda_\beta = \lambda$ and $z_i(a^*, b^*) = 0$ for all i. Summing over i, the first-order conditions imply that for all $i \in N$, x^* uniquely solves

$$f_i(0) u_i'(w_i + x_i^*) - \lambda = 0. \tag{\#}$$

By condition (∗), therefore, x^* maximizes $\sum_{i \in N} f_i(0) u_i(w_i + x_i^*)$ on X, as claimed. That is, both candidates necessarily converge on the policy that maximizes a weighted utilitarian preference aggregation rule, with the weights being defined by individuals' marginal vote-probabilities evaluated at any point of indifference between platforms, $z_i(a, b) = 0$ all i.

The first-order conditions can reveal more about the equilibrium platform than that it maximizes a Benthamite aggregation rule. For instance, suppose all individuals share identical preferences over wealth, $u_i(\cdot) = u(\cdot)$ all $i \in N$, and suppose further that every person's initial endowment of wealth w_i is either high ($w_i = H$), middle ($w_i = M$) or low ($w_i = L$); let N_t denote the set of voters with endowment t and $|N_t| = n_t$. Then the first-order conditions (#) yield for all $t \in \{H, M, L\}$,

$$\frac{1}{n_t} \sum_{i \in N_t} f_i(0) u'(t + x_i^*) = \lambda.$$

Now assume that individuals' bias distributions, F_i, are common within, but not across, wealth groups: $w_i = t$ implies $F_i = \bar{F}_t$, all i, t. Then the preceding equalities imply

$$\bar{f}_H(0) u'(H + x_H^*) = \bar{f}_M(0) u'(M + x_M^*) = \bar{f}_L(0) u'(L + x_L^*). \qquad (\#\#)$$

Finally, suppose the direction of bias is correlated with wealth. In particular, assume $\bar{f}_M$ is symmetric strictly single-peaked on $\Re$, $\max \bar{f}_M(x) = \bar{f}_M(0)$ and, for all $\eta = (\eta_\beta - \eta_\alpha) \in \Re$,

$$\bar{f}_H(\eta) = \bar{f}_M(\eta - d) \text{ and } \bar{f}_L(\eta) = \bar{f}_M(\eta + d')$$

for some constants $d, d' > 0$. This means the typical rich person, other things being equal, is predisposed toward candidate β, the typical poor person is similarly inclined toward α and the middle class is on average neutral between the candidates. Under these conditions, $\bar{f}_M(0) > \max\{\bar{f}_H(0), \bar{f}_L(0)\}$ in which case concavity of preferences and (§) imply $[M + x_M^*] > \max\{[H + x_H^*], [L + x_L^*]\}$. To see this, suppose $[H + x_H^*] \geq [M + x_M^*]$. Then $u'' < 0$ and $\bar{f}_M(0) > \bar{f}_H(0)$ imply

$$\bar{f}_H(0) u'(H + x_H^*) < \bar{f}_M(0) u'(M + x_M^*)$$

contradicting (##); a similar argument if $[L + x_L^*] \geq [M + x_M^*]$. In other words, the electoral equilibrium outcome involves a redistribution of wealth from both the rich and the poor groups to the middle class to such an extent that the middle class become the wealthiest members of society. More generally, the tendency for majoritarian politics to benefit the middle classes at the expense of the wealthy and the poor is known as *Director's Law*.

7.7 Policy-motivated candidates

We argued earlier that although exploiting candidate uncertainties about voters' decision criteria can provide a formal solution to the equilibrium non-existence problem for multidimensional politics, such a solution is attenuated insofar as it depends on distributions of idiosyncratic aspects of voter decision-making. An alternative, but not mutually exclusive, approach is to focus less on voter uncertainty and more on candidate motivation. The assumption so far is that candidates care exclusively about winning office, having policy concerns only to the extent that such concerns promote electoral success. Although clearly an abstraction, supposing that candidates are purely office-seeking has the virtues of being parsimonious, neutral across both policy-outcomes and candidates, and reflects the fact that winning office is a key component of any agenda for policy-implementation. Nevertheless, politicians do at least claim to have preferences over policy and, when in office, to pursue a more-or-less well defined policy agenda, promoting some positions over others even under circumstances where doing so seems ill-tailored to remaining in office. In this section, then, we explore the consequences for electoral equilibrium of having two policy-oriented candidates compete for office. And although relaxed somewhat in the next chapter, for this section at least we assume that candidates can commit to implement their electoral platforms conditional on winning office. Such an electoral credibility assumption is not too demanding when candidates are presumed to care only about winning office, since there is no reason for them to implement any other platform than the one on which they are elected; when candidates have policy preferences of their own, however, the assumption is far less appealing.

An intuition is that electoral competition with policy-motivated, rather than with purely office-motivated, candidates is likely to exhibit equilibria precisely because such candidates are unwilling to adopt any platform at all to insure election. Similarly, unless both candidates have identical most-preferred policies, the same logic suggests candidates' platforms do not converge in equilibrium. The intuition, however, turns out to be mistaken in general: equilibria are just as hard to come by and, when they do exist, are more often than not convergent. On the other hand, including both policy-motivated candidates and probabilistic voting can (although not always) support two-candidate equilibria with divergent electoral platforms: probabilistic voting supplies existence and policy-motivation yields divergence.

In section 7.1 above, candidate c's preferences $W_c(x, y)$ are defined exclusively in terms of electoral success and failure. If c cares about policy, this is not enough. Let $u_c : X \to \Re$ describe c's policy preferences, where u_c is assumed continuous and strictly quasi-concave on X with most-preferred policy, $x_c \in X$. If we suppose further that candidates might care at least a little about winning elections *per se* then, for any pair of platforms $(a,b) \in X^2$ offered by candidates α and β respectively, candidate α has payoff

$$\hat{W}_\alpha(a,b) = \begin{cases} u_\alpha(a) + \xi_\alpha & \text{if } \alpha P \beta \\ u_\alpha(b) & \text{if } \beta P \alpha \\ \frac{1}{2}[u_\alpha(a) + u_\alpha(b) + \xi_\alpha] & \text{otherwise} \end{cases},$$

where $\xi_\alpha \geq 0$ is α's value of winning office; candidate β's payoff, $\hat{W}_\beta(a,b)$ is defined analogously. A pure policy-oriented candidate c is captured in this setup by setting $\xi_c = 0$ and pure office-seeking candidate is captured by letting ξ_c become arbitrarily large relative to the policy payoff c achieves by implementing his or her most preferred alternative, $u_c(x_c)$. A (pure strategy) *policy-motivated two-candidate equilibrium* is a pair of platforms $(a,b) \in X^2$ such that, for all $y \in X$,

$$E\hat{W}_\alpha(a,b) \geq E\hat{W}_\alpha(y,b) \text{ and } E\hat{W}_\beta(a,b) \geq E\hat{W}_\beta(a,y)$$

where E is expectation operator as usual and we continue to assume no voter abstention.

Theorem 7.11 *Suppose $X \subset \Re^k$ is convex and compact, $u \in \mathcal{R}_{cs}^n$ and $\xi_c > 0$, each $c \in \{\alpha, \beta\}$. A pair of platforms (a,b) is a policy-motivated two-candidate equilibrium under a simple and strong electoral rule f if and only if $\{a,b\} \subseteq C_f(u)$.*

Proof (Necessity) Let $(a,b) \in X^2$ be an equilibrium pair of platforms and, without loss of generality, suppose $a \notin C_f(u)$. There are three cases: either bPa or aRb or $a = b$. Suppose first that bPa; then $E\hat{W}_\alpha(a,b) = u_\alpha(b)$. But $\xi_\alpha > 0$ implies

$$E\hat{W}_\alpha(b,b) = u_\alpha(b) + \frac{1}{2}\xi_\alpha > E\hat{W}_\alpha(a,b)$$

and (a,b) cannot be an equilibrium. Similarly, (a,b) cannot be an equilibrium if aPb. Therefore, aIb and $E\hat{W}_\alpha(a,b) = \frac{1}{2}[u_\alpha(a) + u_\alpha(b) + \xi_\alpha]$. Since f is simple, aIb implies $P(b,a;u) \notin \mathcal{L}(f)$ and therefore, by f strong, $R(a,b;u) \in \mathcal{L}(f)$. Let $z(t) = [(1-t)a + tb]$. Then $u \in \mathcal{R}_{cs}^n$ implies that, for any $t \in (0,1)$ and all $i \in R(a,b;u)$, $u_i(z(t)) > u_i(b)$ so $z(t)Pb$. Therefore,

7.7. POLICY-MOTIVATED CANDIDATES

$\xi_\alpha > 0$ yields that for $t > 0$ sufficiently small, $E\hat{W}_\alpha(z(t), b) > E\hat{W}_\alpha(a, b)$ contradicting the supposition that (a, b) is an equilibrium and $a \notin C_f(u)$. Finally suppose $a = b \notin C_f(u)$. Then $E\hat{W}_\alpha(a, b) = u_\alpha(a) + \xi_\alpha/2$. But since $u \in \mathcal{R}_{cs}^n$ and $a \notin C_f(u)$, there exists an alternative $a' \neq a$ arbitrarily close to a such that $a'Pa$ and, since $\xi_\alpha > 0$, $E\hat{W}_\alpha(a', a) = u_\alpha(a') + \xi_\alpha > E\hat{W}_\alpha(a, a)$. This proves necessity.

(Sufficiency) Let (a, b) satisfy the hypotheses of the claim. Since X is convex and $u \in \mathcal{R}_{cs}^n$, f simple and strong implies $C_f(u)$ is either empty or singleton [Exercise]; hence $a = b = x^*$. Therefore $E\hat{W}_\alpha(a, b) = [u_\alpha(x^*) + \frac{1}{2}\xi_\alpha]$. Without loss of generality, consider a deviation by candidate α to a platform $y \neq x^*$: then $y \notin C_f(u) = \{x^*\}$, in which case bPy [Exercise] and $\xi_\alpha > 0$ yield

$$E\hat{W}_\alpha(y, b) = u_\alpha(x^*) < E\hat{W}_\alpha(a, b)$$

and y cannot be a profitable deviation for α, proving the theorem. $\square$

As is apparent from the sufficiency part of the proof to Theorem 7.11, if (a, b) is a policy-motivated two-candidate equilibrium under a strong simple rule f, then necessarily $a = b$; that is, despite being primarily policy-motivated, if there is any independent value to holding office at all ($\xi_c > 0$), the candidates are drawn to adopt identical platforms in equilibrium. More significant, perhaps, are the implications of the theorem for equilibrium existence. Exactly as in the canonical model with purely office-seeking candidates, the likelihood of a non-empty core is negligible in sufficiently high dimensional spaces; consequently, the likelihood of electoral equilibria with policy-motivated candidates is similarly negligible so long as they also value winning *per se*, even if only an infinitesimally small amount. Thus any equilibrium existence result for pure policy-oriented candidates, $\xi_c = 0$ each c, is unlikely to be robust to such small positive valuations of holding office.

Before looking more closely at the pure policy-oriented case, it is worth noting the role of assuming that f is strong in Theorem 7.11 with a simple example.

Example 7.6 Suppose there are only two voters and f is majority rule. Both voters $i = 1, 2$ and both candidates $c = \alpha, \beta$ have Euclidean preferences over a two-dimensional policy space, with most preferred points as indicated in Figure 7.6.

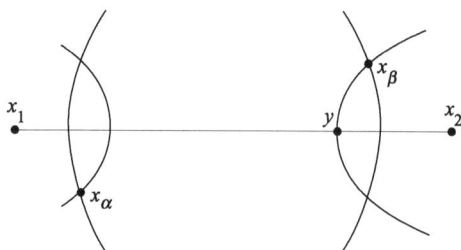

Figure 7.6: Voter and candidate ideal points

With an even number of voters, majority rule is simple but not strong and the majority core in the figure is the set of convex combinations of the voter ideal points, x_1, x_2. It is easy to see that if $\xi_c > 0$ is sufficiently small, then the pair of platforms (x_α, x_β) is an equilibrium: since $x_\alpha I x_\beta$ neither candidate is willing to give up the possibility of winning with their ideal policy for the sure chance of winning on an inferior platform (in the case of $c = \alpha$, for instance, we require $\frac{1}{2}[u_\alpha(x_\alpha) + u_\alpha(x_\beta)] - u_\alpha(y) \geq \frac{1}{2}\xi_\alpha$). Thus Theorem 7.11 does not apply here. □

Whether or not the electoral rule is strong, the existence of a nonempty core for any noncollegial rule is typically constrained to low dimensional spaces, the implications of the theorem for equilibrium existence remain salient. With this in mind, then, consider two-candidate competition with purely policy-motivated candidates, $\xi_\alpha = \xi_\beta = 0$.

If a pair of platforms (a, b) is a pure policy-motivated two-candidate equilibrium for some electoral rule f, then the following must be true of the candidates' and the social preferences:

(.1) $P(b) \subseteq R_\alpha^{-1}(b)$
(.2) $P(a) \subseteq R_\beta^{-1}(a)$.

In words, (.1) says that any policy that defeats β's platform b is weakly less preferred by α to b; (.2) says the same thing with respect to β's preferences over alternatives that beat a. When candidates' preferences are distinct and voters are heterogenous, these necessary properties for an alternative to be part of an electoral equilibrium are demanding, requiring much the same sort of symmetry in the distribution of voter preferences relative to candidate preferences as that needed for the existence of core alternatives [PPTI, Theorem 5.8]. To see this, first consider two possibilities illustrated in Example 7.7.

7.7. POLICY-MOTIVATED CANDIDATES

Example 7.7 In both of the following two examples, every voter $i \in N$ and each candidate $c \in \{\alpha, \beta\}$ is assumed to have Euclidean preferences over a two-dimensional policy space, the election is by simple majority rule and the distribution of voter preferences is such that the majority core is empty.

(1) Let $N = \{1, 2, 3\}$ and suppose voter and candidate ideal points are as illustrated in Figure 7.7.

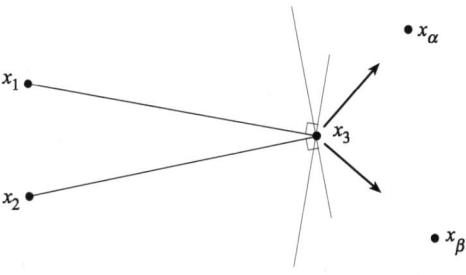

Figure 7.7: Preference distribution for (1)

In this configuration, both candidates are extreme in the same direction relative to voters and properties (.1) and (.2) obtain at a policy on the boundary of the voter Pareto set, PS_N. Specifically, there is a convergent electoral equilibrium at $a = b = x_3$, voter 3's ideal point.

(2) Let $N = \{1, \ldots, 5\}$ and suppose voter and candidate the ideal points are as described in Figure 7.8.

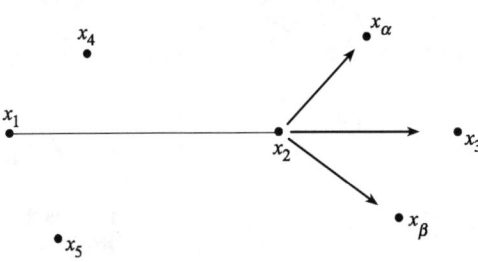

Figure 7.8: Preference distribution for (2)

Unlike for the example illustrated in Figure 7.7, the candidates here are not both extreme in the same direction; in particular, a subset of the Pareto set for the candidates $PS_{\{\alpha,\beta\}}$ (the line connecting x_α and x_β) is strictly interior to the Pareto set for the electorate, PS_N. Nevertheless, there does exist a convergent electoral equilibrium, this time at a policy strictly interior to PS_N: properties (.1) and (.2) hold at $a = b = x_2$. □

Although in Example 7.7(1), illustrated by Figure 7.7, the decisive coalition $\{1, 2\}$ is not blocked by any voters at x_3, it is effectively counterbalanced by the two candidates. Being relatively extreme in the same direction, any alternative strictly preferred to x_3 by voters 1 and 2 is an alternative strictly less preferred to x_3 by both candidates α and β. In effect therefore, the coalition $\{1, 2\}$ is blocked at x_3 by the "coalition" of candidates $\{\alpha, \beta\}$: despite the fact that candidates do not vote, they do exert agenda control. And it is not hard to check that at any policy other than x_3 in Figure 7.7, there is always at least one candidate who prefers to offer a competing platform endorsed by some winning coalition of voters.

The sort of configuration illustrated in Figure 7.7 is not typical. While policy-motivated candidates might well be relatively extreme as compared to the electorate as a whole, they are unlikely to be extreme in the same direction with respect to the distribution of voter preferences. Example 7.7(2) describes such a situation. There are two key features of the preference distribution for existence of the equilibrium depicted in Figure 7.8. First, the Plott symmetry conditions [PPTI, Definition 5.8] are satisfied for a decisive coalition containing voter 2, specifically the coalition $\{1, 2, 3\}$, leaving the coalition $\{1, 4, 5\}$ as the only winning coalition with a non-empty set of policies strictly more preferred to x_2. And second, voter 3's gradient vector at x_2 lies between those of candidates α and β at x_2, which implies that any policy majority preferred to x_2 is preferred by neither candidate to x_2 itself, so properties (.1) and (.2) obtain. Thus a similar symmetry occurs as in Figure 7.7: any direction away from x_2 in which some decisive coalition of voters prefers to move is effectively blocked by the unwillingness of either candidate to move in that direction. If the distribution of voter preferences in Figure 7.8 is perturbed by moving x_2, say, slightly off the line connecting x_1 and x_3, the relevant symmetry in the distribution is upset and it can be checked by inspection that now there is no pair of policies for which properties (.1) and (.2) hold so no electoral equilibrium.

In view of Theorem 7.11 and the fragility illustrated by the example illustrated in Figure 7.8, a more formal development of the propositions underlying Example 7.7 is of limited value here. On the other hand, more can be said regarding the existence and properties of electoral equilibria with purely policy-motivated candidates when voting is probabilistic.

When a candidate $c \in \{\alpha, \beta\}$ is purely policy-oriented and voting is

7.7. POLICY-MOTIVATED CANDIDATES

probabilistic, c's payoff from any pair of competing platforms (a, b) is given by the expected utility,

$$E[u_c(z)|a, b] = \Pr[\alpha \text{ wins } |a, b]u_c(a) + \Pr[\beta \text{ wins } |a, b]u_c(b)$$

where $z \in \{a, b\}$ denotes the platform offered by the winning candidate. Using the notation of section 7.5 and recalling the full participation assumption,

$$\Pr[\alpha \text{ wins } |a, b] = \sum_{M \in \mathcal{L}(f)} \left[\prod_{i \in M} p_i(u_i(a), u_i(b)) \prod_{j \in N \setminus M} [1 - p_j(u_j(a), u_j(b))] \right].$$

This is not a nice expression. Although the probability function $\Pr[\alpha$ wins $|a, b]$ is continuous in platforms a and b, it cannot be expected to inherit any of the concavity properties presumed of individual vote-probabilities and, consequently, the expected payoff $E[u_c(z)|a, b]$ cannot justifiably be presumed concave. So while the argument for the existence of a mixed strategy equilibrium in Theorem 7.9 implies the existence of a mixed strategy equilibrium in the electoral game defined by candidates α and β seeking to maximize their respective expected payoffs, such a result is fairly minimal, offering no explanation for policy choice or the character of equilibrium behavior more generally.

To say anything more than that policy-motivated candidate equilibrium exists under probabilistic voting, therefore, assumptions must be imposed directly on the probability of winning function. In particular, suppressing any consideration of voter behavior, for any pair platforms $(a, b) \in X^2$ let $\Pr_c(a, b) \equiv \Pr[c \text{ wins } |a, b]$ denote the probability that candidate $c \in \{\alpha, \beta\}$ wins the election; with full participation, $\Pr_\beta(a, b) = [1 - \Pr_\alpha(a, b)]$. Then a pure strategy electoral equilibrium with policy-motivated candidates under uncertainty is a pair of platforms $(a^*, b^*) \in X^2$ such that

$$E[u_\alpha(z)|a^*, b^*] \geq E[u_\alpha(z)|a, b^*] \text{ all } a \in X$$

and

$$E[u_\beta(z)|a^*, b^*] \geq E[u_\beta(z)|a^*, b] \text{ all } b \in X.$$

Assume $\Pr_c(a, b)$, $c = \alpha, \beta$, is *unbiased*: $\Pr_c(a, b) = [1 - \Pr_c(b, a)]$ for all $(a, b) \in X^2$. Assuming $\Pr_c(a, b)$ unbiased is tantamount to assuming that voters care only about policy; in effect, therefore, the electoral uncertainty confronting candidates regards some aspect of the distribution of voter preferences. For any alternative $x \in X^\circ$, the interior of X, say that $\Pr_c(x, x)$

is *nondegenerate* at (x,x) if there exists some open neighborhood of x such that, for every pair (a,b) in the neighborhood, $\text{Pr}_c(a,b) > 0$; should there exist no such neighborhood, $\text{Pr}_c(x,x)$ is said to be *degenerate* at (x,x). Thus, if $\text{Pr}_c(x,x)$ is nondegenerate at (x,x) then the probability of c's electoral success is strictly positive for all pairs of platforms in some sufficiently small neighborhood about (x,x). Nondegeneracy is a weak restriction. Finally, a differentiable utility function $u: X \to \Re$ is strictly *pseudo-concave* on X if, for all $x,y \in X$, $u(y) > u(x)$ implies $\nabla u(x) \cdot (y-x) > 0$ [PPTI, Definition 5.7]. A pseudo-concave utility is quasi-concave but not necessarily the converse: if a pseudo-concave utility u has a stationary point, then it must be a global maximum for u (for example, $u(x) = x^3$, $x \in \Re$, is strictly quasi-concave but not, at $x = 0$, strictly pseudo-concave).

Theorem 7.12 *Let $X \subset \Re^k$ be convex and compact. Suppose, for each candidate $c = \alpha, \beta$ and any pair of platforms (a,b), that $\text{Pr}_c(a,b)$ is unbiased and that c's preferences u_c are strictly pseudo-concave on X. Suppose further that candidate ideal points $x_\alpha, x_\beta \in X$ are distinct. Let $(a^*, b^*) \in X^2$ be a pure strategy electoral equilibrium with policy-motivated candidates under uncertainty. Then $a^* = b^* = x \in X^\circ$ only if, for both candidates c, $\text{Pr}_c(x,x)$ is degenerate at (x,x).*

Proof Suppose $(a^*, b^*) = (x,x)$ where x is interior to X. Since $x_\alpha \neq x_\beta$, $x \neq x_c$ for at least one candidate c; without loss of generality, assume $x \neq x_\alpha$. Fix β's platform, $b = x$ and consider α's preferences at x. In particular, let

$$h = \nabla u_\alpha(x)/\|\nabla u_\alpha(x)\|$$

be the direction of α's gradient vector at x. Since $x \neq x_\alpha$ and u_α is strictly pseudo-concave, there exists some $\epsilon_0 > 0$ for sufficiently small such that, for all $\epsilon \leq \epsilon_0$, $u_\alpha(x + \epsilon h) > u_\alpha(x)$. Now suppose $\text{Pr}_\alpha(x,x)$ is nondegenerate at (x,x). Then there exists some $\delta_0 > 0$ sufficiently small such that, for all $\delta \leq \delta_0$, $\text{Pr}_\alpha(x + \delta h, x) > 0$. Let $\gamma = \min\{\delta_0, \epsilon_0\}$. Then

$$\begin{aligned} E[u_\alpha(z)|x + \gamma h, x] \\ = \text{Pr}_\alpha(x + \gamma h, x)u_\alpha(x + \gamma h) + [1 - \text{Pr}_\alpha(x + \gamma h, x)]u_\alpha(x) \\ > u_\alpha(x) \\ = E[u_\alpha(z)|x, x] \\ = E[u_\alpha(z)|a^*, b^*], \end{aligned}$$

which contradicts $(a^*, b^*) = (x,x)$ constituting an interior pure strategy electoral equilibrium. Applying a similar argument to $c = \beta$, proves the theorem. □

Theorem 7.12 is not an existence result for pure strategy equilibria since there is no assurance that any candidate's payoff function, $E[u_c(z)|a, b]$, is appropriately quasi-concave in own platform. Nevertheless, conditional on the existence of a pure strategy equilibrium, the result shows that policy convergence is not to be expected.

7.8 Application: Ideological divergence

In section 7.2 we developed an explanation for ideological convergence under majority voting when candidates care only about winning office. But Theorem 7.12 suggests that such convergence is unlikely when candidates are policy motivated and there is electoral uncertainty. Theorem 7.12, however, does not suggest anything about the extent of equilibrium platform divergence or about whether electoral uncertainty or policy polarization is the more important for driving a wedge between candidates' platforms.

Consider the same basic one-dimensional spatial model described in section 7.2: every voter has symmetric single-peaked preferences over the ideology (policy) dimension, here normalized to $X = [-1, 1]$, and there are sufficiently many voters to justify approximating the electorate as infinite with a continuous distribution of voter ideal points over X; let $\mu \in X$ denote the median voter's most preferred alternative. Electoral uncertainty on the part of candidates α and β is modeled as uncertainty about the true value of μ. In particular, assume both α and β treat μ as a random draw from a uniform distribution F_m with support $[-m, m]$, $m \in (0, 1)$. As usual, each voter has a unique undominated voting strategy of voting for the candidate offering the policy closest to the voter's ideal point; hence the probability that α wins the election when α's and β's platforms are, respectively, a and b with $a < b$ is given by

$$\Pr\nolimits_\alpha(a, b; m) = \begin{cases} 0 & \text{if } \frac{a+b}{2} \leq -m \\ \int_{-m}^{(a+b)/2} dF_m(\mu) & \text{if } \frac{a+b}{2} \in (-m, m) \\ 1 & \text{if } \frac{a+b}{2} \geq -m \end{cases}$$

and $\Pr_\alpha(a, b; m) = 1/2$ if $a = b$. Then $\Pr_\beta(a, b; m) = 1 - \Pr_\alpha(a, b; m)$ and it is easily seen that $\Pr_c(a, b; m)$ is unbiased and, for every policy $x \in (-m, m)$, $\Pr_c(x, x; m)$ is nondegenerate at (x, x). Finally, suppose the two candidates are purely policy-motivated, having strictly pseudo-concave preferences with respect to ideology u_c, $c = \alpha, \beta$, with ideal points

$$-1 < x_\alpha < 0 < x_\beta < 1.$$

For convenience, we refer to this model as the ideology model with electoral uncertainty F_m.

Lemma 7.5 *If $(a^*, b^*) \in [-1,1]^2$ is an electoral equilibrium in the ideology model with electoral uncertainty F_m and pure policy-motivated candidates, then $a^* < b^*$ and $[a^* + b^*]/2 \in (-m, m)$.*

Proof By the assumptions on candidate ideal points and F_m, it is easy to confirm that there exists no equilibrium in which $a^* > b^*$ [Exercise]. So suppose first that $a^* = b^* = x$, in which case $\Pr_c(a, b; m) = \Pr_c(x, x; m) = 1/2$ for both $c = \alpha, \beta$. By Theorem 7.12, $x \notin (-m, m)$; because $\Pr_c(a, b; m)$ is unbiased we can, without loss of generality, assume $x \leq -m$. But then, for sufficiently small $\epsilon > 0$, $\Pr_\beta(x, x + \epsilon; m) \approx 1$. Therefore, since $x < x_\beta$ and u_β is strictly pseudo-concave,

$$E[u_\beta(z)|x, x+\epsilon]$$
$$= [1 - \Pr_\beta(x, x+\epsilon; m)]u_\beta(x) + \Pr_\beta(x, x+\epsilon; m)]u_\beta(x+\epsilon)$$
$$> u_\beta(x)$$
$$= E[u_\beta(z)|x, x],$$

which contradicts $(a^*, b^*) = (x, x)$ constituting an electoral equilibrium. Hence, $a^* < b^*$ in any pure strategy equilibrium.

Now suppose $a^* < b^*$ and $[a^* + b^*]/2 \notin (-m, m)$; again without loss of generality, assume $[a^* + b^*]/2 \leq -m$. Then, $a^* < -m$, $b^* < 1$ and $\Pr_\alpha(a^*, b^*; m) = 0$. Let $\epsilon > 0$ and suitably small. If $b^* \neq x_\beta$ we can repeat essentially the same argument as above to conclude that β's payoff increases with a deviation from b^* to $b^* + \epsilon$ in the case $b^* < x_\beta$ and, in the case $b^* > x_\beta$, from b^* to $b^* - \epsilon$; so suppose $b^* = x_\beta$. In this case (among others), α has a profitable deviation to some platform $a' \in (a^*, 0)$ such that $0 \geq [a' + b^*]/2 > -m$: by definition, $[a' + b^*]/2 \in (-m, m)$ implies $\Pr_\alpha(a', x_\beta; m) > 0 = \Pr_\alpha(a^*, b^*; m)$ and, therefore, $x_\beta > 0$ and u_α strictly pseudo-concave yield

$$E[u_\alpha(z)|a', b^*] = \Pr_\alpha(a', x_\beta; m)u_\alpha(a') + [1 - \Pr_\alpha(a', x_\beta; m)]u_\alpha(x_\beta)$$
$$> u_\alpha(x_\beta)$$
$$= E[u_\alpha(z)|a^*, b^*].$$

The lemma follows. □

The parameter m in the ideology model with electoral uncertainty F_m, is a simple measure of the extent to which the two candidates are uncertain

7.8. APPLICATION: IDEOLOGICAL DIVERGENCE

about the consequences of offering at least some electoral platforms: the greater is m the greater the degree of uncertainty. Lemma 7.5 says that in any (pure strategy) electoral equilibrium to the model, purely policy-motivated candidates will diverge whenever $m > 0$. The question of interest now is what happens to candidate platforms as the electoral uncertainty is resolved, leaving only policy-motivation to support the possibility of platform divergence. The next result answers this question for the ideology model. Recall that $m = 0$ implies the true median of the voter distribution is $\mu = 0$.

Theorem 7.13 *Let $(a(m), b(m)) \in [-1, 1]^2$ be an electoral equilibrium in the ideology model with electoral uncertainty F_m and pure policy-motivated candidates. Then both candidates' platforms converge to the true median ideal point as $m \to 0$: $\lim_{m \to 0} a(m) = \lim_{m \to 0} b(m) = 0$.*

Proof By Lemma 7.5, $\lim_{m \to 0}[a(m) + b(m)] = 0$. Let $x > 0$ and suppose there is a (sub)sequence $(m^t) \to 0$ such that $\lim_{t \to \infty} a(m^t) = -x$. Then $\lim_{t \to \infty} b(m^t) = x$ and, since $\Pr_c(\cdot; m)$ is unbiased, for $c = \alpha, \beta$,

$$\lim_{t \to \infty} \Pr_c(a(m^t), b(m^t); m^t) = \Pr_c(-x, x; 0) = 1/2.$$

Therefore,

$$\lim_{t \to \infty} E[u_\alpha(z) | a(m^t), b(m^t)] = \frac{1}{2}[u_\alpha(-x) + u_\alpha(x)].$$

But for suitably small $\epsilon > 0$ and sufficiently large t,

$$\frac{(a(m^t) + \epsilon) + b(m^t)}{2} \approx \frac{\epsilon}{2} > m^t \approx 0.$$

Figure 7.9 illustrates the argument.

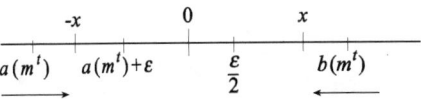

Figure 7.9: Argument for Theorem 7.13

Hence, for sufficiently large t, $\Pr_\alpha(a(m^t) + \epsilon, b(m^t); m^t) = 1$ in which case

$$E[u_\alpha(z) | a(m^t) + \epsilon, b(m^t)] \approx u_\alpha(-x + \epsilon) > \frac{1}{2}[u_\alpha(-x) + u_\alpha(x)],$$

contradicting the supposition that $(a(m^t), b(m^t))$ is an equilibrium for all t. Hence, $\lim_{m \to 0} a(m) = \lim_{m \to 0} b(m) = 0$ as claimed. □

Thus, in the absence of electoral uncertainty, ideological convergence is robust to the introduction of possibly extreme and purely policy-oriented candidates. Small deviations from full certainty induce correspondingly small deviations from full convergence in the ideology model with electoral uncertainty. In effect, policy-motivated candidates prefer to compromise in favor of the median and win for sure rather than risk losing to the less preferred platform offered by their opponent.

7.9 Turnout

So far we have assumed that all individuals vote for one or the other of the two available candidates. In relatively large elections, however, full participation is a woefully poor approximation to any empirical reality. Typically, voter abstention is significant and, even were it not an important feature of observed elections, not voting at all is a legitimate choice for individuals and a satisfactory theory of electoral competition needs to admit this possibility. In this section, therefore, we focus on electoral competition when abstention is an option. And it is worth emphasizing at the outset that our concern is not to explain why people might choose to vote in large elections or to account for observed levels and patterns of turnout (although such topics are necessarily addressed in the discussion to follow). Rather, consistent with the theme of this volume on understanding connections between the (policy) preferences of individuals within a society and the collective (policy) choices of that society, our main concern is to understand the implications of permitting abstention for candidates' selection of electoral platforms, that is, for the policy agenda offered to individuals through electoral competition.

If candidates are seen as indifferent by any voter then there is no reason for that voter to vote at all; in particular, if voters care only about policy and candidates offer identical platforms, then abstention is the best decision whenever there is any opportunity cost at all of casting a vote. Consequently we begin by assuming the candidates' positions are fixed and distinct. Assume also that elections are decided by simple *plurality* voting, whereby the candidate receiving the most votes wins whether or not that candidate receives votes from more than half of the enfranchised population. If there is a tie, the outcome of the election is assumed to be determined by a fair lottery over the two candidates, so each wins with probability $1/2$.

7.9. TURNOUT

Consider a single voter $i \in N$ and, without loss of generality, normalize i's payoffs from the candidates' given platforms (a, b) to satisfy

$$u_i(a) = 1 > u_i(b) = 0.$$

There is also a small opportunity cost to voting κ due, for example, to the time it takes to go to a voting booth and record a vote. Note that voting for b is strictly dominated by voting for a for i; consequently, if i chooses to vote at all then she surely votes for platform a. Treating the participation decisions of the remaining $n-1$ voters as given, there are four events relevant to i's decision on whether to vote or to abstain. *Without* i's vote exactly one of the following occurs:

(LL) a loses by at least two votes;
(L) a loses by exactly one vote;
(T) a and b tie;
(W) a wins by at least one vote.

Individual i cannot affect the outcome of the election in either event (LL) or (W). In both cases i is strictly better off abstaining, so saving the cost of casting an irrelevant vote. On the other hand, i's vote surely matters in each of the remaining two events, (L) and (T). Voter i, that is, is *pivotal* for the election in these events. Given the electoral platforms are fixed and taking it as understood that no individual uses a strictly dominated strategy and votes for her least preferred candidate, a mixed vote strategy for i is a choice $v_i \in [0, 1]$, where v_i is the probability that voter i votes for her most preferred candidate (here, a). If $v_i = 1$ then i votes for her preferred candidate surely; if $v_i = 0$ then i abstains surely.

Let $p_e(n)$ denote the probability that event $e = LL, L, T, W$ occurs conditional on there being n eligible voters. Then i's expected payoff from voting for a, $E[u_i|v_i = 1]$ is

$$p_{LL}(n)u_i(b) + p_L(n)\frac{1}{2}[u_i(a) + u_i(b)] + [p_T(n) + p_W(n)]u_i(a) - \kappa$$
$$= p_L(n)\frac{1}{2} + [p_T(n) + p_W(n)] - \kappa;$$

similarly, i's expected payoff from abstaining, $E[u_i|v_i = 0]$ is

$$[p_{LL}(n) + p_L(n)]u_i(b) + p_T(n)\frac{1}{2}[u_i(a) + u_i(b)] + p_W(n)u_i(a)$$
$$= p_T(n)\frac{1}{2} + p_W(n).$$

Hence i chooses to vote rather than abstain only if

$$E[u_i|v_i = 1] - E[u_i|v_i = 0] = [p_L(n) + p_T(n)]\frac{1}{2} - \kappa \geq 0. \qquad (*)$$

Let $\Pr[piv|n] \equiv [p_L(n) + p_T(n)]$ be the probability of being pivotal. From a purely decision-theoretic perspective, it is plausible and intuitive to suppose $\Pr[piv|n]$ is strictly decreasing in n: the larger is the electorate the less likely it is that any single vote tips the election one way or the other. Indeed, from a typical individual's perspective, we expect $\Pr[piv|n] \to 0$ as $n \to \infty$. But then for any cost $\kappa > 0$ there exists a sufficiently large finite electorate for which the inequality $(*)$ fails so i rationally abstains and, if all individuals are reasoning similarly, the prediction seems to be that nobody votes. However, if all individuals are abstaining then the election must surely be tied in which case the probability of i being pivotal is one, implying $(*)$ holds with strict inequality and it seems everyone should vote; and so on. Apparently, there is an infinite regress: if all others vote, a rational individual should abstain; but then if all individuals are rational, nobody votes and a rational individual, recognizing the probability of being pivotal is now one, should vote; but then ... .

There are two things to note about the preceding logic. First, even at the first step it is *not* true that "if all others vote, a rational individual should abstain"; rather, the conclusion from $(*)$ is that only those with negligible costs choose to vote ($\kappa \approx 0$ or $\kappa < 0$). Whether the proportion of such individuals in any given society is large or small is entirely an empirical matter; to assert on the basis of $(*)$ that rational choice predicts zero turnout in any sizeable election is simply a *non sequitur*. The second thing is that there is no more of a problem with the "infinite regress" than there is with solving any pair of simultaneous equations: all the argument makes clear is that turnout is a function of the probability of being pivotal and the probability of being pivotal is a function of turnout. In equilibrium, the pivot probability and expected turnout must be mutually consistent and mutual consistency almost always implies positive turnout. The rest of the section is devoted to exploring such equilibria, beginning with an extended example in which individuals are identical in every respect save their preferences over the two fixed candidates. Subsequently, we allow voter abstention in a spatial model of electoral competition where preferences vary more widely and candidates are free to choose their respective electoral platforms.

Example 7.8 Suppose there are two candidates with distinct fixed platforms (a, b). Suppose further that the electorate is partitioned into two groups of

7.9. TURNOUT

identical individuals: all those in group L strictly prefer a to b and all those in group M strictly prefer b to a. Let $|L| = l$, $|M| = m$; without loss of generality, assume $0 < l \leq m$ with $l + m = n$. Voter preferences are as described above: for all $i \in L$,

$$u_i(a) = 1 > u_i(b) = 0;$$

and for all $i \in M$,

$$u_i(b) = 1 > u_i(a) = 0.$$

The cost to voting is $\kappa > 0$ for every individual. Individuals choose whether to bear the cost of voting and vote for their most preferred candidate or, at no direct cost, to abstain; as above, $v_i \in [1, 0]$ denotes the probability that voter i chooses to vote for i's most preferred candidate. The election is by plurality rule with ties broken by a fair coin toss. We look for undominated Nash equilibria, $v^* = (v_1^*, \ldots, v_n^*) \in [0, 1]^n$. Following the logic supporting (∗) above and, for any $i \in N$ and $(n-1)$-strategy profile v_{-i}, writing $\Pr[piv|v_{-i}]$ for the probability i is pivotal given the strategies of all other individuals, an individual i's best response decision criterion is

$$\left.\begin{array}{l} v_i = 1 \\ v_i \in [0,1] \\ v_i = 0 \end{array}\right\} \text{ if } \Pr[piv|v_{-i}^*]\frac{1}{2} \gtreqless \kappa. \qquad (**)$$

The existence of equilibria is assured by the Nash existence theorem, Theorem 7.2. Indeed, there are typically a great many equilibria. One fairly apparent exception to the multiplicity is when the cost of voting exceeds $1/2$: referring to the inequality (∗) above, if $\kappa > 1/2$ then the expected payoff of voting is negative even in the case i is surely pivotal. Thus $\kappa > 1/2$ implies there is a unique undominated Nash equilibrium: $v_i^* = 0$ all $i \in N$ so all abstain. Hereafter, therefore, assume $\kappa < 1/2$. Then multiple equilibria are the norm. Rather than enumerate all of the possibilities for $\kappa < 1/2$, we consider three important cases.

(1) *Pure strategy equilibria.* If $l = m$ there is a unique pure strategy equilibrium: $v_i^* = 1$ all $i \in N$ so all vote. Given that the two groups are of the same size, it is immediate that if $n - 1$ others vote then $p_L(n) = 1$. Therefore, if i abstains then i assures herself of a zero payoff but if i votes then i creates a tie yielding a payoff of $1/2 - \kappa > 0$. More interesting, perhaps, is that if $0 < l < m$ then there are no pure strategy equilibria in undominated strategies. To check this, suppose to the contrary that v is a pure strategy equilibrium: $v_i \in \{0, 1\}$ all $i \in N$. Let l^v denote the number

of group L individuals who vote in v and define m^v analogously for group M. There are three cases.

$l^v > m^v + 1$ or $l^v + 1 < m^v$. In both instances no individual is pivotal in which case, given the behavior of the $n-1$ others, every individual $i \in N$ has incentive to abstain. Hence, v cannot be an equilibrium profile.

$l^v = m^v$. Because, $l \neq m$ there exists at least one individual i who abstains in v. But $l^v = m^v$ implies $\Pr[piv|v_{-i}] = 1$ in which case $(**)$ implies i's best response to v_{-i} is to vote, $v_i' = 1$, contradicting v being an equilibrium.

$l^v = m^v - 1$ or $l^v - 1 = m^v$. Let i be a member of the group with smaller turnout. If $v_i = 0$ then $\Pr[piv|v_{-i}] = 1$ and i can create a tie by voting; since $\kappa < 1/2$, this gives a higher payoff to i than does abstention. Hence, if v is an equilibrium, it must be that all individuals of the group with smaller turnout are voting surely. But then no such individual is pivotal and that group's favored candidate loses surely; therefore abstention gives a better payoff than voting, again contradicting the claim that v is an equilibrium.

Thus the existence of pure strategy equilibria with any sort of turnout at all is confined to the case of a perfectly evenly divided electorate. Although clearly special, should this circumstance occur then turnout is 100% irrespective of the size of the two groups or of the cost of voting, so long as this cost is bounded above by one-half of the total benefit of winning. On the other hand, an evenly divided electorate seems to be an empirically unlikely scenario when candidates are commonly seen as being distinct. The remaining two illustrative cases considered, then, involve mixed strategies.

We consider only *quasi-symmetric mixed strategy equilibria*. The term "symmetric" here refers to a restriction on mixed strategies that says that if any member i of a given group uses a nondegenerate mixed strategy $v_i \in (0, 1)$, then every member of that group uses the same strategy; that is, if $v_i \in (0, 1)$ then $v_i = v_j$ for all j in the same group as i. There is no substantive reason why all individuals in a group should adopt the same (nondegenerate) randomization, but the restriction is technically convenient, allows us to make the salient points relatively simply and has some appeal given the homogeneity of preferences among group members. However, as the qualifier "quasi-" suggests, it is not assumed that all voters use mixed strategies, or that individuals in different groups use the same nondegenerate mixed strategy, or that members of the group using pure strategies have to use the same pure strategy. Thus quasi-symmetric mixed strategy equilibria can involve all individuals using mixed strategies, with those of the same group using the same strategy; or they can involve all members of

7.9. TURNOUT

one group mixing, some members of the other group voting surely and the remaining individuals of that group abstain; or (in principle) they can involve all individuals using pure strategies. Given (1), the next case involves individuals from exactly one group using mixed strategies.

(2) *A mixed quasi-symmetric equilibrium.* In this case we look for an equilibrium in which all individuals in group L use the same (nondegenerate) mixed strategy, $v_i = \hat{v} \in (0,1)$ all $i \in L$, voting with probability $\hat{v}$ for a and abstaining with probability $1 - \hat{v}$, and exactly l members of group M vote surely for b with the remaining $m - l \geq 0$ individuals abstaining. Abusing notation, let $v = (\hat{v}; m^v = l)$ denote this strategy profile where, as in (1), m^v is the *ex post* number of individuals from M who vote and write $\hat{v}_{-i}$ to denote the behavior of individuals in L other than i. If individual $i \in L$ is to use a mixed strategy $\hat{v}$ then i must be indifferent between voting for a and abstaining. And since exactly $l = |L|$ members of group M are presumed to vote surely, an individual $i \in L$ is pivotal only in the event that i's vote creates a tie. Therefore, in equilibrium (**) implies we must have for all $i \in L$

$$\Pr[piv|(\hat{v}_{-i}; m^v = l)] = 2\kappa$$
$$\Leftrightarrow \Pr[l^v = l - 1|\hat{v}_{-i}] = 2\kappa$$
$$\Leftrightarrow \hat{v}^{l-1} = 2\kappa,$$

where l^v is the *ex post* number of individuals from L who vote. On the other hand, given that $l - 1$ other members of M are supposed to vote for b, an individual $j \in M$ can be pivotal either by creating or by breaking a tie. Thus, if any individual $j \in M$ is expected to vote surely in equilibrium, (**) requires

$$\Pr[piv|(\hat{v}; m^v = l - 1)] \geq 2\kappa$$
$$\Leftrightarrow \Pr[l^v = l|\hat{v}] + \Pr[l^v = l - 1|\hat{v}] \geq 2\kappa$$
$$\Leftrightarrow \hat{v}^l + l\hat{v}^{l-1}(1 - \hat{v}) \geq 2\kappa.$$

Similarly, if any individual $j \in M$ is expected to abstain surely in equilibrium then necessarily

$$\Pr[piv|(\hat{v}; m^v = l)] \leq 2\kappa$$
$$\Leftrightarrow \Pr[l^v = l|\hat{v}] \leq 2\kappa$$
$$\Leftrightarrow \hat{v}^l \leq 2\kappa.$$

Clearly, if the equality constraint $\hat{v}^{l-1} = 2\kappa$ holds, then necessarily the latter two constraints do not bind. Hence there exists an equilibrium of this sort for every cost $\kappa < 1/2$. Solving for $\hat{v}$ gives $\hat{v} = (2\kappa)^{1/(l-1)}$. Therefore

$$\lim_{l \to \infty} \hat{v} = 1 \text{ and } \left.\frac{d\hat{v}}{d\kappa}\right|_{\kappa < 1/2} > 0$$

so, in direct contrast to the decision-theoretic model of participation with which the section began, this particular equilibrium of the game-theoretic model predicts expected turnout is *increasing*, both in the size of the electorate (with l and m growing at the same rate and $l \leq m$) and in the cost of voting. It follows that the probability of a tied result similarly increases with l and κ.

(3) *A totally mixed quasi-symmetric equilibrium.* The final equilibrium we consider is one in which all individuals are using mixed strategies, with members of different groups adopting different randomizations. Suppose all $i \in L$ use a mixed strategy $\hat{v}$ and all $j \in M$ use a mixed strategy, $\bar{v}$. Following the notational conventions of (2), denote the specified strategy profile as $v = (\hat{v}; \bar{v})$ with $\hat{v}_{-i}$ (respectively, $\bar{v}_{-i}$) denoting the behavior of all individuals in L (respectively, M) other than i. The indifference condition supporting any equilibrium randomization for $i \in L$ is that

$$\Pr[piv|(\hat{v}_{-i}; \bar{v})] = 2\kappa$$
$$\Leftrightarrow \Pr[l^v = m^v|\hat{v}_{-i}; \bar{v}] + \Pr[l^v = m^v - 1|\hat{v}_{-i}; \bar{v}] = 2\kappa$$

where

$$\Pr[l^v = m^v|\hat{v}_{-i}; \bar{v}]$$
$$= \sum_{t=0}^{\min[l-1,m]} \binom{l-1}{t}\binom{m}{t}[\hat{v}^t(1-\hat{v})^{l-1-t}][\bar{v}^t(1-\bar{v})^{m-t}]$$

and

$$\Pr[l^v = m^v - 1|\hat{v}_{-i}; \bar{v}]$$
$$= \sum_{t=0}^{\min[l-1,m-1]} \binom{l-1}{t}\binom{m}{t+1}[\hat{v}^t(1-\hat{v})^{l-1-t}][\bar{v}^{t+1}(1-\bar{v})^{m-1-t}].$$

A similar condition holds for any individual $j \in M$, where we require $\Pr[piv|(\hat{v}; \bar{v}_{-j})] = 2\kappa$. Although there are several possibilities within this class of behavior, we look at the case in which all $i \in L$ use $\hat{v}$ and all $j \in M$ use the complementary mixed strategy, $\bar{v} \equiv 1 - \hat{v}$. Then, noting

7.9. TURNOUT

that $l \leq m$ by assumption, the two indifference conditions characterizing the equilibrium profile $(\hat{v}; \bar{v}) = (\hat{v}; 1 - \hat{v})$ simplify: for $i \in L$,

$$[\hat{v}^m(1-\hat{v})^{l-1}]\left[\sum_{t=0}^{l-1}\binom{l-1}{t}\binom{m}{t} + \frac{1-\hat{v}}{\hat{v}}\sum_{t=0}^{l-1}\binom{l-1}{t}\binom{m}{t+1}\right] = 2\kappa$$

and, for $j \in M$,

$$[\hat{v}^m(1-\hat{v})^{l-1}]\left[\sum_{t=0}^{l-1}\binom{l}{t+1}\binom{m-1}{t} + \frac{1-\hat{v}}{\hat{v}}\sum_{t=0}^{\min[l,m-1]}\binom{l}{t}\binom{m-1}{t}\right] = 2\kappa.$$

A standard identity in combinatorics (see Tucker [198]) states

$$\sum_{t=0}^{T}\binom{T}{t}\binom{S}{t+s} = \binom{T+S}{T+s}. \qquad (\dagger)$$

Let $T = l - 1$ and $S = m$; then setting $s = 1$ and applying the identity $(\dagger)$ yields

$$\sum_{t=0}^{l-1}\binom{l-1}{t}\binom{m}{t+1} = \binom{l+m-1}{l}.$$

Now set $s = 0$ to obtain

$$\sum_{t=0}^{l-1}\binom{l-1}{t}\binom{m}{t} = \binom{l+m-1}{l-1}.$$

Substituting into the indifference condition for $i \in L$ then gives a further simplification to

$$[\hat{v}^m(1-\hat{v})^{l-1}]\binom{l+m-1}{l-1} + [\hat{v}^{m-1}(1-\hat{v})^l]\binom{l+m-1}{l} = 2\kappa. \qquad (\ddagger)$$

Rehearsing a similar argument for $j \in M$ shows that exactly the same indifference condition holds [Exercise]; hence $(\ddagger)$ describes the equilibrium (given $\kappa < 1/2$). It is easiest to understand the properties of the equilibrium by treating the cost of voting as the dependent variable and solving for the value of κ, say $\kappa(\hat{v})$, that rationalizes a mixed strategy $\hat{v}$. In particular, $\kappa(0) = \kappa(1) = 0$ and

$$\frac{d\kappa}{d\hat{v}} \gtreqless 0 \Leftrightarrow \hat{v} \lesseqgtr \frac{\sqrt{m(m-1)}}{\sqrt{l(l-1)} + \sqrt{m(m-1)}} \equiv \hat{v}^+.$$

Thus the relationship between expected turnout and the cost of voting is not monotonic, equilibria of the sort being considered exist only for voting costs $\kappa \leq \kappa(\hat{v}^+)$ and there can be multiple equilibria for a given cost, κ. These observations are illustrated in Figure 7.10 for $l = m = 2$.

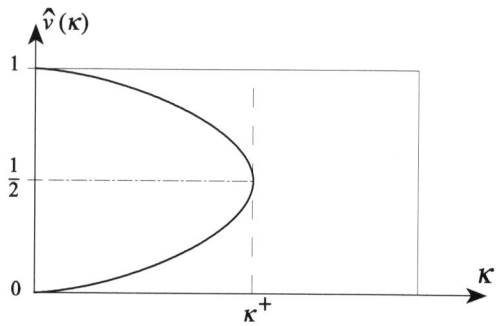

Figure 7.10: Expected turnout and cost of voting

For $\kappa < \kappa^+ = \kappa(\hat{v}^+)$ in the figure, there are two equilibria of the $(\hat{v}; 1 - \hat{v})$ sort. When $\kappa > \kappa^+$, however, there is no $(\hat{v}; 1 - \hat{v})$ equilibrium. There are two continuous selections for $\hat{v}$ as a function of $\kappa \leq 1/2$. Assuming $\hat{v}$ does change continuously in voting cost, expected turnout in this example with $l = m$ is constant in κ: $[\hat{v}l + (1 - \hat{v})m] = n/2$. If a similar figure applies to asymmetric electorates with $l < m$, then aggregate expected turnout is increasing in κ for the continuous selection $\hat{v}(\kappa) > 1/2$ and decreasing in κ for the selection $\hat{v}(\kappa) < 1/2$. □

Example 7.8 shows that the decision-theoretic intuitions derived from (∗) may not apply in a strategic setting. On the one hand, individuals face the familiar collective action free-riding problem whereby a single vote is deemed sufficiently unlikely to matter in the aggregate but, on the other hand, there is an incentive to coordinate behavior within a given group to promote the group's electoral interests.

Before going on it is worth remarking that the conflicting incentives of free-riding and coordination are not peculiar to voting. Indeed, the participation problem of Example 7.8 is an instance of a general class of *threshold public good* problems. In these problems the group M is typically empty, $L = N$, and the alternative b is a status quo with a being a costly but universally preferred alternative. This alternative is implemented only if sufficient individuals each contribute an amount κ to cover the cost, say $\underline{n}\kappa > Cost$.

7.9. TURNOUT

In the electoral context, the public good ("good", at least, for the winning group) is the successful candidate and the threshold for implementation, $\underline{n}$, is endogenously defined to be one more than the number of contributors (voters) from the opposing group.

Example 7.8 illustrates various strategic issues in the theory of participation when the candidates' platforms are fixed and distinct and when voters differ only in their qualitative preference over these platforms. But the main concern of the chapter is with elections in which the two platforms are strategically chosen by office or policy motivated individuals or parties. The rest of the section, therefore, considers some implications of admitting voter abstention in a general spatial model of two-candidate electoral competition under plurality rule.

Subject to two modifications, we use the canonical multidimensional spatial model with two purely office-seeking candidates, as described in sections 7.1 and 7.3 above. The first modification is straightforward: rather than assume candidates are vote-maximizers, assume they choose platforms to maximize expected plurality. As Example 7.1 makes clear, the distinction between plurality and majority voting can matter when voting is an option and, in the presence of abstention, vote-maximizing and plurality-maximizing behavior need not coincide. With full participation, any change in candidate c's platform that increases c's vote total necessarily reduces her opponent's vote total, implying c's plurality increases also. Without full participation, however, an increase in c's votes can be generated by a reduction in the number of individuals who abstain, in which case the same change in c's platform might simultaneously induce more abstainers to vote for her opponent, resulting in a reduction in c's plurality. Example 7.9 illustrates the possibility.

Example 7.9 There are three voters $i = 1, 2, 3$, each with single-peaked preferences defined over a one-dimensional issue space $X = [-1, 1]$, and two candidates α, β. For any policy $z \in X$, let $u_i(z) = -(z - x_i)^2$ be voter i's utility from z and assume $x_1 = -1 < x_2 = 0 < x_3 = 1$. Suppose there is a common cost of voting $\kappa = 0.01$. An individual i is assumed to vote (whatever the pivot probability) for platform y against z if and only if

$$u_i(y) - u_i(z) > \kappa.$$

Let both candidates α, β converge on the median voter's ideal point, respectively offering platforms, $a^* = b^* = 0$. At (a^*, b^*) both candidates receive zero votes because all voters abstain. Now suppose β seeks to maximize her

vote total and consider a unilateral deviation from b^* to a platform $b = 0.11$. Then
$$u_3(b) - u_3(a^*) \approx 0.208 > \kappa$$
and candidate β receives one vote, since now $i = 3$ votes surely for β against α; thus β's vote total at (a^*, b) exceeds that at (a^*, b^*). But at the same time, β's unilateral deviation from b^* to b induces voters $j = 1, 2$ to participate and vote surely for α against β:
$$[u_1(a^*) - u_1(b)] > [u_2(a^*) - u_2(b)] \approx 0.012 > \kappa.$$
Hence, β's plurality strictly decreases from zero at (a^*, b^*) to -1 at (a^*, b). Under plurality rule, β loses the election surely by making the deviation despite increasing her vote share. Given candidates are interested in winning office, therefore, it is unreasonable to assume vote rather than plurality maximizing behavior. □

When abstention is not an option and there are only two candidates, knowing the size of the electorate is largely irrelevant for voters: the unique undominated strategy is to vote surely for the preferred candidate. In turn, this decision rule pins down the mapping between electoral platforms and expected votes, a mapping that constrains the policy choices of strategically rational candidates. When abstention is a possibility, however, the elimination of dominated voting strategies still leaves voters with a choice between participating and abstaining. Consequently, the mapping between candidate platforms and vote shares is not so straightforward, depending as it now does (and as is illustrated by the analysis of Example 7.8) on the computation of various multinomial probabilities defining expected turnout, the probability of winning and so forth. And it is this complexity that in part motivates the second, somewhat less straightforward, modification to the canonical model.

Hitherto the number of voters has been presumed known for sure. Although largely a convenient approximation, the assumption that every individual is aware of the exact size of the electorate is implausible. It turns out that, at least for the present purpose, relaxing the assumption is not only a move toward empirical realism but it also makes the formal analysis of equilibrium voting behavior less cumbersome. The appropriate framework is provided by the Poisson voting model and it is useful first to describe this model in a little generality before applying it to the problem of two-candidate electoral competition with abstention.

Rather than assume the size of the electorate is known to be some number n, suppose that the actual number of potential voters is a random variable

7.9. TURNOUT

distributed according to a Poisson distribution with mean n, where n is presumed large. Then the probability that there are l voters in the society is

$$\Pr[l|n] = \frac{e^{-n} n^l}{l!}.$$

As a statistical model underlying the true size of any electorate, the Poisson distribution uniquely exhibits a very useful technical property, *environmental equivalence*: under the Poisson distribution, any individual in the realized electorate believes that the number of other individuals in the electorate is also a random variable distributed according to a Poisson distribution with the same mean. On the one hand, if the individual thinks there are n voters and the individual is one of them, then his estimate of the number of other individuals present is $n-1$ and this exerts a downward bias on his assessment of the true size of the electorate; on the other hand, the very fact that the individual is in the electorate constitutes evidence in favor of a larger rather than a smaller number of voters and this exerts an upward bias on his assessment of the true size of the electorate. Under the assumption that the distribution of electorate sizes is Poisson, these two biases cancel out exactly [145].

Because the number and therefore the identity of realized individuals in the electorate is a random variable, it is appropriate to drop the individual-specific labels (e.g. $i \in N$) and instead identify voters by *type*. An individual's type describes all of the strategically relevant characteristics of the individual and is summarized as a realization t from a given set of feasible types T. Although all that is required for the theory is that T is a compact metric space, for our purposes it suffices to assume T is a compact subset of a multidimensional Euclidean space, $T \subset \Re^d$: for example, T might be a set of parameters characterizing an agent's utility function over the policy space or perhaps a closed interval of voting costs or both. Each individual's type $t \in T$ is a random variable, drawn independently according to a distribution F on T; assume F has full support with a strictly positive probability density everywhere. Individuals know their own types, the distribution F and that the population size is a random draw from a Poisson distribution with mean n, but do not know surely either the number or identity of other types in the polity.

Let Z be a finite set of feasible actions (pure strategies) that any individual might take. Specifically, for the (possibly m-candidate) voting model, Z is the set of permissible ballots from which an individual may choose, including that in which he or she abstains. For example, voters in the realized electorate for a two-candidate competition between α and β have three feasible actions, $Z = \{\alpha, \beta, \emptyset\}$: vote for α (with platform a) or β (with platform b) or abstain $\emptyset$. When there are several candidates or parties, the set Z can be more complicated; the important thing here is that Z is finite. Then for any type $t \in T$, action (or ballot) $z \in Z$ and policy outcome $x \in X$, $U(x, z, t) \in \Re$ is the individual's payoff from choosing z and ending up with an outcome x. Assume U is jointly continuous in x and t for any z, and bounded on $X \times Z \times T$.

Because the size of the electorate is a random draw from a Poisson distribution with mean n and comprises individuals whose types are also randomly chosen, a strategy here is properly defined as depending on voter type rather than voter identity. Let $\sigma_n : T \to \Delta Z$ be the mixed strategy, mapping types into a probability distribution over the set of feasible actions in an election involving a Poisson electorate with mean size n. For any set $S \subseteq T$, write $\sigma_n(z; S)$ to denote the probability that a randomly chosen individual chooses ballot $z \in Z$ conditional on having a type $t \in S$. Although the equilibrium concept can be defined in terms of σ_n as usual, it is easier to work instead with distributional strategies. A *distributional strategy* τ_n is a probability distribution over ballots and types such that the marginal distribution of τ_n on T is precisely the distribution F. Thus each strategy σ_n defines a unique distributional strategy τ_n (and conversely) as follows: for all $(z, S) \in Z \times 2^T$ such that $\int_S dF > 0$,

$$\tau_n(z; S) = \sigma_n(z; S) \int_S dF(t);$$

hence $\tau_n(z; S)$ is the probability that a randomly chosen individual is of type $t \in S$ and chooses ballot z. Clearly,

$$\sum_{z \in Z} \tau_n(z; S) = \sum_{z \in Z} \sigma_n(z; S) \int_S dF(t)$$
$$= \int_S dF(t)$$

and, for each action z, we can write $\tau_n(z) = \tau_n(z; T)$ for the marginal probability that z is chosen under τ_n.

If all individuals' behavior is defined by the distributional strategy τ_n and the Poisson distribution with mean n governs the choice of electorate size, the number of individuals in the electorate taking action $z \in Z$ is itself a Poisson random variable with mean $n\tau_n(z)$. Moreover, this number can be shown independent of the number of other individuals taking actions $z' \neq z$

7.9. TURNOUT

[145]. Consequently, letting $v(z) \in \{0, 1, 2, \ldots\}$ denote the (random) number of individuals in an electorate who choose ballot $z \in Z$, the probability that any possible profile of realized ballot totals $\mathbf{v}(\mathbf{z}) = (v(z_1), \ldots, v(z_{|Z|}))$ occurs is given by

$$\Pr[\mathbf{v}(\mathbf{z})|n\tau_n] = \prod_{z \in Z} \left(\frac{e^{-n\tau_n(z)}(n\tau_n(z))^{v(z)}}{v(z)!} \right).$$

Invoking the environmental equivalence property, the expected utility of a type t individual from action z given that all others use the strategy τ_n is

$$E[U(x, z, t)|\tau_n] = \sum_{\mathbf{v}(\mathbf{z})} \Pr[\mathbf{v}(\mathbf{z})|n\tau_n] U(x(\mathbf{v}(\mathbf{z})), z, t)$$

where $x(\mathbf{v}(\mathbf{z})) \in X$ is the winning platform (policy outcome) at $\mathbf{v}(\mathbf{z})$.

The *Poisson voting model* (n, T, Z, U) is then the random electorate model just described, in which (1) the size of the electorate is a random draw from a Poisson distribution with mean n; (2) the set of types T is a compact metric space; (3) the set of actions, or permissible ballots, Z is finite; and (4) preferences U are continuous and bounded.

Given τ_n and an action $z \in Z$, define those types $t \in T$ for which z is an expected utility-maximizing action:

$$S^*(z, n\tau_n) = \{t \in T : \forall z' \in Z,\ E[U(x, z, t)|\tau_n] \geq E[U(x, z', t)|\tau_n]\}.$$

Let $(a_1, \ldots, a_m) \in X^m$ be a list of candidate platforms. A *Poisson voting equilibrium* for any given set of feasible ballots Z is a distributional strategy $\tau_{n|(a_1,\ldots,a_m)}$ such that, for all actions $z \in Z$,

$$\tau_{n|(a_1,\ldots,a_m)}(z; S^*(z, n\tau_{n|(a_1,\ldots,a_m)})) = \tau_{n|(a_1,\ldots,a_m)}(z).$$

In words, given the electorate size is a random variable with a Poisson distribution having mean n and given individuals' preferences are determined in the manner described above, a Poisson voting equilibrium for a fixed list of candidate platforms $(a_1, \ldots, a_m)$ is a distributional strategy $\tau_{n|(a_1,\ldots,a_m)}$ such that, for all feasible actions z', the only types who choose a particular action z are those types for which z is a maximal choice conditional on all others following $\tau_{n|(a_1,\ldots,a_m)}$. A proof for the following result can be found in Myerson [147, Theorem 0].

Lemma 7.6 *There exists a Poisson voting equilibrium $\tau_{n|(a_1,\ldots,a_m)}$ for every list of platforms $(a_1, \ldots, a_m) \in X^m$ and all finite n.*

We now apply the Poisson voting model to two-candidate electoral competition under plurality rule with costly voting and abstention. First suppose candidates α and β, respectively, have chosen platforms $(a, b) \in X^2$. Then the set of feasible actions for any voter is $Z = \{\alpha, \beta, \emptyset\}$: vote for α, vote for β, or abstain $\emptyset$. An individual's type is an ordered pair $t = (\theta, \kappa)$, where $\theta \in \Theta$ is a vector of parameters characterizing the individual's policy preferences over the policy space $X \subset \Re^k$ and $\kappa \in [0, 1]$ is the cost of voting the individual must bear to participate actively in any election. So $T \equiv \Theta \times [0, 1]$, where $\Theta \subset \Re^l$ is compact and the restriction of voting costs to the unit interval is simply a normalization. Each component of an individual's type $(\theta, \kappa) \in T$ is a random variable, with θ drawn independently according to a distribution H on Θ and κ drawn independently according to a distribution G on $[0, 1]$; G and H have full support with strictly positive densities everywhere. Individuals' types are drawn independently; individuals know their own types and know G and H. Define the joint distribution F on T by $F(\theta, \kappa) \equiv H(\theta)G(\kappa)$.

Individual payoffs are assumed quasi-linear in policy and costs: the payoff to a type (θ, κ) when platform $x \in X$ wins the election is $u(x, \theta) - \kappa$ if the individual votes and $u(x, \theta)$ otherwise, $u(\cdot, \theta)$ is continuous, strictly quasi-concave and bounded on X for all $\theta \in \Theta$. Hence,

$$U(x(\mathbf{v}(\mathbf{z})), z, (\theta, \kappa)) = \begin{cases} u(x(\mathbf{v}(\mathbf{z})), \theta) - \kappa \text{ if } z \in \{\alpha, \beta\} \\ u(x(\mathbf{v}(\mathbf{z})), \theta) \text{ if } z = \emptyset \end{cases}.$$

Under the assumptions on u, preferences U are continuous and bounded. Thus all the requirements of a Poisson voting model obtain and Lemma 7.6 applies.

Fix (a, b) and let $\tau(z) = \lim_{n \to \infty} \tau_n(z)$, where $\tau_n \equiv \tau_{n|(a,b)}$ is a mean n Poisson voting equilibrium. Let the probability a vote for candidate $c \in \{\alpha, \beta\}$ is pivotal under τ_n be $piv(c|n\tau_n)$.

Lemma 7.7 *Assume $\tau(\alpha) + \tau(\beta) > 0$. Then*

$$\lim_{n \to \infty} \frac{piv(\alpha|n\tau_n)}{piv(\beta|n\tau_n)} = \lim_{n \to \infty} \sqrt{\frac{\tau_n(\beta)}{\tau_n(\alpha)}}.$$

A proof for this lemma can be found in Myerson [147]. The result implies that for sufficiently large n, the probability a vote for α is pivotal, $piv(\alpha|n\tau_n)$, exceeds that of a vote for β, $piv(\beta|n\tau_n)$, if the expected vote total going to α, $n\tau_n(\alpha)$, is less than that for β, $n\tau_n(\beta)$. The reason for this is intuitive: if α is anticipated to receive fewer votes under τ_n than β, then

7.9. TURNOUT

the conditional likelihood that α is behind by one vote is greater than the conditional likelihood that β is behind by one vote. The lemma constitutes an important step in the argument for the next result, which states that if the policy platform of candidate c has a higher expected payoff for the electorate than that of c's opponent then, for sufficiently large societies, c almost surely wins the election.

Theorem 7.14 *Suppose candidates α, β respectively propose platforms $a, b \in X$ such that*

$$\int_\Theta u(b,\theta)dH(\theta) > \int_\Theta u(a,\theta)dH(\theta).$$

Then the probability that β wins the election in a Poisson voting equilibrium $\tau_{n|(a,b)}$ converges to one as n goes to infinity.

Proof Lemma 7.6 insures there exists a voting equilibrium $\tau_n \equiv \tau_{n|(a,b)}$ for every finite n. Fix such an equilibrium and define the subsets of voter types

$$\Theta_\alpha = \{\theta \in \Theta : u(a,\theta) > u(b,\theta)\},$$
$$\Theta_\beta = \{\theta \in \Theta : u(a,\theta) < u(b,\theta)\}.$$

Excluding strictly dominated strategies, a voter never votes for his or her least preferred candidate. By environmental equivalence, an individual of type $(\theta, \kappa) \in \Theta_\alpha$ strictly prefers to vote for α rather than abstain if and only if

$$(u(a,\theta) - u(b,\theta))piv(\alpha|n\tau_n) > \kappa.$$

Hence the probability a randomly chosen individual votes for α in equilibrium is

$$\tau_n(\alpha) = \int_{\Theta_\alpha} G((u(a,\theta) - u(b,\theta))piv(\alpha|n\tau_n))dH(\theta). \quad (i)$$

Similarly, the probability a randomly chosen individual votes for β in equilibrium is

$$\tau_n(\beta) = \int_{\Theta_\beta} G((u(b,\theta) - u(a,\theta))piv(\beta|n\tau_n))dH(\theta). \quad (ii)$$

The expected total number of votes is therefore $n[\tau_n(\alpha) + \tau_n(\beta)]$. Suppose

$$\lim_{n \to \infty} n[\tau_n(\alpha) + \tau_n(\beta)] < \infty.$$

Then $\lim_{n\to\infty} n\tau_n(c)$ must be finite for both candidates $c \in \{\alpha, \beta\}$ and, further, the associated pivot probabilities $piv(c|n\tau_n)$ must converge to the positive pivot probabilities associated with these finite limits. But $piv(\alpha|n\tau_n) <$

∞ means that the right hand side of (i) must be finite; hence, $\lim_{n\to\infty} \tau_n(\alpha)$ is finite so $\lim_{n\to\infty} n\tau_n(\alpha) = \infty$, a contradiction. Therefore, the expected total number of votes must go to infinity as n goes to infinity; in particular, at least one candidate c's expected vote total $n\tau_n(c)$ must be going to infinity with n. Hence, by Lemma 7.7, it must be that for both candidates c, $\lim_{n\to\infty} piv(c|n\tau_n) = 0$. By assumption, the density of voting costs exists and is strictly positive at $\kappa = 0$; therefore, $\lim_{n\to\infty} piv(\alpha|n\tau_n) = 0$ implies that for n large,

$$\int_{\Theta_\alpha} G((u(a,\theta) - u(b,\theta))piv(\alpha|n\tau_n))dH(\theta)$$
$$\approx piv(\alpha|n\tau_n) \int_{\Theta_\alpha} G'(0)(u(a,\theta) - u(b,\theta))dH(\theta)$$

and similarly for $c = \beta$. Using (i) and (ii) yields

$$\frac{\tau_n(\alpha)}{\tau_n(\beta)} \approx \frac{piv(\alpha|n\tau_n)}{piv(\beta|n\tau_n)} \frac{\int_{\Theta_\alpha}(u(a,\theta) - u(b,\theta))dH(\theta)}{\int_{\Theta_\beta}(u(b,\theta) - u(a,\theta))dH(\theta)}.$$

Applying Lemma 7.7 gives

$$\frac{\tau_n(\alpha)}{\tau_n(\beta)} \approx \sqrt{\frac{\tau_n(\beta)}{\tau_n(\alpha)}} \frac{\int_{\Theta_\alpha}(u(a,\theta) - u(b,\theta))dH(\theta)}{\int_{\Theta_\beta}(u(b,\theta) - u(a,\theta))dH(\theta)}.$$

Collecting terms we obtain

$$\frac{\tau_n(\alpha)}{\tau_n(\beta)} \approx \left(\frac{\int_{\Theta_\alpha}(u(a,\theta) - u(b,\theta))dH(\theta)}{\int_{\Theta_\beta}(u(b,\theta) - u(a,\theta))dH(\theta)}\right)^{\frac{2}{3}}. \quad (iii)$$

By hypothesis, $\int_\Theta u(b,\theta)dH(\theta) > \int_\Theta u(a,\theta)dH(\theta)$ and H has full support with strictly positive density everywhere. Therefore, the right hand side of (iii) lies strictly between zero and one and the expected vote total for β must be going to infinity with n. Then (iii) implies that, at least in the limit, the expected number votes for α falls short of β's expected vote total by a positive fraction of that total. Now, the variance and mean of any random variable with a Poisson distribution are the same number and, consequently, the standard deviation of such a random variable becomes a negligible fraction of the mean as the mean becomes arbitrarily large. But this means the expected difference in vote totals, $n\tau_n(\beta) - n\tau_n(\alpha)$, must become infinitely large as n goes to infinity which proves the theorem. □

7.9. TURNOUT

The significance of Theorem 7.14 lies in its implications for spatial candidate competition. So now suppose the two candidates are free to choose any feasible policy platform and understand that voting behavior conditional on any chosen pair of platforms is described by a Poisson voting equilibrium. As usual, candidates are presumed to maximize their respective expected pluralities, taking the position of their opponent as given. (In fact, at least for sufficiently large electorates, maximizing a candidate's probability of winning given his opponent's electoral platform similarly maximizes the candidate's expected plurality; proving this claim is left as an exercise.) More formally, a *Poisson electoral equilibrium* is a pair of policy positions $(a^*, b^*) \in X^2$ and a Poisson voting equilibrium $\tau_{n|(a^*,b^*)}$ such that, for all $a \in X$

$$[\tau_{n|(a^*,b^*)}(\alpha) - \tau_{n|(a^*,b^*)}(\beta)] \geq [\tau_{n|(a,b^*)}(\alpha) - \tau_{n|(a,b^*)}(\beta)]$$

and, for all $b \in X$

$$[\tau_{n|(a^*,b^*)}(\alpha) - \tau_{n|(a^*,b^*)}(\beta)] \leq [\tau_{n|(a^*,b)}(\alpha) - \tau_{n|(a^*,b)}(\beta)].$$

Corollary 7.4 *If $(a^*, b^*) \in X^2$ is a Poisson electoral equilibrium then, for sufficiently large n,*

$$\{a^*, b^*\} \subseteq \arg\max_{x \in X} \int_\Theta u(x, \theta) dH(\theta).$$

In particular, if there exists a unique policy x^* that maximizes expected aggregate utility in the electorate then $a^* = b^* = x^*$ and turnout is zero.

Proof Follows immediately from Theorem 7.14 and the definition of a Poisson electoral equilibrium. □

Assuming a unique aggregate expected utility maximizing policy, x^*, Corollary 7.4 says that if candidates are office-motivated and unconstrained in the platforms they can adopt (save by X), then two-candidate competition in the spatial model with abstention and costly voting results in both candidates converging on x^* and, consequently, nobody votes. The threat of inducing counter-productive turnout is enough of an incentive for neither candidate to deviate unilaterally from x^* in an effort to secure a positive plurality: those induced to vote should a candidate so deviate to a platform $x \neq x^*$ are not surely those who prefer the platform x over x^*.

Although the underlying story is quite different, the strategically coherent model of electoral competition with rational abstention yields the same implication with respect to candidate convergence as the typical full-participation models and, with respect to turnout, yields (in this case, coherently) the same implication as the decision-theoretic models with policy-motivated voters.

7.10 Discussion

Elections are important for (more-or-less) democratic polities. Although possibly most elections involve multiple candidates and complicated electoral rules, the simplest, non-trivial, form of election is a two-candidate competition for a single office. Furthermore, leaving aside questions of candidate entry, two-candidate electoral competition is a plausible approximation to electoral systems dominated by two political parties. Thus two-candidate competition has some claim to be fundamental to any understanding of more complex electoral systems.

This chapter develops the spatial theory of two-candidate elections at a fairly high level of abstraction, focusing in particular on questions of the existence and characterization of equilibrium policy platforms proposed by candidates who are constrained only by the technical feasibility constraints on the set of available positions. Of course, in any concrete election, the competing candidates or parties face many constraints imposed by history, convention or voter beliefs. It would not, for instance, be possible (or credible) for a party long-associated with laissez faire economic policies to run for election on a platform of full state ownership of industry. Including asymmetries of this sort is entirely appropriate for modeling electoral environments with enough structure to specify the relevant constraints closely. But, from a general theoretical perspective, imposing constraints at the outset is unsatisfactory. Ideally, asymmetries across candidates should be explained rather than assumed and presuming their existence leaves open the extent to which results derived are peculiar to the specification of those constraints. It is appropriate, therefore, to develop the abstract theory of elections assuming that candidates are essentially symmetric and free to adopt any feasible platform on which to compete for electoral office, leaving the inclusion of candidate asymmetries and constraints for subsequent analysis.

Given a preference aggregation rule f, the central questions addressed in the spatial preference model concern the relationship between the distribution of individuals' preferences over the (policy) space and the existence and character of "best", or core, alternatives relative to that rule. Introducing two candidates responsible for proposing alternatives in the spatial model,

7.10. DISCUSSION

requiring individuals to record their preferences over pairs of proposals by actively voting and aggregating such revealed preferences by applying the rule f to the recorded votes, then yields an abstract and parsimonious model of electoral competition. In effect, the spatial voting model of electoral competition is a binary voting game in which the two alternatives are chosen endogenously by agents (candidates) within the polity.

In common with the spatial preference model, the central questions for the spatial voting model regard the existence and character of particular sorts of alternative; in this case, however, the focus is not on subsets of alternatives that are "best" with respect to the underlying voting rule but, rather, on pairs of alternatives that are equilibrium proposals in a strategic game between the two candidates competing for individuals' votes. In general, there is no reason to expect there to be a direct connection between the answers to these two sets of question. Nevertheless, if candidates are concerned only with winning office, if voting is costless so all individuals rationally vote, and if there is no uncertainty about preferences or proposals, then it turns out that in fact the two sets of question share the same answer: the set of core alternatives in the spatial preference aggregation model is exactly the set of alternatives that constitute pure strategy two-candidate equilibrium platforms in the spatial voting model of electoral competition (Theorem 7.1). It follows that core characterization results for the preference aggregation model describe electoral equilibria in the spatial voting model, making clear the role of the voting rule in promoting centrally located candidates (Corollary 7.1). In particular, when the core is singleton, then the electoral equilibrium involves both candidates converging to the same platform. So while, in equilibrium, the identity of the winner is uncertain, the identity of the winning platform is known surely. Unfortunately, with respect to equilibrium existence, the equivalence of core alternatives and pure strategy electoral equilibria also implies the existence of such electoral equilibria in higher dimensional policy spaces is likely to be fragile at best (Corollary 7.2).

The absence of a positive and general equilibrium existence result for the canonical model that does not hinge on the details of how indifferent voters choose to vote is problematic for a general theory of electoral competition. Before further complicating the model, however, it is worth asking what if anything can be said about candidate behavior in the framework of Theorem 7.1, when pure strategy equilibria do not exist. In the spatial preference aggregation model without candidates or any concerns with voting as an act, the answer to the analogous question is provided by the so-called chaos theorems [PPTI, ch.6]: if the core of the preference aggregation rule is empty then almost every alternative is in the top-cycle set (Definition 4.2). But in the spatial voting model of elections, alternatives are offered by strategically rational candidates and it is unreasonable to expect that any alternative at all might in principle be chosen as an electoral platform. In fact, under the assumptions of Theorem 7.1 and Corollary 7.2, those platforms that could possibly be chosen by rational candidates, that is, those platforms in the support of any equilibrium *mixed* strategy, lie within a subset of the Pareto set of policies for the electorate, the uncovered set, that converges continuously to the core when the latter exists (Theorems 7.4 through 7.7). Unlike the core, however, the value of these results for applied work is severely limited by the considerable practical complexity of identifying the uncovered set for an arbitrary distribution of voter preferences. Pragmatic concerns notwithstanding, Theorems 7.4, 7.5 and 7.6 show that the properties of the spatial voting theory of elections do not coincide with those of the spatial preference aggregation theory, despite the equivalence result (Theorem 7.1).

To a large extent, the equilibrium existence problem in the spatial voting model is technical. The Nash existence theorem for mixed strategy equilibria (Theorem 7.2) applies if the policy space is approximated with a finite grid, irrespective of how fine the grid might be. Furthermore, in the finite case with two purely office-motivated candidates, the mixed strategy equilibrium is unique and symmetric (Theorem 7.3): both candidates adopt the same mixed strategy and thus, *ex ante*, the candidates are equivalent from a policy perspective, just as they are in the convergent pure strategy equilibria when these exist. The difficulty in proving a general mixed strategy equilibrium existence result for the spatial voting model with a continuum of alternatives lies in the absence of sufficient continuity in the mapping that connects pairs of policy positions to vote shares: a small unilateral change in one candidate's position can result in the candidate's vote share changing from less to more than one-half of the electorate, thus inducing a discrete jump in her payoff. But these discontinuities often arise as a result of the presumption that indifferent individuals in the spatial model necessarily vote for each candidate with probability one-half. If this assumption is relaxed to presuming only that indifferent individuals use a symmetric voting strategy, thus allowing the probability of indifferent individuals voting for one or other candidate to be sensitive to the platforms offered, then existence of a mixed strategy equilibrium is guaranteed (Theorem 7.8).

Establishing the existence of electoral equilibria with symmetric voting is important, as it insures the internal coherence of the multidimensional spatial model of elections. Nevertheless, a compelling empirical interpretation of candidates' using mixed strategies to decide on their electoral platforms

7.10. DISCUSSION

(and, therefore, under the assumptions of the model, the platform to be implemented conditional on being elected) is hard to construct. It remains true, then, that a satisfactory theory of elections seems to demand more structure than that offered by the minimal perturbation from the pure spatial theory of preference aggregation to which Theorem 7.1 applies. Among the most obvious substantive assumptions to relax in this regard are those concerning candidates' information about voters' preferences and those concerning candidates' motivations.

It is unreasonable to expect candidates for electoral office to know surely the details of every individual's preferences or voting criteria. Including some idiosyncratic characteristic to voters' decisions, and assuming candidates know at best the distribution from which these characteristics are drawn, can induce sufficient continuity in candidates' assessments of how policy positions map into vote shares to admit a general equilibrium existence result (Theorem 7.9). Furthermore, if the uncertain characteristic concerns a non-policy bias of voter behavior and pure strategy equilibria exist, then such equilibria involve platforms that maximize weighted sums of voter policy preferences (Theorem 7.10). Thus assuming some uncertainty on the part of candidates is both substantively plausible and technically productive. And voters clearly do exhibit candidate biases that appear predicated on non-policy features such as race and religion; given such biases are consequential in the aggregate, therefore, as presumed in probabilistic voting theory, candidate uncertainty can provide a useful structure for more applied problems.

On the other hand, exactly how the uncertainty over voters' decisions is introduced can matter: if it is with respect to policy preferences, then the requisite continuity is not assured (Example 7.5); if it is with respect to some non-policy characteristics, then the theory is typically silent about why the relevant characteristics are independent of policy positions or why policy-oriented voters should care which candidate implements a given platform (Example 7.4). An empirical justification for this apparently *ad hoc* component of the probabilistic voting model is available. Namely, when estimating aggregate vote or plurality functions using historical data, the analyst has no possibility of learning surely what voters' policy preferences happen to be. Therefore, even if the underlying theory is based exclusively on a fully rational and policy-oriented electorate, operationalizing the theory for empirical estimation requires explicit introduction of a statistical error component and doing this essentially amounts to specifying a probabilistic voting model. Although, from this perspective, the pragmatic value of probabilistic voting is high, a general theoretical argument deriving from the limitations of statistical estimation is not very compelling. First, theory is in principle what constrains empirical work rather than the reverse and, second, the "statistical estimation" argument is unnecessary in similar informationally constrained environments such as, for example, consumer demand theory; applying it here is itself somewhat *ad hoc*.

The assumption that candidates are purely office-motivated is instrumental. The argument is that either candidates really are motivated by winning office or they in fact have policy preferences but, because they are incapable of implementing such preferences unless they win office, their electoral behavior is directed to winning. In both cases, presuming candidates choose electoral platforms primarily to promote electoral success is appropriate. Yet it is not clear that policy-motivated candidates would in fact be willing to adopt any platform at all to win office because policy compromise may be more distasteful than electoral failure. But if so, this is largely irrelevant: in the absence of any candidate uncertainty regarding voter behavior, it takes only a small valuation of holding office *per se* for otherwise purely policy-motivated candidates to be essentially indistinguishable from purely office-motivated candidates (Theorem 7.11). If there is uncertainty about voter decisions and voting is probabilistic, however, policy-motivated candidates offer distinct platforms in equilibrium (Theorem 7.12). In other words, probabilistic voting and policy-motivated candidates result in electoral equilibria in which the candidates offer divergent platforms; thus it is possible in this framework for both the identity of the winning candidate and the identity of the winning policy to be uncertain at the time of the vote.

The focus of the theory of two-candidate electoral competition is on the behavior of candidates: what platforms should we expect to observe in equilibrium? With only two candidates who are committed to implementing their respective electoral platforms conditional on winning office, strategically rational voters have a simple problem when voting is costless: always vote for a more preferred candidate. Consequently, we have assumed throughout that voting is costless and that nobody abstains; in this setting, candidate decisions are not clouded by any concerns with turnout. But voting is costly at times, albeit minimally, and turnout varies more or less systematically with things like the weather, the perceived closeness of elections, the significance of the salient issues and so forth. It is important, therefore, to explore the implications of admitting abstention for candidate behavior.

The decision-theoretic approach to voter turnout suggests only those with negligible voting costs can be expected to vote in large elections.

7.10. DISCUSSION

Whether or not such individuals constitute a significant proportion of the electorate is purely an empirical question. Irrespective of the facts, however, as a model of turnout the decision-theoretic approach is incomplete: a rational individual would recognize that if all other potential voters assume their particular vote is irrelevant in the aggregate and so abstain, then the probability that the individual is pivotal is one, implying he or she should (given the benefits of surely determining the winner exceed the cost of doing so by voting) surely vote. Voting is (at least in part) an instrumentally strategic act and a satisfactory theory of voting recognizes this fact. In particular, when voters are instrumentally rational and strategic, pretty much any voting equilibrium when candidates are distinct must involve some positive number of votes cast (Example 7.8). The relevant question here, therefore, concerns whether office-motivated candidates offer distinct equilibrium platforms when turnout is endogenous, depending on individuals' costs of voting and their expected benefits of so doing, defined in part by the platforms themselves and in part by the behavior of other voters. Addressing the question, however, is analytically complicated when the size of the electorate is finite and presumed known surely to every voter and candidate. Consequently, we exploit the Poisson voting model which assumes (plausibly) that candidates and individuals are uncertain of the total number of possible voters along with their respective preferences. Under these assumptions it turns out that equilibrium platforms generally exist and must, as in the probabilistic voting model, involve candidates adopting expected aggregate utility maximizing platforms (Corollary 7.4). If there is a unique such platform, therefore, candidates converge in equilibrium and, given costly voting, everybody abstains. While empirical turnout in large elections can be very low indeed, it is virtually never zero and candidates do not always appear to converge on a given platform. As a predictive result, that is, Corollary 7.4 is not obviously successful. As a normative result on the abstract theory of spatial voting, however, it is a subtle and important finding, providing an electoral efficiency property comparable to the classical efficiency theorem for general economic equilibrium.

Much of the theory of two-candidate elections developed in this chapter is deliberately abstract, deriving quite explicitly from the theory of direct preference aggregation in the spatial model. The claim is that much of the deeper intuition regarding voter preferences, candidate incentives and the electoral institutions through which they interact is revealed through an understanding of this theory. And to a greater or lesser degree, more applied models of electoral behavior reflect the imposition of more structure and detail on the abstract model.

7.11 Exercises

7.1 Check the claims of Example 7.3.

7.2 Prove Claims *(3)* and *(4)* of Lemma 7.1.

7.3 Check that any Nash equilibrium strategy must survive the iterated deletion of strictly dominated strategies (Definition 4.1).

7.4 (a) Prove that for any weakly Paretian collective preference relation $f(\rho) = R$ on X, where $\rho \in \mathcal{R}^n$,

$$C_f(\rho) \subseteq U(f(\rho)) \subseteq PS_N(\rho).$$

(b) Construct an example in which the core is not empty and both inclusions are strict.

7.5 Prove that for any strong simple rule [PPTI, Definition 3.6] $f(u)$ on X,

$$C_f(u) \neq \emptyset \Rightarrow [U(f(u)) = C_f(u)].$$

7.6 (a) For the pure distribution model with linear and selfish voter preferences, prove that the uncovered set coincides with the interior of the Pareto set.

(b) In case the collective preference relation is strict everywhere on X, show that Definition 7.2 coincides with that of Definition 4.5.

7.7 Provide an example to show that the statement "x covers y" does not imply "x deep covers y".

7.8 (a) Check the quasi-concavity and comparative static claims in section 7.4.

(b) Prove or provide a counterexample to the claim that, for any individual, the individual's most preferred level of tax-revenue under progressive taxation is identical to that under proportional taxation where the same rate is applied to both high and low earnings.

7.9 Let $X = [0,1]$ and let $\Pr(a,b) \in [0,1]$ denote the probability that platform $a \in X$ is preferred by a plurality to $b \in X$. Assume (1) $\Pr(a,b) = 1 - \Pr(b,a)$, and (2) for $a < b$ (respectively, $a > b$) $\Pr(a,b)$ is non-decreasing (respectively, non-increasing) in a and in b. Prove that if Pr is continuous

7.11. EXERCISES

at every point $(a,b) \in [0,1]^2$ such that $a = b$, then $\Pr(a,b) = 1/2$ for all $(a,b) \in [0,1]^2$.

7.10 Assume no probabilistic voting and no abstention. Prove that the sets of two-candidate electoral equilibria under plurality rule are independent of whether candidates $c \in \{\alpha, \beta\}$ maximize the expected value, $EW_c(a,b)$ as specified in section 7.1 or maximize expected plurality as specified in section 7.5.

7.11 Prove the two claims made in the Sufficiency argument for Theorem 7.11.

7.12 For Lemma 7.5, check that the assumptions on candidate ideal points and F_m imply there exists no equilibrium in which $a^* > b^*$.

7.13 *Prove:* $u \in \mathcal{R}_{cs}^n$, f simple and X convex imply $C_f(u)$ is convex; if f is also strong and $C_f(u)$ nonempty, then $C_f(u) = \{x^*\}$ and, for all $y \neq x^*$, $x^* P y$.

7.14 (a) Using a one-dimensional spatial model of two-candidate competition under plurality rule with abstention and a continuum of voters, each of whom has symmetric single-peaked preferences, discuss the relationships between the following candidate objectives: choose platforms to maximize (1) probability of winning, (2) expected plurality and (3) expected vote-share.

(b) Show that, for sufficiently large electorates, maximizing candidate α's probability of winning given candidate β's electoral platform similarly maximizes the candidate's expected plurality. [Hint: consider each vote v_i as a random draw from $\{-1, 0, 1\}$, where -1 indicates a vote for β, 0 is abstention and 1 indicates a vote for α; now observe that for n large, the probability α wins is the probability that $\sum_i v_i/n > 0$; finally, exploit the law of large numbers to obtain the result.]

7.15 (a) Establish the unproven claims of Example 7.8 (in (3), note that $l \leq m$ and $l > m - 1$ implies $l = m$ and that $\binom{2l-1}{l} = \binom{2l-1}{l-1}$).

(b) Show that if $l = m$ and $\kappa > \kappa^+$, there exist equilibria in which all individuals of both groups use exactly the same mixed strategy; that is, for all $i \in N$, $v_i = v'$.

(c) Find some additional equilibria to the participation game of Example 7.8.

7.16 Consider a multidimensional probabilistic voting model with policy-motivated candidates. Let $X \subset \Re^k$ be the compact and convex policy space.

Let $\Pr(a,b) \in [0,1]$ be the probability candidate α with platform $a \in X$ defeats candidate β with platform b; suppose Pr is twice-differentiable in all arguments. Assume candidate c's utility from platform z being the winning policy is $u_c(z)$, $c = \alpha, \beta$, where u_c is twice-differentiable and strictly concave on X. Show that if both candidates maximize expected payoff from the election and that if (a^*, b^*) is an interior equilibrium, then $a^* \neq b^*$.

7.12 Further reading

The literature on two-party electoral competition is huge. Early formal models of one-dimensional spatial elections are described in Hotelling [101] and Smithies [195]. The classic reference for political science, however, is Downs [61]. Davis and Hinich [54], [55], [56] introduced the multidimensional spatial model of voting and electoral competition; the early theory is elaborated in Davis, Hinich and Ordeshook [57] and Ordeshook [152]. The fundamental properties of majority rule for aggregating (sincere) preferences in the spatial model are discussed at length in Austen-Smith and Banks [13]; key references include Plott [166], Davis, de Groot and Hinich [53], Kramer [105], Cohen [44], McKelvey [122], [123], Schofield [183], [184], Matthews [120] and McKelvey and Schofield [127]. Hinich and Ordeshook [98], Aranson, Hinich and Ordeshook [3] and Hoyer and Mayer [102] compare the implications of alternative candidate objectives.

Theorem 7.2 is due to Nash [151]. There are multiple texts describing the basic theory of constant sum games and, more generally, Nash equilibrium: Fudenberg and Tirole [82], Myerson [144] and Osborne and Rubinstein [155] are three excellent examples. Theorem 7.3 was proved independently by Laffond, Laslier and Le Breton [111], who also proved Theorem 7.4, and Fisher and Ryan [81]; Theorem 7.5 is due to Banks, Duggan and Le Breton [24]. McKelvey [124] provided Theorem 7.6 and a version of Theorem 7.7; the version here is due to Banks, Duggan and Le Breton [25]. See also Cox [47]. Under restrictive assumptions (a continuum of voters and a concave distribution of ideal points), Kramer [107] establishes existence of a mixed strategy equilibrium for the two-candidate, multidimensional, spatial model in which indifferent voters vote with probability one-half for each candidate and candidates maximize vote-shares. The idea of "deep covering" is due to John Duggan and Theorem 7.8 is due to Duggan and Jackson [64].

The term "probabilistic voting" refers to a variety of models of elections in which either candidates treat voter decisions probabilistically, the approach introduced by Enelow and Hinich [66] and pursued by Hinich [95],

[96] and Enelow and Hinich [67], [68], or voters are modeled literally as voting stochastically, on which see Coughlin [45] who synthesizes and reviews a great deal of the relevant literature. Hinich and Ordeshook [97] consider a probabilistic (from the candidates' perspective) model of abstentions in the basic one-dimensional framework and Hinich, Ledyard and Ordeshook [99], [100] extend the idea to a multidimensional setting; Slutsky [194] observed some difficulties with their formulation. Coughlin and Nitzan [46] prove a version of Theorem 7.10. The formal development of the theory in section 7.5 relies heavily on Banks and Duggan [23]; Ball [16] observed some difficulties, illustrated by Exercise 7.9, with probabilistic voting models in which the source of uncertainty included voters' policy preferences. The application of section 7.6 is adapted from Lindbeck and Weibull [117].

Kramer [106] and Wittman [203] explore a dynamic spatial model of policy-motivated candidates; Wittman [204], Calvert [39] and Duggan and Fey [63] consider the canonical static model of two-candidate competition with policy-motivated candidates. Versions of Theorem 7.11 can be found in the latter two papers. Example 7.7 is due to Duggan and Fey [63]; Theorem 7.12 and Theorem 7.13 follow Calvert [39] and Wittman [204]. *Inter alia*, Roemer [175] offers an original theory of policy-motivated parties, rather than candidates, centering on a model of intra-party competition.

Downs [61] discussed the problem of accounting for turnout in large elections with costly voting. The rational choice literature attempting to account for observed voting patterns in such elections is extensive; a useful overview is Feddersen [73]. Riker and Ordeshook [174] assume an exogenous benefit to voting (the "D term", where D is for Duty), thus changing the relative costs and benefits of going to the polls directly; Ferejohn and Fiorina [77] change the presumed decision theory, assuming voters are not expected utility maximizers but rather take actions to minimize the maximum regret (formally defined) of an action; Palfrey and Rosenthal [160], [162] and Ledyard [116] treat turnout as a strategic, rather than a purely decision-theoretic, problem; Feddersen and Pesendorfer [74], [75] explore an informationally-grounded theory; Morton [135], [136] and Uhlaner [199] develop group-based models of turnout, effectively reducing the large-n problem to a small-n problem by assuming the existence of blocks of voters who behave the same way. Example 7.8 is adapted from Palfrey and Rosenthal [160]; Palfrey and Rosenthal [161] develop a more general theory of threshold contribution games and collective action. The theory of large Poisson games is due to Myerson [145], [147], [148]. Corollary 7.4 was first proved by Ledyard [116] using a combinatorial argument; the argument presented in the text, exploiting Theorem 7.14, is due to Myerson [147].

Chapter 8

Multicandidate Elections

Although theoretically significant, elections with exactly two candidates are relatively unusual. In general there are at least two candidates and the possibility of multiple electoral competitors raises a variety of substantive and analytic issues, issues that are finessed or largely irrelevant when considering elections with two given candidates seeking a single office. For example, the concept of the "wasted vote" and questions of candidate participation, or the number of candidates, in an election are finessed by assuming a given two-candidate contest. Similarly, proportional representation schemes for determining electoral success are irrelevant when only one office is at stake. As a result, important comparative questions regarding the relative merits of various electoral rules simply cannot be addressed. Furthermore, if the election is for a legislature and legislative policy decisions require, as is typical, majority support of the elected legislators, then rational voters and candidates make their respective electoral decisions taking account of the subsequent legislative bargaining and committee decision-making. Addressing these issues, among others, requires admitting a more general class of electoral rule for multicandidate competition and providing a more complex analysis of voter behavior.

In the case of exactly two candidates competing for a single office, we assumed that individuals could vote for at most one candidate with the electoral rule being defined by a simple preference aggregation rule applied to recorded profiles of votes. In effect, the winner of a two-candidate election for one position is defined under a simple electoral rule by the candidate receiving sufficient votes, where "sufficient" is defined by the rule and is not restricted to "most". When there are multiple candidates or parties, however, possibly competing for multiple elected offices or legislative seats, the restriction to casting at most one vote is too limiting and proportional representation schemes can be important. In this chapter, therefore, the class of electoral rules considered is that of *rank scoring rules*. Rank scoring rules (defined below) include many of the simple electoral rules of Chapter 7 but in principle allow individuals to cast multiple votes and admit proportional representation where relevant.

When a choice involves voting for one of two candidates, individuals' are either indifferent or have a unique undominated voting decision: vote for the candidate offering the most preferred platform, that is, vote "sincerely". Multiple candidates, however, imply multiple pivot events for a rational voter to consider in completing a ballot and confining attention to undominated strategies often provides relatively little if any analytical purchase. In particular, there is no reason to suppose sincere voting by all individuals constitutes undominated Nash equilibrium behavior at every distribution of candidate platforms. This is illustrated by the following example.

Example 8.1 Let the policy space be $X = [0, 1]$; assume $N = \{1, ..., 11\}$ and that there are three candidates identified with platforms $(a, b, c) = (\frac{1}{11}, \frac{6}{11}, \frac{9}{11})$. Suppose all individuals have Euclidean preferences on X with ideal points $x_i = i/11$, all $i \in N$. Finally, assume the election is for a single office and the winner is decided by plurality vote with ties being broken by a fair random device. Then if all $i \in N$ vote sincerely, $i = 1, 2, 3$ vote for a; $i = 4, ..., 7$ vote for b; and $i = 8, ..., 11$ vote for c. This results in a tie between b and c, so each of these candidates wins the election with probability $1/2$ and a loses for sure. However, individual $i = 1$ (for example) strictly prefers b to win surely than to have a 50% chance of ending up with c. Consequently, given all $i > 1$ vote sincerely over $\{a, b, c\}$, individual 1's best response is to vote for b; that is, voting sincerely is not an undominated strategy for 1 since to do so here is to "waste" her vote on a sure loser. □

Empirically, the extent to which voters can be expected to adopt rational, or best response, voting strategies rather than simply vote sincerely in multicandidate elections is unclear. However, as Example 8.1 makes apparent, the equilibrium electoral outcome in such contests can be highly sensitive to the presence of a tiny number of strategically rational voters. Consequently, even if the empirical incidence of strategically rational voting amongst a large electorate is small, an assumption that all voters vote sincerely is not necessarily innocuous. On the other hand, sincere voting behavior is analytically tractable and provides a useful benchmark from which to develop a deeper theory of multicandidate elections with strategically rational voters. So we begin by considering the strategic incentives facing a given set of candidates contesting an election for a single office under sincere voting.

8.1 Sincere voting in multicandidate elections

The simplest benchmark model for analysing competitive elections with more than two candidates is defined by fixing the number of candidates and assuming voters record their preferences directly, or sincerely, rather than strategically over any list of candidate platforms. Specifically, assume there are $m \geq 2$ office-seeking candidates competing for votes from a (typically) large set of policy-oriented voters, $N = \{1, \ldots, n\}$; let $M = \{1, \ldots, m\}$ denote the set of candidates. As usual, we assume throughout the chapter that the policy space $X \subset \Re^k$ is convex and compact. In particular, suppose for now that X is a closed interval on the real line, $X \subset \Re$. Each voter $i \in N$ has policy preferences on X representable by a strictly single-peaked utility function $u_i : X \to \Re$ with ideal point $x_i \in X$. The election is assumed decided by a normalized rank scoring rule without abstention.

Definition 8.1 *A normalized rank scoring rule for a fixed number of candidates m is defined by a vector $s = (s_1, \ldots, s_m)$ such that $1 = s_1 \geq s_2 \geq \ldots \geq s_{m-1} \geq s_m = 0$ and a mapping that assigns a set of winners for any profile of permissible ballots, where a permissible ballot is any permutation of the vector $(1, s_2, \ldots, s_{m-1}, 0)$.*

The normalization here refers to the joint restrictions $s_1 = 1$ and $s_2 = 0$ and is purely a convenience; the defining characteristics of rank scoring rules are that $s_t \geq s_{t+1}$ for all $t = 1, \ldots, m-1$ and $s_1 > s_m$. Not all rules of interest are rank scoring rules. For instance, *approval voting* is a scoring rule but not a rank scoring rule; under approval voting, the restriction that $s_1 > s_m$ is not required so voters may vote for, or approve of, any and all candidates should they so choose. Example 8.2 describes some special cases of (normalized) rank scoring rules.

Example 8.2 (1) *Single nontransferable vote.* Set $s_2 = \ldots = s_{m-1} = 0$; then the permissible ballots are permutations of the vector $(1, 0, \ldots, 0)$ and individuals must vote for exactly one of the m candidates with the $l < m$ winners being the candidates receiving the l most votes (all l^{th}-place ties being broken according to a fair random device).

(2) *Simple plurality rule.* Identical to single nontransferable vote with $l = 1$.

(3) *Single negative voting.* Set $s_2 = \ldots = s_{m-1} = 1$; then the permissible ballots are permutations of the vector $(1, \ldots, 1, 0)$ and individuals must vote for all but one of the m candidates with the $l < m$ winners being the candidates receiving the l most votes (all l^{th}-place ties being broken according to a fair random device).

(4) *The Borda rule.* Set $s_2 = (m-2)/(m-1), \ldots, s_{m-1} = 1/(m-1)$. The $l < m$ winners are the candidates receiving the l highest aggregate vote scores (all l^{th}-place ties being broken according to a fair random device). □

As Example 8.2 suggests, rank scoring rules generalizes the class of anonymous simple electoral rules for two-candidate elections; that is, simple electoral rules for which the numbers of votes for each candidate suffices to determine the electoral preference rather than exactly who cast what vote.

In this section we consider elections for a single office (making concerns with proportional representation moot) and, given the assumption of sincere voting, the relevant strategic concerns are with respect to equilibrium lists of candidate platforms. Let $a_c \in X$ denote candidate c's platform, $c \in M$. For each individual $i \in N$, for any list of candidate platforms $a = (a_1, \ldots, a_m)$ and rank scoring rule vector $s = (1, s_2, \ldots, s_{m-1}, 0)$, let $s^i(a) = (s_1^i(a), \ldots, s_m^i(a))$ denote i's sincere ballot. By definition, $s^i(a)$ is a permutation of the vector s such that

$$\forall c' \neq c, \ u_i(a_c) > u_i(a_{c'}) \Rightarrow s_c^i(a) = s_1 = 1,$$
$$\forall c' \neq c, \ u_i(a_c) < u_i(a_{c'}) \Rightarrow s_c^i(a) = s_m = 0$$

and for all candidates c, c',

$$u_i(a_c) \geq u_i(a_{c'}) \Rightarrow s_c^i(a) \geq s_{c'}^i(a).$$

In case $u_i(a_c) = u_i(a_{c'})$, the individual is assumed to use a fair lottery to determine $s_c^i(a)$ and $s_{c'}^i(a)$, subject to the preceding constraints.

Suppose that the electorate N is sufficiently large that it can be approximated as an infinite set. In particular, given the assumption of sincere voting and that preferences are strictly quasi-concave and continuous over X, the electorate can be sufficiently described by a cumulative distribution function $F : X \to [0, 1]$ where $F(x)$ is the proportion of the electorate with ideal points $x_i \leq x$. Assume F has full support, $F(0) = 0$, $F(1) = 1$ and the density dF is strictly positive and continuous on $(0, 1)$. Thus $u \in \mathcal{R}_{cs}^n$ implies

8.1. SINCERE VOTING IN MULTICANDIDATE ELECTIONS

the set of individuals who are indifferent between any two distinct policies in X is a negligible proportion of the electorate relative to the proportion of individuals having a strict preference between the two alternatives. Finally, to exclude some pathologies, suppose that for any distinct positions $a < b$, there exists a proper subset $A \subset [a, b]$ such that $x_i \in A$ implies $u_i(a) > u_i(b)$, $x_i \in [a, b] \setminus A$ implies $u_i(a) < u_i(b)$ and $\int_A dF(x) > 0$ and $\int_{[a,b] \setminus A} dF(x) > 0$. If individuals' preferences are symmetric about their ideal points, for example, then this exclusion property is automatically satisfied given $dF(x) > 0$ at every $x \in X$. Figure 8.1 illustrates the sort of pathology precluded by the assumption.

For all $x_i \in (a,b)$, $u_i(a) > u_i(b)$

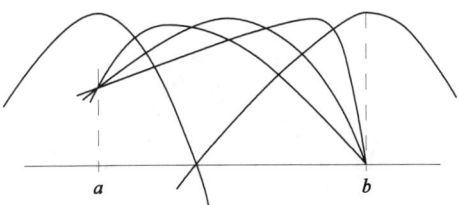

Figure 8.1: Example of excluded profiles

Candidates are assumed to maximize their respective expected pluralities, taking the platforms of others as fixed. With multiple candidates, c's expected plurality at a is defined by

$$\Pi_c(a) = V_c(a) - \max_{c' \neq c}\{V_{c'}(a)\},$$

where $V_c(a)$ is c's expected (sincere) vote share at the vector of platforms $a \in X^m$. Given that the proportion of individuals indifferent between any pair of distinct policies is negligible, $V_c(a)$ can be defined in terms of two sets of voters. For each candidate c, any list of platforms $a \in X^m$ and rank $j \in M$, let

$$\ell_c^j(a) = \{i \in N : x_i < a_c \text{ and } \Pr[s_c^i(a) = s_j] > 0\}$$

and

$$r_c^j(a) = \{i \in N : x_i > a_c \text{ and } \Pr[s_c^i(a) = s_j] > 0\}.$$

The union of $\ell_c^j(a)$ and $r_c^j(a)$, therefore, is the set of individuals who, with some positive probability, rank c's platform j^{th} best on their sincere ballots over the alternatives $\{a_1, \ldots, a_m\}$; individuals with ideal points to the left of a_c fall in $\ell_c^j(a)$ and those with ideal points to the right of a_c fall in $r_c^j(a)$. Now for any $a \in X^m$, let $K_c(a) \geq 1$ denote the number of candidates with platforms at a_c. Then for all $c \in M$ and all $a \in X^m$,

$$V_c(a) = \frac{1}{\left[K_c(a) \sum_{j=1}^{j=m} s_j\right]} \sum_{j=1}^{j=m} s_j \left[\int_{\ell_c^j(a)} dF(x) + \int_{r_c^j(a)} dF(x)\right].$$

A (sincere voting) *multicandidate electoral equilibrium* under a rank scoring rule, is a list of platforms $a^* = (a_1^*, \ldots, a_m^*) \in X^m$ such that, for all $c \in M$ and all $a_c \in X$,

$$\Pi_c(a_c^*, a_{-c}^*) \geq \Pi_c(a_c, a_{-c}^*).$$

Theorem 8.1 *If $a^* \in X^m$ is a multicandidate electoral equilibrium under a rank scoring rule, then*

$$a_c^* \in \left\{\min_{c' \in M}\{a_{c'}^*\}, \max_{c' \in M}\{a_{c'}^*\}\right\} \Rightarrow K_c(a^*) \geq 2$$

with equality for simple plurality rule.

Proof Without loss of generality, label candidates such that $a_1^* \leq a_2^* \leq \ldots \leq a_m^*$ and suppose the claim is false for some rank scoring rule; in particular, suppose without loss of generality that $K_1(a^*) = 1$. Then

$$V_1(a^*) = \frac{1}{\left[\sum_{j=1}^{j=m} s_j\right]} \left[s_1 F(a_1^*) + \sum_{j=1}^{j=m} s_j \int_{r_1^j(a^*)} dF(x)\right].$$

Let $a_1 \in (a_1^*, a_2^*)$. By assumption, u_i is single-peaked on X, all $i \in N$, and $a_1^* = \min_c\{a_c^*\}$. Hence, the maintained assumptions on the distribution function F imply $F(a_1) > F(a_1^*)$ and, for all $j = 1, \ldots, m$, $\int_{r_1^j(a_1, a_{-1}^*)} dF(x) \geq \int_{r_1^j(a^*)} dF(x)$. Therefore, $V_1(a_1, a_{-1}^*) > V_1(a^*)$ and, for all $c = 2, \ldots, m$, $V_c(a_1, a_{-1}^*) \leq V_c(a^*)$ with strict inequality for at least one candidate $c \neq 1$. But this contradicts a^* being a multicandidate equilibrium under the rule. A proof for the remaining claim, that if a^* is a multicandidate equilibrium under simple plurality rule then $K_1(a^*) = K_m(a^*) = 2$, is left as an exercise. □

8.1. SINCERE VOTING IN MULTICANDIDATE ELECTIONS

In words, Theorem 8.1 asserts that if all voters report sincere ballots under the given rank scoring rule and if a^* is a Nash equilibrium profile of candidate platforms when all candidates seek to maximize their own pluralities, then there must be at least two candidates adopting each of the extreme positions offered to the electorate at a^*. Furthermore, if the scoring rule is simple plurality then there must be exactly two candidates offering each of the extreme platforms. The intuition is familiar from the analysis of two-candidate competition with plurality maximizing candidates: if the candidates diverge and there is no abstention, then both candidates have an incentive to close the distance between them slightly since, by doing so, they can only increase their own vote share at the expense of that of their opponent. With only two candidates, both must offer the extreme platforms at any profile of platforms $a \in X^2$ and so Theorem 8.1 predicts candidate convergence in equilibrium, consistent with Corollary 7.1. With more than two candidates, however, the existence of electoral equilibria in which all candidates converge on a given platform is not guaranteed. Indeed, the theorem implies there exists no multicandidate equilibrium under simple plurality rule with three candidates.

Fix a normalized rank scoring rule with vector $s = (1, s_2, \ldots, s_{m-1}, 0)$. The *Cox threshold* for s is defined by

$$\mathcal{C}(s; m) = \frac{1}{m} \sum_{j=1}^{j=m} s_j,$$

the average score assigned under s.

Example 8.3 Assume $m \geq 2$. Then, under
  (1) *simple plurality rule,* $s = (1, 0, \ldots, 0)$, $\mathcal{C}(s; m) = 1/m$;
  (2) *single negative vote,* $s = (1, \ldots, 1, 0)$ and $\mathcal{C}(s; m) = (m-1)/m$;
  (3) *the Borda rule,* $s = (1, (m-2)/(m-1), \ldots, 1/(m-1), 0)$ and $\mathcal{C}(s; m) = 1/2$. □

It is important to note that the Cox threshold depends exclusively on the scoring vector s and not at all on either the rules governing how ballots are aggregated or the number of elected offices to be decided. For instance, given the number of candidates m, the Cox threshold for simple plurality rule applied to an election for one legislative seat is the same as that for the single nontransferable vote rule for multiple seats.

Theorem 8.2 provides an interpretation of the Cox threshold. For any number $t \in [0, 1]$, let F_t be the quantile implicitly defined by $\int_0^{F_t} dF(x) = t$.

CHAPTER 8. MULTICANDIDATE ELECTIONS

Theorem 8.2 *A convergent list of platforms $a^* = (F_t, F_t, \ldots, F_t) \in X^m$ is a multicandidate electoral equilibrium under a rank scoring rule if and only if $[1 - \mathcal{C}(s; m)] \leq t \leq \mathcal{C}(s; m)$.*

Proof Let $a^* = (F_t, F_t, \ldots, F_t)$. Then for all $c \in M$, $V_c(a^*) = \mathcal{C}(s; m)$ and $\Pi_c(a^*) = 0$. Consider the payoff to candidate c from a unilateral deviation to $a_c(\epsilon) = F_t + \epsilon$; there are two possibilities.

(1) If $\epsilon > 0$, then

$$\lim_{\epsilon \downarrow 0} V_c(a_c(\epsilon), a^*_{-c}) = s_1 \int_{F_t}^1 dF(x) + s_m \int_0^{F_t} dF(x) = s_1(1-t)$$

and, for all $c' \neq c$,

$$\lim_{\epsilon \downarrow 0} V_{c'}(a_c(\epsilon), a^*_{-c}) = \frac{1}{m-1} \left[t \sum_{j=1}^{j=m-1} s_j + (1-t) \sum_{j=2}^{j=m} s_j \right].$$

(2) If $\epsilon < 0$, then

$$\lim_{\epsilon \uparrow 0} V_c(a_c(\epsilon), a^*_{-c}) = s_1 \int_0^{F_t} dF(x) + s_m \int_{F_t}^1 dF(x) = s_1 t$$

and, for all $c' \neq c$,

$$\lim_{\epsilon \uparrow 0} V_{c'}(a_c(\epsilon), a^*_{-c}) = \frac{1}{m-1} \left[t \sum_{j=2}^{j=m} s_j + (1-t) \sum_{j=1}^{j=m-1} s_j \right].$$

Therefore, a^* can be a multicandidate electoral equilibrium if and only if, for all $c, c' = 1, \ldots, m$,

$$\lim_{\epsilon \downarrow 0} \left[V_c(a_c(\epsilon), a^*_{-c}) - V_{c'}(a_c(\epsilon), a^*_{-c}) \right] \leq 0$$

and

$$\lim_{\epsilon \uparrow 0} \left[V_c(a_c(\epsilon), a^*_{-c}) - V_{c'}(a_c(\epsilon), a^*_{-c}) \right] \leq 0.$$

Substituting for the relevant vote shares, collecting terms and using the normalization $s_1 = 1 > s_m = 0$, the left side of the first inequality can be written

$$s_1(1-t) - \frac{1}{m-1} \left[t \sum_{j=1}^{j=m-1} s_j + (1-t) \sum_{j=2}^{j=m} s_j \right] = \frac{1}{m-1} \left[m(1-t) - \sum_{j=1}^{j=m} s_j \right].$$

8.1. SINCERE VOTING IN MULTICANDIDATE ELECTIONS

Hence

$$\lim_{\epsilon \downarrow 0} \left[V_c(a_c(\epsilon), a^*_{-c}) - V_{c'}(a_c(\epsilon), a^*_{-c}) \right] \leq 0 \Leftrightarrow 1 - \mathcal{C}(s; m) \leq t.$$

Similarly derive

$$\lim_{\epsilon \uparrow 0} \left[V_c(a_c(\epsilon), a^*_{-c}) - V_{c'}(a_c(\epsilon), a^*_{-c}) \right] \leq 0 \Leftrightarrow t \leq \mathcal{C}(s; m).$$

Together, these inequalities prove the theorem. □

Theorem 8.2 implies that the smaller is $\mathcal{C}(s; m)$, the smaller is the incentive for all candidates to converge in equilibrium on a given platform, and conversely. In effect, the Cox threshold defines the largest share of the electorate whose preferences can be "ignored" in any convergent equilibrium. Suppose, for example, that $t > \mathcal{C}(s; m)$ and some candidate c unilaterally deviates by adopting a platform slightly to the left of F_t. Such a unilateral deviation induces voters to the left of F_t to move c to the top, and voters to the right of F_t to move c down, in their sincere ballots. But, as the proof of the theorem makes clear, the threshold $\mathcal{C}(s; m)$ defines the point at which the net gain is exactly zero and, therefore, $t > \mathcal{C}(s; m)$ implies c's deviation improves her expected payoff. On the other hand, if $t < \mathcal{C}(s; m)$ then any such deviation results in a net fall in the candidate's vote share relative to that of any candidate located at F_t. Thus the larger is the threshold, the more are candidates driven together in the policy space. From this perspective, the Cox threshold is a measure of the extent to which different rank scoring rules induce candidates to adopt divergent platforms in equilibrium. When the threshold is low, candidates can profitably campaign on platforms that appeal only to a relatively small percentage of the electorate whereas, when the threshold is high, candidates need to appeal to a broader segment of the population.

The following implications for existence of convergent multicandidate equilibria are immediate from Theorem 8.2.

Corollary 8.1 *(1) $\mathcal{C}(s; m) < 1/2$ implies there exist no convergent multicandidate equilibria;*

(2) $\mathcal{C}(s; m) = 1/2$ implies there exists a unique convergent multicandidate equilibrium, $(F_{1/2}, \ldots, F_{1/2})$;

(3) $\mathcal{C}(s; m) > 1/2$ implies there exist multiple convergent multicandidate equilibria.

Examples for each of the three cases are easy to find: from Example 8.3, if $m > 2$ then Corollary 8.1(1) applies to simple plurality rule, Corollary 8.1(2) applies to the Borda rule and Corollary 8.1(3) applies to single negative voting. And note that under simple plurality rule, $\mathcal{C}(s;2) = 1/2$ so Theorem 8.2 generalizes the classical median voter result for two-candidate elections. Furthermore, as the number of candidates increases, $\mathcal{C}(s;m)$ is strictly decreasing under plurality rule, constant under the Borda rule, and strictly increasing under single negative voting.

8.2 Application: Comparing electoral rules

An important set of questions for political analysis concerns the choice of an electoral rule for a society. Although there are a great many normative and positive criteria against which various rules might be compared, any choice is plausibly going to depend in part on an understanding of the policy consequences associated with the different rules. And Theorems 8.1 and 8.2, along with the concept of the Cox threshold, are useful in this regard.

Let $\bar{s} = \sum s_j/m$ denote the average score for a normalized rank scoring rule with score vector s. Then the Cox threshold can be written

$$\mathcal{C}(s;m) \equiv 1 - \left[\frac{s_1 - \bar{s}}{s_1 - s_m}\right].$$

Hence, $\mathcal{C}(s;m)$ is strictly decreasing in the ratio of the difference between the top- and the average-rank scores to the difference between the top- and the bottom-rank scores. When candidates have a strong incentive under some rule to be first rather than average relative to being last, the Cox threshold is low and, by Theorem 8.2, there is a corresponding incentive for candidates to distinguish themselves in the election. Conversely, when the rule is such that there is only a small difference between being top-ranked and being average relative to being last, the Cox threshold is high and Theorem 8.2 implies that candidates have an incentive to converge on a particular policy, although not necessarily a majoritarian platform.

For example, suppose all individuals in a large electorate have Euclidean preferences and assume the distribution of voter ideal points over the policy space is uniform. Three rank scoring rules for choosing a single legislative seat are under consideration: simple plurality rule, single negative voting and the Borda rule. The Cox thresholds for these three rules are, respectively, $1/m$, $(m-1)/m$ and $1/2$. Let $A^*(s,m) \subseteq X = [0,1]$ be the set of multicandidate electoral equilibria when the scoring vector is s and there

8.2. APPLICATION: COMPARING ELECTORAL RULES

are m candidates for the office. Then Theorems 8.1 and 8.2 can be used to show [Exercise]:

(1) under simple plurality rule, $A^*(s,4) = \{(1/4, 1/4, 3/4, 3/4)\}$;
(2) under single negative voting, $A^*(s,4) = \{(z, z, z, z) : z \in [1/4, 3/4]\}$;
(3) under the Borda rule, $A^*(s,4) = \{(1/2, 1/2, 1/2, 1/2)\}$.

Thus the only (sincere voting, multicandidate) equilibrium under simple plurality rule is divergent with candidates seeking the support of minorities: whichever candidate wins, there is a feasible policy that a majority of voters strictly prefers to the electoral outcome. Under single negative voting, there is a continuum of equilibria, all of which are convergent and almost all of which result in an electoral outcome that some majority strictly dislikes. Finally, the unique equilibrium policy under the Borda rule is the median policy, so with this rule there exist no majorities that strictly prefer some other alternative to the electoral outcome. Figure 8.2 illustrates the various equilibria.

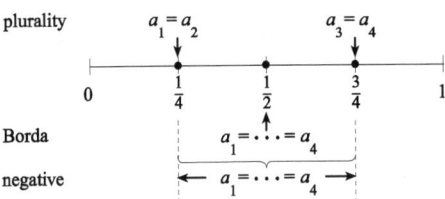

Figure 8.2: Four-candidate equilibria under three rules

Now suppose the number of candidates increases by two to $m = 6$. Then the sets of equilibria $A^*(s, 6)$ for each of the three rules are described in Figure 8.3.

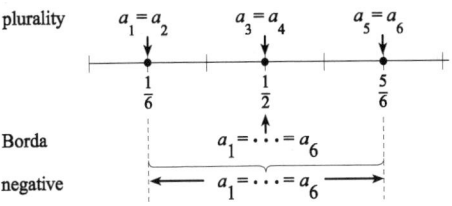

Figure 8.3: Six-candidate equilibria under three rules

As predicted in Theorem 8.2, since an increase in m results in a fall in the Cox threshold for simple plurality rule, the incentive for any one candidate to appeal to a minority of the electorate is reinforced, driving extreme candidates further toward the edges of the policy space. Under single negative voting, however, an increase in m increases the Cox threshold which in turn widens the interval over which convergent equilibria exist, leading to the possibility of a yet worse policy outcome from a majoritarian perspective. But since the Cox threshold for the Borda rule is constant in the number of candidates, the median policy remains the unique equilibrium outcome (given $m \geq 2$).

8.3 Strategic voting

Theorem 8.2 is not a general equilibrium existence theorem for multicandidate electoral equilibria: if $\mathcal{C}(s;m) < 1/2$ then any multicandidate equilibrium must involve at least some diversity in platform and the existence of such non-convergent equilibria is typically contingent on details of the distribution of voter preferences and the particular number of candidates, m. For example, Theorems 8.1 and 8.2 directly imply that there exist no multicandidate equilibria under simple plurality rule when $m = 3$. But as illustrated in the previous section, if $m = 4$, if individual preferences are all Euclidean and if the distribution of ideal points F is uniform on the policy space $X = [0, 1]$, then there is a unique (up to permutations) multicandidate equilibrium under simple plurality rule, $a^* = (1/4, 1/4, 3/4, 3/4)$. In view of the sensitivity to distributions of voter preferences and the number of candidates, a general existence result for pure strategy equilibria is likely unavailable. Although disappointing, the value-added to Theorems 8.1 and 8.2 of such a result is unclear, however, as a closer consideration of the four candidate, simple plurality rule example with a uniform voter distribution suggests.

Example 8.4 Assume there is a large but finite number of voters, each with quadratic preferences over the policy space $[0, 1]$. Voter ideal points are uniformly distributed on $[0, 1]$. There are four candidates, $c = 1, 2, 3, 4$, for a single office competing under simple plurality rule. Then, as above, there is a unique distribution of multicandidate equilibrium platforms, $a^* = (1/4, 1/4, 3/4, 3/4)$. By definition, in a multicandidate electoral equilibrium all voters are presumed to vote sincerely. Consequently, candidate 3, say, offering the platform $a_3^* = 3/4$ has no incentive to deviate unilaterally to a policy $a_3' < a_3^*$ closer to the median, $\mu = 1/2$: given a uniform preference

8.3. STRATEGIC VOTING

distribution and sincere voting, any gain in relative moderates' votes from such a move is exactly offset by a loss in relative extremists' votes and, further, the votes lost from extremists are picked up by candidate 4 offering $a_4^* = 3/4$; therefore $\Pi_3(a_3', a_{-3}^*) < \Pi_3(a^*)$. But although sincere voting over the list of platforms a^* is easily seen to be rational, in the sense that every individual is casting a best-response ballot given the decisions of others, this is not true of all voters at every list of platforms.

Specifically, suppose candidate $c = 3$ unilaterally deviates to the median platform $a_3' = \mu$, yielding a list of alternatives $a' = (1/4, 1/4, 1/2, 3/4)$. If, as presumed for multicandidate equilibria, all individuals vote sincerely at a', symmetric preferences and a uniform distribution of ideal points imply

$$V_1(a') = V_2(a') = \frac{3}{16} < V_3(a') = \frac{1}{4} < V_4(a') = \frac{3}{8}$$

so $\Pi_4(a') > 0 > \Pi_c(a')$ for all candidates $c \neq 4$ and the sincere voting outcome is surely $a_4' = 3/4$. But all voters with ideal points $x_i < 5/8$ strictly prefer $a_3' = 1/2$ to $a_4' = 3/4$. Moreover, the vote profile in which individuals with ideal points $x_i < 5/8$ vote surely for $c = 3$ and all those with ideal points $x_i \geq 5/8$ vote surely for $c = 4$ constitutes undominated Nash equilibrium behavior at a'. So although general sincere voting at a' is Nash behavior, it is not clear why such voting behavior is the most reasonable prediction for this distribution of platforms. And presumably rational office-seeking candidates (like $c = 3$) can appreciate voter incentives and respond accordingly, upsetting the sincere multicandidate electoral equilibrium. □

Unlike Example 8.1, no individuals in Example 8.4 are "wasting their vote" by voting sincerely at the symmetric list of platforms, a^*; indeed, given a^*, voting sincerely is an undominated best response for every voter. Instead, the issue highlighted by Example 8.4 concerns out-of-equilibrium voting. A strategy profile is only an equilibrium if no agent, voter or candidate, can improve his or her payoff by a unilateral deviation from that profile. Whether profitable deviations exist for an electoral candidate depends on how voters are expected to respond to a change in platform. By definition, a multicandidate electoral equilibrium prescribes sincere voting at every list of m platforms and it this that supports a^* constituting such an equilibrium. But Examples 8.1 and 8.4 suggest that the sincere voting prescription is inappropriate and possibly misleading: if voters do in fact vote sincerely then this is something to be explained, not assumed.

Understanding strategic voting in multicandidate elections with a large finite electorate can be very hard. Existence of undominated voting equilibria is not the concern: Theorem 7.2 insures that undominated equilibria exist for any list of candidate platforms and any finite number of voters. The concern, rather, is to *identify* the set of voting equilibria for any distribution of candidate platforms and any electoral rule. For without a characterization of voting equilibria, comparative results on the relative merits of various ways of conducting elections are necessarily contingent, depending on exactly how individuals are presumed to respond to alternative candidate proposals. Intuitively, an instrumentally rational voter does not waste votes on sure losers or sure winners, but allocates them as permitted to preferred candidates in close or pivotal electoral races. Whether or not a particular race, or contest, is close, however, depends on the distribution of votes across candidates and it is this endogeneity coupled with the multiplicity of candidates, and hence the multiplicity of conceivably close races, that gives rise to the analytical complexity of the problem. Such complexity can arise in a two-candidate election with well-defined platforms only if voting is costly, as the only issue is whether, and not which, competition is close. But even if voting is not costly, when there are multiple candidates there are multiple possible close races and rational voters have to assess the relative likelihoods of being pivotal in each instance. For this reason, a general characterization theorem, that is, a theorem that describes the set of voting equilibria for any electoral rule or slate of alternatives, is almost surely unavailable. Instead, we look for more limited results casting light on classes of rule for empirically important environments.

It is convenient to use the Poisson voting model (n, T, Z, U), introduced in section 7.9 above, in which the realized size of the electorate is determined by a random draw from a Poisson distribution with mean n, individuals are characterized by their types $t \in T$, there is a finite set of feasible actions (ballots) Z, and U describes individuals' preferences as a function of outcome, action and type.

Suppose m candidates compete under single nontransferable vote for $1 \leq l < m$ elected offices, or seats. Then the set of actions or permissible ballots, Z, is the set of permutations of the scoring vector $(1, 0, \ldots, 0)$ and the winning l candidates are those receiving the most votes, with ties for the marginal l^{th} place winner being decided by a fair lottery: see Example 8.2(1). Assume the candidates' electoral platforms have been chosen and are fixed. Given fixed positions, there is no ambiguity in identifying candidates with their platforms and, for the rest of the section, we write "candidate $c \in X$" as a shorthand for "candidate c's platform, $a_c \in X$", and so on. Further, there is no reason here to insist that X is one-dimensional.

Voters are characterized by their von Neumann-Morgenstern utilities over the given list of candidates, $M = \{1, \ldots, m\}$. An individual's type

8.3. STRATEGIC VOTING

$t \in T$ is a specification of that individual's preferences over M, described by a vector of utilities, $u_t = (u(1, t), \ldots, u(m, t))$. Assume no individual is indifferent over any pair of candidates and that T is finite; since the electorate is presumed large, these restrictions involve a negligible loss of generality. Normalize utilities such that, for all $t \in T$,

$$\max_{c \in M} u(c, t) = 1 \text{ and } \min_{c \in M} u(c, t) = 0$$

and $c \neq c'$ implies $u(c, t) \neq u(c', t)$. For any elected subset L of l candidates, a type t voter's payoff from L is just the arithmetic sum of his or her payoffs from each elected candidate. Therefore, for any profile of ballot totals $\mathbf{v}(\mathbf{z})$ yielding an elected set of l candidates $L(\mathbf{v}(\mathbf{z})) \subset M$, a type t voter's payoff from reporting a ballot z under (costless) single nontransferable voting is

$$U(L(\mathbf{v}(\mathbf{z})), z, t) = \sum_{c \in L(\mathbf{v}(\mathbf{z}))} u(c, t).$$

By Lemma 7.6, there exists a Poisson voting equilibrium in distributional strategies, $\tau_{n|M}$. Because an individual ballot under single nontransferable voting reports a vote for exactly one of the m available candidates, we can let $\tau_n(c)$ denote the equilibrium vote share of candidate $c \in M$ at $\tau_n \equiv \tau_{n|M}$ and write

$$\tau_n = (\tau_n(1), \ldots, \tau_n(m)).$$

We are interested in large elections and so focus on the limit of an infinite convergent sequence of voting equilibria,

$$\lim_{n \to \infty} \tau_n = (\tau(1), \ldots, \tau(m)).$$

Call such a limiting profile of vote shares a *limit Poisson voting equilibrium*.

As remarked earlier, a rational individual seeks to vote for his or her preferred candidate in a close or pivotal race; the difficulty is that while a voter can vote for exactly one of m candidates under single nontransferable voting, there can be multiple close races in an election for $l < m$ legislative seats. Moreover, just as in the case of two-candidate elections, the probability that in fact *any* race is close in a large election rapidly decreases in the size of the electorate. For sufficiently large electorates, therefore, it is not so much the likelihood of a close race that is critical, for this becomes negligible as n goes to infinity, but the relative likelihoods of the various candidates being in close races conditional on the existence of a close race at all that matter most.

The preceding observations suggest the following intuition. Consider a sincere voting profile over m candidates for l seats and suppose the candidates can be strictly ranked according to sincere vote shares from most to least. Then the most important race is that between the lth and the $(l+1)^{\text{th}}$ ranked candidates, since this race determines the marginal elected candidate. Consequently, rational voters might be expected to switch votes as necessary to their favored alternative between this pair of candidates, inducing a relative fall in the vote shares of other candidates. Other things equal, therefore, those ranked below $(l+1)$ become even less likely winners and those ranked above l find their vote shares converging; hence it becomes relatively less likely that (sincerely) lower-ranked candidates are in close races but relatively more likely that (sincerely) top-ranked candidates find themselves in a close race. In principle, these adjustments settle down when the top $(l+1)$ candidates are receiving approximately the same expected vote share and the remaining $(m-l-1)$ candidates are out of contention for elected office. Theorem 8.3 justifies the spirit of this intuition, although it falls short of providing a formal justification for the argument as a whole.

Theorem 8.3 *Let $(\tau(1),\ldots,\tau(m))$ be a limit Poisson voting equilibrium to an election with m candidates and l seats under single nontransferable voting, $1 \leq l < m$; relabeling candidates as necessary, suppose $\tau(1) \geq \ldots \geq \tau(m)$. Then $\tau(1) = \ldots = \tau(l)$ and, for all $c \in \{l+1,\ldots,m\}$, $\tau(c) \in \{0, \tau(l+1)\}$.*

In words, the theorem states that in large single nontransferable vote elections with m candidates competing for $l < m$ elected offices, or seats, exactly l candidates are expected to tie for first place and any candidate c among the remaining $m-l$ competitors either receives the same expected vote share as that of the $(l+1)^{\text{th}}$ ranked candidate, $\tau(c) = \tau(l+1) \leq \tau(l)$, or receives nothing at all, $\tau(c) = 0$. Thus, the first part of the intuition underlying strategic voting sketched above is supported by the result: the top l candidates are expected to tie with expected vote shares greater than the remaining candidates. On the other hand, the theorem leaves open the possibility of equilibria in which lesser-ranked candidates, that is, those ranked below $(l+1)$, nevertheless receive a strictly positive expected vote share in the limit, so remaining viable for elected office once realized votes are tallied. Exactly what this might mean for understanding multicandidate elections is deferred to section 8.4, below. First however, the theorem needs to be proved.

8.3. STRATEGIC VOTING

The proof of Theorem 8.3 uses some new concepts. Given voters vote for exactly one of the m candidates under single nontransferable voting, the set of permissible ballots Z is equivalent to the set of candidates $\{1,\ldots,m\}$ and a profile of ballot totals $\mathbf{v}(\mathbf{z}) = (v(z))_{z \in Z}$ can be written equivalently as a profile of vote totals for each candidate,

$$\mathbf{v} = (V_1, \ldots, V_m) \in \{0, 1, 2, \ldots\}^m,$$

and, because ties are decided by a fair lottery, the probability a particular candidate c is elected at $\mathbf{v}$, $\omega(c|\mathbf{v})$, satisfies

$$\omega(c|\mathbf{v}) > 0 \Leftrightarrow |\{c' \neq c : V_{c'} > V_c\}| < l.$$

A candidate c is said to be *winning* at $\mathbf{v}$ if $\omega(c|\mathbf{v}) > 0$. In other words, c is winning if there are at least $m - l$ candidates receiving strictly smaller numbers of votes than c, in which case $\omega(c|\mathbf{v}) = 1$, or if c is tied as the lth largest vote recipient, in which case $\omega(c|\mathbf{v})$ is one divided by the number of candidates tied for l^{th} place.

Let $\mathcal{V} = \{0, 1, 2, \ldots\}^m$. At any distributional strategy profile τ_n, the vote total of any candidate is random variable and, given an expected number of voters n, an *event* is a subset of profiles, $B \subseteq \mathcal{V}$. We are especially interested in events in which individual votes can be pivotal in the limit. In particular, for any pair of candidates $\{i, j\}$, say that the race between i and j is close if adding one extra vote to one of these candidates can make one winning at the expense of the other. Formally, an $\{i, j\}$ race is *close* at $\mathbf{v} \in \mathcal{V}$ if and only if either

$$\omega(i|V_i + 1, \mathbf{v}_{-i}) > \omega(i|\mathbf{v}) \text{ and } \omega(j|V_i + 1, \mathbf{v}_{-i}) < \omega(j|\mathbf{v})$$

or

$$\omega(j|V_j + 1, \mathbf{v}_{-j}) > \omega(j|\mathbf{v}) \text{ and } \omega(i|V_j + 1, \mathbf{v}_{-j}) < \omega(i|\mathbf{v}).$$

Let $\Omega(i, j) \subset \mathcal{V}$ denote the event that the $\{i, j\}$ race is close and let $\Omega = \cup_{\{c,c'\}} \Omega(c, c')$ be the union of all such events over every pair of candidates.

Not all close races are equally important in sufficiently large electorates, however; for instance, a close race between the last and the second-to-last ranked vote recipients is irrelevant if the number of candidates is at least three more than the number of available seats. So define an $\{i, j\}$ race to be *serious* at $\mathbf{v} \in \mathcal{V}$ if and only if, given a convergent sequence of Poisson voting equilibria, $(\tau_n)_n$, the probability of the race being close conditional on there being at least one close race is strictly positive in the limit:

$$\limsup_{n \to \infty} \frac{\Pr[\Omega(i,j)|n\tau_n]}{\Pr[\Omega|n\tau_n]} > 0.$$

A candidate c is *serious* if and only if there exists at least one serious race involving c: it turns out that if a race is not serious, then it becomes irrelevant for a rational voter's decision as the expected electorate becomes arbitrarily large and, consequently, any vote for a candidate who is not serious is wasted. It remains to identify which races are serious, taking account of the fact that the probability of any race being close typically vanishes as the expected size of the electorate goes to infinity. The relevant concept here is that of the magnitude of an event: given a convergent sequence of Poisson voting equilibria $(\tau_n)_n$, the *magnitude* of an event $B \subseteq \mathcal{V}$ is

$$mag[B] = \lim_{n \to \infty} \frac{\ln(\Pr[B|n\tau_n])}{n}.$$

Loosely speaking, $mag[B]$ is a measure of the rate at which the likelihood of the event B vanishes as n goes to infinity. Therefore if, for two events A and B, $mag[A] > mag[B]$ then, in the limit as $n \to \infty$, the likelihood of event B becomes negligible relative to that of event A. In particular, if $mag[\Omega(c,c')] > mag[\Omega(d,d')]$ then the $\{d,d'\}$ race is not serious.

Lemma 8.1, a proof of which can be found in Myerson [147], [148], is the key fact underlying the argument below for Theorem 8.3. For $c,c' \in \{i,j\}$, $c \neq c'$, let $\Phi_c(i,j) \subset \mathcal{V}$ be the event defined by $V_c + 1 \geq V_{c'}$.

Lemma 8.1 *For any two candidates i,j such that $\tau(i) > \tau(j)$ in the limit Poisson voting equilibrium,*

$$mag[\Phi_j(i,j)] = -(\sqrt{\tau(i)} - \sqrt{\tau(j)})^2.$$

We are now in a position to prove the theorem.

Proof of Theorem 8.3 Let $(\tau(1),\ldots,\tau(m))$ be a limit Poisson voting equilibrium; without loss of generality assume $\tau(1) \geq \ldots \geq \tau(m)$. Because a vote cast in a race that is already decided leaves a voter's expected payoff unaffected, a strategically rational individual of type t chooses a ballot in the set

$$\arg\max_{c \in Z} E[U(L(\mathbf{v}^{(c)}),c,t)|\tau_n]$$
$$= \arg\max_{c \in Z} \sum_{\mathbf{v}^{(c)} \in \mathcal{V}} \Pr[\mathbf{v}^{(c)}|n\tau_n] \sum_{j \in L(\mathbf{v}^{(c)})} \omega(j|\mathbf{v}^{(c)})u(j,t)$$
$$= \arg\max_{c \in Z} \sum_{\mathbf{v}^{(c)} \in \Omega} \Pr[\mathbf{v}^{(c)}|n\tau_n] \sum_{j \in L(\mathbf{v}^{(c)})} \omega(j|\mathbf{v}^{(c)})u(j,t)$$

8.3. STRATEGIC VOTING

where, for any candidate c, $\mathbf{v}^{(c)} = (V_c + 1, \mathbf{v}_{-c}) \in \mathcal{V}$. Let $\Omega^* \subseteq \Omega$ be the set of serious races. Then, by definition of a serious race,

$$\lim_{n \to \infty} \left[\arg\max_{c \in Z} \sum_{\mathbf{v}^{(c)} \in \Omega} \Pr[\mathbf{v}^{(c)} | n\tau_n] \sum_{j \in L(\mathbf{v}^{(c)})} \omega(j|\mathbf{v}^{(c)}) u(j,t) \right]$$
$$= \arg\max_{c \in Z} \sum_{\mathbf{v}^{(c)} \in \Omega^*} \Pr[\mathbf{v}^{(c)} | n\tau_n] \sum_{j \in L(\mathbf{v}^{(c)})} \omega(j|\mathbf{v}^{(c)}) u(j,t).$$

It follows that in any limit Poisson voting equilibrium, if a candidate c is not serious then $\tau(c) = 0$.

Consider any $c > l + 1$. Candidate c can be in a close race with some candidate $i \leq l$ only if there exists $i \in \{1, \ldots, l\}$ such that $V_c + 1 \geq V_i$. By Lemma 8.1,

$$\begin{aligned} mag[\Phi_c(i,c)] &= -(\sqrt{\tau(i)} - \sqrt{\tau(c)})^2 \\ &\leq -(\sqrt{\tau(l)} - \sqrt{\tau(c)})^2 \\ &= mag[\Phi_c(l,c)]. \end{aligned}$$

Hence, for all candidates $c' \neq c$, $mag[\Omega(c,c')] \leq mag[\Phi_c(l,c)]$. Therefore, $\tau(c) < \tau(l+1)$ implies that for all $c' \neq c$,

$$\begin{aligned} mag[\Omega(c,c')] &< -(\sqrt{\tau(l)} - \sqrt{\tau(l+1)})^2 \\ &= mag[\Omega(l,l+1)]. \end{aligned}$$

It follows that, for all $c > l + 1$, if $\tau(c) < \tau(l+1)$ then c is not serious. Therefore, $c > l + 1$ and $\tau(c) \leq \tau(l+1)$ imply $\tau(c) \in \{0, \tau(l+1)\}$.

Now consider any $c < l$. Arguing similarly as before, if c is in a close race with a candidate $i > l$, there must exist $i \in \{l+1, \ldots, m\}$ such that $V_i + 1 \geq V_c$: for otherwise c wins whether or not she receives an extra vote; that is, $\omega(c|\mathbf{v}^{(c)})|_\tau = \omega(c|\mathbf{v})|_\tau = 1$. By Lemma 8.1, if the $\{c, i\}$ race is close, $i > l$, then

$$\begin{aligned} mag[\Phi_i(c,i)] &= -(\sqrt{\tau(c)} - \sqrt{\tau(i)})^2 \\ &\leq -(\sqrt{\tau(c)} - \sqrt{\tau(l+1)})^2 \\ &= mag[\Phi_{l+1}(c,l+1)]. \end{aligned}$$

Hence, for all candidates $c' \neq c$, $mag[\Omega(c,c')] \leq mag[\Phi_{l+1}(c,l+1)]$. Therefore, $\tau(c) > \tau(l)$ implies that for all $c' \neq c$,

$$\begin{aligned} mag[\Omega(c,c')] &< -(\sqrt{\tau(l)} - \sqrt{\tau(l+1)})^2 \\ &= mag[\Omega(l,l+1)]. \end{aligned}$$

It follows that, for all $c < l$, if $\tau(c) > \tau(l)$ then c is not serious. But then $\tau(c) = 0$, contradicting $\tau(c) > \tau(l) \geq 0$. Therefore, $c < l$ and $\tau(c) \geq \tau(l)$ imply $\tau(c) = \tau(l)$.

Collecting the preceding arguments, we have that if $(\tau(1), \ldots, \tau(m))$ is a limit Poisson voting equilibrium then

$$\tau(1) = \ldots = \tau(l) \geq \tau(l+1)$$

and, for all $c > l+1$, $\tau(c) \in \{0, \tau(l+1)\}$. And this is exactly what the theorem claims. $\square$

8.4 Application: Duverger's Law

At least at the district level, if not so clearly at the national level, it seems that simple plurality rule elections for a single winner are associated with two viable candidates. Even if the election should begin with multiple candidates, by the time votes are cast only two candidates have any real chance of success. Setting l equal to one in Theorem 8.3 provides a rationale for this observation, known as *Duverger's Law*. As stated, however, the theorem is not a full explanation: although there are equilibria with only $l+1$ serious candidates, as Duverger's Law suggests, Theorem 8.3 also admits the possibility of equilibria with more than $l+1$ serious candidates. A more complete explanation grounded on instrumentally rational voting needs an equilibrium refinement proscribing those equilibria with more than $l+1$ serious candidates. Equilibrium stability considerations suggest such a refinement.

Suppose $\tau = (\tau(1), \ldots, \tau(m))$ is a limit Poisson voting equilibrium. From the proof to the theorem, if $\tau(c) < \tau(l+1)$ for a candidate $c > l+1$, then c is not serious and c's expected vote share is negligible, $\tau(c) \approx 0$. Consequently, if there are more than $l+1$ serious candidates at τ, there must exist $c > l+1$ for whom $\tau(c) = \tau(l+1)$. Now suppose there is a small stochastic shock to the system resulting in a perturbed vector of vote shares,

$$\tilde{\tau} = (\tau(1) + \epsilon_1, \ldots, \tau(m) + \epsilon_m)$$

where, for all serious candidates j, $\epsilon_j \in (-\eta, \eta)$, $\eta > 0$ and, for all non-serious candidates j, $\epsilon_j = [0, \eta)$. Then $\tilde{\tau}$ is (almost surely) not a limit Poisson equilibrium. However, although, for sufficiently small η, the l top-ranked candidates at τ remain serious at $\tilde{\tau}$ and the non-serious candidates at τ remain non-serious at $\tilde{\tau}$, the perturbation (almost surely) results in

8.5. CANDIDATE ENTRY

some candidate $c > l + 1$ for which

$$\tau(c) + \epsilon_c > \max_{\substack{j > l+1 \\ j \neq c}} [\tau(j) + \epsilon_j].$$

But then candidates $j > l + 1$, $j \neq c$, are no longer serious and we expect the equilibration process to drive their vote shares to zero. In other words, equilibria involving more than $l + 1$ serious candidates appear fragile with respect to arbitrarily small stochastic shocks, whereas those with at most $l+1$ serious candidates seem robust. Having said this, it should be emphasized that the preceding argument is at most plausible, not rigorous.

Single nontransferable voting is the extension of simple plurality rule to multi-seat elections. So while Duverger's Law was formulated as a property of plurality rule, single seat, elections, Theorem 8.3 shows the intuition applies more generally to elections under single nontransferable voting for multiple seats. Duverger's Law, that is, is a consequence of rational voters with only one vote to cast seeking to avoid wasting that vote on candidates who are either sure to be successful or sure to be losers and this incentive is not confined to single seat elections.

8.5 Candidate entry

If, as Theorem 8.3 suggests, some candidates in any election are almost sure to lose, why are they contesting the election at all? More generally, the assumption of a fixed number of electoral candidates or parties needs to be relaxed for a more complete theory of electoral competition. In this section, then, we look at candidate entry for a single-winner election under plurality rule with strategically rational voters.

One immediate answer to the question of why candidates run for office could be that contesting an election is costless, so there is no reason *not* to run; but such a response is hardly compelling. The assumption of costless campaigns implicitly adopted hitherto is justified almost entirely by the presumption that the list of candidates in a race is fixed, with any campaign expenses incurred at the (historically given) decision to enter. Once the decision to enter is itself subject to strategic consideration, the assumption of costless campaigns becomes less tenable. Therefore, in view of the canonical model of electoral competition developed in the previous chapter, a reasonable starting point for developing any understanding of the number of candidates contesting an election is to maintain the assumption that candidates are only interested in winning office but introduce at least a minimal cost to running for election.

Suppose the policy space is one-dimensional, say $X = [0,1]$, and that individuals' preferences on X are single-peaked and risk-averse everywhere: $u \in \mathcal{R}_{cs}^n$ and, for all $x \in X$ and all $i \in N$, $u_i''(x) < 0$. As usual, for all $i \in N$, let $x_i \in X$ denote i's most preferred policy and let $\mu \in X$ denote a median voter's most preferred policy; assume μ is unique and strictly interior to X. The electorate is assumed finite and there is also a finite set of potential candidates, $M = \{1, \ldots, m\}$; assume $m \le n$. Later, we identify the set of potential candidates with the set of voters, thus rationalizing an assumption of policy-motivated candidates. Here, however, candidates are assumed purely office-motivated and any policy concerns the potential candidates may have are irrelevant in comparison to the desire to win the election. A (potential) candidate c's strategy is a choice

$$a_c \in X \cup \{\emptyset\}$$

where $a_c = \emptyset$ denotes that $c \in M$ chooses not to enter the election and $a_c \in X$ if and only if c enters the race where, as usual, a_c is the platform on which c contests the election. Voters are strategically rational and the election is under plurality rule for one office with no abstention. Hence voter i's strategy is a decision

$$v_i : (X \cup \{\emptyset\})^m \to \mathbf{S} = \{(s_1, \ldots, s_m) : s_j \in \{0,1\} \; \forall j; \; \sum_{j=1}^{j=m} s_j = 1\}.$$

Let $v_i(a) = (v_{i1}(a), \ldots, v_{im}(a)) \in \mathbf{S}$ be i's vote given candidate decisions $a \in (X \cup \{\emptyset\})^m$ and write $v(a) = (v_1(a), \ldots, v_n(a)) \in \mathbf{S}^n$. By convention, assume $a_c = \emptyset$ implies $v_{ic}(a) = 0$: individuals only vote for a candidate who enters and cannot declare support for any undeclared potential entrant.

Candidates are only interested in winning and the election is for exactly one seat under plurality rule, with ties broken by a fair lottery. Recall that

$$\Pi_c(a) = \sum_{i \in N} v_{ic}(a) - \max_{c' \ne c} \sum_{i \in N} v_{ic'}(a)$$

is candidate c's plurality given a profile of platforms a and a distribution of votes $v(a)$, let $L(a, v(a)) \subseteq M$ be the set of winning candidates:

$$L(a, v(a)) = \{c \in M : \forall c' \ne c, \; \Pi_c(a) \ge \Pi_{c'}(a)\}.$$

Where there is no ambiguity, we write $L(a, v)$ for $L(a, v(a))$. Then candidate c's preferences are described by a function $W_c : (X \cup \{\emptyset\})^m \to \Re$ such that, for all $(a, v) \in (X \cup \{\emptyset\})^m \times \mathbf{S}^n$,

8.5. CANDIDATE ENTRY

$$W_c(a_c, a_{-c}) = \begin{cases} \frac{B}{|L(a,v)|} - d & \text{if } a_c \neq \emptyset \text{ and } c \in L(a,v) \\ -d & \text{if } a_c \neq \emptyset \text{ and } c \notin L(a,v) \\ 0 & \text{if } a_c = \emptyset \end{cases}$$

where $B > 1$ is the benefit of election and $d \in (0, B)$ is a given cost of choosing to run for election. Assuming (justifiably, as shown below) at least one potential candidate always runs for office, voter i's preferences are simply

$$E[u_i|a, v] = \frac{1}{|L(a,v)|} \sum_{c \in L(a,v)} u_i(a_c).$$

Clearly, $d < B$ is a necessary condition for at least one candidate to have any incentive at all to run for office. On the other hand, if $d = 0$ and $m = 2$, the preferences of both candidates and voters are identical to those assumed in the canonical model of two-candidate elections with office-motivated candidates (section 7.1). Not surprisingly, therefore, the equilibrium concept here generalizes that of a two-candidate electoral equilibrium. Specifically, a *multicandidate electoral equilibrium with entry* is a pair $(a^*, v^*) \in (X \cup \{\emptyset\})^m \times \mathbf{S}^n$ such that

(1) for all $c \in M$ and all $a_c \in X$,

$$W_c(a_c^*, a_{-c}^*) \geq W_c(a_c, a_{-c}^*);$$

(2) for all $i \in N$ and all $v_i \in \mathbf{S}$,

$$E[u_i|a^*, (v_i^*, v_{-i}^*)] \geq E[u_i|a^*, (v_i, v_{-i}^*)];$$

(3) no candidate or individual uses a weakly dominated strategy.

Thus, in the case that $m = 2$ and $d = 0$, a multicandidate electoral equilibrium is exactly a two-candidate electoral equilibrium as promised.

With risk-averse and strategic voters, the assumptions that running for office is costly and that purely office-motivated potential candidates have the option not to contest the election at all have a striking implication.

Theorem 8.4 *Assume* $u \in \mathcal{R}_{cs}^n$ *with a unique median μ and, for all $x \in X = [0,1]$ and all $i \in N$, $u_i''(x) < 0$. A pair $(a^*, v^*) \in (X \cup \{\emptyset\})^m \times \mathbf{S}^n$ is a multicandidate electoral equilibrium with entry if and only if*

(1) $a_c^* \in X$ *implies* $c \in L(a^*, v^*)$, $1 \leq |L(a^*, v^*)| \leq B/d$ *and* $n/|L(a^*, v^*)|$ *is an integer;*

(2) for all individuals $i \in N$, $v_i^*(a^*)$ *is sincere over* $L(a^*, v^*)$;

(3) $a_c^* \in X$ *implies* $a_c^* = \mu$.

Proof (Necessity) Part *(1)* follows directly from the definition of equilibrium and the assumption that $B > \max\{1,d\}$. To check this, first note that if $|L(a,v)| > B/d$ then each candidate does better by not entering at all; therefore, for all $c \in M$, $a_c^* \in X$ implies $c \in L(a^*,v^*)$. Further, since $B/d > 1$, $1 \leq |L(a^*,v^*)|$; hence $1 \leq |L(a^*,v^*)| \leq B/d$. Finally, if $|L(a^*,v^*)| = 1$ then clearly $n/|L(a^*,v^*)|$ is an integer. Suppose $|L(a^*,v^*)| \geq 2$. Then definition of $L(a^*,v^*)$ implies $\Pi_c(a^*) = 0$ for all $c \in L(a^*,v^*)$; that is, for all $c,c' \in L(a^*,v^*)$, $\sum_{i \in N} v_{ic}^*(a^*) = \sum_{i \in N} v_{ic'}^*(a^*)$ and this is possible only if $n/|L(a^*,v^*)|$ is an integer.

The proof that *(2)* is necessary in any equilibrium is left as an Exercise. It remains to check *(3)*. To do this, we first show that there can be no more than two distinct platforms offered in equilibrium. Suppose to the contrary that there are three winning candidates $j,k,l \in L(a^*,v^*)$ and $a_j^* < a_k^* < a_l^*$. Without loss of generality, assume $a_j^* = \min\{a_c^* : c \in L(a^*,v^*)\}$ and $a_l^* = \max\{a_c^* : c \in L(a^*,v^*)\}$. Define the expected policy outcome,

$$\bar{a}^* = \frac{1}{|L(a^*,v^*)|} \sum_{c \in L(a^*,v^*)} a_c^*.$$

Then either

$$a_j^* < a_k^* \leq \bar{a}^* < a_l^*$$

or

$$a_j^* < \bar{a}^* \leq a_k^* < a_l^*.$$

Without loss of generality, assume the first possibility obtains. By *(2)*, all individuals vote sincerely over $L(a^*,v^*)$. Therefore, there must exist some $i \in N$ for whom

$$u_i(a_j^*) \geq u_i(a_k^*) > E[u_i|a^*,v^*]$$

where the final inequality follows from strict concavity of u_i: Figure 8.4 illustrates the situation.

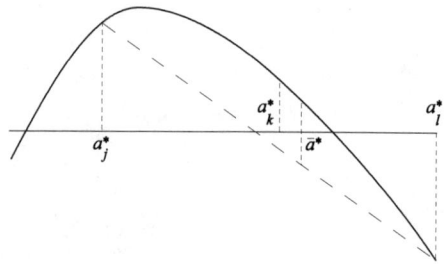

Figure 8.4: i's preferences over platforms

8.5. CANDIDATE ENTRY

But by full participation, i must be voting for some candidate and, by *(1)*, $\Pi_c(a^*) = 0$ for all $c \in L(a^*, v^*)$. Hence, because $j, k \in L(a^*, v^*)$ by hypothesis, it follows that if $v_{ik}^*(a^*) = 0$ then i strictly improves her expected payoff by deviating to vote surely for k; on the other hand, if $v_{ij}^*(a^*) = 0$, then i strictly improves her expected payoff by deviating to vote surely for j. In either case, such profitable deviations contradict the supposition that i's sincere voting strategy is equilibrium behavior. Therefore, the original supposition that there can exist three distinct winning platforms in equilibrium must be false. We now show that in fact there must be exactly one equilibrium platform.

Suppose $j, k \in L(a^*, v^*)$ and $a_j^* < a_k^*$. If $L(a^*, v^*) = \{j, k\}$, *(1)* and *(2)* imply $a_j^* < \mu < a_k^*$ for otherwise $\sum_{i \in N} v_{ij}^*(a^*) \neq \sum_{i \in N} v_{ik}^*(a^*)$. But then $W_j(\mu, a_k^*) > W_j(a_j^*, a_k^*)$, contradicting $a_j^* < \mu < a_k^*$ being equilibrium strategies. So $|L(a^*, v^*)| > 2$. By previous reasoning, all winning candidates must adopt platform a_j^* or a_k^*; without loss of generality, assume there is a candidate $l \in L(a^*, v^*) \backslash \{j, k\}$ with $a_l^* = a_j^*$. Similarly, the previous reasoning also implies there can exist no voter i for whom $u_i(a_j^*) = u_i(a_l^*) > E[u_i|a^*, v^*]$; therefore, if $i \in N$ votes for candidate j or l, we must have $u_i(a_j^*) = u_i(a_l^*) = E[u_i|a^*, v^*]$, in which case $a_j^* < x_i < a_k^*$. In turn, this last fact implies that if k is the only candidate adopting platform $a_k^* > \mu$, then k entering at a platform $a_k = a_j^* + \varepsilon > a_j^*$ is a profitable deviation, $W_k(a_k, a_{-k}^*) > W_k(a_k^*, a_{-k}^*)$, because risk-aversion implies that all voters strictly prefer a_k to a lottery over the platforms $\{a_j^*, a_k^*\}$. On the other hand, if multiple candidates entered the contest at a_k^*, the preceding argument implies that for all voters $i \in N$,

$$u_i(a_j^*) \equiv u_i(a_l^*) = u_i(a_k^*) = E[u_i|a^*, v^*]$$

and $a_j^* < x_i < a_k^*$. But then any candidate c entering at some platform $a_j^* < a_c < a_k^*$ wins surely since, for all $i \in N$,

$$u_i(a_c) > u_i(a_j^*) = u_i(a_k^*).$$

So in either case we obtain a contradiction of the supposition that $j, k \in L(a^*, v^*)$ and $a_j^* < a_k^*$. Thus the argument for necessity is proved if we can show $c \in L(a^*, v^*)$ implies $a_c^* = \mu$. But since exactly one platform can be offered in any equilibrium, if that platform is not the median, any candidate can enter at the median and win surely because the only undominated voting strategy with two platforms is sincere voting. Hence *(3)* is necessary.

(Sufficiency) The only possible equilibrium (a^*, v^*) involves all entering candidates to adopt the median voter's most preferred policy, μ. Suppose a candidate chooses to enter at a platform $a_c \neq \mu$. Then all voters who strictly prefer a_c to μ vote (rationally) for him; to insure that such an entering platform is unprofitable, suppose all other voters vote surely for exactly one of the candidates offering the median platform, say candidate j with $a_j^* = \mu$. By definition of the median, therefore, $\sum_{i \in N} v_{ij}^*(a_c, a_{-c}^*) > \sum_{i \in N} v_{ic}^*(a_c, a_{-c}^*)$ and $W_c(\emptyset, a_{-c}^*) > W_c(a_c, a_{-c}^*)$. Hence no candidate finds it profitable to enter off the median platform and, since $B/d > 1$, at least one candidate always enters. □

The assumption that voters are risk-averse, $u_i'' < 0$ all i, carries a lot of weight in the proof of Theorem 8.4. It is not, however, necessary. With single-peaked preferences, a voter is risk-averse with respect to many gambles involving alternatives that span the voter's ideal point. Consequently, there exist non-pathological distributions of voter preferences for which the arguments supporting the theorem apply. Similarly, although the strong convergence claim fails if there are multiple median voters, it is easy to check in this case that $a_c^* \in X$ implies a_c^* is a median platform.

Corollary 8.1(1) above implies that if $m > 2$ candidates have entered an electoral contest for a single seat and if all voters invariably vote sincerely, then there exist no convergent multicandidate equilibrium under simple plurality rule. In contrast, Theorem 8.4 says that if voters are strategically rational and candidates have the option not to enter the race at all, then the only possible equilibrium is convergent. In other words, the implications of sincere voting models with a given number of candidates are not robust to instrumentally rational voting and the option for candidates not to run for office.

Although Theorem 8.4 addresses candidates' decisions on whether to enter a race, it says nothing at all about where the set of potential candidates might originate and, for a theory of entry, this is a limitation. Constitutionally, as well as for pragmatic reasons, candidates for office are citizens of the polity and are thus eligible to vote. It is natural, therefore, to treat the set of potential candidates as being exactly the set of voters, $M \equiv N$. And modeling potential candidates as citizens rationalizes the policy preferences of candidates. Of course, the very fact that citizens care about policy does not preclude them from having preferences over winning office *per se*, even to the extent that the latter overwhelms any influence their intrinsic policy preferences might otherwise exert. But, other things equal and conditional on being elected, a successful candidate has no incentive to implement any platform other than his or her most preferred policy. In turn, rational voters recognize that whatever a candidate drawn from the electorate might

8.5. CANDIDATE ENTRY

promise in the campaign, should the candidate be elected then that person's ideal policy is the final outcome. When the set of potential candidates coincides with the set of voters, therefore, there is no essential difference between the problem of electoral platform selection and the problem of candidate entry: explaining the distribution of electoral policy platforms is equivalent to explaining the distribution of citizens who choose to run for electoral office.

To explore the implications of thinking about candidate entry directly in terms of individual voters' decisions to declare a candidacy for elected office, we essentially use the framework above. However, voters are no longer assumed to be risk-averse and the policy space X can be multidimensional. Specifically, suppose $X \subset \Re^k$ is compact and assume voter i has policy preferences on X representable by a strictly quasi-concave utility function $u_i \in \mathcal{R}_{cs}$ with ideal point $x_i \in X$, all $i \in N$. Each individual voter is a potential candidate, so $M = N$. Because (we assume) individuals' preferences are known or, at least, made public conditional on choosing to run for elected office, and as there is no reason for an elected candidate to implement anything other than his or her most preferred policy, any individual i who enters the election does so on the platform x_i. The election is for a single seat under simple plurality rule, ties being broken by a fair lottery. If no individual decides to run for office, we suppose a reversion, or status quo, policy $x_0 \in X$ is the outcome; otherwise the elected candidate implements his or her ideal point. It follows immediately that unless all individuals share the same ideal point, any contested election exhibits platform divergence: candidates do not converge in any policy space because no winning candidate can credibly commit to implement any platform other than his or her ideal point.

Since the set of potential candidates is exactly the set of eligible voters, N, and since individuals who choose to run for office necessarily do so on the platform defined by their ideal points, a mixed entry strategy for any $i \in N$ is a choice $\pi_i \in [0,1]$, where π_i is the probability that i enters the election. Let $\pi = (\pi_1, \ldots, \pi_n)$ denote a profile of entry strategies and, for each $i \in N$, let $a_i(\pi_i) \in \{x_i, \emptyset\}$ be the realization of the lottery π_i, where $a_i(\pi_i) = x_i$ if i chooses to run for office and $a_i(\pi_i) = \emptyset$ if i's decision is not to enter the election. Then

$$a(\pi) = (a_1(\pi_1), \ldots, a_n(\pi_n)) \in (X \cup \{\emptyset\})^n$$

is the realized profile of candidate decision over which all individuals $i \in N$ vote. An individual i's voting strategy is essentially as defined for the entry model with a given set of potential candidates with $M = N$, although abstention is allowed; that is,

$$v_i : (X \cup \{\emptyset\})^n \to \mathbf{S} \cup \{\emptyset\}$$

where $\mathbf{S}$ is the set of feasible ballots under plurality rule, defined above, and $v_i(a) = \emptyset$ indicates abstention. As before, assume $a_j = \emptyset$ implies $v_{ij}(a) = 0$. There is no assumption, however, that an individual necessarily votes for herself should she also choose to run as a candidate.

For all $i \in N$, i's preferences conditional on a pair of strategy profiles (π, v) are described by

$$E[u_i | \pi, v] =$$

$$\sum_{a(\pi) \in (X \cup \{\emptyset\})^n} \Pr(a(\pi)) \left[\frac{1}{|L(a(\pi), v(a(\pi)))|} \sum_{j \in L(a(\pi), v(a(\pi)))} u_i(x_j) - \pi_i d \right]$$

where, by convention, $a(\pi) = (\emptyset, \ldots, \emptyset)$ implies $|L(a(\pi), v)| = 1$ with the "winning" platform being x_0; $d > 0$ is the cost of entering the election. A *citizen-candidate electoral equilibrium* is a pair $(\pi^*, v^*) \in (X \cup \{\emptyset\})^n \times (\mathbf{S} \cup \{\emptyset\})^n$ such that

(1) for all $i \in N$, all $\pi_i \in [0, 1]$ and all $v_i \in \mathbf{S} \cup \{\emptyset\}$,

$$E[u_i | (\pi_i^*, \pi_{-i}^*), (v_i^*, v_{-i}^*)] \geq E[u_i | (\pi_i, \pi_{-i}^*), (v_i, v_{-i}^*)];$$

(2) no individual uses a weakly dominated strategy.

Consistent with earlier notation, if π is a pure strategy profile, $\pi_i \in \{0, 1\}$ all $i \in N$, write $a = (a_1, \ldots, a_n)$, leaving the dependency on π understood. And in this case, let

$$M(a) = \{i \in N : a_i = x_i\}$$

be the set of individuals choosing to enter; that is, the set of declared candidates at pure strategy profile a.

General sufficient conditions for the existence of citizen-candidate equilibria with particular numbers of candidates running are hard to come by, depending on details of the underlying preference distribution. Necessary conditions for any pure strategy citizen-candidate equilibrium, however, are fairly readily available directly from the definition of equilibrium *per se*. In particular, the following is true.

8.5. CANDIDATE ENTRY

Theorem 8.5 *Assume $u \in \mathcal{R}_{cs}^n$ and $X \subset \Re^k$ compact. There exists a citizen-candidate equilibrium (π^*, v^*). Furthermore, if $(\pi^*, v^*) = (a^*, v^*)$ is a pure strategy equilibrium then*

(1) for all individuals $i \in N$, $v_i^*(a^*)$ is sincere over $L(a^*, v^*)$;

(2) for all $l \in L(a^*, v^*)$ and all $i \in N$ with $u_i(x_l) \geq \max_{c \in M(a^*)} u_i(x_c)$,

$$\frac{1}{|L(a^*, v^*)|} \sum_{c \in L(a^*, v^*)} u_i(x_c) \geq \max_{c \in L(a^*, v^*) \setminus \{l\}} u_i(x_c);$$

(3) for all $m \in M(a^*) \setminus L(a^*, v^*)$, $L((\emptyset, a_{-m}^*), v^*(\emptyset, a_{-m}^*)) \neq L(a^*, v^*)$;

(4) for all $m \in M(a^*) \setminus L(a^*, v^*)$, there exists $j \in M(a^*)$ such that

$$\frac{1}{|L(a^*, v^*)|} \sum_{c \in L(a^*, v^*)} u_m(x_c) - d > u_m(x_j).$$

Proof By assumption, the set of potential candidates coincides with the finite set of voters, N. And, as already observed, the credibility constraint implies that any declared candidate $i \in N$ is effectively limited to running for office exclusively on his or her most preferred policy at $u \in \mathcal{R}_{cs}^n$, $x_i = \arg\max_{z \in X} u_i(z) \in X$; that is, $Supp[\pi_i] = \{x_i, \emptyset\}$. Furthermore, because $M(a) \subseteq N$ for all $a \in \prod_{i \in N}\{x_i, \emptyset\}$ and $\mathbf{S}$ is finite, $Supp[v_i] = \mathbf{S} \cup \{\emptyset\}$ is finite for every individual i. Hence, for all $i \in N$, i's pure strategy set is finite and Theorem 7.2, the Nash existence theorem, applies directly to insure the existence of citizen-candidate equilibria. Now let (a^*, v^*) be any pure strategy equilibrium.

By definition, $L(a^*, v^*)$ is the set of winning candidates and the election is by plurality rule for a single office. Therefore, for all $c, j \in L(a^*, v^*)$, $\sum_{i \in N} v_{ij}^*(a^*) = \sum_{i \in N} v_{ic}^*(a^*)$. If there exists $i \in N$ who is not voting for a most preferred candidate in $L(a^*, v^*)$, then i can switch her vote to such a candidate to insure that candidate's election and strictly increase her own payoff. Hence, in equilibrium, all individuals must vote sincerely over winning candidates. This is *(1)*. Claim *(2)* follows similarly: let $l \in L(a^*, v^*)$ and consider $i \in N$ such that $u_i(x_l) \geq \max_{c \in M(a^*)} u_i(x_c)$; if

$$\frac{1}{|L(a^*, v^*)|} \sum_{c \in L(a^*, v^*)} u_i(x_c) < \max_{c \in L(a^*, v^*) \setminus \{l\}} u_i(x_c) = u_i(x_j)$$

then i can vote (not sincerely) for $j \in L(a^*, v^*) \setminus \{l\}$ to insure j wins the election, increasing i's payoff.

Suppose $m \in M(a^*)\backslash L(a^*, v^*)$ and $L((\emptyset, a^*_{-m}), v^*(\emptyset, a^*_{-m})) = L(a^*, v^*)$; then $d > 0$ implies

$$\begin{aligned}
E[u_m|(x_m, a^*_{-m}), v^*(x_m, a^*_{-m})] &= \frac{1}{|L(a^*, v^*)|} \sum_{j \in L(a^*, v^*)} u_m(x_j) - d \\
&< \frac{1}{|L(a^*, v^*)|} \sum_{j \in L(a^*, v^*)} u_m(x_j) \\
&= E[u_m|(\emptyset, a^*_{-m}), v^*(\emptyset, a^*_{-m})],
\end{aligned}$$

contradicting $a^*_m = x_m$ being an equilibrium best response entry strategy for $m \in N$. This proves *(3)*.

Finally, for any $m \in M(a^*)\backslash L(a^*, v^*)$, let $L^*_{-m} \equiv L((\emptyset, a^*_{-m}), v^*(\emptyset, a^*_{-m}))$. By definition of $a^*_m = x_m$ being a best response,

$$\begin{aligned}
\frac{1}{|L(a^*, v^*)|} \sum_{j \in L(a^*, v^*)} u_m(x_j) - d &\geq \frac{1}{|L^*_{-m}|} \sum_{j \in L^*_{-m}} u_m(x_j) \\
&\geq \min_{c \in L^*_{-m}} u_m(x_c) \\
&\geq \min_{c \in M(a^*)} u_m(x_c),
\end{aligned}$$

confirming *(4)* and completing the proof. □

Before going on, it is worth remarking that assuming $u \in \mathcal{R}^n_{cs}$ for Theorem 8.5 is stronger than necessary. In fact, the only required conditions on preferences are that they are weak orderings over X with unique ideal policies: presuming $u \in \mathcal{R}^n_{cs}$ suffices and is convenient for the exposition but far from necessary for the result.

The first two properties of Theorem 8.5 concern equilibrium voting behavior. Condition (1) rehearses Theorem 8.4(2): if the set of winning candidates $L(a^*, v^*)$ is not singleton, then each must be receiving exactly the same number of votes; consequently every individual is pivotal in equilibrium, implying that individuals vote sincerely over $L(a^*, v^*)$. Condition (2) exploits the same pivotal voting logic to show that not only must voting be sincere with respect to the set of winning candidates, each individual must also (weakly) prefer the lottery induced by $L(a^*, v^*)$ to obtaining the payoff associated with the sure election of their second most preferred declared winning candidate. Figure 8.5 illustrates the distinction between the Theorem 8.5(1) and 8.5(2). In the figure, all three candidates are winning if i votes sincerely for candidate 1, $L(a, v) = \{1, 2, 3\}$; but given v_{-i}, sincere voting over $L(a, v)$ yields expected outcome $\bar{a}$, which implies that i's

8.5. CANDIDATE ENTRY

expected payoff induced by $L(a,v)$ is strictly less than the certain payoff i obtains from voting strategically for candidate 2.

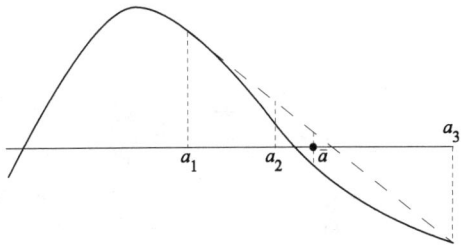

Figure 8.5: i's incentive to vote strategically for a_2

Technically, the remaining two conditions identified in Theorem 8.5 are fairly immediate consequences of the equilibrium property that an individual contests the election only if the opportunity cost of not doing so is too high. Substantively, the conditions show that, unlike when potential candidates are purely office-motivated and free to implement any feasible platform from the policy space X, the set of winners $L(a^*, v^*)$ in a citizen-candidate equilibrium is not necessarily the entire set of declared candidates $M(a^*)$. Individuals can choose to enter an election despite being sure of losing because, by doing so, they affect the lottery over the final policy outcome sufficiently to warrant bearing the campaign cost. Such a possibility is clearly precluded when candidates care solely about winning.

Example 8.5 Assume $X \subset \Re^2$ and $u \in \mathcal{R}_{cs}^n$. Suppose the set of voters N is partitioned into subsets $\{N_1, \ldots, N_5\}$ such that

$$\forall i \in N_1, \ u_i(y) > u_i(z) > u_i(x);$$
$$\forall i \in N_2, \ u_i(z) > u_i(y) > u_i(x);$$
$$\forall i \in N_3, \ u_i(z) > u_i(x) > u_i(y);$$
$$\forall i \in N_4, \ u_i(x) > u_i(z) > u_i(y);$$
$$\forall i \in N_5, \ u_i(x) > u_i(y) > u_i(z).$$

Then, for all $i \in N$, $x_i \in \{x, y, z\}$ and, by the credibility constraint, the strategically relevant set of electoral platforms is simply the set of ideal points $X^* = \{x, y, z\}$. For each $t = 1, \ldots, 5$, let $n_t = |N_t|$ and suppose

(i) $n_1 > \max\{n_2 + n_3, n_4 + n_5\} + 1$;
(ii) $n_2 + n_3 + n_4 > n_1 + n_5$;
(iii) $n_3 + n_4 + n_5 > n_1 + n_2$.

Then, for $d > 0$ sufficiently small, there exists a pure strategy citizen-candidate equilibrium (a^*, v^*) in which $M(a^*) = \{l, m, r\}$, $l \in N_1$, $m \in N_2$ and $r \in N_5$, and v^* is such that

$$i \in N_1 \Rightarrow v^*_{il}(a^*) = 1;$$
$$i \in N_2 \cup N_3 \Rightarrow v^*_{im}(a^*) = 1;$$
$$i \in N_4 \cup N_5 \Rightarrow v^*_{ir}(a^*) = 1.$$

It is straightforward to check that $v^*(a^*)$ is undominated equilibrium voting behavior [Exercise]. Therefore, by *(i)*,

$$L(a^*, v^*) = \{l\} \subset M(a^*) = \{l, m, r\}.$$

If the N_5-type individual r drops out of the election and leaves a two-way race between the N_1-type and N_2-type candidates, then sincere voting is the unique undominated voting strategy and *(ii)* implies $m \in N_2$ wins surely. But since $u_r(y) > u_r(z)$ and $x_m = z$, r is clearly better off remaining a (surely losing) candidate. Similar reasoning justifies why the N_2-type individual m prefers not to drop out of the election and, given $M(a^*) = \{l, m, r\}$, no other individual finds it worthwhile to enter the election [Exercise]. □

In contrast to the canonical multidimensional theory of electoral competition, Theorem 8.5 shows that the citizen-candidate theory surely possesses equilibria for any distribution of voter preferences over the policy space. Although the policy space is in principle a multidimensional continuum X in $\Re^k$, the credibility constraint reduces the strategically relevant set of platforms from X to the finite collection of individual ideal points, $\{x_i \in X : i \in N\}$. On the other hand, the impossibility of any sort of compromise platform being implemented is extreme. Unless, for instance, only one individual enters the electoral race, platform convergence is made impossible by fiat and, further, the credibility constraint implies that a necessary condition for a Condorcet winner $x^* \in X$ to be offered to the electorate is that $x^* = x_i$ for some individual $i \in N$ [Exercise].

An alternative approach within the citizen-candidate framework that avoids both the extreme of no compromise induced by the credibility constraint and the extreme of uninhibited platform choice by given candidates is to remove candidates altogether and assume a completely open agenda under which individuals are free to vote directly for any single alternative from the feasible policy space X, with the policy receiving the most votes being the implemented outcome. In other words, the set of potential candidates M is not assumed to be some relatively small set of exogenously given

8.5. CANDIDATE ENTRY

agents, $M = \{1, \ldots, m\}$ as supposed in Theorem 8.4, or the set of all voters, $M = N$ as supposed in Theorem 8.5, but the set of all feasible policies, $M = X$.

To obtain explicit analytical results, it is convenient to strengthen the maintained assumption of a compact and convex set of feasible policies a little and suppose X is a closed hypersphere in $\Re^k$, normalized to have center 0 and radius 1; specifically, $X = \{x \in \Re^k : \|x\| \leq 1\}$. Similarly, we again suppose that all individuals are risk-averse and, in particular, assume all individuals' have quadratic preferences on X: for all $i \in N$ and all $y \in X$,

$$u_i(y) = -\|y - x_i\|^2.$$

For the same reasons as offered in discussing Theorem 8.4, although convexity of the set of feasible policies and a sufficient degree of risk-aversion among the electorate are required for some of the arguments to follow, neither the assumption that X is a hypersphere nor the assumption that preferences are quadratic are essential. They are, as the intuition developed shortly makes clear, technically useful rather than substantively relevant restrictions.

There are no parties or candidates; the set of alternatives over which individuals vote is the set of feasible policies, X. Individuals either abstain or, at a small cost $\kappa > 0$, vote for at most one alternative from X. The policy receiving the most votes is the policy outcome, with ties being broken by a fair lottery. To avoid trivialities arising from prohibitive voting costs or unusually concentrated distributions of voter preferences on X, assume that, for every feasible policy y, there exists an individual i who prefers to vote for x_i, her ideal point, and induce a lottery between y and x_i rather than see y implemented surely: that is, for all $y \in X$, there exists $i \in N$ such that

$$\frac{1}{2}[u_i(x_i) + u_i(y)] - \kappa > u_i(y) \Leftrightarrow$$
$$-2\kappa > u_i(y).$$

There is full information and voting is strategically simultaneous. A pure voting strategy for $i \in N$ is a choice $v_i \in X \cup \{\emptyset\}$; as before, $v_i = \emptyset$ denotes that i abstains from voting. Note that because X is a hypersphere from $\Re^k$, each voter has an continuum of policy alternatives from which to choose. The equilibrium concept is simply undominated Nash: an *open-agenda electoral equilibrium* is an undominated vote profile $v^* \in (X \cup \{\emptyset\})^n$ such that, for all $i \in N$ and all $v_i \in X \cup \{\emptyset\}$,

$$E[u_i(y)|v_i^*, v_{-i}^*] \geq E[u_i(y)|v_i, v_{-i}^*].$$

Let $L(v^*) \subset X$ be the set of winning policies under v^*:

$$L(v^*) = \{x \in X : \forall y \neq x, |\{i \in N : v_i^* = x\}| \geq |\{i \in N : v_i^* = y\}|\}.$$

As described, the open-agenda model of an election is extremely parsimonious. In effect, the only two assumptions that matter are that individuals exhibit some risk-aversion and face a small cost to voting. Beyond that, voters may vote for any one of a continuum of feasible policies and have full information about the preferences of all individuals in the electorate. Despite the relative absence of any structure on the collective choice process, the following remarkable result is available.

Let $\mathcal{F}$ be the set of distributions of voter ideal points on X such that, for every ball $B \subseteq X$ with diameter $3\kappa/8$ and for every distribution $F \in \mathcal{F}$, there exists an individual $i \in N$ such that $x_i \in B$ and, for all $i \neq j$, $x_i \neq x_j$. Restricting attention to distributions from $\mathcal{F}$ implies that the electorate is large and dispersed over X because, for any given finite number of voters n, the restriction becomes impossibly demanding as the cost of voting becomes negligible. However, since our concern is precisely with large finite electorates, the assumption that the cost of voting $\kappa > 0$ is small yet the distribution of ideal points is described by some distribution $F \in \mathcal{F}$ is weak. Moreover, it is important to note that there is no reason to expect an arbitrary distribution $F \in \mathcal{F}$ to admit a nonempty majority core. Recall that $X°$ denotes the interior of X in $\Re^k$ [PPTI, sect.5.4].

Theorem 8.6 *Assume, for all $i \in N$, u_i is quadratic on $X = \{x \in \Re^k : \|x\| \leq 1\}$ and that the cost of voting $\kappa > 0$ is small. Then for any distribution of voter ideal points $F \in \mathcal{F}$, there exists an open-agenda electoral equilibrium and, for every such equilibrium v^*, $|L(v^*)| = 2$. Moreover, in equilibrium, individuals either abstain or vote sincerely over the set of winning alternatives and, if $L(v^*) \subset X°$ for some open-agenda equilibrium v^*, then there exists a continuum of open-agenda electoral equilibria.*

Although every individual can vote for any single alternative from the feasible set of "candidates" $M = X$, only two alternatives are winning in equilibrium and only winning alternatives receive any votes at all. In effect, Theorem 8.6 is an extreme form of the strategic voting result for fixed-platforms, Theorem 8.3. With an infinite number of fixed alternatives, rational (strategic) voting in a plurality rule election for a single-seat results in exactly two serious candidates, the only candidates to have positive support. Theorem 8.6, therefore, is an argument for Duverger's Law.

8.5. CANDIDATE ENTRY

That only winning alternatives receive votes in open-agenda equilibria is a straightforward consequence of costly voting and the fact that, unlike in the citizen-candidate framework, the set of candidates in the election is fixed. Nevertheless, it is important to note that there is surely positive turnout, even with n large and costly voting, and that those who vote in equilibrium vote sincerely over the set of winning alternatives. The intuition underlying the claim that only two alternatives receive votes in any equilibrium is essentially that underlying Theorem 8.4: first, given a distribution of risk-averse voters $F \in \mathcal{F}$, there is always some voter who prefers to vote surely for a less preferred alternative rather than accept a lottery over three or more policies; and second, the assumption that the cost of voting is small insures that, for any alternative y, there is always a voter willing to induce a lottery over his or her ideal point and y rather than accept y for sure. Thus equilibria cannot involve fewer or greater than two alternatives receiving votes.

Before making the intuition precise and proving the theorem, it is useful to illustrate the result with an explicit example.

Example 8.6 Suppose $X = [-1, 1]$ and $N = \{1, \ldots, 7\}$ with individual ideal points

$$x_1 = -x_7 = -1; x_2 = -x_6 = -\frac{2}{3}; x_3 = -x_5 = -\frac{1}{3}; x_4 = 0.$$

Let the cost of voting $\kappa = 1/6$. Then $F \in \mathcal{F}$ and, for all $y \in X$, there is an individual i for whom $u_i(y) < -2\kappa$, implying there can be no equilibria with only one winning alternative. In fact, by Theorem 8.6, all open-agenda equilibria involve exactly two alternatives receiving the same number of votes and no other alternative receiving any votes. Let $\{x, y\} \subset X$ be a typical pair of winning policies, $x < y$.

Because n is an odd number and winning policies have equal votes, at least one individual must abstain in any equilibrium v^*. In particular, at least $i = 4$ must abstain: for if, say, $v_4^* = x$ then quadratic preferences and $x < y$ imply $v_j^* = x$ for all $j = 1, 2, 3$ and, therefore, y is not winning, a contradiction. And since $i = 4$ must abstain, $x_4 = 0$ cannot be an equilibrium winning alternative in which case, by the quadratic preferences and the symmetry of the distribution of ideal points, all equilibria involve $x < 0 < y$.

Similarly, each winning alternative must get at least two votes in equilibrium. Suppose to the contrary that only one person votes for x and only one person votes for y. By quadratic preferences and $x < 0 < y$, if anyone votes for x (respectively, y) then it must be individual $i = 1$ (respectively,

$i = 7$). Given only individuals 1 and 7 vote, individuals 2 and 6 must abstain and $v_2^* = v_6^* = \emptyset$ are best responses if and only if both of the following inequalities obtain:

$$\frac{1}{2}[u_2(x) + u_2(y)] \geq u_2(x) - \kappa;$$
$$\frac{1}{2}[u_6(x) + u_6(y)] \geq u_6(y) - \kappa.$$

Substituting for $u_i(\cdot)$ and κ and collecting terms, these two inequalities can be written, respectively, as

$$(y - x)(\frac{4}{3} + x + y) \leq \frac{1}{3};$$
$$(y - x)(\frac{4}{3} - x - y) \leq \frac{1}{3}.$$

Adding and collecting terms then yields $(y - x) \leq 1/4$. Therefore, since $x < 0 < y$, we must have $x > -1/4$ and $y < 1/4$. But then individual 7, say, can profitably deviate from voting as supposed, $v_7^* = y$, and vote for her ideal point $x_7 = 1 > y$; given $v_j = \emptyset$ for all $j \in \{2, \ldots, 6\}$, such a deviation yields

$$\begin{aligned} E[u_7(z)|x_7, v_{-7}^*] &= \frac{1}{2}[u_7(x) + u_7(x_7)] - \kappa \\ &> \frac{1}{2}[u_7(x) + u_7(y)] - \kappa \\ &= E[u_7(z)|y, v_{-7}^*]. \end{aligned}$$

It follows from the preceding remarks that there are only two possible sorts of equilibria: those in which exactly one individual abstains, $v^I = (x, x, x, \emptyset, y, y, y)$, and those in which three individuals abstain, $v^{II} = (x, x, \emptyset, \emptyset, \emptyset, y, y)$. To identify the set of policy pairs for which v^I is equilibrium voting behavior it suffices, by quadratic preferences and symmetry of the distribution of ideal points, to find those pairs of platforms $(x, y) \in X^2$ such that $x < 0 < y$ and for which a marginal voter $i \in \{3, 5\}$ is willing to bear the cost of voting rather than abstain. That is, taking $i = 5$ without loss of generality and noting that $E[u_5(z)|y, v_{-5}^I] = \frac{1}{2}[u_5(x) + u_5(y)] - \kappa$, it is enough to find the family of ordered pairs (x, y) such that

$$E[u_5(z)|y, v_{-5}^I] \geq E[u_5(z)|\emptyset, v_{-5}^I] = u_5(x).$$

Similarly, to identify the set of policy pairs for which v^{II} is equilibrium voting behavior it suffices to find those pairs $(x, y) \in X^2$ such that $x < 0 < y$ and

8.5. CANDIDATE ENTRY

for which
$$E[u_6(z)|y, v^{II}_{-6}] \geq E[u_6(z)|\emptyset, v^{II}_{-6}] = u_6(x).$$

Doing the relevant computations for the parameterization of the example yields Figure 8.6.

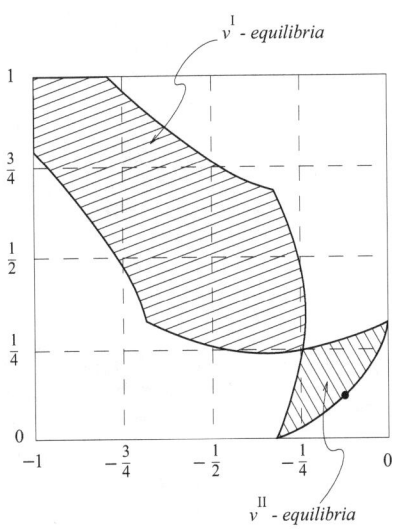

Figure 8.6: Equilibria for Example 8.6

Any pair (x, y) in the larger shaded region to the north-west of the diagram is a v^I-equilibrium winning pair, and any pair (x, y) in the smaller shaded region to the south-east of the diagram is a v^{II}-equilibrium winning pair. It is worth observing that equilibrium winning platforms are at least a distance $1/4$ apart at $(x, y) = (-\frac{1}{8}, \frac{1}{8})$ but can be maximally divergent at $(x, y) = (1, 1)$; and since the former is strictly interior to the policy space, there is, as predicted by the theorem, a continuum of equilibrium policy pairs. □

We now prove the theorem. The argument uses two preliminary results, neither of which depends on any limitations on the distribution of individual ideal points. The first of these, Lemma 8.2, provides an equivalence result that holds only when there are at least three winning alternatives, $|L(v^*)| \geq 3$. In particular, the lemma says that the following statements are equivalent when (and only when) $|L(v^*)| \geq 3$:

For any $i \in N$ and $a \in L(v^*)$,

○ Paying the cost of voting κ to obtain the sure utility from a is strictly preferable to the lottery over all winning alternatives;
  ○ Voting for a is a best response to v_{-i}^*;
  ○ In equilibrium, i's expected payoff from voting for a is at least as great as that from abstaining.

Lemma 8.2 *Suppose v^* is an open-agenda equilibrium and $|L(v^*)| \geq 3$. Then the following statements are equivalent. For any $i \in N$ and $a \in L(v^*)$,*

(S1) $u_i(a) > \frac{1}{|L(v^*)|-1} \left[\sum_{y \in L(v^*) \setminus \{a\}} u_i(y) + |L(v^*)|\kappa \right]$;

(S2) $v_i^* = a$;

(S3) $u_i(a) \geq \frac{1}{|L(v^*)|-1} \sum_{y \in L(v^*) \setminus \{a\}} u_i(y) + |L(v^*)|\kappa$.

Furthermore, if $|L(v^*)| = 2$ then (S1) $\Rightarrow$ (S2) $\Rightarrow$ (S3) but (S3) does not imply (S1).

Proof Assume (S1) is true. Collecting terms, the inequality (S1) is precisely the inequality

$$u_i(a) - \kappa > \frac{1}{|L(v^*)|} \sum_{y \in L(v^*)} u_i(y).$$

Now suppose, contrary to the claim, that (S2) fails and $v_i^* = \emptyset$. Then

$$\begin{aligned} E[u_i(z)|a, v_{-i}^*] &= u_i(a) - \kappa \\ &> \frac{1}{|L(v^*)|} \sum_{y \in L(v^*)} u_i(y) \\ &= E[u_i(z)|\emptyset, v_{-i}^*] \end{aligned}$$

contradicting $v_i^* = \emptyset$ being a best response to v_{-i}^*. On the other hand, if $v_i^* \neq \emptyset$ then

$$\begin{aligned} E[u_i(z)|v_i^*, v_{-i}^*] &= \frac{1}{|L(v^*)|} \sum_{y \in L(v^*)} u_i(y) - \kappa \\ &< u_i(a) - \kappa. \end{aligned}$$

Hence the supposition must be false and (S1) $\Rightarrow$ (S2) as claimed.

By definition of $L(v^*)$ and of a best response strategy, $v_i^* = a$ implies

$$\begin{aligned} E[u_i(z)|a, v_{-i}^*] &= \frac{1}{|L(v^*)|} \sum_{y \in L(v^*)} u_i(y) - \kappa \\ &\geq \frac{1}{|L(v^*)|-1} \sum_{y \in L(v^*) \setminus \{a\}} u_i(y) \\ &= E[u_i(z)|\emptyset, v_{-i}^*]. \end{aligned}$$

8.5. CANDIDATE ENTRY

Therefore, $(S2) \Rightarrow (S3)$. To complete the argument for equivalence, it remains to check $(S3) \Rightarrow (S1)$. But given the hypothesis that $|L(v^*)| \geq 3$, this last implication follows on inspection of the two relevant inequalities.

Likewise, setting $|L(v^*)| = 2$ it is clear that $(S3)$ no longer implies $(S1)$; on the other hand, the argument that $(S1)$ implies $(S2)$ which in turn implies $(S3)$ does not depend on $|L(v^*)| - 1 > 1$. And this observation completes the proof. □

Along with showing that individuals either abstain or vote sincerely over the set of equilibrium winning alternatives, the second preliminary result, Lemma 8.3, now argues that any equilibrium must involve at least two winning alternatives, $|L(v^*)| \geq 2$.

Lemma 8.3 *Let v^* be any open-agenda equilibrium. Then*
(1) $\infty > |L(v^*)| \geq 2$;
(2) $a \notin L(v^*)$ implies $v_i^* = a$ for no $i \in N$;
(3) $a, y \in L(v^*)$ implies $v_i^* = a$ only if $u_i(a) \geq u_i(y)$.

Proof Let v^* be an equilibrium vote profile. To prove (1), first observe that $v^* = (\emptyset, \ldots, \emptyset)$ cannot describe equilibrium behavior. To see this, suppose the contrary. Then the implemented policy outcome is the result of a uniform lottery over X. Since X is a hypersphere with center 0, the expected outcome of the lottery is $\bar{x} = 0$. By risk-aversion, for all $i \in N$, $u_i(\bar{x}) > E[u_i(y)|v^*]$. By assumption, for all $y \in X$, there exists some $i \in N$ such that $u_i(y) < -2\kappa$; let $j \in N$ be such that $u_j(\bar{x}) < -2\kappa$. Then

$$\begin{aligned} E[u_j(y)|\emptyset, v_{-j}^*] &< u_j(\bar{x}) \\ &< -2\kappa \\ &< -\kappa \\ &= E[u_j(y)|x_j, v_{-j}^*]. \end{aligned}$$

Hence $v_j^* = \emptyset$ is not a best response to $v_i^* = \emptyset$ for all $i \neq j$. It follows that $1 \leq |L(v^*)| < \infty$.

Now suppose $L(v^*) = \{z\}$. Suppose $v_i^* = v_j^* = z$; then $L(z, v_{-i}^*) = L(\emptyset, v_{-i}^*)$ and

$$\begin{aligned} E[u_i(y)|z, v_{-i}^*] &= u_i(z) - \kappa \\ &< u_i(z) \\ &= E[u_i(y)|\emptyset, v_{-i}^*]. \end{aligned}$$

So exactly one individual $i \in N$ can be voting for z; without loss of generality, suppose $v_1^* = z$ and, for all $i > 1$, $v_i^* = \emptyset$. By assumption, there exists some individual j for whom $u_j(z) < -2\kappa$. Either $j = 1$, in which case

$$\begin{aligned} E[u_1(x_1)|x_1, v_{-1}^*] &= -\kappa \\ &> u_1(z) - \kappa \\ &= E[u_1(z)|z, v_{-1}^*]; \end{aligned}$$

or $j > 1$ and

$$\begin{aligned} E[u_j(x_j)|x_j, v_{-1}^*] &= \frac{1}{2}u_j(z) - \kappa \\ &> u_j(z) \\ &= E[u_j(y)|\emptyset, v_{-j}^*]. \end{aligned}$$

In both cases, we find a contradiction to the supposition that v^* is an equilibrium with $L(v^*) = \{z\}$. Therefore, $|L(v^*)| \neq 1$ and so, by the previous step, we must have $\infty > |L(v^*)| \geq 2$ for any equilibrium v^*.

To confirm (2), let $a \notin L(v^*)$. Then $\kappa > 0$ and $a \notin L(v^*)$ imply

$$\begin{aligned} E[u_i(y)|a, v_{-i}^*] - \kappa &= E[u_i(y)|\emptyset, v_{-i}^*] - \kappa \\ &< E[u_i(y)|\emptyset, v_{-i}^*] \end{aligned}$$

in which case $v_i^* = a$ cannot be a best response.

Finally, let $a, y \in L(v^*)$ and suppose there exists $i \in N$ with $v_i^* = a$ but $u_i(a) < u_i(y)$. By Lemma 8.2, $v_i^* = a$ implies

$$u_i(a) \geq \frac{1}{|L(v^*)| - 1} \sum_{y \in L(v^*) \setminus \{a\}} u_i(y) + |L(v^*)|\kappa.$$

Therefore

$$u_i(a) - \frac{u_i(y)}{|L(v^*)| - 1} \geq \frac{1}{|L(v^*)| - 1} \sum_{z \in L(v^*) \setminus \{a,y\}} u_i(z) + |L(v^*)|\kappa.$$

By part (1) of the lemma, $|L(v^*)| \geq 2$; hence $u_i(a) < u_i(y)$ implies

$$u_i(y) - \frac{u_i(a)}{|L(v^*)| - 1} > u_i(a) - \frac{u_i(y)}{|L(v^*)| - 1}.$$

Therefore,

$$u_i(y) > \frac{1}{|L(v^*)| - 1} \sum_{z \in L(v^*) \setminus \{y\}} u_i(z) + |L(v^*)|\kappa.$$

8.5. CANDIDATE ENTRY

Now

$$\frac{1}{|L(v^*)| - 1} \sum_{z \in L(v^*) \setminus \{y\}} u_i(z) + |L(v^*)|\kappa$$

$$\geq \frac{1}{|L(v^*)| - 1} \left[\sum_{z \in L(v^*) \setminus \{y\}} u_i(z) + |L(v^*)|\kappa \right]$$

and consequently

$$u_i(y) > \frac{1}{|L(v^*)| - 1} \left[\sum_{z \in L(v^*) \setminus \{y\}} u_i(z) + |L(v^*)|\kappa \right].$$

By Lemma 8.2, therefore, $v_i^* = y$: contradiction. $\square$

The theorem is proved by exploiting the breakdown in the equivalence relation identified in Lemma 8.2 when $|L(v^*)| = 2$, to show that there can be at most two winning alternatives in any equilibrium, $|L(v^*)| \leq 2$. This last step requires insuring that there always exists a voter who strictly prefers to break a tie between at least three alternatives in favor of some winning alternative, rather than accept a lottery over more than two alternatives; the distributional restriction to $F \in \mathcal{F}$ fulfills this role and suffices to show the existence of open-agenda equilibria.

Proof of Theorem 8.6 Lemma 8.3(2) and (3) confirm the claims about equilibrium voting behavior. It remains to show $|L(v^*)| = 2$ and confirm the existence claims for open-agenda equilibria; consider these in turn.

In view of Lemma 8.3(1), to prove $|L(v^*)| = 2$ it suffices to show $|L(v^*)| \leq 2$. And to do this, it proves useful to rewrite statements $(S1)$ and $(S3)$ of Lemma 8.2 in a somewhat different form. Specifically, for any $a \in L(v^*)$, let

$$q(a, v^*) = \frac{1}{2} \left[(a \cdot a) - \frac{1}{|L(v^*)| - 1} \sum_{y \in L(v^*) \setminus \{a\}} (y \cdot y) \right]$$

and

$$Q(a, v^*) = a - \frac{1}{|L(v^*)| - 1} \sum_{y \in L(v^*) \setminus \{a\}} y.$$

To understand these definitions, note that $\sum_{y \in L(v^*) \setminus \{a\}} (y \cdot y) / [|L(v^*)| - 1]$ is the average squared length (i.e. distance from the origin) of winning alternatives other than a and, similarly, $\sum_{y \in L(v^*) \setminus \{a\}} y/[|L(v^*)| - 1]$ is the average winning alternative excluding a. Thus, $q(a, v^*) \in \Re$ is a scalar defined by (half of) the difference between the squared length of a and the average squared length of winning alternatives other than a; and $Q(a, v^*) \in X$ is an alternative defined by the difference between the winning alternative a and the average winning alternative excluding a.

Expanding $u_i(z)$ for any $i \in N$ and $z \in X$,

$$u_i(z) = -(x_i \cdot x_i) + 2(x_i \cdot z) - (z \cdot z).$$

Then substituting for $u_i(a)$ and collecting terms, statements $(S1)$ and $(S3)$, respectively, of Lemma 8.2 may be written

$$(x_i \cdot Q(a, v^*)) > q(a, v^*) + \frac{|L(v^*)|}{2(|L(v^*)| - 1)} \kappa \qquad (S1')$$

and

$$(x_i \cdot Q(a, v^*)) \geq q(a, v^*) + \frac{1}{2}|L(v^*)|\kappa. \qquad (S3')$$

Now suppose $|L(v^*)| \geq 3$. Taking v^* and $a \in L(v^*)$ as understood, let $|L(v^*)| = \lambda$, $q(a, v^*) = q$ and $Q(a, v^*) = Q$. Without loss of generality, define a basis for the policy space such that $Q = (Q_1, 0, \ldots, 0)$ and $Q_1 \geq 1$ (for example, if $Q(a, v^*) = (Q'_1, \ldots, Q'_k)$ with respect to the usual basis $e = (e_1, \ldots, e_k)$, then choose a new basis $\hat{e} = (\hat{e}_1, \ldots, \hat{e}_k)$ such that every point $y \in X$ with respect to e becomes the point $\hat{y} = y - (Q'_1 - 1, Q'_2, \ldots, Q'_k)$ with respect to $\hat{e}$; in particular, with respect to $\hat{e}$, the origin is the point $-(Q'_1 - 1, Q'_2, \ldots, Q'_k)$ and $Q = (1, 0, \ldots, 0)$). By Lemma 8.2 and $\lambda \geq 3$, there can exist no individual $i \in N$ and alternative $a \in L(v^*)$ such that statements $(S1)$ and $(S2)$ obtain, but not statement $(S3)$. That is, using the forms $(S1')$ and $(S3')$, the set $T \subseteq N$ must be empty, where

$$T = \{i \in N : \frac{1}{Q_1}(q + \frac{\lambda}{2}\kappa) > x_{i1} > \frac{1}{Q_1}(q + \frac{\lambda}{2(\lambda - 1)}\kappa)\}.$$

If $Q_1 = 0$ then T is not defined. However, $Q_1 = 0$ implies $Q = 0$ in which case, either $(S1')$ fails for every $i \in N$ implying $a \notin L(v^*)$, or it holds for every $i \in N$ implying $\{a\} = L(v^*)$. In both cases, we have a contradiction, so in fact $Q_1 > 0$ and T is well-defined. Geometrically, the ideal points of individuals $i \in T$, if any, lie between two parallel hyperplanes, as illustrated in Figure 8.7.

8.5. CANDIDATE ENTRY

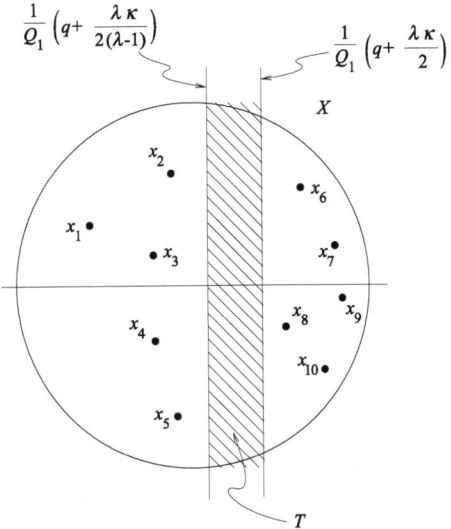

Figure 8.7: The set T

Under the supposition that $\lambda \geq 3$, there can be no individuals with ideal points between these two hyperplanes. But, by definition,

$$Q_1 = (a_1 - \frac{1}{|L(v^*)| - 1} \sum_{y \in L(v^*) \setminus \{a\}} y_1) < 2;$$

hence the distance between the hyperplanes defining T is

$$\frac{\lambda(\lambda - 2)\kappa}{(\lambda - 1)2Q_1} > \frac{3}{8}\kappa$$

and, by assumption, $F \in \mathcal{F}$. Therefore, if both hyperplanes intersect X there must exist at least one individual $j \in T$, contradicting Lemma 8.2. The only remaining possibility is that at most one of the two hyperplanes intersects X. But in this case, either no individual votes for a, contradicting $a \in L(v^*)$, or all individuals vote for a, contradicting Lemma 8.3(1). Thus $\lambda \leq 2$ as required.

The argument that equilibria exist for any $F \in \mathcal{F}$ and that, typically, there is a continuum of equilibria, is by construction. For any real number $\xi \in \Re$ and vector $y \in \Re^k$, let

$$H_{y,\xi} = \{x \in \Re^k : x \cdot y = \xi\}$$

be the hyperplane defined by y and ξ, and let

$$H_{y,\xi}^+ = \{x \in \Re^k : x \cdot y > \xi\}$$

and

$$H_{y,\xi}^- = \{x \in \Re^k : x \cdot y < \xi\}$$

be the open halfspaces defined by $H_{y,\xi}$. A *median hyperplane* through $y \in \Re^k$ for F is a hyperplane $H_{y,\xi}$ such that

$$|\{i \in N : x_i \in H_{y,\xi}^+\}| \leq n/2$$

and

$$|\{i \in N : x_i \in H_{y,\xi}^-\}| \leq n/2.$$

Median hyperplanes generalize the idea of a median line [PPTI, Example 6.7]; it is easily checked that for any $y \in \Re^k$ there exists at least one median hyperplane $H_{y,\xi}$ for any distribution of Euclidean (*a fortiori*, quadratic) preferences on X [Exercise]. Now, by definition of $F \in \mathcal{F}$, no two individuals share the same ideal point. Therefore, by n finite and large, there must exist at least one point $y \in \Re^k$ and number $\xi \in \Re$ such that $H_{y,\xi}$ is a median hyperplane with the property

$$n/2 \geq |\{i \in N : x_i \in H_{y,\xi}^+\}| = |\{i \in N : x_i \in H_{y,\xi}^-\}| \geq 2.$$

To see that such a hyperplane exists, suppose not: then every median hyperplane through every point y must divide the population into uneven parts; hence, by the assumption that all individuals' ideal points are distinct, every median hyperplane through every point y contains the ideal points of at least two individuals (if a median H through some y contains a unique ideal point then n must be even, in which case distinct ideal points implies there is another hyperplane through y sufficiently close to H that contains no ideal points and thus must divide the population exactly in half). But since there is an uncountable number of points $y \in \Re^k$ and, therefore, an uncountable number of median hyperplanes, this is possible only if n is also uncountable, contradicting n finite and confirming the existence of the hyperplane $H_{y,\xi}$. Figure 8.8 illustrates the situation in $\Re^2$ for $n = 7$ and $H = H_{y,\xi}$.

8.5. CANDIDATE ENTRY

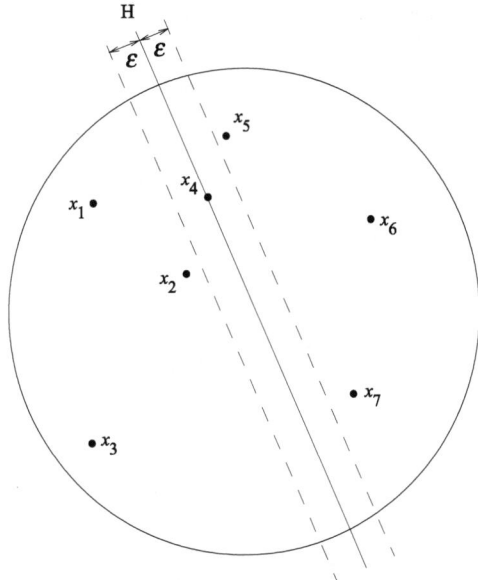

Figure 8.8: The median hyperplane, $H = H_{y,\xi}$

Moreover, because $H_{y,\xi}^+$ and $H_{y,\xi}^-$ are open halfspaces, n is finite and all individuals' ideal points are distinct, there exist $\varepsilon > 0$ such that, as shown in Figure 8.8,

$$x_i \in H_{y,\xi}^+ \Rightarrow x_i \in H_{y,\xi+\varepsilon}^+$$

and

$$x_i \in H_{y,\xi}^- \Rightarrow x_i \in H_{y,\xi-\varepsilon}^-.$$

By construction, the hyperplanes $H_{y,\xi+\varepsilon}$ and $H_{y,\xi-\varepsilon}$ are parallel (they may or may not be median hyperplanes however). We use $H_{y,\xi+\varepsilon}$ and $H_{y,\xi-\varepsilon}$ to define an open-agenda equilibrium. To save notation, write $\underline{H} \equiv H_{y,\xi-\varepsilon}$ and $\overline{H} \equiv H_{y,\xi+\varepsilon}$.

Without loss of generality, suppose $y = (1, 0, \ldots, 0)$. Then

$$\begin{aligned} \underline{H} &= \{(z_1, \ldots, z_k) \in \Re^k : z_1 = \xi - \varepsilon\}, \\ \overline{H} &= \{(z_1, \ldots, z_k) \in \Re^k : z_1 = \xi + \varepsilon\}. \end{aligned}$$

Now define the alternatives, $a, b \in X$ by

$$\begin{aligned} a &= (a_1, 0, \ldots, 0) = ((\xi - \frac{\kappa}{2\varepsilon}), 0, \ldots, 0), \\ b &= (b_1, 0, \ldots, 0) = ((\xi + \frac{\kappa}{2\varepsilon}), 0, \ldots, 0). \end{aligned}$$

By assumption, the cost of voting κ is small; in particular, it suffices to assume $\kappa/\varepsilon > 0$ sufficiently small to insure $\{a, b\} \subset X^\circ$. Let $N(\overline{H}^+) = \{i \in N : x_{i1} > \xi + \varepsilon\}$ and $N(\underline{H}^-) = \{i \in N : x_{i1} < \xi - \varepsilon\}$. Now consider the strategy profile, v^* defined by

$$\forall i \in N(\underline{H}^-), \ v_i^* = a;$$
$$\forall i \in N(\overline{H}^+), \ v_i^* = b;$$

and

$$\forall i \notin N(\underline{H}^-) \cup N(\overline{H}^+), \ v_i^* = \emptyset.$$

Figure 8.9 illustrates the strategy: all individuals to the left of $\underline{H}$ vote for a, all individuals to the right of $\overline{H}$ vote for b, and the remaining individuals, if any, abstain.

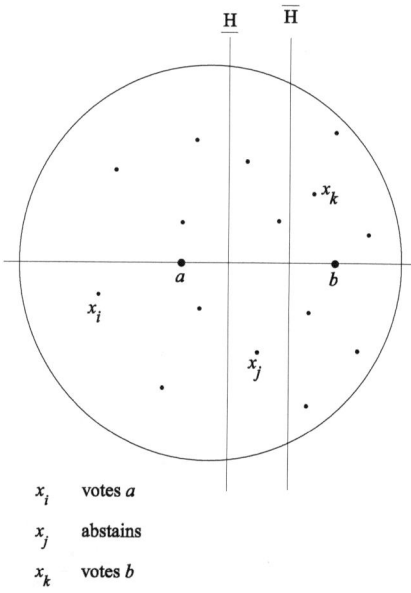

Figure 8.9: Equilibrium voting

By construction, $L(v^*) = \{a, b\}$. Let $i \in N(\underline{H}^-)$ and $v_i^* = a$. We wish to check $v_i^* = a$ is a best response. Suppose i deviates to a strategy $v_i \in \{b, \emptyset\}$; then $E[u_i(z)|v_i, v_{-i}^*] \leq u_i(b)$. Hence

$$E[u_i(z)|v_i^*, v_{-i}^*] - E[u_i(z)|v_i, v_{-i}^*] \geq 0$$

if
$$\frac{1}{2}[u_i(a) + u_i(b)] - \kappa \geq u_i(b).$$

Substituting for u_i quadratic and collecting terms, this inequality obtains iff

$$\frac{1}{2}((b_1 - a_1)(b_1 + a_1)) - \kappa \geq x_{i1}(b_1 - a_1).$$

By definition, $(b_1 - a_1) = \kappa/\varepsilon$ and $(b_1 + a_1) = 2\xi$. Therefore, $v_i^* = a$ is a best response if

$$x_{i1} \leq \xi - \varepsilon;$$

that is, if $i \in N(\underline{H}^-)$ which is the case. Similar arguments apply to individuals $j \in N(\overline{H}^+)$ and individuals $j \notin N(\underline{H}^-) \cup N(\overline{H}^+)$, completing the proof of existence.

Suppose v^* is as defined above with $L(v^*) = \{a, b\} \subset X^\circ$. Choose a policy pair $a', b' \in X^\circ$ such that

$$a' = (a_1, t, 0, \ldots, 0),$$
$$b' = (b_1, t, 0, \ldots, 0)$$

and $t \in (-s, s)$, $s = \min\{1 - \|a\|, 1 - \|b\|\}$. Then for each $z \in \{a, b\}$, $q(z, v^*) = q(z', v^*)$ and $Q(z, v^*) = Q(z', v^*)$. Therefore, replacing a by a' and b by b' throughout, v^* is an equilibrium vote profile with $L(v^*) = \{a', b'\} \subset X^\circ$: thus there exist a continuum of equilibria if there exists any open-agenda equilibrium with strictly interior winning alternatives. This completes the proof. □

8.6 Application: Duverger and divergence

Given a fixed and distinct set of candidates, Theorem 8.3, as observed previously (section 8.4), provides a purely strategic voting explanation for the focus on only two candidates in a multicandidate competition for a single office under plurality (single nontransferable vote) rule. The theorem offers no account, however, of why the candidates hold the differentiated positions with which they are associated by the electorate, or of why almost surely losing candidates would choose to run for office at all. Theorems 8.4, 8.5 and 8.6 address these concerns. To fix ideas, suppose for the discussion to follow that the policy space is the interval $X = [0, 1]$, that there is a large (finite) number of risk-averse voters with symmetric single-peaked preferences, that all voters' ideal points $\{x_i\}$ are distinct and distributed over X, and that the median voter's most preferred alternative is $\mu \in X^\circ$.

380   CHAPTER 8. MULTICANDIDATE ELECTIONS

Theorem 8.4 assumes there is a given number of potential candidates, all of whom are office-motivated, and that entry into an electoral competition is costly. Although the theorem can provide conditions under which exactly two, purely office-motivated, candidates enter a plurality rule election, it hardly constitutes a compelling explanation for Duverger's Law and no explanation at all for candidate divergence. Specifically, the theorem implies

Corollary 8.2 *Under the hypotheses of Theorem 8.4, there exists a multicandidate electoral equilibrium with entry in which exactly two candidates enter if and only if both candidates converge on the median μ, there is an even number of voters, and the benefits of winning office are at least twice as great as the cost of entering the election.*

Proof Follows immediately from Theorem 8.4. □

Theorem 8.4 is less an empirical claim about electoral competition, and more a conceptual critique of theories of multicandidate elections with platform divergence in which individuals are presumed to vote sincerely and candidates are presumed to be purely office-motivated. Assuming that candidates are themselves citizens automatically induces policy-motivated candidates and, with strategically rational voting, supports equilibria in which electoral platforms necessarily diverge if there is any competition at all. Thus Theorem 8.5 can be used to prove Corollary 8.3.

Corollary 8.3 *Under the hypotheses of Theorem 8.5 with status quo policy $x_0 = 0$, there is a citizen-candidate equilibrium in which exactly two candidates enter if and only if their electoral platforms are their respective ideal points, the mean of their ideal points is precisely the median μ, and the distance between their ideal points is at least twice the cost of entering the election.*

Proof [Exercise.] □

Unlike in Corollary 8.2, therefore, the result here insists that two-candidate equilibria similarly involve two distinct equilibrium platforms being offered to the electorate, although the expected policy outcome, μ, is identical to that predicted by Corollary 8.2. Purely policy-motivated candidates suffice here to yield platform divergence in contested elections. On the other hand, a concern with the corollary as a rationale for Duverger's Law is that there may exist other equilibria with more than two candidates in exactly the same setting. Thus the result offers some justification for Duverger's

8.6. APPLICATION: DUVERGER AND DIVERGENCE

claim but it is certainly not sufficient. Furthermore, the policy divergence property is to some extent hard-wired by the fundamental hypothesis that the set of candidates is the electorate itself. As a consequence, the usual assumption of monopoly control over final policy by the elected official insures that any elected citizen implements her most preferred policy irrespective of the electoral platform on which she ran; rational voters recognize this and ignore the campaign rhetoric when deciding how to vote.

Any difficulties with endogenous entry of citizen-candidates as an explanation of multicandidate electoral competition are moot when there are no candidates at all, only policies. Moreover, if the available policies for selection are precisely those of the feasible set, there is no sense in which equilibrium platform divergence is hard-wired. The insight reflected in Theorem 8.6, in which the set of potential "candidates" is simply the (infinite) set of feasible policies, is that strategic and costly voting with risk-averse individuals is enough to yield equilibria involving only two distinct winning alternatives; indeed, these are the only equilibria and, as such, the result offers an embryonic theory of political parties.

Corollary 8.4 *Under the hypotheses of Theorem 8.6, the only open-agenda electoral equilibria that exist are those in which exactly two distinct platforms obtain votes. Furthermore, the expected equilibrium policy outcome need not be the median μ.*

Proof Follows immediately from Theorem 8.6. □

From the perspective of Theorem 8.6, therefore, Duverger's Law is as much about simple plurality rule elections resulting in two *position* equilibria as it is about such elections resulting in two *candidate* equilibria.

Insofar as Duverger's Law says that plurality rule elections tend to result in competitions between only two serious candidates or parties, any account of the claim that takes plurality rule as given is at best incomplete. It might be, for instance, that conditions justifying Duverger's Law under plurality voting are also conditions under which at most two serious candidates exist for electoral systems other than plurality rule. In other words, Duverger's Law is to a large extent a comparative static claim, connecting the number of serious contenders for electoral office to the electoral rule used to decide between them. Simply identifying conditions under which all (suitably defined) equilibria involve but two candidates with any chance of election under plurality rule is an important but not sufficient part of any explanation. A complete (or, at least, more complete) theory needs to show that, other things equal, variations in the electoral system *per se* are associated with variations in the number of serious electoral contenders with plurality rule in particular supporting only two-candidate races. From this perspective, none of the results presented here offer a complete account of Duverger's Law; they do, however, contribute to an understanding of the incentives and behavior that support the claim under plurality rule.

8.7 Discussion

By the time voters vote, the number of candidates competing for office is fixed. The number of candidates is not, however, fixed by fiat but as a result of strategic decisions by individuals and political parties. In principle, the incentives to run for elected office depend at least in part on the electoral rule and on the anticipated behavior of voters conditional on any distribution of platforms offered by the set of declared candidates. To develop an understanding of the number and policy distribution of candidates and parties in any election, therefore, it is useful first to explore the implications of electoral competition among a fixed set of candidates.

With only two candidates competing for a single office and conditional on voting at all, voters have a unique undominated voting strategy: vote sincerely for the candidate offering the preferred policy platform. When there are more than two distinct candidates competing for a single office, voters' decisions are more complicated because a restriction to undominated strategies in this case serves only to rule out individuals voting for their least preferred candidate or policy platform. Sincere voting over multiple candidates, therefore, is not something that can be properly assumed but, to the extent it exists at all, something to be explained. Indeed, the common observation that voters avoid casting a "wasted vote" in three-or-more alternative elections is an observation that sincere voting is surely not universal. And Example 8.1 shows that strategic voting need not be widespread for such behavior to have significant electoral consequences. Nevertheless, along with the number of candidates, we begin this chapter by restricting individuals to sincere voting and focus exclusively on the strategic selection of (one-dimensional spatial) policy platforms by office-motivated candidates in elections with scoring rules.

Given a scoring rule, full information and costless voting, there is no reason for any individual to abstain. Thus sincere voting provides an incentive, familiar from the analysis of two-candidate elections under plurality rule, for extreme candidates in a one-dimensional policy space to choose platforms

8.7. DISCUSSION

arbitrarily close to that adopted by their nearest rival. Individuals have single-peaked preferences and, therefore, sincere voting and full participation insures that the extreme platforms offered in a multicandidate electoral equilibrium are not offered by only one candidate (Theorem 8.1). In the case that there are exactly two candidates, the incentive necessarily results in a convergent equilibrium. With more than two candidates, however, convergence is not assured and it is important to identify the environments in which convergence can be expected. In particular, if all electoral rules lead to convergent equilibria, then details of the rules themselves and of the number of candidates competing for office can affect the final policy outcome only to the extent that the particular policy on which candidates converge is sensitive to these data. At least under sincere voting, such universal convergence turns out not to occur (Theorem 8.2).

Every scoring rule uniquely defines a Cox threshold (but different rules might define the same threshold) as a (possibly constant) function of the number of competing candidates. For instance, under plurality rule with m candidates, the Cox threshold is $1/m$ whereas it is always one half for the Borda rule (Example 8.3). The Cox threshold for a rule essentially describes the largest proportion of the electorate that a candidate can ignore without damaging his or her prospects for winning office under sincere voting. Intuitively, we might expect multicandidate elections using rules with low thresholds to induce relatively more diffuse distributions of electoral equilibrium platforms than those using rules with high thresholds; and (again, given sincere voting) this is exactly the case (Corollary 8.1). In effect, platform convergence is more likely the more important it is for a candidate not to be ranked least under the relevant scoring rule, while nonconvergence follows when candidates are more concerned to be ranked first than about their showing conditional on not being first. Thus plurality rule induces nonconvergence with multiple candidates whereas the Borda rule drives candidates to the same policy position (section 8.2). Furthermore, at least for the case of plurality rule, the multicandidate equilibrium prediction is precisely the median voter theorem when $m = 2$. In one respect, therefore, multicandidate equilibrium generalizes the concept of two-candidate electoral equilibrium (section 7.1). However, it is important to recognize that the generalization is limited by the assumption of sincere voting: with $m = 2$ sincere voting is the unique undominated best response strategy for individuals but this is not so for $m > 2$.

In sum, both details of the electoral institution and the number of competing candidates or parties for office influence the equilibrium distribution of platforms offered to a sincere electorate. There is no assurance, however, that multicandidate equilibria invariable exist or, more importantly from a substantive perspective, that sincere voting is either a sensible restriction or a reasonable approximation to empirical reality. Certainly, theoretical support for universal sincere voting is at best fragile and there is reason to believe it is consequential (Examples 8.1 and 8.4).

The study of simultaneous strategic voting over several distinct candidates is technically complex. The main complication is that there can be multiple pivot events. Suppose the election is for a single office under plurality rule with m candidates. Ignoring any distinction between making and breaking a tie, if $m = 2$ there is exactly one pivot event and its resolution fixes the winner; consequently, an individual's best vote decision is independent of what others do. With $m > 2$, however, there are many possible pivot events defined by the various combinations of candidates involved and the ranking for which they are tied. Thus, any one voter's belief about where best to allocate his or her vote depends on the vote-decisions of others. A general claim about strategic voting is therefore unlikely. Nevertheless, a more limited, albeit empirically important, result is available. Specifically, if there are several, say $l > 1$, distinct elected positions to be decided by single nontransferable voting and more candidates than positions are contesting the election, $m > l$, then precisely the same intuition behind the idea that people try not to waste their vote in winner-takes-all, plurality rule elections seems to apply. And because a vote for somebody almost sure to lose is a wasted vote, a plausible conjecture is that in any strategic election with single nontransferable voting, almost all votes are (in equilibrium) concentrated on $l + 1$ candidates. This turns out to be true (Theorem 8.3) and thus provides, as a special case, a purely strategic voting rationale for Duverger's Law, which states that plurality rule voting for a single office leads to at most two 'serious' candidates. But if it is right that (an extended version of) Duverger's Law obtains, then there is a question about why candidates almost certain to lose an election bother to enter the race at all, especially if running a campaign is costly. One answer might simply be that the identity of exactly which $l + 1$ candidates, for instance, are perceived as "serious" by voters is unclear *ex ante*, so at the time of any decision to run for office, potential candidates assess a sufficient chance of success to warrant entering the race. Although such an explanation is not *prima facie* very compelling, even if correct there remain questions about candidates' platform selections in the presence of strategic voters (Example 8.4). Addressing these questions requires a theory of candidate entry.

In view of the canonical model of electoral competition, one natural starting point for understanding candidate entry is to fix a set of potential

8.7. DISCUSSION

candidates, assume each candidate is concerned only with winning office, and ask what platforms such candidates would adopt if entry is costly and voters are strategically rational. It is apparent that purely office-motivated candidates have no incentive to enter an electoral contest if they are sure to lose; it is less apparent what exactly this fact implies for the equilibrium distribution of platforms offered to voters. The answer is that the number of entrants is constrained only by the ratio of benefits from holding office to the costs of entry and all entrants adopt the median voter's most preferred policy as their platform (Theorem 8.4). This result is in stark contrast to the implications of assuming a fixed number of competing candidates and sincere voting (Theorems 8.1 and 8.2). As such, the value of this benchmark entry model derives less from its appeal as a reflection of any empirical reality (which is limited at best) and more as an analytical robustness check on models of multicandidate elections that presume fixed numbers of candidates and sincere voting. While the latter certainly illuminate some incentives facing strategic candidates with several competitors, equilibrium predictions supported by the models appear fragile.

The theory of the electoral competition developed over the preceding two chapters is a theory in which candidates are either given exogenously and endowed with various motivations for seeking office or, as just discussed, come from an exogenously fixed pool of potential candidates distinct from the electorate. But candidates are citizens too. The fixed pool of potential candidates, therefore, is more plausibly taken to be exactly the electorate itself: every individual voter is eligible to run for office should he or she so choose. And from this perspective, candidate preferences derive directly from individual policy preferences, implying that the entry decision and the decision on which platform to run for office conditional on entering an election, are equivalent. At least in the static setting considered here, citizens who enter the race implement their respective ideal policies should they win office; it is immediate that if multiple citizens declare a candidacy, then policy convergence is impossible unless all such individuals share the identical ideal point. Furthermore, once candidates are also citizens with policy preferences, there are more circumstances under which it is rational for an individual to contest a costly election than when individuals are concerned only with winning office. Specifically, despite being sure that they will not win, an individual might enter an electoral race to affect the expected policy outcome by implicitly blocking the entry or exit of other potential or declared candidates (Theorem 8.5 and Example 8.5).

The citizen-candidate perspective on political competition is quite intuitive and simultaneously gives rise to a theory of candidate entry and a theory of candidate preferences. On the other hand, the implication that, other things being equal, declared candidates are locked into implementing their ideal points should they win is restrictive. As a matter of fact, candidates do credibly adjust their policy positions and, even should they not do so, a theory of platform selection predicated exclusively on an individual's exogenously given policy preferences effectively reduces any account of collective policy outcomes to an account of which particular individuals choose to run for office. Although understanding who chooses to seek election is clearly important to a full theory of electoral politics, providing an account of collective choice based entirely on such a foundation seems unwise.

A somewhat different approach within the spirit of the citizen-candidate theory is to eschew candidates and parties altogether. Instead, the set of 'potential candidates' is assumed to be the full set of feasible policy outcomes, with each individual permitted to vote for any one policy or not at all. Assuming away candidates as agents or, equivalently, assuming there is a candidate for every possible alternative in the policy space, seems, at least *prima facie*, to be unreasonable for any sort of theory of electoral competition with a large number of voters. Insofar as the focus of a model of elections is on understanding the behavior of particular agents with given objectives (e.g. maximizing the probability of winning), or on understanding the behavior of historically established political parties in a constrained (e.g. two-party) environment, such a presumption is justified. However, if the focus is on understanding the deeper implications of using a given vote (rather than preference) aggregation rule to determine collective policy choices, then dispensing at the outset with the intermediary steps involved in candidates choosing platforms is eminently sensible. And in this respect, the implications of plurality rule under costly voting and abstention are subtle and striking: in every open-agenda equilibrium with risk-averse voters and a multidimensional policy space, exactly two divergent policy positions receive any votes at all (Theorem 8.6). Despite the absence of candidates or parties, strategic and costly voting under plurality rule leads to equilibria with two distinct platforms and positive turnout. The precise location of any given pair of equilibrium platforms, however, is in general indeterminate (Example 8.6).

Of course, the result that costly plurality voting alone generates two-position equilibria does not imply that candidates or parties are irrelevant to electoral competition. There are typically many open-agenda equilibria and the realization of any equilibrium at all is a distinctly non-trivial matter, requiring a high degree of coordination even among a fully aware electorate. In more applied environments, voters cannot be assumed to be so informed

8.8. EXERCISES

and, at the very least, candidates and parties provide a coordination role, directing attention to salient issues and alternatives. Nevertheless, the open-agenda perspective exposes some important properties of strategic voting and suggests a theory of party formation in terms of coordinating voters on particular policies.

Relatively few elected officials have any authority to make unilateral policy decisions, yet the theory of electoral competition developed in this and the previous chapter concerns choosing agents who, conditional on winning office, exert essentially dictatorial control over policy. At the same time, the theory of legislative decision-making explored in earlier chapters at best left implicit any reelection concerns of legislators. But insofar as voters care more about outcomes than about process *per se*, a satisfactory theory of policy choice requires integrating both the electoral and the legislative stages of collective decision-making.

8.8 Exercises

8.1 Complete the proof of Theorem 8.1: if a^* is a multicandidate equilibrium under simple plurality rule then $K_1(a^*) = K_m(a^*) = 2$.

8.2 Prove that for the model of section 8.1, the only multicandidate electoral equilibria under single negative voting are convergent.

8.3 (a) Prove assertions (1), (2) and (3) in section 8.2.

(b) For the same specification (Euclidean preferences and uniform voter distribution), prove that there exists no pure strategy multicandidate equilibrium under plurality rule if $m = 3$.

8.4 Prove, as claimed in Theorem 8.4, that sincere voting over $L(a^*, v^*)$ is a necessary condition for any multicandidate electoral equilibrium with entry.

8.5 Confirm the unproven claims made in Example 8.5.

8.6 Consider a citizen-candidate model in which $X = [0, 1]$ and the status quo policy is $x_0 = 0$. There is an odd (large) number of individuals; each individual $i \in N$ has single-peaked preferences on X given by, $u_i(y) = -|x_i - y|$, $x_i, y \in X$. Let $\mu \in X$ be median ideal point and let $d > 0$ be the cost of entering the election.

(a) *Prove*: There exists a citizen-candidate equilibrium with only $i \in N$ running for office if and only if (i) $x_i \geq d$ and (ii) there is no individual $j \in N \backslash \{i\}$ such that either $2\mu - x_i < x_j < x_i - d$ or $x_i + d < x_j < 2\mu - x_i$.

(b) Under what circumstances is the ideal point of the sole candidate in (a) surely the median voter?

(c) *Prove*: There exists a citizen-candidate equilibrium with only $i, j \in N$ running for office if and only if (i) $[x_i + x_j]/2 = \mu$ and (ii) $|x_i - x_j| \geq 2d$.

8.7 Construct a counter-example to show that citizen-candidate equilibrium policy outcomes need not be core outcomes even when the latter exist.

8.8 Let the radius of X in Theorem 8.6 be $t > 0$. Give a utility interpretation of t. Show that the existence claim now needs the diameter of B to be $3\kappa/8t$. Discuss the implications of changing t for Theorem 8.6.

8.9 Show that there exists a median hyperplane for any distribution of Euclidean preferences through every point $y \in \Re^k$. [Hint: think of a line through a point in $\Re^2$ with all ideal points on one side; rotating the line sufficiently puts all the points on the other side; by continuity, there must be a line that divides the population in half.]

8.10 Assume there is a one-dimensional policy space $X = [0, 1]$ over which a continuum of voters with Euclidean preferences is distributed uniformly; normalize the size of the electorate to one. There are two "large" candidates who surely compete under plurality rule (with no abstention) for a single office; there is also a third, "small", candidate. All three candidates seek to maximize their respective vote-shares and all voters vote sincerely for the candidate with their most preferred policy of those offered. Assume the two large candidates first choose (and commit to) their platforms simultaneously; having so chosen, the third, small, candidate decides on his or her platform; finally, voters vote.

(a) Write down the various agents' strategies and find the undominated subgame perfect Nash equilibrium to the game.

(b) Discuss whether the implications of your answer to (a) seem reasonable. What are the implications of strategic voting, or of adding a cost to entering a race and losing, or of changing candidate objectives to plurality maximization?

8.11 Prove Corollary 8.3.

8.9 Further reading

Theorems 8.1 and 8.2 are due to Cox [48], [49], the seminal positive theory contributions to the topic; see also Cox [51] and Denzau, Katz and Slut-

8.9. FURTHER READING

sky [58]. Myerson first named the Cox threshold, $\mathcal{C}(s;m)$, as such and, in [146], demonstrates the importance and value of the concept for comparing electoral systems; the discussion here benefits from Myerson's insights. Cox [50] extended Duverger's Law to multiple-seat elections under single non-transferable voting, Theorem 8.3. The Poisson game approach and proof for the result presented in section 8.3, however, are due to Myerson (personal communication). Myerson and Weber [149] and Myerson [148] study strategic voting equilibria for multicandidate elections under a variety of electoral rules. Although anticipated by Riker [170], Duverger's Law, that simple plurality rule elections for a single seat tend to lead to two viable parties, originates in Duverger [65] and is further explored in Riker [172], [173]. Subsequent contributions include Palfrey [158], Feddersen [72] and Fey [80]. Theorem 8.4 is due to Feddersen, Sened and Wright [76]; see also Palfrey [157] (on which Exercise 8.10 is based) and Osborne [153] for sequential models of candidate entry. The citizen-candidate model was introduced by Osborne and Slivinski [156] and Besley and Coate [33] (where some help on Exercise 8.6 can be found). Osborne and Slivinsky assume sincere voting, compare plurality rule with a runoff electoral system, and are responsible for the term "citizen-candidate"; Besley and Coate allow preferences to depend on candidate names and for feasible policy alternatives to depend on winning candidates' identities and so forth. Theorem 8.5 and Example 8.5 are due to Besley and Coate. Theorem 8.6 and Example 8.6 are due to Feddersen [72]. Greenberg and Weber [87], Greenberg and Shepsle [86] and Sugden [196] look at more cooperative game-theoretic models of entry under proportional representation. See also Schofield [188]. Shepsle [192] reviews much of the early literature.

Chapter 9
Legislative Elections

More-or-less independent theories of committee choice, coalition building or electoral behavior surely contribute to our understanding of how the details of political institutions affect policy choice, yet most policy outcomes are the result of a legislative coalition or committee decision procedure (such as those studied in earlier chapters) involving elected representatives from several geographic districts or political parties. Thus, rational policy-motivated voters take into account the likely legislative consequences of voting one way rather than another in elections. In turn, rational candidates or parties take account of such deliberations when deciding on their electoral strategies and subsequent legislative behavior, conditional on winning at least some degree of representation in the legislature. To explain the distributions of party platforms and electoral votes in legislative elections, therefore, it is necessary first to characterize how such distributions map into final legislative policy outcomes.

Although surely relevant to any multimember legislative election, the preceding remarks are especially salient with respect to parliamentary systems. Whereas, in almost all such systems, simple majority or plurality rule is predominantly used for making decisions within the elected legislature, the election of the legislature *per se* from among the various competing parties and candidates is decided by some form of proportional representation rule. While a party may indeed secure an overall majority within the elected legislature, this is only one of many possible distributions of legislative seats, most of which involve no one party winning a clear majority. And in the absence of a single party with a legislative majority, policy decisions are not necessarily electoral platforms but rather the result of bargaining among members of some post-election coalition government.

There are a myriad ways, both in principle and in fact, for elections and legislatures to be organized. Nevertheless, in this chapter we consider a stylized sequential model of parliamentary democracy in which three homogenous parties compete for legislative representation in a pure proportional voting election; once the composition of the elected legislature is determined, legislative bargaining under a given protocol determines the governing coalition and consequent policy choice. Much of the subtlety inherent in institutional variation is clearly finessed by such a stylized model, as is our earlier concern with candidate entry. The goal, however, is not to provide a comprehensive positive theory of representative democracy, but to connect some of the central themes of earlier chapters and develop a broader intuition for how legislative and electoral incentives interact.

9.1 Elections, government and policy

Three homogenous parties, l, m, r, compete for legislative representation over a one-dimensional policy space, $X = [\underline{x}, \bar{x}]$. An *electoral strategy* for $c \in \{l, m, r\}$ is a platform choice, $a_c \in X$. To avoid complications with integer problems in allocating a finite number of legislative seats, we suppose the election is by pure proportional representation with no abstention. Given any profile of electoral policy platforms $a = (a_l, a_m, a_r) \in X^3$ and party $c \in \{l, m, r\}$, let $V_c(a) \in [0, 1]$ denote c's realized electoral vote share. It is both unreasonable and implausible that simply voting for oneself suffices for a seat in the post-election legislature. Consequently, to achieve any positive level of legislative influence, a party is assumed to require at least a minimal proportion of electoral support, $s \in (0, 1/4)$, where s is supposed bounded away from zero. So for each party c and distribution of vote shares $V = (V_l, V_m, V_r)$, let $\omega_c(V) \in [0, 1]$ be c's *legislative weight*; then $\omega_c(V) = 0$ if $V_c < s$ and, if $V_c \geq s$,

$$\omega_c(V) = \frac{V_c}{\sum_{j=l,m,r}\{V_j : V_j \geq s\}}.$$

Write $\omega = (\omega_l, \omega_m, \omega_r)$.

Unlike the election, legislative decision-making is by weighted majority rule. Thus the family of decisive coalitions in the legislature, $\mathcal{L} \subseteq 2^{\{l,m,r\}}$, is described by

$$\mathcal{L} = \{L \subseteq \{l, m, r\} : \sum_{c \in L} \omega_c > \frac{1}{2}\}.$$

9.1. ELECTIONS, GOVERNMENT AND POLICY

Clearly, if $\omega_c > 1/2$ for some party c, then $\{c\} \in \mathcal{L}$ and c constitutes the government, controlling all legislative decisions. But in case no party is decisive on its own then, by full participation, all parties must have legislative representation ($V_c \geq s$ for all c) and any government involves a coalition of at least two parties.

Following an election, government formation and legislative decisions are decided through a fixed sequential bargaining protocol involving only those parties with positive weight, $\omega_c > 0$. As discussed in some detail in Chapter 6, there are many possible bargaining protocols. Here, we adopt a particular finite bargaining sequence that reveals the relevant incentives in an analytically tractable way without doing obvious damage to empirical reality. Specifically, given a list of legislative weights $\omega > 0$, the protocol gives the party with the highest weight (ties invariably being broken by a fair lottery) the first opportunity to form a government by proposing a legislative policy outcome $y^1 \in X$ and a distribution of a fixed amount of transferable private benefits, the perks of office, across the parties, $b^1 = (b_l^1, b_m^1, b_r^1) \in \mathbf{B}$ where

$$\mathbf{B} = \{b \in [0, B]^3 : \sum_{c=l,m,r} b_c \leq B\}.$$

Should the largest party's proposal be rejected by a decisive legislative coalition $L \in \mathcal{L}$, the sequence moves to the second bargaining period and the party with the next highest weight has an opportunity to form a government, proposing a pair $(y^2, b^2) \in X \times \mathbf{B}$; if this too fails to receive legislative approval, the sequence goes to the third period and the remaining party has a last chance to form a government with a proposal $(y^3, b^3) \in X \times \mathbf{B}$. In the event that all legislative parties fail to form a government, the protocol implements a fixed "caretaker government" decision $(y^0, b^0) \in X \times \mathbf{B}$.

For any party $c \in \{l, m, r\}$ with positive legislative weight, $\omega_c > 0$, a *legislative strategy* for c is a pair $\lambda_c = (\pi_c, \delta_c)$ consisting of a proposal $\pi_c = (y^c, b^c) \in X \times \mathbf{B}$ to be offered conditional on being asked to form a government, and a decision strategy δ_c describing the set of other parties' proposals that c is willing to support,

$$\delta_c : X \times \mathbf{B} \times \{1, 2, 3\} \to [0, 1],$$

where $\delta_c(y^j, b^j, t) \in [0, 1]$ is the probability that c votes for party j's proposal (y^j, b^j) offered at the tth legislative bargaining period. In principle, both components of a legislative strategy, (π_c, δ_c), are conditional on the profile of electoral platforms, details of the vote distribution and the history of the legislative bargaining process. However, for the (subgame perfect) equilibrium analysis to follow, including such dependencies explicitly adds nothing but notation; up to the dependency on the bargaining period itself, legislative strategies are therefore assumed ahistorical at the outset.

To solve the legislative bargaining game requires endowing parties with preferences over $X \times \mathbf{B}$. Let $a = (a_l, a_m, a_r) \in X^3$ be the profile of electoral platforms; then for any $(z, b) \in X \times \mathbf{B}$ and $c \in \{l, m, r\}$, party c's payoff is given by

$$W_c(z, b; a_c) = \begin{cases} b_c - (z - a_c)^2 & \text{if } \omega_c > 0 \\ -d & \text{if } \omega_c = 0 \end{cases}.$$

Conditional on having legislative representation, parties have quasi-linear preferences over the perks of office, b_c, and the final policy outcome, z; if a party fails to win enough votes to have any weight in the legislature, then it suffers a nontrivial cost of running an unsuccessful campaign, $d > 0$. Implicitly, we assume such costs are recovered if a party wins any legislative seats. A party's (legislative) policy preferences depend on the distance between the final legislative outcome and the platform on which a party contested the election. The specification reflects two empirical intuitions: first, that legislators elected on a platform in fact care about the policy on which they fought the election; and second, that the electorate treats a party's campaign statements and position on policy sufficiently seriously that it penalizes the party in subsequent (here, unmodeled) elections to the extent that final outcomes deviate from that position, thus affecting the party's opportunities for, say, acquiring the perks of office in later legislatures. In both cases, a party's payoff from holding legislative office is decreasing in the distance between that party's electoral platform and the final legislative policy decision.

Given a list of party platforms $a \in X^3$ and a profile of legislative strategies, let $W_c^t(\lambda; a_c)$ denote party c's continuation value under λ from voting against the proposal λ_j offered by party $j \in \{l, m, r\}$ in the tth bargaining period, $t = 1, 2, 3$ (see section 6.5, for example). Then a *legislative equilibrium* at $a \in X^3$ is a list of undominated legislative strategies $\lambda^* = (\lambda_l^*, \lambda_m^*, \lambda_r^*)$ such that, for all $c \in \{l, m, r\}$,

(1) for all $(z, b, t) \in X \times \mathbf{B} \times \{1, 2, 3\}$,

$$\delta_c^*(z, b, t) > 0 \Rightarrow W_c(z, b; a_c) \geq W_c^t(\lambda^*; a_c),$$

(2) for all $\pi_c \in X \times \mathbf{B}$,

$$E[W_c(z, b; a_c) | a, (\pi^*, \delta^*)] \geq E[W_c(z, b; a_c) | a, (\pi_c, \pi_{-c}^*, \delta^*)].$$

9.1. ELECTIONS, GOVERNMENT AND POLICY

Legislative equilibria are simply subgame perfect Nash equilibria in undominated strategies $\lambda^* = (\pi^*, \delta^*)$. The first condition requires parties to support another's proposal only if rejection leads to a worse expected outcome along the equilibrium path; and the second condition insists that parties choose a best response proposal conditional on being asked to form a government and on the responses of the other legislative parties.

To avoid dealing with some tedious corner cases in identifying legislative equilibria in the model, assume B is sufficiently large to insure that the caretaker government decision (z^0, b^0) can always be chosen such that, for all $a \in X^3$, $W_c(z^0, b^0; a_c) = 0$ with $\sum_c b_c^0 \leq B$ (with quadratic policy preferences, $B \geq |X|^2$ suffices).

Individuals are assumed purely policy-motivated with quadratic preferences on X:

$$\forall z \in X, \ u(z; x) = -(z - x)^2$$

describes the payoff from policy z to any voter with ideal point $x \in X$. Although the electorate N is finite (so, in particular, there can be positive probability that an individual vote is pivotal), we suppose $|N|$ is sufficiently large that the distribution of ideal points on X is well-approximated by a continuous cumulative distribution function $F : X \to [0,1]$ with full support on X. Hereafter, therefore, the names of the voters are ignored. Assume that the distribution of ideal points is symmetric about the median voter's ideal policy, μ. All individuals vote for exactly one party. A *voting strategy* is a map

$$v : X^4 \to \Delta\{l, m, r\}$$

such that, for any individual with ideal point $x \in X$ and any list of electoral platforms $a \in X^3$, $v(a; x) = (v_l(a; x), v_m(a; x), v_r(a; x))$ is a probability distribution over parties; that is, for any party c, $v_c(a; x) \in [0,1]$ is the probability that a voter with ideal point x votes for party c and $\sum_c v_c(a; x) = 1$. Write $v(a) = (v(a; x))_{x \in X}$.

Given an electoral threshold $s \in (0, 1/4)$ and a symmetric distribution of voter ideal points F, a *legislative election equilibrium* is a list of undominated party strategies $(a^*, \lambda^*) = ((a_l^*, \lambda_l^*), (a_m^*, \lambda_m^*), (a_r^*, \lambda_r^*))$ and an undominated voting strategy v^* such that

(1) λ^* is a legislative equilibrium at $a^* \in X^3$;

(2) for all $c \in \{l, m, r\}$ and all $a_c \in X$,

$$E[W_c(z, b; a_c^*)|v^*, a^*, \lambda^*] \geq E[W_c(z, b; a_c)|v^*, (a_c, a_{-c}^*), \lambda^*];$$

(3) for all $x \in X$, all $a \in X^3$ and all $v(\cdot; x) \in \Delta\{l, m, r\}$,

$$E[u(z;x)|v^*,(a,\lambda^*)] \geq E[u(z;x)|(v(a;x),v^*),(a,\lambda^*)].$$

In words, condition (1) says that parties use legislative equilibrium strategies conditional on attracting sufficient votes to have positive legislative weight; condition (2) likewise insists that parties select their respective electoral platforms taking account of both voters' strategies and other parties electoral and subsequent legislative strategies; and condition (3) requires that every voter's strategy is an undominated best response to other voters' strategies at *every* vector of electoral platforms $a \in X^3$, taking account of the expected legislative consequences of his or her decision conditional on parties' legislative strategies. As such, (3) rules out problems of the sort illustrated earlier in Example 8.4, where the sincere voting assumption was consistent with strategically rational decision-making in equilibrium, but not so consistent off the equilibrium path. Together, properties (1), (2) and (3) imply legislative election equilibria are subgame perfect, with party and voter decisions interlinked across both the electoral and legislative stages of the collective choice process.

To identify legislative election equilibria, we first solve for legislative equilibria conditional on a list of electoral platforms $a \in X^3$ and a distribution of votes $V(a) = (V_l(a), V_m(a), V_r(a))$; without loss of generality, and as suggested by the notation, assume hereafter that $a_l \leq a_m \leq a_r$. Theorem 6.4 implies there exists a no-delay equilibrium to the legislative bargaining subgame and, therefore, the largest party's opening proposal is accepted in such an equilibrium. Moreover, because the policy space is one-dimensional and party preferences (conditional on a) are quasi-linear, any equilibrium proposal must involve a policy lying between the ideal points of the proposer and a potential coalition partner, along with a distribution of perks that offers nothing to the residual party.

Lemma 9.1 below provides details of the proposals and shows that, subject to an innocuous refinement for one case (presumed to hold throughout), the legislative bargaining protocol induces a function connecting any pair $(a, V(a))$ to final policy outcomes $x \in X$. The one case requiring a refinement to insure a unique policy outcome occurs if the third proposer in the bargaining sequence, that is, the smallest party, is indifferent over which other party to propose as a governing coalition partner, conditional on the out-of-equilibrium event that both preceding proposals are rejected. However, the equilibrium payoff to the smallest party depends precisely on expectations regarding its third period proposal. In such a case, therefore,

9.1. ELECTIONS, GOVERNMENT AND POLICY

we assume the third period proposer commits to making the proposal that induces its highest equilibrium payoff. And given that following through on such a promise strictly improves the smallest party's utility, the commitment is surely credible.

The lemma is established using familiar backwards induction arguments. By assumption, the caretaker government decision, conditional on no party successfully forming a government, leaves all parties with a zero payoff, thus fixing the continuation values for the third and final bargaining period; given these values, the smallest (last-proposing) party has a well-defined optimization problem, the solution to which induces the continuation values for the second bargaining period. In turn, these values imply the middle (second-proposing) party too has a well-defined problem that yields the first bargaining period continuation values; finally, the largest (first-proposing) party selects a utility-maximizing proposal subject to meeting these first-period continuation values and it is this proposal that describes the equilibrium coalition government, policy outcome and perq-distribution.

If two parties receive the same vote share in an election, their legislative weights are likewise the same and, in this case, the order in which the two parties make proposals in the bargaining is decided by fair lottery. With this in mind, the statement of Lemma 9.1 abuses notation somewhat and writes "$\omega_c > \omega_{c'}$" to mean either "$V_c > V_{c'}$" or "$V_c = V_{c'}$ and the realization of the lottery results in party c taking precedence in the bargaining sequence over party c'". Thus, there are six cases to consider depending on the possible sequence of proposals; by symmetry, it suffices to consider only three: (1) $\omega_m > \omega_l > \omega_r$; (2) $\omega_l > \omega_m > \omega_r$; and (3) $\omega_l > \omega_r > \omega_m$. The remaining three cases follow simply from interchanging the relative weights of parties l and r.

Some further notation is useful for stating the result. Given electoral platforms $a_l \leq a_m \leq a_r$, define

$$\ell_l = (a_m - a_l) \text{ and } \ell_r = (a_r - a_m);$$

also, for any two parties c, c', write

$$a_{cc'} = \frac{a_c + a_{c'}}{2}.$$

Let $(z^*, b^*) \in X \times \mathbf{B}$ denote an equilibrium policy and perq-distribution outcome.

Lemma 9.1 *Fix a list of electoral platforms $a_l \leq a_m \leq a_r$ and legislative weights $(\omega_l, \omega_m, \omega_r)$. Then the following is true of any legislative equilibrium*

λ^*. If $\omega_c > 1/2$ for some $c \in \{l,m,r\}$ then c forms the government on its own and implements the outcome $(z^*, (b_c^*, b_{-c}^*)) = (a_c, (B, 0, 0))$. If $\omega_c \leq 1/2$ for all $c \in \{l, m, r\}$ then the government is a two-party coalition consisting of the largest and the smallest parties with outcomes as follows.

(1) If $\omega_m > \omega_l > \omega_r$ then $(z^*, (b_m^*, b_{-m}^*)) = (a_m, (B, 0, 0))$.

(2) If $\omega_l > \omega_m > \omega_r$ and

  (2a) $\ell_l \leq \ell_r$ then $(z^*, (b_l^*, b_{-l}^*)) = (a_m, (B, 0, 0))$;

  (2b) $\ell_l > \ell_r$ then $z^* = a_{lr}$, $b_l^* = B - b_r^*$, $b_r^* = \frac{1}{4}(a_l - a_r)^2$ and $b_m^* = 0$.

(3) If $\omega_l > \omega_r > \omega_m$ and

  (3a) $\ell_l > \ell_r$ then $z^* = a_{lm}$, $b_l^* = B - b_m^*$, $b_m^* = \frac{1}{4}(a_l - a_m)^2 - \frac{1}{4}(a_{rm} - a_m)^2$ and $b_r^* = 0$;

  (3b) $2\ell_l \geq \ell_r \geq \ell_l$ then $z^* = a_{lm}$, $b_l^* = B - b_m^*$, $b_m^* = \frac{1}{4}(a_l - a_m)^2 - (a_{lr} - a_m)^2$ and $b_r^* = 0$;

  (3c) $2\ell_l < \ell_r \leq 3\ell_l$ then $z^* = 2a_{lm} - a_{lr}$, $(b_l^*, b_{-l}^*) = (B, 0, 0)$;

  (3d) $3\ell_l < \ell_r$ then $(z^*, (b_l^*, b_{-l}^*)) = (a_l, (B, 0, 0))$.

Proof That a party with a strict legislative majority, $\omega_c > 1/2$, implements its ideal policy and allocates all perks of office to itself is evident. So assume there is no such party; then $0 < \omega_c \leq 1/2$ for all $c \in \{l, m, r\}$. Recall that $W_c^t(\lambda; a_c)$ is party c's continuation value under a legislative strategy profile λ from voting against the proposal π_j offered by party $j \in \{l, m, r\}$ in the tth bargaining period, $t = 1, 2, 3$. We prove only case (3b), leaving the arguments for the remaining possibilities as exercises.

(3b) Suppose $\omega_l > \omega_r > \omega_m$ and $2\ell_l \geq \ell_r \geq \ell_l$. By construction, for all strategy profiles λ and all parties c, $W_c^3(\lambda; a_c) = 0$. Working back from the $t = 3$ bargaining period therefore, subgame perfection requires that the smallest party, party m, choose a proposal $(y^m, b^m) \in X \times \mathbf{B}$ to maximize $W_m(y, b; a_m)$ subject to the proposal being acceptable to at least one other party. By assumption, $a_l \leq a_m \leq a_r$ and preferences are quasi-linear; hence it is not immediately obvious to which party m should make a proposal. To resolve this issue, it is first necessary to identify m's best payoff from seeking the support of each party separately, and then to compare them. Consider m's best proposal to attract l as a coalition partner. Because preferences are increasing in perks, if m makes a proposal directed toward party l then that proposal necessarily involves no private goods to party r. Moreover, by earlier arguments (from Chapters 5 and 6), subgame perfection implies that l surely accepts any proposal that leaves it indifferent between accepting and rejecting that proposal. Thus, conditional on choosing l as a coalition

9.1. ELECTIONS, GOVERNMENT AND POLICY

partner, m solves the following Lagrangian maximization problem:

$$\max_{y,b_l,\zeta^m} \Lambda^m(y, b_l; \zeta^m) = B - b_l - (y - a_m)^2 + \zeta^m[b_l - (y - a_l)^2]$$

where we have substituted for the legislative utilities W_c and ζ^m is the Lagrange multiplier. By concavity and the assumption that B is sufficiently large to permit all coalitions to form for all $a \in X^3$, the first-order conditions suffice for an interior solution:

$$\frac{d\Lambda^m}{dy} = -2(y - a_m) - \zeta^m 2(y - a_l) = 0;$$

$$\frac{d\Lambda^m}{db_l} = \zeta^m - 1 = 0;$$

$$\frac{d\Lambda^m}{d\zeta^m} = b_l - (y - a_l)^2 = 0.$$

Solving yields

$$y = a_{lm}; \quad b_l = \frac{1}{4}(a_m - a_l)^2.$$

Hence

$$W_m(a_{lm}, b_l; a_m) = B - \frac{1}{4}(a_m - a_l)^2 - (a_{lm} - a_m)^2$$
$$= B - \frac{1}{2}(a_m - a_l)^2.$$

Similarly, conditional on choosing r as a coalition partner, m makes a proposal

$$y' = a_{rm}; \quad b_r = \frac{1}{4}(a_m - a_r)^2$$

yielding a payoff

$$W_m(a_{rm}, b_r; a_m) = B - \frac{1}{2}(a_m - a_r)^2.$$

Therefore

$$W_m(a_{lm}, b_l; a_m) \gtreqless W_m(a_{rm}, b_r; a_m) \Leftrightarrow$$
$$(a_m - a_r)^2 \gtreqless (a_m - a_l)^2 \Leftrightarrow$$
$$\ell_r^2 \gtreqless \ell_l^2.$$

By assumption, $\ell_r \geq \ell_l \geq 0$. Assuming the inequality is strict, m's best proposal at $t = 3$ is to suggest a coalition with party l by making the proposal $(y^m, (b_l^m, B - b_l^m, 0))$ with $y^m = a_{lm}$ and $b_l^m = \frac{1}{4}(a_m - a_l)^2$. And in case $\ell_r = \ell_l$ then, as shown momentarily, the refinement discussed in the text above implies m surely makes this proposal to l. Hence, the $t = 2$ continuation values are

$$W_l^2(\lambda; a_l) = W_l^3(\lambda; a_l) = 0;$$
$$W_m^2(\lambda; a_m) = B - \frac{1}{2}(a_m - a_l)^2;$$
$$W_r^2(\lambda; a_r) = -(a_{lm} - a_r)^2.$$

Now consider party r's $t = 2$ proposal and suppose, first, that r proposes to include l as a coalition partner. Then $W_l^2(\lambda; a_l) = 0$ implies r's optimization problem looks exactly like that facing m when m chooses the proposal to offer l. Omitting the details, we obtain $(y, (b_l, B - b_l, 0))$ with $y = a_{lr}$ and $b_l = \frac{1}{4}(a_r - a_l)^2$. In this case,

$$W_r(a_{rl}, b_l; a_r) = B - \frac{1}{2}(a_l - a_r)^2.$$

On the other hand, if r proposes to m rather than to l at $t = 2$ then, for the proposal to be accepted, m must be offered at least $W_m^2(\lambda; a_m) = B - \frac{1}{2}(a_m - a_l)^2$. Thus r solves

$$\max_{y', b_m, \zeta^r} \Lambda^r(y', b_m; \zeta^r) = B - b_m - (y' - a_r)^2 + \zeta^r[b_m - (y' - a_m)^2 - W_m^2(\lambda; a_m)].$$

From the first-order conditions we obtain r's $t = 2$ proposal $(y', (b_m, B - b_m, 0))$ where $y' = a_{rm}$ and

$$b_m = B + \frac{1}{4}(a_r - a_m)^2 - \frac{1}{2}(a_m - a_l)^2.$$

Thus

$$W_r(a_{lr}, b_l; a_r) \gtreqless W_r(a_{rm}, b_m; a_r) \Leftrightarrow$$
$$B - \frac{1}{2}(a_l - a_r)^2 \gtreqless \frac{1}{2}(a_m - a_l)^2 - \frac{1}{2}(a_r - a_m)^2$$
$$= (a_m - a_{lr})(a_r - a_l).$$

By assumption, $2\ell_l \geq \ell_r \geq \ell_l$ and so $a_{lr} \in [a_m, a_{rm}/2]$. Therefore, the right-hand side of the inequality is at most zero whereas, by assumption on the relative size of B, the left-hand side of the inequality is at least zero.

9.1. ELECTIONS, GOVERNMENT AND POLICY

Consequently, the most profitable coalition for r to propose in $t=2$ is a coalition with l. Hence,

$$W_l^1(\lambda; a_l) = W_l^2(\lambda; a_l) = W_l^3(\lambda; a_l) = 0;$$
$$W_m^1(\lambda; a_m) = -(a_{lr} - a_m)^2;$$
$$W_r^1(\lambda; a_r) = B - \frac{1}{2}(a_l - a_r)^2.$$

Clearly, l's best proposal is to include m, the smallest party, in the governing coalition (so justifying m's $t=3$ proposal to l when indifferent) since m is in a weaker bargaining position than is r at $t=1$ and $a_l \leq a_m \leq a_r$. Thus l solves

$$\max_{y, b_m, \zeta^l} \Lambda^l(y, b_m; \zeta^l) = B - b_m - (y - a_l)^2 + \zeta^l[b_m - (y - a_m)^2 - W_m^1(\lambda; a_m)].$$

The first-order conditions are

$$\frac{d\Lambda^l}{dy} = -2(y - a_l) - \zeta^l 2(y - a_m) = 0;$$
$$\frac{d\Lambda^l}{db_m} = \zeta^l - 1 = 0;$$
$$\frac{d\Lambda^l}{d\zeta^l} = b_m - (y - a_m)^2 + (a_{lr} - a_m)^2 = 0.$$

Solving, we obtain l's $t=1$ proposal $(y^l, (b_m^l, B - b_m^l, 0))$,

$$y^l = a_{lm}; \quad b_m^l = \frac{1}{4}(a_l - a_m)^2 - (a_{lr} - a_m)^2.$$

This proves (3b). Establishing the remaining cases is left as an exercise. □

It follows from the lemma that, at the electoral stage of the decision sequence, voters and parties can predict the policy implications associated with any profile of party platforms and distribution of votes and thus face well-defined electoral decision problems. Given a voting strategy v, electoral platforms $a \in X^3$ and a realized vector of weights $\omega(v(a))$ (that is, given the realization of any legislative tie-breaking lottery), the legislative equilibrium λ^* described in Lemma 9.1 induces a policy outcome $z^* = z(\omega(v(a))) \in X$.

Although the details of the policy locations and perq-distributions identified in Lemma 9.1 depend on the assumption that parties' preferences are quadratic in policy and linear in perks, the qualitative properties of the equilibrium outcomes depend only on policy preferences being single-peaked and preferences over perks being strictly increasing. Similarly, the prediction that it is always the largest and the smallest parties that form a governing coalition in equilibrium depends on the assumption that the order of proposals matches the order of legislative weights. But it is readily checked that so long as the bargaining protocol fixes a three-step sequence *ex ante*, then any legislative equilibrium involves the first and the final proposers constituting the equilibrium government. Example 9.1 illustrates this fact and makes clear that, although the relative location of parties' legislative ideal points surely affects the location of the final policy outcome, it is irrelevant to the composition of the governing coalition.

Example 9.1 Assume $X = [0, 1]$, $B = 1$ and $(a_l, a_m, a_r) = (0, \varepsilon, 1)$, where $\varepsilon > 0$ and small. Suppose all parties have a positive legislative weight and no party has a strict majority; suppose also that the bargaining protocol specifies the order of proposals to be l, m, r, with the "caretaker" outcome (z^0, b^0) being chosen to insure all parties receive a payoff equal to zero if no proposal is accepted: for ε small, $z^0 \approx \varepsilon/3$ and

$$(b_l^0, b_m^0, b_r^0) \approx (\frac{\varepsilon}{3}, (\frac{\varepsilon^2}{9}, \frac{\varepsilon}{3}(\frac{1}{3} - \varepsilon), 1 - \frac{\varepsilon}{9}(1 - 2\varepsilon))$$

yields $W_c^3(\lambda, a_c) = 0$, all c. The $t = 3$ proposal is made by r. Party r surely does best by proposing to m, its ideologically closest party. The optimal proposal solves

$$\max_{y,b}(1 - b) - (y - 1)^2$$

subject to

$$b - (y - \varepsilon)^2 \geq 0.$$

The solution is $y^r = (1 + \varepsilon)/2$ and

$$(b_l^r, b_m^r, b_r^r) = (0, \frac{1}{4}(1 - \varepsilon)^2, 1 - \frac{1}{4}(1 - \varepsilon)^2)$$

yielding continuation values

$$\begin{aligned} W_l^2(\lambda; 0) &= -\frac{1}{4}(1 + \varepsilon)^2; \\ W_m^2(\lambda; \varepsilon) &= 0; \\ W_r^2(\lambda; 1) &= 1 - \frac{1}{2}(1 - \varepsilon)^2. \end{aligned}$$

9.1. ELECTIONS, GOVERNMENT AND POLICY

Given these values, party m's optimal proposal in $t = 2$ is to offer its ideal outcome,

$$(y^m, (b_l^m, b_m^m, b_r^m)) = (\varepsilon, (0, 1, 0)),$$

since $W_l(y^m, b^m; 0) > W_l^2(\lambda; 0)$ and so the proposal passes. And because $\varepsilon \in (0, 1/2)$, it is immediate that l's optimal proposal at $t = 1$ is to attract party r as a coalition partner by proposing $(y^l, (b_l^l, b_m^l, b_r^l)) = (\varepsilon, (1, 0, 0))$. Under this proposal,

$$W_r(y^l, b^l; 1) = W_r^1(\lambda; 0) = -(1 - \varepsilon)^2$$

and therefore, by subgame perfection, r accepts the proposal.

Thus the legislative equilibrium outcome is a coalition government consisting of the first and last proposers, $\{l, r\}$, implementing a policy outcome $z^* = a_m$ and a distribution b^* that allocates all perks of office to the first proposer, l. Moreover, the equilibrium coalition government is $\{l, r\}$ for any $a_m \in (a_l, a_r) \subseteq [0, 1]$. □

Lemma 9.1 predicts that governing coalitions in the case that no party has a legislative majority consist of the largest and the smallest parties. Final policy outcomes, therefore, are not monotonic in vote shares and there exist no dominated voting strategies at the electoral stage of the process. This fact is justified with an example.

Example 9.2 Suppose $X = [0, 16]$ and, for the convenience, assume the electorate is small, $N = \{1, \ldots, 15\}$. Suppose the electoral threshold is $s = 1/5$; thus parties must receive at least three votes to insure positive legislative representation. Let voter ideal points be such that, for all $i \in N$, $x_i = i$ and write $u(y; x_i) \equiv u_i(y)$ etc. Assume $a_l = a_m = 11 < a_r = 12$. Then $u_1(a_l) = u_1(a_m) > u_1(a_r)$. We wish to show that individual $i = 1$ voting for party r is not a dominated strategy. To do this, suppose individuals $i = 2, \ldots, 5$ vote for l; individuals $i = 6, \ldots, 11$ vote for m; and individuals $i = 12, \ldots, 15$ vote for r. All voters $2, \ldots, 15$ are voting sincerely relative to the electoral positions $(a_l, a_m, a_r) = (11, 11, 12)$. Furthermore, each party $c \in \{l, m, r\}$ is receiving sufficient votes that $\omega_c > 0$, however $i = 1$ votes. If individual 1 votes sincerely for either party l or m, then no party has an overall majority but the legislative weights are $\omega_m > \omega_l > \omega_r$ if $i = 1$ votes for l and $\omega_m > \omega_l = \omega_r$ if $i = 1$ votes for m. By Lemma 9.1, if $i = 1$ votes for l, the legislative bargaining equilibrium policy outcome is

$$\frac{1}{2}(a_m + a_r) = 11\frac{1}{2};$$

and if $i = 1$ votes for m, the equilibrium policy outcome (in expectation) is

$$\frac{1}{2}(a_m + a_r) + \frac{1}{2}a_m = 11\frac{1}{4}.$$

On the other hand, if $i = 1$ votes for r then $\omega_m > \omega_r > \omega_l$ and the equilibrium policy outcome is $a_m = 11$ for sure. In this case, therefore, $i = 1$ has a best response to vote for party r. □

The absence of any dominated voting strategies complicates the analysis of equilibrium voting behavior. With many voters and three parties there are a great many undominated Nash voting equilibria for almost any triple of electoral platforms. To motivate a selection that precludes *prima facie* absurd predictions (for example, all voters invariably vote for the left-most candidate), we first invoke the symmetry assumption on the distribution of ideal points and look only for symmetric legislative election equilibria to the process as a whole, although not necessarily to any particular subgame, and then impose a nontriviality restriction on individual votes in such equilibria. Specifically, the vote-strategy profile in a symmetric legislative equilibrium must be such that, given all others' votes, every individual's vote must be pivotal with respect to the final policy outcome; at the electoral stage, that is, each voter in a symmetric legislative election equilibrium can affect the legislative outcome by switching his or her vote. With these remarks in mind, consider the following specification of voting behavior as a function of the electoral platform vector.

Let $a \in X^3$ and assume, without loss of generality, that $a_l \leq a_m \leq a_r$. For any individual with ideal point $x \in X$, say that the voting strategy v is *sincere at* a if $v(a;x)$ specifies that the individual votes surely for the candidate offering his or her most preferred alternative from the set $\{a_l, a_m, a_r\}$, breaking indifference over any subset of candidates with a fair lottery as necessary. Recall that μ is the median voter's ideal policy and let $\epsilon > 0$ be small.

(v1a) If $\mu = a_l = a_m = a_r$ then all individuals vote for m with probability one;

(v1b) If $\mu = a_l = a_m < a_r$ (respectively, $\mu = a_r = a_m > a_l$) then all individuals vote sincerely at a over $\{a_m, a_r\}$ (respectively, $\{a_m, a_l\}$), setting $v_l(a;x) = 0$ (respectively, $v_r(a;x) = 0$);

(v1c) If either $\mu \leq a_l$ or $\mu \geq a_r$ and (v1a) or (v1b) do not obtain, then all individuals vote sincerely at a;

9.1. ELECTIONS, GOVERNMENT AND POLICY

(v2) If $\mu \in (a_l, a_r)$ and there exists $a_c \in \{a_l, a_m, a_r\}$ such that, for all $c' \neq c$,

$$\int_{\{x \in X : u(a_c; x) > u(a_{c'}; x)\}} dF(x) > 1/2,$$

then all individuals vote sincerely at a;

Now suppose $a_l < \mu < a_r$ and (v2) does not apply.

(v3a) If $\mu > a_m$ then, for all $x \in X$

$$x < \min\{\mu - \epsilon, a_{mr}\} \Rightarrow v_m(a; x) = 1$$
$$x \geq \min\{\mu - \epsilon, a_{mr}\} \Rightarrow v_r(a; x) = 1;$$

(v3b) If $\mu < a_m$ then, for all $x \in X$

$$x \leq \max\{\mu + \epsilon, a_{ml}\} \Rightarrow v_l(a; x) = 1$$
$$x > \max\{\mu + \epsilon, a_{ml}\} \Rightarrow v_m(a; x) = 1;$$

(v4) If $\mu = a_m$ and $\ell_l < \ell_r$ (respectively, $\ell_l > \ell_r$) then all individuals vote sincerely at a over $\{a_l, a_m\}$ (respectively, $\{a_r, a_m\}$), setting $v_r(a; x) = 0$ (respectively, $v_l(a; x) = 0$);

(v5) If $\mu = a_m$ and $\ell_l = \ell_r < 8\ell^*/3$, then all individuals vote sincerely at a over $\{a_l, a_r\}$, setting $v_m(a; x) = 0$, where ℓ^* is implicitly defined by $\int_\mu^{\mu+\ell^*} dF(x) = [F(\mu + \ell^*) - F(\mu)] = s/2$;

(v6) If $\mu = a_m$ and $\ell_l = \ell_r \geq 8\ell^*/3$, then, for all $x \in X$

$$x < \mu - \ell^* \Rightarrow v_l(a; x) = 1$$
$$x > \mu + \ell^* \Rightarrow v_r(a; x) = 1$$
$$x \in [\mu - \ell^*, \mu + \ell^*] \Rightarrow v_m(a; x) = 1.$$

The strategy v defined by (v1) through (v6) is exhaustive: voting behavior is fully specified for every possible vector of electoral platforms $a \in X^3$. There are two things to note about the strategy. First, it results in a symmetric distribution of (expected) votes only in those cases that a is symmetric about the median ideal point μ, (v5), (v6), or that all three parties adopt the same platform, (v1); in all other instances, the voting strategy provides incentives for at least one party to adjust its platform. And second, when parties are symmetrically located but not too tightly clustered, (v6), the distribution of votes implies the middle party receives just enough to insure legislative representation and the two more extreme parties share the remaining votes equally. Thus every voter is pivotal here.

In a legislative election equilibrium, the voting strategy must describe Nash behavior at every distribution of electoral platforms, irrespective of whether or not a particular distribution is itself part of a legislative election equilibrium. Lemma 9.2 confirms that this is true of the strategy defined by (v1)-(v6).

Lemma 9.2 *Define the voting strategy v^* by properties (v1)-(v6). Then for all $a \in X^3$ and all $x \in X$,*

$$E[u(z(\omega(v^*(a))); x)|(a, \lambda^*)] \geq E[u(z(\omega(v(a;x), v^*(a))); x)|(a, \lambda^*)]$$

where λ^* is the legislative equilibrium described in Lemma 9.1 and $z(\omega(\cdot))$ is the final policy outcome conditional on realized weights $\omega(\cdot)$.

Proof Let $a_l \leq a_m \leq a_r$ and consider each case in turn.

(v1a) Obvious.

By symmetry, it suffices to consider only the case in which $\mu \leq a_l$ to check the claim for (v1b) and (v1c).

(v1b) Assume $\mu = a_l = a_m < a_r$; then sincere voting over $\{a_m, a_r\}$ with $v_l^*(a; x) = 0$ for all $x \in X$ implies $v_m^*(a; x) > 1/2$. Therefore, by Lemma 9.1, $z(\omega(v^*(a))) = a_m$ surely and sincere voting is clearly a best response strategy.

(v1c) Now assume $\mu \leq a_l$ and (v1a) does not obtain. There are three cases to check.

If $\mu \leq a_l < a_m \leq a_r$, $v^*(a)$ implies $\omega_l(v^*(a)) > 1/2$. Therefore, by Lemma 9.1, $z(\omega(v^*(a))) = a_l$ and no voter is pivotal over the set of possible legislative equilibrium policy outcomes; so sincere voting is a best response for all individuals.

If $\mu < a_l = a_m < a_r$, sincere voting implies that, for all $x \leq (a_l + a_r)/2$, $v_l^*(a^*; x) = v_m^*(a^*; x) = 1/2$ and, for all $x > (a_l + a_r)/2$, $v_r^*(a^*; x) = 1$. Since the threshold $s < 1/4$ and $\mu < a_r$, $\omega_l(v^*) = \omega_m(v^*) > 0$. Now, either $\omega_r(v^*) = 0$, in which case Lemma 9.1 yields $z(\omega(v^*(a))) = a_l = a_m$ and sincere voting is a best response strategy for all x at a; or $\omega_r(v^*) > 0$. If $\omega_r(v^*) > 0$, it is possible that $\omega_r(v^*) > \omega_l(v^*) = \omega_m(v^*)$ or that $\omega_l(v^*) = \omega_m(v^*) \geq \omega_r(v^*)$. In the latter situation, Lemma 9.1 yields $z(\omega(v^*(a))) = a_l = a_m$ and sincere voting is a best response as before; in the former situation, however, Lemma 9.1 yields $z(\omega(v^*(a))) = a_{lr}$. By definition,

9.1. ELECTIONS, GOVERNMENT AND POLICY

$v_r^*(a^*; x) = 1$ if and only if $x > a_{lr}$; hence no individual with ideal point $x > a_{lr}$ prefers to switch their vote and support either of the other two parties and, likewise, no voter with ideal point $x \leq a_{lr}$ prefers to switch their vote and support r. Thus, sincere voting is again a best response strategy for all x at a.

If $\mu < a_l = a_m = a_r$ the final policy outcome $z(\omega(v^*(a))) = a_l$ is invariant to the distribution of votes, so sincere voting is trivially a best response.

(v2) $\mu \in (a_l, a_r)$ implies $a_l < a_r$ and, given the hypothesis defining this case, essentially the same argument as for the first case under (v1c) applies.

(v3) Suppose $a_r > \mu > a_m \geq a_l$. By construction, $v^*(a)$ insures $\omega_r(v^*(a)) > 1/2$ and no individual is pivotal in the subgame and, therefore, $v^*(a)$ describes best response voting at a. Exactly the same argument (*mutatis mutandis*) applies when $a_r \geq a_m > \mu > a_l$.

(v4) Suppose $\mu = a_m$ and $\ell_l < \ell_r$. By quadratic preferences and $a_l < \mu = a_m < a_r$, sincere voting over $\{a_l, a_m\}$ (setting $v_r(a; x) = 0$) insures $\omega_m(v^*(a)) > 1/2$ and $z(\omega(v^*(a))) = a_m$. Thus a strict majority prefers the outcome a_m to any other equilibrium policy outcome and no voter is pivotal. Hence $v^*(a)$ is a best response strategy. The same argument applies if $\ell_l > \ell_r$.

(v5) If $\mu = a_m$ and $\ell_l = \ell_r < \ell^*$ and all individuals vote sincerely at a over $\{a_l, a_r\}$, setting $v_m(a; x) = 0$, $u(\cdot)$ quadratic implies $\omega_l(v^*(a)) = \omega_r(v^*(a)) > \omega_m(v^*(a)) = 0$. By Lemma 9.1, therefore, the expected final outcome is $[a_l + a_r]/2 = a_m$. All individuals are pivotal with respect to $\{a_l, a_r\}$ and $s > 0$ implies (given the large electorate) that no individual can induce any third possible outcome by voting for m. Hence sincere voting over $\{a_l, a_r\}$ is a best response for all individuals.

(v6) Suppose $\mu = a_m$ and $\ell_l = \ell_r \geq \ell^*$. Given $v^*(a)$, $\omega_m(v^*(a)) = s$ and

$$\omega_l(v^*(a)) = \omega_r(v^*(a)) = (1-s)/2.$$

By Lemma 9.1, therefore, $z(\omega(v^*(a))) \in \{a_{lm}, a_{rm}\}$, where each occurs with probability $1/2$, and (recalling the electorate is large but finite) all individuals are pivotal. By supposition, $\ell_l = \ell_r = \ell > 0$. Hence, the expected policy outcome is $[a_l + a_r]/2 = a_m$ and, by $u(\cdot; x)$ quadratic for all $x \in X$,

$$E[u(z(\omega(v^*)); x)] = -(a_m - x)^2 - \left(\frac{\ell}{2}\right)^2,$$

where dependency of payoffs and outcomes on a and λ^* is suppressed. By symmetry, it suffices to check that individuals with ideal points $x \geq \mu$ are making best response decisions under v^*. So consider first an individual with ideal point $x \in [\mu, \mu + \ell^*]$; then $v_m^*(a; x) = 1$. Suppose the individual deviates and votes surely for r rather than m, $v_r = 1$. Then

$$V_r(v(a;x), v^*) > V_l(v(a;x), v^*) = (1-s)/2$$

and

$$V_m(v(a;x), v^*) < s.$$

Therefore m fails to attract sufficient votes for legislative representation and $\omega_r(v(a;x), v^*) > 1/2$. By Lemma 9.1, $z(\omega(v(a;x), v^*)) = a_r$ for sure and the individual's payoff is

$$E[u(z(\omega(v(a;x), v^*)); x)] = -(a_r - x)^2.$$

Hence, $a_r - a_m = a_r - \mu = \ell$ implies

$$
\begin{aligned}
E[u(z(\omega(v^*)); x)] &\geq E[u(z(\omega(v(a;x), v^*)); x)] \Leftrightarrow \\
(a_r - x)^2 - (a_m - x)^2 - \left(\frac{\ell}{2}\right)^2 &\geq 0 \Leftrightarrow \\
(a_r - a_m)(a_r + a_m - 2x) - \left(\frac{\ell}{2}\right)^2 &\geq 0 \Leftrightarrow \\
\frac{a_r + a_m}{2} - x - \frac{\ell}{8} &\geq 0 \Leftrightarrow \\
\mu + \frac{\ell}{2} - x - \frac{\ell}{8} &\geq 0 \Leftrightarrow \\
\mu + \frac{3}{8}\ell &\geq x.
\end{aligned}
$$

But by hypothesis, $\ell \geq 8\ell^*/3$ and $x \leq \mu + \ell^*$. Therefore, $v_m^*(a; x) = 1$ is a best response vote. The same argument also shows $v_r^*(a; x) = 1$ is best response for any $x > \mu + \ell^*$. Finally since it is clearly unprofitable for an individual with $x > \mu$ to vote for l at v^*, this completes the proof. □

With the exception of distributions of electoral platforms falling under (v1), (v2) or (v6), there is little that is particularly compelling or empirically plausible in the description of the voting strategy of Lemma 9.2. But as discussed earlier, it is necessary to specify voting behavior both in and out of (in this case) legislative election equilibria and, furthermore, the demand

9.1. ELECTIONS, GOVERNMENT AND POLICY

that such equilibria be undominated subgame perfect in turn requires voting behavior to be Nash best responses at every logically possible list of platforms $a \in X^3$. However, it turns out that the less plausible distributions of votes occur exclusively off the equilibrium path. And it is worth noting that simply assuming sincere voting everywhere is not enough. Indeed, because legislative decision-making is majoritarian in that a party with legislative weight exceeding one-half controls the chamber, insisting on sincere voting here effectively makes the subgame in which parties' choose electoral platforms equivalent to three-party simple plurality election in which the winner takes all [Exercise]. Therefore, at least some strategic voting is necessary to support legislative electoral equilibria under proportional representation.

Recall that $\ell^* > 0$ is implicitly defined by $[F(\mu + \ell^*) - F(\mu)] = s/2$ and define $\hat{\ell} \geq \ell^*$ similarly by $[F((\mu + \hat{\ell})/2) - F(\mu)] = 1/4$; for any $a \in X^3$, assume $a_l \leq a_m \leq a_r$. If a party fails to attract the threshold vote-share then it bears a nontrivial cost $d > 0$. The requirement that this cost be "nontrivial" is used only to establish the necessity claim of the result to follow and, in terms of parameters defined above, "nontrivial" amounts to assuming $d \geq 8(\ell^*)^2/3$.

Theorem 9.1 *Let λ^* and v^* be defined by Lemmas 9.1 and 9.2, respectively. Then $((a^*, \lambda^*), v^*)$ is a legislative equilibrium if and only if $\ell_l = \ell_r = \ell$ and $\ell \in [\frac{8}{3}\ell^*, \hat{\ell})$.*

Proof (Sufficiency) Assume $a^* \in X^3$ satisfies the hypothesis. Lemma 9.2 implies $v^*(a^*)$ is defined by (v6) under which parties l and r attract equal vote shares of $(1 - s)/2$ and the middle party m, located at the median's ideal point, $a_m^* = \mu$, receives the remaining vote share, s. By Lemma 9.1, therefore, the final legislative outcome is

$$(z(\omega(v^*(a^*))), b(\omega(v^*(a^*)))) \in \{(a_{lm}^*, (B - b_m^*, b_m^*, 0)), (a_{rm}, (0, b_m^*, B - b_m^*))\}$$

where each outcome occurs with probability one-half and

$$b_m^* = \frac{1}{4}(a_l^* - a_m^*)^2 - (a_{lr}^* - a_m^*)^2 = \frac{1}{4}\ell^2.$$

For any $a \in X^3$ and $c \in \{l, m, r\}$, write $EW_c^*(a) \equiv E[W_c(z, b; a_c)|v^*, a, \lambda^*]$; then, for each $c, c' \in \{l, r\}, c \neq c'$,

$$EW_c^*(a^*) = \frac{1}{2}[B - b_m^* - (a_{cm}^* - a_c^*)^2] + \frac{1}{2}[-(a_{cm}^* - a_c^*)^2]$$

$$= \frac{1}{2}B - \frac{11}{8}\ell^2;$$

and

$$EW_m^*(a^*) = b_m^* - \frac{1}{2}[(a_{lm}^* - a_m^*)^2 + (a_{rm}^* - a_m^*)^2]$$
$$= 0.$$

By assumption on the size of B, $EW_c^*(a^*) > 0$, $c = l, r$. To check sufficiency, we show that any unilateral deviation in a party c's platform resulting in a vector of electoral platforms $a = (a_c, a_{-c}^*)$ leads to an expected payoff $EW_c^*(a) < EW_c^*(a^*)$. Consider each party in turn.

By definition of the middle party, it suffices to look only at deviations by m to platforms $a_m \in [a_l^*, a_r^*]$, $a_m \neq \mu$. Without loss of generality, suppose $a_m < \mu$; then case (v3) obtains and $v^*(a)$ insures

$$\omega_r(v^*(a)) > 1/2 > \omega_m(v^*(a)) > 0.$$

Hence, by Lemma 9.1, the outcome is $(z, (b_l, b_m, b_r)) = (a_r^*, (0, 0, B))$ so

$$EW_m^*(a) = -(a_r^* - a_m)^2 < EW_m^*(a^*).$$

Now suppose l deviates to a platform $a_l \neq a_l^*$; by definition of the leftmost party, only deviations to platforms $a_l \leq a_m^*$ need to be checked. There are three cases. Assume first that $a_l < a_l^*$. Then $\ell_l > \ell_r = \ell$ and (v4) obtains. Hence $v^*(a)$ is such that $\omega_l(v^*(a)) = 0$ and

$$EW_l^*(a) = -d < EW_l^*(a^*).$$

If $a_l \in (a_l^*, a_m^*)$, $\ell_l < \ell_r = \ell$ and (v4) again obtains; in this case, however, $v^*(a)$ yields

$$\omega_m(v^*(a)) > 1/2 > \omega_l(v^*(a)) > 0.$$

By Lemma 9.1, the outcome is $(a_m^*, (0, B, 0))$ so

$$EW_l^*(a) = -(a_m^* - a_l)^2 < EW_l^*(a^*).$$

Finally, suppose $a_l = a_m^*$. Then (v1a) holds with $\mu = a_l = a_m^* < a_r^*$ and $v^*(a)$ gives l no votes at all, so

$$EW_l^*(a) = -d < EW_l^*(a^*).$$

Because symmetric arguments apply to any unilateral deviation by party r, this completes the argument for sufficiency.

(Necessity) We first show that if $a \in X^3$ falls under any case (v1) through (v5) defining the voting strategy v^*, then a cannot be an equilibrium list of

9.1. ELECTIONS, GOVERNMENT AND POLICY

platforms. To do this, first note that no list of platforms with $\mu \notin [a_l, a_r]$ can constitute equilibrium behavior [Exercise]. So assume $\mu \in [a_l, a_r]$ hereon.

If $\mu = a_l = a_m \leq a_r$ then, depending on whether the inequality is strict, (v1a) or (v1b) with $a_l = a_m < a_r$ applies; in both cases, however, $EW_l^*(a) = -d$. But $a' = (a_m - \varepsilon, a_m, a_r)$, $\varepsilon > 0$, falls under either (v1b) with $a_l < a_m = a_r$ or (v4). In both cases, Lemma 9.1 yields $EW_l^*(a') = -\varepsilon^2 > EW_l^*(a)$ for ε sufficiently small so the deviation is profitable. By symmetry, $a_l \leq a_m = a_r = \mu$ cannot be an equilibrium list of platforms.

If $\mu = a_l$ and cases (v1a) and (v1b) do not apply, then (v1c) applies with $a_l < a_m \leq a_r$; consequently, $v^*(a)$ yields $\omega_l(v^*(a)) > 1/2$. Therefore, by Lemma 9.1, $z(\omega(v^*(a))) = a_l$, $b_l = B$ and so $EW_m^*(a) = -(a_l - a_m)^2$. But if m deviates unilaterally to $a'_m = a_{lm}$, (v1c) continues to obtain and $EW_m^*(a') = -(a_l - a_{lm})^2 > EW_m^*(a)$. By symmetry, $a_l \leq a_m < a_r = \mu$ cannot be an equilibrium list of platforms.

Together, the preceding arguments imply that (v1) is inconsistent with equilibrium behavior under v^*; in particular, $a_l < \mu < a_r$ is a necessary property of legislative election equilibrium platforms here.

If $\mu \in (a_l, a_r)$ and there is a Condorcet winner, say a_c, among the set of platforms, then (v2) applies and sincere voting yields the policy outcome a_c and perq distribution b with $b_c = B$. Suppose $c = l$; then $u(\cdot)$ symmetric and $a_l < \mu < a_r$ imply $a_{lm} \geq \mu$ and $a_m > \mu$. Suppose m deviates to platform $a'_m = \mu$; then (v4) obtains at $a' = (a_l, a'_m, a_r)$ and, by definition of v^*, λ^*, we have $EW_m^*(a') = B > EW_m^*(a)$. A similar argument applies if the Condorcet winning platform at a is offered by party $c = r$. So if a describes equilibrium platform choices, it must be that $c = m$. But then either $a_m > \mu$ and l can deviate to $a'_l = \mu$ to give a' such that (v1c) applies and obtain a payoff

$$EW_l^*(a') = B > -(a_m - a_l)^2 \geq EW_l^*(a);$$

or $a_m < \mu$ and a symmetric argument applies for r. Hence, $a_m = \mu$ here, in which case party l can deviate to $a'_l = \mu - \varepsilon$, $\varepsilon > 0$ and small so that (v4) applies and gives $EW_l^*(a') = -\varepsilon^2 > EW_l^*(a)$. So no profile a such that (v2) obtains supports a legislative election equilibrium.

Suppose $a_l < \mu < a_r$ and (v2) does not apply. If $a_m \neq \mu$ then (v3) applies and similar reasoning as above yields the desired contradiction: at least one of the extreme parties can profit by deviating to a platform $a'_v = \mu$. So assume $a_m = \mu$. If $\ell_l < \ell_r$, (v4) holds and $v^*(a)$ implies $\omega_r(v^*(a)) = 0$ and $EW_r^*(a) = -d$. Suppose r deviates to any policy $a'_r \in (\mu, a_r)$ such that $(a'_r - a_m) < \ell_l$. Then (v4) applies again with the roles of l and r reversed

and
$$EW_r^*(a') = -(a_m - a'_r)^2 > EW_r^*(a).$$

By symmetry, therefore, no profile a for which (v4) holds can be an equilibrium list of platforms.

Suppose a falls under (v5): $\mu = a_m$ and $\ell_l = \ell_r < 8\ell^*/3$. Then $\omega_m(v^*(a)) = 0$ and $EW_m^*(a) = -d$. However, if m deviates to $a'_m = \mu - \varepsilon$, $\varepsilon > 0$ and small, a' is such that (v3a) obtains so

$$EW_m^*(a') = -(a_r - a'_m)^2 = -(\ell_r + \varepsilon)^2.$$

Hence
$$EW_m^*(a') - EW_m^*(a) = d - (\ell_r + \varepsilon)^2.$$

By assumption, $d \geq 8(\ell^*)^2/3$ and, by supposition, $\ell_r < 8\ell^*/3$. Therefore, $EW_m^*(a') > EW_m^*(a)$ for ε sufficiently small.

It follows that if $a \in X^3$ is an equilibrium list of platforms, (v6) must apply. To complete the argument for necessity, note that by symmetry of $u(\cdot)$ and F, the distribution of ideal points, $\mu = a_m$ and $\ell_l = \ell_r \geq \hat{\ell}$ imply (v2) obtains with a_m being a Condorcet winner among $\{a_l, a_m, a_r\}$. □

Legislative election equilibria supported by v^*, therefore, involve a distribution of party platforms with the middle party, m, adopting the median voter's ideal policy and the two relatively extreme parties, l and r, located symmetrically about the median, neither too close to nor too far from, the median ideal policy. The legislative weights are then $\omega_l = \omega_r > \omega_m$ with m attracting exactly the threshold vote share s. It follows from Lemma 9.1, therefore, that the equilibrium policy outcome is either a_{lm} or a_{rm}, with expected outcome $[a_{lm} + a_{rm}]/2 = \mu$. And it is worth noting that while no voter votes for his or her least preferred party in equilibrium, there are surely voters who vote for their second best platform from the three offered. Specifically, there are individuals who rank the middle party platform best of the three, but for whom it is nevertheless rational to vote for an extreme party to insure a balance at the legislative bargaining stage. Should such an individual, say with ideal point $x > a_m = \mu$, deviate and vote sincerely for m rather than for r, then, given others' decisions, the individual's least preferred party l ends up with the largest legislative weight and Lemma 9.1 implies the outcome is a_{lm} for sure; and a_{lm} for sure is clearly worse for the individual than a fair lottery over a_{lm} and a_{rm}. Figure 9.1 illustrates the equilibrium.

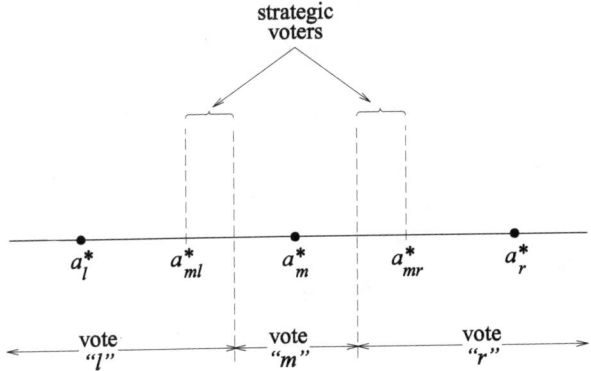

Figure 9.1: Legislative election equilibrium

9.2 Application: Representative legislatures

An argument often advanced in support of electing representatives to a majoritarian legislature by proportional representation rather than by simple plurality rule runs as follows. At least for reasonably-sized legislatures and unlike under plurality rule, proportional representation results in a distribution of representatives' preferences that reflects the distribution of voter preferences. Furthermore, legislative decisions from majoritarian legislatures elected under proportional representation almost always have to be determined through a coalition bargaining process, resulting in policy outcomes that are more-or-less weighted averages of representatives' ideal points. Therefore, since representatives' legislative weights reflect their relative vote-shares and thus the distribution of voter preferences, final policy outcomes from polities using proportional elections are superior compromises than those from polities using simple plurality elections under which a single party almost always dictates policies that reflect only the preferences of its supporters.

Whatever the empirical validity of claims for proportional representation that rest at least in part on the argument sketched above, the results of the preceding section, albeit developed around a limited model with three parties and one-dimensional politics, suggest that their theoretical basis is obscure.

First, the fact that legislative decision-making is majoritarian implies that some strategic voting is necessary to support legislative election equilibria in which all three parties are represented: from Theorem 9.1 and

Lemma 9.2, there are two blocks of individuals who, in equilibrium, vote for their second most preferred party rather than their most favored party. The premise that vote-shares reflect the distribution of preferences in the electorate, therefore, is suspect. Moreover, it follows from the theorem that the *lower* is the minimal vote-share threshold ($s > 0$) required for legislative representation, the *larger* is the equilibrium proportion of the electorate voting strategically [Exercise]. In other words, with a fixed number of parties competing for votes, relatively low barriers to legislative entry are associated with relatively high degrees of strategic voting and a correspondingly weaker association between voters' and representatives' policy preferences.

Second, sequential legislative bargaining need not result in policy outcomes that reflect the relative legislative weights (essentially, vote-shares) of elected representatives. For the particular bargaining protocol analyzed here, Lemma 9.1 makes clear that for arbitrary distributions of legislative weights, the coalition government is minimum winning but need not be of minimal size: in legislative equilibrium, the governing coalition comprises the largest and smallest parties. Nor need this coalition be connected in the sense that the ideal points of parties are adjacent. In the full, legislative election equilibrium, however, where party platforms and thus legislative objectives are defined, the *de facto* government does indeed comprise a minimally sized and connected coalition. But precisely because of this, the final policy outcome implemented by the government is surely not a compromise among all representatives but only among coalition members with compromise policies lying all to one side of the policy space. Although the expected policy outcome is the median voter's ideal point μ, the realized policy outcome lies either to the left or to the right of μ. For example, with a uniform distribution of voters distributed over the policy space $X = [0, 1]$, Theorem 9.1 implies there is a legislative equilibrium in which the final policy outcome is $z^* \in \{1/4, 3/4\}$ whereas the median is $\mu = 1/2$.

Among the possible legislative equilibrium party platforms predicted by Theorem 9.1, the least diverse distribution (a_l^*, a_m^*, a_r^*) is the most (Pareto) efficient. To see this, note that all agents' preferences are quadratic over policy and, therefore, every agent strictly prefers a lottery with a given expected outcome and variance to a lottery with the same expected outcome but greater variance. Since the expected policy outcome, the median voter's ideal policy μ, is invariant across legislative election equilibria, as is the expected distribution of perks among parties, it follows that the distribution of platforms with least variance is most preferred. Furthermore, at least on these grounds, simple plurality elections with two parties in fact dominate the proportional election system with three parties here: the two-party plurality system yields the median voter's ideal point μ for sure in equilibrium and sincere voting is the unique undominated voting strategy.

Conceptual concerns arising out of limited models are more often than not suggestive rather than compelling. Nevertheless, it is worth noting that West German politics over the two decades 1970-1990 broadly corresponds to the framework here: proportional rule elections with a 5% vote-share threshold, majoritarian legislature and three significant parties. In all five legislative elections during that period, two large parties (SPD and CDU) were evenly balanced and (for the most part) spanned the third, smaller, party (FDP) on an ideological dimension. The SPD and CDU each attracted around 40% to 45% vote-shares and the FDP attracted around a 7% to 10% vote-share. In three of the five legislative elections during that period, 1972, 1983 and 1987, the governing coalition consisted of the FDP and one of the larger two parties. Although these observations hardly constitute a test of the predictions of Theorem 9.1, they do at least provide reason to think the conceptual concerns suggested by the theorem are empirically germane.

9.3 Discussion

The preceding five chapters concerned legislatures and elections, considered largely as independent decision-making arenas. To develop a deeper understanding of how individuals' preferences map into collective choices through representative political systems, however, requires integrating the two arenas, for legislators' decisions over outcomes depend in part on the electoral implications of those decisions and citizens' decisions over candidates for legislative office depend in part on the legislative implications of voting one way or another. Comparative evaluations of, say, two or more electoral rules absent any account of the legislative policy outcomes induced by each are necessarily subject to qualification. It is possible, for example, for a proportional election rule to appear superior to plurality rule on a criterion of maximizing the dispersion of legislator preferences, but to induce legislative incentives that lead to less desirable final policy decisions from the electorate's perspective. Indeed, this is essentially the argument of the previous section: at least in the case of a one-dimensional policy space, a three-party proportional election system supports a *prima facie* inferior outcome relative to a two-party plurality election.

The model considered in this chapter explicitly links legislative and electoral behavior through voters' understanding of how post-election legislative bargaining, and thereby the final policy outcome, depends upon electoral vote-shares. The model does not, however, consider the incentives for parties to enter the election as a function of expected subsequent behavior or address questions arising from the prevalence of multidimensional policy spaces. Yet both features appear critical to a full understanding of both proportional election systems and coalition government more generally.

9.4 Exercises

9.1 Complete the proof of Lemma 9.1.

9.2 Example 9.2 suggests that even if two parties adopt an identical electoral platform, distinct from the third party, the actual location of the legislative policy outcome can depend on the relative legislative weights of these two parties. Explain the intuition for this result.

9.3 Show (or provide a counterexample) that insisting on sincere voting at the electoral stage of the model developed in the chapter effectively makes the political system equivalent to three-party simple plurality election in which the winner takes all.

9.4 Show that no list of platforms with $\mu \notin [a_l, a_r]$ can constitute equilibrium behavior (given λ^*, v^*).

9.5 Use Theorem 9.1 to show that, other things equal, the lower is the minimal vote-share threshold ($s > 0$) required for legislative representation, the larger is the equilibrium proportion of the electorate voting strategically.

9.6 The model of party preferences in the chapter assumes parties' policy payoffs are not contingent on whether or not the party belongs to the governing coalition. Consequently, a legislative party excluded from government is presumed to be penalized by voters for the government's policy decision. One suggestion for why such a penalty is not unreasonable is that being excluded from a government coalition is itself something requiring explanation by the party, perhaps indicating legislative ineffectiveness to voters with the extent of such ineffectiveness being positively correlated with the gap between electoral and final policy. Briefly evaluate this suggestion. Write down a model of party policy preferences that are contingent on whether the party is in the governing coalition. To what extent are the results of the chapter sensitive to your proposed variation?

9.5 Further reading

This chapter rests on Austen-Smith and Banks [10]. Baron and Diermeier [31] consider a closely related model in a two-dimensional policy space; Austen-Smith [9] integrates an economic model of occupational choice with a political system of the sort studied here to compare redistributive tax policies in political economies under proportional representation and plurality rule. Austen-Smith [8], surveys earlier models of legislative elections, including multidistrict models under plurality rule and, in Austen-Smith [7], offers a formal criticism of the sincere voting assumption for understanding legislative elections in general. Laver and Schofield [113] is a comprehensive overview of coalition theory applied to post-WWII parliamentary governments in Europe; the data cited in section 9.2 is taken from this book.

The literature on coalition government formation, abstracting from electoral concerns, is relatively advanced. Contributions include Baron [30] who applies the legislative bargaining model to a two-dimensional model of coalition formation; Merlo [128] who explores a sequential model of coalition formation with uncertainty; and Diermeier, Eraslan and Merlo [60] who construct and estimate a structural model of government coalition formation. Cooperative game theory offers a natural alternative approach to understanding coalitional government. The idea of the minimum winning coalition was introduced by Riker [171], the seminal contribution for political science, both to the theory of coalition formation and positive political theory *per se*; Axelrod [14] augmented the theory to require minimum winning *connected* coalitions. Cooperative game-theoretic models have been applied to government formation by, among others, Schofield [185], [186], [187].

Chapter 10

Summary and Conclusions

A central task for political science is to understand how the preferences of individuals comprising a society map into the collective choices of that society. The development of such an understanding constitutes the organizing principle for this volume and its precursor, *Positive Political Theory I: Collective Preference*.

In the Preface to the first volume, we distinguished two approaches to thinking about how preferences are aggregated to arrive at collective decisions. The *direct* (collective preference) approach is motivated by an essentially decision-theoretic methodology: individual preferences are directly aggregated into a collective preference which, as in individual decision theory, is maximized to yield a set of best (relative to the maximand) alternatives, the collective choices. The *indirect* (game-theoretic) approach recognizes that the preferences individuals choose to reveal need not coincide with the preferences with which they are endowed: an individual may have a clear ranking of candidates for electoral office, for example, yet choose to vote strategically or to abstain. Thus, while individual preferences surely influence individual decisions and actions, it is individual actions (in particular for our purposes, voting and agenda-selection), not individual preferences *per se*, that are aggregated to arrive at collective choices.

Formally, let $\mathcal{R}^n$ be the usual domain of individual preference profiles over a set of alternatives X for a society $N = \{1, \ldots, n\}$. Let $\varphi : \mathcal{R}^n \rightrightarrows X$ be a collective choice rule; for any profile $\rho \in \mathcal{R}^n$, $\varphi(\rho) \subseteq X$ denotes the outcomes chosen by society. Now define a preference aggregation rule $f : \mathcal{R}^n \to \mathcal{B}$, where $\mathcal{B}$ is the set of all complete binary relations over X [PPTI, ch.2], and define the mapping $m : \mathcal{B} \rightrightarrows X$ such that, for all $\rho \in \mathcal{R}^n$,

$$m(f(\rho)) = \{x \in X : \forall y \in X, \, x f(\rho) y\}$$

is the maximal set of alternatives in X with respect to the binary relation $f(\rho) \in \mathcal{B}$, the *core* of f at ρ. Then the direct approach to preference aggregation is summarized as the analysis of the collective choice rule defined by the composition of m and f, $\varphi \equiv m \circ f$. The indirect approach, however, begins with a description of the actions, or pure strategies, $\mathcal{M}_i$ an individual $i \in N$ can take and a rule $g : \mathcal{M} \to X$ that associates an alternative $g(s) \in X$ with every feasible profile of actions $s \in \mathcal{M} \equiv \Pi_{i \in N} \mathcal{M}_i$. A pair $(\mathcal{M}, g)$ is a mechanism. An abstract theory of how individuals choose their respective actions under a given mechanism is a mapping $\beta : \mathcal{R}^n \rightrightarrows \mathcal{M}$ where, for any $\rho \in \mathcal{R}^n$, $\beta(\rho) \subseteq \mathcal{M}$ is the set of action profiles consistent with the theory β at preference profile ρ. Defining the composition of g and β by

$$g(\beta(\rho)) = \{x \in X : x = g(s) \text{ for some } s \in \beta(\rho)\},$$

all $\rho \in \mathcal{R}^n$, the indirect approach to preference aggregation is then summarized as the analysis of the collective choice rule $\varphi \equiv g \circ \beta$. Figure 10.1 depicts the various links and suggests, rather than being mutually exclusive, that the direct and indirect approaches are complementary.

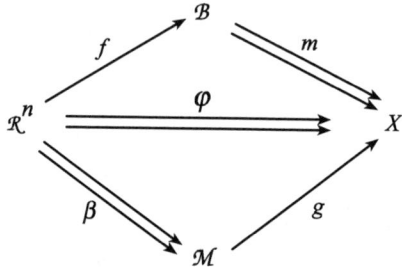

Figure 10.1: Linking preferences to collective choices

Positive Political Theory I explores the direct approach to preference aggregation. In that volume we argue that a key distinction between the collective preference and game-theoretic tacks lies in an implicit tradeoff each makes between the general existence of well-defined collective choices and a mild normative condition, minimal democracy, which requires that no individual i can unilaterally veto an alternative x in favor of an alternative y if all individuals other than i strictly prefer x to y. While insuring general existence proves elusive for collective preference theory (the set $m(f(\rho))$ is typically empty under all but the most constrained conditions) but largely unproblematic for game theory (the set $g(\beta(\rho))$ is typically nonempty in all

10.1. RETROSPECTIVE

but the most unstructured settings), the reverse is true in regard to collective choices that respect minimal democracy. Indeed, by [PPTI, Corollary 7.1], there exists no approach to preference aggregation that, in the absence of additional restrictions on the domain of application, is consistent with insuring the existence of well-defined collective choices that invariably satisfy minimal democracy.

Collective preference theory insists on minimal democracy and the argument of *Positive Political Theory I* is that, as a consequence of such insistence, a general theory of political behavior analogous to the decision-theoretic model of maximizing individual choice is unavailable. This conclusion both informs and motivates exploring the indirect approach to preference aggregation through the aggregation of equilibrium actions. We know that existence of well-defined equilibrium predictions within game-theoretic models typically comes at the expense of a violation of minimal democracy; what is not known, however, is how severe a violation is required, or what these equilibrium predictions might be, or how the predictions might depend on institutional details. Such concerns are the subject-matter of the preceding chapters.

10.1 Retrospective

From the theoretical perspective of preference aggregation, dictatorships are trivial: collective choice simply reflects what the dictator wants. Of course, the implementation of such wants is often far from trivial and there is much to be learned about the behavior of dictatorial polities. But given we are interested in indirect preference aggregation mediated by political institutions in more-or-less democratic polities, the emphasis lies on representative systems, loosely described by a two-stage process: elections and legislative decision-making. The lower half of Figure 10.1, that is, can be decomposed, with the legislature intervening between electoral decisions and policy outcomes. Such a decomposition is shown in Figure 10.2, below.

In Figure 10.2, $(\mathcal{M}_E, g_E)$ is an electoral mechanism, where $\mathcal{M}_E$ describes the possible profiles of individuals' votes and g_E maps votes into legislatures; and $(\mathcal{M}_L, g_L)$ is a legislative mechanism, where $\mathcal{M}_L$ describes the possible profiles of legislators' actions and g_L maps these actions into policy outcomes. (All individuals, voters or elected members of the legislature are assumed to behave according to the theory β.) Thus voters choose legislators (and, possibly, the executive) and legislators choose policies.

CHAPTER 10. SUMMARY AND CONCLUSIONS

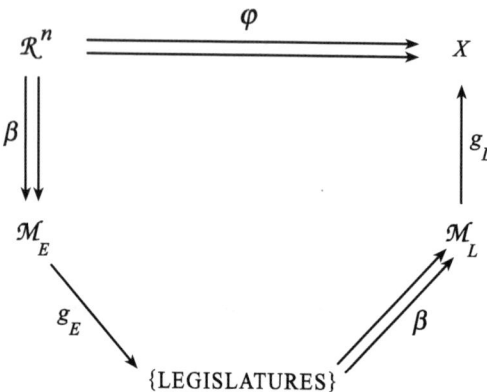

Figure 10.2: An abstract representative political system

Before worrying about either elections or legislatures, however, it is important to ask whether there need be any concern at all with strategic or manipulative behavior on the part of individuals. If individuals typically find it in their interest to reveal their preferences when asked to do so, then analytical and normative complications with strategic choice are moot and we can (in principle) make collective choices through a direct democracy by applying the relevant collective choice rule (the mapping φ in Figure 10.2) to the list of reported preferences. In this case, the institutions of indirect, or representative, democracy are essentially pragmatic, facilitating the collection and processing of individual preferences to yield collective choices.

Chapter 2 addresses the extent to which direct preference aggregation rules are susceptible to manipulation through individual strategic behavior. Perhaps unfortunately, it turns out (at least in principle) that strategic behavior is endemic. Subject to some mild technical conditions, if a collective choice rule is defined on a sufficiently unrestricted domain, single-valued and nondictatorial, then it surely offers incentives for individuals to misrepresent their true preferences (Theorem 2.1 and Theorem 2.5). Although this somewhat negative result disappears in the important case of single-peaked preference profiles (Theorem 2.4), the likelihood of such profiles obtaining over any but the simplest sets of policy alternatives is small. The institutions of indirect democracy, that is, are necessarily more than ciphers translating sincerely revealed individual preferences into collective choices.

In view of the pessimistic results of Chapter 2, Chapter 3 explores the extent to which any distortions (suitably defined) in collective choice intro-

10.1. RETROSPECTIVE

duced by individual strategic behavior might be attenuated through careful institution, or mechanism, design. And here the results depend in large part on what is presumed about individual behavior (Corollary 3.1, Theorem 3.5 and Theorem 3.6) and the domain of application (Theorem 3.8). It seems that the more general is the environment within which individual strategic behavior can be mitigated with a suitable institutional design, the more arcane and empirically implausible must be that design (Theorem 3.7). Collective decision-making institutions found in the world, however, although on occasion somewhat arcane, are surely not empirically implausible. So, rather than pursue a normative theory of institutional design, the remainder of the discussion concerns a positive analysis of strategically rational behavior within (abstractions of) empirically salient political institutions or mechanisms.

Although both of the electoral and legislative stages of a representative democratic system are concerned with choosing a subset of outcomes from among those available, elections involve large numbers of individuals choosing among candidates for office while legislative decisions involve a relatively small number of individuals choosing among policies. Insofar as rational, policy-oriented individuals are consequentialist, they evaluate candidates exclusively with respect to the likely policy implications of electing some rather than others to office. And insofar as the interests of electoral candidates depend on the choices of citizens, candidates likewise evaluate their various decisions with respect to how they influence citizens' choices through final policy outcomes. Analytically, therefore, it is appropriate to begin by developing an understanding of the incentives and constraints governing legislative decision-making before going on to develop theories of legislative or executive elections.

Chapters 4, 5 and 6 concern legislative decision-making. Policy-making within legislatures involves many things and we abstract considerably, focusing on committee voting over a fixed agenda, agenda-setting and legislative bargaining. Committee voting is typically sequential: an agenda is an ordering of the given feasible set of alternatives and a specification of the rules under which voting proceeds. In the language developed earlier, agendas are mechanisms, with a most important class of such mechanisms being binary agendas whereby voting is invariably over pairs, either of alternatives or of subsets of alternatives. Binary agendas exhibit a remarkable and extremely useful property: they are dominance solvable, which implies that they yield unique, well-defined and easily computed equilibrium outcomes (Theorem 4.1). If there is no constraint other than to binary agendas on how an agenda can be organized, the set of equilibrium policy outcomes consistent with strategically rational voting is exactly the top-cycle set of alternatives for the committee (Theorem 4.3). By itself, therefore, the use of a binary agenda for collective choice fails to impose sufficient structure on decision-making to say anything more concrete than what can be said with an abstract direct preference aggregation model. Narrowing the class of admissible mechanisms to some subset of binary agendas helps considerably. Amendment agendas (among others) are widely used and refine the predictions regarding committee decisions (Theorem 4.5, Theorem 5.4 and Theorem 5.5). Similarly, especially when policies have a spatial representation and any feasible agenda is a (possibly endogenous) finite selection from some underlying policy space, issue-by-issue agendas yield clear predictions irrespective of whether there is a nonempty core for the relevant voting rule and committee preference profile (Theorem 5.1, Corollary 5.1 and Theorem 5.2).

Not all legislative agenda setting is centered on voting although voting is, more often than not, an important component of any final decision. A complementary perspective is legislative bargaining. Rather than build a full agenda prior to voting over that agenda to determine a legislative policy decision, bargaining theory considers agenda setting as an ongoing process whereby alternatives are offered from various individuals and put up for consideration immediately: acceptance of a proposal defines the policy decision and terminates the process; rejection of a proposal entails some other committee member offering a new proposal, and so on. Because the underlying set of alternatives is a multidimensional policy space, there are nontrivial questions regarding equilibrium existence for bargaining protocols. However, existence can be assured under some reasonable assumptions (Theorem 6.4). More interesting, however, are the characterizations of equilibrium proposals and outcomes (Theorem 6.2, Theorem 6.3, Theorem 6.5 and Theorem 6.7) where it is clear that having proposal rights, especially the right to offer the first proposal, is advantageous.

It is worth noting that a recurrent theme of Chapters 4, 5 and 6 is that details of committee structure and of the rules governing voting and agenda-selection can greatly affect the character of final policy decisions. To some extent this is to be expected. We have already observed that equilibrium predictions from models falling under the rubric of indirect preference aggregation are achieved in part by not insisting on a condition of minimal democracy; it follows that some individuals in some settings are capable of unilaterally affecting collective decisions in their favor and, whenever possible, can be expected to do so.

Legislative decisions are taken by those elected to legislative office. Chap-

10.1. RETROSPECTIVE

ters 7 and 8, therefore, explore electoral decision-making with, respectively, two and more than two candidates or parties. To a large extent, the theory developed in these chapters is a theory of executive rather than legislative elections: all winning candidates are presumed to have monopoly control of the legislative decision-making apparatus and to implement the platforms on which they compete for office. With only two candidates and no uncertainty about what the policies the candidates would implement conditional on reaching office, individuals have a clear voting decision when voting costs are negligible: vote "sincerely" for the candidate offering the most preferred platform. Recognizing that voters vote sincerely then renders the analysis of the two candidates' strategic platform choices relatively straightforward. Unfortunately, when the candidates care only about winning and there is no abstention, the set of equilibrium electoral platforms is precisely the set of core alternatives for the underlying vote (equivalent in this case to preference) aggregation rule (Theorem 7.1). While such a result has predictive content for one-dimensional politics, it has limited predictive content for multidimensional politics beyond the observation that the status quo is invariably vulnerable to replacement, even without any shift in the underlying distribution of voter preferences. On the other hand, two-candidate electoral competition with no abstention or uncertainty and purely office-motivated candidates is formally representable as a two player constant sum game. Thus an equilibrium, at least in mixed strategies, surely exists for any finite set of policy alternatives or finite approximation to a spatial policy space (Theorem 7.2); indeed, the support of any mixed strategy equilibrium must lie within the uncovered set (Theorem 7.4 and Theorem 7.5). And changing the electoral equilibrium concept slightly to permit indifferent voters to choose how to vote as a function of the platforms *per se,* rather than insisting such voters invariably vote for each candidate with probability one-half, yields existence of mixed strategy equilibria in the continuum case also (Theorem 7.8).

Mixed strategy predictions in the spatial model of elections, however, are typically both hard to identify and hard to interpret. These difficulties motivate considering the electoral implications of admitting alternative, arguably more empirically grounded, assumptions on candidate objectives (in particular, candidates might care about policy itself) and information (assuming candidates know everything about the distribution of voter preferences is unreasonable). Doing so turns out to yield more descriptive results (Theorem 7.9, Theorem 7.10 and Theorem 7.12). The situation is complicated by the possibility of voter abstention. While there are problems with understanding patterns of turnout, the concern in the text is on understanding how policies and preferences are connected and, therefore, we focus on the implications of abstention on candidate competition. And the key theoretical result is that turnout drives office-motivated candidates to a utilitarian optimal policy rather than to a median policy (Corollary 7.4).

Two-candidate elections are a focal case but relatively unusual in the world at large. Moreover, assuming only two candidates at the outset leaves unaddressed any explanation of why only two candidates compete for office at all. At least some consideration of multicandidate elections is therefore essential. Assuming individuals vote sincerely as in the two-candidate case results in electoral equilibria in which the relative dispersion of candidates over a one-dimensional issue space is closely connected to the electoral rule in place; the more important it is not to come in last the greater is the incentive for clustering (Theorem 8.2). The value of this result, however, is mitigated by the fact that sincere voting is rarely equilibrium behavior at every multicandidate distribution of platforms. Indeed, with strategically rational voters and a given set of m distinct candidates competing for $l < m$ political offices under single nontransferable voting, equilibrium voting typically entails only $l+1$ candidates having any serious chance of election (Theorem 8.3). And in this case, there is a question regarding why more than $l+1$ candidates choose to run for office in such elections. There are a variety of possible answers to this question, depending in part on the electoral rule in place, the pool of possible candidates and their objectives (Theorem 8.4, Theorem 8.5 and Theorem 8.6).

Indirect preference aggregation connects individuals' preferences over a feasible set of policy alternatives to a collective choice through the political institutions of elections and legislatures. Rational agents within any institution are in principle sensitive to the consequential implications of any intermediate action or decision. Thus voters evaluate candidates for legislative office on the basis of their expected impact on subsequent legislative decision-making; in turn, when selecting electoral platforms or choosing whether to enter an election at all, candidates for legislative office pay attention to the implications of their decisions for electoral success. Explicit consideration of the connections between electoral and legislative decision-making thus requires an integrated model of the representative process. At least for the illustrative model of Chapter 9, in which an election under proportional rule is followed by legislative policy choice under coalitional bargaining, it is clear how voters' appreciation of the induced mapping between electoral vote distributions and legislative policy outcomes affects the qualitative predictions of both electoral and legislative behavior (Theorem 9.1).

10.2 A conclusion

Given almost any profile of individuals' preferences over feasible outcomes, variations in details of the preference aggregation rule influence the collective choices associated with that profile. Similarly, variations in details of the political institutions influence the collective choices induced through strategic behavior of individuals with those same preferences. Unlike with the direct preference aggregation approach, however, collective choices induced through the equilibrium behavior of strategically rational agents acting within political institutions (here, voting and agenda-setting in elections and legislatures) are almost always well-defined in that such equilibria exist. In some settings, it is possible to show that the two aggregation schemes, direct and indirect, yield the same outcomes (for example, Corollary 4.3, Theorem 6.6 and Theorem 7.1); and similarly, when the core is empty for some preference aggregation rule, the sets of equilibrium outcomes of at least some focal indirect schemes are (in a suitably defined sense) sufficiently continuous in preferences that they yield collective choices "close to" where the core would be when the preference profile is "close to" supporting a nonempty core (for example, Theorem 6.7 and Theorem 7.7). Thus the gain offered by the indirect approach to preference aggregation lies in its flexibility with respect to the analysis of specific institutions for collective choice and the absence of any fundamental difficulty in insuring the existence of well-defined outcomes. On the other hand, the cost of the indirect approach lies in its violation of minimal democracy and its sensitivity to sometimes small changes in assumptions regarding individual behavior (compare, for instance, Theorem 3.3 and Theorem 3.6) and in assumptions regarding institutional design (compare Theorem 4.3 and Theorem 4.5 for example).

Politics is complicated and to make any progress toward unraveling the complexity requires abstraction. Formal models are inherently abstractions, providing an effective way of developing some intuition for, and a cumulative understanding of, how political institutions and environments influence individual behavior and collective choice. Not all formal models fall within a single theoretical framework. In this and the preceding volume, however, we focus exclusively on strategic, rational choice-theoretic models. Although surely not the only useful or necessarily the most appropriate framework in all conceivable cases, rational choice theory provides a coherent set of assumptions applicable to any setting in which purposive individuals interact, respond to incentives and constraints, and take instrumental decisions to promote their respective individual or collective objectives. Politics, we believe, is quintessentially such a setting.

Bibliography

[1] Abreu, D. and H. Matsushima 1992. Virtual implementation in iteratively undominated strategies. *Econometrica, 60:993-1008*.

[2] Aliprantis, C.D. and K.C. Border 1999. *Infinite Dimensional Analysis: A Hitchhiker's Guide (2nd. ed)*. New York: Springer.

[3] Aranson, P., M. Hinich and P. Ordeshook 1974. Election goals and strategies: equivalent and nonequivalent election strategies. *American Political Science Review, 68:135-152*.

[4] Arrow, K.J. 1963. *Social Choice and Individual Values (2nd. ed.)*. New Haven: Yale University Press.

[5] Arrow, K.J. 1970. *Essays in the Theory of Risk Bearing*. Chicago: Markham.

[6] Austen-Smith, D. 1987. Sophisticated sincerity: voting over endogenous agendas. *American Political Science Review, 81:1323-1329*.

[7] Austen-Smith, D. 1989. Sincere voting in models of legislative elections. *Social Choice and Welfare, 6:287-299*.

[8] Austen-Smith, D. 1996. Electing legislatures. In N. Schofield (ed) *Collective Decision-Making: Social Choice and Political Economy*. New York: Kluwer-Nijhoff.

[9] Austen-Smith, D. 2000. Redistributing income under proportional representation. *Journal of Political Economy, 108:1235-1269*.

[10] Austen-Smith, D. and J.S. Banks 1988. Elections, coalitions and legislative outcomes. *American Political Science Review, 82:405-422*.

[11] Austen-Smith, D. and J.S. Banks 1990. Stable governments and the allocation of policy portfolios. *American Political Science Review*, 84:891-906.

[12] Austen-Smith, D. and J.S. Banks 1991. Monotonicity in electoral systems. *American Political Science Review*, 85:531-537.

[13] Austen-Smith, D. and J.S. Banks 1999. *Positive Political Theory I: Collective Preference*. Ann Arbor: University of Michigan Press.

[14] Axelrod, R. 1970. *Conflict of Interest*. Chicago: Markham.

[15] Baliga, S., L.C. Corchon and T. Sjostrom 1997. The theory of implementation when the planner is a player. *Journal of Economic Theory*, 77:15-33.

[16] Ball, R. 1999. Discontinuity and nonexistence of equilibrium in the probabilistic spatial voting model. *Social Choice and Welfare*, 16:533-556.

[17] Banks, J.S. 1985. Sophisticated voting outcomes and agenda control. *Social Choice and Welfare*, 1:295-306.

[18] Banks, J.S. 1989. Equilibrium outcomes in two-stage amendment procedures. *American Journal of Political Science*, 32:25-43.

[19] Banks, J.S. and G. Bordes 1988. Voting games, indifference and consistent sequential choice rules. *Social Choice and Welfare*, 5:31-44.

[20] Banks, J.S. and J. Duggan 2000. A bargaining model of collective choice. *American Political Science Review*, 94:733-788.

[21] Banks, J.S. and J. Duggan 2001. Existence of Nash equilibria on convex sets. *Working Paper*, Department of Political Science, University of Rochester.

[22] Banks, J.S. and J. Duggan 2002. A bargaining model of legislative policy-making. *Quarterly Journal of Political Science*, 1: 49–85.

[23] Banks, J.S. and J. Duggan 2003. Probabilistic voting in the spatial model of elections: the theory of office-motivated candidates. In D. Austen-Smith and J. Duggan (eds.), *Social Choice and Strategic Decisions: Essays in Honor of Jeffrey S. Banks*. Berlin: Springer.

[24] Banks, J.S., J. Duggan and M. Le Breton 2002. Bounds for mixed strategy equilibria and the spatial model of elections. *Journal of Economic Theory, 103:88-105.*

[25] Banks, J.S., J. Duggan and M. Le Breton 2006. Social choice and electoral competition in the general spatial model. *Journal of Economic Theory, 126:194-234.*

[26] Banks, J.S. and F. Gasmi 1987. Endogenous agenda formation in three person committees. *Social Choice and Welfare, 54:133-152.*

[27] Barbera, S. 1977. Manipulation of social decision functions. *Journal of Economic Theory, 15:226-278.*

[28] Barbera, S., F. Gul and E. Stacchetti 1993. Generalized median voter schemes and committees. *Journal of Economic Theory, 61:262-289.*

[29] Baron, D.P. 1991a. Majoritarian incentives, pork barrel programs, and procedural control. *American Journal of Political Science, 34:57-90.*

[30] Baron, D.P. 1991b. A spatial bargaining theory of government formation in parliamentary systems. *American Political Science Review, 85:137-164.*

[31] Baron, D.P and D. Diermeier. 2001. Elections, governments and parliaments in proportional representation systems. *Quarterly Journal of Economics, 116:933-967.*

[32] Baron, D.P. and J.A. Ferejohn 1989. Bargaining in legislatures. *American Political Science Review, 83:1181-1206.*

[33] Besley, T. and S. Coate 1997. An economic model of representative democracy. *Quarterly Journal of Economics, 112:85-114.*

[34] Billingsley, P. 1968. *Convergence of Probability Measures.* New York: John Wiley & Sons.

[35] Black, D. 1958. *The Theory of Committees and Elections.* Cambridge: Cambridge University Press.

[36] Black, D. and R.A. Newing 1951. *Committee Decisions with Complementary Valuations.* London: William Hodge.

[37] Border, K.C. 1985. *Fixed Point Theorems with Applications to Economics and Game Theory.* Cambridge: Cambridge University Press.

[38] Border, K.C. and J. Jordan 1983. Straightforward elections, unanimity and phantom voters. *Review of Economic Studies, 50:153-170.*

[39] Calvert, R. 1985. Robustness of the multidimensional voting model: candidate motivations, uncertainty and convergence. *American Journal of Political Science, 29:69-95.*

[40] Calvert, R. 1989. Reciprocity among self-interested actors: uncertainty, asymmetry, and distribution. In P.C. Ordeshook (ed.), *Models of Strategic Choice in Politics.* Ann Arbor: University of Michigan Press.

[41] Camerer, C. and M. Weber 1992. Recent developments in modelling preference: uncertainty and ambiguity. *Journal of Risk and Uncertainty, 5:325-370.*

[42] Ching, S. 1998. Strategy-proofness and "median voters." *International Journal of Game Theory, 26:473-490.*

[43] Clarke, E. 1971. Multipart pricing of public goods. *Public Choice, 11:17-33.*

[44] Cohen, L. 1979. Cyclic sets in multidimensional voting models. *Journal of Economic Theory, 20:1-12.*

[45] Coughlin, P. 1992. *Probabilistic Voting Theory.* Cambridge: Cambridge University Press.

[46] Couglin, P. and S. Nitzan 1981. Electoral outcomes with probabilistic voting and Nash social welfare maxima. *Journal of Public Economics, 15:113-121.*

[47] Cox, G.W. 1987a. The uncovered set and the core. *American Journal of Political Science, 31:408-422.*

[48] Cox, G.W. 1987b. Electoral equilibrium under alternative voting institutions. *American Journal of Political Science, 31:82-108.*

[49] Cox, G.W. 1990. Centripetal and centrifugal incentives in electoral systems. *American Journal of Political Science, 34:903-935.*

[50] Cox, G.W. 1994. Strategic voting equilibria under the single nontransferable vote. *American Political Science Review, 88:608-621.*

[51] Cox, G.W. 1997. *Making Votes Count.* Cambridge: Cambridge University Press.

[52] Dasgupta, P., P. Hammond and E. Maskin 1979. The implementation of social choice rules: some general results on incentive compatibility. *Review of Economic Studies, 46:185-216.*

[53] Davis, O.A., M.H. DeGroot and M.J. Hinich 1972. Social preference orderings and majority rule. *Econometrica, 40:147-157.*

[54] Davis, O.A. and M.J. Hinich 1966. A mathematical model of policy formation in a democratic society. In J. Bernd (ed.), *Mathematical Applications in Political Science II.* Dallas: Southern Methodist University Press.

[55] Davis, O.A. and M.J. Hinich 1967. Some results related to a mathematical model of policy formation in a democratic society. In J. Bernd (ed.), *Mathematical Applications in Political Science III.* Dallas: Southern Methodist University Press.

[56] Davis, O.A. and M.J. Hinich 1968. On the power and importance of the mean preference in a mathematical model of democratic choice. *Public Choice, 5:59-72.*

[57] Davis, O.A., M.J. Hinich and P.C. Ordeshook 1970. An expository development of a mathematical model of the electoral process. *American Political Science Review, 64:426-448.*

[58] Denzau, A., R. Katz and S. Slutsky 1985. Multi-agent equilibria with market share and ranking objectives. *Social Choice and Welfare, 2:95-118.*

[59] Denzau, A. and R. MacKay 1983. Gatekeeping and monopoly power of committees: an analysis of sincere and sophisticated behavior. *American Journal of Political Science, 27:740-761.*

[60] Diermeier, D., H. Eraslan and A. Merlo 2003. A structural model of government formation. *Econometrica, 71:27-70.*

[61] Downs, A. 1957. *An Economic Theory of Democracy.* New York: Harper.

[62] Duggan, J. 2003. Endogenous amendment agendas. *Social Choice and Welfare, 27: 495–530.*

[63] Duggan, J. and M. Fey 2005. Electoral competition with policy-motivated candidates. *Games and Economic Behavior*, 51:490-522.

[64] Duggan, J. and M. Jackson 2004. Mixed strategy equilibrium and deep covering in multidimensional electoral competition. *Working Paper*, Department of Political Science, University of Rochester.

[65] Duverger, M. 1954. *Political Parties*. London: Methuen.

[66] Enelow, J. and M.J. Hinich 1981. A new approach to voter uncertainty in the Downsian spatial model. *American Journal of Political Science*, 25:483-493.

[67] Enelow, J. and M.J. Hinich 1982a. Ideology, issues and the spatial theory of elections. *American Political Science Review*, 76:493-501.

[68] Enelow, J. and M.J. Hinich 1982b. Nonspatial candidate characteristics and electoral competition. *Journal of Politics*, 44:115-130.

[69] Epstein, L. 1992. Behaviour under risk: recent developments in theory and application. In J.J. Laffont (ed.), *Advances in Economic Theory: Sixth World Congress I*. Cambridge: Cambridge University Press.

[70] Eraslan, H. 2002. Uniqueness of stationary equilibrium payoffs in the Baron-Ferejohn model. *Journal of Economic Theory*, 103:11-30.

[71] Farquharson, R. 1969. *Theory of Voting*. New Haven: Yale University Press.

[72] Feddersen, T.J. 1992. A voting model implying Duverger's Law and positive turnout. *American Journal of Political Science*, 36:938-962.

[73] Feddersen, T.J. 2004. Rational choice theory and the paradox of not voting: a review. *Journal of Economic Perspectives*, 18:99-112.

[74] Feddersen, T.J. and W. Pesendorfer 1996. The swing voter's curse. *American Economic Review*, 86:408-424.

[75] Feddersen, T.J. and W. Pesendorfer 1999. Abstentions in elections with asymmetric information and diverse preferences. *American Political Science Review*, 93:381-398.

[76] Feddersen, T.J., I. Sened and S.G. Wright 1990. Rational voting and candidate entry under plurality rule. *American Journal of Political Science*, 34:1005-1016.

[77] Ferejohn, J.A. and M.P. Fiorina 1975. Closeness counts only in horseshoes and dancing. *American Political Science Review, 69:920-925.*

[78] Ferejohn, J.A., M.P. Fiorina and R.D. McKelvey 1987. Sophisticated voting and agenda independence in the distributive politics setting. *American Journal of Political Science, 30:169-193.*

[79] Ferejohn, J.A. and K. Krehbiel 1987. The budget process and the size of the budget. *American Journal of Political Science, 31:296-320.*

[80] Fey, M. 1997. Stability and coordination in Duverger's Law: a formal model of preelection polls and strategic voting. *American Political Science Review, 91:135-147.*

[81] Fisher, D. and J. Ryan 1992. Optimal strategies for a generalized "scissors, paper, stone" game. *American Mathematical Monthly, 99:935-942.*

[82] Fudenberg, D. and J. Tirole 1991. *Game Theory.* Cambridge, MA: MIT Press.

[83] Gibbard, A. 1973. Manipulation of voting schemes. *Econometrica, 41:587-602.*

[84] Glicksberg, I. 1952. A further generalization of the Kakutani Fixed Point Theorem with application to Nash equilibrium points. *Proceedings of the American Mathematical Society, 3:170-174.*

[85] Green, J. and J.-J. Laffont 1979. *Incentives in Public Decision Making.* Amsterdam: North Holland.

[86] Greenberg, J. and K. Shepsle 1987. The effects of electoral awards in multiparty competition with entry. *American Political Science Review, 81:525-537.*

[87] Greenberg, J. and S. Weber 1985. Multiparty equilibria under proportional representation. *American Political Science Review, 79:693-703.*

[88] Gretlein, R.J. 1983. Dominance elimination procedures on finite alternative games. *International Journal of Game Theory, 12:107-113.*

[89] Groseclose, T. and K. Krehbiel 1993. On the pervasiveness of sophisticated sincerity. In W.A. Barnett, M.J. Hinich and N.J. Schofield (eds.), *Political Economy: Institutions, Competition and Representation.* Cambridge: Cambridge University Press.

[90] Groves, T. 1973. Incentives in teams. *Econometrica, 41:617-631*

[91] Groves, T. and J. Ledyard 1977. Optimal allocation of public goods: a solution to the "free rider" problem. *Econometrica, 45:783-809.*

[92] Harris, C. 1985. Existence and characterization of perfect equilibrium in games of perfect information. *Econometrica, 53:613-628.*

[93] Harsanyi, J.C. 1973. Games with randomly disturbed payoffs: a new rationale for mixed strategy equilibrium points. *International Journal of Game Theory, 2:1-23.*

[94] Hellwig, M., W. Leininger, P. Reny and A. Robson 1990. Subgame perfect equilibrium in continuous games of perfect information: an elementary approach to existence and approximation by discrete games. *Journal of Economic Theory, 52:406-422.*

[95] Hinich, M.J. 1977. Equilibrium in spatial voting: the median voter result is an artifact. *Journal of Economic Theory, 16:209-219.*

[96] Hinich, M.J. 1978. The mean vs the median in spatial voting games. In P.C. Ordeshook (ed.), *Models of Strategic Choice in Politics.* Ann Arbor: University of Michigan Press.

[97] Hinich, M.J. and P.C. Ordeshook 1969. Abstentions and equilibrium in the electoral process. *Public Choice, 7:81-106.*

[98] Hinich, M.J. and P.C. Ordeshook 1970. Plurality maximization vs vote maximization: a spatial analysis with variable participation. *American Political Science Review, 64:772-791.*

[99] Hinich, M.J., J. Ledyard and P.C. Ordeshook 1972. Nonvoting and the existence of equilibrium under majority rule. *Journal of Economic Theory, 4:144-153.*

[100] Hinich, M.J., J. Ledyard and P.C. Ordeshook 1973. A theory of electoral equilibrium: a spatial analysis based on the theory of games. *Journal of Politics, 35:154-193.*

[101] Hotelling, H. 1929. Stability in competition. *Economic Journal, 39:41-57.*

[102] Hoyer, R. and L. Mayer 1974. Comparing strategies in a spatial model of electoral competition. *American Journal of Political Science, 18:501-523.*

[103] Jackson, M. 1992. Implementation in undominated strategies: a look at bounded mechanisms. *Review of Economic Studies*, 59:757-776.

[104] Kramer, G. 1972. Sophisticated voting over multidimensional choice spaces. *Journal of Mathematical Sociology*, 2:165-180.

[105] Kramer, G. 1973. On a class of equilibrium conditions for majority rule. *Econometrica*, 41:285-297.

[106] Kramer, G. 1977. A dynamical model of political equilibrium. *Journal of Economic Theory*, 16:310-334.

[107] Kramer, G. 1978. Existence of electoral equilibrium. In P.C. Ordeshook (ed.), *Game Theory and Political Science*. New York: New York University Press.

[108] Krehbiel, K. 1985. Obstruction and representativeness in legislatures. *American Journal of Political Science*, 29:643-659.

[109] Krehbiel, K. 1987. Sophisticated committees and structure-induced equilibria in Congress. In M.D. McCubbins and T. Sullivan (eds.), *Congress: Structure and Policy*. Cambridge: Cambridge University Press.

[110] Kreps, D.M. 1988. *Notes on the Theory of Choice*. Boulder: Westview Press.

[111] Laffond, G., J.-F. Laslier and M. Le Breton 1993. The bipartisan set of a tournament game. *Games and Economic Behavior*, 5:182-201.

[112] Laslier, J.-F. 1997. *Tournament Solutions and Majority Voting*. Berlin: Springer.

[113] Laver, M. and N.J. Schofield 1991. *Multiparty Government: The Politics of Coalition in Europe*. Oxford: Oxford University Press.

[114] Laver, M. and K.A. Shepsle 1990. Coalitions and cabinet government. *American Political Science Review*, 84:873-890.

[115] Laver, M. and K. Shepsle 1996. *Making and Breaking Governments*. Cambridge: Cambridge University Press.

[116] Ledyard, J. 1984. The pure theory of large two-candidate elections. *Public Choice*, 44:7-43.

[117] Lindbeck, A. and J.W. Weibull 1987. Balanced-budget redistribution as the outcome of political competition. *Public Choice, 52:273-297.*

[118] Maskin, E. 1985. The theory of implementation in Nash equilibrium: a survey. In L. Hurwicz, D. Schmeidler and H. Sonnenschein (eds.), *Social Goals and Social Organization: Essays in Memory of Elisha Pazner.* Cambridge: Cambridge University Press.

[119] Maskin, E. 1999. Nash equilibrium and welfare optimality. *Review of Economic Studies, 66:23-38.*

[120] Matthews, S.A. 1980. Pairwise symmetry conditions for voting equilibria. *International Journal of Game Theory, 9:141-156.*

[121] McGarvey, D. 1953. A theorem on the construction of voting paradoxes. *Econometrica, 21:608-610.*

[122] McKelvey, R.D. 1976. Intransitivities in multidimensional voting models and some implications for agenda control. *Journal of Economic Theory, 12:472-482.*

[123] McKelvey, R.D. 1979. General conditions for global intransitivities in formal voting models. *Econometrica, 47:1086-1112.*

[124] McKelvey, R.D. 1986. Covering, dominance and institution-free properties of social choice. *American Journal of Political Science, 30:283-314.*

[125] McKelvey, R.D. 1996. Social choice. *Unpublished lecture notes,* California Institute of Technology.

[126] McKelvey, R.D. and R.G. Niemi 1978. A multistage game representation of sophisticated voting for binary procedures. *Journal of Economic Theory, 18:1-22.*

[127] McKelvey, R.D. and N.J. Schofield. 1987. Generalized symmetry conditions at a core point. *Econometrica, 55:923-934.*

[128] Merlo, A. 1997. Bargaining over governments in a stochastic environment. *Journal of Political Economy, 105:101-131.*

[129] Miller, N.R. 1977. Graph-theoretical approaches to the theory of voting. *American Journal of Political Science, 21:769-803.*

[130] Miller, N.R. 1980. A new solution set for tournaments and majority voting. *American Journal of Political Science, 24:68-96.*

[131] Miller, N.R. 1995. *Committees, Agendas and Voting.* Chur: Harwood Academic Publishers.

[132] Moore, J. 1992. Implementation, contracts and renegotiation in environments with complete information. In J.J. Laffont (ed.), *Advances in Economic Theory: Sixth World Congress I.* Cambridge: Cambridge University Press.

[133] Moore, J. and R. Repullo 1988. Subgame perfect implementation. *Econometrica, 66:1191-1220.*

[134] Morelli, M. 1999. Demand competition and policy compromise in legislative bargaining. *American Political Science Review, 93:809-820.*

[135] Morton, R. 1987. A group majority model of voting. *Social Choice and Welfare, 4:117-131.*

[136] Morton, R. 1991.Groups in rational turnout models. *American Journal of Political Science, 35:758-776.*

[137] Moulin, H. 1979. Dominance-solvable voting schemes. *Econometrica, 47:1337-1351.*

[138] Moulin, H. 1980. On strategy-proofness and single-peakedness. *Public Choice, 35:437-456.*

[139] Moulin, H. 1986. Choosing from a tournament. *Social Choice and Welfare, 3:271-291.*

[140] Moulin, H. 1988. *Axioms of Cooperative Decision Making.* Cambridge: Cambridge University Press.

[141] Muller, E. and M.A. Satterthwaite 1977. The equivalence of strong positive association and strategy-proofness. *Journal of Economic Theory, 14:412-418.*

[142] Muller, E. and M.A. Satterthwaite 1985. Strategy-proofness: the existence of dominant strategy mechanisms. In L. Hurwicz, D. Schmeidler and H. Sonnenschein (eds.), *Social Goals and Social Organization: Essays in Memory of Elisha Pazner.* Cambridge: Cambridge University Press.

[143] Muthoo, A. 1999. *Bargaining Theory with Applications.* Cambridge: Cambridge University Press.

[144] Myerson, R.B. 1991. *Game Theory: Analysis of Conflict.* Cambridge, MA: Harvard University Press.

[145] Myerson, R.B. 1998. Population uncertainty and Poisson games. *International Journal of Game Theory, 27:375-392.*

[146] Myerson, R.B. 1999. Theoretical comparisons of electoral systems. *European Economic Review, 43:671-697.*

[147] Myerson, R.B. 2000. Large Poisson games. *Journal of Economic Theory, 94:7-45.*

[148] Myerson, R.B. 2002. Comparison of scoring rules in Poisson voting games. *Journal of Economic Theory, 103:217-251.*

[149] Myerson, R.B. and R. Weber 1993. A theory of voting equilibria. *American Political Science Review, 87:102-114.*

[150] Nash, J.F. 1950. The bargaining problem. *Econometrica, 18:155-162.*

[151] Nash, J.F. 1951. Noncooperative games. *Annals of Mathematics, 54:289-295.*

[152] Ordeshook, P.C. 1971. Pareto optimality and electoral competition. *American Political Science Review, 65:1141-1145.*

[153] Osborne, M.J. 1993. Candidate positioning and entry in a political competition. *Games and Economic Behavior, 5:133-151.*

[154] Osborne, M.J. and A. Rubinstein 1990. *Bargaining and Markets.* San Diego: Academic Press.

[155] Osborne, M.J. and A. Rubinstein 1994. *A Course in Game Theory.* Cambridge, MA: MIT Press.

[156] Osborne, M.J. and A. Slivinski 1996. A model of political competition with citizen-candidates. *Quarterly Journal of Economics, 111:65-96.*

[157] Palfrey, T.R. 1984. Spatial equilibrium with entry. *Review of Economic Studies, 51:139-156.*

[158] Palfrey, T.R. 1989. A mathematical proof of Duverger's Law. In P.C. Ordeshook (ed.), *Models of Strategic Choice in Politics*. Ann Arbor: University of Michigan Press.

[159] Palfrey, T.R. 1992. Implementation in Bayesian equilibrium: the multiple equilibrium problem in mechanism design. In J.J. Laffont (ed.), *Advances in Economic Theory: Sixth World Congress I*. Cambridge: Cambridge University Press.

[160] Palfrey, T.R. and H. Rosenthal 1983. A strategic calculus of voting. *Public Choice, 41:7-53*.

[161] Palfrey, T.R. and H. Rosenthal 1984. Participation and the provision of discrete public goods: a strategic analysis. *Journal of Public Economics, 24:171-193*.

[162] Palfrey, T.R. and H. Rosenthal 1985. Voter participation and strategic uncertainty. *American Political Science Review, 79:62-78*.

[163] Palfrey, T.R. and S. Srivastava 1991. Nash implementation using undominated strategies. *Econometrica, 59:479-501*.

[164] Pattanaik, P.K. 1978. *Strategy and Group Choice*. Amsterdam: North Holland.

[165] Peleg, B. 1984. *Game Theoretic Analysis of Voting in Committees*. Cambridge: University of Cambridge Press.

[166] Plott, C.R. 1967. A notion of equilibrium and its possibility under majority rule. *American Economic Review, 57:787-806*.

[167] Pratt, J.W. 1964. Risk aversion in the small and in the large. *Econometrica, 32:122-136*.

[168] Repullo, R. 1985. Implementation in dominant strategies under complete and incomplete information. *Review of Economic Studies, 52:223-229*.

[169] Repullo, R. 1987. A simple proof of Maskin's Theorem on Nash implementation. *Social Choice and Welfare, 4:39-41*.

[170] Riker, W.H. 1953. *Democracy in the United States*. New York: Macmillan.

[171] Riker, W.H. 1962. *The Theory of Political Coalitions.* New Haven: Yale University Press.

[172] Riker, W.H. 1976. The number of political parties: a reexamination of Duverger's Law. *Comparative Politics, 9:93-106.*

[173] Riker, W.H. 1982. The two-party system and Duverger's Law: an essay on the history of political science. *American Political Science Review, 76:753-766.*

[174] Riker, W.H. and P.C. Ordeshook 1968. A theory of the calculus of voting. *American Political Science Review, 62:25-43.*

[175] Roemer, J.E. 2001. *Political Competition: Theory and Applications.* Cambridge MA: Harvard University Press.

[176] Romer, T. and H. Rosenthal 1978. Political resource allocation, controlled agendas and the status quo. *Public Choice, 33:27-45.*

[177] Rothschild, M. and J. Stiglitz 1970. Increasing risk I: a definition. *Journal of Economic Theory, 2:225-243.*

[178] Rubinstein, A. 1982. Perfect equilibrium in a bargaining model. *Econometrica, 50:97-109.*

[179] Saijo, T. 1987. On constant Maskin monotonic social choice functions. *Journal of Economic Theory, 42:382-386.*

[180] Satterthwaite, M.A. 1975. Strategy-proofness and Arrow's conditions: existence and correspondence theorems for voting procedures and social welfare functions. *Journal of Economic Theory, 10:187-217.*

[181] Savage, L.J. 1954. *The Foundations of Statistics.* New York: John Wiley & Sons.

[182] Schmeidler, D. and H. Sonnenschein 1978. Two proofs of the Gibbard-Satterthwaite Theorem on the possibility of a strategy-proof social choice function. In H. Gottinger and W. Leinfellner (eds.), *Decision Theory and Social Ethics: Issues in Social Choice.* Dordrecht: Reidel.

[183] Schofield, N.J. 1978. Instability of simple dynamic games. *Review of Economic Studies, 45:575-594.*

[184] Schofield, N.J. 1983. Generic instability of majority rule. *Review of Economic Studies, 50:695-705.*

[185] Schofield, N.J. 1987. Stability of coalition governments in Western Europe. *European Journal of Political Economy, 3:555-591.*

[186] Schofield, N.J. 1993. Political competition and multiparty coalition governments. *European Journal of Political Research, 23:1-33.*

[187] Schofield, N.J. 1995. Coalition politics: a formal model and empirical analysis. *Journal of Theoretical Politics, 7:245-281.*

[188] Schofield, N.J. 1997. Multiparty electoral politics. In D.C. Mueller (ed.), *Perspectives on Public Choice.* Cambridge: Cambridge University Press.

[189] Selten, R. 1965. Spieltheoretishe behandlung eines oligopolmodells mit Nashfrägetraheit. *Zeitschrift fur die Gesamle Staatswissenschaft, 12:310-324.*

[190] Selten, R. 1975. Reexamination of the perfectness concept for equilibrium points in extensive form games. *International Journal of Game Theory, 4:25-55.*

[191] Shepsle, K.A. 1979. Institutional arrangements and equilibrium in multidimensional voting models. *American Journal of Political Science, 23:27-59.*

[192] Shepsle, K.A. 1991. *Models of Multiparty Competition.* Chur: Harwood Academic Publishers.

[193] Shepsle, K.A. and B.R. Weingast 1984. Uncovered sets and sophisticated voting outcomes with implications for agenda institutions. *American Journal of Political Science, 28:49-74.*

[194] Slutsky, S. 1975. Abstentions and majority equilibrium. *Journal of Economic Theory, 11:292-304.*

[195] Smithies, A. 1941. Optimum location in spatial competition. *Journal of Political Economy, 49:423-439.*

[196] Sugden, R. 1984. Free association and the theory of proportional representation. *American Political Science Review, 78:31-44.*

[197] Sundaram, R. 1996. *A First Course in Optimization Theory.* New York: Cambridge University Press.

[198] Tucker, A. 1984. *Applied Combinatorics (2nd. ed.)*. New York: John Wiley & Sons.

[199] Uhlaner, C. 1989. Rational turnout: the neglected role of groups. *American Journal of Political Science, 33:390-422*.

[200] Von Neumann, J. and O. Morgenstern. 1944. *Theory of Games and Economic Behavior*. Princeton: Princeton University Press.

[201] Walker, M. 1980. On the nonexistence of a dominant strategy mechanism for making optimal public decisions. *Econometrica, 48:1521-1540*.

[202] Winter, E. 1996. Voting and vetoing. *American Political Science Review, 90:813-823*.

[203] Wittman, D. 1977. Candidates with policy preferences: a dynamic model. *Journal of Economic Theory, 14:180-189*.

[204] Wittman, D. 1983. Candidate motivation: a synthesis of alternatives. *American Political Science Review, 77:142-157*.

[205] Zhou, L. 1991. Impossibility of strategy-proof mechanisms in economies with pure public goods. *Review of Economic Studies, 58:107-120*.

Index

Abreu, D., 110
abstention in elections, 253, 304
acyclic
    preference aggregation rule, 4
agenda
    amendment, 29
    binary, 113
        defined, 116
    endogenous, 166
    issue-by-issue, 62
agenda independence, 139
agenda-setting game
    equilibrium, 174
        and majority core, 182
        and sincere voting, 185
        existence, 177
Aliprantis, C.D., 231
Allais Paradox, 14
allocation, 94
amendment agenda
    admissible, 138
    and status quo, 138
    as a collective choice rule, 29, 52
    defined, 132
    endogenous, 173
    two-stage, 144
    voting tree representation, 115
appropriations process, 189
Aranson, P., 330
Arrovian aggregation rule, 30
Arrow Possibility Theorem, 22
Arrow, K.J., 18, 68

augmented median voter rule, 37
Austen-Smith, D., 18, 110, 190, 191, 330, 417
Axelrod, R., 417

backwards induction, 205
Baliga, S., 110
Ball, R., 331
Banks set, 146
Banks, J.S., 18, 110, 146, 190, 191, 251, 271, 330, 331, 417
Barbera, S., 68
bargaining
    axiomatic, 252
    demand, 252
    legislative, 392
bargaining theory
    and impatience, 196
    and recognition probabilities, 195
    distributive, 204, 225
    over policy, 225
    sequential, 194
    two-person, 193
Baron, D.P., 251, 252, 417
battle of the sexes, 202
Besley, T., 389
best response, 85
Black, D., 68, 190
Borda rule
    and Maskin monotonicity, 85
    as scoring rule, 336
    defined, 19

Border, K.C., 68, 153, 231
Bordes, G., 146
budget process, 189

Calvert, R., 252, 331
Camerer, C., 18
candidate uncertainty, 283
    over policy-independent bias, 284
    over voter policy preferences, 284
candidates, 254
    and agenda control, 298
    and entry, 353
    benefit of winning, 355
    cost of entry, 355
    office-motivated, 255
    policy-motivated, 293
    potential, 354
    serious, 350
    winning, 354
    winning at $\mathbf{v}$, 349
caretaker government, 393
chaos theorems, 323
Ching, S., 68
citizen candidates, 360
citizen sovereignty, 36
Clarke, E., 111
classical efficiency theorem, 327
close race, 349
closed rule, 189
coalition government, 158, 163, 244, 395
Coate, S., 389
Cohen, L., 330
collective choice function
    anonymous, 52
    citizen sovereignty, 36
    constant, 80
    defined, 8
    dictatorial, 21
    full range, 31
    manipulable, 21
    peak monotonic, 49
    peak only condition, 42
    respects unanimity, 22
    self-implementable, 74
    strategy-proof, 21
    strongly monotonic, 109
    unanimity condition, 42
    uncompromising, 49
collective choice rule
    anonymous, 8
    defined, 8
    implementable, 72
    neutral, 68
    no veto property, 82
    path independence, 146
    property α, 145
    property ϵ, 146
    resolute, 8
    strategy resistant, 89
    truthfully implementable, 72
committee, 159
    assignment, 159
    delegation, 190
    jurisdiction, 159
    system, 159
committee equilibrium, 160
    sequential, 161
compact set
    general definition, 231
    in Euclidean space, 2
Condorcet
    consistent, 162
    criterion, 42
    winner, 52
        as sophisticated outcome, 130
continuation value, 209
contour sets
    of a preference relation, 2
    of a utility function, 2

INDEX

convex preferences, 2
convex set
   set, 2
Corchon, L., 110
core
   and bargaining, 236
   issue-by-issue
      and sophisticated voting, 156
      defined, 149
      existence of, 153
   majority, 62
   of a preference aggregation rule, 7
   portfolio allocation, 190
correspondence
   closed graph property, 151
   continuous, 151
   lower hemi-continuous, 150
   upper hemi-continuous, 150
costless campaign, 353
Coughlin, P., 331
covering relation
   deep covering, 278
   in the finite model, 134
   in the spatial model, 269
Cox threshold, $\mathcal{C}(s;m)$, 339
Cox, G.W., 330, 388, 389

D term, 331
Dasgupta, P., 110
Davis, O., 330
de Groot, M., 330
decisive coalitions
   defined, 4
   minimum winning, 199
   monotonic, 4
   of a preference aggregation rule, 4
   proper, 4
decisive structure, 5

deep uncovered set, 278
Denzau, A., 190, 388
dictator
   for collective choice, 21
   for preference aggregation, 4
Diermeier, D., 417
Director's Law, 292
domain
   continuous and convex, $\mathcal{R}_{cs}^n$, **3**
   separable, $\mathcal{R}_{sep}^n$, 65
   unrestricted, $\mathcal{R}^n$, 3
   weighted Euclidean, $\mathcal{W}^n$, **54**
dominance solvability
   and binary voting trees, 124
   of game forms, 122
Downs, A., 330, 331
Duggan, J., 191, 251, 271, 279, 330, 331
Duverger's Law, 352
   as two-position equilibria, 381
Duverger, M., 389

elections
   multicandidate, 333
   two-candidate, 253
electoral equilibria
   and the uncovered set, 268, 271
   uniqueness in finite games, 265
electoral equilibrium
   and the core, 257, 294
   citizen-candidate, 360
   in symmetric voting, 279
   multicandidate, 338
      convergence, 341
      with entry, 355
   open-agenda, 365
   Poisson, 321
   policy-motivated candidate, 294
   probabilistic voting, 285
   two-candidate, 257

electoral rule, 90, 253
    as a mechanism, 91
    dictatorial, 92
    plurality, 285
    preference monotonic, 92
    rank scoring, 334
    simple, 255
    vote monotonic, 91
electoral uncertainty, 301
Enelow, J., 330
Epstein, L., 18
equilibrium
    β-equilibrium, 71
    dominant strategy, 75
    legislative, 394
    legislative election, 395
    Nash, 78
    no-delay, 211, 231
    Poisson voting, 317
    quasi-symmetric mixed, 308
    stationary, 209
        uniqueness in distributive bargaining games, 214
    subgame perfect Nash, 171
    undominated Nash, 85
    undominated subgame perfect
        in stationary strategies, 203
Eraslan, H., 251, 417
Euclidean distance, 228
    and continuity, 228
    between sets, 277
Euclidean preferences
    simple, 54
    weighted, 54
expected plurality in
    multicandidate elections, 337
    two-candidate elections, 285
expected utility theory, 8
    and subjective probability, 18
    axiomatic justification, 13

Farquharson, R., 146
Feddersen, T.J., 331, 389
Ferejohn, J.A., 146, 191, 251, 331
Fey, M., 331, 389
Fiorina, M.P., 146, 331
Fisher, D., 330
folk theorem, 207
free-riding, 312
Fudenberg, D., 330
full participation assumption, 285
full range, 31

game, 71
    binary voting, 117, 128
    extensive form, 169
    subgame of, 170
    zero-sum, 264
game form, 71
    binary voting, 117
    dominance solvable, 122
game tree, 169
Gasmi, F., 191
Gibbard, A., 68
Gibbard-Satterthwaite Theorem, 21
    connection to Arrow Possibility
        Theorem, 32
    for the spatial model, 53
Glicksberg Fixed Point Theorem, 231
Green, J., 111
Greenberg, J., 389
Gretlein, R.J., 146
Groseclose, T., 191
Groves mechanism, 98
    defined, 100
Groves, T., 111
Gul, F., 68

Hammond, P., 110
Harris, C., 191
Harsanyi, J., 251

INDEX

Hellwig, M., 191
Hinich, M.J., 330, 331
Hotelling, H., 330
Hoyer, R., 330

ideal point, 33
    induced, 7, 61
ideological convergence, 259
implementation
    in β-equilibrium, 72
    in dominant strategy equilibrium, 76, 78
    in Nash equilibrium, 78, 82
    and monotonicity, 82
    in subgame perfect equilibrium, 110
    in undominated Nash equilibrium, 86
    in undominated strategies, 89
    self, 74, 94, 96, 98
    virtual, 110
implementation problem, 20, 69
    with incomplete information, 110
independence of irrelevant alternatives
    preference aggregation rule, 4
issue allocation, 163
    ω-monopoly equilibrium, 164
issue-by-issue agenda
    and agenda independence, 140
    and status quo, 154
    as a collective choice rule, 62
    defined for the spatial model, 155
    in the spatial model, 148
    sophisticated voting equilibrium
        characterized, 156
        defined, 156
        existence, 158
    voting, 147

Jackson, M., 110, 279, 330

Jordan, J., 68

Kakutani Fixed Point Theorem, 153
Katz, A., 388
Kramer, G., 146, 190, 330, 331
Krehbiel, K., 190, 191
Kreps, D., 18

Laffond, G., 330
Laffont, J.-J., 111
Laslier, J.-F., 146, 330
Laver, M., 190, 191, 417
Le Breton, M., 271, 330
Ledyard, J., 111, 331
legislative election equilibrium, 395
legislative elections, 391
legislative equilibrium, 394
legislative representation, 392
legislative weight, 392
Leininger, W., 191
Lindbeck, A., 331
lower semi-continuous function, 178

MacKay, R., 190
magnitude of an event, 350
majority rule
    defined, 3
    for committee voting, 114
manipulable choice function, 21
Maskin monotonicity
    defined, 79
Maskin, E., 110
matching pennies, 201
Matsushima, H., 110
Matthews, S.A., 330
maximal set, 6, 30
maximum regret, 331
Maximum Theorem, 165
Mayer, L., 330
McGarvey, D., 146
McKelvey, R.D., 111, 146, 330

mechanism, 71
  bounded, 88
  direct, 71
    decision efficient, 100
    independent of individual utilities, 100
    extensive form, 168
    Groves, 98
    pivotal, 98
median
  induced, 7, 149
median hyperplane, 376
Median Voter Theorem, 240, 259
Merlo, A., 417
message, 70
message profile, 71
metric space, 231
Miller, N.R., 146
minimal democracy constraint, xiii
monotonicity, 79
  and strategy-proofness, 68
  Maskin, 79
    and Nash implementation, 82
  of electoral rules, 90
  preference, 92
  strong, 109
  vote, 91
  weak, 31, 79
Moore, J., 110
Morelli, M., 252
Morgenstern, O., 18
Morton, R., 331
Moulin, H., 68, 111, 146
Muller, E., 68
Muthoo, A., 251
Myerson, R., 317, 318, 330, 331, 350, 389

Nakamura number
  defined, 5, 258

Nash equilibrium, 70
  best response property, 85
  defined, 78
  subgame perfect
    defined, 171
  undominated, 85, 117
Nash Existence Theorem, 263
Nash, J.F., 110, 252, 330
Newing, R.A., 190
Niemi, R., 146
Nitzan, S., 331
no-delay equilibrium, 211, 231

ω-monopoly equilibrium
  and issue-by-issue median, 166
  defined, 164
  existence, 165
open rule, 189
Ordeshook, P.C., 330, 331
Osborne, M.J., 251, 252, 330, 389
outcome function, 71

Palfrey, T.R., 110, 331, 389
Pareto efficient, 7
Pareto extension rule
  and Maskin monotonicity, 84
  defined, 3
Pareto set
  defined, 7
parliament, 163, 244
  governing coalition, 163
party policy preferences, 394
Pattanaik, P.K., 68
peak monotonicity, 49
peak only, 42
Peleg, B., 68
perks of office, 244, 393
Pesendorfer, W., 331
pivot probability, 306
pivotal vote, 305

INDEX

in legislative elections, 404
in multicandidate elections, 334, 346
in two-candidate elections, 256
Plott symmetry conditions, 298
Plott, C., 330
plurality rule
 and Maskin monotonicity, 85
 as a scoring rule, 336
 defined, 3
Poisson electorate, 316
Poisson voting equilibrium, 317
 and aggregate utility, 321
 limit, 347
Poisson voting model, 314, 346
 and close races, 349
 and serious races, 349
 defined, 317
 distributional strategy, 316
 environmental equivalence, 315
 events, 349
  magnitudes of, 350
policy polarization, 301
pork barrel politics, 221
potential candidates, 354
 as citizens, 358
 as set of alternatives, 365
Pratt, J.W., 18
preference aggregation
 direct, xiii, 419
 indirect, xiv, 419
preference aggregation rule
 acyclic, 4
 Arrovian, 30
 Benthamite utilitarian, 289
 Borda rule, 19
 collegial, 5
 defined, 3
 dictatorial, 4

independent of irrelevant alternatives, 4, 22
majority rule, 3
noncollegial, 5
Pareto extension rule, 3
plurality, 3
q-rule, 3
quasi-transitive, 17
simple, 5, 148
transitive, 4
unrestricted domain, 3
voting, 6
weakly monotonic, 31
weakly Paretian, 3, 22
preference distribution, 260
preference profile, 3
 restriction to $L \subseteq N$, 20
 restriction to $S \in \mathcal{X}$, 3
 single-peaked, 34
preference relation, 1
 complete, 1
 continuous, 2
 over lotteries, 9
  continuity, 9
  independence, 9
 reflexive, 1
 separable, 64, 157
 transitive, 2
probabilistic voting, 285
 and aggregate utility maximization, 287
 and distributive politics, 289
 and policy-motivated candidates, 298
probability of winning function, 299
 degenerate, 300
 nondegenerate, 300
 unbiased, 299
progressive taxation, 281
Prohorov distance, 229

proportional representation, 244, 392
  and legislative elections, 413
proportional taxation, 328
pseudo-concave, 300

q-rule
  defined, 3
quasi-concave, 2
quasi-linear preferences
  defined, 94
quasi-transitive, 17

rank scoring rule
  defined, 335
  sincere ballot for, 336
rank scoring rules, 334
reciprocity, 204
rectangular set of alternatives, 154
Reny, P., 191
Repullo, R., 110
revelation principle, 76
Riker, W.H., 331, 389, 417
Robson, A., 191
Roemer, J., 331
Romer, T., 191
Rosenthal, H., 191, 331
Rothschild, M., 18
Rubinstein, A., 251, 252, 330
Ryan, J., 330

Saijo, T, 110
Satterthwaite, M., 68
Savage, L.J., 18
Schmeidler, D., 68
Schofield, N.J., 330, 389, 417
Selten, R., 191
Sened, I., 389
separable preferences, 64, 157
sequential rationality, 199
serious race, 349
Shepsle, K.A., 146, 190, 191, 389

simple rule
  collegial, 255
  defined, 5
  strong, 275
single negative voting, 336
single nontransferable vote, 335
single-peaked preferences
  defined, 33
  in electoral competition, 260
  symmetric, 260
Sjostrom, T., 110
Slivinski, A., 389
Slutsky, S., 331, 389
Smithies, A., 330
Sonnenschein, H., 68
sophisticated agenda, 133
sophisticated equivalent, 118
  and amendment agendas, 119
  and successive elimination, 120
sophisticated outcome, 118
  and weak monotonicity, 131
  as a collective choice rule, 131
  characterized
    for amendment agendas, 137
    for binary agendas, 129
sophisticated sincerity, 184
spatial voting model, 254
Srivastava, S., 110
Stacchetti, E., 68
stationary equilibrium, 209
  and upper-hemicontinuity, 242
  no-delay, 211, 232
  static, 235
Stiglitz, J., 18
strategic voting
  in multicandidate elections, 345
strategy, 71
  best response, 85
  distributional, 316
  dominant, 74

INDEX 453

electoral, 392
history-dependent, 196
history-independent, 203
iterated deletion of dominated, 122
legislative, 393
mixed, 71, 199
and purification, 200, 251
proposal, 174
pure, 71, 199
stationary, 203, 225
defined, 208
undominated, 74, 117
vote, 117, 174
weakly dominant, 74
strategy profile, 71
stationary, 208
strategy-proof, 20
collective choice rules, 68
defined, 21
subgame, 170
proper, 170
subgame perfection, 168
successive elimination agenda, 120
Sugden, R., 389

tail chasing, 88
threshold public good, 312
Tirole, J., 330
top cycle set, 73, 128
transitive
preference aggregation rule, 4
preference relation, 2
truthfully implementable
in β-equilibrium, 72
in dominant strategy equilibrium, 76
in Nash equilibrium, 78
Tucker, A., 311
turnout in elections, 306

two-step principle, 135

Uhlaner, C., 331
unanimity, 22, 42
uncompromising, 49
uncovered set
and continuity, 274
in the finite model, 134
in the spatial model, 269
uniform convergence, 274
utility bias, 283
policy-independent, 284
voter-specific, 284
utility function, 2
concave, 194
pseudo-concave, 300
quasi-concave, 2
von Neumann-Morgenstern, 9

von Neumann, J., 18
von Neumann-Morgenstern utility
defined, 9
existence, 13
indices of local risk-aversion, 18
risk-acceptant, 16
risk-averse, 16
vote
sincere, 117
sophisticated, 118
symmetric, 278
vote aggregation rule, 254
collegial, 256
vote profile
in two-candidate elections, 255
vote share
in multicandidate elections, 337
in two-candidate elections, 261
voter type, 315
voting cost
negligible, 256

positive, 305
voting rule, 5
   defined, 6
voting tree
   and dominance solvability, 124
   binary, 115
      defined, 116
   node
      decision, 115
      initial, 115
      sophisticated equivalent, 118
      terminal, 115
   precedence relation, 115

Walker, M., 111
wasted vote, 333
weak convergence, 229
   and continuity, 229
weak preference order, 1
weakly Paretian
   collective choice function, 22, 38
   preference aggregation rule, 3
Weber, M., 18
Weber, R., 389
Weber, S., 389
Weibull, J., 331
Weierstrass' Theorem, 165
Weingast, B.R., 146
Winter, E., 252
Wittman, D., 331
Wright, S.G., 389

Zhou, L., 68
Zorn's Lemma, 274